Saudi Arabia Enters
the Twenty-First Century

Other Books by Anthony H. Cordesman

The Lessons of Afghanistan: War Fighting, Intelligence, and Force Transformation (Washington, DC: CSIS, 2002)

Iraq's Military Capabilities in 2002: A Dynamic Net Assessment (Washington, DC: CSIS, 2002)

Strategic Threats and National Missile Defenses: Defending the U.S. Homeland (Westport, CT: Praeger, 2002)

A Tragedy of Arms: Military and Security Developments in the Maghreb (Westport, CT: Praeger, 2001)

Peace and War: The Arab-Israeli Military Balance Enters the 21st Century (Westport, CT: Praeger, 2001)

Terrorism, Asymmetric Warfare, and Weapons of Mass Destruction: Defending the U.S. Homeland (Westport, CT: Praeger, 2001)

Cyber-threats, Information Warfare, and Critical Infrastructure Protection: Defending the U.S. Homeland, with Justin G. Cordesman (Westport, CT: Praeger, 2001)

The Lessons and Non-Lessons of the Air and Missile Campaign in Kosovo (Westport, CT: Praeger, 2000)

Transnational Threats from the Middle East: Crying Wolf or Crying Havoc? (Carlyle, PA: Strategic Studies Institute, 1999)

Iraq and the War of Sanctions: Conventional Threats and Weapons of Mass Destruction (Westport, CT: Praeger, 1999)

Iran's Military Forces in Transition: Conventional Threats and Weapons of Mass Destruction (Westport, CT: Praeger, 2000)

U.S. Forces in the Middle East: Resources and Capabilities (Boulder, CO: Westview, 1997)

Perilous Prospects: The Peace Process and Arab-Israeli Military Balance (Boulder, CO: Westview, 1996)

The Lessons of Modern War, Volume IV: The Gulf War, with Abraham R. Wagner (Boulder, CO: Westview, 1995; paperback 1999).

US Defence Policy: Resources and Capabilities (London: RUSI Whitehall Series, 1993)

After the Storm: The Changing Military Balance in the Middle East (Boulder, CO: Westview, 1993)

Weapons of Mass Destruction in the Middle East (London: Brassey's, 1991)

The Lessons of Modern War, Volume I: The Arab-Israeli Conflicts, with Abraham R. Wagner (Boulder, CO: Westview, 1990)

The Lessons of Modern War, Volume II: The Iran-Iraq Conflict, with Abraham R. Wagner (Boulder, CO: Westview, 1990)

The Lessons of Modern War, Volume III: The Afghan and Falklands Conflicts, with Abraham R. Wagner (Boulder, CO: Westview, 1990)

The Gulf and the West: Strategic Relations and Military Realities (Boulder, CO: Westview, 1988)

NATO's Central Region Forces: Capabilities, Challenges, Concepts (London: RUSI/Jane's, 1987)

Western Strategic Interests in Saudi Arabia (London: Croom Helm, 1986)

The Gulf and the Search for Strategic Stability: Saudi Arabia, the Military Balance in the Gulf, and Trends in the Arab-Israeli Military Balance (Boulder, CO: Westview, 1984)

Jordanian Arms and the Middle East Balance (Washington, DC: Middle East Institute, 1983)

Imbalance of Power: An Analysis of Shifting U.S.-Soviet Military Strengths, with John M. Collins (Monterey, CA: Presidio, 1978)

Saudi Arabia Enters the Twenty-First Century

The Military and International Security Dimensions

ANTHONY H. CORDESMAN

Published in cooperation with the
Center for Strategic and International Studies,
Washington, D.C.

Westport, Connecticut
London

Library of Congress Cataloging-in-Publication Data

Cordesman, Anthony H.
   Saudi Arabia enters the twenty-first century: The military and international security
dimensions / Anthony H. Cordesman.
   Includes bibliographical references (p.) and index.
      p. cm.
   ISBN 0–275–97997–0 (alk. paper)—ISBN 0–275–98091–X (set : alk. paper)
   1. National security—Saudi Arabia.   2. Saudi Arabia—Armed Forces.   3. Saudi
Arabia—Defenses.   4. Saudi Arabia—Military policy.   I. Title: Military and international
security dimensions.   II. Title: Saudi Arabia enters the 21st century.   III. Title.
   UA853.S33C665   2003
   355′.0330538—dc21   2002044978

British Library Cataloguing in Publication Data is available.

Library of Congress Catalog Card Number: 2002044978
ISBN: 0–275–98091–X (set)
        0–275–97997–0 [Military]
        0–275–97998–9 [Political]

First published in 2003

Praeger Publishers, 88 Post Road West, Westport, CT 06881
An imprint of Greenwood Publishing Group, Inc.
www.praeger.com

Printed in the United States of America

The paper used in this book complies with the
Permanent Paper Standard issued by the National
Information Standards Organization (Z39.48–1984).

10 9 8 7 6 5 4 3 2 1

Contents

Illustrations

Preface

This book is a product of the Saudi Arabia Enters the 21st Century Project of the Center for Strategic and International Studies (CSIS). This project has been supported by the Smith Richardson Foundation and builds on the work done for the CSIS Strategic Energy Initiative, the CSIS Net Assessment of the Middle East, and the Gulf in Transition Project. It is being conducted in conjunction with a separate—but related—study called the Middle East Energy and Security Project.

The project uses a net assessment approach that looks at all of the major factors affecting Saudi Arabia's strategic, political, economic, and military position and attempts to foresee future implications of current trends. It examines the internal stability and security of Saudi Arabia, social and demographic trends, and the problem of Islamic extremism. It also investigates the changes taking place in the Saudi economy and petroleum industries, the problems of Saudisation, changes in export and trade patterns, and Saudi Arabia's new emphasis on foreign investment.

The assessment of Saudi Arabia's strategic position in this volume includes an analysis of Saudi military forces, defense expenditures, arms imports, military modernization, readiness, internal security forces, and war-fighting capability. It also examines the implications of the conventional military buildup and creeping proliferation of weapons of mass destruction in the Gulf and the resulting changes in Saudi Arabia's security position.

Another object of this volume is to examine the implications of change within Saudi Arabia, their probable mid- and long-term impacts, and the most likely changes in the nature or behavior of Saudi Arabia's current ruling elite. It attempts to project the possible implications for both Gulf stability and the U.S. position in the Gulf. A future volume will look beyond the military dimension and a narrow definition of political stability and study the implications of the shifts in the pattern of the Gulf and changes in Saudi external relations, such as changes in Saudi policy toward Iran and Iraq. It will examine the cooperation and tensions between Saudi Arabia and the other Southern Gulf states and the security and strategic implications of the steady expansion of Saudi Arabia's oil, gas, and petrochemical exports.

This later volume will also examine the succession issues in the royal family, the immediate political probabilities, and the generational changes that are occurring in the royal family and Saudi Arabia's technocrats. At the same time, it examines the future political, economic, and social trends in Saudi Arabia and possible strategic futures for the Kingdom through the year 2010.

The overall examination of the strategic future of Saudi Arabia includes Saudi Arabia's possible evolution in the face of different internal and external factors—including changes in foreign and trade policies by the West, Japan, and the Gulf states. Key issues affecting Saudi Arabia's future, including its economic development, relations with other states in the region, energy production and policies, and security relations with other states will be examined as well.

Future work on the project will focus on the development of working documents that will be revised on the basis of outside comment. As a result, new material will be provided under the "Saudi Arabia Enters the 21st Century" heading of the CSIS Web page at *www.csis.org*. This material will change in response to comments received from policymakers and outside experts. To comment, provide suggestions, or note corrections, please contact Anthony H. Cordesman at the address shown on each report, or e-mail him at *Acordesman@aol.com*. Related material can be found in the "Gulf and Transition" and "Middle East Energy and Security" sections of the CSIS Web page.

SOURCES

The text of this book makes it clear that many of the statements and statistics used in the text are highly uncertain. Where possible, a range of views, figures, and sources are shown, and major uncertainties are described in detail. It is important that the reader understand, however, the basic approach to gathering data used in this book and the special role played by the Internet and informal comments by Saudi officials, private individuals, and other experts on Saudi Arabia. As the notes make clear, this book relies heavily on both Saudi and U.S. government publications and on material from the World Bank and UN. It also relies on material from leading research institutes like the International Institute for Strategic Studies and Jane's. While extensive review has been made of academic and private estimates of key data and trends, few such sources and data are incorporated in the text. This was done both to ensure some degree of consistency and comparability in the data, and to ensure that the data involved were as up to date and reliable as possible.

The text also relies heavily on interviews. The author has frequented Saudi Arabia for several decades, and was able to visit the Kingdom several times over a three-year period during the drafting of this book. During each of these visits, various drafts of the manuscript were circulated to Saudi officials, military, academics, and other experts, as well as U.S., British, and French officials who were serving in Saudi Arabia or had served in it in the past. In addition, the book was placed on the CSIS Web site for comment, and copies were sent to various U.S., British, and French officials, military officers, intelligence officers, and other experts. Some provided detailed comments on the text, and the text was constantly revised as a working document on the basis of such input.

These interviews and comments are not cited because most of those involved did not want their contributions acknowledged in any form. The few exceptions are made at the request of those contributing. It should be noted, however, that most of the updates covering the period from 1999 onward depend heavily on field research, interviews, and outside comments, rather than on formal written sources.

Media sources, including Internet material, translations of broadcasts, newspapers, magazine articles, and similar materials, have also been used extensively. These are referenced in most cases, but some transcribed broadcasts and much of the Internet material did not permit detailed attribution. The use of media sources presents obvious problems in terms of reliability, but the author has not found that academic or official sources are more reliable than media sources, and extensive cross-comparisons have been made of most such material.

The Internet and several online services were used to retrieve data on U.S. and Saudi government reporting and policy. Since most of the databases involved are dynamic and either change or are deleted over time, there is no clear way to footnote much of this material. Recent press sources are generally cited, but are often only part of the material consulted.

As the text makes clear, the sources drawn upon in writing this analysis do not provide any consensus over the details of demographic data, budget data, military expenditures and arms transfers, force numbers, unit designations, or weapons types. While the use of the computer database developed for this study allowed some cross-correlation and checking of such sources, reporting on factors like force strengths, unit types and identities, and tactics often could not be reconciled and citing multiple sources for each case is often not possible.

In many cases, the author adjusted figures and data on a "best guess" basis, drawing on some thirty years of experience in the field. In some other cases, the original data provided by a given source were used without adjustment to ensure comparability, even though this leads to some conflicts in dates, place names, force strengths, and so forth, within the material presented—particularly between summary tables surveying a number of countries and the best estimates for a specific country in the text. In such cases, it seemed best to provide contradictory estimates to give the reader some idea of the range of uncertainty involved.

Personal and location names also presented a consistent problem. No standardization emerged as to the spelling of various names, and differences emerged in the transliteration of the same terms and names into English even within the Saudi government. A limited effort has been made to standardize some of the spellings used in this text, but many names are tied to a database where the preservation of the original spelling is necessary to identify the source and tie it to the transcript of related interviews that cannot be referenced in the notes because of the agreement not to reveal the source.

METHODS

This book deliberately focuses on military capabilities, security issues, and military economics, rather than on the internal politics of Saudi defense and the Saudi military. It also deliberately provides details on such issues, even at the cost of length and occasional repetition. The analysis is intended primarily to provide detailed analysis and background for those who must assess Saudi military and internal security developments, their impact on the military balance, and their full implications for peace negotiations and arms control, rather than provide summary policy recommendations.

Most of the value judgments regarding military effectiveness are made on the basis of American military experience and standards. Although the author has lived in the Middle East, and worked as a U.S. advisor to several Middle Eastern governments, he feels that any attempt to create some Middle Eastern standard of reference is likely to be far more arbitrary than basing such judgments on his own military background.

Anthony H. Cordesman
Arleigh A. Burke Chair in Strategy
Center for Strategic and International Studies

Acknowledgments

The author would like to thank Kevin Wein, Uzma Jamil, Carolyn Mann, Daniel Berkowitz, Andrew Li, Jeffery Leary, and Jennifer Moravitz for their assistance in researching and editing this study, and John Duke Anthony, David Long, Natif Obeid, and Saint John Armitage for their comments and insights. He would also like to thank the many Saudis who made comments and suggestions that cannot be formally attributed to them, as well as the officials in the U.S., British, and French governments.

Chapter 1

Saudi Strategic Challenges

Saudi Arabia faces many security challenges, including major strategic challenges from Iran and Iraq. While Iran has a divided government with important elements of political moderation, it is still a major proliferator, continues to build up its capability to threaten Gulf shipping, and may well have played a role in the bombing of the U.S. Air Force barracks in Al-Khobar. It is far too soon to know whether Iran will be a true moderate state or will seek to become the kind of military power than can intimidate or dominate its neighbors. Iraq remains a major conventional military threat to Kuwait and Saudi Arabia, and is covertly building up its capability to use weapons of mass destruction. If Saddam Hussein continues to survive, and sanctions weaken, Iraq is certain to rearm and acquire a significant stock of chemical, biological, and possibly nuclear weapons. If the United States and Britain remove Saddam from power, Saudi Arabia could face years of instability until (and if) Iraq emerges as a stable and moderate state.

Saudi Arabia faces challenges from its allies as well as its potential enemies. It must forge a better approach to collective security with its Gulf allies, and create more stable long-term security arrangements with the United States and the West. The Southern Gulf has made slow progress toward creating a serious collective defense capability. More important, Saudi Arabia's security ties to the United States present growing problems due to the backlash from the fact that so many Saudis participated in the al Qaeda attacks on the United States on September 11, 2001, the tensions that have grown out of the Second Intifada and the near-breakdown in the

Arab-Israeli peace process, and the problems created by Islamic extremism in Saudi Arabia.

Finally, Saudi Arabia faces serious challenges in transforming and modernizing its military and internal security forces. It has made significant progress in developing its military forces, but progress has slowed badly since the end of the Gulf War in 1991 and there are still serious weaknesses in each of its military services. It faces major obstacles in encouraging its military to spend more effectively. It needs to restructure its force development plans, limit its modernization spending, and fund training and sustainment on a much sounder basis.

The Saudi military badly needs a new kind of leadership, and one that focuses on military effectiveness and not major arms buys or force expansion. Since the mid-1990s, Saudi Arabia has failed to spend the money necessary to sustain its readiness and training capabilities. It has not managed its equipment purchases well, and has sometimes overspent on the wrong equipment. When it has made the right equipment purchases, it has often failed to support some with adequate manpower management, operations and maintenance, training, and sustainability. It has failed to give its forces effective capability and interoperability for joint action with Kuwait in defending against Iraq and to redeploy and concentrate truly combat-capable Saudi land forces to defend the Kingdom's northern border.

None of the strategic challenges Saudi Arabia faces seriously threaten the Kingdom's security as long as relations with Iran continue to improve, Iraq stays weak, and the United States maintains a strong military presence in the region. All of Saudi Arabia's current military problems can be corrected by focusing on the proper strategic priorities, and by giving higher priority to manpower management and funding operations, maintenance, and sustainability. In fact, most of its problems can be solved by changing the focus of the Kingdom's military development from "buy, buy, and buy" to "train, maintain, and sustain." Saudi Arabia could accomplish even more by focusing its current manpower, equipment, and support resources on high-priority missions. Such mission-oriented planning would improve the Kingdom's overall military effectiveness, and reduce the strain that military spending is putting on the Saudi budget and economy.

KEY POTENTIAL THREATS

The main strategic challenge Saudi Arabia faces is the need to plan for its forces to deal with its two major threats in the Northern Gulf, plus a residual threat in the south from Yemen. In addition, the Kingdom must defend the security of its imports and exports and find ways to help ensure the security of its Southern Gulf neighbors. Bahrain and Kuwait are both particularly vulnerable, yet are critical allies in shielding the Kingdom's territory and oil facilitation from any attack by Iran or Iraq.

The balance of military forces in the region does not favor Saudi Arabia, unless it has the aid of the United States and its Southern Gulf allies. Table 1.1 provides a brief overview of Saudi Arabia's strategic position relative to other Gulf states, and Table 1.2 provides a detailed picture of its force strength in comparison with that of each of its neighbors. It is clear from the data in both of these tables that Saudi Arabia is a major military power by Gulf standards and that Saudi forces make up a great deal of the total military strength of the Arab Gulf Cooperation Council (GCC). At the same time, it is also clear that Saudi Arabia cannot hope to match the total force strength of Iran or Iraq.

The Challenge from Iran and Iraq

Iran and Iraq are two very different powers, with different political systems and objectives, geographic positions, and military force structures. Iran is currently by far the less threatening power, but it still poses a threat to the Kingdom and could still become the greater threat over time. Iraq is a more immediate threat and the one that Saudi forces must plan to defend against most urgently. Both Iran and Iraq, however, are major proliferators and Saudi Arabia must deal with the threat of weapons of mass destruction as well as the threat of conventional attacks and asymmetric warfare.

The Military Threat from Iran

In the case of Iran, Saudi Arabia has chosen to improve relations and create a tacit strategic partnership in "checking" Iraq. Iran, however, is developing long-range missile forces, has chemical and probably biological weapons, and is seeking nuclear weapons. It has developed a carefully tailored mix of naval, air, submarine, mine, anti-ship missile, and Revolutionary Guard forces in the lower Gulf, with bases near the main shipping channels. This gives Iran the ability to threaten traffic through the Strait of Hormuz.

Iran's Conventional Forces

U.S. experts in Washington feel that the regular Iranian land forces have around 175,000 to 180,000 men, the air and air defense forces have 30,000 to 35,000, and the navy has around 18,000. They estimate that the Revolutionary Guards have around 120,000 men with a naval branch of 18,000 to 20,000. Iran also has around 300,000 men in various militia, paramilitary, and national police forces. The U.S. Central Command (USCENTCOM) provides somewhat different figures. The regular army is estimated to have around 300,000 actives. The Revolutionary Guards have a total strength of around 170,000. The air force and air defense force are

Table 1.1
The Size and Military Capabilities of the Gulf States in 2002

Country	Total Active Manning	Total Active Army Manning	Tanks	OAFVs/APCs	Artillery	Combat Aircraft	Armed Helicopters
Iran	513,000	475,000	1,565	1,455	3,284	283	104
Iraq	424,000	375,000	2,200	2,700	2,250	316	100
Bahrain	11,000	8,500	106	306	93	34	40
Kuwait	15,500	11,000	385	406	68	82	20
Oman	43,400	31,150	117	219	120	40	0
Qatar	12,330	8,500	35	302	44	18	19
Saudi Arabia	201,500	150,000	1,055	5,427	568	348	33
UAE	65,000	59,000	411	1,400	308	101	49
Yemen	54,000	49,000	910	880	614	71	8
Djibouti	9,600	8,000	0	31	6	0	0
Eritrea	171,900	170,000	100	80	155	17	5
Ethiopia	252,500	250,000	300	220	370	51	26
Somalia	—	—	—	—	—	—	—
Sudan	117,000	112,500	200	661	1,060	35	10
Turkey	515,900	402,000	4,205	2,966	2,953	505	37

Sources: Adapted by Anthony H. Cordesman from CIA, *World Factbook* and IISS, *Military Balance.*

estimated to have 35,500, and the navy to have 18,000. This gives Iran's land forces a total strength of 470,000 actives.

The International Institute for Strategic Studies (IISS) estimates that Iran's military forces total 513,000 actives in 2002, with approximately 220,000 conscripts. The regular army has about 325,000 actives, including 220,000 conscripts. The Revolutionary Guards have a total strength of around 125,000, roughly 100,000 of which are assigned to the land branch. The Iranian Air Force and Air Defense Force have around 45,000, and the IISS reports strength of the air branch of the Revolutionary Guards as part of the land branch, but they may have up to 5,000 men. The regular Iranian Navy is estimated to have 18,000 to 20,600 men, and the Iranian Naval Guards total an additional 20,000 (including 2,000 in IRGC naval air and marine forces). The IISS also estimates that Iran has roughly 200,000 personnel assigned to the Basij (Population Mobilization Army), with about 90,000 full-time actives. The law-enforcement forces include a total of around 150,000, with more than 40,000 paramilitary Gendarmerie and border guards.[1]

The Iranian army and IRGC have a total of around 450,000 men— including roughly 125,000 Revolutionary Guards—and an inventory of some 1,135 main battle tanks, 1,200 other armored vehicles, and 1,950 towed, 290 self-propelled, and 665+ MRL major artillery weapons. The army has large numbers of mortars, 1,700 AA guns, and AT-3, AT-5, and TOW anti-tank guided weapons. It has UAVs, 100 AH-1J attack helicopters, and over 400 utility and lift helicopters; the readiness of these aircraft, however, is low.[2]

Iran's 45,000-man air force has over 280 combat aircraft with potential operational status. It has about 150 aging and worn U.S. fighters, which include 66 F-4D/E and 25 F-14A/B that are about 60% serviceable. It has 24 Su-24 and 30 MiG-29 Soviet-made fighters and Chinese F-7Ms. These are believed to be about 80% serviceable. It has 14 RF-4E reconnaissance aircraft, and 5 P-3F and 5 C-130H-MR maritime reconnaissance aircraft. It has significant transport aircraft and limited tanker capability. Its land-based surface-to-air missile defenses are an awkward blend of U.S.-made sensors and one hundred IHawk missile launchers and Russian/Chinese-made sensors, and ten SA-5, forty-five HQ-21, thirty Rapier, fifteen Tigercat, and an unknown number of FM-80 missile launchers.

Unlike Iraq, Iran has significant naval forces, with 18,000 regulars and 20,000 naval guards. Over the last decade, it has made major improvements in its ability to threaten maritime traffic through the Gulf, and its ability to conduct unconventional warfare. It has five submarines, three aging missile frigates, and two aging corvettes. Additionally, it has ten Kaman missile patrol boats, and ten Houdong missile patrol boats, most of which are equipped with C-802 anti-ship missiles. Other Iranian naval assets include two mine-layers and five mine countermeasure vessels, as well as large stocks of mines.

Table 1.2
Gulf Military Forces in 2002

	Iran	Iraq	Bahrain	Kuwait	Oman	Qatar	Saudi Arabia*	UAE	Yemen
Total Active	513,000	424,000	11,000	15,500	43,400	12,330	201,500	65,000	54,000
Regular	325,000	375,000	11,000	15,500	33,300	12,330	126,500	65,000	54,000
National Guard & Other	125,000	0	0	0	6,400	0	75,000	0	0
Reserve	350,000	650,000	0	23,700	0	0	20,000	0	40,000
Paramilitary	40,000	42,000+	10,160	5,000	4,400	0	15,500+	1,100	70,000
Army and Guard Manpower	450,000*	375,000	8,500	11,000	31,500	8,500	150,000	59,000	49,000
Regular Army Manpower	325,000	375,000	8,500	11,000	25,000	8,500	75,000	59,000	49,000
Reserve	350,000	650,000	0	0	0	0	20,000	0	40,000
Total Main Battle Tanks***	1,565	2,200	106	385	117	35	1,055	411	910
Active Main Battle Tanks	1,565	1,900	106	293	117	35	710	330	910
Active AIFV/Recce, Lt. Tanks	865	1,300	71	355	78	112	1,270+	780(40)	440
Total APCs	590	2,400	235	151	189	190	3,440	620	440
Active APCs	550	1,800	205	111	103	172	2,630	570	240
ATGM Launchers	75	100+	15	118	48	124+	480+	305	71
Self Propelled Artillery	310	150	62	68 (18)	24	28	200	181	55
Towed Artillery	2,085	1,900	22	0	96	12	238(58)	80	395
MRLs	889+	200	9	27	0	4	60	72(24)	165
Mortars	5,000	2,000+	21	78	101	45	400	155	502
SSM Launchers	51	56	0	0	0	0	10	6	30

Light SAM Launchers	?	1,100	78	0	72	0	650	100	800
AA Guns	1,700	6,000	27	0	26	0	10	62	530
Air Force Manpower	30,000	30,000	1,500	2,500	4,100	2,100	20,000	4,000	3,500
Air Defense Manpower	15,000	17,000	0	0	0	0	16,000	0	0
Total Combat Aircraft	283	316	34	82	40	18	348	101	71(40)
Bombers	0	6	0	0	0	0	0	0	0
Fighter/Attack	163+	130	12	40	12	18	100	43	40
Fighter/Interceptor	74+	180	22	14	0	0	181	22	25
Recce/FGA Recce	6	5	0	0	12	0	10	8	0
AEW C4I/BM	1	0	0	0	0	0	5	0	0
MR/MPA**	5	0	0	0	0	0	0	0	0
OCU/COIN/CCT	0	0	0	28	16	0	14	28	0
Other Combat Trainers	35	157	0	0	0	0	50	0	6
Transport Aircraft****	68	12	3	4	16	6	61	21	18
Tanker Aircraft	4	2	0	0	0	0	16	0	0
Total Helicopters	628	375	47	28	30	23	137	105	25
Armed Helicopters****	104	100	40	16	0	19	21	49	8
Other Helicopters****	524	275	7	12	30	4	116	56	17

continued

Table 1.2 (Continued)

	Iran	Iraq	Bahrain	Kuwait	Oman	Qatar	Saudi Arabia*	UAE	Yemen
Major SAM Launchers	250+	400	15	84	40	9	106	39	57
Light SAM Launchers	?	1,100	—	60	28	90	309	134	120
AA Guns	—	6,000	—	60	—	—	340	—	—
Total Naval Manpower	38,000*	2,000	1,000	2,000	4,200	1,730	15,500	2,000	1,500
Regular Navy	15,400	2,000	1,000	2,000	4,200	1,730	12,500	2,000	1,500
Naval Guards	20,000	0	0	0	0	0	0	0	0
Marines	2,600	—	—	—	—	—	3,000	—	—
Major Surface Combatants									
Missile	3	0	3	0	0	0	8	4	0
Other	0	0	0	0	0	0	0	0	0
Patrol Craft Missile	10	1	6	10	6	7	9	8	4
(Revolutionary Guards)	10	—	—	—	—	—	—	—	—
Other	42	5	4	0	7	—	17	6	5
Revolutionary Guards (Boats)	40	—	—	—	—	—	—	—	—
Submarines	6	0	0	0	0	0	0	0	0
Mine Vessels	7	3	0	0	0	0	7	0	6
Amphibious Ships	9	0	0	0	1	0	0	0	1
Landing Craft	9	—	4	2	4	0	8	5	5
Support Ships	22	2	5	4	4	—	7	2	2

Naval Air	2,000	—	—	—	—	—	—
Naval Aircraft							
Fixed Wing Combat	5	0	0	0	0	0	0
MR/MPA	10	0	(7)	0	0	0	0
Armed Helicopters	19	0	0	0	21	(8)	0
SAR Helicopters	—	0	0	0	4	(6)	0
Mine Warfare Helicopters	3	0	0	0	0	0	0
Other Helicopters	19	2	—	—	6	—	0

Note: Equipment in storage shown in the higher figure in parenthesis or in range. Air Force totals include all helicopters, including army operated weapons, and all heavy surface-to-air missile launchers.

*Iranian total includes roughly 100,000 Revolutionary Guard actives in land forces and 20,000 in naval forces.

**Saudi totals for reserve include National Guard Tribal Levies. The total for land forces includes active National Guard equipment. These additions total 450 AIFVs, 730(1,540) APCs, and 70 towed artillery weapons.

***Total tanks include tanks in storage or conversion.

****Includes navy, army, national guard, and royal flights, but not paramilitary.

*****Includes Air Defense Command.

Sources: Adapted by Anthony H. Cordesman from interviews; IISS, *Military Balance*; *Jane's Sentinel*; *Periscope*; and Jaffee Center for Strategic Studies, *The Middle East Military Balance*.

It has anti-submarine warfare (ASW) and mine warfare helicopters, and large stocks of land-based anti-ship missiles, including Silkworms. In addition, the Iranian air force can deliver C-801 anti-ship missiles.

Iran is seeking to acquire modern Soviet combat aircraft and modern surface-to-air missiles, like the Russian S-300 series. It has 120 export versions of the T-72 and 440 BMPs, and is seeking to import or produce more modern armor; however, Iran has not been able to offset the obsolescence and wear of its overall inventory of armor, ships, and aircraft. Additionally, Iran has not been able to modernize key aspects of its military capabilities, such as airborne sensors and combat, command, control, communications and intelligence/battlefield management (C^4I/BM), electronic warfare, land-based air defense integration, beyond-visual-range air-to-air combat, night warfare capabilities, stand-off attack capability, armored sensors and fire control systems, artillery mobility and battle management, combat ship systems integration, and so on.

Even without such modernization, Iran has substantial conventional forces, but it cannot project power against Saudi Arabia by land unless it can cross Iraq. Today, this seems to be a virtually impossible contingency. Iran and Iraq remain hostile and deploy much of their total force strength along their mutual border. Iran is not organized to support and sustain land force maneuvers at any distance from Iran's major bases and lacks the artillery mobility and overall armored strength to conduct rapid maneuvers and deep attacks into Saudi Arabia.

Iran's Amphibious Capabilities

Iran can carry out small amphibious operations. Iran's amphibious ships theoretically give Iran the capability to deploy about 1,000 troops, and about 30 to 40 tanks in an amphibious assault, but Iran has not practiced amphibious operations using heavy weapons and has never demonstrated that it has an effective "forced entry" and across-the-beach over-the-shore capability. Iran might use commercial ferries and roll-on-roll-off ships if it felt they could survive. Iran has also built up its capability to hide or shelter small ships in facilities on its islands and coastline along the Gulf, and the ability to provide them with defensive cover from anti-air and anti-ship missiles. However, all of Iran's training to date has focused on amphibious raiding or largely unopposed transit operations and not on operations using heavy weapons or larger combat operations.

Iran has held several amphibious warfare exercises every year since 1992. The first major exercise following the Iran-Iraq War seems to have been the Great Khaibar exercise in September 1995, which centered on operations near the Strait of Hormuz and Hengam Island, and which involved IRGC naval and marine units and Navy commands operating from Iranian Navy landing ships. There have since been large-scale exercises in every year that has followed.[3]

This amphibious capability allows Iran to pose a tacit or active threat to the southern Gulf states, particularly small, vulnerable states like Bahrain and the UAE. However, Iran's capability to conduct such amphibious and across-the-Gulf operations is currently limited. Unless the Southern Gulf states and the United States permit Iran to use ferries or commercial ships to conduct unopposed landings or transfers of troops, the Iranian Navy and IRGC would have very limited capability. Iran lacks the air and surface power to move its amphibious forces across the Gulf in the face of significant air/sea defenses, or to support a landing in a defended area, and would be highly vulnerable unless its forces achieved total surprise.

Iran's capability to carry out conventional attacks on a southern Gulf state is unlikely to change as long as the United States maintains a major military presence in the Gulf. If Iran was to strike across the Gulf in force, the Iranian Navy and Naval Guards would need much more effective air cover, a stronger surface fleet, and better night vision and targeting systems for their small craft, as well as additional amphibious ships and hovercraft. Large-scale assaults would also require Iran to use commercial ships with roll-on roll-off capability and to practice over-the-beach operations using heavy equipment and armor—training that now is totally lacking.

At the same time, Iran can already use small elements of its naval forces to deploy mines and other unconventional warfare forces covertly, to supply arms to radical movements in the Southern Gulf, seize undefended islands, and threaten or attack offshore oil operations, ports, and desalinization facilities.

Iran's Focused Threat to Gulf Shipping

Iran can also take advantage of the long, vulnerable shipping routes through the Gulf. It has the ability to launch mines, naval or air strikes, and anti-ship missile strikes from positions along the entire length of the Gulf and the Gulf of Oman and to threaten or harass Gulf shipping. While strategists sometimes focus on the threat that Iran could "close the Straits," a bottle does not have to be broken at the neck. Low-level Iranian mine and unconventional warfare strikes on shipping designed to harass and intimidate might allow Iran to achieve at least limited political and economic objectives much more safely than escalating to all-out attacks on the flow of oil.

Iran is funding a carefully focused mix of military capabilities to threaten shipping in the Gulf. This capability already includes the purchase of three Russian submarines with mine-laying capabilities and advanced naval mines. It includes the deployment of a wide range of anti-ship missiles on small craft and in land bases near the main shipping channels through the Gulf. It includes the creation of a large force of Revolutionary Guards equipped for anti-ship and amphibious warfare. As a result, Iran now has enough naval capability stationed along the Gulf coast, in the Strait of Hormuz, and deployable in the Gulf of Oman to harass shipping and require a major Saudi and U.S. response if Iran should take offensive action. Iran has also focused its resources on obtaining long-range missiles and weapons of mass destruction and the ability to fight unconventional warfare.

Gulf shipping not only is vital to the Saudi economy in spite of the fact that it has pipelines and ports on the Red Sea; it also has great strategic importance. Nearly 90% of all the oil exported from the Gulf transits by tanker through this Strait of Hormuz. That is the only passage to the Indian Ocean and world shipping routes. The Strait is the world's most critical oil "chokepoint," and nearly 40% of all the oil traded on world markets transits through a passage between Oman and Iran that is only thirty-seven miles wide at its narrowest point. Tankers and other ships must move through two-mile-wide channels for inbound and outbound tanker traffic, as well as a two-mile-wide buffer zone. In 2002, more than 14 million bbl/d of oil transited the Strait to serve the global economy, much of it going eastwards to Asia—particularly to Japan, China, and India. Other key shipments moved westwards via the Suez Canal, the Sumed Pipeline, and around the Cape of Good Hope in South Africa to Western Europe and the United States.[4]

Any closure of the Strait of Hormuz would require use of much longer alternate routes with limited capacity and higher transportation costs. Such routes include the 5 million bbl/d–capacity East-West Pipeline and the Abqaiq-Yanbu natural gas liquids line pipeline, across Saudi Arabia to Yanbu and ports on the Red Sea. Saudi Arabia has considered creating other pipelines to the Indian Ocean across the UAE and Oman, and even through Yemen to the Gulf of Aden. However, no plans currently exist to fund such facilities.

The security of the Strait of Hormuz is further complicated by a long-standing struggle between Iran and the UAE over the ownership of three islands near the main shipping channels through the lower Gulf: Abu Musa, Greater Tunb Island, and Lesser Tunb Island. The Shah of Iran seized de facto control of these islands when Britain left the Gulf and Iranian troops occupied them in 1992. The Iranian Foreign Ministry claimed that the islands were "an inseparable part of Iran" in 1995.

Iran has rejected proposals first made by the GCC in 1996 for disputer resolution by the International Court of Justice; these proposals were supported by the UAE. Iran has also taken additional steps to strengthen its position on the islands. It set up a power plant on Greater Tunb, opened an airport on Abu Musa, and announced plans for construction of a new port on Abu Musa. Iran did state its willingness to resume talks with the UAE in September 2000, however, and it has not fortified the islands or deployed major forces on them.[5]

Saudi Arabia's position in the Gulf is also vulnerable to Iranian air and missile attacks because its major oil ports and many of its desalination and electric power facilities are open to attack. In addition, its offshore oil fields are vulnerable. These include Khafji and Hout, which are connected to Safaniyah, the world's largest offshore oilfield (with estimated reserves of 19 billion barrels). Other Saudi offshore production includes Arab Medium crude from the Zuluf (over 500,000 bbl/d capacity) and Marjan (270,000 bbl/d capacity) fields, and Arab Heavy crude from the Safaniya field. This vulnerability could grow with time. Saudi Arabia has resolved a long-standing offshore Gulf border dispute with Kuwait, which may lead to the development of the 13-Tcf Dorra gas field, which lies in waters that cross Iranian, Saudi, and Kuwaiti territory.[6]

Iran can also pressure Saudi Arabia with the threat of support for Shi'ite extremists in both Saudi Arabia's Eastern Province and Bahrain, or by using pilgrims to embarrass the Kingdom with riots or protests during the Hajj. In fact, the overt or tacit threat of force—so-called "wars of intimidation"— are currently a more practical option for Iran than actual conflict.

This "focused threat" allows Iran to get the maximum amount of re-gional influence and intimidation per Iranian Rial, and with total military spending that has averaged well under $10 billion a year since 1990. At the same time, it scarcely gives Iran much war fighting capability against any regional coalition that involves the United States, and Iran has good reasons not to become involved in such a war. Iran is highly dependent on its oil export revenues and has no way to export any significant volume of oil except through the Gulf. It cannot defend its oil facilities against U.S. missile and stealth bomber attacks, and its naval and anti-ship missile forces cannot survive for more than a few days to weeks in the face of U.S. mili-tary action. Iran's mine warfare capabilities may pose a threat in terms of long-term harassment, but they cannot block the Gulf. Iran lacks modern land-based air defenses, has limited modern fighter strength, has only about thirty modern attack aircraft (the Su-24), and has no modern airborne sen-sors and command and control assets. Its military forces and bases are open to U.S. retaliation.

Iran and Asymmetric Wars

Iran may be able to counter Saudi, U.S., and allied capabilities—and achieve some of its objectives—through other forms of asymmetric warfare. One such method of attack would be to use direct and indirect threats rather than carry out actual attacks. Iran's ability to fight such "wars of intimi-dation," will improve steadily in the near- to mid-term, in spite of its mili-tary weakness. In many cases, Saudi Arabia's neighbors may be willing to react to such intimidation by accommodating Iran to some degree. This is particularly true of those Southern Gulf states whose gas and oil resources are most exposed—like Qatar—or who perceive Iraq as a more serious threat—like Kuwait.

Iran has steadily improved the capabilities of the Iranian Revolutionary Guard Corps (IRGC), and the Quds Force for other forms of unconventional warfare, including the potential use of chemical and biological weapons. Iran has also demonstrated that it is steadily improving its ability to conduct "proxy wars" by training, arming, and funding movements like the Hezbollah.

Iran is steadily improving capabilities for information warfare and cyber-terrorism, although it seems unlikely that it is capable of advanced attacks on protected U.S. military and U.S. government computer, information, and battle management systems. Iran probably has more capability to attack the United States' private sector and the systems of Gulf States. It also is almost certainly improving the defense of its own systems, which often are land-based and require little more than isolation from netted or open systems to provide a first line of defense.

These capabilities may allow Iran to conduct the kind of low-level and/or covert asymmetric warfare where the "revolution in military affairs" and America's conventional military superiority would be of more limited value. At the same time, any use of such forces is unlikely to drive the United States out of the Gulf, and would risk alienating the Southern Gulf without defeating them. The November 1995 bombing of the National Guard training center and June 1996 bombing of the Al-Khobar Towers in Saudi Arabia demonstrated American vulnerabilities in the Gulf long before September 11. As for proxy wars, it is unclear which terrorist movements are willing to accept such Iranian support and pay the probable political price tag, but the risk can scarcely be ignored.

Iran and Weapons of Mass Destruction

Iran's efforts to acquire chemical, biological, and nuclear weapons—and suitable long-range strike systems—are a more serious threat and are described in detail in Chapter 10. Iran has significant numbers of Scud missiles, extended-range North Korean Scuds, and Chinese CSS-8 missiles, and is developing (and may be deploying) a longer-range Shehab 3 missile. It has extensive stocks of chemical weapons, including mustard and nerve gases, and possibly blood agents. Although it has bought extensive equipment for biological warfare, its capabilities remain unclear. Iran has had a nuclear weapons program since the time of the Shah, but does not seem to have any active enrichment capabilities. It can probably design efficient implosion weapons and produce every component except for the fissile material.

At the same time, weapons of mass destruction do not necessarily make radical changes in Iran's contingency capabilities. Iran's current success in proliferation does give Iran a post–Gulf War edge over Iraq, and inevitably affects Saudi, U.S., British, Israeli, and Southern Gulf perceptions of the risks inherent in any military encounter with Iran.

Much depends upon the collective willingness of Saudi Arabia, the United States, Britain, and Southern Gulf states to take the risk of engaging Iran in the face of such threats, refuse its demands, and respond to Iranian escalation and/or retaliation. It seems unlikely that Iran's "creeping proliferation" will reach the point in the near-term where Iran's capabilities will be great enough to limit or paralyze Saudi, U.S., and allied military action. Further, it seems unlikely that Iran can continue to build up its capabilities without provoking even stronger U.S. counterproliferation programs, including retaliatory strike capabilities. The same is true of a response from Iraq and the Southern Gulf states. As a result, Iran's "creeping proliferation" may end in provoking a "creeping arms race" rather than giving Iran any clear political or military edge.

Such arms races do not, however, always bring deterrence and stability. There are at least four ways that Iran could challenge Saudi security:

- A successful Iranian attempt to buy significant amounts of weapons-grade material that suddenly shifts proliferation from "creeping" to an active and regionally destabilizing threat and potential counter to U.S. conventional capabilities.

- Iranian acquisition of highly lethal biological weapons and/or change in the U.S. and regional perception of biological weapons.

- A case of lateral escalation in which Iraq finds a way to end UN sanctions and/or reveal a substantial break-out capability of its own, creating the risk of a new Iran-Iraq war using weapons of mass destruction that could affect two countries with over 15% of the world's oil reserves and that could spill over into other Gulf states.

- Iranian use of such weapons through proxies or in covert attacks where it had some degree of plausible deniability.

Iran may also become much more threatening in the future. An Iran with large, modern, long-range missile forces armed with biological and/or nuclear weapons would have far more leverage and be far more threatening. There are no short-term missile defense options, and U.S. and Gulf support would be at least somewhat less credible. As is the case with Iraq, weapons of mass destruction may not fundamentally change the military balance in the Gulf, but they will certainly change the Kingdom's perception of risk.

The Military Threat from Iraq

Iraq presents a threat of a very different kind from Iran, although much depends on whether the United States and Britain use force to overthrow Saddam Hussein's regime. While Iran has only limited amphibious capability and has no land borders with Saudi Arabia, Iraq can invade Saudi

Arabia through Kuwait or directly across the flat Saudi-Iraqi border to the west of Kuwait. Saudi Arabia's main oil fields, oil ports, and many of the Kingdom's refinery and petrochemical facilities are near the Upper Gulf coast and within relatively short strike distance from Iraq.

The Iraqi Army and Key Security Elements

In late 2002, the International Institute of Strategic Studies (IISS) estimated that the Iraqi army still could deploy some 375,000 men, organized into seven corps, with two Republican Guards corps and five regular army corps. These forces included six Republican Guards divisions (three armored, one mechanized, and two infantry) plus four Special Republican Guards brigades. The regular army had some sixteen divisions; while eleven were relatively low-grade infantry divisions, three were armored divisions and three were mechanized divisions. The regular army also had five commando and two special forces brigades. While these units lacked modern training, and the regular army units were heavily dependent on conscripts, over one-third were full-time regulars or long-service reservists.

Estimates by U.S. Central Command (USCENTCOM) indicate that the Iraqi land forces have a total strength of 700,000 personnel, including reserves. These estimates indicate that Iraq's major combat formations include seventeen regular army divisions (six heavy and eleven light), and six Republican Guards Divisions (three heavy and three light). USCENTCOM also estimates that the total Iraqi Army order of battle includes six armored divisions, four mechanized divisions, ten infantry divisions, two special forces divisions, one Special Republican Guards or Presidential Guard division, nineteen reserve brigades, fifteen People's Army Brigades, and twenty-five helicopter squadrons.[7]

USCENTCOM and other U.S. experts estimate that Iraqi divisions have an authorized strength of about 10,000 men, and that about half of the twenty-three Iraqi divisions have manning levels of around 8,000 men, and "a fair state of readiness." Republican Guards divisions have an average strength of around 8,000 to 10,000 men. Brigades average around 2,500 men—the size of a large U.S. battalion.[8] Both sets of estimates give Iraq a total force, today, of approximately twenty to twenty-three division-equivalents, versus thirty-five to forty division-equivalents in the summer of 1990, and sixty-seven to seventy division-equivalents in January 1991— just before the Coalition offensives began in the Gulf War.[9]

The Iraqi Army relies on large numbers of combat-worn and obsolescent weapons, but it does have some 700 relatively modern T-72 tanks, 900 BMP-series armored infantry fighting vehicles (AIFVs), 150 self-propelled artillery weapons, and 200 multiple-rocket launchers. It has extensive stocks of AT-3, AT-4, Milan, and High-subsonic Optically Teleguided (HOT) anti-tank guided weapons, and roughly one hundred attack and 275 utility/transport helicopters. The mobile elements of Iraq's 17,000-man Air Defense

Command can deploy large numbers of manportable surface-to-air missiles, plus SA-7, SA-8, SA-9, and Roland vehicle-mounted surface-to-air missiles.

Iraq also has extensive internal security and paramilitary forces. The entire police and law enforcement system performs internal security functions and there are parallel internal security services with units in virtually every town and city. The Republican Guards and Special Republican Guards units are specially trained for urban warfare and security operations as well as conventional military operations, and there are three paramilitary forces. The security troops have some 15,000 men, the border guards around 9,000, and Saddam's Fedayeen consist of 18,000 to 20,000 men.

To put these figures in perspective, the United States had a total force of 55,000 military personnel from all services in the entire theater in June 2002. Many were assigned to the Afghan conflict, with 7,500 in Afghanistan, 1,000 in Pakistan, 1,000 in Kyrgyzstan, 1,700 in Uzbekistan, and 13,000 afloat. In addition, the United States had 5,100 personnel in Saudi Arabia, 3,900 in Qatar, 3,500 in Oman, 4,500 in Bahrain, 850 in the UAE, and 64 in Yemen. (The Gulf numbers had dropped since April because of movements into the theater, and because of cuts in the naval presence that dropped the personnel afloat by 9,000.) The United States had a total of 570 aircraft for the entire CENTCOM area, including the Afghan conflict, which included 195 fixed-wing shooters, 40 attack helicopters, 125 support helicopters, 110 fixed-wing cargo aircraft, 40 ISR aircraft, 60 tankers, and 90 allied coalition aircraft.[10]

The United States did not have any major combat units forward deployed, although it had some combat elements in Kuwait. It had the major combat equipment prepositioned for two mechanized brigades in Kuwait and Qatar and was prepositioning a third in the UAE. These sets, however, did not have first line combat equipment in a number of cases, and did not include support and logistic equipment that required up to another thirty days to deploy. Prepositioning ships at Diego Garcia had the equivalent of another brigade set plus substantial support equipment and supplies, but required eleven to seventeen days to make ready and move. The United States did, however, have substantial supplies and basing facilities in Bahrain, Qatar, the UAE, and Oman plus the air units in forces enforcing the southern no-fly zone in Saudi Arabia.

The Deployment of Iraqi Army and Security Elements

USCENTCOM experts indicate that Iraq's divisions were arrayed north-to-south in 2001, with a mix of regular and Republican Guards divisions. All of the divisions near the Kuwait border are regular, although some Republican Guard divisions could move to the border relatively rapidly. U.S. experts indicate that Iraqi land forces have a total of fourteen divisions in the north, three divisions in central Iraq, and six divisions south of An Najaf. The Republican Guards had a total of three armored divisions deployed in the vicinity of Baghdad—one near Taji, one near Baghdad, and one near As Suwayrah.[11] All Republican Guards divisions are located above the 32-degree line. Additional Republican Guards divisions are located around Baghdad to play a major role in internal security. Several more Republican Guards divisions were located north of Baghdad, closer to the Kurdish area.[12]

Estimates by Jane's indicate that the regular army is organized into five major corps, with seventeen main force division equivalents and major bases at Baghdad, Basra, Kirkuk, and Mosul. There are major training areas west of Baghdad, near Mosul, and in the Marsh areas in the south. The training area southwest of Basra has had only limited use because of the no-fly zones.[13] If one exempts the forces deployed near Baghdad dedicated to the security of the regime, and similar internal security garrisons in Basra and Kirkuk, the army forces were deployed as follows in 2002, before Iraq began to regroup its forces to deal with the risk of a U.S. and British attack:

- Northern Iraq: The 1st Corps is headquartered at Kirkuk and the 5th Corps at Mosul. They guard the Turkish border area and deploy on the edge of the Kurdish enclave and guard the oilfields in the north.

  - The 1st Corps includes the 2nd Infantry Division headquartered at Alrabee, the 5th Mechanized division headquartered at Shuwan, the 8th Infantry Division headquartered at Shuwan, and the 38th Infantry Division headquartered at Quader Karam.

  - The 5th Corps has units defending the border area with Syria. It includes the 1st Mechanized Division headquartered at Makhmur, the 4th Infantry Division headquartered at Bashiqa Maonten, the 7th Infantry Division headquartered at Alton Kopri Castle, and the 16th Infantry Division headquartered near the Saddam Dam and Mosul.

- Eastern Iraq: The 2nd Corps is headquartered at Deyala and is deployed east of Baghdad to defend against Iran or any attack by Iranian-backed Iraqi opposition forces. It includes the 3rd Armored Division headquartered at Jalawia, the 15th Infantry Division headquartered at Amerli, and the 34th Infantry Division headquartered near Khanaqin.

- Southern Iraq has two corps that play a major role in securing Shi'ite areas and suppressing Shi'ite dissidents.

  - The 3rd Corps is headquartered in the Nasseria area, and is positioned near the Kuwaiti border. It includes the 6th Armored Division headquartered near Majnoon and Al Nashwa, the 11th Infantry Division headquartered at Al Naserria, and the 51st Mechanized Division headquartered at Zubair.

  - The 4th corps is headquartered at Al Amara and defends the border with Iran. It includes the 10th Armored Division headquartered near Al Teab and Al Amarra, the 14th Infantry Division headquartered south of Al Amara, and the 18th Infantry Division headquartered near Al Amara and Al Musharah.

The Republican Guards add two more corps, with seven divisions, to this list. The Special Republican Guards add four brigades, which are located largely within Baghdad, are organized to defend the regime:

- *The Northern Corps of the Republican Guards* can act to defend against Iran and operate against the Kurds, but its primary mission seems to be the defense of the greater Baghdad area and Tikrit. The four brigade-sized al Madina al Munawara Armored Division is located at the Al Rashedia and Al Taji camps, and plays a key role in defending the outer Baghdad area. The Special Republican Guards provide protection and defense within the city. The Northern Corps also includes the 1st Adnan Mechanized Division at Mosul, the 2nd Baghdad Infantry Division at Maqloob Maontin-Mosul, and the Al Abed Infantry Division at Kirkuk-Khalid Camp.

- *The Southern Corps of the Republican Guards* is headquartered at Al Hafreia and the Al Fateh al Mubin Command Center. It helps defend against Iran in the south, as well as any U.S.-led attacks, and acts as a deterrent force to suppress any Shi'ite uprisings. Its forces include the Nabu Khuth Nusser Infantry Division at Al Husseinia-al Kutt, the Hamurabi Mechanized Division in the Al Wahda area, and the Al Nedaa Armored Division near Baaquba-Deyla.

The Special Republican Guards had four infantry/motorized brigades with fourteen battalions, an armored brigade, and an air defense command with elements to secure Baghdad's ground-based air defenses against any coup attempt. It had a total active strength of about 12,000 to 15,000, but can rapidly mobilize to 20,000 to 25,000. It was the only force stationed in central Baghdad and in the Republican Palace, although there were also brigades of the Special Security Service (SSO), the Iraqi Intelligence Service (IIS), and secret police in the city.

- The First Brigade is headquartered at Hayy Al-Qadisiyeh in Baghdad and has five battalions, including ones stationed in the Republican palace and at Saddam International Airport. Additional battalions, including plainclothes units, are assigned to protect Saddam while he is in transit, and are assigned to guard other palaces and facilities.

- The Second Brigade is headquartered at the Al Rashid military base and has combat-experience elements outside Baghdad and in the Mosul area.

- The Third Brigade is headquartered at Taji and has four combat battalions to defend Taji and the approaches to Baghdad.

- The Fourth Brigade is motorized and is located at Al Harithiyeh and Al Quadisiyeh, and defends the southern outskirts of Baghdad.

- The Armor Command (Fourth Armored Brigade) has T-72s, BMP-1 and BMP-2s, and two armored regiments—one located at the Abu-Ghraib Camp and another near the Al-Makasib village. They provide armored forces to defend the major entrance points to the city.

An estimate by Amatzia Baram put the total number of men involved in the various internal security and intelligence organizations at over 100,000, and possibly as high as 150,000, excluding the Republican Guards but including some 30,000 in the police forces and 20,000 border guards.[14] The Military Intelligence Service, or Al Estikhbarat al Askariyya, alone was a 3,000- to 5,000-man element with a major complex in the Aladhamia area of Baghdad. It also had a base at the Al Rashid Camp, and elements in Kirkuk, Mosul, and Basra. The Special Branch was organized to carry out covert operations, infiltrate opposition movements, and provide internal security operations within the military. The Military Security Service, or al Amn al Askariyya, reported directly to the Presidential Palace, and deals with subversion within the military forces.

These Iraqi forces have significant limitations. The army and internal security forces have lost many of their personnel with combat experience, have had limited exercise training, and have never mastered combined arms and joint operations by Western standards. They have, however, had ongoing low-level combat experience against the Shi'ite opposition in Southern Iraq, and often deploy to positions opposite Iran and the Kurdish security zone. They do conduct static fire training and limited maneuver training, and the Special Republican Guards, Republican Guards, and security forces are trained for urban warfare and to put down uprisings. The Republican Guards units never broke during the Gulf War, and the army's regular armored, mechanized, and commando/special forces units have generally fought with considerable determination when ordered to do so.

There are other problems. Saddam Hussein exercises tight central control in his self-appointed role as field marshall, and innovation and initiative are often discouraged. Saddam's rotation of commanders to ensure their loyalty; promotion for loyalty or because of tribal origin; the ruthlessness of the security services; and tensions between the regular forces, Republican Guards, Special Republican Guards, and various security services create additional problems. While a number of seemingly convincing reports of security problems, defections, and coup attempts have proved false, at least some seem to be correct. Saddam has also tried on several occasions to create a parallel popular force that would act as a further check on the regular forces. Such forces failed dismally during the Iran-Iraq War, but the latest such effort is the so-called Jerusalem Army, which has been created since the start of the Second Intifada and is under General Iyad Futayyih Khalifa al-Rawi, a former Republican Guards commander. This force is reported to have a goal of twenty-one divisions, but Iraq lacks the experienced cadres, equipment, supplies, and manpower input to build up anything like such a force except at the cost of its other land-force units.[15]

The Iraqi Air Force

The Iraqi Air Force has around 30,000 men. It still has some 316 combat aircraft, although only about 50 to 60% are serviceable. There are other serious readiness problems. The air force has had no new aircraft, missiles, or major combat systems since mid-1990 because of the UN arms embargo resulting from its invasion of Kuwait, and only irregular deliveries of smuggled spare parts and munitions. Senior pilots still fly 60 to 120 hours a year depending on the aircraft, but junior pilots fly as few as 20.

The IISS estimates that the air force has six obsolete H-6D and Tu-22 bombers, and 130 attack aircraft. These include Mirage F-1EQs, Su-20s, forty Su-22s, two Su-24s, and two Su-25s. Iraq still has extensive stocks of short-range air-to-ground missiles and cluster bombs. It also has 180 air defense fighters, including twelve MiG-25s, fifty Mirage F-1EQs, and ten MiG-29s, plus five MiG-25 reconnaissance aircraft. Additionally, the air force has extensive stocks of MiG-21s, training aircraft, and drones, and has experimented with using them as unmanned aerial vehicles (UAVs) and unmanned combat aerial vehicles (UCAVs). It still has two IL-76 tankers and large numbers of transport aircraft. Jane's provides a different estimate with the following key combat types; the number estimated to be in service are shown in parentheses: 40 (0) F-7, 30 (13) Mirage F-1EQ, 36 (15–25) MiG-21, 35 (15–20) MiG-23, 6 (3–6) MiG-25, 17 (1) MiG-29, 33 (15–18) Su-20/22, 21 (6–11) Su-25, 2 T-22, and 3 Tu-16s.[16]

Iraqi Air Force air-to-air and air-to-ground training is limited and unrealistic. In the past, command and control has been over-centralized and mission planning has often set impossible goals. The two no-fly zones have further limited air training and combat experience. There are no modern airborne sensor, command and control, or intelligence capabilities, other than a small number of UAVs. Air control and warning is still heavily dependent on outdated ground-based intercept capabilities. The air force has, however, practiced penetration raids by single low-flying aircraft, and has shown that it can conduct independent offensive operations at the small formation level.

The heavy surface-to-air missile forces of the Iraqi Air Defense Command are still organized into one of the densest defensive networks in the world. There are four regional air defense centers at Kirkuk (north), Kut al Hayy (east), Al Basra (south), and Ramadia (west). Major command facilities are underground and hardened. Additionally, there is a network of redundant radars and optical fiber command links. The system is backed by extensive low-altitude anti-aircraft (AA) guns, and SA-8b, SA-11, and SA-13 short and medium range missiles. The Sterla 2 and 10 (SA-7 and SA-10) are used for terminal defense of key buildings. Iraq has learned to move its fire units and sensors rapidly, and to use urban cover and decoys, "pop-on radar" guidance techniques, and optical tracking. Its mix of SA-2s, SA-3s, and SA-6s is badly outdated, but some modifications have been made.

Iraqi air capabilities have also been heavily impacted by the northern and southern no-fly zones, which have limited Iraqi air operations to the middle of the country since the early 1990s, and which have led to repeated attacks on Iraqi land-based air defense since the expulsion of UNSCOM from Iraq. The expansion of the no-fly zones in September 1996 from the 32nd parallel to the 33rd parallel—to deny Iraqi air movements over most of northern and southern Iraq—and the creation of a de facto no-drive zone south of the 32nd parallel have been particularly important in the case of "Southern Watch."[17] It has sharply limited Iraq's ability to hold land, air, and joint exercises of the kind that could improve Iraqi readiness; allow it to react to the lessons of the Gulf War; and prepare for war against Kuwait and Saudi Arabia. It has given Saudi Arabia, Kuwait, and the United States strategic depth that extends deep into southern Iraq, and made any major Iraqi land and air movements south of the northern boundary of the southern no-fly zone both strategic warning of a possible attack and a potential reason for the United States to begin a military campaign.

The Iraqi Navy

The 2,000-man Iraqi Navy has never been an effective force and was devastated during the Gulf War. It now has only six obsolete Osa and Bogomol guided missile patrol craft, and three obsolete Soviet inshore mine-sweepers. Iraq does, however, retain all of the shore-based Silkworm and other anti-ship missiles it had at the time of the Gulf War, and extensive stocks of mines—some of them relatively modern and sophisticated. (The United States never succeeded in targeting land-based Iraqi anti-ship missiles during the Gulf War, and the U.S. and British navies entered Iraqi mine fields without detecting their presence.)

Iraqi Operational Capabilities

Iraq has demonstrated that it can still carry out significant ground force movements and fly relatively high peak sortie rates. It has not, however, demonstrated training patterns in any part of the country that show its army has consistent levels of training, can make effective use of combined arms above the level of some individual brigades, or has much capability for joint land-air operations. It also has not demonstrated that it can use surface-to-air missiles in a well-organized way as a maneuvering force to cover its deployed land forces.

Iraq's infrastructure is now better than its combat forces. Iraq has been able to rebuild many of the shelters and facilities it lost during the Gulf War, and much of the air force C4I/BM system. This C4I/BM system included an extensive net of optical fiber communications net, a TFH 647 radio relay system, a TFH tropospheric communications system, and a large mix of radars supplied by the Soviet Union. Iraq has rebuilt most of the air bases damaged during the Gulf War, and a number of bases received only limited damage. This gives Iraq a network of some 25 major operating bases, many with extensive shelters and hardened facilities.[18]

Most experts do not believe Iraq has nuclear weapons or has any significant domestic ability to produce fissile materials. Ex-IAEA inspectors do believe, however, that Iraq retains all of the technology needed to rapidly make moderately sized implosion weapons if it can obtain fissile material. It has developed its own initiators, HE lenses, and switching devices. Iraq retains significant capabilities to use and manufacture chemical and biological weapons, and is believed to have anywhere from fifteen to eighty Scud missile assemblies of various types.

Iraq and the Problem of Sanctions and Equipment Modernization

UN sanctions and the Gulf War have had a major impact on Iraqi war fighting capabilities. Iraq has not been able to fund and/or import any major new conventional warfare technology to react to the lessons of the Gulf War, or to produce any major equipment—with the possible exception of limited numbers of Magic "dogfight" air-to-air missiles. Iraq's inability to recapitalize and modernize its forces means that much of its large order of battle is now obsolescent or obsolete, has uncertain combat readiness, and will be difficult to sustain in combat. It also raises serious questions about the ability of its forces to conduct long-range movements or maneuvers, and then sustain coherent operations.

Iraq has maintained much of the clandestine arms-purchasing network that it set up during the time of the Iran-Iraq War. It has prior experience in buying from some 500 companies in 43 countries, and has set up approximately 150 small purchasing companies or agents. Intelligence experts feel that Iraq also has an extensive network of intelligence agents and middlemen involved in arms purchases. Iraq has probably obtained some air defense equipment from countries like the Ukraine and China, and may have been able to smuggle in some spare parts through Syria, Turkey, and Jordan.

Nevertheless, Iraq has not been able to restructure its overall force structure to compensate for its prior dependence on an average of $3 billion a year in arms deliveries. It has not visibly deployed any major new weapon system since 1991, or been able to recapitalize any aspect of its force structure. About two-thirds of its remaining inventory of armor and aircraft is obsolete by Western standards. Iraq has lacked the funds, spare parts, and production capabilities to sustain the quality of its consolidated forces. While it has domestic military production facilities, it is limited to the production of guns and ammunition, and has never succeeded in mass-producing more advanced weapons. Many of its modernization efforts have shown some technical skill, but others have been little more than unintentional technical practical jokes.

In contrast, Saudi Arabia has taken delivery on over $66 billion worth of new arms since 1991, Kuwait has received $7.6 billion, Iran $4.3 billion, Bahrain $700 million, Oman $1.4 billion, Qatar $1.7 billion, and the UAE $7.9 billion. Equally important, the United States has made major upgrades in virtually every aspect of its fighter avionics, attack munitions, cruise missile capabilities, intelligence, reconnaissance, and targeting capabilities.

The Threat of Invasion

At this writing, Iraq seems more likely to be invaded than invade, but it still poses a strategic threat to Saudi Arabia, Kuwait, and the Southern Gulf. Like Iran, Iraq can use the threat of force to conduct "wars of intimidation" if it can avoid the threat of U.S.- and British-led military action, break out of military containment, rebuild its conventional capabilities, and acquire strong missile forces and biological and nuclear weapons. Iraq's ability to intimidate Saudi Arabia could force the Kingdom to change its oil production and pricing policies and to support Iraqi ambitions in the Gulf area. While Saudi Arabia improved its relations with Iraq at the Arab Summit meeting in March 2002, Saudi Arabia fears both Iraqi conventional military capability and Iraq's ongoing covert effort to proliferate and deploy CBRN weapons.

The threat of an actual Iraqi invasion of Saudi Arabia and Kuwait does exist, but should not be exaggerated. Clashes like Desert Fox have shown that Iraq would have to be willing to take extreme risks to engage in any conflict that involves U.S. air forces, and Iraq cannot rebuild its conventional forces quickly even if it breaks out of UN sanctions. It will be years after sanctions on arms imports are finally lifted before any credible combination of Iraqi arms imports, domestic military production efforts, and retraining and reorganization of Iraqi forces can give Iraq enough capability to deliberately initiate a conflict with Saudi Arabia—as long as Saudi Arabia is allied with Britain and the United States.

Nevertheless, Iraq has some near-term contingency capabilities that might allow it to exploit the limits of Saudi and U.S. capabilities and the "revolution in military affairs," particularly if no military effort to overthrow Saddam occurs, and the Saudi-U.S. military relationship should deteriorate. Iraq's forces still retain significant war fighting capabilities and much of the force structure that made Iraq the dominant military power in the Gulf after its victory over Iran. Iraqi forces can still seize Kuwait in a matter of days or occupy part of Saudi Arabia's Eastern Province if they do not face immediate opposition from U.S., Kuwaiti, and Saudi forces.

U.S. experts estimated in June 2002 that a total of twelve Iraqi divisions were effective enough to be used in an attack on Kuwait and/or Saudi Arabia. There were five regular divisions—three relatively combat-ready—in the southern border region north of Kuwait. There were two Republican Guards divisions that could be rapidly deployed to support the three more capable regular divisions in an attack on Kuwait, which USCENTCOM labeled the "Basrah breakout." Iraq could also draw upon four special Republican Guard Brigades, seven commando brigades, and two Special Forces brigades.[19]

Iraq would, however, encounter major problems in assembling and deploying its forces into any kind of coherent invasion force. It would lack both modern air defense weapons and high-quality air support. The Iraqi Air Force had a total of roughly 35,000 to 40,000 men in 2002, including some 15,000 to 17,000 air defense personnel. U.S. estimates indicate that the Iraqi Air Force had 330 to 370 combat aircraft in inventory, while IISS estimates indicate that Iraq had at least 316 combat aircraft, including 6 bombers, 130 fighter-ground attack aircraft, and 180 fighters. Virtually all experts agree, however, that many of the Iraqi aircraft counted in this total had limited or no operational combat capability and Iraqi training and readiness standards were poor.

In fact, some aspects of Iraq's military infrastructure are now better than its combat forces. Iraq has been able to rebuild many of the shelters and facilities it lost during the war, and much of the air force's C4I/BM system. This C4I/BM system included an extensive net of optical fiber communications, a TFH 647 radio relay system, a TFH tropospheric communications system, and a large mix of radars supplied by the Soviet Union. Iraq has rebuilt most of the air bases damaged during the Gulf War, and a number of bases received only limited damage. This gives Iraq a network of some 25 major operating bases, many with extensive shelters and hardened facilities.[20]

The Problem of Kuwait

If the United States and Britain do not take military action to overthrow the regime of Saddam Hussein, Kuwait will be the main potential area of weakness in any defense of the Saudi border area by a Saudi-U.S. coalition. The Saudi-Iraqi border area does not have any major cities or oil facilities and Iraq would have to invade deep into the desert to reach any major Saudi target. An Iraqi seizure of Kuwait, however, would put Iraqi forces on the Saudi border at a point much nearer Saudi Arabia's critical oil facilities and population centers and astride major roads into Saudi Arabia.

USCENTCOM and U.S. experts indicated in June 2002 that Iraq could assemble and deploy five heavy divisions south into Kuwait in a matter of days; it had a total of five Republican Guards divisions within 140 kilometers of Kuwait. Iraqi divisions had an authorized strength of about 10,000 men, and about half of the Iraqi army's twenty-three divisions had manning levels of around 8,000 men and "a fair state of readiness." Republican Guards divisions had an average of around 8,000 to 10,000 men. Brigades averaged around 2,500 men—the size of a large U.S. battalion.

A force of five Iraqi divisions would compare all too favorably with total Kuwaiti forces of about four brigades, with only about a brigade equivalent combat-ready, and with a total forward-deployed U.S. strength that normally did not include a single forward-deployed land brigade. The Saudi forces at Hafr al Batin were at most the equivalent of one combat-effective brigade that was trained and exercised to fight defensively near its peacetime base; this brigade could require two weeks to fully deploy forward to the Kuwait and Saudi borders in sustainable, combat-ready form. The so-called GCC rapid deployment force is largely a political faction, with little meaningful real-world combat capability against Iraqi heavy divisions. Moreover, the new agreements that the GCC signed in 2000, 2001, and 2002 to strengthen this force, promise to produce little substantive action to change what is little more than a military façade.

USCENTCOM indicates that Kuwait could only deploy less than two brigade-equivalent battalions to defend its territory, and Saudi Arabia would take days to deploy even one heavy brigade into areas north of Kuwait City. The tyranny of geography, Kuwait's small size, and Saudi Arabia's widely dispersed army would give Iraq an advantage in land combat in any sudden or surprise attack. The failure of Kuwait and Saudi Arabia to make more than limited cooperative defense efforts compounds the problem, as does Saudi Arabia's poor performance in modernizing its land forces and giving its air force offensive capability.

Kuwait dreamed of a twelve-brigade force after the Gulf War, but it only has two under-strength active brigades and two reserve brigades. Its land forces total only 11,000 personnel, and this total includes 1,600 foreign contract personnel, most of whom are noncombatants. The total manpower of the Kuwaiti armed forces, including the air force and navy, totals about one U.S. brigade "slice" (combat manpower plus support). The Kuwaiti army has an active tank strength of only about 75 M-84s (Yugoslav T-72s) and 174 M-1A2s.

As discussed in detail later in this analysis, Saudi forces also have important weaknesses. The Saudi army has reverted to a static defensive force that has limited effectiveness above the company and battalion level. Although according to Saudi reports, it has 75,000 full time regulars in the army, plus 75,000 active members of the National Guard, actual manning levels are significantly lower. Some of its M-1A2 tanks are still in storage, plus about 145 of its 290 obsolescent AMX-30s. As a result, Saudi Arabia relies heavily on its active M-1A2s and 450 M-60A3s. This is still a significant amount of armor, but it is dispersed over much of the Kingdom, and Saudi Arabia lacks the training; manpower quality; sustainability; and command, control, communications, computer, intelligence/surveillance and reconnaissance (C^4I/SR) capabilities for effective aggressive maneuver warfare and forward defense.

The United States built up its forces in the Gulf significantly in 2002 in preparation for a major military action to overthrow Saddam Hussein. Before that time, however, the United States only had elements of one heavy brigade prepositioned in Kuwait, but it took at least fourteen to twenty-one days to fully man, deploy, and sustain this brigade. The U.S. Army was able to deploy another two relatively light brigades in full combat-ready form in eighteen to thirty days, but the brigade set prepositioned in Qatar took several weeks to deploy to the Kuwaiti border area, and the division support set propositioned in Qatar normally could not deploy in full combat-effective form until M+27 to M+35. The U.S. Army brigade set prepositioned on ships near Diego Garcia took nearly a month to deploy in sustainable combat form. The U.S. Marine Corps has another light division equivalent and air wing that it could deploy as a Marine Expeditionary Force, but this force took at least three weeks to fully deploy. It also lacked heavy armor and the Marine Corps' readiness has been seriously underfunded in recent years.

Iraq remains acutely vulnerable to U.S. and British air power and cannot match Saudi Arabia in air combat capability. Unless there are weeks of strategic warning, however, Kuwait, Saudi Arabia, and the United States will lack the land forces to stop Iraq without immediately committing massive amounts of air and missile strikes against the advancing Iraqi forces and Iraqi strategic targets.

There is no way to predict whether the United States and British military buildup in Iraq will remove Saddam Hussein's regime from the equation, or what force capabilities will exist in the Gulf in the future. Even if U.S. and British force levels drop and Saddam is not replaced, Iraqi land forces might be able to penetrate into Kuwait City—despite strikes by U.S., Saudi, and Kuwaiti air power—if Iraq was willing to take very high losses in reaching and seizing the city. If Iraq then attempted to take the Kuwaiti population hostage, it might succeed. USCENTCOM experts privately speculate that the United States would at best have a 50-50 chance of preventing Iraq from occupying Kuwait City. The only way that Iraqi forces could then be dislodged would be through a combination of another land buildup in Saudi Arabia by the United States and allied forces, and a massive strategic/interdiction air campaign against targets on Iraqi territory.

If Saddam Hussein's regime does survive, any coalition's ability to deal with a sudden Iraqi attack on Kuwait is likely to depend on U.S. ability to mass offensive air and missile power and use it immediately against

Iraq the moment major troop movements begin, without first seeking to win air superiority or air supremacy. It will depend on U.S. willingness and ability to couple strikes against Iraqi leadership and strategic targets to this offensive in an effort to force Iraq to halt its offensive, and U.S. ability to deter, defend, and retaliate against any Iraqi use of weapons of mass destruction.

Even then, preventing an Iraqi occupation of Kuwait City could be a difficult task if Iraq were willing to absorb the damage done by U.S. and allied air and missile power. A Saudi-U.S. coalition could be confronted with an asymmetric war in which Iraq ruthlessly exploited the suffering of the Iraqi people to force a halt to U.S. military action. Kuwaiti government security experts have, in fact, postulated a far worse case in which Iraq uses overt or covert attacks with biological weapons to effectively destroy Kuwait as a nation and create new facts on the ground.

In such a worst-case contingency, the essential dilemma in any "second liberation" of Kuwait would be U.S., Saudi, and Kuwaiti willingness to act in the face of potential massacres of Kuwaiti civilians, versus the willingness of an Iraqi regime to accept massive damage to Iraq. It seems likely that the United States and Saudi Arabia would show the necessary ruthlessness if the Kuwaiti government supported such action. Oil is too strategically important to cede such a victory to a leader like Saddam Hussein.

Once again, much depends on whether Saddam Hussein survives the threat of U.S.- and British-led action. Defending Kuwait will also become an increasingly "close run thing" if Iraq can escape the effect of sanctions and improve its ability to modernize and rebuild its war fighting capability. There are a number of ways in which Iraq might then increase the challenge it could pose to U.S. capabilities and the "revolution in military affairs" without acquiring similar military technologies and capabilities:

- Iraq may somehow obtain nuclear weapons, or demonstrate the possession of highly lethal biological weapons.
- The United States might be forced to reduce its forward presence and readiness in the Gulf to the point where it could not rapidly deploy air power and/ or reduce its overall power projection capabilities. This could occur either as a result of U.S. domestic political and funding issues or added Iranian and Iraqi success in their diplomatic campaigns to limit the U.S. role in the region.
- Iraq may choose a more limited and "acceptable" objective like restoring its pre–Gulf War border or demanding access to Bubiyan, Warbah, the Kwar Abdullah, and the Gulf. This might make it harder for the United States to obtain support from its other regional allies and/or nations outside the Gulf.
- Improvements in relations with Saudi Arabia might create a situation in which Saudi Arabia may not immediately and fully support U.S. action and commit its own forces.

- Kuwait's government may feel it faces so serious an increase in the Iraqi threat that it would refuse to accept the cost of continuing to fight in the face of ruthless Iraqi action against a "hostage" Kuwaiti people.

Iraq's Capabilities in Other Contingencies

The situation would be far more favorable to a Saudi-U.S. coalition in any contingency that did not involve Kuwait. Iraq has almost none of the assets necessary to win a naval-air battle against U.S. forces in the Gulf, and has no prospect of acquiring these assets in the foreseeable future. It would have to rebuild, modernize, and massively expand both its regular navy and air force to levels of strength and capability it is unlikely to achieve for the next half-decade. Alternatively, Iraq could develop its capabilities to deliver weapons of mass destruction to the point where it could support its conventional military capabilities with a threat that might seriously inhibit U.S. military action and/or the willingness of Southern Gulf states to support the United States and provide air and naval facilities.

Unlike Iran, Iraq cannot conduct meaningful surface ship, naval air force, or amphibious operations. Currently, the Iraqi navy can only conduct limited mine warfare and land-based anti-ship missile attacks, and surprise raids on offshore facilities. Its air force may be able to conduct limited anti-ship missile attacks using its Mirage F-1s, but would have to find a permissive environment to survive. Iraqi Mirage F-1s burdened with the AM-39 Exocet would be unlikely to survive Kuwaiti, Saudi, or Iranian air defenses without a level of air escort capability that Iraq cannot currently provide.

Iraq also faces the counterthreat posed by the United States. Iraq has little ability to intimidate its neighbors into accepting such operations as long as the United States has the ability to use its air and missile power to inflict enough strategic damage on Iraq to create a massive deterrent to any Iraqi escalation to chemical or biological weapons, and can back these capabilities with the ultimate threat of U.S. theater nuclear escalation. There is little near-term prospect that Iraq will develop enough power projection capability—and supporting power from its navy, air force, and weapons of mass destruction—to win any conflict in the Southern Gulf where it did not attack by land into Kuwait or across the Saudi border. The only exception might be a case in which it operated in support of a coup or uprising, as when Iraqi volunteers operated in southern Yemen in 1994. Any Iraqi attack on a Southern Gulf state is also the contingency most likely to unite the United States and the Southern Gulf states and to ensure European and other support for a strong U.S.–Southern Gulf response.

This does not mean that Iraqi air and/or naval forces could not score some gains from a sudden, well-planned raid in the Gulf, or challenge U.S. military capabilities in some ways. Iraq could not sustain any initial success, however, and would probably accomplish nothing more than provoking a

U.S., Southern Gulf, or Iranian reaction that would far offset any advantages Iraq could gain. The only exception might be a proxy unconventional or terrorist attack that would allow Iraq to preserve some degree of plausible deniability.

Like Iran, however, Iraq is not limited to the war fighting capabilities of conventional military forces. Iraq may be able to achieve some of its objectives through intimidation and/or direct and indirect threats. Iraq certainly understands that asymmetric warfare is a potential counter to U.S. superiority and the "revolution in military affairs." It has steadily sought to improve its capabilities in these areas since 1991. Iraq's neighbors have already increasingly accommodated Iraq to some degree in the face of tacit Iraqi threats and overt political pressure, and this includes even those neighbors that see Iraq as a more serious threat—like Kuwait and Saudi Arabia.

Unlike Iran, Iraq has not demonstrated much recent capability to conduct "proxy wars" by training, arming, and funding Arab extremist movements. Iraq does sponsor some extremist and terrorist groups, but the end result has done little for Iraq. Iraq also lacks Iran's bases, training centers, and staging facilities in other countries, and the political support of third nations like the Sudan and Syria, which are close to the scene of such proxy conflicts. Similarly, Iraq can only hope to win proxy wars fought against vulnerable governments. Attempts to fight such wars will have little impact on a successful Arab-Israeli peace settlement or in sustaining civil conflict in the face of a government that demonstrates that it has the capacity to govern and deal with its social problems.

Iraq has some capability for information warfare and cyber-terrorism, but it seems very unlikely that it is capable of advanced attacks on protected U.S. military and U.S. government systems. Iraq also probably has little capability to attack the U.S. private sector and the systems of Gulf states. It is, however, steadily improving the defense of its own systems. Most are redundant, rely heavily on buried land-links and optical fibers, and are isolated from netted or open systems.

At the same time, any dramatic failure of the peace process or instability in the regimes in the Gulf and the region might allow a hostile Iraq to make more successful use of proxy wars in the future. So too would the creation of a radical Arab regime in Jordan, Egypt, or Syria, which might turn to Iraq for support. Iraq also has a strong revanchist motive to use proxy warfare against Israel, Saudi Arabia, and the United States. Similarly, Iraq may seek to improve its capabilities for unconventional warfare, including the use of chemical and biological weapons. The practical problem that Iraq faces will be to find a place and contingency where it could exploit such capabilities that offer more return than using proxies, and which allows Iraq to act at an acceptable level of risk so that the United States and its allies would not retaliate.

Much will depend upon regional perceptions of the long-term resolve of the United States, the ability of the Southern Gulf states to avoid major divisions, and the willingness of those states to show that they will support a firm U.S. response to Iraq, even at some risk. Much will also depend on the ability of Iraq's leadership to set achievable demands and avoid open confrontation.

Iraq and Weapons of Mass Destruction

Iraq has seen proliferation as a counter to conventional superiority since the late 1960s. It sought weapons of mass destruction long before the Gulf War showed it what the "revolution in military affairs" (RMA) and U.S. conventional superiority could accomplish. As a result, it is hardly surprising that Iraq sees proliferation as its key potential method of countering the U.S. advantage in conventional forces and the RMA, and has been willing to pursue such options in the face of massive economic costs, UNSCOM and IAEA efforts to destroy its remaining capabilities, and the extension of UN sanctions.

In spite of the Gulf War, and nearly eight years of UNSCOM efforts before Iraq forced an end to UN inspections, Iraq still presents a major threat in terms of proliferation. It is all too clear that Iraq may have increased this threat since active UNSCOM and IAEA efforts ended in December 1998. At the same time, Iraq's present holdings of chemical and biological weapons may well be too limited to seriously constrain U.S. military freedom, or to seriously intimidate Iraq's neighbors.

As a result, even if Saddam Hussein's regime survives, it seems unlikely that Iraq can reach the point, before 2005–2007, where its capabilities are great enough to change Saudi, U.S., British, Iranian, Israeli and/or Southern Gulf perceptions of risk to the point where they would limit or paralyze military action in response to any serious Iraqi threats or attacks. Furthermore, it seems unlikely that Iraq can openly build up major production and deployment capabilities without provoking strong U.S. counterproliferation activity, including preemptive military action. They are also likely to provoke a response in kind by Iran and the Southern Gulf states. As a result, Iraq's acquisition of weapons of mass destruction may end simply in provoking an arms race even if UN sanctions should fail.

Nevertheless, Iraq's possession of weapons of mass destruction inevitably affects U.S., British, Israeli and Southern Gulf perceptions of the risks inherent in attacking Iraq at some level. Moreover, if UN sanctions on Iraq are lifted, Iraq may be able to rebuild its strategic delivery capabilities relatively quickly, and any sustained conflict involving weapons of mass destruction could have drastic consequences. This would be particularly true if Iraq could develop advanced biological weapons with near-nuclear lethality, or assemble nuclear devices with weapons-grade fissile material bought from an outside source. There might be little or no warning of such strategic developments, and the United States might not be willing to counter by extending theater nuclear deterrence to protect its Southern Gulf allies.

As is the case with Iran, there are several other developments that might allow Iraq to use proliferation to pose a near-term threat to U.S. conventional capabilities in the region:

- A successful Iraqi attempt to buy significant amounts of weapons-grade material. This could allow Iraq to achieve a nuclear breakout capability in a matter of months. Both the United States and the region would find it much harder to adjust to such an Iraqi effort than to the slow development of nuclear weapons by creating fissile material in Iraq. It seems likely that the United States could deal with the situation by extending a nuclear umbrella over the Gulf, but even so, the Southern Gulf states might be far more responsive to Iraqi pressure and intimidation. Most, after all, are so small that they are virtually "one-bomb states."

- A change in the United States and regional perception of biological weapons. Biological weapons are now largely perceived as unproven systems of uncertain lethality. Regardless of their technical capabilities, they have little of the political impact of nuclear weapons. Iraq might, however, conduct live animal tests to demonstrate that its biological weapons have near-nuclear lethality or some other power might demonstrate their effectiveness in another conflict. The successful mass testing or use of biological weapons might produce a rapid paradigm shift in the perceived importance of such weapons and of Iraq's biological warfare programs.

- Iraq might break out of UN sanctions and reveal a more substantial capability than now seems likely. Paradoxically, such an Iraqi capability would help to legitimize Iran's and Israel's nuclear, biological, and chemical programs and the escalation to the use of such weapons.

- Iraq might use such weapons through proxies or in covert attacks with some degree of plausible deniability. Terrorism and unconventional warfare would be far more intimidating if it made use of weapons of mass destruction.

PLANNING FOR A FULL RANGE OF THREATS

The Kingdom cannot plan its military forces around the certainty of a moderate Iran or a contained Iraq. Even if Saddam Hussein's regime is driven from power or moderate elements do come to dominate Iranian politics, it cannot predict their future rate of convention of modernization and it faces a serious risk that either or both states will have extremely lethal weapons of mass destruction and effective delivery systems. Iran and Iraq can also threaten other Southern Gulf states and have at least some capability to conduct "proxy wars" against the Kingdom by providing funds, arms, and training to extremists inside Saudi Arabia. The Kingdom must plan for both current and future threats, and for both conventional and asymmetric wars.

The Challenge from the Red Sea

One threat has eased: Saudi Arabia has greatly improved its relations with Yemen in recent years, and Yemen has failed seriously to modernize its shrinking military forces for nearly half a decade. Nevertheless, Yemen is a poor and highly populated nation with a population roughly equal to that of Saudi Arabia, and has claimed Saudi Arabia's southeastern Asir region in the past. Saudi military planners still quietly regard Yemen as one of the three major threats it must shape its forces to deal with.

More generally, Saudi Arabia must plan to protect its Red Sea coast against other potential threats. Major port and desalination facilities on the coast and major Saudi oil export and petrochemical facilities that are served by the Saudi East-West pipeline to the port of Yanbu, Jeddah, Makkah, and Medina are also linked to Red Sea security. While the stability of Yemen, Somalia, Eritrea, Ethiopia, and the Sudan have improved since the late 1990s, all are troubled and somewhat unstable states.[21]

The entrances to the Red Sea have two major potential chokepoints that could affect Saudi security. Tankers heading west from the Gulf must pass through the Bab al-Mandab, which is located between Djibouti and Eritrea in Africa, and Yemen on the Arabian Peninsula. Any closure of the Bab al-Mandab could keep tankers from reaching the Suez Canal/Sumed Pipeline complex and force them to divert around the southern tip of Africa. After tankers move through the Bab al-Mandab, they must pass either through the Suez Canal or the Sumed Pipeline complex in Egypt that connect the Red Sea and Gulf of Suez with the Mediterranean Sea. In 2001, roughly 3 million bbl/d of Gulf oil exports passed through the Suez Canal/Sumed complex. Any closure of the Suez Canal and/or Sumed Pipeline would again divert tankers around the southern tip of Africa (the Cape of Good Hope), greatly increasing transit time and cost and sharply reducing available tanker capacity.[22]

The Challenge from Israel, Jordan, and Syria

It is difficult to foresee a contingency that could lead to a direct conflict between Saudi Arabia and Israel. Israel has nuclear weapons, missiles, and an overwhelming conventional superiority or "edge." In 2002, Saudi Arabia led the Arab world in proposing a comprehensive peace settlement with Israel. It is not organized to project military power into an Arab-Israeli conflict and Israel has no incentive to broaden a conflict to include Saudi

Arabia. At the same time, Saudi Arabia cannot ignore that fact that conflicts and escalation are always unpredictable, or leave its Western territory unshielded. It needs some level of air defense and ability to discourage Israeli overflights.

Saudi Arabia may be able to plan for little or no military involvement in any Arab-Israeli conflict, but it cannot avoid some risks. Those include involvement in limited clashes, over border areas, and air space. They included Arab demands for at least token Saudi military involvement in any major escalation of the Second Intifada or new Arab-Israeli conflict, and they include serious problems in military relations with the United States. Israel presents a serious indirect threat to Saudi Arabia. Its continuing struggle with the Palestinians and Syria means that Saudi Arabia faces constant pressure from the Arab world and many Saudis to reduce its ties to the United States—Israel's closest ally. At the same time, Israel has often put pressure on U.S. administrations or Congress to limit U.S. arms sales to Saudi Arabia or to pressure Saudi Arabia to limit its support to Palestinians.

Saudi Arabia also has to be concerned about the future stability of Jordan if the Second Intifada continues to escalate. There could be demands on Jordan to end its peace with Israel or allow some presence from Iraqi forces and other volunteers in support of the Palestinians. As a worst-case scenario, Saudi Arabia must consider the risk of the collapse of Hashemite rule and the threat that a radical Palestinian state could emerge on its western border. Saudi Arabia also cannot totally distance itself from developments in Syria and Lebanon. Any major military escalation on Israel's northern front would again exacerbate the problems in Saudi military fees to Israel's closest allies.

The Challenge of Saudi and Egyptian Military Relations

Saudi Arabia does not face any military threat from Egypt. It is generally a political and diplomatic ally, although it is a past enemy and sometimes a rival. Egypt is, however, the only Arab military power potentially strong enough to land the Kingdom in a serious conflict with Iran and Iraq. The Gulf War showed, however, that Egyptian forces have limited power projection capability. Egyptian forces were slow to advance against Iraq for political reasons, and Egypt made requests for aid that Saudi military planners felt exceeded the value of the contributions they could make.

THE CHALLENGE FROM THE UNITED STATES AND THE WEST

Saudi relations with the United States pose a growing strategic challenge of a very different kind. Saudi Arabia is caught up in the dilemma that it has no current prospect of being able to develop forces strong enough to meet its regional strategic challenges alone. This makes it dependent on a foreign power—the United States. The United States, however, is non-Muslim and Israel's closest ally. The U.S. view of how to deal with the political and security issues in the Middle East often differs from that of Saudi Arabia.

The U.S. military presence in Saudi Arabia also presents problems for the Kingdom in terms of cultural differences and a hostile reaction to U.S. foreign policy and support of Israel in the Second Intifada, and from those Saudis who oppose a Western presence of any kind. Many Islamists resent any U.S. presence on Saudi soil, and many Saudi officials and officers question the U.S. approach to Iran and Iraq. Above all, the Second Intifada has led to steadily growing resentment of U.S. ties to Israel within the Saudi population as a whole and in the rest of the Arab and Islamic world.

Saudi Arabia initially reacted to the Gulf War by expanding its security arrangements with the United States. The United States and Saudi Arabia expanded the U.S. Military Training Mission (USMTM) agreement to increase U.S. access to Saudi air and seaports, including Jubail, and improved the joint warfare capabilities of their AWACS force.[23] Saudi Arabia allowed the U.S. Air Force (USAF) to regularly rotate combat units in and out of Saudi air bases, and the USMTM increased its peacetime manning to roughly seventy military, five civilian, and ten local personnel. Saudi Arabia increased its stocks of selected spares and electronics to support U.S. force deployment—including enough parts and supplies to support fifteen USAF tactical fighter equivalents. It increased the number of joint exercises with U.S. forces.[24] It standardized key aspects of its C⁴I system to make them interoperable with U.S. C⁴I systems, including theater missile defense arrangements for Saudi Arabia's Patriot missiles. Saudi Arabia also ordered $1.6 billion worth of U.S. military construction services between 1991 and 1995.[25]

Yet, significant problems emerged in U.S. and Saudi cooperation that affected the size and nature of the U.S. presence on Saudi soil. Saudi Arabia rejected U.S. proposals to preposition two division sets of ground combat equipment in Saudi Arabia—although the United States could have left such equipment there when its forces completed their withdrawal from the Gulf at the end of 1991.[26] This rejection was partly a result of Saudi concern with the opposition from Islamic fundamentalists and partly a result of an unrealistic Saudi sensitivity to the nuances of sovereignty. At the same time, the United States was slow to understand a Saudi emphasis on informal cooperation and low-profile activities rather than the kind of formal and highly visible arrangements that the United States preferred. Saudi internal and external stability has long depended on keeping strategic cooperation as quiet as possible, while the United States has long been insistent on formal and public arrangements.

According to some reports, Saudi Arabia did offer to allow U.S. Army prepositioning of major armor, artillery, and other equipment in Saudi warehouses at Saudi cost, and under joint U.S.-Saudi guard. The United States insisted on a formal status of forces agreement, flying the U.S. flag, total U.S. control of the facility, and large numbers of U.S. personnel. It presented a U.S. plan, complete with lengthy computer lists of additional equipment. Saudi officials have privately indicated that the Kingdom then rejected the U.S. plan because of the way in which it was presented, and because the United States insisted on an overt basing facility that openly violated the royal family's pledge to the Islamic clergy not to grant bases or formally base non-Muslim forces in the Kingdom. The U.S. plan would almost certainly have resulted in a crisis with hard-line Islamic fundamentalists.

These problems did not block improvements in other forms of cooperation. Saudi Arabia reached an agreement for joint U.S. and Saudi land force training in September 1991, and exercises have been held regularly since that time. This cooperation has proved vital to maintaining the interoperability of the Saudi and U.S. air forces, as has continued cooperation in training, exercises, acquiring stockpiles of munitions and supplies, designing repair and maintenance facilities, improving C^4I/BM systems, and a host of other factors.[27]

During the 1990s, the United States strengthened Saudi-U.S. cooperation by reshaping its strategy and force plans to rely more on informal cooperation, concentrate the U.S. military presence in areas with less political visibility, and rely more on prepositioning outside the Kingdom. While such efforts have accelerated since the beginning of the Second Intifada and September 11, they are not new. They were first reflected in the recommendations made during the "Bottom Up Review" of U.S. defense plans for fiscal years 1995–1999 that Secretary of Defense Les Aspin made public on September 1, 1993.

The United States dealt with its problems in land-force prepositioning by maintaining a seven-ship maritime prepositioning squadron at Diego Garcia, and by expanding its presence in Kuwait, Bahrain, Qatar, the UAE, and Oman—rather than Saudi Arabia. The United States is now prepositioning equipment on land for one brigade in Kuwait, one in Qatar, and one in the UAE. The United States prepositioned one "swing" brigade set at sea that would normally be deployed afloat near the Gulf, but which could go to Asia or elsewhere in the world. Once complete, this prepositioning will allow at least one U.S. heavy division to deploy against Iraq within fourteen to twenty-one days.

The United States concluded, however, that Saudi sensitivities to a large-scale U.S. land presence, even in the form of centers with prepositioned equipment, would force the United States to rely on more limited prepositioning in other countries and on the periodic deployment of U.S. forces in exercises and other training activity.[28] As a result, the United States emphasized cooperation with Saudi Arabia in maintaining a limited presence of U.S. air units, in improving Saudi-U.S. C⁴I/BM capabilities, in making Saudi air and land forces interoperable with U.S. forces, and in improving Saudi basing and infrastructure to support both Saudi and U.S. forces in defending Kuwait and meeting other defensive needs in the Gulf.

This approach paid off for both Saudi Arabia and the United States in August 1992, when the United States, Britain, and France established a no-fly zone over Iraq. Saudi Arabia not only allowed U.S. aircraft to operate, but also provided refueling tankers, combat air defense patrols, and support from Saudi AWACs. This support was critical to the United States, Britain, and France since it allowed them to establish the no-fly zone over Iraq with less than 150 aircraft—they would have had to provide roughly 100 more aircraft without Saudi support. At the same time, it contained Saddam Hussein at minimum risk to Saudi Arabia.

Saudi Arabia continued to provide the United States with extensive host nation support and defense cost sharing equal to 86% of the cost of stationing U.S. forces in the Kingdom. It provided over $2 million in direct support in 2000, and nearly $80 million in indirect support.[29]

During the late 1990s, the United States also began to make major adjustments in the "visibility" of its military presence in Saudi Arabia in response to terrorist attacks, and did so long before the attacks on the World Trade Center and the Pentagon in September 2001. The United States not only reduced its overall manpower presence in the Kingdom; it relocated much of its presence in Saudi Arabia to an isolated base in the desert south of Riyadh after the Islamic extremist attacks on the Saudi National Guard headquarters and on the USAF barracks in Al Khobar.

The events of September 11, 2001, have, however, made the problems in Saudi and U.S. military cooperation much worse, as have unresolved differences between Saudi Arabia and the United States over the need to overthrow Saddam Hussein's regime by force. The fact that Saudis were the leading participants in the attack on the World Trade Center and the Pentagon came as a shock to both nations. So did the level of Saudi Islamist extremist participation in al Qaeda and the fighting in Afghanistan. Media reaction in both countries degenerated into a mud-slinging contest, and a Saudi political tendency to deny the facts interacted with sweeping congressional charges that often seemed to attack all Saudis and Islam. By mid-2002, U.S. calls to remove Saddam Hussein's regime had added new problems: Saudi Arabia saw Iraq as a threat that could be dealt with by continuing containment.

At the same time, the deterioration of the Second Intifada has increased Saudi popular hostility to U.S. support of Israel as well as that of the Saudi government. These were issues long before September 11, and had already undercut the U.S.-Saudi alliance. So, at a different level, have Saudi and U.S.

tensions over the U.S. military presence in Saudi Arabia. The United States
felt Saudi Arabia was too slow and too grudging in allowing the United
States to use its facilities for the war in Afghanistan. Saudi Arabia, however, was still irritated by the fact that the United States had unilaterally
reinforced its forces in the Kingdom in 1998 and had used them to strike
Iraq in Operation Desert Fox without Saudi Arabia's permission. Similarly,
U.S. forces in Southern Watch had struck well north of the 33rd parallel
in the first major strike on Iraqi air defenses on February 16, 2001, in spite
of an agreement not to strike north of the 32nd parallel without Saudi permission. This fear of U.S. unilateralism was compounded by the fact that
the United States kept some 25,000 short tons of air munitions prepositioned in Saudi Arabia in spite of repeated calls by Prince Sultan to
reduce these stockpiles to levels around 5,000 short tons.

Terrorist attacks on U.S. forces in Saudi Arabia had already led the
United States to cut its presence in Saudi Arabia sharply during the late
1990s and move much of its manpower and facilities to other Southern Gulf
states or back to the United States. The United States had only 4,861 military personnel in Saudi Arabia before the attacks on the World Trade Center
and the Pentagon in September 2001, out of a total of 10,317 in all of the
GCC states. While it has made major temporary increases in its deployments
in Kuwait, Bahrain, the UAE, and Oman after September 2001 to deal with
the war in Afghanistan and a possible strike on Saddam Hussein's regime,
it made minor further reductions in its presence in Saudi Arabia.[30]

There are sharp limits to how much the United States can continue these
reductions and still meet Saudi security needs. The United States is located
half a world away from Saudi Arabia, and cannot keep its forces "over-
the-horizon." It needs access to Saudi bases, as much standardized and interoperability with Saudi forces as possible, common training, interoperable
command and control systems, and some level of prepositioning. Rapid
power projection is only possible with a forward presence in the Gulf, and
effective coalition warfare capabilities cannot be suddenly improvised in a
crisis. Furthermore, Saudi Arabia needs continuing U.S. support for its
military modernization and joint training.

The United States is not the Kingdom's only Western military partner.
Saudi Arabia has turned to Britain for help in modernizing its air forces in
order to help reduce its dependence on the United States, and the risk that
friction with Israel might lead the U.S. Congress to limit arms transfers to
the Kingdom. It has turned to France as a major supplier of naval weapons. The fact remains, however, that the United States is the only country
with sufficient power projection capability to deter Iran and Iraq and provide Saudi Arabia with security.

Similarly, Saudi interoperability with U.S. forces and U.S. rapid deployment capability are both key factors in regional deterrence and Saudi ability to fight any large-scale joint or combined-arms warfare. There are also

problems in the integrity of the British and French arms sales efforts. Neither Britain nor France put the same kind of controls on their arms sales as the United States does when they are conducted under the Foreign Military Sales (FMS) program managed by the Department of Defense. While U.S. FMS are anything but perfect—and there has been some corruption in the handling of transportation arrangements and offset programs—there is substantially more corruption and waste in non-U.S. programs. This is particularly true of the massive al-Yamamah program that Saudi Arabia has bought from Britain and France.

THE CHALLENGE FROM THE GCC AND THE GULF

Saudi Arabia also faces challenges from its allies in the Southern Gulf. The GCC has tried for more than two decades to create an effective degree of military cooperation and interoperability between all of the Gulf states but has only had limited success. At the same time, Saudi Arabia has made only slow progress in bilateral and multilateral military cooperation with Bahrain and Kuwait.

This lack of effective military cooperation within the Southern Gulf makes Saudi Arabia overdependent on the United States and the West. The GCC is nearly two decades old, but has achieved little in integrating and improving the war fighting capabilities of its member states. The present GCC rapid deployment force, which is stationed in Saudi Arabia near the Iraqi Saudi border, has little or no war fighting capability, and recent GCC agreements to increase this force sharply have been largely symbolic—countries simply agreed to assign more forces to the contingency mission. Saudi Arabia's security is heavily dependent on the security of neighbors like Bahrain, Kuwait, Oman, Qatar, and the UAE. Saudi Arabia, however, cannot provide these states with more than limited additional defense capability and they are far too weak to defend themselves.

The Peninsula Shield Force is deployed in the vicinity of Hafr al Batin. This force has a nominal strength of 5,000, but most of this manpower is not forward deployed and it is little more than a political façade. No meaningful contingency plans exist to rapidly deploy sufficient land and air forces from other Gulf states to meet Saudi needs, and there are problems even in developing close cooperation between Saudi Arabia and Kuwait. The GCC has made progress in data sharing and creating secure military communications links, but even if the GCC fully executes all of its present $C^4I/$ BM programs, the war fighting impact will remain extremely limited. In practice, the United States would still have to provide the C^4I/SR capability to allow Saudi, Kuwaiti, and other Southern Gulf forces to fight effectively. In fact, the United States would have to provide much of this capability simply for Saudi land and air forces to deploy to the right areas and carry out effective combat operations. The Saudi high command is incapable of conducting effective high-tempo combined land-air battle operations without intensive U.S. support.

Kuwait's military weakness was demonstrated in 1990, and far too little improvement has taken place in Kuwait's military posture since the Gulf War. Bahrain and Saudi Arabia cooperate more closely, but Bahrain is too small to develop a meaningful self-defense capability against Iran or Iraq and is even more dependent on the United States than Saudi Arabia. Qatar has only limited self-defense capability. The UAE has an ongoing dispute with Iran over the control of islands in the Gulf, and its military forces are little more than a "Potemkin village." It has large stocks of modern equipment that are not supported by proper manning, training, and sustainment and that have little real military effectiveness. Oman is critical to ensuring the security of the Strait of Hormuz, but there are still residual tensions between Oman and Saudi Arabia and Oman lacks both the size and financial resources to compete with Iran.

Saudi planners are realistic in assessing these problems. They fully recognize that any talk of a Gulf or Arab security structure is likely to be an exercise in political symbolism as long as such problems exist. They are fully aware that neither Egypt nor Syria has serious power projection capabilities. They know that any Iraqi rhetoric about friendship and peaceful relations cannot be trusted, and that it will be years before it will be possible to tell if Iran is truly emerging as a stable and moderate regime. This leaves them, however, with the dilemma of continued dependence on the United States—with all of its advantages and disadvantages.

THE CHALLENGE OF PROLIFERATION

Saudi Arabia faces two major emerging new military challenges. The first is proliferation, and the growing risk that Iran, Iraq, and other regional states will deploy significant numbers of long-range missiles and other delivery systems armed with chemical, biological, and nuclear weapons. Proliferation is now a creeping threat, but Saudi Arabia must eventually face the problem of developing suitable counterproliferation capabilities, providing missile and civil defenses, and redefining its security relationship with the United States to provide a different kind of deterrence and war fighting capability.

Iraqi, Iranian, and other regional proliferation threaten both Saudi military and civil facilities and oil and gas production facilities that are critical to the entire world. The U.S. Energy Information Agency (EIA) estimates that the Gulf contains around 679 billion barrels of proven oil reserves (roughly 66% of total world oil reserves) and 1,918 Tcf of natural gas reserves (35% of the world total). Saudi Arabia alone has 261.7 billion barrels of proven oil reserves (roughly 25% of total world oil reserves) and 214 Tcf of natural gas reserves (4% of the world total).

As of early 2002, the Gulf had roughly 22.7 million bbl/d of oil production capacity (about 31% of the world total), and accounted for 27% of world total oil production. Saudi Arabia accounted for roughly half this total with roughly 10–11 million bbl/d of oil production capacity. The Gulf countries also maintained over 90% of the world's excess oil production capacity.[31] This capacity is critical to dealing with any disruption of supply from a given supplier or sudden increase in world demand, and any broad disruption of supply from the Gulf would leave the world with limited options for compensating for the lack of Gulf production.

Maintaining actual oil production is equally important. The Gulf countries had estimated net oil exports of 16.8 million bbl/d of oil in 2001. Saudi Arabia exported the most oil of any Gulf country in 2001, with an estimated 7.4 million bbl/d (44% of the total). Iran had estimated net exports of around 2.6 million bbl/d (15%), followed by the United Arab Emirates (2.1 million bbl/d—12%), Iraq (2.0 million bbl/d—12%), Kuwait (2.0 million bbl/d—12%), Qatar (0.8 million bbl/d—5%), and Bahrain (0.02 million bbl/d—0.1%). The strategic importance of such production will also grow steadily with time. The EIA estimates that Gulf oil production capacity is expected to reach about 30.4 million bbl/d by 2010, and 44.5 million bbl/d by 2020—compared to about 23 million bbl/d currently. This would increase Gulf oil production capacity to 36% of the world total by 2020.[32]

The second threat is unconventional or asymmetric warfare, and this threat already is changing Saudi security planning. The terrorist attacks on the U.S. Marine Corps barracks in Lebanon, the Saudi National Guard headquarters, and the Al-Khobar Towers; sporadic sabotage of ARAMCO facilities; and occasional Yemeni infiltration across the Saudi border illustrate the fact that Saudi Arabia may face enemies that use special forces, terrorist proxies, and other unconventional means to attack the Kingdom that are sometimes allied with the extremist opponents of the Saudi regime.

These two emerging threats are not yet critical to the Kingdom's survival, and may diminish if Iran continues to moderate and/or Saddam Hussein is driven from power. At the same time, Saudi Arabia must consider the risk that terrorism or proxy warfare that leads to serious U.S. casualties might undermine its security relations with the United States. Further, it must consider the risk that unconventional or terrorist attacks may eventually use chemical, biological, and nuclear weapons.

NOTES

1. IISS, *Military Balance, 2001–2002,* "Iran."

2. These Iranian force estimates are based largely upon Anthony H. Cordesman, *Iran's Military Forces in Transition* (Westport, CT: Praeger, 1999); the IISS, *Military Balance, 2001–2002;* and material in the Internet edition of Jane's *Sentinel* series, accessed in June 2002.

3. IRNA, April 21, 1997, May 2, 1997; Iranian TV, April 26, 1997; *Jane's Defence Weekly*, October 7, 1995, p. 22, April 23, 1997, p. 19, April 30, 1997, p. 6, June 24, 1995, p. 5, November 6, 1996, p. 23, June 25, 1997, p. 14, October 29, 1997, p. 4; *Washington Times*, May 4, 1997, p. A-7, May 12, 1997, p. A-13; Reuters, April 23, 1997, 0818, May 7, 1997, 0452, July 3, 1997, 0452, July 9, 1997, 1655; *The Washington Post*, April 30, 1997, p. 6; April 23, 1997, p. 19, April 30, 1997, p. 6, June 30, 1997, p. A-20; Associated Press, June 30, 1996, 0629; May 7, 1997, 0452, July 3, 1997, 0452, July 9, 1997, 1655.

4. EIA, *Persian Gulf Factsheet*, March 2002, URL: *http://www.eia.doe.gov/cabs/pgulf.html*.

5. Ibid.

6. Ibid.; *BP Statistical Review of World Energy* (Bournemouth, England: BP Distribution Services, 2001).

7. Estimates provided by USCENTCOM in June, 1996 and 1997, plus interviews.

8. USCENTCOM briefing by "senior military official."

9. Estimate first provided by USCENTCOM in June, 1996, plus interviews.

10. U.S. Department of Defense, Public Affairs Office, June 27, 2002.

11. Based on interviews.

12. USCENTCOM briefing by "senior military official."

13. *Jane's Sentinel Security Assessment*, Iraqi Army, online edition, accessed May 7, 2002.

14. Amatzia Baram, "The Iraqi Armed Forces and Security Apparatus," in *Conflict Security Development* (London: Centre for Defence Studies, King's College, 2001), pp. 113–123.

15. Amatzia Baram, "The Iraqi Armed Forces and Security Apparatus," in *Conflict Security Development* (London: Centre for Defence Studies, King's College, 2001), pp. 113–123.

16. *Jane's Sentinel Security Assessment*, Iraqi Air Force, on-line edition, accessed May 7, 2002.

17. Daniel Byman, "After the Storm: U.S. Policy Toward Iraq Since 1991," *Political Science Quartely*, vol.115, no. 4.

18. Many different lists exist of the names of such bases. Jane's lists Al Amarah, Al Asad, Al Bakr, Al Basrah—West Maqal, Al Khalid, Al Kut, Al Qayyarah, Al Rashid, Al Taqaddum, Al Walid, Artawi, As Salman, As Samara, As Zubair, Baghdad-Muthenna, Balada, Bashur, Erbil, Jalibah, Karbala, Radif al Khafi, Kirkuk, Mosul, Mudaysis, Nejef, Qal'at Sikar, Qurna, Rumaylah, Safwan, Shibah, Shyaka Mayhar, Sulyamaniya, Tal Afar, Tallil-As Nasiryah, Tammuz, Tikrit, Ubdaydah bin al Jarrah, and Wadi Al Khirr. Many of the bases on this list are of limited size or are largely dispersal facilities. See *Jane's Sentinel*, The Gulf States, "Iraq" (London: Jane's Publishing, various editions).

19. IISS, *The Military Balance, 2001–2002*.

20. See list provided in note 18.

21. EIA, *Persian Gulf Factsheet*, March 2002, URL: *http://www.eia.doe.gov/cabs/pgulf.html*; *BP Statistical Review of World Energy* (Bournemouth, England: BP Distribution Services, 2001).

22. Ibid.

23. *Jane's Intelligence Review*, November 1, 1994, p. 500.

24. Dale Bruner, "US Military and Security Relations with the Southern Gulf States," Washington, DC: NSSP, Georgetown University, May 8, 1995.

25. Defense Security Assistance Agency (DSAA), *Foreign Military Sales, Foreign Military Construction Sales, and Military Assistance Facts*, Washington, DC, various editions; U.S. Department of State, Congressional Presentation: Foreign Operations Fiscal Year 1996, p. 499.

26. At one point, the United States seems to have considered a plan to preposition enough equipment for an entire corps of three divisions and 150,000 men. *New York Times*, October 15, 1992, p. A-1.

27. It should be noted that the United States already had 300 combat aircraft in Saudi Arabia and 150 on two carriers, and that Saudi Arabia objected to additional deployments, not to cooperate with the United States. *New York Times*, September 25, 1991, p. A-14; September 27, 1991, p. A-1; September 30, 1991, p. A-5.

28. Ibid.

29. Secretary of Defense, *Report on Forces for the Common Defense*, Report to the U.S. Congress, Washington, Department of Defense, March 2001, p. III-27, B-26.

30. Data from the Department of Defense Office of Public Affairs, and *Report on Allied Contributions to the Common Defense*, March 2001, Report to the U.S. Congress by the Secretary of Defense, p. III-26.

31. As of early 2002, world excess oil production capacity had increased to around 7.3 to 7.8 million bbl/d from about 4.4 million bbl/d in 2001.

32. EIA, *Persian Gulf Factsheet*, March 2002, URL: *http://www.eia.doe.gov/cabs/pgulf.html*.

Chapter 2

Saudi Military Leadership, Organization, and Manpower

The Kingdom's military forces are currently divided into five major branches: the Army, the National Guard, the Navy, the Air Force, and the Air Defense Force. Saudi Arabia also has large paramilitary and internal security forces, and a small strategic missile force. While the organization of Saudi forces is relatively modern, it does divide its land forces into two major branches under the control of two major princes and still faces major problems in the leadership of its armed forces at every level. It also has significant problems in manpower numbers, quality, and management.

THE LEADERSHIP OF SAUDI FORCES

Saudi military forces are formally under the direct control of King Fahd bin Abdulaziz al-Saud. King Fahd is the prime minister of Saudi Arabia, Custodian of the Two Holy Mosques (since adopting the title in 1986 to substitute for "His Majesty") and the commander in chief of the Saudi Armed Forces. He is one of the sons of the Kingdom's founder, and assumed power of the Kingdom on June 13, 1982, after the death of King Khalid bin Abdulaziz. Prior to his current appointment, King Fahd became Saudi Arabia's first minister of education in 1953 and was appointed minister of the interior in 1962. He held this post until he became heir apparent in 1975.[1]

The minister of defense takes care of most actual decision-making that affects the regular armed forces. Prince Sultan bin Abdulaziz al-Saud has been the minister of defense and aviation since 1962 and the second deputy prime minister since 1982. Prior to these positions, Prince Sultan held numerous government posts including governor of Riyadh, minister of agriculture, and minister of communications. Prince Sultan has now spent four decades shaping and modernizing Saudi Arabia's armed forces, has made most policy decisions relating to military procurement, and has supervised the construction of modern military bases and cities throughout the Kingdom.[2]

The National Guard is under a separate chain of command. Prince Abdullah bin Abdulaziz bin Abdul Rahman al-Saud, the crown prince and first deputy prime minister, has commanded the National Guard since 1963.

Prince Nayef bin Abdulaziz al-Saud has been the minister of the interior since 1975. He effectively controls the Kingdom's paramilitary and internal security forces, including the Frontier Force, Civil Defense Force, Police, Fire Service, Passport Division and Special Security and Investigation Forces. Like the other senior princes, Prince Nayef has held prior gubernatorial and ministerial posts such as governor of Riyadh, deputy minister of the interior, minister of state for internal affairs, and president of the Supreme Council for Internal Affairs.

Prince Turki bin Faisal was appointed director-general of intelligence by King Khalid bin Abdulaziz in 1977. He held this position until he was replaced by Prince Nawaf bin Abdulaziz on September 1, 2001. Prince Nawaf now monitors internal and external intelligence matters affecting Saudi Arabia. According to some reports, he has focused his mission on gaining a better understanding of the relationship between extremist groups in Saudi Arabia and the flow of currency both within the Kingdom and beyond its borders.[3]

A number of other members of the royal family also play key roles in the military. Prince Khalid bin Sultan, Prince Sultan's son recently became the assistant minister of the defense and aviation and the de facto senior administrator of the regular military service. Prince Abdulaziz bin Abdul-Rahman is the deputy minister of defense and aviation; Prince Turki bin Nasr is the deputy commander of the Royal Saudi Air Force; Prince Badr bin Abd Al Aziz is the deputy commander of the National Guard. Other key officers included General Saleh Al-Mahya, the chief of staff; Lieutenant General Sultan Al-Motairy, the deputy chief of staff; Prince Mitebibn Abdullah, assistant deputy commander of the National Guard; and Prince Mohammed bin Nayef bin Abdulaziz, assistant minister of the interior for security affairs.

Some aspects of this leadership have been consistently effective. Both Saudi experts and American military officers serving in Saudi Arabia have high praise for Crown Prince Abdullah, Prince Miteb, and the leadership of the National Guard. Observers inside the Ministry of Defense and Aviation (MODA), as well as foreign advisors, praise Khalid bin Sultan for bringing a new degree of leadership and initiative to the MODA, for revitalizing the ministry, and for trying to provide the level of maneuver skills and sustainability Saudi Arabia's military forces need.

There is little praise, however, for the recent leadership of Prince Sultan or Prince Nayef. Many observers privately question Prince Sultan's effectiveness in shaping Saudi Arabia's military forces since the end of the Gulf War in 1991, and particularly in coping with the need to restructure Saudi forced to deal with the funding constraints that have affected Saudi forces since 1994. There has also been serious corruption, involving the royal family, in the Saudi Air Force—corruption that has not led to serious punishment and that is a matter of common knowledge in the Saudi military. Prince Nayef is seen as too conservative and slow moving, and Prince Nawaf bin Abdul is widely regarded as an incompetent replacement for Prince Turki.

ORGANIZATION AND LEADERSHIP

The Saudi command structure has slowly improved, but still lacks some of the elements necessary for a modern command structure. It tends to be cautious and over-compartmented, and does not encourage combined arms operations,"jointness," or cooperation between the services. Command relationships are highly personal. Informal relationships often define real authority and promotion, and the Saudi royal family maintains tight control over operations, deployments, procurement, and all other aspects of Saudi military spending.

The role of the royal family in the command structure is a mixed blessing. Senior members of the royal family exert tight control over every important command activity, operation, promotion, planning, and procurement decision. There are al-Sauds in a number of senior command positions, although others have deliberately been given lower ranks to allow officers outside the royal family to hold command slots. Some of these officers have done very well indeed; others, however, have been little more than place-takers, and a few have been corrupt. The royal family does not yet seem to understand that its members must uniformly be judged by the highest standards, and that mediocre or corrupt members of the family are an unacceptable embarrassment.

Promotion and retention in the Saudi high command tends to reward longevity, conservatism, and personal loyalty rather than performance. Many senior commanders are from families with long ties to the Saudi royal family, and many mid-level officers come from families and tribes that are traditionally loyal to the al-Saud family. At the same time, the level of education and experience of Saudi officers has improved strikingly since the mid-1950s—when most officers had a traditional background. The military forces are also less political. Some officers at the time supported Nasser and other Arab radicals, while others were more interested in politics and careerism than military professionalism.

Saudi Arabia still makes many promotions for political reasons and because of nepotism. It has been slow to develop systems of rotation that retire senior officers and systems that modernize the higher levels of command. There are many good high-ranking officers, but there are also many mediocre and overcautious "loyalists." Senior officers often serve far too long and block the promotion of younger and more capable officers below them. Some treat their positions as sinecures or positions they can exploit for profit.

Unless this situation changes, it may eventually produce significant unrest. There have been few signs of political activism in the Saudi military in recent years. Younger Saudi officer corps often still have a traditional cultural background, but they are increasingly well educated and often have considerable technical proficiency. The Saudi military services have also developed relatively modern headquarters and management systems with the support of Western advisors and technicians. As a result, there is a relatively high degree of military proficiency in many areas. This is particularly true at the tactical level and in those junior- to mid-level positions where professionalism is more important in defining power and status than political contacts and family or tribal background.

MANAGEMENT, BUDGETING, AND LEADERSHIP

Some of Saudi Arabia's leadership problems begin at the top. Prince Sultan, the second deputy prime minister and minister of defense and aviation, has made a major and enduring contribution to the Kingdom's military development, but he has not always provided the kind of leadership Saudi Arabia needs. There is no doubt that he is active, intelligent, and often sympathetic to the West. At the same time, he sometimes seems obsessed with new equipment purchases, and has insufficient patience to deal with the manpower management, operations and maintenance, and sustainability issues that shape real-world military effectiveness. In general, he seems to find it easier to make dramatic new arms buys than take the kind of hard, consistent, and systematic decisions necessary to translate strategic ideas into operational and mission-oriented war fighting capability. The end result is that Saudi arms purchases have sometimes done more to disorganize the Saudi military and create conversion problems than they have done to improve it.

Prince Sultan has also failed to adequately recognize the manpower and financial constraints on the expansion of Saudi military forces. In a speech in 1996, he announced plans to modernize the Saudi armed forces:

> We have great plans to modernize the armed forces during the next five-year plan. The broad headlines have been made starting with the training of the individual to securing modern equipment. The sixth plan for our armed

forces, which may begin next year, will be, God willing, a plan of expansion not only in purchases but in men and attracting Saudi school and university graduates.[4]

Perhaps fortunately, the financial constraints imposed by low oil revenues curbed such modernization plans. Unfortunately, Prince Sultan and the MODA failed to react to these constraints by adequately downsizing and slowing Saudi procurement plans, and by creating more realistic annual budgets and five-year plans that stressed investing in balanced war fighting capabilities rather than procurement.

After 1995, key military activities like manpower quality, training and exercises, sustainment, and maintenance were underfunded. The MODA also failed to exert central management over the services to ensure that they maintained readiness and converted effectively to new equipment, and allowed each service to develop very different levels of capability by branch. Far too little effort was made to develop cohesive plans to ensure suitable progress in interservice cooperation or "jointness," in combined arms, and in balancing the development of combat arms with suitable sustainment and support capabilities. Economies were made in many of these areas to fund equipment orders that should have been downsized and renegotiated, and when years of high oil revenues did occur, the ministry sometimes sharply overspent its budget by making new arms purchases.

Prince Khalid bin Sultan's appointment may be a key first step in giving the MODA the leadership it has lacked since the end of the Gulf War, but he faces a series of difficult challenges. The ministry needs to shift from a focus on force buildup to a focus on force effectiveness, and introduce tight top-down budget and program management. It has failed to develop effective planning, programming, and budgeting systems that ensure that there are effective fiscal controls, and needs to work on its procurement, manpower, and operating and maintenance systems. This makes it difficult to plan and control cash flow for major arms buys. It encourages "stovepiped" funding of different elements of the military forces, and makes it harder to control waste and corruption. There are no stable force modernization and force expansion goals or efforts to shape and fund balanced war fighting capabilities. There seems to be no centralized system to honestly assess the war fighting capability and readiness of Saudi forces and monitor measures of effectiveness. There also is no public transparency of the kind that ensures funds are spent effectively, or that allows Saudis inside and outside the MODA to assess what the five-year plan is, how the budget is allocated, or how money is actually spent.

In fairness, these same problems affect every military force in the Middle East to some degree, including Israel. A combination of outdated paternalism, exaggerated and pointless secrecy, and the treatment of defense as a virtual fiefdom of the ruling elite is the rule in the region and not the exception. Nevertheless, there are a number of high-level Saudis, including some junior members of the royal family, who hope that when Prince Abdullah becomes king, he will reduce Saudi new equipment buys, concentrate on military effectiveness, and fund the sustainment for the Army and Air Force so as to minimize waste. Prince Abdullah may find this difficult because of his natural rivalry with his half brother and putative successor. Saudi Arabia does, however, need to reshape its priorities and the planning and management of the National Guard has been significantly better than that of the MODA.

There is a similar need for better direction and leadership in the upper echelons of the Saudi military in each military service, and for changes in command and doctrine that will make Saudi military thinking and operational plans less static, improve every aspect of force planning and management, and prune the upper levels of command. Saudi Arabia needs to move from a nation whose military forces are static and defensive in character to one with military forces that are oriented toward maneuvering, speed of concentration, and joint warfare. It also needs to match its close collective security ties to the United States with much more effective efforts to developing coalition war fighting capabilities with the other Southern Gulf states—most notably Bahrain and Kuwait.

These problems in organization and high command are compounded by the fact that Saudi Arabia has one of the most complex force postures of any developing nation, while operating some of the most advanced military technology in the world. In several cases, this technology is more advanced than that in many developed NATO countries. Furthermore, Saudi Arabia has just completed the final stages of massive infrastructure programs that have created some of the world's most modern facilities out of empty desert. It is beginning to produce its second generation of ranks with modern military training; only a little more than a generation ago most of its troops were Bedouin with only limited education and technical background.

Still, all of these challenges and problems need to be kept in perspective. The Saudi military forces have often been criticized by those who have little appreciation of the challenges they face and how much they have already accomplished. Saudi Arabia's military planning and management may have been imperfect, but so has every other country that has tried to cope with the ongoing revolution in military affairs. Saudi Arabia has already overcome massive challenges in terms of manpower, infrastructure, and technology transfer. It has a very solid mix of infrastructure and existing equipment holdings to build on, and a relatively high level of overall tactical proficiency for a developing nation.

The Kingdom can draw on military support from the West, and Saudi Arabia has been fortunate in its potential enemies. Iran has never fully rebuilt its conventional forces since it experienced massive losses at the end of the Iran-Iraq War. Iraq suffered a devastating defeat in the Gulf, and UN sanctions have blocked any major arms imports since the summer of 1990. Yemen's forces have been weakened by civil war, and it has had few major arms imports since the end of the Cold War. Saudi Arabia may have its military problems, but its most serious potential threats have had military disasters.

MILITARY MANPOWER

The quality and quantity of military manpower has been one of the most important challenges that Saudi Arabia has faced since it first decided to create modern military forces in the 1960s, and it is a challenge that the Kingdom will continue to face until well after the year 2010. Saudi Arabia can buy modern military equipment and infrastructure from other countries, but it must rely on its own manpower base to make these assets effective and develop deterrent and war fighting capabilities.

This manpower challenge is not easy to meet. The Saudi military faces the same problems in recruiting suitable manpower that are faced by the Saudi civil sector. Advanced military equipment requires increasingly higher levels of education and experience, and military forces require tight discipline, a strong work ethic, merit-based promotion, training standards that reject those that fail, and modern, service-wide manpower management. Military forces that rely on civilian support for routine military tasks in peacetime have no capability to perform them in war. It is far easier to train soldiers at the tactical level than it is to develop suitable cadres of specialists and technicians and the kind of middle to senior officers that can lead in peacetime and command in war.

MANPOWER POOL AND MANPOWER PROBLEMS

Saudi Arabia now has a manpower pool that can meet all of its needs, if it manages the pool effectively. In the past, Saudi Arabia's total population has been limited relative to that of Northern Gulf neighbors like Iran and Iraq, but this situation is changing. In 2002, Iran had a population of over 68 million. At the same time, Saudi Arabia's total population was over 22 million—nearly equal to that of Iraq, which had a population of 22.3 million. While Saudi population data are uncertain and vary accordingly to source, Saudi Arabia had a male population of over 1.3 million in 2002 in the age group from eighteen to twenty-two years of age, and the Saudi Central Department of Statistics reported that there were 1.93 million native Saudi males in the age group from fifteen to twenty-nine years in 1999.[5]

Regardless of exactly which population figures are correct, all sources now give Saudi Arabia a substantial pool of military-age manpower to draw on. For example, CIA estimates indicate that Saudi Arabia's total pool was around 5.7 million men of military age in 2001. This compares with a pool of roughly 17.8 million males of military age in Iran, 5.6 million males of military age in Iraq, and 3.9 million males of military age in Yemen.[6] (See Table 2.1 for a comparison of Saudi demographics with those of other Middle Eastern countries.) No country, however, comes close to drawing on its total eligible manpower pool in peacetime.

Saudi Arabia has not, however, mobilized its manpower as effectively as Iran and Iraq, both of which were able to place nearly 1 million men under arms during the Iran-Iraq War. Saudi Arabia only had about 126,500 men in its regular forces in early 2002, plus 75,000 to 100,000 full-time regulars in its National Guard.[7] These totals compare with 513,000 actives for Iran and 424,000 for Iraq, which has a total population almost equal to that of Saudi Arabia.[8] The broader trends in Gulf military manpower levels are shown in Chart 2.1, and it is clear that Iran and Iraq's regular forces have long had a much larger active strength than Saudi Arabia.[9]

Saudi Arabia does face several serious internal problems in mobilizing its manpower resources. There were 942,000 foreign males in the age group from fifteen to twenty-nine years in 1999, out of a total of 2.87 million including Saudi males. Continuing tribal and regional rivalries have also affected the recruiting base. Saudi Arabia has had to be cautious about recruiting from regions, such as the Hijaz, which opposed the Saudi conquest in the 1920s and 1930s, and from rival tribes. The rise of Islamic fundamentalism among the poorer and more tribal Saudis, coupled with long-standing hostility among a number of tribes and the Hijaz, have placed additional limits on the Saudi recruiting base and the groups it can conscript from. As a result, the armed forces drew heavily on most of the tribal and regional groupings on which they can count for political support.

Past Methods of Reducing Dependence on Foreign Military Manpower

In the past, Saudi Arabia tried to compensate for its manpower problems by:

- Placing heavy dependence on foreign support and technicians (which reached a maximum of over 14,000 personnel).
- Using small elements of foreign forces in key specialty and technical areas—such as combat engineers—to "fill in" the gaps in Saudi land forces. It formerly had some 10,000 Pakistani troops to fill out one brigade (the 12th Armored Brigade) at Tabuk. These Pakistani forces have not been replaced, although some contingency arrangements may exist with Egypt.[10]
- Selectively undermanning its forces while building up its training and manpower base.

- Concentrating on building a fully effective air force as a first-line deterrent and defense.
- A de facto reliance on over-the-horizon reinforcement by the United States and Western allies to deal with high-level or enduring conflicts.

Some of these techniques are still useful, but they are now far less necessary because of the rapid growth of the Saudi population, and other factors have helped Saudi recruiting.

Current Manpower Quantity and Quality Problem

Employment in military jobs has become steadily more important to the families of those who do serve. Some Saudi units estimate, for example, that every enlisted man now supports an average of eleven dependents. Although most Saudi recruits tend to make the military a career once they join (there is only about a 10 to 15% loss after the first full enlistment), urbanization, labor migration, and intermarriage have also done a great deal to break down traditional tribal and regional recruiting problems. Even the National Guard now mixes Saudis from a wide range of tribes and areas in the Kingdom.

At the same time, the Kingdom has not provided sufficient money to train, hire, and retain all of the regular and skilled manpower it needs. It has no conscription program, and recruiting has sometimes been erratic because money has been a problem—recruiting had to be suspended during the worst moments in the "oil crash" in the late 1990s—a time when Crown Prince Abdullah was also forced to freeze hiring for civil departments. As a result of funding constraints, many units are still well short of their authorized levels of manpower. The systematic underfunding of operations, maintenance, training equipment, and sustainment since the mid-1990s has also meant that Saudi officers and technicians have not gotten the exposure they need in the form of on-the-job training and work activity.

The armed forces face the same broader problems with manpower quality as Saudi society. Despite Saudi population growth and the expansion of Saudi educational facilities, skilled manpower with practical experience and a work ethic remains at a premium, far too much use is made of rote learning, far too little training stresses initiative and problem solving, foreign language and technical training are often inadequate, and men who fail or fall short of the required standard are passed or promoted. The Kingdom has steadily tried to reduce its overall dependence on foreign manpower as part of its "Saudisation" policy, and has accelerated this process since 1997. Saudisation, however, has been as much of a mixed blessing in the MODA as in the Saudi civil economy as a whole. It has sometimes replaced competent foreign technicians and support personnel with Saudis who are not equally competent in the position.

Table 2.1
Saudi Military Demographics versus Those of Neighboring States in 2001

Country	Total Population	Males Reaching Military Age Each Year	Males Between the Ages of			Males Between 15 and 49	
			13 and 17	18 and 22	23 and 32	Total	Medically Fit
Iran	68,281,000	823,040	4,587,000	3,827,000	5,771,000	18,318,000	10,872,000
Iraq	22,300,000	274,035	1,498,000	1,281,000	1,894,000	5,902,000	3,302,000
Bahrain	626,000	5,926	33,000	26,000	40,000	222,000	122,000
Kuwait	2,065,000	18,309	120,000	103,000	147,000	781,000	466,000
Oman	2,674,000	26,469	131,000	106,000	154,000	771,000	430,000
Qatar	610,000	6,797	25,000	21,000	35,000	312,000	164,000
Saudi Arabia	22,205,000	233,402	1,348,000	1,133,000	1,670,000	5,894,000	3,291,000
UAE	2,571,000	25,482	86,000	84,000	143,000	778,000	420,000
Yemen	18,885,000	238,690	974,000	788,000	1,293,000	4,103,000	2,303,000

Afghanistan	22,567,000	252,869	1,451,000	1,178,000	2,014,000	6,645,000	3,562,000
Djibouti	783,000	—	41,000	34,000	55,000	108,000	64,000
Eritrea	3,905,000	—	246,000	205,000	311,000	—	—
Ethiopia	63,659,000	703,625	3,843,600	3,083,000	4,617,000	14,538,000	7,582,000
Somalia	10,317,000	—	607,000	494,000	707,000	1,825,000	1,011,000
Sudan	29,632,000	398,294	1,948,000	1,644,000	2,471,000	8,436,000	5,195,000
Turkey	67,652,000	674,805	3,266,000	3,254,000	6,098,000	18,882,000	11,432,000
Egypt	70,615,000	712,983	3,634,000	3,218,000	5,067,000	18,563,000	12,020,000
Gaza	1,132,000*	—	—	—	—	—	—
Israel	6,336,000	49,206	281,000	270,000	526,000	1,522,000	1,246,000
Jordan	6,869,000	57,131	274,000	245,000	4,447,000	1,459,000	1,034,000
Lebanon	3,578,000	—	213,000	195,000	391,000	980,000	605,000
Palestine	3,000,000*	—	163,000	140,000	233,000	—	—
Syria	16,493,000	200,859	1,042,000	853,000	1,210,000	4,385,000	2,449,000
West Bank	1,700,000*	—	—	—	—	—	—

Sources: Adapted by Anthony H. Cordesman from CIA, *World Factbook*, and IISS, *Military Balance.*

Chart 2.1
Trends in Total Gulf Military Manpower

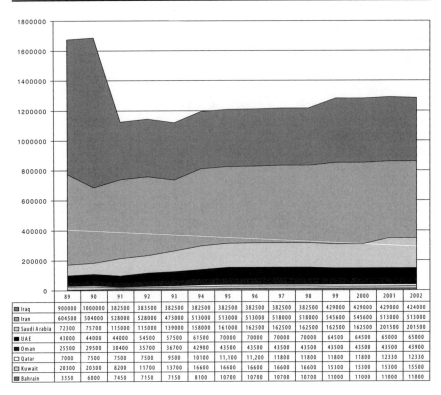

	89	90	91	92	93	94	95	96	97	98	99	2000	2001	2002
Iraq	900000	1000000	382500	383500	382500	382500	382500	382500	382500	382500	429000	429000	429000	424000
Iran	604500	504000	528000	528000	473000	513000	513000	513000	518000	518000	545600	545600	513000	513000
Saudi Arabia	72300	75700	115000	115000	139000	158000	161000	162500	162500	162500	162500	162500	201500	201500
UAE	43000	44000	44000	54500	57500	61500	70000	70000	70000	70000	64500	64500	65000	65000
Oman	25500	29500	30400	35700	36700	42900	43500	43500	43500	43500	43500	43500	43500	43900
Qatar	7000	7500	7500	7500	9500	10100	11,100	11,200	11800	11800	11800	11800	12330	12330
Kuwait	20300	20300	8200	11700	13700	16600	16600	16600	16600	16600	15300	15300	15300	15500
Bahrain	3350	6000	7450	7150	7150	8100	10700	10700	10700	10700	11000	11000	11000	11000

Sources: Estimated by Anthony H. Cordesman using data from various editions of the IISS
Military Balance, Jane's Sentinel, and *Military Technology*. Note that Saudi includes full-
time active National Guard, Oman includes Royal Guard, Iran includes Revolutionary
Guards, and Iraq includes Republican Guards and Special Republican Guards.

Reductions in the role of training and education abroad also affect the
ability of the armed forces to reach the proper skill levels, and foreign language skills are becoming a problem. Saudi military training in the United
States, for example, now averages about 15% of the levels in the early
1990s. Senior U.S. advisors feel this lack of training in the United States is
a particularly serious problem for the Saudi Air Force. Such advisors believe that the United States needs to provide for more international military education and training (IMET) aid and reduce the premiums it has
charged Saudi military personnel training in the United States. The appro-
priation for $25,000 for such training in 2002 is at least a first step in re-
ducing the added fees and surcharges the United States has applied in the
past, and reflects the U.S. priority for profiteering over partnership.

Current and Future Saudi Military Manpower Levels

Comparative estimates of the buildup of Saudi active military manpower are shown in Chart 2.2. The buildup of total full-time active manpower by service is shown in Chart 2.3. According to the IISS, Saudi Arabia had approximately 75,000 full-time uniformed actives in its Army in 2001, plus 15,500 in its Navy, 20,000 in its Air Force, and 16,000 in its Air Defense Force. It has 100,000 more full-time actives in its Royal Guards and National Guard, 10,500 in its Frontier Forces, 4,500 in its Coast Guard, and up to 500 more men in its Special Security Forces and other special units.

Chart 2.2
Saudi Active Military Manning, 1980–2002 (1,000s of Personnel)

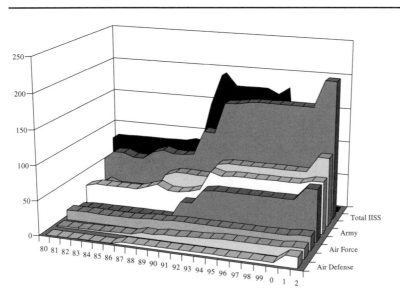

	80	81	82	83	84	85	86	87	88	89	90	91	92	93	94	95	96	97	98	99	0	1	2
☐ Air Defense								4	4	4	4	4	4	4	4	4	4	4	4	4	4	16	16
☐ Navy	1.5	2.2	2.2	2.5	2.5	3.5	3.5	3.5	7.8	7.2	9.5	9.5	11	11	12	14	14	14	14	14	14	16	16
▣ Air Force	15	15	15	14	14	14	14	15	17	17	18	18	18	18	18	18	18	18	18	18	18	20	20
▣ National Guard -Active	8	10	10	10	10	10	10	10	10	10	10	35	35	55	57	57	57	57	57	57	57	75	75
☐ Army	31	35	35	35	35	35	40	45	38	38	40	45	73	68	70	70	70	70	70	70	70	75	75
☐ National Guard - Total	20	30	25	25	25	25	25	50	56	56	55	55	75	77	77	77	77	77	77	77	77	100	100
▣ Total IISS	55	67	67	62	62	73	78	74	74	76	113	112	157	158	161	163	163	163	163	163	163	202	202
■ Total ACDA	79	79	80	80	80	80	80	80	84	82	146	191	172	172	172	172	164	175	-	-	-		

Sources: Adapted by Anthony H. Cordesman from various editions of ACDA, *World Military Expenditures and Arms Transfers* (Washington: ACDA/GPO); U.S. State Department, *World Military Expenditures and Arms Transfers* (Washington: Bureau of Arms Control); IISS, *Military Balance*; JCSS, *The Middle East Military Balance*; and material provided by U.S. experts.

Chart 2.3
Total Saudi Active Military Manning by Military Service, 1980–2002 (1,000s of Personnel)

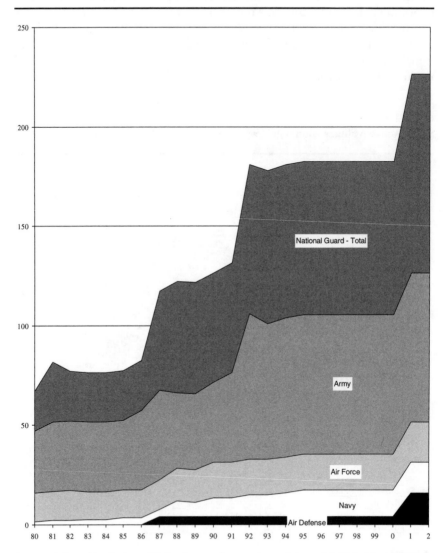

Sources: Adapted by Anthony H. Cordesman from various editions of ACDA, *World Military Expenditures and Arms Transfers* (Washington: ACDA/GPO); U.S. State Department, *World Military Expenditures and Arms Transfers* (Washington: Bureau of Arms Control, 1999); IISS, *Military Balance*; JCSS, *The Middle East Military Balance*; and material provided by U.S. experts.

These figures produce a maximum of about 178,000 active men, although Saudi Arabia reports another 20,000 part-time levies in the National Guard—an estimate confirmed by U.S. advisors in the Kingdom. The data in Charts 2.2 and 2.3 understate the true nature of the Saudi manpower buildup because Saudi regulars and National Guardsmen are now far more reliable and less likely to take unauthorized leave.[11]

The U.S. State Department has provided a somewhat different, if somewhat dated, estimate of Saudi military manning, including irregulars:[12]

- 191,500 uniformed troops in the armed forces, including:
  - Royal Saudi Navy (RSNF) (including Marines)   15,500
  - Royal Saudi Air Force (RSAF)   20,000
  - Royal Saudi Air Defense Forces (RSADF)   16,000
  - Royal Saudi Land Forces (RSLF)   75,000
  - Reservists   0
- Saudi Arabian National Guard (SANG):
  - Uniformed troops   65,000
  - Paramilitary/Irregular Troops   35,000
  - Total, Including Irregulars   226,500

Whatever the exact total may be, Saudi Arabia does maintain far larger forces than it did in the past. Its regular active forces only totaled 65,700 men before Iraq invaded Kuwait, with some 38,000 in the Army, 6,000 in the Navy, an additional 1,200 Marines, 16,500 in the Air Force, and 4,000 in the Air Defense Forces. The National Guard had a nominal strength of 56,000, but only 10,000 men were active, another 20,000 were assigned to the regular reserve, and 26,000 in the part-time tribal irregulars.[13]

Even today, however, the Saudi force of full-time regulars remains under 130,000 men. This simply is not enough active manpower to meet the needs of Saudi Arabia's current force structure, or to properly fight and sustain the equipment and weapons that the Kingdom has already purchased for its regular forces. Saudi Arabia has a force structure equivalent to about three divisions, a Navy with some seventeen major surface combatants plus seven mine countermeasure vessels, an Air Force with 417 combat aircraft on hand and 348 "active in combat units," and Air Defense Forces with some thirty-three surface-to-air missile batteries.

There are no magic formulas that set the military manpower requirements for such a force structure and equipment strength, but Saudi Arabia probably needed some 200,000 to 250,000 actives to make its force structure fully effective. The alternatives are to (a) increase the manpower pool, (b) restructure its National Guard to take over some of the functions of the Army, (c) shift men from the National Guard into the Army, and/or (d) abolish many of its units with older equipment.

Saudi Arabia explored doubling its forces and expanding its total regular military forces to 200,000 men shortly after the Gulf War. Prince Sultan reiterated this goal in May 1996. As noted earlier in this chapter, he stated: "The sixth plan for our armed forces, which may begin next year, will be, God willing, a plan of expansion not only in purchases but in men and attracting Saudi school and university graduates."[14] It is far from clear, however, that Saudi Arabia can reach 200,000 full-time actives of reasonable quality by the year 2005, and it is virtually certain that it cannot do so with men of the proper quality.

While Saudi Arabia certainly has a large enough manpower pool in its total population to draw upon, it has emphasized new equipment purchases over manpower, and its growing budgetary problems since 1991 have led it to sacrifice manpower numbers and quality in order to pay for arms imports. As a result, the Saudi regular forces have serious problems. It is necessary for them to make reforms in their recruiting and training to compensate for past neglect and Saudi Arabia will find it difficult to deal with these problems before 2005–2010 unless it restructures its present pattern of defense investment.

Current Manpower Management Problems

Effective manpower management is also an issue. If there is also meaningful effort to create force-wide manpower management in the MODA, it is certainly not apparent from the results. Each service seems to manage its own manpower intake, promotion, career development, and retention with little overall effort to manage military manpower resources and with insufficient supervision of the effectiveness of the result. These problems are then further complicated by the fact that the National Guard makes up about one-third of total full-time active Saudi military manpower, and runs a totally separate recruiting, training, and retention system with little communication with the ministry and equally little effort to develop common policies or economies of scale in training, recruiting, and other military manpower activities.

The regular services need to refocus training and promotion on quality and performance. Nepotism, family contacts, and tribal status often still determine which men are selected for skilled positions or appointments. Time in service determines many aspects of promotion, as does seniority within a given rank. Selection out is still rare, and senior officers often stay in given positions far too long. There has been little incentive for middle-grade officers to be innovative or take chances, and senior officers who show limited leadership capability are often retained. More effort needs to be made to aggressively promote high-quality junior- and middle-ranking officers, to reward the best officers with top positions, or to prune midlevel and senior officers who fail to demonstrate outstanding performance.

There is a cultural reluctance to promote on the basis of merit. Saudi officers are the first to say that the quality of the officer corps suffers because "Saudis do not fail Saudis" in training programs, and promotion often comes through seniority. One officer made a comment about the promotion process that goes against the grain of much Western thinking on this issue, but that was supported by a number of other officers:

> You [U.S. observers] always ask if the royal family interferes in promotions. They are not the problem. In fact, they often force the promotion of younger and more competent officers. The problem is that no one is really selected out because they are not good enough, people stay far too long in positions at the top, and promotion is a matter of age and seniority. Our problem is not interference from Princes or outsiders. It is what we do to ourselves.

There is also a cultural unwillingness to insist on competence at the expense of social relations. As one Saudi general put it, "You have to understand that one of our most basic problems in training and promotion is that no Saudi officer will ever fail another Saudi officer, and that to reject the son or nephew of a friend is an insult." This helps explain why "Saudisation" presents problems, why the regular military services remain over-dependent on foreign technicians and support personnel, and why fewer foreign support personnel are being asked to do more and more. One long-term British military advisor put it this way: "Saudi military forces have always threatened to become a static display. Now they are threatening to become a static display with rust."

The Saudi National Guard faces fewer problems in these areas. The Guard does not use advanced weapons and requires less technical skills and ability to deal with advanced tactics, joint operations, and combined arms. Ironically, the Guard may be more traditional in some respects, but is more demanding in terms of performance in training and has a more merit-based promotion system. It probably has the basic manpower numbers it needs today, but it does need more trained manpower, and it will have problems obtaining all of the skilled career manpower necessary to make it fully effective as it becomes more technically sophisticated. Creating new National Guard brigades and filling out its support forces will require a further buildup of skilled manpower and any such effort would compete directly with recruiting for the regular armed forces.[15]

Most Saudi military manpower problems could be eliminated during the next decade *if* the MODA develops more effective military manpower and management capabilities and *if* the ministry and National Guard can do a better job in coordinating how the Kingdom uses its military manpower. Saudi Arabia's high population growth rate is rapidly increasing the number of eligible men, its educational system is becoming better, and younger Saudis now realize that the days of guaranteed jobs and high salaries in the civil sector are over. Military service is relatively popular, at least among young males with rural and tribal backgrounds. Saudi Arabia has begun to pay more for new entrants and the expectations of young Saudis are more modest than they were in the 1970s and 1980s. During the late 1990s, for example, unemployment among Saudi men entering the workforce began to approach or exceed 30% and recruiting and retention improved to the point that there were more qualified applicants than the National Guard could absorb. Nevertheless, it will take a sustained and expensive recruiting drive, better training and retention incentives, and better education and manpower management to give Saudi Arabia the military manpower it needs.

Much will depend on popular perceptions of the threats to the Kingdom, and of the real-world value of the Saudi military in defending it, but the Gulf War has already shown that Saudi Arabia could expand its manpower base when Saudis believe that military service is necessary. The Kingdom called for volunteers for the first time, expecting some 25,000 volunteers at most; it got 200,000 to 250,000. This shows that Saudi Arabia can probably expand its manpower significantly in future years if it can convince Saudi youth that a military career is rewarding and that military service is really necessary to defend and help the country.[16] The situation will be very different, however, if young Saudis feel the military forces are sinecures, if they do not believe they are combat effective, and if they believe the Kingdom relies on U.S. forces to defend it rather than using the United States as a military partner.

RELIANCE ON WESTERN FORCES AND REINFORCEMENTS

Saudi Arabia relies heavily on the United States, and to some extent Britain and France, to supplement its own military capabilities. This reliance on the United States makes good strategic sense in many ways. Saudi Arabia cannot hope to develop anything approaching the U.S. level of C⁴I/SR capability, or its ability to exploit the "revolution in military affairs" during the next decade. Saudi and U.S. strategic interests coincide so closely in defending against any overt threat from the Northern Gulf that the Kingdom can count on massive U.S. reinforcements from over-the-horizon capabilities if it, Kuwait, or Bahrain face any such threats, as well as similar U.S. efforts to check any overt aggression against any of the lower Gulf countries.

An ongoing U.S.-British-Saudi partnership actively enforces Operation Southern Watch and the no-fly zone in southern Iraq. As discussed in Chapter 1, this partnership both contains Iraq and deters Iran. The Gulf War demonstrated that Saudi and U.S. forces can fight well in coalition operations, and the United States has maintained a strong mix of F-15, F-16, and other combat, reconnaissance, intelligence, tanker, and support aircraft in

Saudi Arabia since that war. These U.S. forces were originally concentrated in Dhahran on the Gulf coast, but were relocated to Prince Sultan Air Base, some eighty kilometers south of Riyadh, after the bombing of the U.S. Air Force barracks in Al-Khobar on June 25, 1996. The United States also relocated much of the 25,000 short tons of Air Force equipment it had prepositioned in Saudi Arabia, although much of this stockpile may since have been reduced.

The United States also deploys a Patriot PAC-2 anti-air/anti-tactical ballistic missile battery in Saudi Arabia, and is helping the Kingdom to activate its own force as it grows to six PAC-2 battalions. Saudi air bases are sized to allow the United States to rapidly reinforce the Kingdom, and its Air Defense forces and the C^4I system can rapidly integrate two further U.S. Patriot battalions units into Saudi Arabia's land-based air defenses. The United States has also reestablished its presence in the Saudi central air command and control facilities in Riyadh. (It temporarily withdrew this presence after the bombing of Al-Khobar.) These arrangements allowed Saudi Arabia to give the United States substantial—if quiet—tactical support during the war in Afghanistan in 2001–2002. In September 2002, Saudi Arabia also agreed to resume exercises with the United States as well as to broaden the ability of Southern Watch forces to strike across the Iraqi border.

Aside from the equipment for its Patriot unit, the United States has not prepositioned any land force equipment in Saudi Arabia. The fact that the Saudi Army operates so much U.S. equipment does, however, ensure that many of the support facilities the U.S. Army would need are present in the Kingdom. Saudi holdings of U.S. munitions would also allow the Kingdom to sustain intensive U.S. air and land operations until the United States could resupply by sea. The U.S. Air Force, Army, Marine Corps, and Navy also conduct exercises and training with Saudi forces, as well as provide advisors serving with Saudi units.

The U.S. presence in the rest of the Gulf varies with time, but the United States has long prepositioned most of a U.S. Army brigade set in Kuwait, another such set in Qatar, and has a third brigade set on ships at Diego Garcia. It is creating a prepositioning facility in the UAE. It has another brigade equivalent of Marine equipment deployed at sea, and usually has elements of this joint land-air Marine Expeditionary Force deployed on ships in the Gulf. The United States can also move at least two light Army divisions to Saudi Arabia by air and deploy a third, heavier Army division and all of the elements of a Marine division by sea within thirty days. The United States prepositions substantial war fighting supplies for land and air operations in Bahrain, Kuwait, and Oman. It has port facilities in the UAE, bases its 5th fleet in Bahrain, and has contingency arrangements to base air units in Bahrain, Kuwait, Qatar, and the UAE. These arrangements now allow the United States to keep its permanent presence in Saudi Arabia at levels around 5,000 men—a token presence compared to the total forces deployed by Iran or Iraq—while minimizing the impact of a U.S. military presence on Saudi society.

Nevertheless, Saudi dependence on U.S. arms, advisors, and military support clearly presents problems for the Kingdom. As has been touched on in Chapter 1, these problems include the backlash from U.S. ties to Israel and the Second Intifada, the opposition of some Saudi Islamists to a U.S. presence on Saudi soil, and Saudi concern that a U.S. presence in the Kingdom leads the United States to use its forces to serve its own regional interests rather than those of Saudi Arabia.

The Kingdom faces other risks and problems because of its military ties to the West. It now depends on many joint command and C⁴I/SR functions being performed by the United States in any major conflict. Saudi forces need better and integrated Saudi battle management capabilities to enable its Army, National Guard, Air Force, Air Defense Force, and Navy to conduct modern, high-tempo operations against a large opponent like Iran or Iraq. It places de facto reliance on U.S. C⁴I/SR capabilities to integrate and coordinate Saudi joint operations.

As a result, Saudi Arabia must both find ways to reshape its strategic dependence on the United States to make it more politically acceptable, and to strengthen its own C⁴I/SR capabilities. "Reshaping," however, does not mean "abandoning" or "weakening." Saudi Arabia has no alternative to some degree of dependence, which has not weakened—particularly as the threat from weapons of mass destruction grows.

Europe's role in providing military support is limited. Britain is now the only European power truly capable of sustaining advanced air-land-naval combat in the Gulf. It cannot deploy anything like the forces the United States can, but it does maintain a limited RAF strength in Saudi Arabia with a nominal average strength of 200 men, six Tornado GR. Mk 1 attack aircraft, and two VC-10 K2/3 tankers. The Saudi Air Force also operates the Tornado and can support rapid RAF deployments to Saudi Arabia. The Royal Navy has deployed in the Gulf for well over a decade, and although the British Armilla Patrol only consists of a few combat ships, the Royal Navy plays a role in exercise training and improving Saudi and other Gulf naval performance out of any proportion to the size of its normal deployments. Britain could quickly deploy light land forces to the region and up to one mechanized brigade in thirty days.

France also plays a role in the Gulf region, and has a base in Djibouti on the southern coast of the Red Sea. It has maintained a limited air presence of Mirage 2000C fighters, tankers, and transport aircraft in Saudi Arabia, although it ceased to participate in Southern Watch and other operations against Iraq in 1998. The French Army, Air Force, and Navy could provide limited reinforcements in Saudi Arabia and conduct training exercises with the Kingdom and other GCC forces, and some Saudis feel that the Kingdom should increase its reliance on France as a way of reducing its problems in dealing with the United States in regard to September 11 and the Second Intifada.

France, however, has never funded the mix of C^4I/SR, power projection, and sustainment capabilities that French forces would need for a major deployment, and such French reinforcements would be far less effective in actual war fighting than their equipment and tactical readiness would indicate. Major French reinforcement would probably be so dependent on U.S. and Saudi aid in C^4I/SR and sustainment that they would have to take the place of substantially more effective U.S. reinforcements.

As for the rest of Europe, more than three decades of European debates over creating effective European out-of-area power projection capabilities have created institutions, but only token actual war fighting capabilities.

LIMITS TO ISLAMIC AND ARAB REINFORCEMENTS

While some Saudi, Arab, and Western analysts have argued that Saudi Arabia should use Arab forces to reduce or replace its dependence on U.S. and other Western forces and reinforcements, this is not a practical option. There are no other Arab or Islamic countries that have effective power projection and sustainment capabilities, the ability to carry out the required C^4I/SR activity, or anything approaching the advanced tactics and war fighting technology of the United States. Aside from small elite elements, no such country could provide units with even a fifth of the ability to sustain joint or combined arms combat of their U.S. or British counterparts. No such capability can handle the targeting and force management burdens of advanced, interoperable air and land combat, or offer any hope of providing some degree of missile defense and ability to suppress and destroy the weapons of mass destruction and major delivery systems of powers like Iran and Iraq.

Moreover, the Kingdom has not had good experiences in trying to use Arab and Islamic forces to supplement its own. The countries involved have invariably had political and economic agendas that have conflicted with those of Saudi Arabia and their forces have proven to be ineffective and/ or unreliable. Efforts to use Jordanian contract officers led to defections and political problems in the 1950s and 1960s. Pakistani forces serving in the army refused to deploy as requested during the Iran-Iraq War, and no Pakistani battalion-level forces have existed in the Saudi army since that time.

Syria deployed divisions against Iraq in 1990, but they did not fight. Egyptian troops fought as well as they were allowed to, but were slow to advance for political reasons and showed they were weakly organized and lacked the technology and joint warfare capabilities need for such expeditionary missions.[17] This explains why there has never been a serious Saudi attempt to follow up on the Saudi-Egyptian-Syrian "Damascus Accords" signed at the time of the Gulf War. Saudi Arabia saw such an "alliance" as involving an Egyptian-Syrian command presence in the Kingdom and as a largely political and cosmetic symbol of lasting solidarity against Iraq. Egypt and Syria saw it as involving the continued deployment of major combat units and as a way to obtain substantial military and economic aid as well as prestige.

Since 1991, Syria's forces have steadily declined in modernization and relative war fighting capability and no longer be regarded as anything approaching a serious option. Egypt's combat units have steadily improved, but still have limited power projection and sustainment capability. Saudi Arabia also still sees Egypt as something of a rival for power and prestige in the Arab world.

PROGRESS IN OBTAINING SUPPORT FROM THE GCC

The GCC has been discussing military cooperation since it was formed in May 1981, but it has made relatively limited real-world progress. As mentioned in Chapter 1, the GCC has deployed a Peninsula Shield Force in Hafr al Batin in northeastern Saudi Arabia since 1984. This force is deployed in a strategic area roughly sixty-five kilometers from the Kuwaiti border and has a nominal strength of 5,000 men. Leading Saudi commanders and members of the royal family make it clear that the only real war fighting capabilities of this force consist of a Saudi Army brigade that was deployed in the area long before the Peninsula Shield Force existed, that the so-called composite brigade with manpower and equipment from other GCC states is understrength and has only token defensive war fighting capability, and that the plans the GCC ministers announced to strength the Peninsula Shield Force after their meeting in December 2000 are cosmetic rather than real. These problems have been compounded by reliance on GCC exercises that are largely unrealistic showpieces involving token reinforcements from other Southern Gulf states. Unfortunately, the only realistic joint warfare and combined arms exercises that bring even Saudi and Kuwait land and air forces together have been relatively low-level (battalion equivalent–sized) exercises led by the United States.

The GCC does, however, have the potential to do far more in the future, and some progress is being made. Naval cooperation is improving faster than cooperation in air and land forces, with significant contributions from the British, French, and U.S. navies. This involves steadily more realistic exercises in critical missions like mine warfare.

The GCC took twenty years to do so, but it put the first phase of a joint air defense command and control system called Hizam Al Taaun (HAT-Belt of Cooperation) into operation in early 2001. This system provides secure communications between the national air defense command and control centers of the GCC states, rather than truly integrating air defense. However, it can provide early warning and some intercept and land-based air defense data in the event of an air attack by Iran or Iraq. (It would not provide useful data in a ballistic missile, low-altitude air, or cruise missile attack.) However, future plans call for a combination of a Raytheon-developed integrated air battle management system and an Ericson secure optical fiber communications system, which should allow the GCC to finally develop capabilities that should have been in place well over a decade ago.

FUTURE RELIANCE ON FOREIGN MANPOWER AND ADVISORS

The Kingdom has cut back steadily on foreign manpower and contractor support since the early 1990s—both for cost reasons and as part of its Saudisation policies. As a result, it is difficult to make any estimate of the degree to which Saudi Arabia currently offsets its manpower shortages by the direct use of foreign troops and advisors. Further, the separation between formal military advisors and Western contractors is often more a matter of clothing than function. It is clear, however, that there are still significant numbers of U.S., British, and French military advisors serving with Saudi forces, and there are still significant numbers of Western contract personnel—many handling critical service and support functions for Saudi Arabia's most modern weapons. There are small cadres from Brazil and other arms sellers, and at least several hundred PRC personnel servicing and operating Saudi Arabia's CSS-2 long-range surface-to-surface missiles.

At the same time, the Kingdom lacks the financial resources it had in the past to buy the level of Western foreign contractor support it needs to perform routine force-wide functions like maintenance and training. It has also found that using large numbers of foreign contract personnel to provide key skills leads to enduring dependence in areas where Saudi Arabia should have its own capabilities, and leads to problems in training personnel to work well with their Saudi counterparts and then stay in country.

Saudi planners have concluded that foreign contract manpower must be carefully chosen if is expected to maintain and sustain combat forces in an actual war in which Saudi bases and facilities are at risk. As a result, relatively small cadres of Western personnel with long experience in the Kingdom continue to provide critical support and expertise, but Saudi Arabia makes far less use of Western personnel than it did in the past. It does still use more substantial numbers of foreign contract personnel and seconded or ex-military personnel. Saudi Arabia has found, however, that manpower from other Arab or Islamic states can be hard to train to the levels needed for skilled technical support jobs, and hard to retain once it is trained.

As a result, Saudi Arabia has further reasons to carefully examine any future plans to expand its forces or purchase large numbers of additional weapons systems. It is clear that simply creating units on paper and buying large numbers of weapons does not make the required manpower quantity or quality appear. As is the case with training, sustainment, and maintenance, Saudi Arabia needs to concentrate on creating real-world war fighting capability and not force numbers. This means focusing on a future force structure it can actually supply with manpower with the right training and skills and giving the proper manning of support forces the same priority as combat arms.

NOTES

1. David E. Long, *The Kingdom of Saudi Arabia* (Gainesville: University Press of Florida, 1997), pp. 35–38.

2. Royal Embassy of Saudi Arabia, "Government Official's Biographies: His Royal Highness Prince Sultan bin Abdulaziz Al Saud," URL: *http:// www.saudiembassy.net/gov_profile/bio_sultan.html.* Accessed on May 30, 2002.

3. Joseph A. Kechichian, *Succession in Saudi Arabia* (New York: Palgrave, 2001), p. 79.

4. Reuters, May 14, 1996; *Jane's Defence Weekly*, May 22, 1996, p. 4.

5. IISS, *Military Balance, 2001–2002*, "Saudi Arabia"; SAMA, *Thirty-Sixth Annual Report*, 1421H, Table 16.3.

6. CIA, *World Factbook, 2001*, "Iran," " Iraq," "Saudi Arabia," and "Yemen."

7. Some estimates of National Guard regulars go as low as 75,000. Guard officials sometimes use a figure of 150,000, but this seems to include tribal irregulars.

8. IISS, *Military Balance, 2001–2002*.

9. Unless otherwise specified, the military data quoted here are taken from the relevant country sections of various annual editions of the IISS, *Military Balance*; CIA, *The World Factbook*; and Jaffee Center for Strategic Studies, *The Middle East Military Balance* (Tel Aviv: Tel Aviv University).

10. These Pakistani forces left the Kingdom in 1988 and 1989.

11. Based on interviews, IISS estimates, and the *Jane's Sentinel* series for 1999– 2001.

12. Department of State, *Annual Report on Military Expenditures, 1999*, Submitted to the Committee on Appropriations of the U.S. Senate and the Committee on Appropriations of the U.S. House of Representatives, July 27, 2000, in accordance with section 511(b) of the Foreign Operations, Export Financing, and Related Programs Appropriations Act, 1993.

13. IISS, *Military Balance, 1990–1991*.

14. *Jane's Defence Weekly*, May 22, 1996, p. 4.

15. *Jane's Pointer*, September 1996, p. 5; *Defense News*, April 14, 1997, p. 3.

16. Saudi government officials again raised the possibility of instituting a draft in late 1994. See Reuters, 11-23-94 00:39 AET.

17. The data available to the author were so much in conflict that it proved impossible to provide even a useful range.

Chapter 3

Saudi Military Expenditures and Arms Transfers

S audi Arabia faces equally difficult challenges in determining and providing the proper levels of military spending in effectively managing its funds and in deciding on the proper level of arms imports. Uncertain oil revenues and steadily expanding civil demands for entitlements and civil investment have greatly reduced the ease with which the Kingdom can sustain high levels of defense expenditures. At the same time, Saudi Arabia can still afford to spend far more on its military forces than the other Southern Gulf states, Iraq's military spending has been severely restricted by UN sanctions, and Iran's economic problems have sharply limited what it can spend on military forces.

SAUDI MILITARY EXPENDITURES

Chart 3.1 provides a U.S. government comparison of Saudi military expenditures with those of other Gulf states. One point is very clear: Saudi Arabia has spent far more on military forces than any other Gulf state, and is the only major country to have sustained high levels of expenditure since the mid-1990s. A similar comparison of Saudi expenditures with those of Kuwait and its two main threats—Iraq and Iran—is shown in Chart 3.2. A comparable IISS estimate of more recent expenditures by Gulf states is shown in Chart 3.3.

The levels of spending in these charts often differs significantly according to source, but they all show that Saudi military spending dwarfs that of the other Gulf states, although the comparability of the data are somewhat

Chart 3.1
Comparative Military Expenditures of the Gulf Powers, 1984–1999 (Constant $U.S. 1999 Millions)

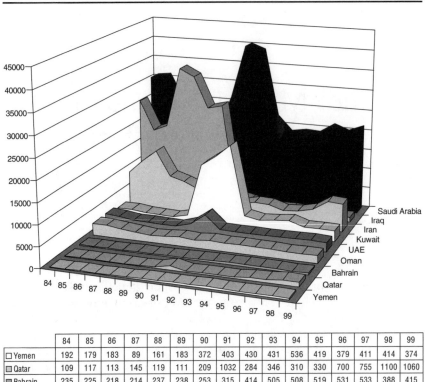

	84	85	86	87	88	89	90	91	92	93	94	95	96	97	98	99
☐ Yemen	192	179	183	89	161	183	372	403	430	431	536	419	379	411	414	374
☐ Qatar	109	117	113	145	119	111	209	1032	284	346	310	330	700	755	1100	1060
▨ Bahrain	235	225	218	214	237	238	253	315	414	505	508	519	531	533	388	415
☐ Oman	2911	2855	2389	2020	1710	1890	2230	1890	2230	2060	2130	2080	1940	1820	1780	1780
▣ UAE	3000	2666	2187	2120	2010	1930	3030	5550	2330	2290	2270	2250	2250	2310	2410	2180
☐ Kuwait	2190	2160	1768	1630	1560	2310	15200	17800	20700	3810	3190	3550	3900	2760	2730	2690
☐ Iran	9386	12680	15320	9350	8330	6820	7160	6710	4170	4950	4770	3640	3940	4730	7150	6880
▨ Iraq	25890	18670	20050	35000	33200	25500	26400	3500	2800	2000	1750	1750	1500	1440	1270	1250
■ Saudi Arabia	30500	30900	24010	21600	17200	17900	27100	40200	38800	22100	18400	19100	18800	21100	19800	21200

Sources: Adapted by Anthony H. Cordesman from ACDA, *World Military Expenditures and Arms Transfers, 1995* (Washington: GPO, 1996) and U.S. State Department, *World Military Expenditures and Arms Transfers, 1999–2000* (Washington: Bureau of Arms Control, 2001).

more uncertain than the figures provided by the U.S. government. Since the mid-1990s, Saudi Arabia has spent almost four times as much on military forces as Iran and nearly ten times more than Iraq. It has spent roughly eight times as much as any of its Southern Gulf allies. Iran does seem to have increased its military spending as a result of the boom in oil revenues in 2000, but it is far from clear that this is sustainable.

Chart 3.2

Comparative Military Expenditures of the High Expenditure Gulf Powers, 1983–1999 (Constant $U.S. Millions)

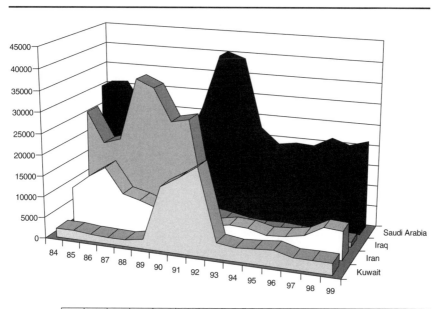

	84	85	86	87	88	89	90	91	92	93	94	95	96	97	98	99
☐ Kuwait	2190	2160	1768	1630	1560	2310	15200	17800	20700	3810	3190	3550	3900	2760	2730	2690
☐ Iran	9386	12680	15320	9350	8330	6820	7160	6710	4170	4950	4770	3640	3940	4730	7150	6880
▨ Iraq	25890	18670	20050	35000	33200	25500	26400	3500	2800	2000	1750	1750	1500	1440	1270	1250
■ Saudi Arabia	30500	30900	24010	21600	17200	17900	27100	40200	38800	22100	18400	19100	18800	21100	19800	21200

Sources: Adapted by Anthony H. Cordesman from ACDA, *World Military Expenditures and Arms Transfers, 1995* (Washington: GPO, 1996) and U.S. State Department, *World Military Expenditures and Arms Transfers, 1999–2000* (Washington: Bureau of Arms Control, 2001).

Chart 3.4 extends these comparisons by showing the burden military spending imposes as a percentage of GNP and of total central government expenditures (CGE). It also shows arms imports as a percent of total imports. Saudi Arabia does not have the highest percentages in every category, and these figures are a "snapshot"—not an average over an extended period of time. Nevertheless, Saudi Arabia clearly has the highest overall military spending burden of any nation in the Middle East. While these estimates illustrate the extent to which Saudi Arabia has been able to buy its way out of its military problems in the past, they also show that Saudi military expenditures have placed a massive burden on the Saudi budget. Only the UAE compares with the Saudi level of effort, and it has done so only in recent years.

Chart 3.3
Comparative Military Expenditures in the Gulf Region, 1995–2001 (Current $U.S. Millions)

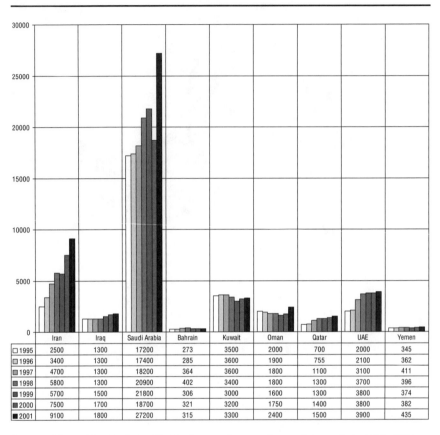

	Iran	Iraq	Saudi Arabia	Bahrain	Kuwait	Oman	Qatar	UAE	Yemen
☐ 1995	2500	1300	17200	273	3500	2000	700	2000	345
▨ 1996	3400	1300	17400	285	3600	1900	755	2100	362
▥ 1997	4700	1300	18200	364	3600	1800	1100	3100	411
▦ 1998	5800	1300	20900	402	3400	1800	1300	3700	396
▩ 1999	5700	1500	21800	306	3000	1600	1300	3800	374
▧ 2000	7500	1700	18700	321	3200	1750	1400	3800	382
■ 2001	9100	1800	27200	315	3300	2400	1500	3900	435

Source: Adapted by Anthony H. Cordesman from various editions of the IISS, *Military Balance*. The author has adjusted a number of figures and has provided trend estimates for the year 2000.

Different Estimates of Saudi Military Expenditures and Their Burden on the Economy

There are a number of different estimates of Saudi expenditures, and of the burden they impose on the Saudi economy, but they agree in terms of broad pattern. Chart 3.5 shows U.S. State Department, U.S. Department of Defense, and IISS estimates of total Saudi spending. Even allowing for differences in constant and current dollars, there are very significant differences in the various estimates.

Chart 3.4
Military Expenditures and Arms Transfers as an Aspect of "Statism" (Military Spending as a Percent of Central Government Expenditures [CGE], Gross National Product [GNP], and Arms Imports as a Percent of Total Imports)

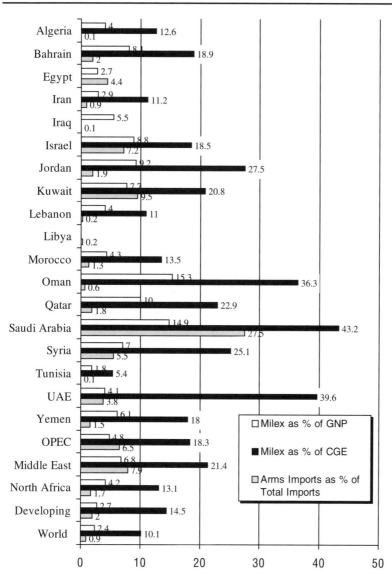

Source: Adapted by Anthony H. Cordesman from U.S. State Department, *World Military Expenditures and Arms Transfers, 1999–2000* (Washington: Bureau of Arms Control, 2001).

Chart 3.5

Comparative Estimates of Saudi Military Spending, 1990–2000 (Current $U.S. Billions)

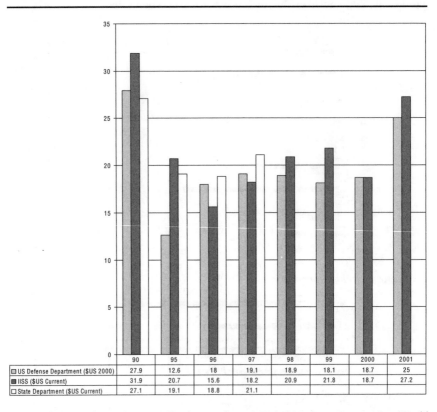

	90	95	96	97	98	99	2000	2001
US Defense Department ($US 2000)	27.9	12.6	18	19.1	18.9	18.1	18.7	25
IISS ($US Current)	31.9	20.7	15.6	18.2	20.9	21.8	18.7	27.2
State Department ($US Current)	27.1	19.1	18.8	21.1				

Sources: Adapted by Anthony H. Cordesman from ACDA, U.S. State Department, *World Military Expenditures and Arms Transfers, 1999–2000* (Washington: Bureau of Arms Control); Report to the U.S. Congress by the Secretary of Defense, *Report on Allied Contributions to the Common Defense, March 2001*, p. E-5; and various editions of the IISS, *Military Balance.*

Chart 3.6 shows a Saudi estimate, along with the trends in the total Saudi national budget and the trends in the GDP. The massive military and civil costs of the Gulf War emerge quite clearly in both charts. Saudi figures in Chart 3.6 indicate that defense and security expenditures remain a very high percentage of the total national budget and GNP.

The Department of Defense (DOD) estimates show that Saudi spending peaked during the Gulf War, then dropped in the mid-to-late 1990s as Saudi Arabia came under increasing financial pressure because of comparatively low oil revenues and increased civil spending burdens caused by major

Chart 3.6
Saudi Estimates of Saudi National Security Spending, 1981–2000 (Current Millions of Saudi Riyals)

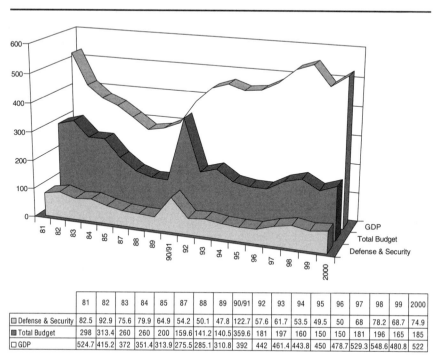

	81	82	83	84	85	87	88	89	90/91	92	93	94	95	96	97	98	99	2000
☐ Defense & Security	82.5	92.9	75.6	79.9	64.9	54.2	50.1	47.8	122.7	57.6	61.7	53.5	49.5	50	68	78.2	68.7	74.9
■ Total Budget	298	313.4	260	260	200	159.6	141.2	140.5	359.6	181	197	160	150	150	181	196	165	185
☐ GDP	524.7	415.2	372	351.4	313.9	275.5	285.1	310.8	392	442	461.4	443.8	450	478.7	529.3	548.6	480.8	522

Source: Adapted by Anthony H. Cordesman from material provided by the Saudi Arabian
　　Monetary Agency.

population increases. The figure for 1995 seems too low in view of Saudi military efforts during that year, but 1995 was a year of Saudi fiscal crisis. Nevertheless, Saudi spending did drop by 33% between 1990 and 2000. What is equally striking, however, is that other DOD sources indicate that Saudi expenditures leaped back up in 2001 as a result of a sudden "boom" in oil expenditures.

Other reporting by the U.S. State Department indicates that Saudi Arabia spent $8.3 billion on defense during January 1 to December 31, 1999.[1] It notes, however, that the Saudi government does not have separate line-item budgets for defense and national security. Because they do not identify them separately, defense spending includes Ministry of Interior expenditures and is therefore somewhat misleading. According to this estimate, Saudi Arabia spent 13% of its GDP and 41.65% of its national budget on military forces during this period.[2]

The State Department estimates that 1999 defense spending was 12% lower than in 1998. Defense spending as a percentage of the budget increased, however, because the overall budget decrease (from $52.3 billion in FY 1998 to $44 billion in 1999) was greater than the decrease in the military budget. This trend reversed sharply in FY 2000 because there was a significant recovery in oil prices, beginning in April 1999. This contributed significantly to a rise in Saudi government budgetary spending, and the nominal GDP, as well as a moderate decrease in the 1999 budget deficit. As yet, however, the United States government has not provided unclassified estimates.[3]

In contrast, the IISS estimates that the Saudi military budget totaled $18.4 billion (69 billion riyals) in 1999, $18.7 billion (70 billion riyals) in 2000, and $27.2 billion (102 billion riyals) in 2001. It estimates actual spending at $21.8 billion (81 billion riyals) in 1999, and $18.7 billion (70 billion riyals) in 2000. The IISS does not explain the sudden estimated leap in planned Saudi spending in 2001. Saudi military sources state that this rise did not occur, and feel the IISS is confusing expenditures on a major security force and sensor system on the Yemen border with added defense spending. However, some DOD sources indicate that part of the rise in 2000 resulted from trying to compensate for underspending in previous years and part resulted from an unfortunate Saudi tendency to rush into spending increases the moment oil revenues rise, regardless of whether they are really needed or whether the money can be spent effectively. Several Saudi civil sources also indicate that this latter explanation is correct and that unplanned and highly wasteful procurement and support contracts were signed that had a major impact in increasing Saudi Arabia's budget deficit problems in ways Crown Prince Abdullah never approved.

Estimating the Burden of Saudi Military Spending

It is hard to assess in detail how Saudi military expenditures are spent. The Saudi budget is vague at best in describing defense and security expenses and provides no particulars of any kind. Furthermore, it does not include all purchases of military equipment, construction, and services. Saudi Arabia does not report all of the relevant costs in its budget documents—particularly costs of defense relating to the purchase of foreign defense goods and services. Saudi Arabia has often increased its defense expenditures after the budget was issued without reporting them, and has never publicly reported the actual cash flow it has spent on arms imports or on the value of the oil it has sometimes used in complex barter deals.

As noted earlier, this lack of transparency in the Ministry of Defense and Aviation (MODA), National Guard, and other Saudi security-related budgets reflects serious problems in the management of Saudi defense resources. It makes it impossible for Saudis inside and outside military and security activities to provide intelligent criticism of the way the Kingdom spends its resources. Perhaps more important, it seems to disguise a critical lack of effective planning, programming, and budgeting in the MODA. If the ministry has anything approaching a five-year plan to keep procurement, manpower, and operations and maintenance expenditure in the proper balance, it certainly is not clear from Saudi actions. This lack of transparency also seems to disguise serious problems in exerting the proper fiscal controls and reviewing, particularly in regard to arms orders and procurement spending.

Some additional data are available, however, on the burden that Saudi military expenditures place on the entire national budget and the economy and on Saudi arms imports. Chart 3.7 supplements that data provided in Chart 3.6 by providing an unclassified estimate by the U.S. intelligence community of how Saudi military spending compares with the trends in the Saudi gross national product, central government spending, total exports, and arms imports. This chart shows that the trend patterns in U.S. estimates do not differ radically from those of the Saudi government. It also shows that the Saudi GNP plunged after the "oil crash" that occurred in 1986, but has since grown faster than total central government expenditures and much faster than military spending and arms purchases.[4] Chart 3.8 provides a somewhat similar estimate by the DOD. The basic trends are similar, although the differences between Charts 3.7 and 3.8 again illustrate how difficult it is to make precise estimates of the economics of Saudi defense.

Export, Economic, and Demographic Impacts

Charts 3.9 to 3.11 show the impact of export, economic, and demographic problems in more detail. While the permutations shown may be of interest largely to economists and budget analysts, the net effect of these charts is to show that the demographic pressures on the Saudi economy, a lack of economic diversification, and major unpredictable swings in oil export revenues have increasingly limited Saudi ability to fund both "guns" and "butter."

- Chart 3.9 analyzes the military spending burden as a percent of GNP and CGE. It shows military manning as a percent of thousands in the total population, and arms imports as a percent of total imports. As might be expected, spending as a percent of CGE shows the same upward "spike" as in Chart 3.6. At the same time, Chart 3.9 shows that the rise in oil prices and the volume of Saudi oil exports that occurred during the war help limit the increase in military spending as a percent of GNP.

- The percentages for military manpower per thousand in the population show an increase from a little over five men per thousand in the population before the Gulf War to around nine per thousand in the late 1990s. On the one hand, the Saudi figures compare with well over thirty men per thousand in Israel

Chart 3.7
State Department Estimate of Saudi Gross National Product, Central Government Expenditures, Military Expenditures, Total Exports, Total Imports, and Arms Import Deliveries, 1984–1999 (Constant $U.S. 1999 Millions)

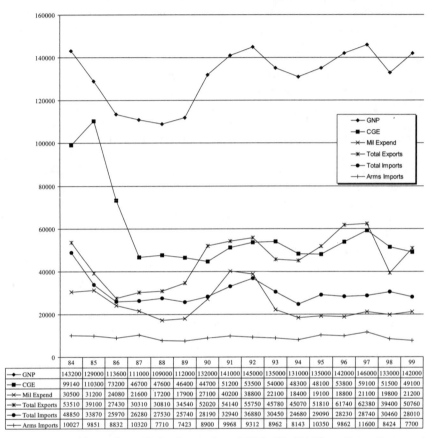

	84	85	86	87	88	89	90	91	92	93	94	95	96	97	98	99
GNP	143200	129000	113600	111000	109000	112000	132000	141000	145000	135000	131000	135000	142000	146000	133000	142000
CGE	99140	110300	73200	46700	47600	46400	44700	51200	53500	54000	48300	48100	53800	59100	51500	49100
Mil Expend	30500	31200	24080	21600	17200	17900	27100	40200	38800	22100	18400	19100	18800	21100	19800	21200
Total Exports	53510	39100	27430	30310	30810	34540	52020	54140	55750	45780	45070	51810	61740	62380	39400	50760
Total Imports	48850	33870	25970	26280	27530	25740	28190	32940	36880	30450	24680	29090	28230	28740	30460	28010
Arms Imports	10027	9851	8832	10320	7710	7423	8900	9968	9312	8962	8143	10350	9862	11600	8424	7700

Sources: Adapted by Anthony H. Cordesman from ACDA, *World Military Expenditures and Arms Transfers, 1995* (Washington: GPO, 1996) and various editions of U.S. State Department, *World Military Expenditures and Arms Transfers* (Washington: Bureau of Arms Control).

and twenty in Iraq. On the other hand, Saudi military manpower per thousand has nearly doubled since the Iraqi invasion of Kuwait and the Saudi manpower percentages are almost exactly the same as Iran's.

- Chart 3.10 provides additional insight into a critical period in Saudi military spending—the Gulf War—and shows that the popular perception that the cost of the war to Saudi Arabia was driven by massive arms imports is completely wrong. It was the cost of Saudi aid to the United States and other Gulf War

Chart 3.8
Department of Defense Estimate of Saudi Gross National Product, Central Government Expenditures, Military Expenditures, Total Exports, Total Imports, and Arms Import Deliveries, 1990–2000 (Constant $U.S. 2000 Billions)

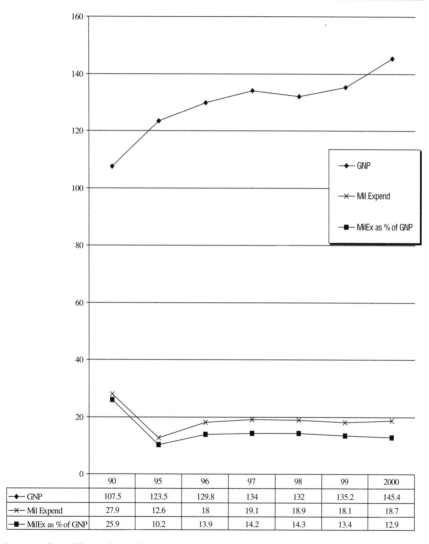

	90	95	96	97	98	99	2000
GNP	107.5	123.5	129.8	134	132	135.2	145.4
Mil Expend	27.9	12.6	18	19.1	18.9	18.1	18.7
MilEx as % of GNP	25.9	10.2	13.9	14.2	14.3	13.4	12.9

Source: Adapted by Anthony H. Cordesman from Report to the U.S. Congress by the Secretary of Defense, *Report on Allied Contributions to the Common Defense, March 2001*, p. E-5.

Chart 3.9
Saudi Military Efforts as a Percent of GNP, Government Expenditures, and Imports and Military Personnel per 1,000 in Total Population, 1972–1999 (All Percentages Are Measured in Absolute Manpower and Constant $U.S. 1999)

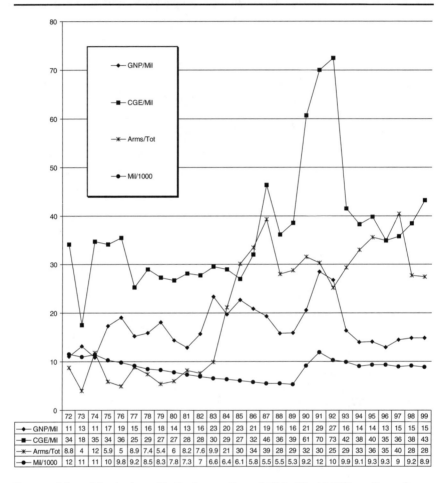

	72	73	74	75	76	77	78	79	80	81	82	83	84	85	86	87	88	89	90	91	92	93	94	95	96	97	98	99
GNP/Mil	11	13	11	17	19	15	16	18	14	13	16	23	20	23	21	19	16	16	21	29	27	16	14	14	13	15	15	15
CGE/Mil	34	18	35	34	36	25	29	27	27	28	28	30	29	27	32	46	36	39	61	70	73	42	38	40	35	36	38	43
Arms/Tot	8.8	4	12	5.9	5	8.9	7.4	5.4	6	8.2	7.6	9.9	21	30	34	39	28	29	32	30	25	29	33	36	35	40	28	28
Mil/1000	12	11	11	10	9.8	9.2	8.5	8.3	7.8	7.3	7	6.6	6.4	6.1	5.8	5.5	5.5	5.3	9.2	12	10	9.9	9.1	9.3	9.3	9	9.2	8.9

Sources: Adapted by Anthony H. Cordesman from ACDA, *World Military Expenditures and Arms Transfers, 1995* (Washington: GPO, 1996) and various editions of U.S. State Department, *World Military Expenditures and Arms Transfers* (Washington: Bureau of Arms Control).

coalition members, the cost of building up Saudi forces, and aid to Kuwait that drove up costs. This pattern is also shown in Chart 3.6, but more of the expenditures are shown outside the national security sector because Saudi definitions differ from those used by the United States.

• Finally, Chart 3.11 shows how the pressures Saudi Arabia faces in terms of guns and butter affected the trends in per capita income and spending. The

Chart 3.10
**Shift in Saudi Military Expenditures and Arms Deliveries as a Percent of 1984 Total,
1984–1997 (Constant $U.S. 1997 Millions)**

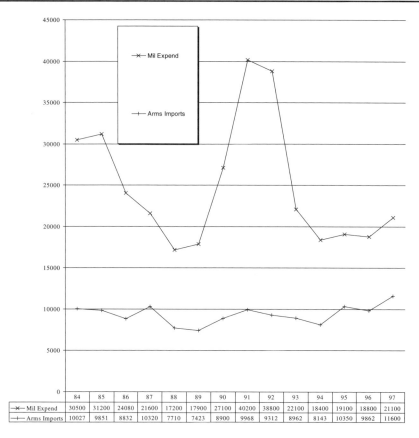

	84	85	86	87	88	89	90	91	92	93	94	95	96	97
—✖— Mil Expend	30500	31200	24080	21600	17200	17900	27100	40200	38800	22100	18400	19100	18800	21100
—+— Arms Imports	10027	9851	8832	10320	7710	7423	8900	9968	9312	8962	8143	10350	9862	11600

Sources: Adapted by Anthony H. Cordesman from ACDA, *World Military Expenditures and Arms Transfers, 1995* (Washington: GPO, 1996) and U.S. State Department, *World Military Expenditures and Arms Transfers, 1998* (Washington: Bureau of Arms Control, 1999).

burden of military spending in per capita terms has not increased since the mid-1980s. However, the era in which Saudi Arabia had a vast surplus of per capita income relative to per capita military spending ended with the "oil crash" in 1986. Since that time, military spending has taken up a significant share of total per capita income even though it is lower in real terms.

The message that emerges from this complex mix of trends is just how much Saudi Arabia now needs to reexamine the burden that military spending now puts on its economy and society and find ways to reduce that

Chart 3.11
Saudi GNP per Capita versus Military Expenditures per Capita, 1983–1999
(Constant $U.S. 1999 Millions)

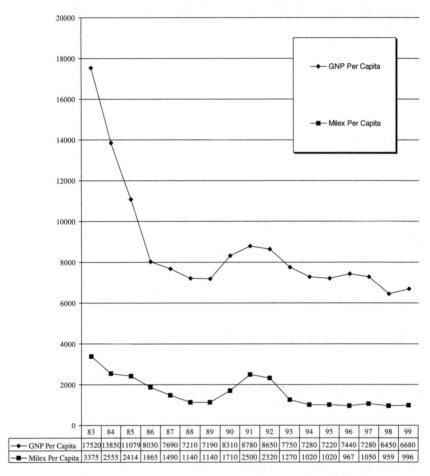

	83	84	85	86	87	88	89	90	91	92	93	94	95	96	97	98	99
GNP Per Capita	17520	13850	11079	8030	7690	7210	7190	8310	8780	8650	7750	7280	7220	7440	7280	6450	6680
Milex Per Capita	3375	2555	2414	1865	1490	1140	1140	1710	2500	2320	1270	1020	1020	967	1050	959	996

Sources: Adapted by Anthony H. Cordesman from ACDA, *World Military Expenditures and Arms Transfers, 1995* (Washington: GPO, 1996) and various editions of U.S. State Department, *World Military Expenditures and Arms Transfers* (Washington: Bureau of Arms Control).

spending if it can possibly do so. Saudi Arabia clearly needs to budget in ways that reflect the fact that its force structure is maturing, that the pressure on spending is for force quality and not increased force quantity, and that spending on modernization and "recapitalization" needs to be carefully balanced against manpower and sustainment. More than the "oil boom" is over; Saudi military development needs to shift from its boom days of expansion to a stable and affordable structure.

Finding the Proper Level of Expenditure

The total cost of Saudi military efforts since the early 1970s has exceeded several hundred billion dollars, even if one excludes the cost of the Gulf War. The Kingdom spent from $14 to $24 billion a year on defense during the late 1970s and the 1980s and its full-time active military manpower increased from 79,000 to 126,500.[5] Much of this expenditure—probably on the order of 60 to 65%—was spent on infrastructure, foreign services and maintenance, and basic manpower training. Saudi Arabia had to create entire military cities, new ports, and major road networks. It had to create modern military bases in the middle of its deserts, and pay for far more extensive training than most of the military manpower in the Third World receives.

There were good reasons for many of these expenditures during Saudi Arabia's period of modernizing its military force. Saudi recruits, whether nomad or "townie," had to be brought to the point where they could operate modern military equipment, and the Kingdom had to buy a pool of equipment and munitions large and modern enough to give Saudi Arabia the ability to deter Iran and Iraq. Since the mid-1980s, Saudi Arabia has been able to shift from creating basic military capabilities and infrastructure to a slower and less expensive buildup of combat capabilities. The cost of the Gulf War placed a massive new burden on the Kingdom, however, and such expenses had to take place at the cost of "butter" and helped lead to chronic Saudi budget deficits.[6]

As the previous charts have shown, the Gulf War pushed Saudi military and security expenditures to the crisis level. Saudi security expenditures rose from 36% of the total national budget in 1988, and 39% in 1989, to nearly 60% in 1990. Although any such estimates are highly dependent on exactly which aspects of the cost of Saudi support to allied military forces during the Gulf War should be included, the percentage rose to around 70% in 1991–1992—including the cost of aid to allied governments during Desert Storm. It declined to around 30% after 1992, and has remained at the 30 to 40% level ever since. There is no question that Saudi military expenditures have continued to contribute to the Saudi deficit, to limit expenditure on civil development, and limit funds for social services throughout the 1990s and early 2000s.[7]

What is far less clear is why Saudi military expenditures have remained so high since the Gulf War, or why some sources report that they suddenly rose in 2001. The long pipeline of arms deliveries ordered in reaction to the war explains some of the high expenditures in the early-to-mid-1990s, but they should have tapered off more rapidly after the mid-1990s than the data available indicates. In fact, both the size of Saudi arms deliveries and the ratio of deliveries to new agreements after 1995 are much higher than can easily be explained by the volume of actual arms deliveries or Saudi needs.

Similarly, military construction expenditures remain too high. The Kingdom completed most of its infrastructure and basic force development expenditures by the late 1980s. This should have led to sharper cuts in such expenditures during the period after the Gulf War, which is particularly true given the systematic underfunding of manpower quality and sustainment from the mid-1990s onward. Once again, the explanation seems to be poor planning, programming, and budgeting by the MODA.

Saudi military expenditures have also remained too high as a percent of GDP and as a percent of total government expenditures. The U.S. State Department estimates indicate that Saudi Arabia spent about 20% of its GDP on defense during 1983–1986. It ranged from 16% to 23% of the GNP during the 1980s, peaked at 27% to 29% in 1990 to 1992, and has since dropped to around 14%. The percentage was only about 8.5% in 1996, however, if GDP is measured in purchasing power parity.[8] The DOD has somewhat different estimates. It indicates that Saudi expenditures peaked at 26% to 28% in 1990–1992, dropped to 10.2% in 1995, rose to around 14% through 1996–1998, and settled around 13% in 1999 and 2000.[9]

Saudi military expenditures averaged around 40% of all central government expenditures (CGE) before the Gulf War, and rose to a peak of 60% to 73% during the Gulf War. They then dropped back to around 35% to 40%; this, however, was still an exceptionally high percentage for a Saudi government that must fund so large a mix of welfare, entitlement, and civil investment expenditures. At the same time, Saudi military expenditures per capita dropped at roughly the same rate as the Saudi per capita GNP. U.S. officials estimate that Saudi expenditures accounted for approximately 35% to 40% of CGE and 12.9% of the GNP in 2000.[10]

There is no way to establish a "golden rule" as to what share of the GNP or total budget Saudi military and security expenditures should consume. It is clear that recent spending has placed an increasing strain on the Saudi budget and economy. At the same time, these percentages are not easy to cut. Saudi Arabia must spend about $13 to $15 billion a year (in 2002 dollars) if it is to maintain its present forces and rate of modernization. It should be noted that the military is making an effort to save some money by taking such steps as increasing its repair capabilities, which would reduce the number of spares normally required to be stockpiled while systems are en route for overseas repair.[11]

SAUDI ARMS IMPORTS

Saudi Arabia has long been dependent on other nations for virtually all of its arms and military technology. It is making slow progress in developing an indigenous arms industry, although it has made progress in the support, supply, and operations and maintenance areas. It can produce some small arms, automatic weapons, and munitions, but much of the Saudi portion of the work consists of assembling imported parts rather than real manufactures.

A number of other programs consist of efforts in which a foreign arms supplier has agreed to set up a defense-related industrial site in Saudi Arabia to "offset" Saudi spending on arms imports. Some of these "offset" efforts have been useful in reducing the need to import technology, services, and parts, but many others are more symbolic efforts to employ Saudis than substantive efforts to aid the Saudi military or industrial base. Some are little more than rackets that benefit Saudi princes and officers, and often the foreign contractors involved. It is scarcely surprising, therefore, that Saudi Arabia's military buildup and modernization has led to massive expenditures on military imports.[12]

These spending patterns also help explain why Saudi Arabia has ranked as one of the world's ten largest military importers in every year for the last two decades. It ranked first in both new arms agreements and in actual arms deliveries during 1989–1992 and 1993–1996. It ranked first in arms deliveries during 1996–1999, although it ranked third in terms of new orders—behind the UAE and India and only marginally above Egypt.[13]

The Volume of Saudi Arms Imports

Until the late 1980s, the dollar value of Saudi military imports did not involve as high a proportion of expenditures on actual weapons as did the arms imports of most other countries. Much of the total cost of Saudi military imports included an exceptionally large percentage of construction services, service support costs, and goods other than weapons and munitions that were imported from other nations. These expenditures are classified as arms imports in the estimates made by the U.S. government even when they do not include weapons.

Since the late 1980s, however, Saudi Arabia has spent roughly the same proportion of its military import dollars on arms as other Middle Eastern countries. It also seems to have spent on arms even if this meant inadequate spending on foreign contract services related to training and sustainment, with particularly severe results in underfunding Air Force readiness. As has been touched upon earlier, the figures on Saudi spending after the Gulf War also reflect more spending on arms than the Kingdom needed or could sustain.

It is not easy to make an accurate analysis of Saudi arms buys. Saudi Arabia does not provide statistics on its military imports, and most outside estimates are of limited analytic reliability. Two useful sources of unclassified intelligence estimates are, however, available from the U.S.

government: The Bureau of Arms Control in the U.S. State Department (formerly the Arms Control and Disarmament Agency [ACDA]) and the Congressional Research Service. These estimates are based on unclassified intelligence data that make a detailed effort to include all weapons and produce comparable estimates.

Those still present uncertainties, but they provide a much more reliable picture than academic and non-governmental organization (NGO) estimates of arms sales. They are certainly accurate in reflecting the steady increase in Saudi arms imports that has taken place in reaction to the massive buildup of Iraqi and Iranian forces, the threats and uncertainties posed by the Iran-Iraq War, the cost of fighting the Gulf War, and other current threats.[14]

Patterns in Saudi Arms Imports, 1973–1990

Chart 3.12 shows the patterns in total arms deliveries to Saudi Arabia from 1973 to 1997. It is clear that the Kingdom embarked on a major military buildup following the October War in 1973, although it is important to note that this buildup was driven by the arms race in Iran, Iraq, and Yemen, and was made possible by the leap in their oil revenues that took place after early 1974. Saudi Arabia never took part in the Arab-Israeli arms race or attempted to create significant military forces on its western border.

Chart 3.12 also shows a further major leap in Saudi arms imports after the fall of the Shah in 1979 and the start of the Iran-Iraq War in 1980 created a very different threat from the north. The growing risk that Iran would defeat Iraq between 1984 and 1987 led to another massive surge in Saudi arms deliveries during 1987–1991, which was caused by orders placed earlier in the Iran-Iraq War, but many of which were delivered after the war's end in 1988. A similar lag in deliveries explains another surge in arms deliveries in 1995 to 1997. Although the Gulf War with Iraq took place in 1990–1991, the surge in orders during and immediately after the war did not result in massive deliveries until the mid-1990s.

If one looks at total transfers to the developing world, Saudi Arabia was the largest arms importer during 1984–1987 ($27.5 billion), 1988–1991 ($26.8 billion), 1991–1994 ($29.8 billion), and 1995–1998 ($67.8 billion).[15] It must again be stressed, however, that these figures for Saudi Arabia arms imports, substantial amounts of services, and the value of actual weapons transfers was around half the total reported.

One other striking aspect of Chart 3.12 is the number of different countries from whom Saudi Arabia purchased arms. There were good reasons to diversify the Kingdom's arms purchases. Saudi Arabia found it could not rely on the United States because of U.S. ties to Israel and internal political pressure from Israel's supporters. It made sense for the Kingdom not to become too dependent on one supplier. Second, major arms purchases were a diplomatic tool in ensuring support from supplier nations. Finally,

Chart 3.12
Trends in Arms Deliveries to Saudi Arabia ($U.S. Current Millions)

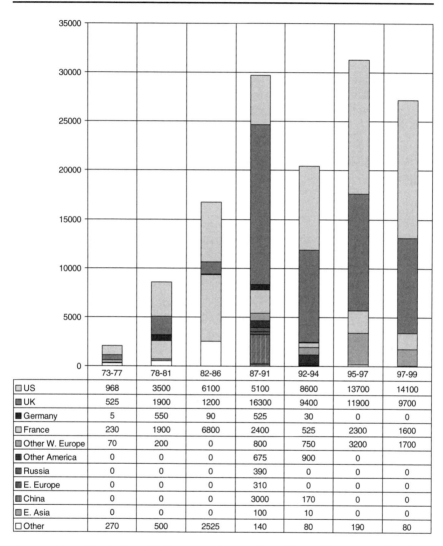

	73-77	78-81	82-86	87-91	92-94	95-97	97-99
US	968	3500	6100	5100	8600	13700	14100
UK	525	1900	1200	16300	9400	11900	9700
Germany	5	550	90	525	30	0	0
France	230	1900	6800	2400	525	2300	1600
Other W. Europe	70	200	0	800	750	3200	1700
Other America	0	0	0	675	900	0	
Russia	0	0	0	390	0	0	0
E. Europe	0	0	0	310	0	0	0
China	0	0	0	3000	170	0	0
E. Asia	0	0	0	100	10	0	0
Other	270	500	2525	140	80	190	80

Sources: Adapted by Anthony H. Cordesman from various editions of ACDA, *World Military Expenditures and Arms Transfers* (Washington: GPO) and various editions of U.S. State Department, *World Military Expenditures and Arms Transfers* (Washington: Bureau of Arms Control).

arms imports were a way of "recycling" oil export revenues and preserving market share.

At the same time, the Kingdom failed to pay proper attention to interoperability and standardization. Like most Gulf countries, it often focused on buying the most effective or advanced system, and paid little attention to the practical problems of integrating weapons from different suppliers into overall force structures that minimized the problems in operating systems designed by different countries, the maintenance problems involved, and the difficulties in supplying and sustaining systems with different maintenance and ammunition needs in combat.

The National Guard aside, the Kingdom paid too little attention to the training burden involved, problems in combined arms and joint operations, and difficulties in command and control. It also underestimated the inevitable rivalry between foreign military advisory teams and the natural competitive bias of foreign contract support teams toward systems made by their companies or countries. Saudi Arabia also underestimated the tendency of supplier countries to focus on sales per se and ignore the Kingdom's strategic interests, even though most supplier countries were dependent on the security of Saudi oil exports.

The Impact of the Gulf War

Chart 3.13 shows the patterns in Saudi arms orders and deliveries before and after the Gulf War. It also shows that Saudi Arabia's investment in arms imports peaked well before Iraq invaded Kuwait. In fact, if one looks further back into the 1980s, Saudi Arabia took delivery on $48.1 billion worth of arms during 1983–1989, and purchased 14.1% of all Third World military import agreements during 1982–1989.[16]

The Gulf War did, however, lead Saudi Arabia to make major additional purchases of military imports. Chart 3.14 shows the size of Saudi Arabia's annual new orders and actual arms deliveries during 1990–1999, and traces the rise in deliveries from the orders placed during the Gulf War. At the same time, it reflects the decline in new orders after the early 1990s caused by the Kingdom's growing economic problems.

Saudi Arabia ordered $18.6 billion worth of military imports in 1990 and took delivery on $6.749 billion worth. Saudi Arabia cut its new orders to $7.8 billion in 1991, but deliveries rose to $7.1 billion as its backlog of increased orders began to raise deliveries. Both new orders and deliveries dropped to $4.5 billion in 1992. Saudi military imports then began to rise again because of the perceived threat from Iran and Iraq. Saudi Arabia ordered $9.6 billion worth of arms in 1993, and took delivery on $6.4 billion. In 1994, it ordered $9.5 billion worth of military imports and took delivery on $5.2 billion.

The end results of these orders were a bill that strained Saudi Arabia's financial capabilities at a time when its oil revenues were declining, and a massive "pipeline" of ongoing arms deliveries that Saudi Arabia could not effectively absorb. The Kingdom had problems with meeting its payment schedules for both U.S. and British arms. Saudi Arabia had signed a multistage deal with Britain and France called al-Yamamah that cost the King-

Chart 3.13
Saudi Arabian New Arms Agreements versus Arms Deliveries, 1990–1999 ($U.S. Current Millions)

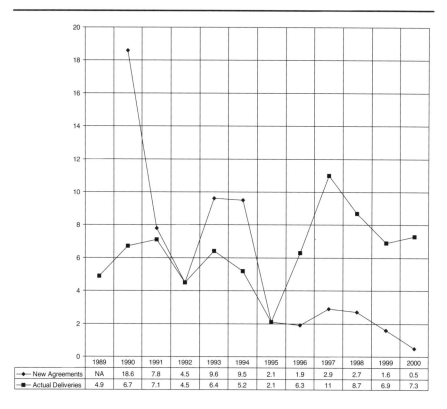

	1989	1990	1991	1992	1993	1994	1995	1996	1997	1998	1999	2000
—◆— New Agreements	NA	18.6	7.8	4.5	9.6	9.5	2.1	1.9	2.9	2.7	1.6	0.5
—■— Actual Deliveries	4.9	6.7	7.1	4.5	6.4	5.2	2.1	6.3	11	8.7	6.9	7.3

Source: Adapted by Anthony H. Cordesman from various editions of Richard F. Grimmett, *Conventional Arms Transfers to Developing Nations* (Washington: Congressional Research Service).

dom up to $3 billion per year, but that was not integrated into its normal budget process. While the Kingdom could meet some of its obligation with oil, the deal still imposed a major financial burden; the United States had to be paid in cash, which imposed even more of a burden. The program is a large financial liability, particularly in view of Saudi Arabia's structural budget deficits.

The Kingdom's problems in paying for its existing arms orders in 1994 led it to make much more modest new purchases after this time. The Kingdom ordered $2.1 billion worth of arms in 1995 and took delivery on $2.1 billion. New orders totaled $1.9 billion in 1996 and deliveries totaled $6.3 billion. Saudi Arabia placed $2.7 billion in new orders in 1997 and took $11 billion worth of deliveries.

Chart 3.14
Saudi Total Exports, Total Imports, and Arms Import Deliveries (Constant $U.S. Millions)

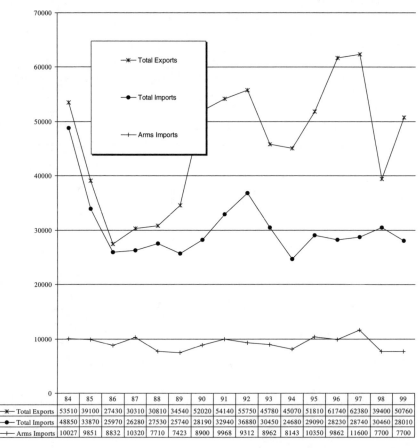

	84	85	86	87	88	89	90	91	92	93	94	95	96	97	98	99
—*— Total Exports	53510	39100	27430	30310	30810	34540	52020	54140	55750	45780	45070	51810	61740	62380	39400	50760
—•— Total Imports	48850	33870	25970	26280	27530	25740	28190	32940	36880	30450	24680	29090	28230	28740	30460	28010
—+— Arms Imports	10027	9851	8832	10320	7710	7423	8900	9968	9312	8962	8143	10350	9862	11600	7700	7700

Sources: Adapted by Anthony H. Cordesman from ACDA, *World Military Expenditures and Arms Transfers, 1995* (Washington: GPO, 1996) and various editions of U.S. State Department, *World Military Expenditures and Arms Transfers* (Washington: Bureau of Arms Control).

The oil crash in late 1997 then reinforced the need for Saudi Arabia to limit its new arms imports. As a result, it placed $2.9 billion in new orders in 1998 and took $8.7 billion worth of deliveries, and placed $1.6 billion in new orders in 1999 and took $6.9 billion worth of deliveries.[17] The scale of the decline in new Saudi arms import agreements is indicated by the fact that new orders during 1991–1994 were only about two-thirds of the total during 1987–1990. Saudi new orders for the four-year period from 1994 to 1997 were substantially less than half the new orders Saudi

Arabia placed during the four-year period before the Gulf War, even measured in current dollars.[18]

The strains the Kingdom faced are illustrated by the fact that Saudi Arabia missed a major FMS payment to the United States in March 1999. Although Pentagon officials insisted that Saudi Arabia had enough funds to cover its future bills as they became due, the Kingdom was slow in making its $150 million monthly deposits as was stipulated in the earlier payment restructuring deal it had made in 1994. In May 1999, the U.S. government also had to devise new financing options to justify the renewal of the $850 million Peace Sun F-15 support contract and the estimated $300 million Peace Shield airspace command and control program.[19]

These pressures led the Kingdom to make massive cuts in its new arms orders after 1995. Chart 3.17 shows just how sharp this decline in new orders was and that it continued despite a major rise in oil prices in the spring of 1999, and a massive increase in oil revenues in 2000. The Kingdom seems to have wisely concluded that this was a "bubble" that could not be counted on to sustain new arms orders. Chart 3.14 shows that Saudi arms imports became a steadily smaller share of its total export revenues and total imports, and declined sharply as a percent of total imports since their peak in the mid-1980s.

At the same time, Chart 3.13 shows that the cost of arms deliveries from past orders was still extraordinarily high even in 2000, and that cuts in new arms agreements have been very slow to cut the actual annual cost of arms imports. This history helps explain how many Saudis outside the MODA often have an exaggerated impression of the size of the Kingdom's actual arms imports and the pace of new orders because they are not aware of the difference between new orders and deliveries and during the late 1990s. Many Saudis confused deliveries with orders and felt that the Kingdom was making massive arms purchases at a time when its oil revenues and export earnings were limited.

In fact, many of Saudi Arabia's problems were self-inflicted wounds. The Kingdom's new arms orders after 1995 were poorly managed and reinforced several major problems in Saudi military sustainment and modernization.

- First, the Kingdom focused on major new arms purchases during the period immediately after the Gulf War rather than sustainment, and then did not shift its purchases to focus on sustainment when it had to make major cutbacks after the mid-1990s. As a result, Saudi Arabia was flooded with weapons but seriously underfunded in terms of the investment in maintenance and sustainment that was necessary to keep its existing weapons effective and properly absorb its new ones.

- Second, the flood of new deliveries during the 1990s added to the Kingdom's problems in effectively recapitalizing and maintaining its overall force posture. As a rough rule of thumb, every major weapons system costs at least as much in terms of the arms imports needed to maintain and upgrade it during its life cycle as it does to buy, and often twice as much. The Kingdom now faces a major future cost problem in making and in keeping its new weapons effective, which will add to the problem of sustaining its existing weapons. While no precise figures are available, some U.S. advisors estimate that the Kingdom needed to restructure its arms import program to focus on sustainment half a decade ago, and now needs to spend three to four times more on support equipment, training systems, and so on, than it does today, even if this means major additional cuts in spending on new arms.

• Third, the Kingdom never really developed a clear strategy for both improving interoperability and setting affordable long-term force goals. It went from year to year, solving its payment problems as they occurred. It did not develop effective future-year plans, and the spending fixes it adopted for any one year tended to compound its overall problems in standardization and interoperability.

Comparisons of Saudi and Other Gulf Arms Buys

Saudi Arabia's procurement difficulties should not be exaggerated. No country in the world has yet succeeded in creating a highly efficient system to manage military procurement and modernization. Success is also relative, and Saudi Arabia's problems with arms imports during the 1990s were minor in comparison to those of its three greatest potential threats: Iran, Iraq, and Yemen.

The overall patterns in Gulf arms imports are shown in Charts 3.15–3.18. Chart 3.15 compares Saudi total arms deliveries to the total deliveries of all of the other Gulf countries. It shows that Saudi arms imports came to dominate the total level of Gulf arms imports during years after the Iran-Iraq and Gulf Wars. If conventional arms imports alone were a measure of war fighting capability, it is clear that Saudi Arabia would be the superpower of the Gulf.

Chart 3.16 compares Saudi arms import deliveries to those of Iran, Iraq, and Yemen. It shows a virtual halt in Iraqi arms imports, and a massive decline in Iranian and Yemeni imports. The trend is even more striking in terms of new agreements. Saudi Arabia signed some $21.8 billion worth of new arms agreements during 1992–1995, while Iran signed $1.1 billion worth of new agreements, Iraq signed none, and Yemen signed $300 million. Saudi Arabia signed some $5.7 billion worth of new arms agreements during 1997–2000, while Iran signed $1.3 billion, Iraq smuggled in less than $50 million worth, and Yemen signed $400 million worth.[20] Chart 3.17 shows, however, that Saudi arms imports make up a far higher percent of total imports than those of any other Gulf state.

Sources of Saudi Arms Imports

Chart 3.12 revealed that Saudi Arabia has depended on the West for virtually all of its military modernization. It is not surprising that its main

Chart 3.15
Cumulative Saudi Arms Imports Relative to Those of the Other Gulf States, 1984–
1997 (Value of Deliveries in Constant $U.S. Millions)

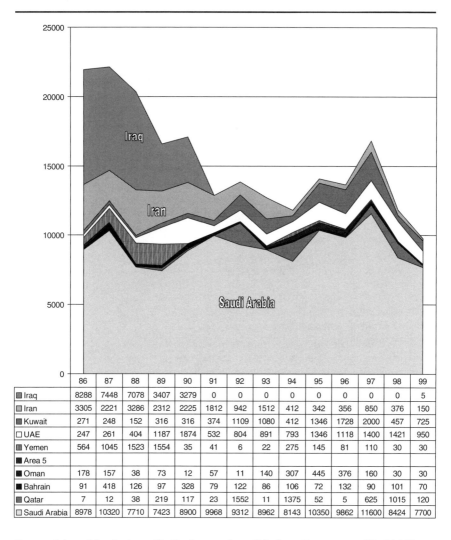

	86	87	88	89	90	91	92	93	94	95	96	97	98	99
▨ Iraq	8288	7448	7078	3407	3279	0	0	0	0	0	0	0	0	5
▨ Iran	3305	2221	3286	2312	2225	1812	942	1512	412	342	356	850	376	150
■ Kuwait	271	248	152	316	316	374	1109	1080	412	1346	1728	2000	457	725
▢ UAE	247	261	404	1187	1874	532	804	891	793	1346	1118	1400	1421	950
▨ Yemen	564	1045	1523	1554	35	41	6	22	275	145	81	110	30	30
■ Area 5														
■ Oman	178	157	38	73	12	57	11	140	307	445	376	160	30	30
■ Bahrain	91	418	126	97	328	79	122	86	106	72	132	90	101	70
▨ Qatar	7	12	38	219	117	23	1552	11	1375	52	5	625	1015	120
▢ Saudi Arabia	8978	10320	7710	7423	8900	9968	9312	8962	8143	10350	9862	11600	8424	7700

Source: Adapted by Anthony H. Cordesman from U.S. State Department, *World Military Expenditures and Arms Transfers* (Washington: GPO, various editions).

suppliers are the United States and Europe. Similarly, Saudi Arabia has developed close military relations with the United States, while balancing its dependence on the United States with major imports of arms from Britain and France; Britain has been a major supplier of aircraft and France has been a major supplier of ships and naval weapons.

Chart 3.16
Saudi Arms Deliveries versus Deliveries to Iran and Iraq, 1986–1999 ($U.S. Constant Millions)

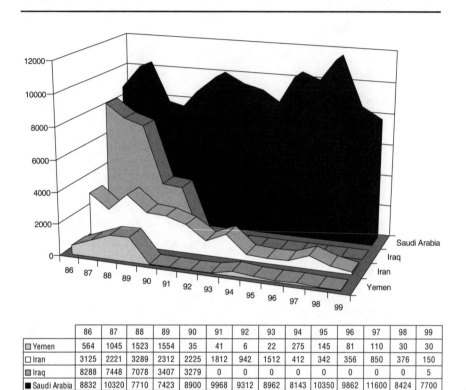

	86	87	88	89	90	91	92	93	94	95	96	97	98	99
☐ Yemen	564	1045	1523	1554	35	41	6	22	275	145	81	110	30	30
☐ Iran	3125	2221	3289	2312	2225	1812	942	1512	412	342	356	850	376	150
▨ Iraq	8288	7448	7078	3407	3279	0	0	0	0	0	0	0	0	5
■ Saudi Arabia	8832	10320	7710	7423	8900	9968	9312	8962	8143	10350	9862	11600	8424	7700

Source: Adapted by Anthony H. Cordesman from ACDA, *World Military Expenditures and Arms Transfers* (Washington: GPO, various editions).

Chart 3.18 shows deliveries by major supplier from 1973 to 1997. What is most striking about this chart is the variation in suppliers over time, which has created many of the interoperability and standardization problems discussed earlier. Part of this pattern was driven by the reluctance of the U.S. Congress to sell the Kingdom arms at a time when Saudi Arabia was perceived to be a threat to Israel. This encouraged Saudi Arabia to turn to France as a major supplier to its Navy, and led the Saudi Air Force to make its massive Al Yamamah buy of Tornadoes and Hawks instead of the F-15. It is interesting to note that in terms of total sales in current dollars, Britain sold more arms to Saudi Arabia during 1973–1997 than did the United States.

Chart 3.17
Arms Imports as a Percent of Total Imports in Middle Eastern Countries

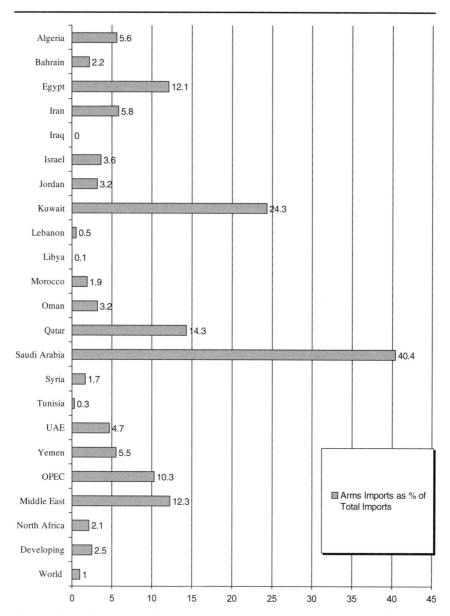

Source: Adapted by Anthony H. Cordesman from U.S. State Department, *World Military Expenditures and Arms Transfers, 1999–2000* (Washington: Bureau of Arms Control, 2001).

Chart 3.18
Arms Deliveries to Saudi Arabia by Major Supplier, 1973–1997 ($U.S. Current Millions)

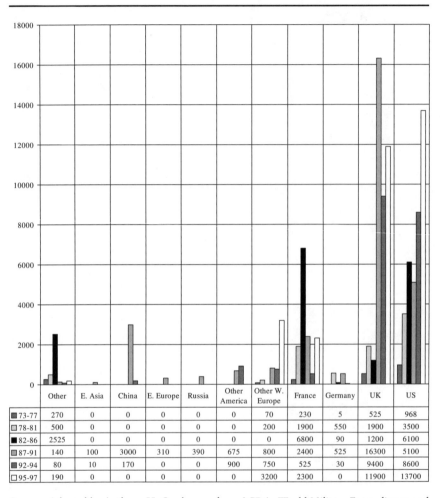

	Other	E. Asia	China	E. Europe	Russia	Other America	Other W. Europe	France	Germany	UK	US
■ 73-77	270	0	0	0	0	0	70	230	5	525	968
□ 78-81	500	0	0	0	0	0	200	1900	550	1900	3500
■ 82-86	2525	0	0	0	0	0	0	6800	90	1200	6100
■ 87-91	140	100	3000	310	390	675	800	2400	525	16300	5100
■ 92-94	80	10	170	0	0	900	750	525	30	9400	8600
□ 95-97	190	0	0	0	0	0	3200	2300	0	11900	13700

Sources: Adapted by Anthony H. Cordesman from ACDA, *World Military Expenditures and Arms Transfers* (Washington: GPO, various editions) and U.S. State Department, *World Military Expenditures and Arms Transfers, 1998* (Washington: Bureau of Arms Control, 1999).

- If one examines ACDA reporting for the period from 1979 to 1983, which covers the period from the fall of the Shah of Iran through the early years of the Iran-Iraq War, Saudi Arabia took delivery on $12.125 billion worth of military imports. This included $5.1 billion worth of military imports from the United States, $2.5 billion from France, $1.9 billion from the UK, $525 million from West Germany, $200 million from Italy, and $1.9 billion from other countries.[21]

- Saudi Arabia took delivery on $19.53 billion worth of military imports during 1984–1988. This included $5.8 billion worth of military imports from the United States, $7.5 billion from France, $2.5 billion from the PRC, $2.1 billion from the UK, $30 million from Italy, and $1.6 billion from other countries.[22]

- During the period from 1985 to 1989, which covers the period from the most intense fighting in the Iran-Iraq War through the cease-fire in 1988, Saudi Arabia imported $23.04 billion worth of military goods, including $5 billion from the United States, $7 billion from France, $7.7 billion from the UK, $2.5 billion from the PRC, $40 million from West Germany, $250 million from other European countries, $140 million from other East Asian states, $390 million from Latin America, and $20 million from other countries in the world.[23]

- During 1992–1994, the period immediately after the Gulf War, Saudi Arabia imported $20.465 billion worth of military goods, including $8.6 billion from the United States, $525 million from France, $9.4 billion from the UK, $170 million from the PRC, $30 million from Germany, $670 million from other European countries, $10 million from other East Asian states, $70 million from Russia, and $90 million from other countries in the world.[24] These totals are somewhat misleading, however, because they only reflect deliveries and were heavily influenced by past orders of British aircraft. Most new Saudi orders were placed with the United States.

- During 1995–1997, Saudi Arabia imported $31.32 billion worth of military goods, including $13.7 billion from the United States, $2.3 billion from France, $11.9 billion from the UK, $1 billion from other NATO countries, $2.2 billion from other Western countries, and $190 million from other countries in the world.[25] These totals are again somewhat misleading, however, because they only reflect deliveries and are still heavily influenced by past orders of British aircraft. Once again, most new Saudi orders were placed with the United States.

More recent reporting by Richard F. Grimmett, which is summarized in Charts 3.19 and 3.20, indicates that Saudi Arabia bought most of its arms from Europe during the four years before the Gulf War, and that its new agreements with the United States during this period only amounted to about 31% of the total. This was partly the result of the political difficulties the United States faced in selling to Saudi Arabia at a time when U.S. supporters of Israel still opposed the sale of advanced weapons. This situation changed significantly after Iraq's invasion of Kuwait, however, and many supporters of Israel suddenly came to regard Saudi Arabia as more of an ally than a threat to Israel.

At the same time, both the United States and Saudi Arabia had every conceivable incentive to cooperate in both building up Saudi forces and making them as interoperable with U.S. forces as possible. Saudi Arabia

Chart 3.19
Total Saudi Arabian Arms Agreements and Deliveries Before and After the Gulf War, 1987–2000 ($US Current Millions)

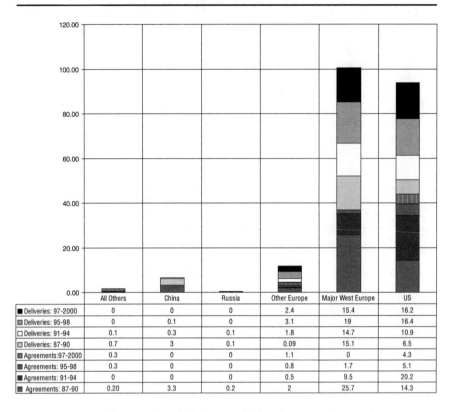

	All Others	China	Russia	Other Europe	Major West Europe	US
■ Deliveries: 97-2000	0	0	0	2.4	15.4	16.2
▤ Deliveries: 95-98	0	0.1	0	3.1	19	16.4
☐ Deliveries: 91-94	0.1	0.3	0.1	1.8	14.7	10.9
☐ Deliveries: 87-90	0.7	3	0.1	0.09	15.1	6.5
■ Agreements:97-2000	0.3	0	0	1.1	0	4.3
■ Agreements: 95-98	0.3	0	0	0.8	1.7	5.1
■ Agreements: 91-94	0	0	0	0.5	9.5	20.2
■ Agreements: 87-90	0.20	3.3	0.2	2	25.7	14.3

0 = less than $50 million or nil, and all data rounded to the nearest $100 million.
Source: Richard F. Grimmett, *Conventional Arms Transfers to Developing Nations* (Washington: Congressional Research Service, various editions).

placed major orders in the United States, and Saudi orders from the United States rose from $14.3 billion during 1987–1990 to $20.2 billion during 1991–1994, and reached 67% of total Saudi new agreements. New orders from Europe dropped from $25.7 billion during 1987–1990 to only $9.5 billion during 1991–1994—31% of the total.[26]

The sources of Saudi arms deliveries were different—reflecting the lag between orders and deliveries. Saudi Arabia received a total of $38 billion in deliveries of military imports during 1995–1998. These deliveries were still dominated by Europe ($21.6 billion versus $16.4 billion from the United States) because of the long lead times in the delivery of past orders. Saudi Arabia only ordered a total of $7.9 billion worth of new arms dur-

Chart 3.20
Declining Orders, Rising Deliveries: Saudi Arabian New Arms Agreements and Deliveries by Major Supplier Before and After the Gulf War, 1987–2000 ($US Current Millions)

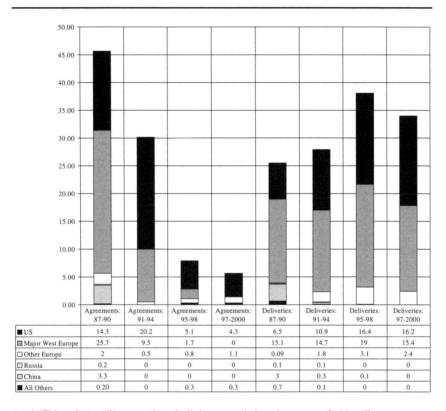

	Agreements: 87-90	Agreements: 91-94	Agreements: 95-98	Agreements: 97-2000	Deliveries: 87-90	Deliveries: 91-94	Deliveries: 95-98	Deliveries: 97-2000
■ US	14.3	20.2	5.1	4.3	6.5	10.9	16.4	16.2
▦ Major West Europe	25.7	9.5	1.7	0	15.1	14.7	19	15.4
☐ Other Europe	2	0.5	0.8	1.1	0.09	1.8	3.1	2.4
☐ Russia	0.2	0	0	0	0.1	0.1	0	0
☐ China	3.3	0	0	0	3	0.3	0.1	0
■ All Others	0.20	0	0.3	0.3	0.7	0.1	0	0

0 = less than $50 million or nil, and all data rounded to the nearest $100 million.
Source: Richard F. Grimmett, *Conventional Arms Transfers to Developing Nations* (Washington: Congressional Research Service, various editions).

ing 1995–1998, however, and most of these new orders were placed in the United States ($5.1 billion versus $2.5 billion from the United States). If one compares the slightly different four-year period from 1996 to 1999, new Saudi orders from the United States totaled $5.5 billion while orders from Europe only totaled $1.3 billion. In contrast, European deliveries totaled $16.6 billion versus $15.5 billion from the United States, Saudi Arabia only received minor deliveries from other countries, and the only major weapons system they supported were the Chinese long-range missiles that Saudi Arabia had bought before the Gulf War.

The patterns since Saudi Arabia's funding crunch in the mid-1990s have been different. The Kingdom signed only $5.7 billion worth of new agreements during 1997–2000, versus $18.8 billion worth during 1993–1996. It signed $4.3 billion worth of agreements with the United States during 1997–2000, versus $11.8 billion during 1993–1996. New agreements with major European states totaled less than $50 million during 1997–2000, versus $6.5 billion during 1993–1996, while new orders from other European states rose from $500 million to $1.1 billion. There were no new Saudi arms agreements with Russia and China from 1993 to 2000, and orders from all other states rose from less than $50 million to $300 million.

In sharp contrast, Saudi Arabia took delivery on $34 billion worth of military goods during 1997–2000, including $16.2 billion from the United States; $15.4 billion from France, Germany, Italy, and the UK; $2.4 billion from other Western countries; and less than $50 million from all other countries in the world. These figures again reflect the acute imbalance in the funding of new Saudi orders relative to the extremely high cost of deliveries of past orders.[27]

The Changing Nature of Saudi Arms Imports

There have been major qualitative changes in Saudi military imports since the mid-1980s, which have been further accelerated since the Gulf War. Until the mid-1980s, Saudi Arabia concentrated on building up its military infrastructure and basic military capabilities. While it is impossible to make precise estimates, weapons, munitions, and specialized military support equipment probably made up less than one-third of Saudi military imports during this period.

Since the mid-1980s, Saudi military imports have shifted to include a steadily increasing number of first-line weapons systems. Furthermore, many military construction and support activities are now carried out by Saudi firms or the equivalent of joint ventures. As a result, more than 60% of Saudi military imports now include weapons, munitions, and specialized military support equipment.

Some of Saudi Arabia's recent major arms imports are summarized in Table 3.1. It is clear that Saudi military modernization remained broadly based through most of the 1990s. At the same time, it shows that the rate of new procurement and deliveries dropped sharply after the mid-1990s, and will create major modernization, standardization, and interoperability problems in each service.

There also are major uncertainties affecting Saudi Arabia's future modernization of its armored forces. While the Kingdom continues to discuss buying two types of advanced modern tanks, it cannot yet effectively operate its present mix of M-60s and M-1s, and its French-made AMX-30s are obsolete and mostly in storage. It needs to rationalize its mix of other armored vehicles more than it needs to purchase new ones. As is the case with its other regular services, the Army needs to emphasize training and sustainment purchases over new weapons. The Army does, however, need more long-range, self-propelled artillery firepower and advanced anti-tank weapons of the kind that can best help Saudi ground forces defend against an attack by Iraq.

The past modernization of the Saudi Air Force has been very ambitious, as has the modernization of Saudi Arabia's land-based air defense forces. It has created what is still a relatively modern Air Force, and Saudi Arabia continues to buy new systems. For example, it has upgraded its five E-3A AWACS and taken delivery on a total of 12 AB-412TP search and rescue helicopters. At the same time, Saudi Arabia underfunded the support of its F-15 force to the point where its readiness is seriously undermined. It has had to ground its aging F-5s; as a result, it is considering selling them and buying a much smaller number of F-15s to compensate for its losses in training.

Saudi Arabia's main requirement for its Air Defense Force is the need to fund theater ballistic missile defenses at some point in the 2000s. The Kingdom has obtained shared early warning systems with the United States, but U.S. and Saudi Patriots are the only system with anti-missile capabilities currently in Saudi Arabia, and the Saudi Patriots are PAC-2 versions with only limited anti-missile capability. The anti–ballistic missile systems Saudi Arabia would need to deal with more advanced Iranian and Iraqi missiles are not yet available from the United States and are not funded through the Kingdom's projections of its military expenditures.

Saudi Arabia plans only a limited naval modernization program once it takes delivery on the three French Lafayette-class frigates in 2001–2005 that it ordered during the 1990s. Some officers still want to buy submarines, although it is far from clear that the Navy can afford to buy and sustain them. Others would like to shift the Navy's modernization priorities to areas like mine warfare and to concentrate on filling in the gaps in U.S. Navy mission capabilities in the Gulf. This is an important change—past Saudi naval imports often reflected more interest in prestige and in the "glitter factor" of having the best-armed large ships than in Saudi Arabia's mission priorities or real-world military effectiveness.

These issues highlight the problems caused by the fact that Saudi modernization planning and spending lacks coherent central direction and tends to lurch from year-to-year—and from major deal to major deal—rather than be part of a coherent future year plan and program budget. Once again, the quality of programming, planning, and budgeting within the MODA is poor. Force modernization tends to focus on major weapons buys without coherent plans to provide suitable support, training, and sustainment. While Saudi Arabia has long had reasonably well-drafted five-year plans in its civil sector, the MODA is decades behind in practical planning skills and it is uncertain that it has the practical authority to implement coherent plans even if they are drafted.

Table 3.1
Key Saudi Equipment Developments

- During Gulf War bought 315 M-1A2s, 30 M-88A1 tank recovery vehicles, 175 M-998 utility trucks, 224 heavy tactical trucks, 29 heavy equipment transporters, 268 five-ton trucks, spares and support equipment, logistics support, ammunition, facilities design and construction, training aids and devices, and U.S. military training services.

- Discussed plans to buy 235-350 additional M-1A2s, Challenger 2s, or Le Clercs, but funding plan unclear.

- Bought 400 M-2A2s, 200 M-113 armored personnel carriers, 50 M-548 cargo carriers, 17 M-88A1 recovery vehicles, and 43 M-578 recovery vehicles.

- Talked about replacing 110 M-109A/A2s with M-109A6, VSEL AS90, and Giat GCT-1. Funding plan even more uncertain.

- Considered order for 9 Multiple Launch Rocket Systems (MLRS), including vehicle mounted rocket launchers, 2,880 tactical rockets, 50 practice rockets, 9 MV-755A2 command post carriers, training and training equipment, but canceled in 1993. Need to supplement present strength of four 180 mm SS-40s and 127 mm SS-30s.

- Army has 12 AH-64 Apache attack helicopters, 155 Hellfire missiles, 24 spare Hellfire launchers, 6 spare engines and associated equipment. Has discussed possible total of 48 AH-64s.

- Army aviation formed in 1986, and now has 12 S-70As, 22 UH-60s, 6 SA-356Ns, and 15 Bell $06CSs—in addition to AH-64s. Considering buy of 88 Westland WS-70 Black Hawks or similar lift helicopters.

- Building a new military city near Jizan, which is on Red Sea coast near border with Yemen. Some cost estimates range up to $8 billion.

- Negotiated a deal with Spain for the purchase of 200 BMR-600 6×6 armored personnel carriers at a cost of up to $440 million.

- Ordered 12 AS-532 A2 Cougar Mk II search and rescue helicopters from Eurocopter, all due to be delivered by the end of 2001 at a cost of $589 million.

- Ordered 1,827 TOW-2A anti-tank guided weapons from the United States in 2000.

- Saudi National Guard (SANG) has bought 400 to 450 versions of the Piranha light armored vehicle (LAV0.

- SANG bought 1,117 LAV-25s from General Motors of Canada through the U.S. Army Tank Automotive Command (TACOM) at cost of $3.4 billion. Package included 116 TOW launchers with 2000 missiles, 27 M-198 155mm howitzers, support systems, training, and facilities.

- The SANG took delivery of the first of 73 120 mm armored mortar systems in 1998.

- SANG bought 130 Belgian LCTS Mark 8 90mm turret weapon systems, including day-night range sights, for integration into its LAVs.

- Refitting four F-2000 frigates with roughly 50 "item" changes, 40 minor. Are adding NBC protection and improving Otomat missile system to enhance search patterns and add re-attack capability. Not improving Crotale to use latest VT1 rounds, but improving Airsys Castor 2B X-band fire control radar to Castor 2C standard. Will complete during 1997–2001.

Table 3.1 (Continued)

- Buying two new La Fayette–class F-3000 frigates as part of a $3.5 billion November 1994 agreement. To complete delivery by 2005.
- Ordered a third La Fayette–class anti-aircraft frigate equipped with the new Aster 15 missile to complete delivery by 2005.
- Four Sandown minelayers entering service, beginning in 1995.
- Considered buy of several AEGIS-class warships to give it advanced battle management, Harpoon anti-ship missiles, Tomahawk strike capability, ASW, anti-aircraft, and anti-ship missile defense capabilities. Too expensive.
- Refitting two logistic replenishment tankers.
- Considered buying coastal submarines.
- Bought 24 F-15S aircraft designed for air combat, and 48 F-15S aircraft dual-capable in both the air defense and strike/attack missions: 24 spare engines, 48 targeting and navigation pods, 900 AGM-65D/G Maverick air-to-surface missiles, 600 CBU-87 bombs, 700 GBU-10/12 bombs, and special mission planning systems.
- Bought 1,500 upgraded AIM-9 air-to-air missiles for use on the F-15 Eagle at a cost of $115 million.
- Considering upgrade of 1,500 AIM-9L to AIM-9M.
- Bought 20 more Hawk 65 jets and 20 more Swiss Pilatus PC-9 turboprop trainers for delivery during 1996-2000. Needs better trainers than either Hawk or Pilatus.
- Bought upgrade of 5 E-3A AWACS in 1997.
- Examining replacement for roughly 100 F-5s. Reports considered funding 12 to 24 F-15s in an initial buy, and l selling F-5s to help fund its new F-15s. Boeing offer included a major depot maintenance facility involving significant offsets, and hires of Saudis. The facility might improve Saudi capability to service its F-15s, and U.S. F-15s, in combat.
- Upgraded nine F-5E reconnaissance fighters in 1997 with improved sensors, GPS, and inertial navigation systems.
- Longer-term requirements for replacement for 60 F-15s in 2005–2010 time frame. F-22, EF-2000, Rafael possible candidates.
- Examined plans to buy up to 70 C-130J-like transports during next decade, and up to 10 additional airborne tankers to supplement its 8 KC-130Hs.
- Order 44 Italian AB-412TP SAR helicopters in 1998. Order 475 US AMRAAM air-to-air missiles in 2000.
- Examined buying up to 21 Patriot batteries (2 training) with 1,055 missiles. Two units funded, and purchased the Patriot Range Support System (PRSS) in 1999.
- New Peace Shield system becoming fully operational, and installation was completed in November 1995. Has central C^4I center, five regional centers, and 17 long-range radars.
- Upgrading 17 MIM-23B I-Hawk batteries.
- Considering upgrade of 170 Shahine mobile and static light SAMs, possibly with Crotale NG.
- Examining replacement of French AMX-30 SA air defense guns.

Corruption, Waste, and Accountability

As has been mentioned earlier, the lack of transparency and accountability is another major problem in Saudi arms sales, as is the tendency to create very large contract programs that become open-ended purchasing programs. At least some Saudi officials and officers feel that it is virtually impossible for anyone in the Saudi government, whether inside or outside the MODA to understand what is being bought in any detail, who is getting the money, and how the flow of Saudi payments is being accounted for. These problems are compounded by layering service and support contracts in purchasing contracts over procurement contracts, accounting for the cost benefits of grossly overambitious offset contracts, and accounting for soft expenditures like transportation and overhead costs.

Outside critics have often exaggerated the level of waste and corruption in Saudi arms deals and military procurement. The following chapters show that the Kingdom has generally bought the right arms and got a highly effective mix of weapons for its money. As will be discussed later, the terms of U.S. foreign military sales (FMS) programs also place serious limits on the misuse of funds. In addition, European countries maintain audit programs that help to limit such problems.

The fact remains, however, that even relatively limited waste and corruption still involve major amounts of money, given the massive size of Saudi arms purchases. Furthermore, some very large Saudi arms deals like the al-Yamamah program, whichstarted out as an integrated purchase of weapons and services from Britain, were structured in ways that involved complex old deals and that led to charges about massive waste and corruption from the start. They have since been expanded to include buys from France and have layered new purchases on old in ways that have made accountability impossible. The original al-Yamamah program was signed in the mid-1980s, and then expanded to levels costing over $30 to $35 billion, with off-budget outlays of roughly $3 billion a year and additional accountability problems caused by including the barter of oil for weapons and complex offset arrangements. Further spending has taken place since 2000 in ways that have led to new charges of waste and corruption.

Saudi Arabia is scarcely unique in keeping almost all of the military, technical, and financial and management aspects of its arms deals secret. Virtually every country in the developing world does so, and the details of procurement and service contracts of many Western states are almost impossible for outsiders to obtain. The fact is, however, that virtually every war fighting aspect of such contracts soon become public. There is no military or strategic reason for classifying the cost and structure of arms deals. In fact, there is even less reason to classify them than the total defense budget. The actual flow of arms and munitions is so public that attempts at secrecy are futile.

This strongly argues for several reforms in Saudi arms purchases and offset programs. First, for maximum transparency and public exposure of the financial details of contracts and purchase arrangements to encourage public review and trust. Second, for annual public reporting on contract performance and the individual performance of offset programs. Third, for the creation of a major new independent audit function within the MODA, with investigative accounting responsibility, to review such programs. Fourth, for the creation of a body similar to the U.S. General Accounting Office under the prime minister to conduct such audits in the case of suspect or troubled programs. And finally, for the inclusion of detailed procurement data in the kind of public defense program and budget discussed earlier.

Military Imports from the United States

As the previous discussion has shown, the United States is hardly Saudi Arabia's only military supplier. Nevertheless, the United States has been a key supplier, and the interoperability between Saudi and U.S. forces will be of critical importance in any major future war. The United States releases a substantial amount of data on these sales through the Defense Security Cooperation Agency. While these data are not directly comparable to the previous intelligence data on arms sales, they are available in considerably more detail, and provide considerable insight into both Saudi Arabia's military development and its military future.

Saudi Arabia has not received any U.S. military assistance since oil prices rose following the embargo after the October War in 1973. Even before that time, it received only minor levels of aid. It received only $1.8 million in excess articles from the United States Military Assistance program during the entire period from 1950 to 1989. Total grant assistance only equaled $29.9 million over the same period, and Saudi Arabia only drew down on $25.9 million of these funds. Saudi Arabia did receive larger assistance under the Foreign Military Financing Program, but the funds now seem minuscule compared to Saudi arms buys since 1973. Total financing during 1950–1989 was $254.2 million, with $65 million in direct financing and $189.9 million in guarantees. The Kingdom repaid all of this money. Saudi Arabia received only $12.5 million in aid under the International Military Education and Training Program.[28]

Many of the patterns in U.S. sales during the pre–Gulf War period (1950–1989) were the result of the fact that Saudi Arabia had to build up modern forces from a very limited base. For example, Saudi Arabia signed some $16 billion worth of foreign military construction agreements with the United States during 1950–1989, and took delivery on $15.1 billion worth of construction services. This was largely a product of the fact that Saudi Arabia lacked both a modern construction industry and experience with the design and construction of military facilities. As a result, it largely phased out U.S. military construction by the early 1980s. During the period from 1989 to 1999, it signed only $1.8 billion worth of new foreign military construction agreements with the United States and took delivery on only $1.5 billion worth of construction services.[29]

The patterns in U.S. government–managed Foreign Military Sales (FMS), and U.S. commercial arms sales have been different. The combination of the rise in oil revenues after 1973, the arms race in the Northern Gulf, the fall of the Shah in 1979, and the Iran-Iraq War of 1980–1988, led Saudi Arabia to buy $30.98 billion worth of FMS during 1950–1989, and to take delivery on $22.6 billion worth of these orders. A further $1.5 billion worth of commercial arms sales was licensed to Saudi Arabia. To put these orders in perspective, they totaled roughly twice the value of U.S. FMS to Israel during the same period.[30]

There were many problems in the course of U.S. arms transfers to Saudi Arabia before the Gulf War that limited the value of these transfers. The United States added significant surcharges and administrative fees that indicated that it was often more interested in military sales than military partnership. The United States sometimes declined to sell key weapons to Saudi Arabia because the U.S. Congress objected to the potential risk to Israel, or because the United States proposed arms sales packages that met U.S. needs without meeting Saudi needs. Examples of such problems include a covert U.S. arrangement with Britain in which the United States pressured Saudi Arabia into buying British Lightning fighters and surface-to-air missiles so that Britain could afford to buy U.S. F-4 fighters. Other problems included a refusal to sell more U.S. tanks, which led Saudi Arabia to buy low-grade French AMX-30s; a naval advisory and sales effort that sold Saudi Arabia low-grade, used U.S. Navy ships that the United States failed to properly support; and a series of long, bitter debates over the sale of the E-3A AWACS and F-15S. At the same time, the Saudi purchases went on to play a vital role in helping to support the United States in Desert Storm.

The close alliance between the United States and Saudi Arabia during the Gulf War, and the fact that Saudi Arabia was clearly not a military threat to Israel, removed most of the problems the Saudis faced in obtaining the U.S. arms exports the Kingdom wanted. The flow of FMS and commercial sales came to include some of the most advanced conventional arms in U.S. inventory. During and after the Gulf War, Saudi Arabia placed very large arms orders. The Kingdom ordered $38.2 billion worth of new FMS agreements during 1990–1999, and took delivery on $29.9 billion. It signed 1.2 times more new FMS agreements during the decade from 1990 to 1999 than it had in the previous three decades, and took delivery on 1.3 times more new FMS goods. Saudi Arabia also requested a little under $400 million in additional commercial arms export licenses during 1990–1999. It ordered

$1.8 billion worth of new military construction agreements, and took delivery on only $1.5 billion in new military construction services.[31]

Overspending and periods of moderate oil revenues forced Saudi Arabia to reduce its new arms purchases in the mid-1990s, and the Kingdom began to have new problems in obtaining the electronics and munitions it needed to stay interoperable with the United States. In 1994, Saudi Arabia had to delay several major potential military import contracts—including purchases of $64 million worth of U.S. multiple-rocket launchers and a $1 billion contract for 150 more M-1 tanks. Saudi Arabia had to reach an agreement with the United States to restructure and defer some of its payments for past military imports, partly because of unexpectedly low oil revenues and partly because it faced unanticipated major payments to the United States to cover the costs of deploying U.S. forces during the Gulf War.[32] Saudi Arabia faced projected payments for U.S. arms of about $4.1 billion in 1994 and $6 billion in 1995. This would have cost Saudi Arabia $10.1 billion over a period of only two years.

These pressures led to negotiations in which the United States and Saudi Arabia agreed to restructure the Saudi military sales program on January 29, 1994. They did so in ways that avoided the cancellation of any weapons programs, but stretched some purchases out and reduced the monthly procurement rate of F-15 fighters from two to one. This cut Saudi Arabia's total arms purchases during 1994–1995 from $10.1 to $9.2 billion, and Saudi Arabia's payment for 1994 to $3.35 billion. In April, Saudi Arabia also arranged to borrow $1.85 billion of this total from three Saudi banks.[33] The Kingdom was forced to delay or defer a contract with Britain for the purchase of some aviation equipment and the construction of a new air base.[34]

Several senior U.S. officers involved in the United States military sales and advisory program in Saudi Arabia privately welcomed this cutback. They had growing concerns about Saudi Arabia's failure to provide the manpower, training, facilities, and sustainability to make proper use of all of its arms purchases, and were concerned that the United States would get the blame for "pushing" arms on Saudi Arabia. They advocated capping the accumulated balance of U.S. arms sales to Saudi Arabia at $10 billion, and some pushed for levels as low as $8 billion.

The practical problem was that U.S. manufacturers continued to push sales. No other foreign supplier showed any interest in controlling the pace of sales and key Saudis like Prince Sultan kept pushing for more arms purchases and threatened to turn to other suppliers if the United States did not sell. Furthermore, the Clinton White House showed a continued willingness to intervene on the side of higher sales when it came under political pressure from U.S. manufacturers or when the sale involved exports with desirable political visibility. Saudi Arabia faced similar pressures from European suppliers.

The total Saudi FMS debt dropped in FY1997, but Saudi Arabia still owed the United States a great deal for a number of major cases. In mid-1996, it still owed $6.5 billion out of a total of $9 billion for the 72 F-15Ss, $500 million out of $3.1 billion for 315 M-1A2s, $500 million out of $1.5 billion for 400 M-2A2s, and $2.2 billion out of $4 billion for 20 Patriot batteries. Saudi Arabia had not succeeded in bringing its total debt down to $10 billion in FY1988, and still owed the United States over $13 billion. This meant it owed the United States $3.5 billion during the course of calendar 1997, plus $300–$400 million more for maintenance and support on existing contracts.[35]

The oil crash that began in late 1997—which continued through the spring of 1999—forced Saudi Arabia to cut back even further on its arms purchases and reduce its backlog of new orders. It also created new cash flow problems until Saudi oil revenues began to rise in the summer of 1999. In May 1999, the U.S. government had to devise financing options to justify the renewal of the $850 million Peace Sun F-15 support contract and the estimated $300 million Peace Shield airspace command and control program after Saudi Arabia missed a payment in March 1999. These two programs, which were due to expire at the end of May 1999, comprised only a fraction of the $60 billion worth of FMS contracts signed between Saudi Arabia and the United States. However, the suspension of these high-profile contracts could have damaged the relationship between the United States and its largest FMS customer, as well as jeopardized broader geopolitical and strategic cooperation between the two countries.[36]

The recent trends in Saudi orders of U.S. military equipment are summarized in Table 3.2. This table shows a major rise in new FMS orders during the first half of the 1990s, followed by a decline after 1994—reflecting the overall patterns in Saudi arms sales discussed earlier. Similarly, the table shows a predictable rise in deliveries after 1994, stemming from the delay between orders and actual deliveries. The patterns in FMS construction largely reflect the highly specialized construction of facilities associated with specific major arms purchases. Saudi Arabia had long been able to carry out other construction activity on its own.

One interesting aspect of the data in Table 3.2 is the low level of Saudi direct commercial arms sales. The Kingdom initially sought to reduce its level of FMS purchases and to make commercial purchases. It soon became apparent, however, that the fees the U.S. government charged for managing the FMS program were minor compared to the management and planning burden associated with Saudi direct purchases. Moreover, the FMS program was under tight U.S. government control and kept corruption and commissions to a minimum.

Limiting corruption and commissions became a growing issue for the Saudi government during the 1990s as it came under acute pressure from sellers that were not under direct government control to make sales that often led to grossly excessive profit margins, kickbacks, and other problems. It should be noted in this regard that major European governments and military firms were the source of many of these problems, not the Saudi purchasers, and that virtually no such corruption occurred in the arms buys of the Saudi National Guard. Because of U.S. law and controls, most of the abuses in FMS sales were limited to transport costs and some aspects of the offset programs the Kingdom demanded as part of its terms for making arms buys.[37]

Chart 3.21 shows the content and value of recent Saudi FMS arms purchases and deliveries from the United States. Once again, the gap between purchases and deliveries is clear. At the same time, a detailed look at the data in Chart 3.21—and discussions with U.S. and Saudi military experts— reveal a number of other patterns:

- Saudi Arabia has eased the debt burden that presented major problems in the mid-1990s. It paid down its FMS debt burden from a peak of around $24 billion to less than $3 billion in early 2001. It reduced its annual FMS payments to around $1.8 billion.[38]

- There is a steady growth in services to keep equipment maintained and combat capable. The same is true of maintenance, spare parts and modifications. Even so, there is broad agreement that Saudi Arabia has not ordered anything like the total pool of services, spare parts, and maintenance capabilities from the United States that it now needs. This has helped lead to critical readiness problems in some aspects of the Saudi military forces, especially the Air Force. Similar problems affect the equipment provided by other countries and are often worse.

- While training expenditures are significant, the level of program activity is far too low to ensure suitable training. The problems are compounded by Saudisation of a kind that has replaced skilled manpower with underskilled Saudi personnel, and by a decline in performance standards; as noted in Chapter 2, "Saudis will not fail Saudis."

- The modernization of land combat vehicles and tactical and support vehicles has been underfunded since a surge of purchases shortly after the Gulf War.

- Other support equipment has been a major part of Saudi purchases and deliveries, reflecting the increasing sophistication of the Saudi equipment pool and the rising investment necessary to keep it operating.

- Communications equipment and military electronics have been modernized, but not at the rates necessary to support advanced combined arms and maneuver warfare.

- The United States does not provide major new naval systems; virtually all of these systems come from France.

- There have not been many new U.S. aircraft orders, but deliveries of past orders have been a major part of all Saudi arms deliveries.

Table 3.2
The Pace of U.S. Arms Sales Before and After the Gulf War: Annual U.S. Foreign Military Sales (FMS), Commercial Arms Export Agreements, Military Assistance Programs (MAP), and International Military Education and Training (IMET) Programs with Saudi Arabia, FY1985–1996 (Current Millions)

	86	87	88	89	90	91	92	93	94	95	96	97	98	99
Foreign Military Financing Program														
Payment Waived	—	—	—	—	—	—	—	—	—	—	—	—	—	—
DoD Direct	—	—	—	—	—	—	—	—	—	—	—	—	—	—
DoD Guarantee	—	—	—	—	—	—	—	—	—	—	—	—	—	—
FMS Agreements	682	6,350	1,671	1,140	9,120	9,175	936	11,379	1,627	445	1,275	742	2,153	1,369
Commercial Sales	814	183	168	68	912	67	89	53	8	27	48	12	12	8
FMS Construction Agreements	6	—	19	—	563	394	4	632	6	6	14	—	187	20
FMS Deliveries	2,199	2,872	938	619	874	2,742	2,387	3,453	1,992	3,568	3,854	4,660	3,959	3,445
FMS Construction Deliveries	na	na	na	na	263	273	216	121	91	108	49	37	349	88

MAP Program	—	—	—	—	—	—	—	—	—	—	—
MAP Deliveries	—	—	—	—	—	—	—	—	—	—	—
MAP Excess Defense Articles Program	—	—	—	—	—	—	—	—	—	—	—
MAP Excess Defense Articles Deliveries	—	—	—	—	—	—	—	—	—	—	—
IMET Program/Deliveries	—	—	—	—	—	—	—	—	—	—	—

Sources: Adapted from data provided by the U.S. Defense Security Assistance Agency (DSAA), *Foreign Military Sales, Foreign Military Construction Sales and Military Assistance Facts as of September 30, 1996* (Washington: Department of Defense, 1997) and by the Defense Security Cooperation Agency on March 19, 2001.

Chart 3.21
Shaping the Mid-to-Late 1990s: U.S. Arms Sales and Deliveries Transfers to Saudi Arabia by Category from U.S. FY 1996–2000 ($U.S. Current Millions)

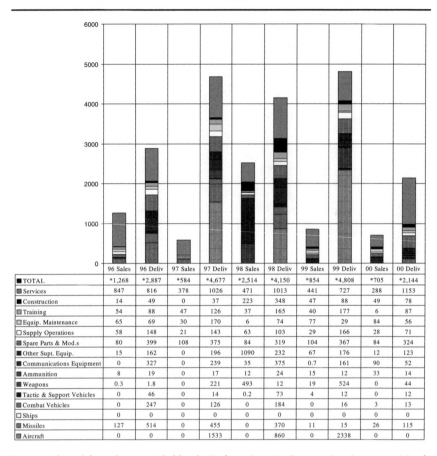

	96 Sales	96 Deliv	97 Sales	97 Deliv	98 Sales	98 Deliv	99 Sales	99 Deliv	00 Sales	00 Deliv
■ TOTAL	*1,268	*2,887	*584	*4,677	*2,514	*4,150	*854	*4,808	*705	*2,144
▨ Services	847	816	378	1026	471	1013	441	727	288	1153
■ Construction	14	49	0	37	223	348	47	88	49	78
▨ Training	54	88	47	126	37	165	40	177	6	87
☐ Equip. Maintenance	65	69	30	170	6	74	77	29	84	56
☐ Supply Operations	58	148	21	143	63	103	29	166	28	71
■ Spare Parts & Mod.s	80	399	108	375	84	319	104	367	84	324
■ Other Supt. Equip.	15	162	0	196	1090	232	67	176	12	123
■ Communications Equipment	0	327	0	239	35	375	0.7	161	90	52
■ Ammunition	8	19	0	17	12	24	15	12	33	14
■ Weapons	0.3	1.8	0	221	493	12	19	524	0	44
■ Tactic & Support Vehicles	0	46	0	14	0.2	73	4	12	0	12
■ Combat Vehicles	0	247	0	126	0	184	0	16	3	13
☐ Ships	0	0	0	0	0	0	0	0	0	0
▨ Missiles	127	514	0	455	0	370	11	15	26	115
▨ Aircraft	0	0	0	1533	0	860	0	2338	0	0

Source: Adapted from data provided by the Defense Security Cooperation Agency on March 19, 2001.

In summary, Saudi purchases from the United States have provided Saudi Arabia with much of the advanced equipment it needs to deter and defend against Iran and Iraq. They have also ensured a higher degree of standardization and interoperability between Saudi and U.S. forces and strengthened Saudi capability for coalition warfare and U.S. contingency capabilities in the Gulf.

These advantages, however, are not a valid argument for further massive Saudi purchases from the United States, or for issuing Saudi Arabia a "blank check" it can use to buy any U.S. weapon or technology without careful review of their impact on the Saudi economy, the urgency of Saudi military needs, and the fact that priority should be given to balance war fighting capability. First, the weapons' effectiveness depends on a large continued U.S. advisory presence over a period of at least a decade, and the facilities and exercises necessary to allow major U.S. reinforcement and effective interoperability. Second, Saudi Arabia is now buying more arms than it can absorb, and has many other social and economic priorities. A stable Saudi Arabia is far more important than a well-armed Saudi Arabia. The Kingdom already has so many arms deliveries that it cannot absorb them properly, and it needs to emphasize training, conversion, and sustainability.

At the same time, the United States has a long history of selling arms with surcharges or special fees that other countries do not pay. Until very recently, it has imposed similar extra charges for training the Saudi military in the United States, and made no effort to ease the cost of training as Saudi Arabia's budget problems increased. It has failed to work with Saudi Arabia to develop true interoperability; FMS managers who have been based in the United States at considerable cost to the Kingdom have been sales-oriented rather than partnership-oriented. There is a clear need for reform from the U.S. as well as the Saudi side of arms sales.

Creating a Balanced and Sustainable Flow of Arms

Saudi Arabia can afford to continue to be a major arms importer, but it faces growing limits. The charts in this chapter have shown that Saudi Arabia can afford to fund larger arms imports and modernization expenditures than any potential threat country. At the same time, the charts communicate another message: unless Saudi oil export revenues are extremely high, Saudi Arabia will not be able to afford to buy and support the kind of massive weapons purchases it made in the past.

Several senior Saudi officers, as well as long-experienced USCENTCOM and British experts, made it clear during interviews in 2000–2002 that they felt Saudi Arabia should carefully limit its future major arms buys and focus on financing the training, facilities, and sustainment capabilities it needs to make them effective. U.S. officers used the slogan "train, maintain, and sustain." At the same time, these same officers pointed out that much of Saudi Arabia's equipment is now aging, and military technology continues to evolve. They noted that Saudi Arabia needs to improve its interoperability with U.S. power projection forces and with the forces of its Gulf allies. They also stressed that it needs to maintain qualitative superiority over the equipment in Iranian and Iraqi forces. It is clear from such interviews that limiting major new arms purchases in no way means a halt in new arms purchases.

The practical challenge Saudi Arabia faces is how to best restructure its arms purchases to create a balanced and sustainable flow of arms, services, and other equipment to both maintain balanced combat forces and support a reasonable degree of modernization. This should not be a problem at levels of annual arms imports well under $3 billion a year *if* Saudi Arabia limits its force expansion and modernization to the levels it can actually man, maintain, and integrate into an effective joint warfare capability. The issue is whether Saudi Arabia can adapt its arms buys to emphasize force quality over force quantity, and mission-effectiveness over the "glitter factor" and prestige provided by buying the most advanced equipment available.

Commissions and Special Fees

There is another reason for keeping arms imports as limited as the growth of potential threats and the technical need for modernization permits. The Saudi MODA and its Western suppliers need to be far more sensitive to the political image of arms imports inside Saudi Arabia. Many Saudis, including some by Saudi ex-ministers and junior members of the royal family, feel that the Kingdom's allies have often pressured or forced it to buy arms that it does not need, and that such arms purchases involve massive favoritism and corruption. Many such charges are unfair. The Saudi National Guard has long had a reputation for managing its arms buys with a very high degree of integrity and the MODA has improved its accounting and fiscal controls.

Favoritism and corruption are hardly unique to Saudi arms purchases. For example, a detailed cross-cultural comparison of the integrity, fiscal management and level of corruption in Saudi and French military procurement might well favor Saudi Arabia. The U.S. has had plenty of its own arms scandals over the years. Britain and France both benefited from the corruption in the al-Yamamah deal. In addition, Saudis are correct in pointing out that there has often been political pressure on Saudi Arabia to buy equipment at the highest levels of Western governments. Moreover, commissions and special fees are scarcely unusual in the region and the developing world—every Gulf state engages in such practices to some degree, including Iran and Iraq. Commissions and special fees are a normal practice in foreign arms sales to the rest of the Middle East, most of the developing world, and even some European countries.

Nevertheless, the larger the volume of sales, the larger the problem. In the case of Saudi Arabia, arms sales involve such massive sums that any problems risk tainting all Saudi military purchases with the image of corruption. It is hardly surprising, therefore, that extremist opposition groups— and many moderate Saudis—are finally convinced that Saudi arms purchases are often made as a result of commissions and bribes, and charge that many of Saudi Arabia's arms buys are simply a waste of money, claiming that billions of dollars in "arms import" expenditures actually go directly to senior members of the royal family.

Saudi Arabia's arms buys have generally bought high-quality and combat-effective equipment, but politics, hidden commissions, special fees, inflated transport contracts, and profiteering through offset arrangements are a problem. Despite efforts to eliminate profiteering in arms sales, many European arms sales to Saudi Arabia involve at least some special payments, kickbacks, commissions and fees, or open bribes. In spite of U.S. law, U.S. companies and firms also find ways to make such payments—sometimes by rigging the offset programs required as part of arms sales to favor firms or agents favored by given princes, or by allowing special transport and delivery contracts that go to firms run by members of the royal family. These commissions and fees are virtually the rule with European arms sales, and sales that are not controlled as part of the U.S. FMS program.

These problems are compounded by a problem discussed earlier: The Saudi national budget—like that of most countries in the developing world—does not provide any detailed public information on Saudi military expenditures and arms purchases, agreements that trade oil for arms, or those that are funded by state funds not integrated into the Saudi national budget. These "off-book" arms buys make orderly accounting extremely difficult, and lead to still further charges of corruption. Further, there is no doubt that many offset programs are overstaffed and expensive, regardless of whether or not they are actually corrupt. In at least some cases, four or more Saudis are hired for every real job while foreigners do the actual work. While it must be stressed that some programs are successful, other offset programs may seem impressive on paper but are little more than a waste of state funds.

Saudi offset programs present an additional problem. Saudi arms purchase contracts require the seller to provide an offset equal to 35% of the technical value or cost of the hardware purchased. There have been some striking successes like AEC, but the practical problem is that there is no way to create effective offset programs or staff them with skilled Saudi labor at the required rate. Since the mid-1980s, U.S. contractors alone have incurred offset obligations totaling over $1.7 billion and only 16% have been realized. British contractors have only realized 8% of some $2 billion in offsets, and French firms have only realized about 6% of $700 million in sales.[39] Worse, some programs that have been created are dummy firms or "sweetheart" deals set up under retired officers and/or the friends of princes and senior officers. Such programs only make an illusory contribution to the Saudi economy and Saudi defense. While offsets are desirable in principle, overambitious programs simply create the illusion of aiding economic development while actually encouraging corruption. The present Saudi offset program is little more than a hollow shell and needs massive restructuring. At a minimum, offset operatives should be treated as business ventures with full disclosure and annual reports and clear standards for penalizing contractor nonperformance and for immediately terminating nonproductive programs.

Both Saudi Arabia and the West need to pay more careful attention to the political image of Saudi arms sales and imports. Today, they damage the credibility and integrity of the Saudi armed forces, the Saudi royal family, and Western governments and arms sellers. They create the image of massive waste of state funds at a time when Saudi Arabia can no longer afford such waste, and Saudi officers are all too aware of political arms buys that undercut Saudi efforts at interoperability and standardization. Transparency is important for political as well as management problems. There is an urgent need to improve Saudi military accounting and contracting procedures at a far more rapid rate than is currently the case, to ruthlessly prosecute Saudis and Westerners who engage in such practices, and to integrate every aspect of Saudi arms purchases fully so they are visible in the regular Saudi national budget and subject to normal Saudi audit procedures and fiscal controls.

NOTES

1. Exchange rate of 3.75 Saudi riyals to $1 U.S. dollar.
2. Department of State, *Annual Report on Military Expenditures, 1999*, Submitted to the Committee on Appropriations of the U.S. Senate and the Committee on Appropriations of the U.S. House of Representatives, July 27, 2000, in accordance with section 511(b) of the Foreign Operations, Export Financing, and Related Programs Appropriations Act, 1993.
3. Ibid.
4. Arms Control and Disarmament Agency (ACDA), *World Military Expenditures and Arms Transfers* (Washington: GPO, various editions), Table I.
5. IISS, *Military Balance, 2001–2002*.
6. The FY1988 budget was planned to have a $10 billion deficit, with $8 billion in foreign borrowing. It involved the first foreign borrowing in twenty-five years and the first increase in taxes in eight years—all on foreign businesses. The actual budget reached a $15 to $17 billion deficit by the year's end, with some $10 billion in financing. *Economist*, January 16, 1988, p. 59; *Defense News*, January 18, 1988, p. 4.
7. Calculations made by the author using various tables provided by the Saudi embassy in Washington in October 1993, and April 1995.
8. Based on various editions of the CIA *World Factbook*. Some of the differences between these estimates may, however, reflect differences in the CIA definition of GDP and military expenditures.
9. *Report on Allied Contributions to the Common Defense*, March 2001, Report to the U.S. Congress by the Secretary of Defense, p. E-6.
10. Interview with official of the Office of the Secretary of Defense, February 2001.
11. *Defense News*, November 20–26, 1995, p. 27.
12. Richard F. Grimmett, *Conventional Arms Transfers to the Third World,*

1985–1992 (Washington: Congressional Research Service, CRS-93-656F, July 19, 1993), pp. 59, 69; *Conventional Arms Transfers to the Third World, 1989–1996* (Washington: Congressional Research Service, CRS-97-778F, August 13, 1997), pp. 53, 65; and *Conventional Arms Transfers to the Third World, 1992–1996* (Washington: Congressional Research Service, CRS-RL30640, August 18, 2000), pp. 47–49, 58–60.

13. Richard F. Grimmett, *Conventional Arms Transfers to the Third World, 1989–1996* (Washington: Congressional Research Service, CRS-97-778F, August 13, 1997), pp. 53, 65–66.

14. Arms Control and Disarmament Agency (ACDA), *World Military Expenditures and Arms Transfers, 1989* (Washington: GPO, 1990), Table II; ACDA printout dated May 14, 1996; ACDA, *World Military Expenditures and Arms Transfers, 1996* (Washington: GPO, 1997), Table II; and U.S. State Department, *World Military Expenditures and Arms Transfers, 1998* (Washington: Bureau of Arms Control, 1999).

15. Based on data provided by Richard F. Grimmett.

16. See ACDA, "High Costs of the Persian Gulf War," *World Military Expenditures and Arms Transfers, 1987* (Washington: GPO, 1988), pp. 21–23; ACDA printout dated May 14, 1996; and Richard F. Grimmett, *Trends in Conventional Arms Transfers to the Third World by Major Supplier, 1982-1989* (Washington: Congressional Research Service, Library of Congress, 90-298F, June 19, 1990).

17. ACDA, *World Military Expenditures and Arms Transfers, 1989* (Washington: GPO, 1990), Table II; ACDA printout dated May 14, 1996; ACDA, *World Military Expenditures and Arms Transfers, 1996* (Washington: GPO, 1997), Table II; and U.S. State Department, *World Military Expenditures and Arms Transfers, 1998* (Washington: Bureau of Arms Control, 1999).

18. These data are all taken from the 1988 to 1996 editions of Richard F. Grimmett, *Conventional Arms Transfers to Developing Nations* (Washington: Congressional Research Service).

19. *Defense Weekly*, May 31, 1999, pp. 1, 20.

20. Richard F. Grimmett, *Trends in Conventional Arms Transfers to the Third World by Major Supplier, 1992–1999* (Washington: Congressional Research Service, Library of Congress, RL-30640, August 18, 2000).

21. ACDA, *World Military Expenditures and Arms Transfers, 1985* (Washington: GPO, 1985), pp. 133–134; and ACDA printout dated May 14, 1996.

22. ACDA, *World Military Expenditures and Arms Transfers, 1989* (Washington: GPO, 1990), pp. 117–118; ACDA printout dated May 14, 1996.

23. The ACDA changed its way of reporting arms sales by source in 1992. ACDA, *World Military Expenditures and Arms Transfers, 1990* (Washington: GPO, 1992), Table III; ACDA printout dated May 14, 1996.

24. Ibid.; ACDA, *World Military Expenditures and Arms Transfers, 1991–1992* (Washington: GPO, 1994), Table III; and ACDA, *World Military Expenditures and Arms Transfers, 1993–1994* (Washington: GPO, 1995).

25. Ibid.

26. Richard F. Grimmett, *Conventional Arms Transfers to Developing Nations, 1987–1994* (Washington: Congressional Research Service, 95-862F, August 4, 1994), pp. 56–57, 68; *Conventional Arms Transfers to the Third World, 1989–1996* (Washington: Congressional Research Service, CRS-97-778F, August 13,

1997), pp. 53, 65; *Conventional Arms Transfers to the Third World, 1989–1996* (Washington: Congressional Research Service, CRS-RL-31083, August 16, 2001), pp. 53, 65.

27. Richard F. Grimmett, *Conventional Arms Transfers to the Third World, 1993–2000* (Washington: Congressional Research Service, CRS-RL31083, August 16, 2001), pp. 47, 58.

28. These figures are based on data provided by the Defense Security Cooperation Agency as of March 19, 2001.

29. Ibid.

30. Ibid.

31. Ibid.

32. *New York Times*, August 22, 1993.

33. Richard F. Grimmett, *Saudi Arabia: Restructuring Arms Payments to the US* (Washington: Congressional Research Service, 94-356F, April 25, 1994); *New York Times*, January 3, 1994, p. A-3, January 18, 1994, p. A-8; Department of Defense, "Saudi Stretch Out," February 1, 1994; *Wall Street Journal*, January 31, 1994, p. A2; Reuters, April 5, 1994; *Defense News*, January 10, 1994, p. 1, May 30, 1994, p. 1; *Aviation Week*, February 7, 1994, p. 22; *Inside the Navy*, January 3, 1994, p. 3; *Christian Science Monitor*, December 20, 1993, p. C-1.

34. *New York Times*, August 22, 1993.

35. *Jane's Defence Weekly*, July 10, 1996, p. 30, February 26, 1997, p. 32; Interviews at USCENTCOM.

36. *Jane's Defence Weekly*, May 31, 1999, pp. 1, 20.

37. U.S. Defense Security Assistance Agency (DSAA), *Foreign Military Sales, Foreign Military Construction Sales and Military Assistance Facts as of September 30, 1994* (Washington: Department of Defense, 1995).

38. Interview with OSD official, February 2001.

39. *Defense News*, March 17, 1997, pp. 1, 40.

Chapter 4

The Saudi Army

The Saudi Army has grown steadily since the 1960s and has become an increasingly modern force. At the time of the October War in 1973, the Saudi Army only had some 36,000 men, 25 medium tanks, and 260 other armored vehicles. By the time the Iran-Iraq War took place in 1980, the Saudi Army had 31,000 men, but had 380 main battle tanks, 600 other armored vehicles, and a significant strength of self-propelled artillery. The year the Gulf War began, the Saudi Army had 40,000 actives, 550 main battle tanks, 1,840 other armored vehicles, and 275 self-propelled artillery weapons.

The Saudi Army emerged as a significant regional military force during the Gulf War. Both Arab task forces—Joint Forces Command (East) and Joint Forces Command (North)—were organized under the command of Lieutenant General Prince Khalid bin Sultan al-Saud.[1] By the time the air-land phase of the war began, the Saudi ground forces in the theater totaled nearly 50,000 men, with about 270 main battle tanks, 930 other armored fighting vehicles, 115 artillery weapons, and over 400 anti-tank weapons.

Today, the Saudi Army has about 75,000 actives, an inventory of 1,055 medium tanks on-hand or in delivery, plus over 3,000 other armored vehicles, and 500 major artillery weapons. It is headquartered in Riyadh, and has five staff branches: G1 Personnel, G2 Intelligence and Security, G3 Operations and Training, G4 Logistics, and G5 Civil and Military Affairs. It also has field commands organized into eight zones under military zone commanders.

In spite of this expansion, the Saudi Army faces major challenges. It must deal with two major potential threats—Iran and Iraq—that both have far larger ground forces. Iraq poses a particularly serious challenge, sharing a common border with few terrain features that aid the Saudi Army in defending the oil-rich areas along the Gulf coast. At the same time, the Saudi Army still faces a potential threat from Yemen and must have some forces to cover its border with Jordan and Syria. This means a relatively small army must defend a territory roughly the size of the United States east of the Mississippi, while there are limits to the extent the Saudi Army can concentrate its forces to meet a single threat.

SAUDI COMBAT UNIT STRENGTH AND DEPLOYMENTS

The Saudi Army has compensated for its lack of force strength and experience in modern military operations by deploying forces in large military cities that can fully house and support its combat units. This both allows them to deploy near possible fronts and minimizes the risk that some coup attempt might be launched near the capital, holy places, or key ports and oil facilities.

These factors explain why the Army has a base near Abha—halfway between Jiddah and Jizan—to cover the Yemeni border, plus King Abdul Aziz Military City at Khamis Mushayt and ten Mechanized Brigade and other combat elements at Shahrurah in the southeast. There are smaller garrisons at Najran and Jezan in the south and Dammam in the east. Another major army facility, King Faisal Military City, is located near Tabuk in the west, which allows Saudi Arabia to cover any potential threat from Israel, Jordan, or Syria.

Saudi Arabia built a large base called King Khalid Military City near Hafr al Batin on the Iraqi and Kuwaiti borders during 1983–1987. This city houses some 65,000 military personnel and civilians. The GCC Peninsular Shield Force is located at this city, which is capable of housing and supporting three full Saudi Army brigades. A fourth major base or military city has been under construction at Jizan, near the western end of the Saudi-Yemeni border, since 1996. A naval port and air base are also under construction at Jizan.

These bases have eased many of the Kingdom's deployment and logistical problems. They also have served the political purpose of keeping Saudi ground forces away from the kingdom's political power centers. At the same time, they now place too many of the Kingdom's ground forces in remote areas near the Yemeni border and in Tabuk to deal with an Israeli ground threat that seems very unlikely to materialize. The bases also have encouraged a static, defensive mentality in the Saudi Army, which has been reinforced by a lack of meaningful emergency and cross-reinforcement exercises. In fact, until Khalid bin Sultan became assistant minister of defense in 2001, Saudi Arabia conducted little more than token set piece exercise activity—and then only with long periods of preparation and warning—between 1992 and 2002.

Saudi Arabia is not yet capable of conducting division-sized operations. In 2002, the combat strength of the Saudi Army consisted of three armored brigades, five mechanized infantry brigades, one airborne brigade, and one Royal Guards regiment. It also had five independent artillery brigades and an aviation command. The Saudi Army deployed the 12th Armored Brigade and 6th Mechanized Brigade at King Faisal Military City in the Tabuk area, the 4th Armored Brigade and 11th Mechanized Brigade at King Abd al-Aziz Military City in the Khamis Mushayt area, the 20th Mechanized Brigade and 8th Mechanized Brigade at King Khalid Military City near Hafr al Batin, and the 10th Mechanized Brigade at Sharawrah, which is near the border with Yemen and about 150 kilometers from Zamak.

A typical Saudi armored brigade had an armored reconnaissance company equipped with Panhard M3s, three tank battalions with forty-two tanks each, two tank companies with a total of thirty tanks, three tank troops with a total of twelve tanks, a mechanized infantry battalion with fifty-four AIFVs/APCs, and an artillery battalion with eighteen self-propelled guns. It also had an army aviation company, an engineer company, a logistic battalion, a field workshop, and a medical company.

A typical Saudi mechanized brigade had an armored reconnaissance company, one tank battalion with thirty-seven to forty-two tanks, three mechanized infantry battalions with fifty-four AIFVs/APCs each, two infantry companies with a total of thirty-three APCs, three infantry platoons with a total of twelve APCs, and an artillery battalion with eighteen self-propelled guns. It also had an army aviation company, an engineer company, a logistic battalion, a field workshop, and a medical company. It had twenty-four anti-tank guided weapons launchers and four mortar sections with a total of eight 81 mm mortars.

The Airborne Brigade and Royal Guard Brigade were deployed near Riyadh. The Airborne Brigade had two parachute battalions and three Special Forces companies.[2] The Special Forces companies report directly to Prince Sultan. The Royal Guard Brigade had three battalions, and was equipped with light armored vehicles. It reports directly to the king and is recruited from loyal tribes in the Najd. The Army also has an Army Aviation Command, formed in 1986, that operated Saudi Arabia's Bell 406 armed helicopters and AH-64s. There also were security garrisons at most major Saudi cities, including Dhahran, Jeddah, and Riyadh.

The Army has a number of major educational facilities. It operates the King Abd al-Aziz Military Academy near Riyadh and an Army Staff College at Riyadh. There are numerous specialized training centers for NCOs and technicians in Saudi Arabia, and Saudi junior officers and other ranks train in specialized areas in Britain, France, and the United States.

THE MANPOWER ISSUE

The trends in the buildup of the manpower in Saudi land forces are shown in Chart 4.1, and the comparative level of Saudi and other Gulf army manpower is shown in Chart 4.2. The Saudi Army has encountered growing problems in expanding to the force levels required to secure the Kingdom's northern borders, to help ensure the security of Kuwait, and to deal with potential problems in the south. Its most serious problem is manpower. The Saudi Army only had a total of 38,000 to 43,000 men in late 1988, with another 56,000 full-time and part-time men in the National Guard. Despite crash efforts to build up the Army's manpower during the Gulf War—efforts that sometimes raised combat unit manning by as much as 20%—the Army's force structure was still undermanned in 1991 by about 20% to 35%. Many individual units had even worse manning levels. As of 2002,

Chart 4.1
Saudi Active Land Force Manning, 1980–2002 (1,000s of Personnel)

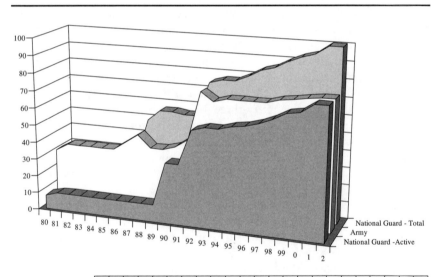

	80	81	82	83	84	85	86	87	88	89	90	91	92	93	94	95	96	97	98	99	0	1	2
National Guard -Active	8	10	10	10	10	10	10	10	10	10	35	35	55	57	57	59	60	62	65	69	70	75	75
Army	31	35	35	35	35	35	40	45	38	38	40	45	73	68	70	70	70	70	72	73	74	75	75
National Guard - Total	20	30	25	25	25	25	25	50	56	56	55	55	75	77	77	80	84	86	90	93	95	100	100

Note: Statistical base differs somewhat from that used for Charts 3.2 and 3.3.

Sources: Adapted by Anthony H. Cordesman from ACDA, *World Military Expenditures and Arms Transfers, 1995* (Washington: GPO, 1996); U.S. State Department, *World Military Expenditures and Arms Transfers, 1999* (Washington: Bureau of Arms Control, 2000); various editions of the IISS, *Military Balance* and the JCSS, *The Middle East Military Balance*; and material provided by U.S. experts.

Chart 4.2

Comparative Trends in Gulf Total Active Military Manpower, 1979–2002 (Total Includes Iranian Revolutionary Guard, Saudi National Guard, and Omani Royal Guard)

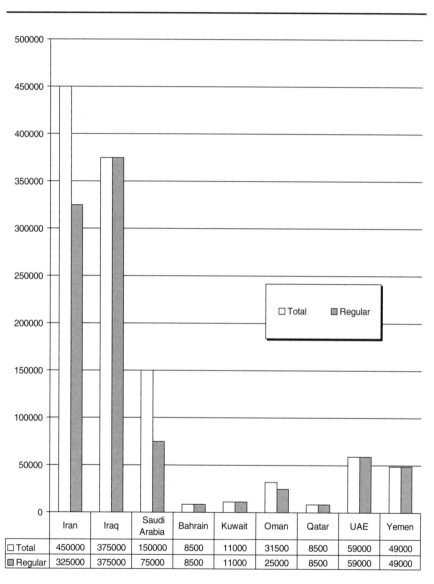

	Iran	Iraq	Saudi Arabia	Bahrain	Kuwait	Oman	Qatar	UAE	Yemen
☐ Total	450000	375000	150000	8500	11000	31500	8500	59000	49000
▓ Regular	325000	375000	75000	8500	11000	25000	8500	59000	49000

Sources: Estimated by Anthony H. Cordesman using data from various editions of the IISS *Military Balance*, *Jane's Sentinel*, and *Military Technology*.

the Saudi Army had still only reached a total of around 75,000 full-time actives for a force structure that required up to twice as many men.

This level of manpower is adequate to man about two U.S. light division "slices," with only minimal manning for combat, combat support, and service support units. In the U.S. Army, it could support a total force with a maximum of around 600 tanks and 1,000 other armored vehicles. In practice, however, the Saudi Army's manpower must be divided into force structure that has an order of battle equivalent to around three heavy divisions, and with an equipment pool at least that size. This requires more manpower than Saudi Arabia has available.

SAUDI ARMY FORCE EXPANSION

Saudi Arabia's manpower problems raise serious doubts about the ambitious force expansion plans that the Kingdom has discussed since the Gulf War, and which it would need to implement to be able to defend against the Iraqi threat if Iraq should succeed in breaking out of UN sanctions. After the Gulf War, Saudi Arabia and the United States carried out a secret Saudi-U.S. Joint Security Review in August 1991 called the Malcor Report that was completed in August 1991. The resulting plan called for a three-corps Saudi force of seven divisions by the year 2000. One option called for a nine-"division" force of 90,000 men, although 90,000 men would normally only be enough to fully man and support a Western force of three two-brigade divisions.[3]

The Saudi Army was soon forced to adopt more modest goals, but even these goals still called for the Army to expand to a total of five divisions by the year 2000. The expansion also called for a conversion from a brigade-oriented command structure to a division-oriented structure. It would provide the ability to deploy up to three divisions in the north to defend Saudi Arabia's Gulf coast and border with Iraq. Another division was to be deployed near Al-Kharj or the capital, and a fifth division in the south, although some sources indicate that one brigade of this latter division was to be in the south and the other would be at Tabuk.

These Saudi force expansion plans called for the use of a relatively unwieldy division structure, rather than the brigade-oriented command structure that better suited the Kingdom. They required a minimum of 105,000 men to create a force that would have had limited combat endurance and sustainability, and they required at least 130,000 men to provide a full mix of sustainability and support forces.

The Saudi Army faced serious problems.

- The only way Saudi Arabia could shift to a true divisional force structure with five divisions was to create two-brigade units instead of the planned three-brigade forces, and leave them without adequate combat support and service support forces. This change, however, threatened to waste manpower and financial resources on administrative staff. A brigade structure remains the most efficient way of organizing Saudi forces as long as they are going to be dispersed widely to the borders of the country.

- The Saudi command structure had not progressed to the point where it could carry out the battle management for integrated combat operations at the divisional level.

- Saudi Arabia would have needed more than nine heavy brigades to provide the combat elements for such a force. A total Saudi force structure of about ten brigades, plus some lighter independent formations, may be as large a force as Saudi Arabia can properly create and sustain until well beyond the year 2000.

- Saudi Arabia did consider creating two to three additional light divisions and adding a mobilization or reserve component to its support forces.[4] Such support forces would have limited manning in peacetime, but would use temporary-duty civilians in their support forces in a major crisis. However, the Saudi Army failed to create such forces and lay the groundwork for a rapid buildup in a crisis.

- Saudi forces lacked the independent combat support and service support forces necessary to sustain and support the existing strength of the Saudi Army.

- Finally, much of Saudi maintenance continued to be performed by foreign contractors, and the quality of much of this work was mixed. Overstretching Saudi military manpower meant further delaying Saudi Army ability to provide an adequate ordinance corps and forces that can properly sustain combat equipment away from major bases, in extensive maneuver, or under conditions where combat repair and recovery are needed.

Although Prince Sultan continued to talked about expanding the Army to at least 90,000 men long after the Gulf War, it became clear by the late 1990s that Saudi Arabia would have serious problems in funding the substantial additional purchases of equipment it would need to equip such a force at a time when funds were becoming increasingly tight. Any such expansion would require additional tanks, infantry fighting vehicles, self-propelled artillery, and mobile air defense systems. Funding these items would also present potential conflicts with the priorities of both existing Army units and the different funding priorities of the Saudi National Guard.

It is not surprising, therefore, that the Saudi Army has kept its brigade-oriented force structure, and that its total forces still remain at under three division equivalents. It also is not surprising that this force structure has serious manpower quality, equipment maintenance and upgrade, sustainability, support, and training problems and needs substantially more well-trained actives. Stretching limited manpower, equipment, and support capabilities to create added combat units would serve little purpose. Many U.S. advisors feel that the Saudi Army should focus on improving its existing force structure rather than force expansion, although some elements of the leadership of the Army would like to add two more light brigades.

One thing is clear: regardless of what the Saudi Army decides, it will not be able to create a force structure that can meet regional threats like Iraq without help from its neighbors and allies like the United States and Britain. The Saudi Army will not be able to defend its territory in the upper Gulf from an all-out attack by Iraq, or to concentrate its forces quickly and effectively to aid Kuwait, unless Saudi Arabia has extensive U.S. support. Further, the threat from the northern Gulf is only part of the threat that Saudi Arabia must deal with. It must provide forces sufficient to guard against the emergence of an Iranian threat and defend its western border area and Red Sea coast, while maintaining forces in the south to deal with a continuing low-level border conflict with Yemen.

THE SAUDI ARMY EQUIPMENT BUILDUP AND THE NEED FOR IMPROVED STANDARDIZATION AND INTEROPERABILITY

The Saudi Army's problems in expansion, planning, manpower, organization, and deployment have been compounded by the need to absorb the massive equipment buildup that took place before and after the Gulf War. The scale of this buildup is shown in Chart 4.3. It should be stressed that the figures in this chart are based on unclassified data, and that the trends shown are not precise. At the same time, they are unquestionably correct in broad terms and the chart shows that buildup through the mid-1990s was extremely large and rapid.

Saudi Army equipment problems are more than a matter of numbers. The Army also faces the need to operate a complex mix of equipment supplied by many nations, and then be able to operate effectively with the equipment mixes in the forces of regional allies, the United States, and Britain. The diversification of the Saudi Army's sources of army equipment has reduced its dependence on the United States, but it has also increased its training and support burden and has raised its operations and maintenance costs. Saudi Arabia has also made some purchases of army equipment from its major oil customers that do not serve the Army's needs.

Saudi Arabia still operates three types of tanks supplied by the United States and France. It has holdings of five different types of major armored fighting vehicles and armored personnel carriers, and an inventory of more than twenty subtypes. It has major artillery holdings from five different countries, anti-tank weapons from four, and helicopters from two. This equipment is broadly interoperable, but each additional type increases the Army's training and sustainability problems.

Saudi Arabia's unique weather, terrain, and desert warfare conditions also create special demands in terms of support and sustainability. Much of the

Chart 4.3
The Growth in Saudi Army Weapons Strength, 1979–2002

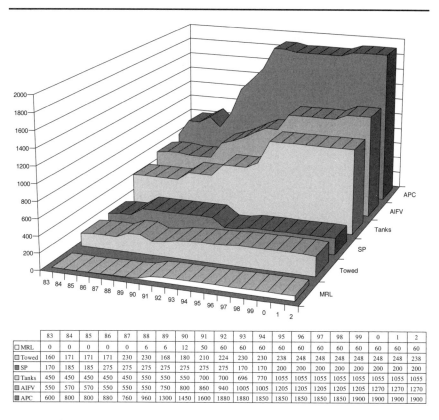

	83	84	85	86	87	88	89	90	91	92	93	94	95	96	97	98	99	0	1	2
☐ MRL	0	0	0	0	0	6	6	12	50	60	60	60	60	60	60	60	60	60	60	60
☐ Towed	160	171	171	171	230	230	168	180	210	224	230	230	238	248	248	248	248	248	248	238
■ SP	170	185	185	275	275	275	275	275	275	275	170	170	200	200	200	200	200	200	200	200
☐ Tanks	450	450	450	450	450	550	550	550	700	700	696	770	1055	1055	1055	1055	1055	1055	1055	1055
☐ AIFV	550	570	570	550	550	550	750	800	860	940	1005	1005	1205	1205	1205	1205	1205	1270	1270	1270
■ APC	600	800	800	880	760	960	1300	1450	1600	1880	1880	1850	1850	1850	1850	1850	1900	1900	1900	1900

Sources: Adapted by Anthony H. Cordesman from various editions of the IISS, *Military Balance*; the JCSS, *The Middle East Military Balance*; and material provided by U.S. experts.

equipment the Saudi Army has purchased has required modification, or extensive changes to its original technical and logistic support plan, before it could be operated in large numbers. As a result, most new systems present major servicing and support problems and will continue to do so until new maintenance procedures are adopted and modifications are made to failure-prone components. These problems will increase strikingly the moment the Saudi Army is force to operate away from its bases, conduct sustained maneuvers, and deal with combat damage.

Contractor support is not a substitute for uniformed Saudi combat support and service support capabilities that can deploy and fight in the field, and the Saudi Army's standardization and interoperability problems are compounded by the need to support equipment in remote and widely dispersed locations. The Saudi Army has tried to reduce such problems by creating an advanced logistic system, but some experts feel this effort has been overly ambitious and has lacked proper Saudi and U.S. advisory management.

SAUDI TANKS

Saudi Arabia has made a massive investment in armor. The growth of Saudi armored strength is shown in Chart 4.4, and the trends shown in this chart reflect a steady increase in total inventory and one that has been too rapid for Saudi Arabia to properly crew or support. The Saudi Army has had to retire its older types like the AMX-30 from service or put them in storage. Saudi holdings are compared to those of other Gulf States in Chart 4.5. It is clear from this chart that Iraq remains the largest armored power in the Gulf, although Iran has a high tank strength and Saudi Arabia has the highest overall level of mechanization.

In 2002, Saudi Arabia had a total inventory of 1,055 main battle tanks and more than 300 tank transporters. Its tanks included 315 M-1A2s, 450 M-60A3s, and 290 French-made AMX-30s. About half of the AMX-30s were in storage, however, and only about 700 to 765 of Saudi Arabia's main battle tanks were operational. The Kingdom was also experiencing major problems in converting to the M-1A1 tanks, which left it with a core strength of around 380 well-manned M-60A3s, about 100 to175 M-1A2s that were combat-ready with good crew proficiency, and a residual force of around 160 to 170 AMX-30s.

The AMX-30

Saudi Arabia's inventory of 290 French AMX-30s is concentrated in the Khamis Mushayt area, and is the Achilles heel of its tank force. The AMX-30 lacks the armor, firepower, and operational availability to keep it in service against threats armed with T-62s, T-72s, and modern tanks like the T-80, M-60, Khalid, Merkava, Chieftain, and Challenger.

While the adoption of newer anti–armor round technology has made up for the lack of penetrating power in the Obus G rounds that France originally sold the Saudi Army, the AMX-30's fire control and range-finding capability is not able to help Saudi tank crews make up for their lack of experience. The AMX-30 also lacks power, cooling, and filtration for desert combat. Saudi Arabia has needed to phase the AMX-30 out of its force structure for nearly half a decade.

In practice, most Saudi AMX-30 tanks never had more than token exercise use during any point in their life cycle, and some have only thirty to

Chart 4.4
The Growth in Saudi Armored Weapons Strength, 1979–2002

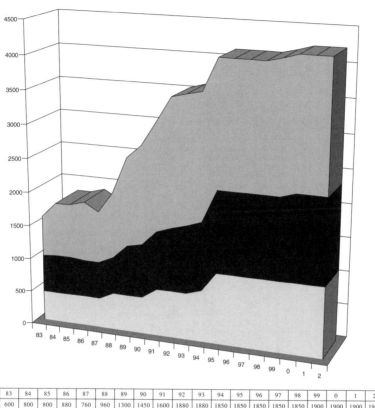

	83	84	85	86	87	88	89	90	91	92	93	94	95	96	97	98	99	0	1	2
▢ APC	600	800	800	880	760	960	1300	1450	1600	1880	1880	1850	1850	1850	1850	1850	1900	1900	1900	1900
■ AIFV	550	570	570	550	550	550	750	800	860	940	1005	1005	1205	1205	1205	1205	1205	1270	1270	1270
▢ Tanks	450	450	450	450	450	550	550	550	700	700	696	770	1055	1055	1055	1055	1055	1055	1055	1055

Sources: Adapted by Anthony H. Cordesman from various editions of the IISS, *Military Balance*; the JCSS, *The Middle East Military Balance*; and material provided by U.S. experts.

fifty miles of total travel. Nearly 50% of Saudi Arabia's 290 AMX-30s are now in storage, but Saudi Arabia is unlikely to fully phase the AMX-30 out of its forces in the immediate future. According to some reports, it is considering selling its AMX-30s and replacing them with the Le Clerc as part of the al-Yamamah deal.

The M-60A3

Charts 4.5 through 4.9 show comparative armor and tank strength in the Gulf region. The Iranian and Iraqi threat is impressive—at least in terms

Chart 4.5
Total Gulf Operational Armored Fighting Vehicle Strength, 2002

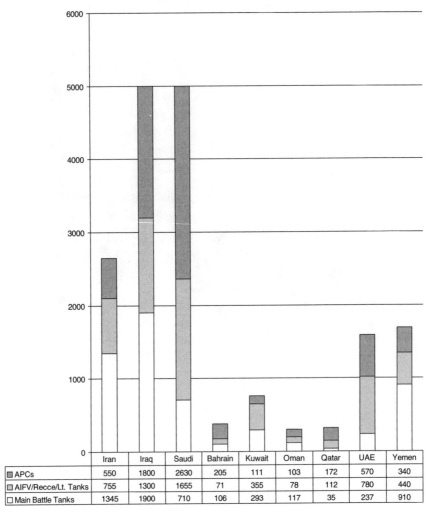

	Iran	Iraq	Saudi	Bahrain	Kuwait	Oman	Qatar	UAE	Yemen
▣ APCs	550	1800	2630	205	111	103	172	570	340
▢ AIFV/Recce/Lt. Tanks	755	1300	1655	71	355	78	112	780	440
☐ Main Battle Tanks	1345	1900	710	106	293	117	35	237	910

Sources: Estimated by Anthony H. Cordesman using data from various editions of the IISS, *Military Balance*, and *Jane's Sentinel*.

of the total numbers—and the Saudi Army's 450 M-60A3s and 315 M-1A2s are the only part of its tank force that really meet Saudi needs. The M-60A3 is not as advanced as the M-1A1, but Saudi Arabia has found the M-60A3 to be a significant advance over the M-60A1 and converted all of its existing M-60A1s to the M-60A3 by 1990. Saudi Arabia's other M-60A3s are

Chart 4.6
Trends in Total Gulf Main Battle Tank Inventory, 1979–2002

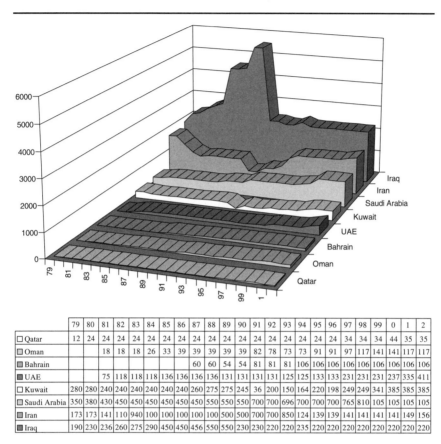

	79	80	81	82	83	84	85	86	87	88	89	90	91	92	93	94	95	96	97	98	99	0	1	2
☐ Qatar	12	24	24	24	24	24	24	24	24	24	24	24	24	24	24	24	24	24	34	34	34	44	35	35
☐ Oman			18	18	18	26	33	39	39	39	39	39	82	78	73	73	91	91	97	117	141	141	117	117
▣ Bahrain									60	60	54	54	81	81	81	106	106	106	106	106	106	106	106	106
▣ UAE			75	118	118	118	136	136	136	136	131	131	131	131	125	125	133	133	231	231	231	237	335	411
☐ Kuwait	280	280	240	240	240	240	240	240	260	275	275	245	36	200	150	164	220	198	249	249	341	385	385	385
▣ Saudi Arabia	350	380	430	450	450	450	450	450	450	550	550	550	700	700	696	700	700	700	765	810	105	105	105	105
▣ Iran	173	173	141	110	940	100	100	100	100	100	500	500	700	700	850	124	139	139	141	141	141	141	149	156
▣ Iraq	190	230	236	260	275	290	450	450	456	550	550	230	230	220	220	235	220	220	220	220	220	220	220	220

Sources: Adapted by Anthony H. Cordesman from the IISS, *Military Balance*; *Periscope*; the JCSS, *The Middle East Military Balance*; *Jane's Sentinel*; and *Jane's Defence Weekly*.

relatively new: the Kingdom bought 150 M-60A3s, along with 15,000 de-pleted uranium 105 mm anti-tank rounds, as part of an emergency order in August 1990.

The M-60A3 has shown that it is still capable of engaging any tank cur-rently deployed in the region. Although they lack a decisive technical superi-ority over the T-72 and the other first-line tanks in potential threat forces, M-60s easily outperformed the export versions of the T-72 in Iraqi forces dur-ing the Gulf War. The M-60 is likely to remain in the Saudi force structure through the year 2005. The M-60A3s have thermal sights, modern fire-control computers, laser range finders, and engine and air intake improvements. The M-60A3 does, however, present some operational problems—the crew

Chart 4.7
Total Operational Main Battle Tanks in All Gulf Forces, 1979–2002

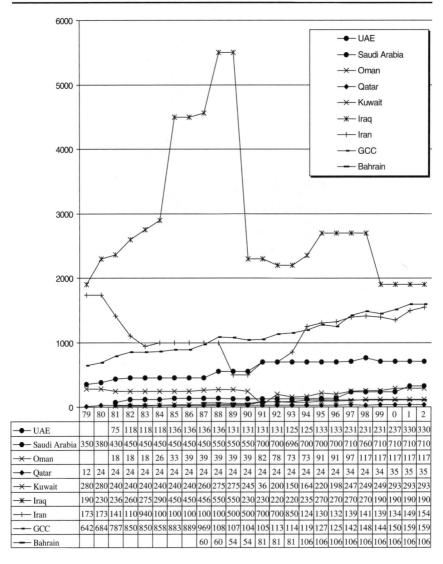

	79	80	81	82	83	84	85	86	87	88	89	90	91	92	93	94	95	96	97	98	99	0	1	2
—●— UAE			75	118	118	118	136	136	136	136	131	131	131	131	125	125	133	133	231	231	231	237	330	330
—●— Saudi Arabia	350	380	430	450	450	450	450	450	450	550	550	550	700	700	696	700	700	700	710	760	710	710	710	710
—✕— Oman			18	18	18	26	33	39	39	39	39	39	82	78	73	73	91	91	97	117	117	117	117	117
—◆— Qatar	12	24	24	24	24	24	24	24	24	24	24	24	24	24	24	24	24	24	34	24	34	35	35	35
—✕— Kuwait	280	280	240	240	240	240	240	240	260	275	275	245	36	200	150	164	220	198	247	249	249	293	293	293
—✳— Iraq	190	230	236	260	275	290	450	450	456	550	550	230	230	220	220	235	270	270	270	270	190	190	190	190
—+— Iran	173	173	141	110	940	100	100	100	100	100	500	500	700	700	850	124	130	132	139	141	139	134	149	154
—— GCC	642	684	787	850	850	858	883	889	969	108	107	104	105	113	114	119	127	125	142	148	144	150	159	159
—— Bahrain									60	60	54	54	81	81	81	106	106	106	106	106	106	106	106	106

Note: Iran includes active forces in the Revolutionary Guards. Saudi Arabia includes active
   National Guard.
Sources: Adapted by Anthony H. Cordesman from the IISS, *Military Balance*; *Periscope*;
   JCSS, *The Middle East Military Balance*; *Jane's Sentinel*; and *Jane's Defence Weekly*.

Chart 4.8
Medium-to-High-Quality Main Battle Tanks by Type, 2002

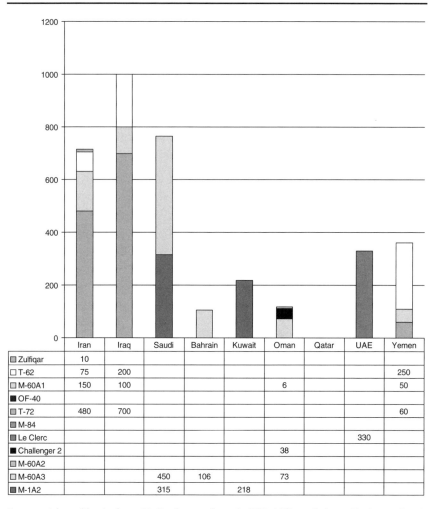

	Iran	Iraq	Saudi	Bahrain	Kuwait	Oman	Qatar	UAE	Yemen
⊟ Zulfiqar	10								
☐ T-62	75	200							250
☐ M-60A1	150	100				6			50
■ OF-40									
⊟ T-72	480	700							60
▨ M-84									
■ Le Clerc								330	
■ Challenger 2						38			
☐ M-60A2									
☐ M-60A3			450	106		73			
▨ M-1A2			315		218				

Sources: Adapted by Anthony H. Cordesman from the IISS, *Military Balance*; *Periscope*; *Jane's Sentinel*; and *Jane's Defence Weekly*.

compartment cannot be cooled effectively in extremely hot weather, and it can develop internal temperatures of well over 120 degrees.[5]

The M-1A2 Upgrade Program

The M-1A2 is currently the most advanced tank in Saudi inventory. Saudi Arabia has sought improved armor since the mid-1980s. It began by seeking

Chart 4.9
Holdings of Low-Quality Main Battle Tanks by Type, 2002

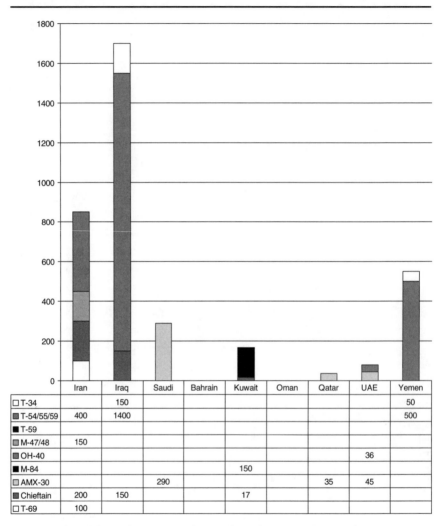

	Iran	Iraq	Saudi	Bahrain	Kuwait	Oman	Qatar	UAE	Yemen
□ T-34		150							50
▨ T-54/55/59	400	1400							500
■ T-59									
▥ M-47/48	150								
▨ OH-40								36	
■ M-84					150				
□ AMX-30			290				35	45	
▨ Chieftain	200	150			17				
□ T-69	100								

Sources: Adapted by Anthony H. Cordesman from the IISS, *Military Balance*; *Periscope*; JCSS, *The Middle East Military Balance*; *Jane's Sentinel*; and *Jane's Defence Weekly*.

to re-equip and expand its armored forces with U.S.-made M-1 tanks. The M-1 offered the Saudi Army one of the world's most effective weapons systems, and one that could be fully supported and upgraded over time by the U.S. Army. It not only offered Saudi Arabia a tank superior to any tank in Iranian and Iraqi forces, but also offered improved interoperability and standardization with the U.S. Army and improved U.S. rapid-deployment capabilities. Saudi Arabia faced major uncertainties, however, over whether the U.S. Congress would permit such sales.

As a result, the Kingdom examined alternative tanks—including Brazilian, British, French, and German models. It announced in February 1988 that it had short-listed the M-1A1 and EE-T1 Osoro for some form of co-production in a purchase that might involve some 315 vehicles and a $1 billion contract. Two issues that then delayed a Saudi decision were uncertainty over whether the United States was willing to sell the M-1A2 with a 120 mm gun, and whether Brazil could actually mass-produce the Osoro, which then only existed in prototype form.

Saudi Arabia finally decided to buy 315 M-1A2s for a total cost of $3.1 billion in September 1989.[6] (One U.S. expert indicates that a total of 395 were in-country in 2001, including spares and war reserves.) The reasons for the Saudi decision become clear from an examination of the M-1A2's performance characteristics. The Saudis bought an advanced version of the 68.5-ton M-1 with a 120 mm gun, advanced armor, and thermal sights. It has full line-of-sight gun stabilization that provides full shoot-on-the-move capability. A digital ballistic computer provides quick aiming correction, based on automatic and manual inputs, such as wind velocity, vehicle cant, and gun tube deflection. A laser range finder provides target data for the ballistic computer. The thermal imaging sight improves target acquisition during both day and night at ranges in excess of 3,000 meters.

The M-1A2 does consume large amounts of fuel, but its 1,500 horsepower engine, automatic transmission, and two final drives give it a top speed of 43 mph on hard-surfaced roads. An advanced torsion bar and long-stroke rotary shock absorber suspension give it cross-country speeds of up to 33 mph. Crew survivability is enhanced by the compartmentalized storage of fuel and ammunition and an automatic fire extinguisher system. The tank has a comparatively low profile and noise signature, and has external grenade launchers for rapid concealment.

Other key features of the M-1A2 tank include:[7]

- Added appliqué armor to protect it against future Soviet-made weapons systems and potential upgradability to active armor.
- A commander's independent thermal viewer that allows him to acquire targets in the dark or haze while the gunner is engaging other targets and hand off such targets independently to the gunner.
- An improved commander's weapon station with excellent visibility and ballistic protection, an enlarged hatch, and protection against directed-energy weapons.
- Precise position navigation and use of the satellite global positioning system (GPS).
- A carbon dioxide laser range-finder that allows all-weather target engagement, reduces the risk of blinding friendly forces, and allows rapid enough calculation to engage helicopters.

- A systems integration package of features to reduce workload and crew fatigue.

Saudi Arabia bought other modifications of the M-1A2 that improved its capability for desert warfare. These included use of a Jaguar radio to improve inter-tank communication (instead of a single channel ground/air system), a driver's thermal viewer to improve visibility through smoke and dust, a two-kilowatt external auxiliary power unit, countermine equipment, and hardware and software capable of displaying English and Arabic text, and Arabic labels.

The Kingdom now has all of its M-1A2s in service, and U.S. advisors report that they have a 95% operational readiness rate. It is using advanced systems like MILES to train its tank crews and is sending some commanders to the National Training Center in the United States. According to a number of experts, this element of the Saudi Army is now the only major element of its combined arms forces with moderate to high effectiveness. Unfortunately, Saudi Arabia concentrates its M-1A2s at Tabuk, to deal with a low probability Israeli invasion, and Saudi tank units have little long-range deployment and sustainment capability and no effective combined arms support.

Supporting the M-1A2 with Additional Armor and Equipment

The Saudi Army's purchase of the M-1A2 was part of a package that included 30 M-88A1 tank recovery vehicles, 175 M-998 utility trucks, 224 heavy tactical trucks, 29 heavy equipment transporters, 268 five-ton trucks, spares and support equipment, logistics support, ammunition, facilities design and construction, training aids and devices, and U.S. military training services.[8] It involved substantial offset programs, including the manufacture of radios, circuit boards, and wiring assemblies for the tank.[9]

Saudi Arabia bought advanced gunnery trainers like the EEC M-1A2 gun trainer and began to train crews at the U.S. Army armored warfare training center at Fort Knox. This training project was called Project Sword and cost $16.7 million. The first of the 178 Saudi troops to be trained to act as instructors in Saudi Arabia arrived in the United States early in 1993. These Saudi troops received language training in San Antonio and exercise training at the U.S. Army proving ground at Aberdeen.[10]

The Kingdom also learned an important lesson from Iraq's experience during the Iran-Iraq War and the movement of armor during the Gulf War: It bought some 300 heavy equipment transporters (HETs) and can now move more than a brigade set of heavy tanks rapidly using tractor trailers. The Saudi Army has practiced at least one such move by deploying a brigade out of Tabuk.

The Ongoing Search for Replacements for the AMX-30

The Saudi Army has never been able to make effective use of the AMX-30 and has needed to replace its AMX-30s for more than a decade. Iraq's invasion of Kuwait led Saudi Arabia to consider further purchases of M-1A2 tanks. On September 27, 1990, it signed a tentative agreement to buy a second armored vehicle package that included 235 M-1A2 tanks, 200 Bradley fight vehicles, a207 M-113 armored personnel carriers, 50 M-548 cargo carriers, 17 M-88A1 recovery vehicles, and 43 M-578 recovery vehicles. This agreement would have brought the total number of M-1A2s on order to 465 tanks, with delivery to begin in April 1993, taking place over a three-year period.

However, Saudi Arabia first delayed its order for 235 additional M-1A2s in late July 1992. It did so because Kuwait's purchase of the M-1A2 kept the M-1A2 production line open longer than had previously been estimated, and Saudi Arabia did not have to place its orders until production for Kuwait was completed. Saudi Arabia was then forced to continue delaying its order for financial reasons. These problems became so serious that it seemed in early 1994 that Saudi Arabia might have to delay taking delivery on its earlier orders of M-1A2s. The delivery of 175 M-1A2s took place in March 1994, with another 140 in August, but these deliveries only went forward after Saudi Arabia rescheduled its arms payments to the United States.[11]

As a result, Saudi Arabia is still debating more than a decade after the Gulf War (a) exactly how many new tanks it will buy to reduce its dependence on the United States, (b) whether it needs and can afford a second type of modern tank, and (c) whether it will buy surplus tanks that will provide de facto prepositioning for U.S. forces.[12] Senior Saudi sources indicated in August 1993, that the Saudi Army still planned to buy the additional 235 tanks, and was planning to create a total tank force of 1,200 tanks, with a total of 700 M-1A2s and 500 M-60A3s.[13] Since that time, however, the Kingdom has been under serious sustained financial pressure, and there have been no indications of major purchase plans.[14]

Saudi tank purchases may continue to be delayed because of their cost, the problems in absorbing and manning the large additional number of modern tanks, and tensions with the United States over the Second Intifada and September 11. In fact, some senior Saudi Army officers see no need for additional tanks in the near future, and would rather use any additional funding for training and sustainment. Nevertheless, there has been a continuing competition for such sales—a competition that has been heightened by Saudi Arabia's history of buying major equipment from a number of suppliers in an attempt to win broad foreign support, the concern of some Saudi officers about becoming overreliant on U.S. supply of the M-1A2, and intense political lobbying efforts by various suppliers and supplier countries.

A number of Saudi officers have advocated the purchase of the French Le Clerc, which completed extensive trials in Saudi Arabia in August 1995, to fill the vacancies left by the retirement of the AMX-30.[15] According to some U.S. experts these trials were successful enough for the Saudi Army to consider replacing its AMX-30 tanks with the Le Clerc.[16] A specially modified version of the Le Clerc underwent field tests in late July 1997 as part of competitive trials between the Le Clerc, the M-1A2, and the British Desert Challenger for a $3 billion contract with the Royal Saudi Land Forces.[17]

The British were also invited to participate in the competition for Saudi tank purchases, and sent the Desert Challenger to the Kingdom for firepower and mobility trials during the summer of 1996. After an initial generator failure, the Challenger completed around 3,000 kilometers of endurance tests.[18] The Desert Challenger has a number of improvements over the original Challenger 2, including a German MTU power pack capable of matching the Le Clerc's 1,500 horsepower. A Challenger Armored Repair and Recovery vehicle also accompanied the Desert Challenger. The British hoped to persuade the Saudi army to move forward with a proposed $4.7 billion contract for 150 to 300 Desert Challengers, and possibly to buy Desert Warrior armored fighting vehicles and AS-90 self-propelled guns for British equipped units.

This competition, and the fact that an entire brigade of AMX-30s was due for early retirement, prompted General Dynamics Land Systems, the manufacturer of the M-1A2, to offer to retrofit the entire Saudi M-1A2 inventory with an auxiliary power unit and crew compartment cooling systems. According to GDSL, the retrofit could be done relatively easily at a facility in the region. GDSL has indicated that it hopes such actions would be followed by the purchase of additional M-1A2s.[19]

The Problems in Buying Several Types of Main Battle Tank

Saudi financial and budget deficit problems have delayed any major procurement decisions, but this competition continues. For example, high Saudi oil revenues in 2000 again led the MODA to consider tank buys, although the drop in revenues in 2001 may again have pushed such decisions several years into the future.

This ongoing competition between the M-1A2, Le Clerc, and Desert Challenger involves more than financial issues. It creates a serious risk that the Saudi Army could eventually end up being equipped with two very different types of advanced main battle tanks—each with significantly different training, support, maintenance and tactical requirements. The U.S. M-1A2 tank may be slightly better than its European counterparts, but the M-1A2, Le Clerc, and Desert Challenger all seem to be excellent tanks. The fact remains, however, that any differences in technical characteristics are likely to be of minor importance in determining Saudi military effectiveness. The real issue is the improved standardization and interoperability that would result from using U.S. equipment.

There also is no question that the U.S. Army is the only Western force that can provide major armored reinforcements to the Saudi Army. The French Army has never had the capability to project armored forces to the Gulf. Recent British force cuts mean that the British Army cannot deploy the kind of armored forces to the Gulf that it deployed in 1990. Purchases of these tanks as an alternative to U.S. armor cannot meet Saudi military needs.

Limiting Main Battle Tank Buys and Numbers, as Well as Those of Other Army Equipment, and Relying on Force Effectiveness, Coalition Warfare, and the Air-Land Battle

One option would be to avoid another major tank buy indefinitely. The Saudi Army already has a total of 765 M-60A3s and M-1A2s in inventory. This is enough for three mechanized divisions, and a limited additional buy of 100 to 150 additional M-1s would give Saudi Arabia enough high-performance tanks to equip two full divisions and still allow it to use the remaining M-60A3s to fully equip the rest of its forces.

Saudi Arabia does not have to size its land forces against Iran because Iran has no "land bridge" to deploy against Saudi Arabia without moving through a hostile Iraq, and Iran only has limited amphibious lift. Staying with a force of roughly 800 to 900 U.S.-supplied tanks would give the Saudi Army the equivalent of three heavy armored divisions or four light divisions worth of tanks that are considerably more advanced than those in Iraqi inventory. Slowly expanding the holdings of its eight heavy brigades would ensure that it developed effective crews and support with a minimum of "turbulence" in terms of manpower, training, and providing adequate support and training.

While the resulting Saudi tank force would not come close to the 2,200-odd tanks in Iraqi forces, Iraqi tank numbers do not reflect Iraqi tank quality. Iraq now must rely on 1,000 obsolescent T-54s, T-55s, T-77s, T-59s, and T-69s, plus some captured Chieftains, M-47s, and M-60s of dubious operational value. Iraq's core tank strength consists of only 200 T-62s and 700 T-72s, none of which have truly modern fire control systems or armor, and Iraq has not been able to substantially modernize any aspect of its tank force since 1990. An effective Saudi Army that could rapidly concentrate to defeat or substantially delay an Iraqi force with five to six of Iraq's best divisions might well be effective in meeting Saudi Arabia's needs. Expanding tank holdings faster than the Kingdom can crew or sustain them will not.

Furthermore, the fact the United States has prepositioned armored brigade sets in Kuwait and Qatar, as well as additional unit sets at sea, makes the issue of parity largely moot. Saudi Arabia should not rely on U.S. reinforcement to the point of failing to fund its own defense. At the same time, a combination of U.S. air and land power does allow the Kingdom to concentrate on making its forces effective rather than simply large. This allows it to downsize its near- and mid-term tank and other arms purchases with considerable safety and to concentrate on improving manpower and sustainability. Saudi Arabia also has the option of developing a more integrated coalition with Kuwait and Bahrain that has detailed contingency plans for U.S., British, and other Southern Gulf country reinforcements. This coalition warfare approach not only would strengthen the land defense of the Kingdom, but would allow the Kingdom to solve many of its future arms buys and Army force expansion plans.

Saudi Arabia also has an additional option. It can count on U.S. and British air reinforcements that can deploy far more quickly than U.S. and British land forces. It also now has large numbers of modern F-15s that can make very effective use of air-to-surface guided missiles and laser- and GPS-guided bombs. It is developing the cadre of an effective attack helicopter force that offers far more range and deployment speed than armor. If Saudi Arabia was to shift toward planning to fight effective joint warfare—rather than leave its Army, Air Force, and National Guard as largely independent services—it could plan on fighting the kind of air-land battle that Iraq and Iran are both now totally unequipped to fight. Heavy armor is not obsolete, but there is no reason that the Kingdom has to rely on the force mixes that were appropriate at the time of the Gulf War. Improvements in offensive air power—and the lack of Iranian and Iraqi air modernization—give the Kingdom an alternative with proven combat effectiveness.

SAUDI OTHER ARMORED FIGHTING VEHICLES (OAFVs)

Saudi Arabia has a large inventory of other mechanized armored equipment. It has roughly 2,600 armored vehicles in addition to its tanks (300 reconnaissance, 970 armored infantry fighting vehicles, and 1,900 armored personnel carriers), and has a ratio of about 27 actives per other armored fighting vehicle (OAFV). In contrast, Iran has 1,455 OAFVs for 325,000 actives (450,000 if the Revolutionary Guards are included), and Iraq has about 2,700 for 375,000 men. These comparisons are shown in more detail in Charts 4.10 to 4.13. The Saudi Army also has large numbers of French- and U.S.-made armored recovery vehicles, armored bridging units, and large numbers of special-purpose armored vehicles.[20]

Problems in Standardization and Modernization

It is not possible to separate all of the Saudi Army's holdings of OAFVs from those of the National Guard, Frontier Force, and other paramilitary forces. As of early 2002, however, the Army's holdings of armored infantry

Chart 4.10

Total Operational Other Armored Fighting Vehicles (Light Tanks, Scout, AIFVs, APCs, Reconnaissance Vehicles) in Gulf Forces, 1990–2002

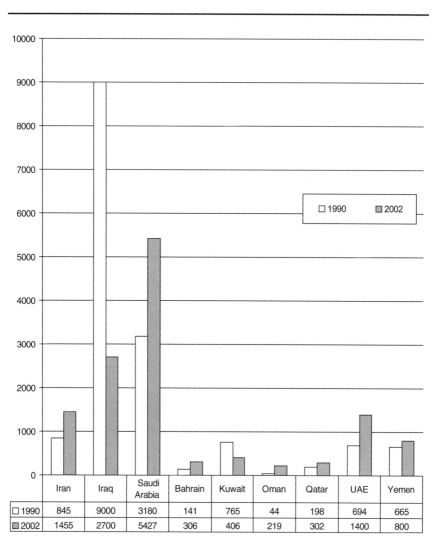

	Iran	Iraq	Saudi Arabia	Bahrain	Kuwait	Oman	Qatar	UAE	Yemen
☐ 1990	845	9000	3180	141	765	44	198	694	665
▨ 2002	1455	2700	5427	306	406	219	302	1400	800

Note: Iran includes active forces in the Revolutionary Guards. Saudi Arabia includes active National Guard.

Sources: Adapted by Anthony H. Cordesman from the IISS, *Military Balance*; *Periscope*; JCSS, *The Middle East Military Balance*; *Jane's Sentinel*; and *Jane's Defence Weekly*.

Chart 4.11
Gulf Active Other Armored Fighting Vehicles (OAFVs) by Major Category, 2002
(Includes National Guard, Revolutionary Guards, and Royal Guards)

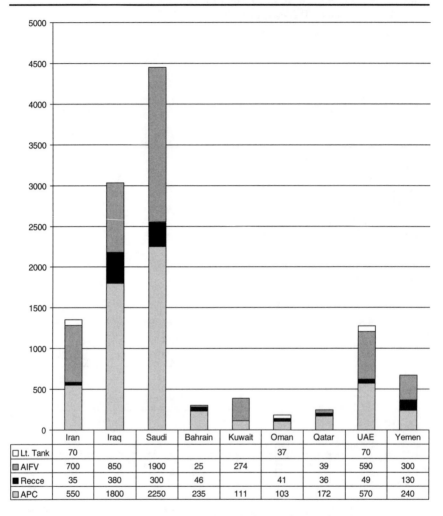

	Iran	Iraq	Saudi	Bahrain	Kuwait	Oman	Qatar	UAE	Yemen
☐ Lt. Tank	70					37		70	
▦ AIFV	700	850	1900	25	274		39	590	300
■ Recce	35	380	300	46		41	36	49	130
☐ APC	550	1800	2250	235	111	103	172	570	240

Sources: Adapted by Anthony H. Cordesman from the IISS, *Military Balance*; *Periscope*; JCSS,
   The Middle East Military Balance; *Jane's Sentinel*; and *Jane's Defence Weekly*.

fighting and command vehicles seem to have included 400 M-2A2 Bradleys,
150 M-577A1s, and 570 AMX-10Ps. It also had 300 to 330 AML-60,
AML-90, and AML-245 reconnaissance vehicles, of which roughly 235 remained in active service.

Chart 4.12
Advanced Armored Infantry Fighting Vehicles, Reconnaissance Vehicles, Scout Vehicles, and Light Tanks by Type, 2002

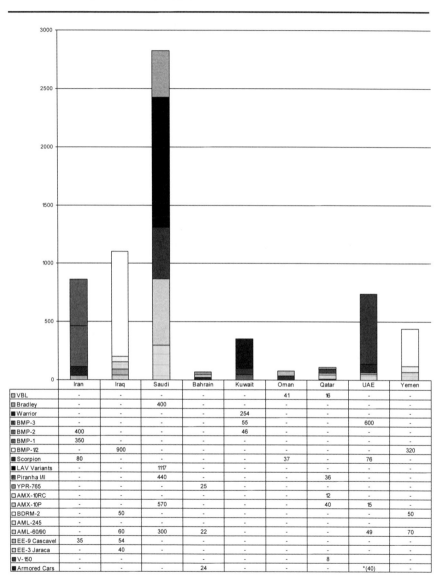

	Iran	Iraq	Saudi	Bahrain	Kuwait	Oman	Qatar	UAE	Yemen
VBL	-	-	-	-	-	41	16	-	-
Bradley	-	-	400	-	-	-	-	-	-
Warrior	-	-	-	-	254	-	-	-	-
BMP-3	-	-	-	-	55	-	-	600	-
BMP-2	400	-	-	-	46	-	-	-	-
BMP-1	350	-	-	-	-	-	-	-	-
BMP-12	-	900	-	-	-	-	-	-	320
Scorpion	80	-	-	-	-	37	-	76	-
LAV Variants	-	-	1117	-	-	-	-	-	-
Piranha III	-	-	440	-	-	-	36	-	-
YPR-765	-	-	-	25	-	-	-	-	-
AMX-10RC	-	-	-	-	-	-	12	-	-
AMX-10P	-	-	570	-	-	-	40	15	-
BDRM-2	-	50	-	-	-	-	-	-	50
AML-245	-	-	-	-	-	-	-	-	
AML-60/90	-	60	300	22	-	-	-	49	70
EE-9 Cascavel	35	54	-	-	-	-	-	-	-
EE-3 Jaraca	-	40	-	-	-	-	-	-	-
V-150	-	-	-	-	-	-	8	-	-
Armored Cars	-	-	-	24	-	-	-	*(40)	-

Sources: Adapted by Anthony H. Cordesman from the IISS, *Military Balance*; *Periscope*; *Jane's Sentinel*; and *Jane's Defence Weekly*.

Chart 4.13
Armored Personnel Carriers (APCs) in Gulf Armies, 2002

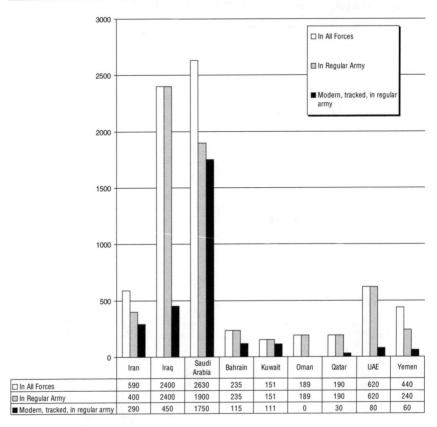

	Iran	Iraq	Saudi Arabia	Bahrain	Kuwait	Oman	Qatar	UAE	Yemen
☐ In All Forces	590	2400	2630	235	151	189	190	620	440
☐ In Regular Army	400	2400	1900	235	151	189	190	620	240
■ Modern, tracked, in regular army	290	450	1750	115	111	0	30	80	60

Note: Iran includes active land forces in the Revolutionary Guards. Saudi Arabia includes the active forces in the National Guard.

Sources: Adapted by Anthony H. Cordesman from the IISS, *Military Balance*; *Periscope*; JCSS, *The Middle East Military Balance*; *Jane's Sentinel*; and *Jane's Defence Weekly*.

The Saudi Army had 1,750 variants of the M-113, including 950-850 M-113A1s and M-113A2s; and 250 to 300 armored mortar carriers, including M-106A1s and M-125s. It also had 30 EE-11 Brazilian Urutus, 110 German UR-416s, 120 Spanish BMR-600s and 270-290 Panhard M-3/VTT armored personnel carriers in inventory; only 150 Panhard M-3s, however, remained in active service.

It is obvious from these totals that the Saudi Army's holdings of OAFVs include enough U.S.-supplied equipment to provide reasonable levels of standardization for all of the Saudi Army's full-time active manpower, as well as a high degree of interoperability with U.S. forces. At the same time, the Saudi Army's total inventory of such weapons includes far too many types of weapons that have been bought from far too many suppliers over the years, and presents serious problems in operability, standardization and modernization. Many types are highly specialized and difficult to properly integrate into Saudi forces in small numbers. Some purchases are also the result of political efforts to give foreign suppliers a share of the Saudi market, regardless of military need.

The end result is that the Saudi Army has so many different types of OAFVs that many are no longer in active service—or even useful as spare parts—and even the equipment that is active is still so diverse that it presents training, maintenance, logistic, maneuver, and readiness problems.

The Bradley M-2A2

Saudi Arabia has attempted to deal with some of its standardization and interoperability problems by buying more modern U.S. armored vehicles—including the M-113 and M-2A2 Bradley. During the Gulf War, it ordered 400 M-2A2 armored fighting vehicles for a cost of $1.5 billion. It also bought 200 M-113 armored personnel carriers, 50 M-548 cargo carriers, 17 M-88A1 recovery vehicles, and 43 M-578 recovery vehicles.[21]

The Bradley is particularly important because it is the only armored fighting vehicle in Saudi Army inventory with the combination of speed, protection, and firepower necessary to support the M-1A2 in battle. By 1997, the Saudi Army had all 400 Bradley M-2A2s in service, in addition to 1,500 to 1,750 M-113 variants in its active force structure. These M-2A2s gave the Saudi Army an OAFV with the speed, protection, and firepower to keep pace with Saudi tanks and outmatch the Soviet armored fighting vehicles in most potential threat armies—many of which have better protection and firepower than many of the armored vehicles in service with Saudi forces. The M-2A2 is heavily armed, equipped with TOW-2 missiles and a 25 mm cannon. It has air conditioning, which provides protection against gas warfare and allows extended operation even at peak desert temperatures. Saudi Arabia has contracted with FMC-Arabia for logistic support of the M-2A2.[22]

Saudi Arabia built a facility to upgrade its M-113 series vehicles that is located near Al-Kharj. In a $413 million contract awarded in early 1997, FMC Arabia is overhauling 523 M-113A1/M-113A2 series full-tracked APCs to the latest M-113A3 standard using U.S. parts. The improved M-113A3 includes a more powerful 6V-53T Detroit diesel engine, Allison X-200-4 automatic transmission, external fuel tanks, and variable-speed cooling fan.[23] This facility may eventually upgrade another 1,000 or more M-113s, as well as the M-2, M-109, and other armored vehicles.

Further Purchases and Force Expansion

Saudi sources indicated as early as August 1993, that the Kingdom might go on to buy a total of 550 to 700 M-2A2s, and then standardize on the M-113A1 for the rest of its armored fighting vehicles. Like the M-1A2 buy, a larger purchase would have improved Saudi army capabilities and provided a higher degree of interoperability and standardization with U.S. Army forces. The M-113, and various combat versions of the M-113, are acceptable armored vehicles, although they lack the speed and armor to fight armored forces equipped with the most modern tanks and armored fighting vehicles.

Saudi Arabia's funding problems, however, make it increasingly unlikely that the Kingdom will make major new buys of M-2A2s in the near future. In fact, Saudi Arabia had problems in properly crewing and supporting its existing M-2A2 force. It now has only 70% of the mechanics it needs, and 15% to 20% of these are misassigned. Further, even if Saudi Arabia did buy more M-2A2s, this would scarcely eliminate its need to support many types of armored vehicles that are dependent for parts and technical support on so many different countries. The upgrading of its M-113s seems far more cost-effective.

Even so, Saudi Arabia has continued to buy other types of OAFVs. It has thirty-six German Fuchsia chemical defense vehicles and additional French armored vehicles in delivery, and is examining possible purchases of other armored vehicles from Brazil, Britain, and Germany.[24] It announced in 1997 that it was also producing a 6 × 6 wheeled armored fighting vehicle called the Peninsula Shield. This system began development in 1977 and entered advanced development in 1998. It is being built at the Abdullah Al-Fairs Heavy Industries factory in Dammam, and Saudi Arabia plans to build 50 in 1997, and then 150 a year later. It is amphibious and has a 450 horsepower engine. It is said to have a land speed of up to ninety kilometers per hour and to go up to sixteen kilometers per hour in water. Saudi Arabia has conducted trials of a version with a two-man turret with a 90 mm gun.[25]

Once again, the Saudi Army needs to give more attention to standardization, interoperability, and ease of training, as well as to stressing force effectiveness over force size, and putting more reliance on coalition warfare and the air-land battle. As in all other areas of Saudi Army equipment, the key priority is not more or better equipment, but rather to "train, maintain, and sustain" the force in ways that make its existing holdings combat effective. It should organize for effective combined arms warfare at the brigade level and for effective joint warfare with both the Saudi Air Force and coalition forces.

If the Army does buy more OAFVs, it needs to emphasize speed and firepower over numbers. The dispersal of the Saudi Army, the speed of the M-1A2, and the need to concentrate on the Iraqi border in an emergency also mean that speed of maneuver and sustainability are critical to success.

Nathan Bedford Forest is unlikely to have had much Saudi blood, but his advice that a force be "Fastest with the mostest!" is far more important than any of the technical differences between various types of other armored vehicles.

SAUDI ANTI-TANK WEAPONS

The Saudi Army has an excellent mix of small arms, light weaponry, and anti-tank weapons. These include massive stocks of mobile, crew-portable, and man-portable TOW, HOT, and Dragon anti-tank guided missiles. In 2001, Saudi Arabia had a total of some 950 TOW launchers, with some 200 TOW launchers mounted on VCC-1 armored fighting vehicles, and an additional 300 mounted on M-113A1s or other U.S.-supplied armored vehicles. It had 100 HOT launchers, and 90 HOT launchers mounted on AMX-10P armored fighting vehicles.

The Army also had large numbers of TOW crew-portable and roughly 1,000 Dragon man-portable anti-tank guided weapons systems. It also had 300 Carl Gustav rocket launchers, 400 M-20 3.5-inch rocket launchers, thousands of M-72 LAWs, and extensive numbers of 75 mm, 84 mm, 90 mm (100) and 106 mm (300) rocket launchers and recoilless rifles. Saudi Arabia had a large number of missiles, including advanced types. It ordered 4,460 TOW-2 missiles in April 1987, 150 more TOW-2A missile launchers with night vision sights and support equipment on September 27, 1990, and still more TOW-2A missiles in the later 1990s.[26] The Saudi Army ordered French Apilas anti-tank weapons in 1991.

Unlike the older anti-tank guided weapons in some Gulf armies, the Saudi Army TOW-2A missiles can kill T-72A, T-72M1, T-80, and other modern tanks. However, there are limitations to Saudi capabilities. The Dragon and HOT missile inventory is becoming obsolescent. Individual crew and operator training for anti-tank weapons has only reached moderate proficiency, although it still lacks consistency and realism. Units equipped with anti-tank weapons mounted on armored vehicles also sometimes lack maneuver and combined arms training. Crews and men using older weapons are often less proficient than those with the latest weapons, and anti-tank units often lack aggressiveness in employing anti-tank weapons in exercises.

SAUDI ARTILLERY

The Saudi Army has large numbers of modern artillery weapons. The trends in Saudi artillery strength are shown in Chart 4.14, and its total artillery strength and artillery quality are compared to that of other Gulf states in Charts 4.15 to 4.19. In 2002, Saudi Arabia had a total inventory of roughly 568 active major artillery weapons. This compares with 3,284 weapons for Iran and 2,250 for Iraq.

Chart 4.14
The Growth in Saudi Artillery Weapons Strength, 1979–2002

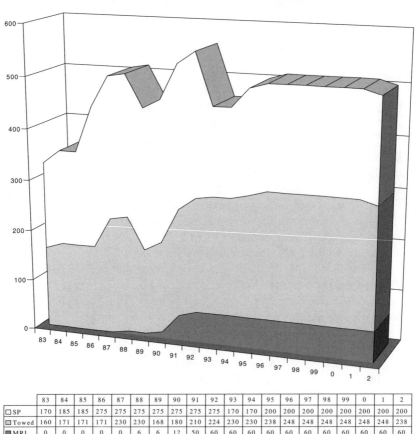

	83	84	85	86	87	88	89	90	91	92	93	94	95	96	97	98	99	0	1	2
☐ SP	170	185	185	275	275	275	275	275	275	275	170	170	200	200	200	200	200	200	200	200
☐ Towed	160	171	171	171	230	230	168	180	210	224	230	230	238	248	248	248	248	248	248	238
■ MRL	0	0	0	0	0	6	6	12	50	60	60	60	60	60	60	60	60	60	60	60

Sources: Adapted by Anthony H. Cordesman from the IISS, *Military Balance*: *Periscope*; JCSS, *The Middle East Military Balance*; *Jane's Sentinel*; *Jane's Defence Weekly*; and material provided by U.S. experts.

In 2002, the Saudi Army inventory included 60-70 Astros II multiple-rocket launchers, and 110 to 120 M-109A1/A2 and 90 GCT 155 mm self-propelled howitzers.[27] The Army had 24 Model 56 and 90 to 100 M-101/M-102 105 mm towed howitzers, and 40 FH-70 105 mm towed howitzers in storage. It had 40 M-198 and 50 M-114 155 mm towed howitzers in service and 5-10 M-115 203 mm towed howitzers and some other older towed weapons in storage. Its total mortar strength included over 400 120 mm and 4.2-inch weapons, over 1,000 81 mm weapons, and large numbers of light 60 mm weapons. It had 70 81 mm, and150 M-30 4.2-inch

Chart 4.15
Total Operational Self-Propelled and Towed Tube Artillery and Multiple Rocket
Launchers in Gulf Forces, 1990–2002

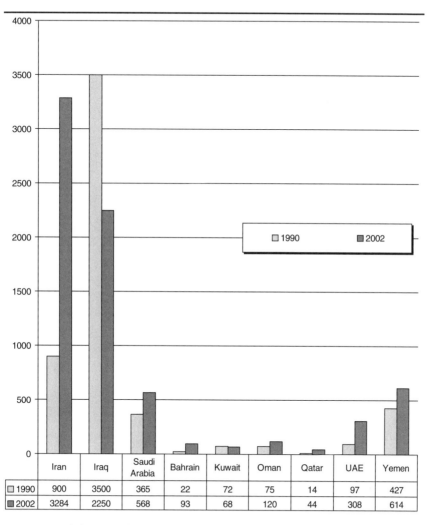

	Iran	Iraq	Saudi Arabia	Bahrain	Kuwait	Oman	Qatar	UAE	Yemen
☐ 1990	900	3500	365	22	72	75	14	97	427
■ 2002	3284	2250	568	93	68	120	44	308	614

Note: Iran includes active forces in the Revolutionary Guards. Saudi Arabia includes active
National Guard.

Sources: Adapted by Anthony H. Cordesman from the IISS, Military Balance; Periscope; JCSS,
The Middle East Military Balance; Jane's Sentinel; Jane's Defence Weekly; and material
provided by U.S. experts.

Chart 4.16
Total Gulf Self-Propelled, Towed, and Multiple Launcher Gulf Artillery by Category, 2002

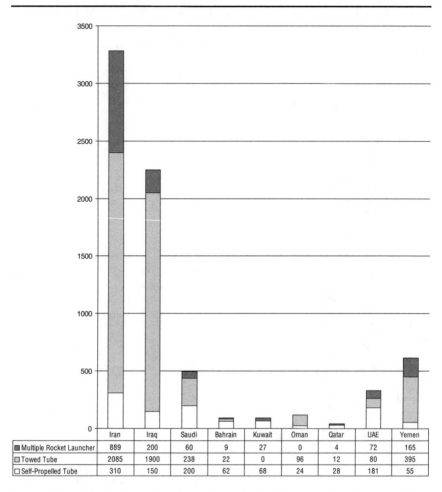

	Iran	Iraq	Saudi	Bahrain	Kuwait	Oman	Qatar	UAE	Yemen
■ Multiple Rocket Launcher	889	200	60	9	27	0	4	72	165
□ Towed Tube	2085	1900	238	22	0	96	12	80	395
□ Self-Propelled Tube	310	150	200	62	68	24	28	181	55

Sources: Adapted by Anthony H. Cordesman from the IISS, *Military Balance*; *Periscope*; JCSS, *The Middle East Military Balance*; *Jane's Sentinel*; *Jane's Defence Weekly*; and material provided by U.S. experts.

mortars on M-106 and M-125A1 armored vehicles, and roughly 200 81 mm to 120 mm towed mortars.[28]

Many Saudi artillery units are, however, what one senior officer terms, "25 years behind the training and effectiveness levels of what is needed." They lack key targeting, command and control, and battle management capabilities, and suffer from manpower quality, mobility, and support

Chart 4.17
Gulf Inventory of Self-Propelled Artillery by Caliber, 2002

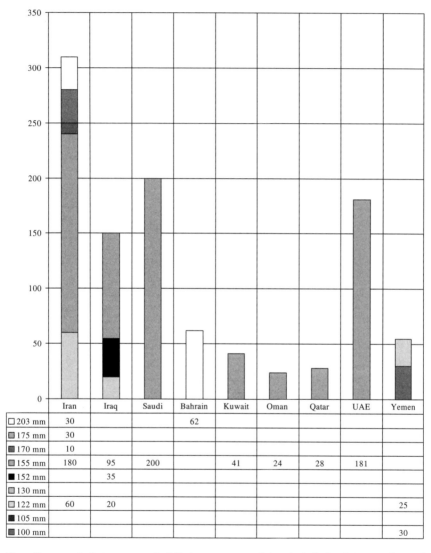

	Iran	Iraq	Saudi	Bahrain	Kuwait	Oman	Qatar	UAE	Yemen
☐ 203 mm	30			62					
▨ 175 mm	30								
■ 170 mm	10								
▨ 155 mm	180	95	200		41	24	28	181	
■ 152 mm		35							
▨ 130 mm									
☐ 122 mm	60	20							25
■ 105 mm									
▨ 100 mm									30

Note: Does not include weapons in full-time storage, and does include Saudi National Guard and Iranian Revolutionary Guards.
Sources: Adapted by Anthony H. Cordesman from the IISS, *Military Balance*; *Periscope*; *Jane's Sentinel*; and *Jane's Defence Weekly*.

Chart 4.18
Gulf Inventory of Towed Artillery by Caliber, 2002

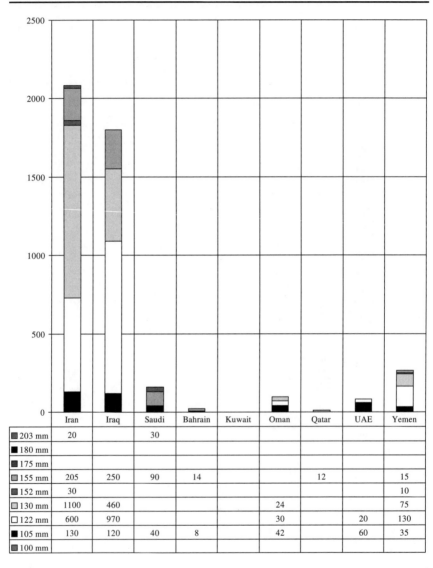

	Iran	Iraq	Saudi	Bahrain	Kuwait	Oman	Qatar	UAE	Yemen
■ 203 mm	20		30						
■ 180 mm									
■ 175 mm									
▥ 155 mm	205	250	90	14			12		15
■ 152 mm	30								10
▢ 130 mm	1100	460				24			75
▢ 122 mm	600	970				30		20	130
■ 105 mm	130	120	40	8		42		60	35
▤ 100 mm									

Note: Does not include weapons in full-time storage, and does include Saudi National Guard and Iranian Revolutionary Guards.

Sources: Adapted by Anthony H. Cordesman from the IISS, *Military Balance*; *Periscope*; *Jane's Sentinel*; and *Jane's Defence Weekly*.

Chart 4.19
Gulf Inventory of Multiple Rocket Launchers by Caliber, 2002

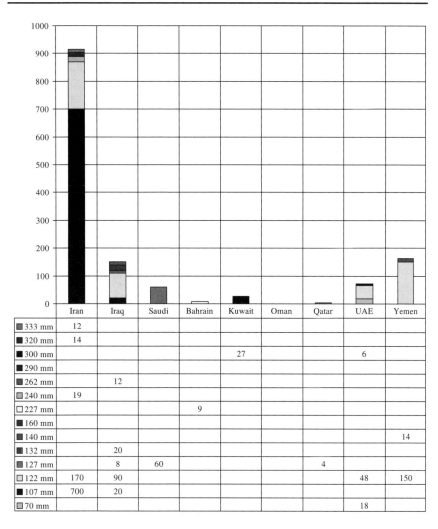

	Iran	Iraq	Saudi	Bahrain	Kuwait	Oman	Qatar	UAE	Yemen
■ 333 mm	12								
■ 320 mm	14								
■ 300 mm					27			6	
■ 290 mm									
■ 262 mm		12							
▨ 240 mm	19								
□ 227 mm				9					
■ 160 mm									
■ 140 mm									14
■ 132 mm		20							
■ 127 mm		8	60				4		
□ 122 mm	170	90						48	150
■ 107 mm	700	20							
▨ 70 mm								18	

Note: Does not include weapons in full-time storage, and does include Saudi National Guard and Iranian Revolutionary Guards.

Sources: Adapted by Anthony H. Cordesman from the IISS, *Military Balance*; *Periscope*; *Jane's Sentinel*; and *Jane's Defence Weekly*.

problems. Training is poor, and many units only shoot in serious training exercises every one-and-a-half years. The Army lacks ballistic computers and mobile fire control and ammunition-supply equipment, and desperately needs new target acquisition radars—such as the AN/PPS-15A, MSTAR, or Rasit 3190B—to replace its vintage 1960 systems. It also needs a modern and fully integrated mix of counter battery radars and fire control systems to rapidly mass and shift fires.[29]

The moderate pace of Saudi Arabia's move from towed artillery to self-propelled artillery that is fully trained and equipped for maneuver and combined arms warfare has left the Saudi Army without sufficient numbers of artillery pieces that have the mobility and firepower to properly support its armored forces. At present, units with M1A2 tanks cannot be sure that their artillery supporter will be combat ready enough, skilled enough, and mobile enough to provide effective combined arms support.

The Saudi Army has only limited-to-moderate ability to use artillery in maneuver and combined arms warfare, to target effectively in counter-battery fire or at targets beyond visual range, and to shift and concentrate fires. Unless the Kingdom takes combined arms and maneuver warfare far more seriously in the future than it has to date, Saudi artillery units will continue to seriously degrade the overall war fighting and defense capabilities of Saudi land forces.

Saudi Arabia also needs more long-range firepower. It has considered ordering the Multiple Launch Rocket Systems (MLRS) to help deal with its fire support problems. On September 27, 1990, it announced its intention to order a package of nine MLRS, including vehicle-mounted rocket launchers, 2,880 tactical rockets, 50 practice rockets, 9 MV-755A2 command post carriers, training and training equipment, and 20 AN/VRC-46 radio sets.

Such an order for the MLRS might have given Saudi Arabia an important potential force multiplier. The MLRS has a highly sophisticated warhead that mixes anti-armor and anti-personnel bomblets. Each MLRS launcher is capable of inflicting more destruction on an area target or large maneuver target than a battalion of regular tube artillery or multiple rocket launchers and can do so at ranges in excess of 40 kilometers, which allows the MLRS to out-range most of the weapons in potential threat forces.[30] The MLRS proved to be too expensive, however, and the Saudi Army has delayed any purchase of the MLRS indefinitely.

As a result, Saudi Arabia is now considering additional buys of self-propelled artillery weapons. Possible candidates include the South African G-6, the U.S. M-109A6, the British AS-90, and the French GCT. These are all excellent artillery weapons, although non-U.S. buys might present some minor standardization and interoperability problems. Saudi Arabia is also considering upgrading 111 of its M-109A2s to the M-109A6 configuration. This would ensure that its artillery can maneuver in ways that keep up with its M-1 tanks.[31] Buying more tube artillery, however, will not meet Saudi Arabia's need for a system that can provide massive anti-armor and anti-personnel capabilities to defeat an attacker like Iraq. As a result, it might end in creating new financial problems that slow down the purchase of higher priority systems like the MLRS.

Saudi Arabia has test-fired its first domestically produced surface-to-surface rocket to mark the inauguration of a new military complex at Al-Kharj, 100 kilometers southeast of Riyadh. The missile has a range of between 35 and 62 kilometers and was produced at the Kingdom's first center for ammunition maintenance at Al-Kharj. The system is a showpiece project, however, with little military significance.

SAUDI ARMY AIR DEFENSE

Saudi Arabia has relatively large numbers of modern air defense weapons by Gulf standards. It is not easy to separate the Saudi Army's air defense assets from those in the Saudi Air Defense Force, and sources disagree over which force operates given systems. However, the Saudi Army seems to have had seventeen anti-aircraft artillery batteries in 2002, and is organized and equipped to protect its maneuver forces in combat.

Total Saudi holdings of short-range air defenses included 73 Crotale (Shahine) radar guided missiles on tracked armored vehicles and 19 shelter-mounted firing units, 36 AMX-30 self-propelled, and 10 shelter-mounted Shahine acquisition units. Saudi Arabia also had large holdings of man-portable surface-to-air missiles. Its holdings included 700 Mistrals, some 200 to 500 Stingers (reporting on numbers is unusually uncertain), and 570 obsolescent Redeye man-portable surface-to-air missiles. Saudi Arabia may have an unknown number of Kolomna KBM Igla (SA-16 Gimlet) weapons. Saudi Arabia bought 50 Stinger launchers and 200 Stinger missiles on an emergency basis in August 1990, and ordered additional Crotales and 700 French Mistral launchers and 1,500 missiles.[32]

It is equally difficult to separate the Army's air defense gun holdings from those of the Air Defense Force and National Guard, but Saudi Arabia's total holdings of light anti-aircraft weapons seems to include 10 M-42 40 mm, and 92 Vulcan M-163 20 mm anti-aircraft guns. It also seems to have 150 Bofors L-60/L-70 40 mm and 128 Oerlikon 35 mm towed guns, and possibly 15 M-117 90 mm towed anti-aircraft guns.

This is a reasonable mix of air defense assets, but training and readiness levels are moderate to low. The separate Saudi Air Defense Force—which controls Saudi Arabia heavy surface-to-air missiles and fixed air defenses—is also a relatively static force that cannot easily support the army in mobile operations.

The Army's air defense units also consist largely of independent fire units, rather than an integrated system of netted C[4]I/BM capabilities, although such capabilities are planned for 2002–2003, and there are problems with secure data links that could transmit data from the E-3A AWACS to disperse Army air defense units. The same is true of Saudi Army air defense assets. As a result, Saudi Arabia must relay largely on a point defense approach in using land-based assets to defend its forces in the field. This makes Saudi land forces remain heavily dependent on air power for air defense.

SAUDI ARMY AVIATION

Saudi Army helicopter forces are key areas for future force improvement. Much of the Saudi Army is now deployed at least 500 miles from the Kingdom's main oil facilities in the Eastern Province, although a brigade is stationed in the new King Fahd Military City in the Eastern Province, and combat elements of another brigade were deployed to the new Saudi Army base at King Khalid City, near Hafr al-Batin, in 1984. For the foreseeable future, the Saudi Army will be dispersed so that much of its strength will be deployed near the Kingdom's borders, with the angles located at Tabuk, Hafr al-Batin, and Sharurah-Khamis Mushayt.

Helicopters offer a partial solution to these deployment problems. They can provide rapid concentration of force and allow Saudi Arabia to make up for its lack of experience in large-scale maneuver. These factors first led the Saudi Army to seek attack helicopters in the early 1980s. In the mid-1980s, the Saudi Army studied plans for developing a sizable helicopter force by the mid-1990s. It initially considered buying 60 to 100 AH-64 attack helicopters, plus additional Blackhawk utility and support, and Chinook CH-47 transport helicopters from the United States.

Saudi Arabia initially experienced political problems in obtaining such helicopters from the United States, however, which led the Saudi Army to obtain an option to buy 88 Sikorsky-designed S-70 Blackhawk helicopters from Westland in Britain. Roughly 80 of these Westlands were to be attack helicopters equipped with TOW-2. The rest were to be configured for SAR missions. The order was divided into batches of 40 and 48 aircraft.

The Gulf War again changed Saudi plans, creating a political condition in which Saudi Arabia could buy the AH-64 from the United States.[33] On September 27, 1990, Saudi Arabia ordered 12 AH-64 Apache attack helicopters, 155 Hellfire missiles, 24 spare Hellfire launchers, 6 spare engines and associated equipment from the United States. At the time, it indicated an interest in buying a total of 48 AH-64s, and was examining the purchase of more attack and support helicopters from the United States, Italy, France, or a Franco-German consortium. The Saudi Army has not placed any additional orders of this kind, but in June 1992, it bought 362 more Hellfire missiles, 3,500 Hydra-70 rockets, and 40 HMMWV vehicles and U.S. support services for its Apaches. It also bought 8 S-70 Sikorsky medevac helicopters.[34]

The AH-64s began to enter Saudi service in 1993, and the Saudi Army now has a helicopter strength that includes 12 AH-64 attack helicopters, 15 Bell 406CS armed helicopters, 12 S-70A1 Sikorsky Blackhawk transport helicopters, 6 SA-365N medical evacuation helicopters, and 10 UL-60 Blackhawk medevac and 12 UH-60 transport helicopters.[35]

The AH-64s are a potential force multiplier for the Saudi Army, and give the it still further interoperability with the U.S. Army. At the same time, 12 AH-64s are not a large force and the Saudi Army needs extensive U.S. support to maintain them, since attack helicopters are as sophisticated as the AH-64 and require as much support and training as a light jet combat aircraft. Even if the comparatively lightly armed Bell 406CSs are included in the total, a force of 27 armed helicopters is too small to make a major impact in solving the Saudi Army's problems in concentrating its forces and maneuvering rapidly to check an Iraqi advance.[36]

In April 2001, Saudi Arabia began preparing a formal request to buy advanced AH-64D equipped with the sensitive Longbow radar. The Pentagon, however, turned down a recent request by Egypt for 35 AH-64Ds. Lieutenant Colonel Shaddah Al-Asmri, Apache operational chief for the Royal Saudi Arabian Army, said on April 5, "We understand it is a priority of the U.S. to protect its technology, but we believe in a matter of time they will support us."[37] Studies indicate that Saudi Arabia needs at least 24 AH-64s, probably closer to 48, to provide the kind of rapid, long-range anti-armor strike capabilities it needs to defend its borders with Iraq and Yemen, and to reinforce Kuwait. It also needs at least twice its present number of transport helicopters.

The Army has had maintenance problems with its helicopter fleet, although standards seem to be much higher than in Iran and Iraq. It also tends to use helicopters more for service and medevac functions than to achieve tactical mobility. This again presents problems in compensating for the dispersal of the Saudi Army and in deploying forward defenses.

SAUDI SUSTAINMENT, INFRASTRUCTURE, AND SUPPORT

The Saudi Army has the facilities, infrastructure, and equipment to support its forces in peacetime and some of its ongoing construction of facilities near Yemen may prove to be excessive before their completion because of the improvement in Saudi-Yemeni relations. The Army has excellent support facilities, although it has progressively underfunded logistic and support vehicles and equipment since the mid-1990s. Nevertheless, the Saudi Army has made major purchases of support equipment, along with the purchase of its M-1A2s and M-2A2s. It is improving its field support vehicle strength and ordered 10,000 support vehicles from the United States on September 27, 1990, including 1,200 High Mobility Multipurpose Wheeled Vehicles (HMMWVs).

The Saudi Army still has extensive foreign support in spite of cutbacks in foreign manpower and support contracts. It has had long-time U.S. Army support for its Ordnance Corps, logistic system, and technical services. This contract was renewed on June 1, 1992, and not only aids Saudi Arabia, but improves the ability of Saudi forces to support U.S. reinforcements and work with them on an interoperable basis.

The key U.S. effort supporting the Saudi Army is the United States Military Training Mission (USMTM). The history of the USMTM dates back to the first twelve-man U.S. military training mission in the Kingdom, which arrived in 1944. Formal accords were signed in 1951 and 1953, and it has been the key U.S. office administering the U.S. side of the Saudi FMS program under accords revised in 1977, having dealt with over $80 billion worth of sales.

In 2001, there were a total of 316 personnel in the USMTM, with 97 U.S. personnel assigned to the Saudi Army. The USMTM also has 10 Marines, 21 Navy, and 81 Air Force personnel, plus 107 civilians. They administered well over 300 sales cases at any one time, and over 100 are for the Saudi Army. The USMTM had advisors in King Khalid Military City, Jubail, Dhahran, Riyadh, Tabuk, Jeddah, Taif, and Khamis Mushayt.

The Saudi Army has not, however, adopted the modern management systems it needs to management sustainment and support under demanding war-fighting conditions, or properly organized to support mobile combat operations in the field. While it made progress toward converting to maneuver warfare during the Gulf War, it then reverted to a largely static and caserne-oriented pattern of peacetime behavior, and has failed to give sustainability the same priority as firepower and mobility.

The lack of standardization within the Saudi Army adds to these problems, as does excessive dependence on base facilities and foreign civilian support. So does the lack of progress in these areas in the rest of the Southern Gulf, and the lack of an effective and integrated organization for the defense of Kuwait and the Saudi border with Iraq. There are exceptions, like attack helicopters and long-range artillery, but the Saudi Army needs the specialized training, organization, and manpower necessary to improve its support structure, and ability to sustain its existing forces in combat, far more than it needs more weapons.

SAUDI ARMY READINESS AND WAR-FIGHTING CAPABILITIES

The Saudi Army showed during the Gulf War that it could fight against Iraqi armored and mechanized forces—the kind of threats it faces in the Gulf region. Nevertheless, the previous analysis has shown that the Saudi Army faces serious problems in many areas. It does not have the manpower and training necessary to operate all of its new major equipment orders properly. The Army does not have a single combat brigade that is now truly combat-ready in terms of the ability to rapidly deploy at full strength and then sustain operations at any distance from its peacetime casernes. Every brigade has shortfalls in its active combined arms strength, usually in artillery and mechanized elements, or both. Every brigade is also short in some elements of combat and service support capability.

The Problem of Training

Training is a problem, and will continue to be a problem in the future. U.S. advisors helped bring Saudi forces to a level of readiness during the Gulf War that they had never before experienced, and gave them their first real experience with large-scale unit and combined-arms training. Many Saudi officers absorbed this training quickly, and the Saudi Army did well during Operation Desert Storm—very well if its low pre-war readiness is considered.

The Saudi Army has continued to make progress at the tactical-small combat unit level since the Gulf War. At the same time, the Army has had continuing problems in converting to the use of constant ongoing deliveries of complex new equipment. Its training plans often have not been properly executed, and maneuver training has been mediocre. Until Khalid bin Sultan forced the army to begin emergency development exercises in 2002, the Army had not conducted any meaningful major rapid-deployment activities since 1992, and when brigades did start to move from Khamis Mushayt and the north toward Tabok, the exercises revealed serious weaknesses.

There is little realistic emphasis on combined arms training involving large formations, and joint land-air training has been ineffective beyond the battalion level, except when organized and led by the United States. As has been discussed earlier, there is far too much favoritism in the selection of personnel for training, and Saudis conducting army training programs often are very reluctant to fail other Saudis.

There has been a lack of support for demanding training and exercises at the higher command level, and little linkage between strategy, overall organization, and force-wide training. The Army's problems have also been compounded by a serious lack of interest in joint warfare training on the part of the Saudi Air Force, and by the Air Force's overall failure to modernize its offensive warfare training and develop effective support and interdiction capabilities.

Saudi Arabia leased the U.S. Army Multiple Integrated Laser Engagement Systems (MILES) for advanced realistic combat training, and took delivery in 1996.[38] This gives the Saudi Army the only advanced land warfare training capabilities in the Southern Gulf, but little effective use has yet been made of the system. The Army is, however, beginning to conduct realistic command post exercises, and is sending bridge commanders to the U.S.

Army National Training Center to gain experience in realistic joint and combined arms warfare. Prince Sultan also reinstituted joint training by the Saudi and U.S. armies in 1999, which began with small command post exercises. This training halted as a result of September 11, but Khalid bin Sultan agreed to reinstate it later in September 2001. The question is whether these developments will eventually result in effective training. The Saudi Army now overemphasizes numbers of combat units and weapons at the expense of training and balanced war fighting capabilities, and does so in ways that are all too common in the Arab world. Both senior Saudi officials and officers do not seem prepared to act on the fact that military manpower and equipment are only effective to the extent they are integrated into forces with realistic war-fighting training.

It is equally unclear that Saudi officials and officers recognize the need to try to integrate realistic war fighting training for Saudi land forces with the coalition warfare training of other GCC land forces. High technology training offers Southern Gulf forces still another potential force multiplier over potential threats from the Northern Gulf. It could provide a way of making up for a lack of combat experience, by standardizing training so as to make Gulf forces more interoperable, and improving interoperability with the U.S. and British armies. The smaller Gulf countries cannot afford such training facilities, but joint use of Saudi facilities would provide them with the capabilities they need and reduce costs to the Saudi Army. The fact that training is often far more important than force numbers and equipment, and that showpiece Saudi and GCC exercises service little practical purpose, is not, however, a reality that any senior Saudi, as yet, seems ready to act on.

Command post and showpiece exercises do not create effective coalition forces, and serious questions exist as to whether major elements of other Southern Gulf armies can fight effectively beside a Saudi force, once it does have adequate training. Effective coalition warfare creates a GCC-wide need for integrated training and field exercises, and for advanced land warfare training facilities for all the land forces in the Southern Gulf. There is a clear need for the kind of automated advanced training capabilities used by the United States at Fort Irwin, and used by Israel in a cheaper and less sophisticated form.

Battle Management and Command and Control

The Saudi Army needs to improve its command, control, communications, and computer (C^4) and battle management capabilities. This is not so much a matter of equipment as a matter of training and leadership, although there are security and integration problems in Saudi Army equipment. Saudi Army command and communications are too rigid and over-centralized, and better long-range communications are needed. It is also essential that promotion at senior command levels should be based on professional merit, not politics.

It is not clear that the Saudi Army is effectively organized, trained, and equipped to provide land-based air defense for its maneuver forces. The creation of a separate Air Defense Force may have had benefits in ensuring that the air defense units would achieve proper attention and suitable amounts of training manpower, but a separate Air Defense Force is best suited to a static and defensive concept of warfare.

Strategic Focus

The strategic focus that the Saudi Army *should* have is clear. The Saudi Army should shape its war fighting concepts around rapid maneuver and sustained high-intensity operations designed to deal with the Iraqi threat and contingency threats from Iran and Yemen. It should emphasize forward defense, the ability to rapidly concentrate, and sustainability in the forward area, which means emphasizing standardization and interoperability. It should make its existing units fully effective before making new major equipment buys and expanding its forces.

The current strategic posture of the Saudi Army, however, falls short of all these goals. The army is too static and defensive in character and lacks strategic focus. It takes days or weeks to move when it needs to be ready in hours or days. It is not capable of rapidly concentrating its armor and artillery to defend Kuwait and its northern border with Iraq. Moreover, its operations remain poorly integrated with those of the Air Force, National Guard, and Air Defense Force. The critical strategic importance of joint operations receives lip service at best.

There is a similar lack of proper attention to the need for effective coalition warfare capability, and efforts to create effective Southern Gulf coalition land forces range from façade to farce. Saudi Arabia clearly needs to both emphasize the ability to rapidly redeploy its forces and meet an attacker as far forward as possible, and emphasize joint operations with Kuwaiti and U.S. land forces against the Iraqi threat. At present, much of the effort to create such coalition warfare capabilities is limited to Saudi participation in small command post exercises in programs like Earnest Leader, although larger exercises are being discussed that would increase in frequency and size and include brigade-sized exercises including U.S. and other GCC forces.

Senior Saudi officials and officers do, however, emphasize interoperability with the United States over interoperability with other Gulf states. They feel there is little meaningful prospect that other GCC countries will contribute major forces capable of defeating Iraqi heavy armored and mechanized units or have forces capable of doing this at any point in the foreseeable future—an impression shared in many other Southern Gulf countries.[39] Even at the highest levels, Saudi officials and officers privately dismiss efforts to create larger "GCC forces" as useful political fictions with little war fighting capability. They see no practical prospect that efforts to persuade the GCC to create effective coalition land forces will succeed. They also see no prospect that other GCC forces will actually go from showpiece exercises to effective training in the foreseeable future. Most notably, some of the most senior officials in the Kingdom privately dismiss Kuwaiti land forces as ineffective and too small to play more than a symbolic role in what they feel must be a de facto U.S.-Saudi coalition.

There is considerable validity in this Saudi position. Regardless of whether the Peninsula Shield Force should be called a façade or a farce, the elements from other Southern Gulf countries that are now forward deployed near King Khalid Military City and Hafr al-Batin seem to have little or no war fighting capability against large formations of heavy Iraqi armor. The "Manama Declaration of the 21st GCC Summit Conference" on December 30–31, 2000, called for increasing the Peninsula Shield Force to some 22,000 men and adding naval and air elements. In practice, however, this again seems to consist of the largely symbolic earmarking of existing units that will be left in their current bases. The practical burden of the land elements of any coalition warfare against Iraq will be left to Kuwait, Saudi Arabia, and the United States.

While Saudi officials are certainly right that it will be years before the GCC as a whole can become a meaningful defensive alliance, this same excuse has deferred any major effort to change the situation for more than a decade. The Saudi Army has also failed to exercise effectively with the National Guard and Saudi Air Force, and its exercises with U.S. and British forces have been far too infrequent, too small, and too command post–oriented.

Until Iraq has stable and moderate leadership, Iran is firmly under moderate leadership, and the future political stability of Yemen is clear, the Saudi Army cannot be left as a façade or a force that would take months or years to be fully combat-effective. Saudi Arabia needs to accept the fact that a Saudi-Kuwaiti-U.S. coalition is critical to its defense and act accordingly to create an effective integrated defense. The failure to accept the fact that the cooperative, integrated defense of Kuwait and the Saudi border with Iraq is the primary mission of the Saudi Army remains a key problem in giving Saudi land forces their proper strategic focus.

NOTES

1. Unless otherwise specified, the military data quoted here are taken from the relevant country sections of various annual editions of the IISS, *Military Balance*;

CIA, *The World Factbook*; Jaffee Center for Strategic Studies, *The Middle East Military Balance*; online editions of *Jane's Sentinel series* and *Periscope, Jane's Intelligence Review*, and *Jane's Defence Weekly*. The cut-off date for such material is January 2002.

Other sources include interviews with Saudi officials and military inside and outside of Saudi Arabia, U.S. experts, and British experts. These are not identified by source by request of those interviewed. They also include the author's publications and other sources mentioned at the start of the section on Saudi Arabia in Dr. Andrew Rathmell, "Saudi Arabia's Military Build-up—An Extravagant Error," *Jane's Intelligence Review* (November 1994), pp. 500–504; Andrew Rathmell, *The Changing Balance in the Gulf*, Whitehall Papers 38 (London: Royal United Services Institute, 1996); Edward B. Atkenson, *The Powder Keg* (Falls Church: NOVA Publications, 1996); Geoffrey Kemp and Robert E. Harkavy, *Strategic Geography and the Changing Middle East* (Washington: Carnegie Endowment/Brookings, 1997); and various editions of USCENTCOM, *Atlas* (MacDill Air Force Base: USCENTCOM); *Jane's Helicopter Markets and Systems*; *Jane's All the World's Armies*; *Jane's Armor and Artillery*; *Jane's Land-Based Air Defense*; and *Jane's Military Vehicles and Logistics*.

2. An airborne ranger battalion is deployed at Tabuk.

3. Major General Dennis Malcor was sent to Saudi Arabia to survey its military requirements after the Gulf War. *Washington Post*, March 15, 1992, p. A-35; *New York Times*, October 15, 1991, p. A-1; *Jane's Defence Weekly*, December 14, 1991, p. 1175.

4. *Defense News*, April 14, 1997, pp. 2, 23.

5. Richard F. Grimmett, *Arms Sales to Saudi Arabia* (Washington: Congressional Research Service, IB91007, August 28, 1991), p. 4.

6. *Inside the Army*, April 6, 1992, p. 1; *Inside the Pentagon*, April 9, 1992, p. 2.

7. Department of Defense, "Sale of Abrams Tanks to Saudi Arabia," Background Information, November, 1, 1989.

8. Department of Defense fax, July 18, 1990; *Defense Week*, March 12, 1990, p. 3.

9. Executive News Service, September 23, 1995, 0557.

10. *Louisville Courier Journal*, November 6, 1992, p. B-3; *Defense News*, June 21, 1993, p. 14; *Jane's Defence Weekly*, February 20, 1993, p. 8.

11. *Jane's Defence Weekly*, February 26, 1994, p. 4.

12. *Jane's Defence Weekly*, February 6, 1988, p. 191, March 7, 1992, July 25, 1992, p. 18, August 15, 1992, p. 5; Grimmett, *Arms Sales to Saudi Arabia*, p. 4; *Defense Daily*, February 14, 1992, p. 251; *Defense News*, March 30, 1992, p. 6.

13. *Jane's Defence Weekly*, February 6, 1988, p. 191, March 7, 1992; *Defense Daily*, February 14, 1992, p. 251; *Defense News*, March 30, 1992, p. 6.

14. *Defense News*, March 30, 1992, p. 6, April 14, 1997, p. 3; *Defense Daily*, February 14, 1992, p. 251; *Jane's Defence Weekly*, February 6, 1988, p. 191, March 7, 1992; *Inside the Army*, April 6, 1992, p. 1; *Inside the Pentagon*, April 9, 1992, p. 2.

15. *Jane's Defence Weekly*, February 6, 1988, p. 191, March 7, 1992; *Defense Daily*, February 14, 1992, p. 251; *Defense News*, March 30, 1992, p. 6; Executive News Service, August 11, 1995, 0625.

16. *Jane's Defence Weekly*, April 17, 1996, p. 10.

17. *Jane's Defence Weekly*, August 6, 1997.

18. *Jane's Defence Weekly*, August 28, 1996, p. 19.

19. *Jane's Defence Weekly*, November 4, 1995, p. 8; *Defense News*, April 14, 1997, p. 3.

20. IISS, *Military Balance*; DMS computer database; interviews in Saudi Arabia; and discussions with U.S. experts. These figures are based largely on Saudi data, and differ significantly from IISS and most Western databases.

21. The first 200 M-2s were produced at a rate of 2 in FY1989, 98 in FY1990, and 100 in FY1991. *Jane's Defence Weekly*, September 9, 1989, p. 452; *Wall Street Journal*, June 2, 1988, p. 56; *Aviation Week*, June 17, 1991, p. 129.

22. *Defense News*, June 6, 1994; *Washington Times*, July 23, 1997, p. A-6.

23. *Jane's Defence Weekly*, August 19, 1998, p.19.

24. DMS computer database; interviews in Saudi Arabia in February 1991; discussions with Saudi experts in December 1990; and *Defense News*, February 22, 1988, p. 3.

25. *Jane's Defence Weekly*, April 9, 1996, p. 14.

26. Grimmett, *Arms Sales to Saudi Arabia*, p. 4.

27. The IISS reports 90 GCT-1s, but Giat only reports the sale of 51.

28. *Aviation Week*, June 17, 1991, p. 129; Grimmett, *Arms Sales to Saudi Arabia*, p. 4; IISS and JCSS military balances; DMS computer database; interviews in Saudi Arabia in February 1991; discussions with Saudi experts in December 1990; and *Defense News*, February 22, 1988, p. 3.

29. *Jane's Defence Weekly*, March 11, 1989, p. 393.

30. Grimmett, *Arms Sales to Saudi Arabia*, p. 4.

31. *Defense News*, April 14, 1997, p. 3.

32. Grimmett, *Arms Sales to Saudi Arabia*, p. 4; *Jane's Defence Weekly*, December 17, 1988, p. 1546, June 25, 1989, p. 1296; Rathmell, "Saudi Arabia's Military Build-up"; Rathmell, *The Changing Balance in the Gulf*; Atkenson, *The Powder Keg*; USCENTCOM, *Atlas, 1996*; *Jane's Sentinel: The Gulf States, 1997*; *Jane's Aircraft Upgrades* (1997–1998); *Jane's Avionics* (1997–1998); *Jane's All the World's Aircraft* (1997–1998); *Jane's World Air Forces* (binder, April 1997); *Jane's Land-Based Air Defense, 1997–1998* (CD-ROM); *Jane's Radar and Electronic Warfare Systems* (CD-ROM); *Jane's Military Communications, 1997–98*; and *Jane's Unmanned Aerial Vehicles and Targets* (binder).

33. *Aviation Week*, April 2, 1990, p. 44; *Jane's Defence Weekly*, November 16, 1991, p. 927; *Wall Street Journal*, October 7, 1991, p. 16.

34. *Jane's Defence Weekly*, December 14, 1991, p. 1175, June 13, 1992, p. 1013. Grimmett, *Arms Sales to Saudi Arabia*, p. 4.

35. *Jane's Defence Weekly*, July 22, 1989, p. 105; IISS, *Military Balance, 1992–1993*, pp. 120–121; *Military Technology, World Defense Almanac, 1992–1993*, Vol. XVII, Issue 1-1993, pp. 157–159.

36. *Journal of Electronic Defense*, February 1994, p. 17.

37. *Defense News*, April 9, 2001, p. 3.

38. Department of Defense Notice Pursuant to Section 62(A) of the Arms Export Control Act, Transmittal No. 9-93, July 19, 1993.

39. These are points normally raised only in private interviews. However, see the comments in *Defense News*, February 5, 2001, p. 5. The broader issues affecting the GCC are laid out in John Duke Anthony's draft of "The GCC's 21st Summit, Part Two: Defense Issues," *Gulf Wire*, Washington, January 2001.

Chapter 5

The Saudi National Guard

Saudi Arabia divides its land force manpower between the Army and the Saudi Arabian National Guard (SANG). The National Guard is the successor of the loyal elements of the Ikhwan, or White Army. It is a tribal force forged out of those elements loyal to the Saud family. It was created in 1956, and was originally administered directly by the king until King Faisal appointed Prince Abdullah its commander in 1962. A year later, Abdullah requested a British Military Mission to help modernize the Guard. Since the late 1970s, however, the U.S.-Saudi Arabian National Guard Program (SANG) and U.S. contractors have provided most of the SANG's advisory functions.[1]

The National Guard is sometimes viewed as a counterweight to any threat from the regular military forces, and a counterbalance within the royal family to Sudairi control over the regular armed forces. Over time, however, it has become a steadily more effective internal security force, as well as a force that can provide rear area security for the Army and can help defend Riyadh. The five major current missions of the Guard are:

- Maintain security and stability within the Kingdom,
- Defend vital facilities (religious sites, oil fields),
- Provide security and a screening force for the Kingdom's borders.
- Provide a combat-ready internal security force for operations throughout the Kingdom, and
- Provide security for Crown Prince Abdullah.

The National Guard was used to deal with the Shi'ite uprising in the Eastern Province, the siege of the Grand Mosque in Mecca in 1979, and put down the Iranian riots in Mecca in 1987. It also helped secure the Eastern Province during the Iran-Iraq War and Gulf War.[2] The National Guard remains under the command of Crown Prince Abdullah, and his half-brother, Prince Badr bin Abdulaziz, the deputy commander in chief.[3]

The assistant deputy commander of the Guard is Sheik Abdulaziz bin Abdul Moshin al-Tuwaijiri, who has served with the Guard since its creation as a modern force. The command structure of the Guard is then divided into three main branches: The primary operational branch is under the lieutenant general, Prince Mit'eb bin Abdulaziz, the assistant deputy commander for military affairs.[4] Lieutenant General Mit'eb is another son of the Crown Prince, and many feel he will replace his father as the commander of the National Guard. He was educated at Sandhurst, and has excellent relations with the British and U.S. armies. He is well liked in the region and is one of the few Saudi officers with good relations with the military in both Jordan and Turkey.

The health affairs branch is under Dr. Fahad Abdul Jabber, and provides some of the most advanced medical care in the Kingdom. A civil deputy, Sheik Abdul Rahman Abu Haimid, controls expenditures and the budget. Sheik Haimid's control over expenditures, and the Guard's reliance on U.S. government–supervised FMS buys, is reported to be a major reason why the National Guard has not been accused of the kind of cronyism and commission-granting that has affected the regular services. One observer, who is a strong proponent of the Guard, estimated that the Guard got 93 cents worth of equipment for every procurement dollar (the United States charges a 3-cent administration fee), while the regular services got only 70 cents worth.

THE MANNING OF THE NATIONAL GUARD

Estimates of the current full-time strength of the National Guard differ sharply. The IISS, for example, reported that the Guard had 57,000 actives and 20,000 tribal levies in 1999, but reported that it had 75,000 actives and 25,000 tribal levies in 2000.[5] A senior U.S. expert quoted a strength of 105,000 in February 2001. Regardless of the exact numbers, it is clear that the Guard is now far larger than it was at the time of the Gulf War, and that it has a full-time active strength approaching that of the Saudi Army.

The Guard's manning now includes a much larger proportion of trained, full-time personnel. In the past, the National Guard recruited largely from loyal tribes in the Najd and Hasa. However, its recruiting base has steadily expanded to include other regions and urban areas, and it now has some Shi'ites. The Guard now deliberately avoids creating active units based around one tribe or region, and recruits on a central basis with much larger numbers of entrants from urban areas. There are far more qualified applicants for its academy and for enlisted positions than the Guard can accept— sometimes over twenty qualified applicants for each opening.

Retention is high, with only 10% to 15% losses after the first tour of duty. Most personnel serve out a career of twenty-five to thirty-five years. This, however, has disadvantages. Even though the Guard tends to promote more on the basis or merit than the other services, key personnel stay too long in given ranks and grades. The Guard needs about 17% attrition annually to keep its personnel in the proper age brackets, and does not come close to this goal—particularly at the more senior levels. Early retirement carries a considerable stigma in some levels of Saudi society, and any retirement means a significant loss in status.

THE ORGANIZATION OF THE NATIONAL GUARD

The SANG does not have a formal mission statement. It is, however, primarily a combat force, and internal security missions like riot control and guard study have secondary and declining importance. It does not provide security for the royal family, except for its commander Crown Prince Abdullah, and most internal security missions are the responsibility of the Ministry of the Interior. ARAMCO has its own active guard force for the Saudi oil fields.

The SANG is headquartered at Riyadh, and has separate regional headquarters for the Eastern and Western Regions at Dammam and Jeddah. The Guard's full-time professional forces have been organized into modern military formations over the two decades. The Guard held its first significant training exercises for its first 6,500-man Mechanized Brigade, the Imam Mohammed bin Saud Brigade, during the early 1980s. It deployed a brigade-sized presence, and a limited oil-field security force in the Eastern Province, and the Mohammed bin Saud brigade held its first major exercise in the desert about 250 miles west of Riyadh in early 1983. Units from other parts of the Kingdom, some as far away as the Eastern Province, moved to join this exercise, and the key mechanized elements performed relatively well. While the Guard experienced problems in translating tribal discipline into regular military discipline and the force was below its authorized manning level, the set-piece maneuvers performed were successful.

Since that time the Guard has steadily expanded its combat capabilities. The National Guard inaugurated its second mechanized "brigade" in a ceremony on March 14, 1985. This new unit was called the King Abd al-Aziz Brigade, which was formed after another relatively successful round of set-piece exercises called "Al Areen," which were held near Bisha. Prince Abdullah then spoke of expanding the Guard to 35,000 men, and succeeded in building up a force of three mechanized brigades by 1989. In the mid-1990s, he discussed expanding the Guard to a total manning of 80,000 to 100,000 by the year 2000, a goal that the SANG largely met.[6]

In 2002, the Guard was organized into four mechanized brigades, with a fifth forming as this book went to press. These brigades had modern light armored vehicles (LAVs), and each brigade had some 800 men each and some 360 vehicles. There were also five light infantry brigades, equipped primarily with V-150s. These forces were deployed so that there were two mechanized brigades, and another forming, near Riyadh, plus one light infantry brigade. The Western Sector had three light infantry brigades, and the Eastern Sector has one mechanized and one light infantry brigade.

There were combined arms battalions near Arar, Rafha, and Hail, and a ceremonial cavalry squadron at Riyadh, with training and support bases headquartered at Riyadh, Jeddah, and Dammam.[7] These Guard battalions were normally assigned only to protect sensitive provincial facilities like power generation, desalination, and communications. There also were tribal force elements (or Fowj) at Arar, Dammam, Rafha, Hail, Buraydah, Hofuf, Medina, Jeddah, Yanbu, Mecca, Taif, Najran, Jizan, Sharawrah, and Riyadh. In early 2002, the Guard had the order of battle shown in Table 5.1.

THE EQUIPMENT OF THE NATIONAL GUARD

The Guard does not have a complex or sophisticated mix of equipment, but has chosen to standardize on some of the best wheeled armored weapons available. In 2002, the Guard's operational forces were equipped with about 1,117 LAVs in its mechanized units. According to the IISS, these included 394 LAV-25s, 184 LAV-Cps, 130 LAV-Ags, 111 LAV-AT, 73 LAV-Ms, 47 LAV, plus 190 LAV support vehicles. It also had 290 V-150 Commando armored vehicles in active service in its light infantry forces, plus 810 more V-150s in storage. The Guard prefers wheeled vehicles because of their superior speed, endurance, and ease of maintenance. The Guard also had a significant number of towed artillery weapons.

The Guard's V-150s have been in service for some time. They are part of an older family of armored vehicles with a number of different configurations and weapons systems, including anti-tank guided missile carriers, cannon turrets, and main guns. While estimates differ, current holdings seem to include 100 to 120 V-150s configured as AIFVs, 20 to 30 with 90 mm guns, 130 to 140 armored command vehicles, 70 to 80 81 mm mortar carriers, 45 to 50 armored recovery vehicles, 30 special purpose vehicles, and 325 to 375 configured as APCs.[8] Other reports indicate that the SANG has 100 TOW fire units mounted on its V-150s, which have been retrofitted with air conditioning.

Some reports indicate that the SANG also had 440 Piranha light, 8 × 8 wheeled armored vehicles. These are designed by FAMAE/MOWAG of

Table 5.1
The Saudi National Guard Order of Battle, Early 2002

Headquarters: Riyadh
- Turki Mechanized Brigade (in formation)
- IMBS Mechanized Brigade
- PSAR Mechanized Brigade
- King Khalid Light Infantry Brigade
- Support brigade
- MP battalion
- King Khalid Light Infantry Brigade support battalion
- Training Base: Signal School, Medical School, NGMS, KKMA, recruiting
- Support Base: Signal Corps, Medical Corps, Weapons and ammunition, Logistics base, and engineers.

Eastern Region Headquarters: Dammam (Brigades at Dammam and Hofuf)
- KAA Mechanized Brigade (in formation)
- Guard Battalion
- MP battalion
- Recruiting
- Support Base: Signal Corps, Medical Corps, Weapons and ammunition, Logistics base, and engineers.

Western Sector Headquarters: Jeddah (Brigades at Jeddah, Medina, and Taif)
- KFB Mechanized Brigade
- KSB Mechanized Brigade
- KOKB Mechanized Brigade
- Guard Battalion
- MP battalion
- Recruiting
- Support Base: Signal Corps, Medical Corps, Weapons and ammunition, Logistics base, and engineers.

Independently deployed light infantry battalions
- Arar (?)
- Yanbu
- Rafha
- Hail (?)

Independent Regular National Guard Element or Presence: Arar, Tabuk, Rafha, Hail, Buraydah, Hofuf, Medina, Yanbu, Mecca, Taif, Khamis Mushayt, Najran, Jizan, Sharawrah.

Independent Tribal Forces or "Fowj" Element or Presence: Arar, Dammam, Rafha, Hail, Buraydah, Hofuf, Medina, Jeddah, Yanbu, Mecca, Taif, Najran, Jizan, Sharawrah, Riyadh.

Source: Author's interviews in Saudi Arabia, April 2000 and February 2001.

Switzerland, and made in Switzerland, Canada, and the UK. They have a combat weight of 16,000 kilograms, a maximum crew of 16, a range of 780 kilometers, and a maximum road speed of 100 kilometers per hour. They can be armed with a wide range of weapons, and configured as support vehicles. They have cross-country mobility roughly equivalent to that of tracked vehicles.

The SANG's most important purchase is a buy of some 1,117 LAV-25s from General Motors of Canada through the U.S. Army Tank Automotive Command (TACOM) at a cost of $3.4 billion. The resulting package included 116 TOW launchers with 2,001 missiles, 27 M-198 155 mm howitzers, support systems, training, and facilities. The LAV-25 is another 8×8 wheeled armored vehicle that can be configured in a number of different ways. It has excellent cross-country mobility, and has been used by the U.S. Marine Corps for some years. It is primarily a combat fighting vehicle, rather than a transport, but also has a number of command, reconnaissance, and support variants.

The National Guard has chosen the Delco 120 mm Armored Mortar System for installation on the LAV-25s. The Saudi National Guard also ordered 130 90 mm turret weapon systems in Cockerill LCTS Mark 8 turrets and 130 M-240 .50 machine guns to upgrade its OAFVs in 1997. It purchased 169,000 rounds of 90 mm ammunition and a full range of spares as part of this buy.[9]

These deliveries are giving the National Guard 10 variants of the LAV-25, including 111 anti-tank weapons vehicles with TOW, 73 armored mortar systems with 120 mm mortars, 182 command vehicles, 71 ambulances, 417 APCs, together with ammunition carriers, recovery vehicles, and engineer vehicles. Some 384 LAVs will be armed with two-man turrets equipped with the 25 mm McDonnell Douglas chain gun and thermal sights. In late April 1997, Saudi Arabia selected the Belgian LCTS Mk 8 90 mm turret, fitted with computerized fire control systems, for the remaining LAVs.[10] The SANG took delivery of the first of 73 120 mm armored mortar systems in 1998.

The Guard plans to standardize its mechanized brigades to use the LAV. Three mechanized brigades already have the LAV, and a fourth is phasing out its gas-powered V-150s. This conversion to the LAV seems to have been completed in 2001, and all five brigades should be fully manned and converted within the next few years. Conversion was so easy that only one battalion set of the LAVs was in storage in the spring of 2000.

The Guard had 30 M-198 howitzers in 2001, plus 40 M-102 105 mm towed artillery weapons and 30 M-198 155 mm howitzers in early2002. It also had 81 mm and 120 mm mortars, including 73 120 mm mortars mounted in LAV-Ms. The Guard needs more weapons and is short of the artillery support it needs, but has found the U.S.-supplied M-198 to be too heavy and is examining weapons from other countries.

The Guard also had 116 TOW launchers with 2,000 missiles and HMMWV light transport vehicles on order. It also had large numbers of TOW anti-tank guided missiles, rocket launchers, and recoilless rifles for its infantry.

The Guard has a limited number of helicopters. Its air defenses consist largely of 30 M-40 Vulcan 20 mm anti-aircraft guns. The Guard has sought to buy the United States' Stinger, but the United States insists that U.S. officers have access to the weapons and count regular formal inventories. Crown Prince Abdullah feels this is a violation of Saudi sovereignty. The Guard has also examined the possibility of using a vehicle-mounted version of the AMRAAM anti–air missile.

The National Guard is steadily improving its communications. It now has advanced SINGARS tactical radios. It has a $52 million contract with the Harris Corporation for RF-5000 Falcon digital high-frequency radios for its vehicles and base stations, and Arabic-language data terminals, turn-key logistical support, and technical assistance.[11]

THE GUARD'S SUPPORT CAPABILITIES

The Guard's support has greatly improved its ability to sustain its deployed forces in recent years, helped in part by its standardization on one basic family of mechanized vehicles for each combat unit, and deliberate attempts to avoid complicating its "train, maintain, and sustain" efforts with oversophisticated or complicated mixes of equipment.

Its full-time active forces do remain dependent on outside contractors for some forms of rear area service support, maintenance, and logistics—although both Saudi and foreign observers note that the foreign advisory and contract support for the SANG has always been performance-oriented, while the advisory and contract support for the regular forces has often been sales-oriented. This support is delivered in part through a modernization program financed by the Saudi government and run by the Office of the Program Manager–Saudi National Guard (OPM-SANG), which is part of the U.S. Army Materiel Command, and by contractors like the Vinnell Corporation. In 2000, the OPM consisted of 95 military personnel, 50 U.S. civilians, 43 third-country civilians, and 95 local hires. There were 400 subcontractor civilian personnel, 280 U.S. and 500 Saudi contractors, and 250 contractor personnel from other countries. These advisory groups were located in Dammam, Hofuf, Riyadh, Jeddah, and Taif.

This advisory, support, and medical services program is now a quarter of a century old and has cost Saudi Arabia well over $6 billion. The headquarters of this program was the target of the car bomb in Riyadh on November 13, 1995. Currently, the program is administered through the OPM-SANG by the U.S. Army Materiel Command and by the Vinnell Corporation, which signed an $819 million, four-year contract to provide support services in January 1994.[12] The Guard signed an additional contract with Vinnell, valued at $163.3 million, for additional training support in 1995.[13]

THE TRAINING OF THE NATIONAL GUARD

The training of the National Guard's full-time forces has improved steadily in recent years, and training activity is considerably higher than in the Army. Training has recently been improved by the use of advanced technology systems like MILES and LAV combat simulators. The United States is helping the SANG set up "mini–National Training Centers" to provide realistic combat training at the battalion level and hopes to expand this program to the brigade level. The light infantry brigades have also begun realistic brigade-level exercises. The artillery is also receiving better training, although SANG units still lack modern digital fire control systems. The maintenance ethic in the SANG has also improved, and training is enhanced.

The men in the Fowj forces have less training but are becoming steadily better trained. The core of the SANG's new training efforts are built around the United States' battle-focused method of training, rather than set-piece exercises.

The SANG uses specially modified Arabic editions of U.S. field manuals, and now has well-organized training schedules. SANG training for key missions and tasks is now tailored to given regions of the Kingdom because the desert warfare conditions and missions in the northeast are very different from the terrain around its cites near the Red Sea, mountains, and border with Yemen. The Guard is now undergoing realistic combat training at the battalion level and is beginning to expand to brigade-sized battle-focused training.

While the SANG has traditional senior leaders, it now has a modern academy for its officers and trains some 300 cadets a year. This academy is popular enough to have some 2,100 applicants in 1999. About 80 SANG officers train in the United States each year, and SANG officers receive extensive English-language training. (They may only go to the United States if they pass the required tests.) Promotion is also increasingly merit-based, and this method of promotion has reached the level of major, although the SANG has a surplus of lieutenants and promotion is slow. The main leadership and promotion problems exist at the top, at general officer level, which has had roughly the same leadership since 1985.

THE READINESS AND EFFECTIVENESS OF THE NATIONAL GUARD

The National Guard has had some operational successes. Guard forces helped secure the Eastern Province during the Iran-Iraq War, but their capabilities were never really tested. They were given special training and additional manning during the Gulf War. The Guard was the first force to meet the initial Iraqi assault on Khafji, and deployed within days while the regular army required weeks. However, the Guard units were not equipped to take on an Iraqi heavy armored brigade and required extensive reinforcement by U.S. air and artillery support during the battle to retake the city. They performed well in rear area and screening missions, but did not play a significant role in the armored advance in the liberation of Kuwait.

The National Guard has done a good job since 1991 in dealing with low-level problems with the Shi'ites in the Eastern Province, extremists, border clashes with Yemeni forces, and Iranian-sponsored riots during the Hajj. There has been little fighting along the Yemeni border since 1997, however, except for incidents with smugglers. Nevertheless, there were still three clashes with armed Yemeni tribesmen in 1999, including one exchange of artillery fire. The Guard has steadily reduced its role in protecting the Hajj as Saudi relations with Iran have improved. The SANG has only had to deal with minor protests since the election of President Khatami, and the Ministry of the Interior now handles most security functions. As a result, the Guard now only deploy one brigade to provide security for the Hajj, rather than the usual two. Reports that the Guard deployed elements in Bahrain in the 1990s during its troubles with the Shi'ites seem to be false.

The SANG has also become a more effective light mechanized force. It has not, however, developed a high capability for sophisticated internal security operations; the forces of the Ministry of the Interior are intended to deal with well-organized cells or sophisticated hostile groups that hide under political cover. As a result, the SANG and Ministry of Interior hold weekly anti-terrorism meetings to coordinate their different activities, and share a common headquarters during the Hajj. The ministry has some 100,000 personnel, including firemen, emergency medical services, and other civil capabilities. It also has anti-terrorist units and forces like SWAT teams. The SANG is just beginning to develop urban SWAT and Special Forces capabilities. It is also still developing its capabilities for military operations in urban terrain (MOUT) and riot and crowd control.

Tribal Forces (Fowj)

The tribal forces of the National Guard, or Fowj, are grouped and deployed where they can defend key regions and cover every critical urban and populated area in the country. They are useful in securing Saudi Arabia against infiltration and terrorists in a way that limits the ability of the Army to conduct a coup, and their leaders are carefully chosen for their loyalty to the regime. They still lack modern combat training, but Prince Abdullah is seeking to correct this situation over the next few years.

The Guard helps key princes maintain close relations with the tribes, and serves as a means of maintaining internal security. The deputy commander of the SANG handles the tribes, although it should be noted that the tribes have changed strikingly in the last decade. Most tribes are now heavily urbanized and many small settlements are all but abandoned. This has helped the SANG recruit, because tribal members from rural areas are often less well-educated and competitive in the Saudi labor force and often need jobs. It also, however, means that the SANG must accept some illiterate recruits, particularly into the Fowj, while the overall intake of tribal youth is better educated and more interested in the full-time forces than in the Fowj.

The Guard balances tribal factions to reduce the risk of feuding, and provides a means through which the royal family can allocate funds to tribal and Bedouin leaders. This organization makes the tribal portion of the Guard politically vital to ensuring the integration of Saudi Arabia's increasingly urbanized and underemployed tribes into its society. The Kingdom's economic problems have greatly improved SANG recruiting in recent years, and SANG soldiers are often the sole breadwinner in extended families. U.S. experts estimate that the SANG now supports up to a million Saudis by providing income, medical support, and education.[14]

Full-Time Forces

The changes in the organization and equipment of the Guard's full-time forces are steadily improving their quality. Unlike the regular Saudi Army, the Guard can deploy rapidly and begin to move the key elements of its brigades in hours. This is one major advantage of its reliance on wheeled vehicles, and Guard units can deploy for a distance of several hundred miles with their existing fuel load without major service support. The Guard has steadily improved the quality of its field and technical training, and has conducted command-post exercises involving up to four brigades. There is some discussion of going to a division-sized structure.

Nevertheless, the Guard has serious force mixture and readiness problems. The Guard's mechanized brigades lack the integral firepower, heavy armor, air defense, and maneuver capability to take on the heavy mechanized infantry or armored forces of Iran and Iraq in head-on combat. The Guard's full-time mechanized and light infantry forces also lack the heavy armor, self-propelled artillery, air mobility, specialized support units, logistics, and maintenance capabilities present in Saudi regular Army units.

The Guard has other limitations. There is little real-world cooperation with the regular forces and the MODA, although there is one token liaison meeting a month. There are no meaningful joint exercises with the Saudi regular Army and Air Force, and there has been no effort to develop a common concept of operations or to see if the Saudi Air Defense Force could support the Guard in some contingencies. The Guard and regular forces use different communications systems, and there are no joint war plans. Any cooperation requires each service to send liaison officers to the other service with radios.

The Guard pays little attention to the GCC, and its leaders have little respect for either the regular Saudi Army, or other Gulf land forces—including Saudi units. They tend to see Egyptian and Jordanian forces as examples of Arab proficiency.

Expansion Options

Prince Abdullah has asked the Guard's foreign advisors to study an expansion beyond 100,000 regulars by the early 2000s. Such manning levels would allow the Guard to create another mechanized brigade and a new mix of battalion-sized formations for its part-time forces. This modest expansion seems well within the SANG's capabilities.[15]

There has also been a series of examinations of possible options for giving the Guard heavier tracked armor and self-propelled artillery. There were media reports after the Gulf War that Prince Abdullah has considered plans to bring the Guard up to a strength of eleven full-time brigades, with tanks, self-propelled artillery, and other heavy equipment. It is unclear, however, that Prince Abdullah ever seriously considered such options. Both Prince Abdullah and the other leaders of the SANG seem to have understood that expansion must proceed slowly, and that the Guard was not ready to move beyond the LAV-25 series of vehicles.

There have been studies of a possible purchase of helicopters. At present, however, there are no plans to "heavy up" the National Guard. It does not have the base of skilled manpower, and its entire infrastructure is sized for LAVs. Moreover, the Guard is paying close attention to the U.S. Army's efforts to "lighten up" its heavy armor and create more rapidly deployable forces.

STRATEGIC ISSUES: THE ROLE OF THE NATIONAL GUARD RELATIVE TO THE ARMY

The National Guard is an effective and well-organized force within the limits imposed by its equipment and organization. It does, however, raise some important strategic issues. While there are no data available on its cost relative to that of the regular Army, it does have roughly the same manpower and has excellent facilities and modern equipment. It does not have a clearly separate mission from that of the Army, however, particularly now that Saudi Arabia has improved its relations with Yemen.

In the past, the National Guard acted as a barrier to a possible coup led by the Army, and gave Prince Abdullah and the rest of the royal family a potential military counterweight to Prince Sultan's control over the regular military forces. It is not clear that these rationales really justify maintaining two parallel ground forces today, particularly when Iran and Iraq pose the most serious threat to the Kingdom and any invasion would require forces capable of dealing with heavy armor. Certainly, Saudi Arabia does not have the budgetary resources to fund a force that is not fully interoperable with the Army, has negligible training in joint operations with the Air Force, and is so compartmented from the regular forces that a very substantial part of the Kingdom's limited resources in trained manpower cannot be used against its most serious enemies with maximum effectiveness.

The time may well have come for Saudi Arabia to look beyond its past fears of coup attempts and the rivalries of its senior princes and to consider how to either bring the regular Army and National Guard under common command or restructure and retrain the Guard so that it can be effective in reinforcing the Army as a light mechanized force in the event of an Iraqi or Iranian attack. The latter solution may be more practical, given Saudi Arabia's history and politics, but the Guard has evolved far beyond the status of a royal guard (which now exists as a separate regiment in any case) and it has done so without evolving to become an effective war fighting force for all of the threats the Kingdom faces.

NOTES

1. David Long, *The Kingdom of Saudi Arabia* (Gainesville: University Press of Florida, 1997).
2. Unless otherwise specified, the military data quoted here are taken from interviews in Saudi Arabia and the relevant country sections of various annual editions of the IISS, *Military Balance*; CIA, *The World Factbook*; JCSS, *The Middle East Military Balance*; the author's publications and other sources mentioned at the start of the section on Saudi Arabia; and Dr. Andrew Rathmell, "Saudi Arabia's Military Build-up—An Extravagant Error," *Jane's Intelligence Review* (November 1994), pp. 500–504; Andrew Rathmell, *The Changing Balance in the Gulf*, Whitehall Papers 38 (London: Royal United Services Institute, 1996); Edward B. Atkenson, *The Powder Keg* (Falls Church: NOVA Publications, 1996); Geoffrey Kemp and Robert E. Harkavy, *Strategic Geography and the Changing Middle East* (Washington: Carnegie Endowment/Brookings, 1997); USCENTCOM, *Atlas, 1996* (MacDill Air Force Base: USCENTCOM, 1997); *Jane's Sentinel: The Gulf States, 1997* and *1999* (London: Jane's Publishing); *Jane's Helicopter Markets and Systems* (CD-ROM); *Jane's All the World's Armies* (CD-ROM); *Jane's Armor and Artillery* (CD-ROM); *Jane's Land-Based Air Defense* (CD-ROM); *Jane's Military Vehicles and Logistics* (CD-ROM).
3. Joseph A. Kechichian, *Succession in Saudi Arabia* (New York: Palgrave, 2001), pp. 175–178.
4. General Mohammed bin Abdullah al-Amr retired in 2000.
5. IISS, *The Military Balance, 1999–2000, 2000–2001,* and *2001–2002* (London: Oxford, 2001), "Saudi Arabia."
6. *Jane's Defence Weekly*, July 10, 1996, p. 33, April 23, 1997, p. 19.
7. Based on interviews in Saudi Arabia in 2000 and 2001. Other sources indi-

cate that the Guard also has an engineer battalion, and a special security battalion. One source suggests that its strength is two mechanized brigades and two Special Forces units. IISS, *Military Balance, 1996–1997, 1999–2000, 2000–2001,* and *2001–2002; Jane's Sentinel: The Gulf States, 1997.*

8. *Jane's Defence Weekly,* July 10, 1996, p. 33, April 23, 1997, p. 19; *Jane's Pointer,* September 1996, p. 5.

9. *Defense News,* June 6, 1994; *Washington Times,* July 23, 1997, p. A-6; *Jane's Defence Weekly,* March 7, 1992, p. 388, January 24, 1996, p. 18, April 23, 1997, p. 19; *Military Technology, World Defense Almanac, 1992–1993,* vol. XVII, no. 1 (1993), pp. 157–159.

10. *Jane's Defence Weekly,* April 23, 1997, p. 19.

11. Author's estimate based on interviews in Saudi Arabia; "Saudi National Guard Fact Sheet," DSAA; FMC data; DMS computer printouts; and the IISS and JCSS military balances.

12. *Chicago Tribune,* November 14, 1995, p. I-1; *Washington Post,* November 14, 1995, p. A-15.

13. *Baltimore Sun,* November 14, 1995, p. 1A; *Chicago Tribune,* November 14, 1995, p. I-1; *Washington Times,* May, 4, 1995, p. B-9.

14. For an interesting Israeli view of the role of the National Guard in the mid-1980s, see Mordechai Abir, "Saudi Security and Military Endeavor," *The Jerusalem Quarterly,* no. 33 (Fall 1984), pp. 79–94. This assessment is based on interviews in Saudi Arabia in April 2000.

15. *Armed Forces Journal* (May 1994), p. 39.

Chapter 6

The Saudi Navy

The Saudi Navy has grown steadily over the last ten years, and now has east and west fleets for its Gulf and Red Sea coasts. The Saudi Navy also has growing effectiveness, particularly in defensive roles like mine warfare.[1] It has expanded from active strength of around 6,000 men in the mid-1980s to much higher levels; in 2002, it had a total active strength of 13,500 to 15,500, including 3,000 marines.[2]

The Saudi Navy is headquartered at Riyadh. Its ranking officers are the chief of naval staff (Vice Admiral Talal Salem al-Mofadhi); commander, east fleet (Rear Admiral al-Hamdi); and commander, west fleet (Rear Admiral Mohammed Abdullah al-Ajalen). The Coast Guard is part of the Frontier Force and has a separate command chain under Lieutenant General Mujib bin Muhammed al-Qahtani.

The Navy has a modern headquarters staff with five major branches— G1 Personnel, G2 Intelligence and Security, G3 Operations and Training, G4 Logistics, and G5 Civil and Military Affairs. Its operational command is divided into two major fleets, plus command of the Marine regiment. The Arabian Gulf Division is headquartered at Al Jubail and has bases at Dammam, Ras Tanura, and Al Qatif, plus a naval aviation element. The Red Sea Division is headquartered at Jeddah, and has bases at Haqi, Al Wajh, and Yanbu. There are small bases at Al Sharmah, Duba, Ras al-Mishab, and Tamwah. The main base of the Coast Guard is at Aziziah.[3]

Saudi Arabia has also begun the construction of a new military city at Jizan, on the Red Sea near the Saudi-Yemeni border. The new facility will include a naval base, an air base, and a dry dock. This adds naval and air capability in an area where Saudi Arabia already has a military city, at Abha, which it uses to base its land forces, and a major air base at Khamis Mushayt.[4]

CURRENT SAUDI NAVAL FORCES

Chart 6.1 shows the manpower strength of the Saudi Navy relative to other Gulf navies. Charts 6.2 to 6.6 show similar data on ship and aircraft strength. Any purely numerical comparisons, however, are misleading. The Iranian Navy has not acquired any major surface ships since the fall of the Shah, although it does have modern missile patrol boats, shore-based long-range anti-ship missiles, and three submarines. The Iraqi Navy was never strong, and was virtually destroyed during the Gulf War. The Omani Navy is the only Southern Gulf navy with relatively high proficiency, but is not equipped with ships anywhere as advanced as those of the Saudi and UAE navies. The key issue in the Gulf is not ship numbers, but ship quality, crew capability, and the ability to employ ships in meaningful missions in combat.

Saudi Navy Combat and Auxiliary Ship Strength

In 2002, the combat strength of the Saudi Navy included four Madina-class (F-2000) frigates, four Badr-class missile corvettes, and nine Al Siddiq-class guided missile ships. It also included three Dammam-class (German Jaguar) torpedo boats, twenty Naja 12 inshore fast craft, seventeen Halter-type coastal patrol craft (some in the Coast Guard), and three Al Jawf (British Sandown) and four Safwa (Addriyah)-class (ex-U.S. MSC-322 Bluebird) mine warfare ships.

There were four Afif-class LCU amphibious craft, four LCMs, two other amphibious craft, two 10,500-ton Boraida-class (French Durance) support ships, four smaller support vessels, fourteen tugboats, and large numbers of small patrol boats including forty Simmoneau Type 51 inshore patrol boats. Auxiliary ships included three Radhwa-class ocean-going tugs, three Radhwa-class coastal tugs, two Buraida-class replenishment oilers (French Durance-class), one Al Riyadh royal yacht, and the Al Azizah hydrofoil yacht tender. The royal yachts are based at Dammam.

Saudi Marine Corps Strength

The 3,000-man Saudi marine forces are organized into one regiment with two battalions. It initially was equipped with 140 BTR-60Ps.[5] It is now equipped with 140 Spanish Santa Barbara SBB BMR-600 6×6 amphibious APCs. It seems to have received nearly 100 Al Fahd 8×8 Armored personnel carriers during 2001.

Chart 6.1
Total Gulf Naval Manpower, 2002

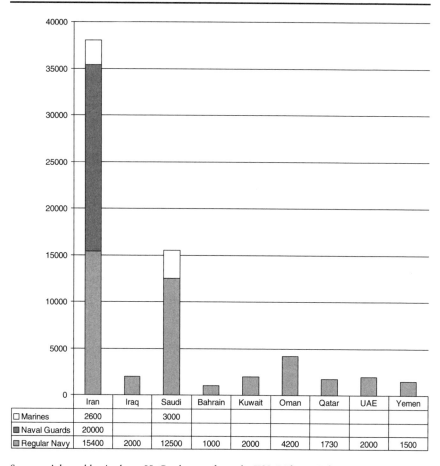

	Iran	Iraq	Saudi	Bahrain	Kuwait	Oman	Qatar	UAE	Yemen
☐ Marines	2600		3000						
▣ Naval Guards	20000								
▣ Regular Navy	15400	2000	12500	1000	2000	4200	1730	2000	1500

Sources: Adapted by Anthony H. Cordesman from the IISS, *Military Balance*; *Periscope*; JCSS, *The Middle East Military Balance*; *Jane's Fighting Ships, 2000–2001*; *Jane's Sentinel*; *Jane's Defence Weekly*; and material provided by U.S. experts.

The basic Al-Fahd can be armed with a cupola-mounted 12.7 mm machine gun, but other weapons systems are being considered, including anti-tank systems armed with the 106 mm recoilless rifle, the Delco 120 mm Armored Mortar system, and the Delco LAV-25/tube-launched optically tracked, wire-guided (TOW) turret system. The LAV-25/TOW turret is armed with a stabilized Boeing 25 mm M242 cannon and 7.62 mm coaxial machine gun. Mounted on either side is a launcher for a Raytheon TOW 3,750 m-range anti-tank guided missile. A total of six TOW missiles are carried.[6]

Chart 6.2
Gulf Naval Combat Ships by Category, 2002

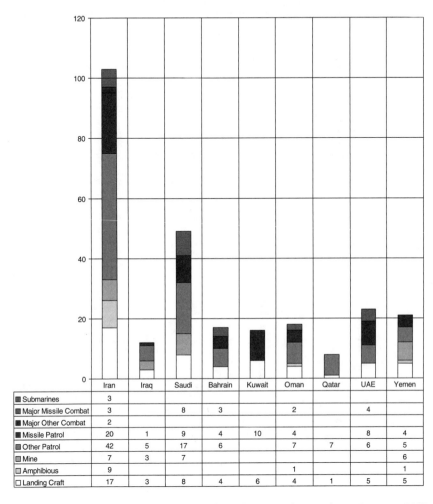

	Iran	Iraq	Saudi	Bahrain	Kuwait	Oman	Qatar	UAE	Yemen
■ Submarines	3								
■ Major Missile Combat	3		8	3		2		4	
■ Major Other Combat	2								
■ Missile Patrol	20	1	9	4	10	4		8	4
■ Other Patrol	42	5	17	6		7	7	6	5
□ Mine	7	3	7						6
□ Amphibious	9					1			1
□ Landing Craft	17	3	8	4	6	4	1	5	5

Sources: Adapted by Anthony H. Cordesman from the IISS, *Military Balance*; *Periscope*; JCSS,
The Middle East Military Balance; *Jane's Fighting Ships, 2000–2001*, *Jane's Sentinel*; *Jane's
Defence Weekly*; and material provided by U.S. experts.

Saudi Naval Aviation

Saudi naval aviation is based at Al Jubail. Various sources report different holdings for Saudi naval aviation. In 2002, it seems to have included
fifteen operational SA-565F Dauphin ASW and anti-ship missile helicopters with AS-15TT missiles, and four SA-565s equipped for the search and

Chart 6.3
Gulf Warships with Anti-Ship Missiles, 2002

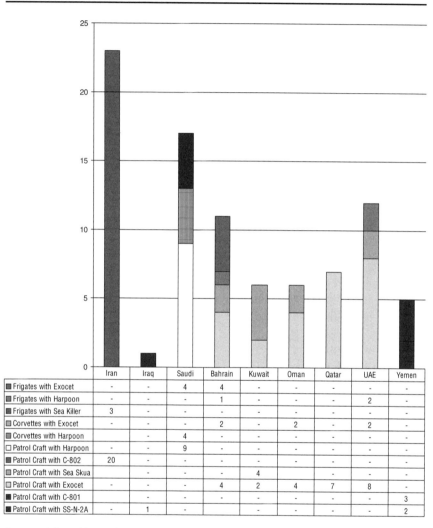

	Iran	Iraq	Saudi	Bahrain	Kuwait	Oman	Qatar	UAE	Yemen
■ Frigates with Exocet	-	-	4	4	-	-	-	-	-
■ Frigates with Harpoon	-	-	-	1	-	-	-	2	-
■ Frigates with Sea Killer	3	-	-	-	-	-	-	-	-
▨ Corvettes with Exocet	-	-	-	2	-	2	-	2	-
▨ Corvettes with Harpoon	-	-	4	-	-	-	-	-	-
▢ Patrol Craft with Harpoon	-	-	9	-	-	-	-	-	-
■ Patrol Craft with C-802	20	-	-	-	-	-	-	-	-
▨ Patrol Craft with Sea Skua	-	-	-	-	4	-	-	-	-
▢ Patrol Craft with Exocet	-	-	-	4	2	4	7	8	-
■ Patrol Craft with C-801	-	-	-	-	-	-	-	-	3
■ Patrol Craft with SS-N-2A	-	1	-	-	-	-	-	-	2

Sources: Adapted by Anthony H. Cordesman from the IISS, *Military Balance*; *Periscope*; JCSS,
The Middle East Military Balance; *Jane's Fighting Ships, 2000–2001*, *Jane's Sentinel*; *Jane's Defence Weekly*; and material provided by U.S. experts.

rescue mission. The SA-365Fs have only limited ASW capability, and are configured primarily for the surface search and attack roles. Each combat-equipped SA-365F carries four missiles and has an Agrion search/attack system. They have Crouzet MAD systems and can carry two Mark 46 torpedoes.

Chart 6.4
Gulf Mine Warfare Ships, 2002

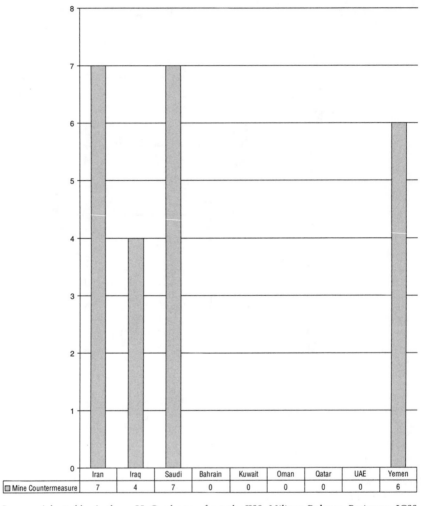

	Iran	Iraq	Saudi	Bahrain	Kuwait	Oman	Qatar	UAE	Yemen
☐ Mine Countermeasure	7	4	7	0	0	0	0	0	6

Sources: Adapted by Anthony H. Cordesman from the IISS, *Military Balance*; *Periscope*; JCSS, *The Middle East Military Balance*; *Jane's Fighting Ships, 2000–2001, Jane's Sentinel*; *Jane's Defence Weekly*; and material provided by U.S. experts.

The Saudi Navy also had three Westland Sea King Mark 47 ASW helicopters, and twelve to twenty-one land-based AS-332SC(B/F) Super Puma helicopters. Some reports indicate the AS-332s included twelve aircraft with Omera search radars, nine with Giat 20 mm cannons, and twelve with Exocet or Sea Eagle air-to-ship missiles. Other reports indicate the AS-332s included only six transport aircraft, plus another six with Exocet air-to-ship missiles.[7]

Chart 6.5
Gulf Amphibious Warfare Ships, 2002

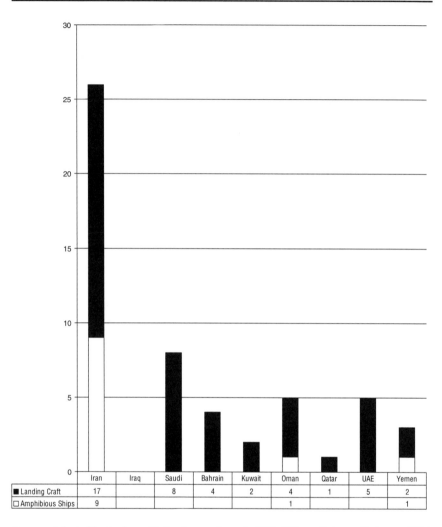

	Iran	Iraq	Saudi	Bahrain	Kuwait	Oman	Qatar	UAE	Yemen
■ Landing Craft	17		8	4	2	4	1	5	2
□ Amphibious Ships	9					1			1

Sources: Adapted by Anthony H. Cordesman from the IISS, *Military Balance*; *Periscope*; JCSS, *The Middle East Military Balance*; *Jane's Fighting Ships, 2000–2001*, *Jane's Sentinel*; *Jane's Defence Weekly*; and material provided by U.S. experts.

The Saudi Coast Guard

The Saudi Coast Guard contains up to 4,500 men and has its main base at Azizam. Its equipment includes two large Yarmouk-class patrol boats, two fast missile attack craft with AS-15TT missiles, four large Al-Jouf-class patrol boats, two large Al Jubatel-class patrol boats, twenty-five Skorpion-

Chart 6.6
Gulf Naval Aircraft and Helicopters Aircraft, 2002

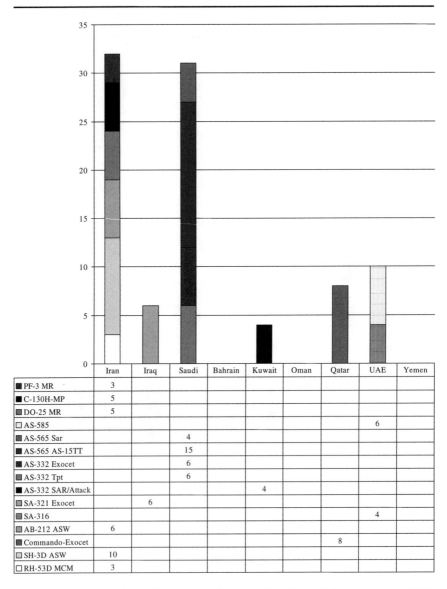

	Iran	Iraq	Saudi	Bahrain	Kuwait	Oman	Qatar	UAE	Yemen
■ PF-3 MR	3								
■ C-130H-MP	5								
■ DO-25 MR	5								
□ AS-585								6	
■ AS-565 Sar			4						
■ AS-565 AS-15TT			15						
■ AS-332 Exocet			6						
■ AS-332 Tpt			6						
■ AS-332 SAR/Attack					4				
■ SA-321 Exocet		6							
■ SA-316								4	
■ AB-212 ASW	6								
■ Commando-Exocet							8		
□ SH-3D ASW	10								
□ RH-53D MCM	3								

Sources: Adapted by Anthony H. Cordesman from the IISS, *Military Balance*; *Periscope*; JCSS, *The Middle East Military Balance*; *Jane's Fighting Ships, 2000–2001*, *Jane's Sentinel*; *Jane's Defence Weekly*; and material provided by U.S. experts.

class patrol boats, thirteen other coastal patrol boats and four SRN-6, Model 4 Hovercraft, sixteen Slingsby SAH 2200 Hovercraft, large numbers of inshore patrol craft, three royal yachts, three small tankers, firefighting craft, and three tugs. Its primary mission is anti-smuggling, but it does have an internal security mission as well.[8]

SAUDI NAVAL DEVELOPMENT

The Saudi Navy began its development by relying on U.S. support and equipment, but now relies on French equipment and support for its larger ships and U.S. support for its smaller weapons systems. The Saudi Navy is making progress in developing combat effectiveness, and exercises with U.S., British, and French forces as well as those of other GCC states. It has cadres of French and U.S. advisors, and coordinates closely with the U.S. Navy Central Command (NAVCENT), which is forward based in Bahrain.

Badr-Class Corvettes and MSC-322 Coastal Mine Sweepers

Major deliveries under the U.S. phase of the Saudi naval expansion effort have been completed for well over a decade.[9] The United States delivered a total of nine 478-ton Al Siddiq-class patrol-gunboat, guided missile (PGG) craft, each armed with two twin Harpoon missile launchers, one 76 mm gun, and light AA weapons. Although the Saudi Navy has lagged behind Saudi air and land forces in the Kingdom's military modernization program, it is now being accorded greater priority partly due to Iran's acquisition of Russian "Kilo"-class submarines.[10]

The United States also delivered four larger patrol-chaser missile (PCG) craft, or Badr-class ships, which the Saudis class as frigates but which most foreign sources class as corvettes.[11] The Badr-class vessels displace 1,038 tons fully loaded, and have two quad Harpoon missile launchers, one 76 mm gun, Vulcan and 20 mm guns, and six 324 mm torpedo tubes. They are being modernized in Saudi Arabia with U.S. assistance.

The Badr-class ships are all based at Jubail on Saudi Arabia's east coast, but they occasionally deploy to the Red Sea. Although the Saudi Navy claims to be a two-sea navy, its forces generally avoid the Indian Ocean and Gulf of Oman, and deploy to either the Gulf or Red Sea.[12]

The United States delivered four MSC-322-class coastal mine sweepers, two large harbor tugs, two utility landing craft, and four LCM-6, four LCU-1610, and four LCM landing craft. Other U.S. deliveries included Harpoon missiles, Mark 46 torpedoes, and ammunition for the Saudi Navy's 76 mm guns and other weapons. The Navy also took delivery of three Dammam-class torpedo boats from Germany, each with four 533 mm torpedo tubes each.

Sawari (Mast) I

Saudi Arabia turned to France as the major source of its naval ships and weapons in the early 1980s, partly because of dissatisfaction with the U.S. Navy advisory effort. Saudi Arabia also turned to France, however, both because of French political pressure and because it felt France could offer ships that were better equipped and better suited to its mission requirements, to provide France with a share of Saudi arms purchases, and to reduce Saudi reliance on the United States. The Saudi Navy did, however, continue to purchase U.S. naval sub-systems for use on its French ships and retained several support contracts with U.S. firms. It also turned to Britain for support in mine warfare and held extensive discussions with Germany regarding the possible purchase of submarines.

The Saudi Navy signed its first major contract with France in 1980 in an effort to accelerate its modernization, and obtain more advanced ships than it could purchase from the United States. The first modernization package was worth $3.4 billion, and Saudi Arabia then signed another contract that effectively made France its primary source of support and modernization for future orders. This follow-on French program, which began in 1982, was called Sawari (Mast) I. It had a minimum value of 14 billion French francs, or $1.9 billion, and may have escalated to $3.2 billion.

The Madina-Class Frigates

France delivered four missile-equipped Madina-class or Type F-2000S frigates by August 1986. These are 2,870-ton vessels when fully loaded. They have eight Otomat 2 missile launchers, eight Crotale surface-to-air missile launchers, one 100 mm gun, four twin Breda 35 mm guns, four 533 mm torpedo tubes, and one SA-365F helicopter.[13] France also delivered two modified Durance-class fuel supply/replenishment vessels (Boraida class), Otomat missiles for the frigates, twenty-four SA-365 Dauphin 2 helicopters (twenty missile-equipped and four SAR-equipped), AS-15 missiles for the helicopters, and additional training services. The Otomat is the longest-range anti-ship missile in Gulf service, with a range of 160 kilometers.[14]

These vessels are all based in Jeddah on Saudi Arabia's Red Sea coast, and so far have had limited operational value. The Saudi west fleet has only token combat readiness and conducts little meaningful exercise activity. Saudi crews trained in France to operate the vessels and helicopters, but the ships are only at sea for a few weeks a year, and at least one ship had a severe engine room fire that has evidently not been fully repaired. These ships will undergo a thirteen-month refit in France at a cost of $1.7 billion.[15] Ship wear and maintenance problems are still a serious problem with this class of Saudi vessels.[16]

The Sawari II Program

The Saudi Navy began to study plans for a Sawari II program in the early 1980s, which was initially estimated to cost $1.6 to $2.12 billion. Prince Sultan met with France's President François Mitterrand and Defense Minister Charles Hernu to discuss this program in May 1983. The program he discussed would have provided Saudi Arabia with at least two more 2,000-ton frigates and possibly 4,000-ton frigates as well. It included selling mine-sweeping helicopters and maritime patrol aircraft as the first step in the procurement of much larger forces, including lift and troop-carrying helicopters, surveillance and intelligence equipment, and special warfare equipment.

While Saudi Arabia ordered twelve Super Pumas and twelve more patrol boats from France in the 1980s, it did not place major additional orders until 1990. Saudi Arabia did not agree to the Sawari II program because of funding problems and because the Saudis experienced growing problems with their French ships that were more severe than those experienced with American vessels. These maintenance and support problems were so serious in the late 1980s that Saudi Arabia even approached the United States to provide support for the French vessels.

The situation slowly improved, however, and Saudi Arabia made a decision to keep France as its major naval supplier. The Saudi Navy signed a new support agreement with France in 1989. The Saudi Navy ordered six additional Super Pumas in 1989, and decided to raise its order for French patrol boats to twenty ships.

SAUDI NAVAL INFRASTRUCTURE AND C⁴I CAPABILITIES

The Saudi Navy C^{4}I system was still unable to support effective combat operations when the Gulf War began. As a result, the Saudi Navy purchased a $307 million upgrade of its C^{4}I system on September 27, 1990.[17] Since that time, Saudi Navy C^{4}I has been upgraded significantly, and it now has commercial data links to improve its interoperability. The Navy has Link 16 secure communications capability and its C^{4}I/BM links are fully compatible with those of the U.S. Navy. Its overall training proficiency and readiness is now capable of supporting a complex combat operation.

Saudi naval facilities are good and its bases are large and well equipped for a force the size of the Saudi Navy. The Jubail base is now the second largest naval base in the Gulf and stretches nearly eight miles along the coast. It already has its own desalinization facility, and is designed to be expandable up to 100% above its present capacity. The Navy is also slowly improving its exercise performance and has begun to conduct joint exercises with the British, Egyptian, and U.S. navies.[18]

The Saudi Navy is procuring an automated logistic system similar to the systems used by its other services, and extensive modern command and control facilities. The first major links in this C^{4}I system became operational, along with hardened command centers at Riyadh, Jubail, and Jeddah, by the end of 1985. The system was supposed to have automated data links to the E-3A by the late 1980s, and be able to transfer data to Saudi ships by secure digital link from the Saudi E-3As as they operated in ocean surveillance mode.

The Navy has purchased other U.S.-designed facilities, including a meteorology laboratory, a Harpoon missile and Mark 46 torpedo maintenance facility, an advanced technical training school, and a Royal Naval Academy. Maintenance, however, is poor to very poor and this problem is compounded by the fact that Saudi Arabia cannot hire foreign maintenance personnel to go to sea, as it can to work at air bases and army depots. The resulting lack of maintenance at sea places a strain on contractor facilities on shore, and leads to the relatively rapid degradation of Saudi naval readiness after ships have been at sea. This situation is not improving.

SAUDI NAVY FORCE EXPANSION PLANS

During the Gulf War, Saudi Arabia placed a tentative order for three F-3000 frigates—*Al Riyadh, Makkah* and *Al Dammal.* These orders were delayed, however, because Saudi Arabia gave priority to new orders for its air and land forces, and because of economic problems. The Saudi Navy only signed firm contracts for two new frigates on November 22, 1994, and did not order a third until May 20, 1997.[19]

Frigate Programs

The resulting program is called Project Mouette in France and Sawari II in Saudi Arabia. It seems to have a total cost of $2.5 billion (19 billion French francs). The first of the three F-3000s, *Al Riyadh,* was launched in August 2000 and is now at an advanced stage of fitting out. Sea trials seem to have begun in late 2001, with handover to the Royal Saudi Naval Forces scheduled for July 2002. *Al Riyadh* will subsequently sail to Toulon to undertake a nine-month program of operational trials under the supervision of NAVFCO, the French Navy's training facilitation organization. *Makkah* was due for launch in late July 2001 and for handover in April 2003. Early steelwork fabrication is underway for the third and final ship, *Al Dammal,* due for delivery in January 2004.[20]

The first two ships will displace 3,700 tons fully loaded, and their design is based on the French La Fayette class of "stealth" frigates, with enhanced air defense capabilities. They have special radar cross-section shaping, IR paint, and reduced heat emission from their funnels. Their magnetic structure has been reduced through degaussing, and their acoustic signature has been reduced with the use of special machines, cradles, and propellers. They are 128 meters long and 16.2 meters wide. They have a crew of 139, with the ability to house a detachment of 25 additional personnel as marines or Special Forces. They have a range of 12,600 kilometers at fifteen knots, and a top speed of twenty-five knots. They are stabilized to allow helicopter operations up to sea state five or six. They have enhanced survivability and damage control capabilities.[21]

The first two frigates will initially carry the Thomson-CSF AirSys Crotale Navale NG surface-to-air missile used in the F-2000S, but are expected to be upgraded to use the vertical launched Aster missile. They will carry eight Exocet missiles, a 100 mm gun, two 20 mm guns, four 324 mm torpedo launchers, and one SA-365F helicopter. The frigates will have decoy launchers, a COMINT suite, and a Thomson-CSF DR 3000 ESM suite and their combat electronics will be much more advanced than those in the F-2000S class. Other features include dual tactical computers, a highly automated combat information center, DRBV-26D long-range surveillance radar, and the DRBV-15C Sea Tiger Mark 2 E/F band two-dimensional surveillance radar. The two frigates will also have special Link 11 and over-the-horizon data link equipment to work with the E-3As in the RSAF, Saudi fighters and strike aircraft, and the Navy's helicopters.[22]

The third ship will come with thirty-two Aster 15 anti-aircraft missiles and the Arabel radar. This same system will be retrofitted to the first two ships by 2005. The third frigate will also be equipped with the Exocet MM-40 Block 2 missile. It will have a more advanced V-26 radar, and will be 500 tons heavier and 10 meters longer than the first two frigates It is not clear what sonar capability they will have, as they were originally ordered without sonar. This makes their capabilities against Iran's submarines somewhat problematic.[23]

Project Mouette and the Overhaul and Modernization of F-2000S-Class Ships

Project Mouette includes the overhaul and modernization of the four F-2000S-class ships, and the two replenishment tankers (LRTs) the Saudi Navy ordered from France in the 1980s. One frigate, the *Madina*, has already been returned to the Navy after a year of refitting and overhaul in Toulon. The last frigate was completed in March 1999.

The modernization involves the improvement of the sonar, the replacement of the MacTaggeart Scott helicopter handling system with the Samahe system, improvements in maintenance and repair subsystems, and improved NBC contamination detection and protection. The NBC enhancement will include an airtight gas citadel and high-performance detection sensors. Missile upgrades primarily concern the OTO Breda/Matra Otomat anti-ship weapon system, which is being given additional capabilities both inside the missiles and in the ship-based control system, including enhanced search patterns to reattack missed targets. The VT1 round for the Crotale will not be provided, but improvements to the Castor 2B X-band radar will bring it up to the 2C standard.[24] France will also provide greatly improved maintenance and overhaul facilities in Jeddah and training for 750 personnel to crew the ships.[25]

Other Modernization and Expansion Options

Saudi Arabia has examined more ambitious programs. These include a SNEP II program that would spend roughly $10 billion to expand and modernize the Saudi Navy over the next ten years. The options also include a $23 billion program to expand its marine and naval special forces during the next ten years—although it seems doubtful that such a program can be implemented.

There are reports that Saudi Arabia has considered the purchase of several AEGIS-class warships to give it advanced battle management, Harpoon anti-ship missiles, Tomahawk strike capability, ASW, anti-aircraft, and anti-ship missile defense capabilities. The AEGIS-class ships are highly effective, but they cost roughly $900 million to $1 billion each, and require highly trained crews. As a result, it would be at least 2003–2005 before such a ship could be delivered. Saudi Arabia would also confront problems in obtaining release of some of the weapons and technologies involved.[26]

While Saudi Arabia may acquire more advanced large-surface ships in the future, such an acquisition is a low priority and is likely to be a waste of Saudi funds. It is extremely doubtful that the Saudi Navy can absorb its existing orders of French frigates effectively until 2005–2010. In the interim, the U.S. Navy and Royal Navy have ample capability to provide such support to Saudi Arabia. Investing similar amounts of money in added air and land capabilities would give Saudi Arabia far more contingency capability.

Mine Warfare Programs

In contrast, the Saudi Navy badly needs to expand its mine warfare capabilities. It now has a total of seven mine warfare ships. However, these include four obsolescent U.S. MSC-322 mine vessels of the Addriyah class that began to phase out in 1997. Its only modern mine warfare vessels are three Al-Jawf-class ships.

The Kingdom began to modernize its mine warfare capability in July 1988, when it agreed to lease two Hunt-class mine vessels from Britain. It did so in response to Iran's successful mining of the Gulf tanker routes during the "tanker war" of 1987–1988. It followed up by placing a tentative order for six to eight Vosper Sandown-class MCMVs, training by the

Royal Navy, and new port facilities for mine warfare vessels from Ballast Nedam, as part of its $18 billion al-Yamamah 2 program.

The Saudi Navy, however, only signed firm contracts for three Sandown-type vessels, which became what the Saudi Navy calls the Al-Jawf class. These vessels are 500-ton ships built by Vosper-Thorneycroft. They have a crew of thirty-four, a range of 3,000 miles, and a speed of twelve knots with diesel engines and six knots using electric engines for minesweeping. They have many advanced features, including vectored thrust with bow thrusters, a remote controlled mine disposal system, a computerized ship positioning system that is accurate to one meter, and a Plessey-Marconi variable depth sonar. It has Saudi enhancements including twin 30 mm Emerson Electric guns and a Contraves fire control system, larger engines, and upgraded Voith-Schneider propulsions.[27]

According to press reports, the Saudi Navy has options to buy three to four more Al-Jawf-class vessels, although it has not yet exercised this option and may be considering purchase of French-built Tripartite mine hunters.[28] Kuwait, Bahrain, Oman, Qatar, and the UAE are also reported to be examining orders of the Sandown or Tripartite mine warfare vessels.[29]

Saudi Arabia is rapidly improving its capability to conduct mine warfare operations, and exercises regularly with the U.S. Navy, which means it could make up a critical gap in U.S. forward-deployed capabilities and perform an important mission. It would take a force of at least fifteen to twenty modern mine warfare vessels in the GCC as a whole, however, to provide security for the main tanker routes used by the Southern Gulf states. While Saudi Arabia is making progress, and the Southern Gulf states are improving their exercise capabilities in mine warfare, the lack of adequate force numbers and combat capability is a major potential vulnerability.

Deferring Coastal Submarines

Saudi Arabia has deferred plans to buy coastal submarines. The Kingdom sought to buy six to eight submarines during the 1980s, and discussed programs costing $4 billion to $6 billion—including one submarine base for each fleet. Saudi Navy representatives visited several European manufacturers in 1986 and 1987, including the builders of the Walrus-class boats in the Netherlands, Vickers Type-2400 in the UK, and ILK 209/2000 and Kockums 471 in West Germany.

This deferral was a wise decision. Iran's deployment of Kilo submarines has increased the submarine threat, but coastal submarines are not ideal hunter-killers, and it is unclear how the Saudis could make cost-effective use of them as a strike force in either the Gulf or Red Sea. Any Saudi purchase of submarines would result in a gratuitous waste of money. Saudi Arabia cannot lack the manpower and maintenance resources to operate submarines. The Gulf and Red Sea are poor operating areas for such vessels,

Saudi Arabia could not use such submarines to fight Iranian submarines effectively, and the high salinity of the Gulf could present problems in terms of long-term operating life.

Deferring Maritime Patrol Aircraft

Saudi Arabia also seems to have deferred an order for two AND-BA Atlantique 2 (ANG) maritime patrol aircraft, and the order of two more Atlantique 2, Fokker F-27 Maritime Enforcers, or Lockheed P-3 Orions as part of a GCC maritime surveillance force. The AND-BA Atlantique 2 (ANG) maritime patrol aircraft proved to be too expensive. The aircraft supplemented the existing maritime surveillance coverage provided by Saudi E-3As and were intended to cover the rest of the Southern Gulf. A Saudi purchase for this mission depended on GCC cooperation, and partial funding of the aircraft. Neither was forthcoming.[30]

Maritime patrol aircraft take a higher priority than submarines, but Saudi Arabia again seems to have made sound decisions. The Kingdom has a valid need for both modern mine warfare and maritime patrol aircraft (MPA), but its E-3A AWACS aircraft have advanced maritime patrol capabilities and Saudi Arabia cannot yet make effective use of its AWACS. It still has the option of substituting its E-3As for maritime patrol aircraft. Unfortunately, the Saudi E-3As will only acquire Link 16 secure data links to the Saudi Navy in the future, and are not really trained for this kind of joint warfare. Ironically, the U.S. E-3As have Link 16 capability and are trained for such a mission. As a result, the USAF can support the Saudi Navy better than the Saudi Air Force.

If the Saudi Air Force develops adequate joint warfare capabilities to support the Saudi Navy, it can provide the necessary maritime patrol coverage, although the defense of the Gulf as a whole would require the UAE or Oman to provide such capabilities in the lower Gulf, and the Saudi E-3As would have problems in covering the entire Red Sea area.

SAUDI NAVAL READINESS AND WAR-FIGHTING CAPABILITIES

The Saudi Navy has enough equipment on hand, and on order, to evolve into a relatively powerful force by regional standards, and U.S. experts feel it is making some progress in becoming an effective force. Its readiness has been helped by intensified training efforts during Operation Earnest Will (1987–1989) and the Gulf War. However, funding has been limited since the mid-1990s. Its overall readiness has dropped and many ships rarely go to sea. Its current equipment mix requires a force of close to 18,000 to 20,000 men, and the Navy is badly undermanned.

The Saudi west or Red Sea fleet has only token military capability. The Eastern Gulf fleet is better and has exercised regularly with the Navy, but is not ready to operate effectively on its own. In spite of these problems, Saudi naval training standards have slowly improved since the early 1990s, as have operating rates and active training and exercise days. The Saudi Navy is working closely with the United States' 5th Fleet and held eleven exercises in 1999, including joint mine warfare task forces. The performance of those ships that participate actively in such exercises received considerable praise from U.S. officers. The Navy remains dependent on foreign maintenance and logistic support, however, and is having problems operating its new French frigates—partly because they are so packed with weapons systems and electronics that they are difficult to fight.

The main threats to Saudi Arabia, as well as the other Arabian Gulf states, are from Iran and Iraq. From a maritime standpoint, there is little threat from Iraq, whose navy was largely destroyed in 1991. Iran, on the other hand, built up some aspects of its naval forces as part of its overall rearmament program. It has taken delivery of two Russian 877EMK Kilo-class diesel-electric submarines since 1993, and a third is expected.

Although the Gulf is too shallow for large-scale underwater warfare, these vessels can fire wake-homing or wire-guided acoustic torpedoes as well as lay mines in strategic shipping lanes, seriously impeding the flow of crude oil and liquefied natural gas exports.[31] Iran has also received ten Hudong-class FACMs from China, and these vessels, along with the older Kaman-class vessels, are being armed with Chinese C-802 anti-ship cruise missiles.

Saudi Arabia scarcely has to meet these threats alone, however, and it is making enough progress that U.S. and British experts feel the Navy can now play at least a limited role in any future naval coalition warfare that does not involve joint warfare with air forces in spite of its manpower and readiness funding problems. The Navy has also taken some steps to bring force expansion back into better balance with readiness. As of June 1999, Saudi Arabia had already earmarked funds for the purchase of three French La Fayette–class frigates, but had shelved its plans to continue its naval expansion due to the decrease in funding.[32]

The key to Saudi success will be to emphasize war-fighting readiness over expansion and modernization, and to keep the Navy's strategic focus on the missions it really needs to perform. It needs to emphasize maritime surveillance, defend offshore facilities and coastal installations, deal with unconventional threats like the naval branch of Iran's Revolutionary Guards and threats to maritime traffic like mine warfare. Seen from this light, putting so substantial a part of its limited resources into frigates that attempt to duplicate the capabilities of large U.S. and British surface ships becomes a low priority. So do efforts to buy submarines, advanced anti-submarine warfare capabilities, and even larger surface ships that do not suit either Saudi Arabia's overall defense needs or the current capabilities of its Navy.

The Saudi Navy can scarcely be expected to compensate for the problems created by the dismal standards of the other Southern Gulf navies (except Oman), but these may not be mission-critical. The Navy should be able to depend heavily on air support and on reinforcement by USCENTCOM and the British, French, and/or U.S. navies.

NOTES

1. Unless otherwise specified, the military data quoted here are taken from the relevant country sections of various annual editions of the IISS, *Military Balance*; CIA, *The World Factbook*; JCSS, *The Middle East Military Balance*; online editions of *Jane's Sentinel series* and *Periscope*, *Jane's Intelligence Review*, and *Jane's Defence Weekly*. The cut-off date for such material is January 2002.

Other sources include interviews with Saudi officials and military inside and outside of Saudi Arabia, U.S. experts, and British experts. These are not identified by source by request of those interviewed. They also include the author's publications and other sources mentioned at the start of the section on Saudi Arabia; and Dr. Andrew Rathmell, "Saudi Arabia's Military Build-up—An Extravagant Error," *Jane's Intelligence Review* (November 1994), pp. 500–504; various editions of *Jane's Sentinel: The Gulf States*; *Jane's Fighting Ships*; *The Naval Institute Guide to the Combat Fleets of the World: Their Ships, Aircraft, and Armament* (Annapolis: U.S. Naval Institute); and online editions of *Periscope*, "Saudi Arabia, Navy/Marines."

2. Based on *Jane's Fighting Ships, 1996–1997, 1999–2000,* and *2000–2001*; IISS, *Military Balance, 1996–1997, 1999–2000,* and *2001–2002*. Some estimates put its total active strength at 13,500 to 17,000 men.

3. Historical sources for the analysis of the Saudi Navy include James Bruce and Paul Bear, "Latest Arab Force Levels Operating in the Gulf," *Jane's Defence Weekly*, December 12, 1987, pp. 1360–1361; and various editions of the "Middle Eastern, North African, and South Asian Navies," sections of the March issue of *Proceedings*.

4. *Jane's Defence Weekly*, May 15, 1996, p. 3.

5. Based on *Jane's Fighting Ships, 1996–1997, 1999–2000,* and *2000–2001*; IISS, *Military Balance, 1996–1997, 1999–2000,* and *2001–2002*.

6. *Jane's Defence Weekly*, April 7, 1999, p. 21.

7. Based on *Jane's Fighting Ships, 1996–1997, 1999–2000,* and *2000–2001*; IISS, *Military Balance, 1996–1997, 1999–2000,* and *2001–2002*.

8. Ibid.

9. These include twenty AS-365N Dauphin helicopters with AS-15TT air-to-surface missiles, and four search-and-rescue versions of the same helicopter.

10. *Jane's Defence Weekly*, July 10, 1998, p. 33.

11. They are Tacoma-class ASUWs, with 2×4 Harpoon launchers, and 2×3 ASTT (Mark 46 lightweight torpedo launchers).

12. Based on *Jane's Fighting Ships, 1996–1997, 1999–2000,* and *2000–2001;* IISS, *Military Balance, 1996–1997, 1999–2000,* and *2001–2002.*

13. These are French F-2000 class vessels with four X 533 mm and two X 406 mm ASTT torpedo launchers, one Dauphin helicopter, one 100 mm gun, and eight Otomat 2 missile launchers.

14. Based on *Jane's Fighting Ships, 1996–1997, 1999–2000,* and *2000–2001;* IISS, *Military Balance, 1996–1997, 1999–2000,* and *2001–2002.*

15. *Jane's Defence Weekly,* July 10, 1996, p. 33.

16. Based on *Jane's Fighting Ships, 1996–1997, 1999–2000,* and *2000–2001;* IISS, *Military Balance, 1996–1997, 1999–2000,* and *2001–2002.*

17. Richard F. Grimmett, *Arms Sales to Saudi Arabia* (Washington: Congressional Research Service, IB91007, August 28, 1991), p. 4.

18. Executive News Service, July 25, 1995, No. 1749.

19. The new contract had a total value of $3.6 billion; 35% to be offset. *Jane's Defence Weekly,* October 8, 1994, p. 1, November 22, 1993, p. 18, December 3, 1994, p. 4, June 26, 1996, p. 26, March 12, 1997, pp. 78–80; *Jane's Intelligence Review,* November, 1996, p. 515, May 28, 1997, p. 4; *Defense News,* February 7, 1994, p. 36; *Financial Times,* January 10, 1994, p. 4; *Middle East Economic Digest,* September 15, 1995, pp. 13–14; Reuters, May 20, 1997, 1611.

20. *Jane's International Defence Review,* June 2001, p. 8.

21. *Jane's Defence Weekly,* December 17, 1988, p. 1546, June 25, 1989, p. 1296, October 8, 1994, p. 1, November 22, 1993, p. 18, December 3, 1994, p. 4, June 26, 1996, p. 26, March 12, 1997, pp. 78–80; *Jane's Intelligence Review,* November 1996, p. 515; *Defense News,* February 7, 1994, p. 36; *Financial Times,* June 13, 1989, p. B-5; *Wall Street Journal,* June 7, 1988, p. 31; *International Defense Review,* 7 (1989), p. 884.

22. Ibid.

23. Reuters, May 20, 1997, 1611; *Jane's Defence Weekly,* June 26, 1996, p. 26, March 12, 1997, pp. 78–80, May 28, 1997, p. 4; *International Defense Review,* 7 (1997), p. 9.

24. *Jane's Defence Weekly,* June 26, 1996, p. 26, March 12, 1997, pp. 78–80; *Jane's Intelligence Review,* November 1996, p. 515

25. *Jane's Defence Weekly,* October 8, 1994, p. 1, November 22, 1993, p. 18, December 3, 1994, p. 4, June 26, 1996, p. 26, March 12, 1997, pp. 78–80; *Jane's Intelligence Review,* November 1996, p. 515; *Defense News,* February 7, 1994, p. 36; *Financial Times,* January 10, 1994, p. 4; *Middle East Economic Digest,* September 15, 1995, pp. 13–14.

26. *Washington Times,* May 27, 1995, p. A-11.

27. The Sandown-class ships have glass-reinforced plastic hulls, Type 2903 Variable Depth Sonar, remote-control mine disposal systems, and Plessey NAUTIS-M command, control, and navigation systems. *Defense News,* March 20, 1989, p. 24, April 24, 1989, p. 28; *Jane's Defence Weekly,* October 26, 1991, p. 770, and February 20, 1993, p. 15; *Jane's Intelligence Review,* November 1996, p. 515.

28. *Jane's Defence Weekly,* July 10, 1996, p. 33; *Military Technology, World Defense Almanac, 1992–1993,* vol. XVII, no.1 (1993), pp. 157–159; *Jane's Intelligence Review,* November 1996, p. 515.

29. *Jane's Defence Weekly*, July 16, 1987, p. 58.

30. *Jane's Defence Weekly*, December 12, 1987, pp. 1360–1361.

31. *Jane's Intelligence Review*, November 1996, p. 514; *Defense News*, June 7, 1999, p. 10.

32. *Defense News*, June 7, 1999, p. 8.

Chapter 7

The Saudi Air Force

S audi Arabia has given the modernization and expansion of the Royal Saudi Air Force (RSAF) a higher priority than that of the Army, Navy, and Air Defense Force. This reflects the fact that the RSAF is the only service that can cover Saudi Arabia's 2.3 million square kilometers of territory. It represents the investment most capable of cross-reinforcement with the other services. It also has had the most impact in terms of regional prestige, and the most credibility in terms of being able to support other GCC states or to operate with USCENTCOM forces in a major crisis, although its quality and real-world strength have declined significantly since the mid-1990s.[1]

The Saudi Air Force is headquartered at Riyadh. Like the Army and Navy, it has a modern headquarters staff with five major branches—G1 Personnel, G2 Intelligence and Security, G3 Operations and Training, G4 Logistics, and G5 Civil and Military Affairs. The RSAF also has a military academy and an extensive system of training schools and support facilities. Its operational command is structured around its air command and operations center and base operations. The main air command and operations center is near Riyadh, and there are sector operating centers at Tabuk, Khamis Mushayt, Riyadh, Dhahran, and Al-Kharj. These centers control air defense operations by fighter aircraft, surface-to-air missiles, and air defense artillery.[2]

The RSAF has shifted from a command structure whose chain of command went from Air Force command to air base command to squadron, to a chain of command going from Air Force command to sector command to base command to wing or group command to squadron. This new command structure is designed to give certain sectors more freedom and flexibility at the local command level.

It has operational command facilities at its air bases in Riyadh (King Faisal Air Academy), Dhahran (King Abdul Aziz), Tabuk, Jeddah, and Khamis Mushayt. There are additional major air bases at Al Jawf, Hafr al Batin, and Taif (King Fahd). There are major Air Defense Force facilities at Al-Kharj, Dhahran, and Khamis Mushayt. Most of Saudi Arabia's fighters and strike aircraft are based at Dhahran, Taif, and Khamis Mushayt. In the past, the RSAF has limited its deployments in Tabuk to minimize vulnerability to Israeli attacks.

THE CURRENT SIZE AND CAPABILITY OF THE SAUDI AIR FORCE

The growth of the Saudi Air Force is summarized in Chart 7.1. While the buildup of the Saudi Air Force's combat strength shown in the chart sometimes seems erratic, until recently the peaks generally represent periods where major new deliveries of combat aircraft took place while the older aircraft were still kept in service. Other peaks represent periods when lower quality and older aircraft were converted to trainers. In general, the modernization and expansion of the Saudi Air Force proceeded relatively smoothly from the time it began to replace its Lightning fighters up to the mid-1990s. Unfortunately, the decline in the late 1990s does reflect a serious drop in force numbers that has been accompanied by a similar drop in warfighting capability.

The IISS estimates that the RSAF had about 20,000 men in 2002, not including another 16,000 men in the Air Defense Force. USCENTCOM estimates the Air Force's strength at a total of 16,500 men. According to one source, the RSAF's combat forces were organized into six wings with a total of fifteen combat squadrons and about 259 operational first-line, fixed-wing combat aircraft, and thirty-nine combat-capable trainers. The IISS estimated that Saudi Arabia had a total inventory of about 432 combat aircraft with about 348 active combat aircraft. The Saudi Army operates an additional force of twelve AH-64 attack helicopters, and the Navy has twenty-one more armed helicopters. These armed naval helicopters include nineteen AS-56 helicopters, of which four are equipped for the search and rescue mission and fifteen have AS-15TT anti-ship missiles, six AS-332B transports, and six AS-332Bs equipped with Exocet anti-ship missiles.[3]

Chart 7.2 shows how the size of the Saudi Air Force manpower compares with that of other Gulf states. Chart 7.3 provides similar data for comparative total fixed- and rotary-wing combat aircraft strength. Chart 7.4 compares relative holdings of advanced types of combat aircraft, and Chart 7.5 compares holdings of low-quality combat aircraft. Chart 7.6 com-

Chart 7.1
Saudi Fixed-Wing and Rotary-Wing Combat Air Strength, 1979–2002

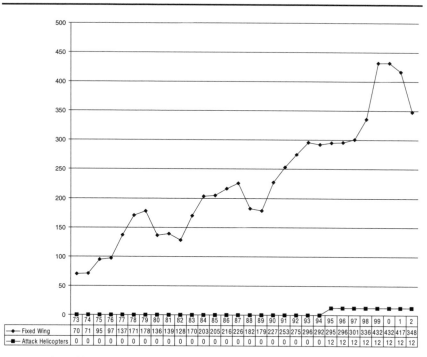

	73	74	75	76	77	78	79	80	81	82	83	84	85	86	87	88	89	90	91	92	93	94	95	96	97	98	99	0	1	2
Fixed Wing	70	71	95	97	137	171	178	136	139	128	170	203	205	216	226	182	179	227	253	275	296	292	295	296	301	336	432	432	417	348
Attack Helicopters	0	0	0	0	0	0	0	0	0	0	0	0	0	0	0	0	0	0	0	0	0	0	12	12	12	12	12	12	12	12

Sources: Adapted by Anthony H. Cordesman from the IISS, *Military Balance*; *Periscope*; JCSS, *The Middle East Military Balance*; *Jane's Sentinel*; *Jane's Defence Weekly*; and material provided by U.S. experts. Does not include armed naval helicopters.

pares reconnaissance aircraft, Chart 7.7 compares sensor aircraft, and Chart 7.8 compares attack helicopter strength.

As these charts show, the Saudi Air Force has benefited from the fact that Iran has not had any major modernization since the fall of the Shah, other than for limited deliveries of MiG-29s and Su-24s, and Iraq has faced an arms embargo since the summer of 1990. As a result, the Iranian Air Force is worn and aging, and the Iraqi Air Force is now at least a decade old and has never had major weapons deliveries to allow it to react to the lessons of its massive defeat during the Gulf War.

This force strength and equipment mix have made the Saudi Air Force the most advanced air force in the Gulf in terms of modern aircraft and weapons. However, it still has major defects, which include:

- An overemphasis on air defense at the expense of offensive air capabilities, particularly capabilities designed to deal with advancing Iraqi armor or the naval threat from Iran.

Chart 7.2
Total Gulf Air Force and Air Defense Manpower, 2002

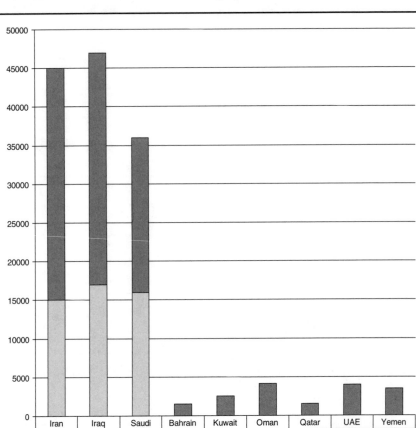

	Iran	Iraq	Saudi	Bahrain	Kuwait	Oman	Qatar	UAE	Yemen
■ Air	30000	30000	20000	1500	2500	4100	1500	4000	3500
□ Air Def	15000	17000	16000	-	-	-	-		

Sources: Adapted by Anthony H. Cordesman from the IISS, *Military Balance*; *Periscope*; JCSS, *The Middle East Military Balance*; *Jane's Sentinel*; *Jane's Defence Weekly*; and material provided by U.S. experts.

- A failure to develop effective joint warfare capabilities and realistic joint warfare training capabilities, and to transform joint warfare doctrine into effective war fighting plans to support the Army, National Guard, and Navy.

- A failure to develop a truly integrated air defense and war fighting capability with other Southern Gulf states.

- A failure to rapidly modernize the RSAF C⁴I/SR and battle management systems, develop high-capacity secure communications, and expand the role of sensor, electronic warfare, and intelligence aircraft to support offensive and joint warfare missions.

Chart 7.3
Total Gulf Holdings of Combat Aircraft, 2002

Fixed-Wing Combat Aircraft

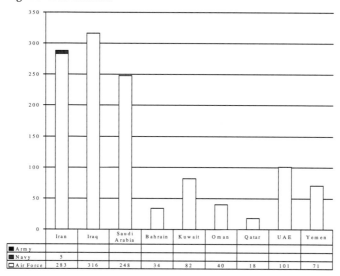

	Iran	Iraq	Saudi Arabia	Bahrain	Kuwait	Oman	Qatar	UAE	Yemen
■ Army									
■ Navy	5								
□ Air Force	283	316	248	34	82	40	18	101	71

Armed and Attack Helicopters

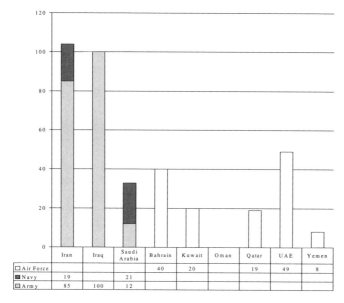

	Iran	Iraq	Saudi Arabia	Bahrain	Kuwait	Oman	Qatar	UAE	Yemen
□ Air Force				40	20		19	49	8
■ Navy	19		21						
□ Army	85	100	12						

Sources: Adapted by Anthony H. Cordesman from the IISS, *Military Balance*; *Periscope*; JCSS, *The Middle East Military Balance*; *Jane's Sentinel*; *Jane's Defence Weekly*; and material provided by U.S. experts.

Chart 7.4
Gulf High- and Medium-Quality Fixed-Wing Fighter, Fighter Attack, Attack, Strike, and Multi-Role Combat Aircraft by Type, 2002

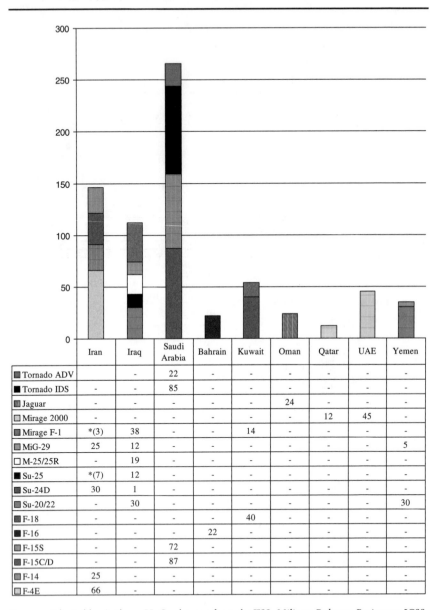

	Iran	Iraq	Saudi Arabia	Bahrain	Kuwait	Oman	Qatar	UAE	Yemen
Tornado ADV		-	22	-	-	-	-	-	-
Tornado IDS	-	-	85	-	-	-	-	-	-
Jaguar	-	-	-	-	-	24	-	-	-
Mirage 2000	-	-	-	-	-	-	12	45	-
Mirage F-1	*(3)	38	-	-	14	-	-	-	-
MiG-29	25	12	-	-	-	-	-	-	5
M-25/25R	-	19	-	-	-	-	-	-	-
Su-25	*(7)	12	-	-	-	-	-	-	-
Su-24D	30	1	-	-	-	-	-	-	-
Su-20/22	-	30	-	-	-	-	-	-	30
F-18	-	-	-	-	40	-	-	-	-
F-16	-	-	-	22	-	-	-	-	-
F-15S	-	-	72	-	-	-	-	-	-
F-15C/D	-	-	87	-	-	-	-	-	-
F-14	25	-	-	-	-	-	-	-	-
F-4E	66	-	-	-	-	-	-	-	-

Sources: Adapted by Anthony H. Cordesman from the IISS, *Military Balance*; *Periscope*; JCSS, *The Middle East Military Balance*; *Jane's Sentinel*; *Jane's Defence Weekly*; and material provided by U.S. experts.

Chart 7.5

Gulf Low-Quality Fixed-Wing Fighter, Fighter Attack, Attack, Strike, and Multi-Role Combat Aircraft by Type, 2002

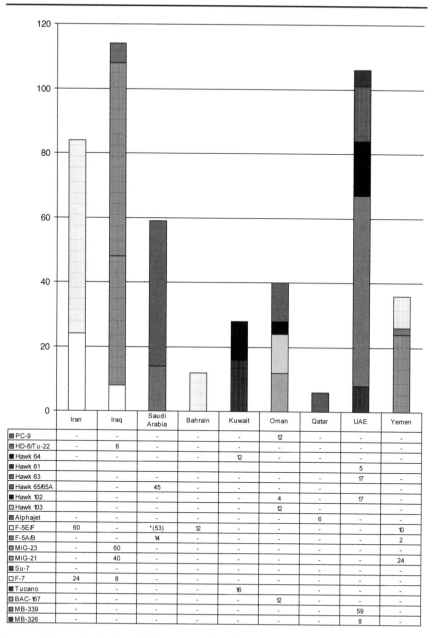

	Iran	Iraq	Saudi Arabia	Bahrain	Kuwait	Oman	Qatar	UAE	Yemen
■ PC-9	-	-	-	-	-	12	-	-	-
■ HD-6/Tu-22	-	6	-	-	-	-	-	-	-
■ Hawk 64	-	-	-	-	12	-	-	-	-
■ Hawk 61								5	
■ Hawk 63	-	-	-	-	-	-	17	-	
■ Hawk 65/65A	-	45	-	-	-	-	-	-	
■ Hawk 102	-	-	-	-	4	-	17	-	
□ Hawk 103	-	-	-	-	12	-	-	-	
■ Alphajet	-	-	-	-	-	6	-	-	
□ F-5E/F	60	-	*(53)	12	-	-	-	-	10
■ F-5A/B	-	-	14	-	-	-	-	-	2
■ MiG-23	-	60	-	-	-	-	-	-	-
■ MiG-21	-	40	-	-	-	-	-	-	24
■ Su-7	-	-	-	-	-	-	-	-	-
□ F-7	24	8	-	-	-	-	-	-	-
■ Tucano	-	-	-	-	16	-	-	-	-
■ BAC-167	-	-	-	-	-	12	-	-	-
■ MB-339	-	-	-	-	-	-	-	59	-
■ MB-326	-	-	-	-	-	-	-	8	-

Sources: Adapted by Anthony H. Cordesman from the IISS, *Military Balance*; *Periscope*; JCSS, *The Middle East Military Balance*; *Jane's Sentinel*; *Jane's Defence Weekly*; and material provided by U.S. experts.

Chart 7.6
Gulf Reconnaissance Aircraft, 2001

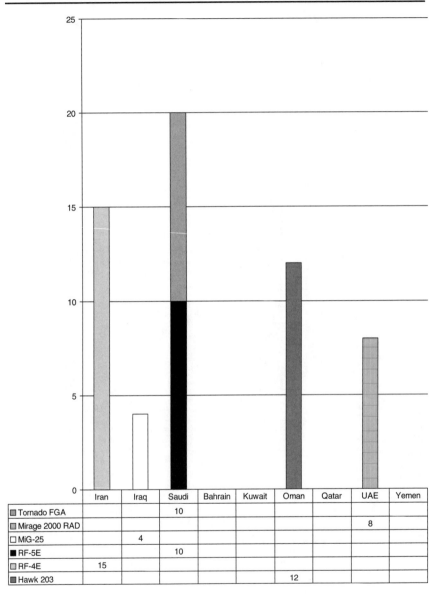

	Iran	Iraq	Saudi	Bahrain	Kuwait	Oman	Qatar	UAE	Yemen
▨ Tornado FGA			10						
▨ Mirage 2000 RAD								8	
☐ MiG-25		4							
■ RF-5E			10						
☐ RF-4E	15								
▨ Hawk 203						12			

Sources: Adapted by Anthony H. Cordesman from the IISS, *Military Balance*; *Periscope*; JCSS, *The Middle East Military Balance*; *Jane's Sentinel*; *Jane's Defence Weekly*; and material provided by U.S. experts.

Chart 7.7
Sensor, AWACS, C⁴I, EW, and Elint Aircraft, 2002

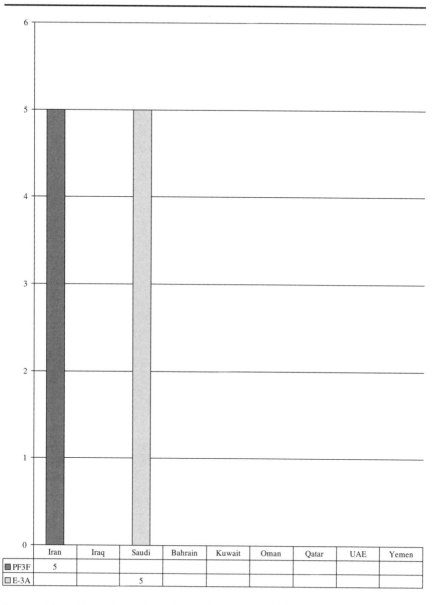

	Iran	Iraq	Saudi	Bahrain	Kuwait	Oman	Qatar	UAE	Yemen
■ PF3F	5								
□ E-3A			5						

Sources: Adapted by Anthony H. Cordesman from the IISS, *Military Balance*; *Periscope*; JCSS, *The Middle East Military Balance*; *Jane's Sentinel*; *Jane's Defence Weekly*; and material provided by U.S. experts.

Chart 7.8
Gulf Attack Helicopters, 2002

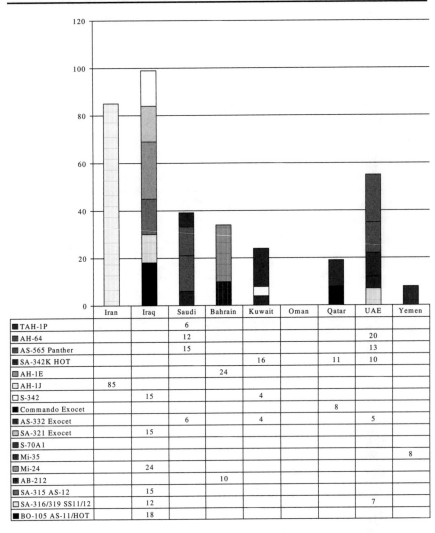

	Iran	Iraq	Saudi	Bahrain	Kuwait	Oman	Qatar	UAE	Yemen
■ TAH-1P			6						
■ AH-64			12					20	
■ AS-565 Panther			15					13	
■ SA-342K HOT					16		11	10	
□ AH-1E			24						
□ AH-1J	85								
□ S-342		15			4				
■ Commando Exocet							8		
■ AS-332 Exocet			6		4			5	
□ SA-321 Exocet		15							
■ S-70A1									
■ Mi-35									8
□ Mi-24		24							
■ AB-212				10					
■ SA-315 AS-12		15							
□ SA-316/319 SS11/12		12						7	
■ BO-105 AS-11/HOT		18							

Sources: Adapted by Anthony H. Cordesman from the IISS, *Military Balance*; *Periscope*; JCSS, *The Middle East Military Balance*; *Jane's Sentinel*; *Jane's Defence Weekly*; and material provided by U.S. experts.

- A lack of overall readiness and poor aircrew and maintenance-to-aircraft ratios, which has forced the near-grounding of its F5s and has severely reduced the effectiveness of its F-15s and Tornados. Since 1994, the poor leadership of the Air Force, the mishandling of overall training and readiness, underfunding, and poorly managed Saudisation have brought readiness to the point of near-crisis and led to a severe increase in the Air Force's accident rate.

- A failure to modernize training to support realistic offensive and joint warfare missions.
- A decline in leadership since the Gulf War, and particularly in focusing the modernization of the RSAF on key missions. Slow promotion and turnover and corruption in the highest ranks have compounded these problems.

Saudi Arabia's mix of aircraft also has its disadvantages as well as its strengths. In 2002, Saudi Arabia's total inventory of major combat aircraft included seventy-two F-15Ss, sixty-seven F-15Cs, twenty F-15Ds, eighty-five Tornado IDSs (ten Tornado GR.1 recce-attack equipped), twenty-two Tornado ADVs, and five E-3A AWACS. Until recently, the RASF also had fifty-six F-5Es, twenty-one F-5Fs, ten RF-5Es, and fourteen F-5Bs. By early 2001, however, most of the F-5s were grounded and in storage. Only fourteen F-5B still seem to be operational in a combat-capable training unit.[4]

The combat-strength RSAF aircraft included four fighter-attack squadrons—three with eighty-five Tornado IDS, and one with fourteen F-15B/F/ RFs. In theory, there were still three squadrons with fifty-three F-5Es, but virtually all of these aircraft were grounded. The IDS squadrons had dual-capable trainer aircraft, and ten had a dual-mission in the reconnaissance role. These squadrons were equipped with a wide range of attack munitions, including AS-15, AS-30, AGM-45 Shrike, and AGM-65 Maverick air-to-surface missiles and the Rockeye, Sea Eagle, and Alarm air-to-ground weapons. Saudi Arabia had MQM-74C Chukar II and Banshee remotely piloted vehicles for reconnaissance and target acquisition.

The Tornado squadrons provided much of the offensive strength of the Saudi Air Force, but were configured more for bombing against fixed targets than joint warfare or operations against armor. The Tornado does, however, have superior low altitude flight performance in attack missions to the F-15S. It was specifically designed to fly nap-of-the-earth missions, while the F-15S is subject to buffeting because of its large wing area. The Tornado also has superior air-to-surface missile armament; it can deliver the ALARM anti-radiation missile and Sea Eagle anti-ship missile. The Saudi F-15S is currently limited to the Maverick, which only has a strike range of around ten miles. Both aircraft can deliver laser-guided bombs and self-illuminate their targets.

The RSAF had nine interceptor squadrons for defensive missions. There were five squadrons with a total of eighty-seven F-15C/Ds (sixty-seven F-15C and twenty F-15Ds), and more squadrons with seventy-two F-15Ss. F-15Ds were deployed to each F-15 squadron to perform both training and operational missions. There was one Tornado ADV squadron with twenty-two aircraft, which also included dual-capable trainer aircraft. Saudi fighters were equipped with modern air-to-air missiles, including AIM-9L and AIM-9P infrared guided missiles and AIM-7F Sparrow and Skyflash radar-guided missiles. The RSAF is acquiring the AMRAAM air-to-air missile, which will give it substantial beyond visual range (BVR) all-weather air combat capability. Saudi F-15 fighter units are capable in the air defense role, but most aircrews now lack adequate advanced-fighter combat training. The Tornado ADS has not proven to be an effective fighter except in a stand-off missile defense role and is being shifted to other missions.

What the Tornado and F-15 squadrons have had in common since the mid-1990s is a lack of adequate pilot training and flight hours, which has led to numerous fatal accidents—all of which have been said to be the result of "pilot error." The truth lies in a combination of those problems and a lack of effective top-level leadership. While far too many Saudi pilots have been allowed to qualify who lacked the necessary skills and language abilities, readiness and training have been underfunded, and responsibility lies with the high command of the RSAF, rather than the pilots.

The RSAF has been the only Southern Gulf air force with meaningful numbers of reconnaissance aircraft. Until recently, the RSAF had two aging reconnaissance squadrons with a total of ten RF-5Es. These aircraft have reached obsolescence in terms of their sensors and survivability, however, and most are now deadlined or in storage. The ten Tornado IDS-Rs in the fighter–ground attack force could probably perform most missions. Saudi Arabia is acquiring reconnaissance and electronic warfare pods for its F-15s and has deployed some of this equipment.

Saudi Arabia had an airborne early-warning squadron with five E-3As early in 2002. These aircraft now have Saudi crews, but the crews have shown only limited capability to manage complex air battles, and the RSAF must rely on the USAF for help in such missions. The Saudi E-3As also lack adequate secure communications and data links, and need to upgrade their software and improve electronic support measures. The remaining multi-purpose squadron with fourteen F-5Bs has both a training and a combat mission, but has had little real operational capability. Most aircraft were "parked" and without real operational capability.

The RSAF also had twenty-five armed Hawk Mark 65 jet trainers, and twenty armed Hawk Mark 65A jet trainers. Saudi holdings of thirty-six BAC-167 turboprop COIN and training aircraft were phased out of service in the late 1990s. The Hawk units were technically capable of performing COIN and light attack functions with machine guns, cannons, and rockets, as well as training missions, but the combat mission training of the Hawk aircrews is limited; the RSAF does not plan to use them in that role. The RSAF also had thirteen Cessna 172s, one Jetstream, and fifty PC-9 aircraft in training units that were not armed for combat.

Some U.S. advisors have argued that the Hawks present problems as training aircraft because they cannot be used to train for supersonic flight or for the kind of demanding mission profiles needed for F-15 training. Others experts note, however, that the United States is the only country to use supersonic trainers (the T-38 Talon), and that such training is normally conducted in supersonic fighters. This includes flight training in the U.S.

Navy—which uses a derivative of the Hawk called the Goshawk—the RAF, and Israeli and Japanese Air Forces.

The combat mission training of the Hawk aircrews is limited and they are vulnerable to short-range air defenses (SHORADS), although they could be useful in securing rear areas. Some experts feel that the Hawk's inability to train aircrews for demanding air-to-air and air-to-combat missions has contributed so much to the problems in Saudi F-15 aircrew proficiency that the aircraft should be replaced, but it is far from clear what better trainer is available.

The RSAF is the only Gulf air force with an effective mid-air refueling capability. In 2002, its support units included a tanker squadron with eight KE-3A tanker/transports, and eight KC-130H tankers. It had three transport squadrons with thirty-eight C-130 cargo-transports (seven E, 29 Hs, and two H-30s), one KE-3B (EW), three L-100-30HS hospital aircraft, and four CN-235s. There were also two helicopter squadrons with twenty-two AB-205s, thirteen AB-206s, seventeen AB-212s, forty AB-41EPs (SAR) and ten AS-5323A2s (SAR). Their AS-532A2 Cougar search and rescue helicopters were ordered from France in September 1996, at a cost of $590 million.[5] The Royal Flight provided substantial additional airlift assets, including two B-747SPs, one B-737-200, four Bae 125-800s, two Gulfstream IIIs, two Learjet 35s, four VC-130Hs, and five utility helicopters.[6]

Saudi Arabia had moderate but aging inventories of air munitions and spares in 2002—a marked decline from the large inventories of cutting-edge munitions and high inventories it had at the time of the Gulf War. For example, the RSAF ordered 101 shipsets of F-15 conformal fuel tanks, 909 AIM-7F and AIM-9P/L air-to-air missiles, 100 Harpoon and 1,600 Maverick air-to-surface missiles, JP-233 and BL-755 bombs and munitions, before Iraq's invasion of Kuwait. It also ordered large numbers of additional Aim-9Ls and Aim-7Fs in August 1990, and 2,000 Mark 84 2,000-pound bombs, 2,100 CBU-87 cluster munitions, 770 AIM-7Fs, and components for laser-guided bombs in July 1991. The Kingdom did not continue to properly maintain and modernize its munitions inventory, however, and has not procured all of the air-to-ground and anti-ship ordnance it needs for joint warfare.[7]

Up until the mid-1990s, the Saudi Air Force had excellent foreign support. During the 1970s and early 1980s, Saudi Arabia was able to draw on USAF and contractor support to create some of the most modern air facilities in the world. These programs have been steadily renewed and expanded ever since; the current contract is worth $2.5 billion and runs from June 1997 through May 31, 2002. There have, however, been growing financing and payment problems since the mid-1990s, which grew worse after the oil crash of late 1997. Saudisation has not helped, nor has adequate use been made of the offset program. Foreign contractors have often been replaced with Saudis selected more for their contacts than their skills, and training programs for Saudis nave not enforced the proper qualification standards.

Facilities remain excellent, however. No U.S. or NATO base has sheltering or hardening equal to the Saudi bases at Dhahran and Khamis Mushayt, and similar facilities will be built at all of Saudi Arabia's main operating bases.

OPERATIONAL HISTORY AND FORCE DEVELOPMENT

The RSAF's history is more impressive than it's present condition. It first proved its effectiveness in Saudi Arabia's border wars with Yemen. In the late 1980s, it created effective air defenses to meet a threat from Iran during the Iran-Iraq War. It established the "Fahd Line," which created an Air Defense Identification Zone and forward air defense system off the Saudi coast. Saudi Arabia defended its air space and shot down an Iranian F-4 that tested Saudi defenses on June 5, 1984.

The Saudi Air Force was the most effective single element of Arab forces in the UN Coalition during the Gulf War. It flew a total of 6,852 sorties between January 17 and February 28, 1991—ranking second after the United States in total air activity and flying about 6% of all sorties flown. These sorties included 1,133 interdiction missions and 523 battlefield air interdiction missions, for a total of 1,656 offensive missions. The RSAF flew 2,050 defensive counter-air missions, 129 offensive counter-air missions, and 102 escort missions for a total of 2,281 air-defense sorties. It also flew 118 reconnaissance sorties, 85 E3-A AWACS sorties, 485 refueling sorties, and 1,829 airlift sorties.[8]

During the slightly longer period from January 16 to February 28, Saudi Air Force F-15C units flew 2,088 sorties (over one-third the total F-15C sorties flown by the USAF) and 451 Tornado ADV sorties. Saudi pilots were as capable in these air defense sorties as most pilots in NATO. The RSAF also flew 665 Tornado GR.1/IDS strike sorties, 1,129 F-5 sorties, and 118 RF-5 sorties. Saudi F-15Cs shot down three Iraqi Mirage F-1s with air-to-air missiles—including the only double kill by a single fighter in the war on January 24, 1991. The RSAF lost only two aircraft—one Tornado GR.1 because of a pilot error in reading the fuel gauge and making an emergency landing, and one F-5 to unknown causes.[9]

Shaping the Saudi Air Force: The "Peace Sun" Program

Much of the capability of the modern Saudi Air Force depends on its ability to make effective use of the F-15 and Tornado. The F-15C/D was the first of these purchases, and had extensive U.S. support. During the early 1980s, spare parts, equipment, and facilities for Saudi Arabia's original

F-15s were provided under an extensive, multi-stage program called "Peace Sun" (Royal Saudi Air Force Technical Support Program).[10] The second stage of Peace Sun (Peace Sun II) involved an $82.5 million contract for spare parts and support equipment for twelve F-15 craft, and this contract was increased by $20.1 million four months later.[11] Under Peace Sun IV, $10.1 million worth of spare components and retrofit kits were provided for modifications and upgrades to the F-15s.[12] Three F-15D and nine F-15C aircraft were purchased from McDonnell Douglas under Peace Sun VI.[13] Also purchased under this contract were two F100 engines for use on the F-15.[14] A follow-up to Peace Sun VI in 1996 included an upgrade of the F-15 software at a cost of $11.5 million.[15]

During the early 1990s, construction work was done at the three bases in the Kingdom where the F-15s are based: Taif, Khamis Mushayt, and Dhahran (Peace Sun IX).[16] Thirty mission support systems were also purchased under this stage for the seventy-two new F-15 aircraft then on order. These systems are capable of flight planning, route planning and threat penetration, weapons delivery and target area tactics, radar predications, mapping and imagery, post-flight analysis, and debriefing and intelligence connectivity.[17] Peace Sun X involved a contract for the LANTIRN terrain-following radar, forward-looking infrared, and laser designator from Martin Marietta.[18] In January 1999, Boeing was awarded a $79.1 million contract to provide for direct manning personnel from January through March 1999 to assist the Saudi Air Force in the operation and maintenance of the F-15.[19] This contract has been renewed regularly since that time, and its total value over time now approaches $1 billion.[20]

The Peace Sun program has been valuable in providing Saudi Arabia with both the F-15 aircraft it needs and the support and upgrade capability necessary to maintain them over the long term. However, the remaining stages of the Peace Sun program are facing the same funding difficulties as other Saudi military contracts. As of May 1999, the United States has considered not renewing the Peace Sun or Peace Shield programs due to Saudi Arabia's inability to make timely payments.[21] The program continues, but evidently at a significantly lower level of effectiveness.

The Saudi Tornado Buy and al-Yamamah Agreement

The RSAF has faced a broad range of additional problems in developing a modern offensive strike capability, and it is important to understand the history of this effort. The RSAF tried for nearly five years to buy more F-15s and acquire an advanced attack mission capability from the United States during the early 1980s. In July 1985, however, President Reagan sent King Fahd a letter stating that he could not obtain congressional approval for the sales Saudi Arabia sought. As a result, the Saudi Air Force initiated talks with Britain. These talks led to a Saudi-UK agreement in September

1985 for sixty Tornado ADV air defense fighters, sixty Tornado IDS/GR.1 attack strike-fighters, light attack aircraft, trainers, helicopters, munitions, and British support services.

That same month, Saudi Arabia signed a series of memorandums of understanding (MOUs) with Britain that gave Saudi Arabia the option of turning each MOU into an individual contract. These MOUs were called the al-Yamamah agreement. Saudi Arabia's first major contract under the MOUs cost $8 billion, but the total value grew to a total of $29 billion by 1992. This figure included training, support, construction, and naval vessels. It was worth roughly $4 billion a year to Britain by the early 1990s.

Saudi Arabia agreed to pay for al-Yamamah by bartering 600,000 barrels of oil per day. This gave the Kingdom a guaranteed market and allowed it to bypass some of the constraints imposed by OPEC quotas.[22] Revenue from the sale of oil has been channeled into a Saudi account at the Bank of England that the British Ministry of Defense uses for payments to contractors.[23] This arrangement created serious payment problems when oil prices were low, however, particularly during the oil crash that began in late 1997.

The first phase of the al-Yamamah program called for the purchase of twenty-four Tornado ADV air defense fighters, forty-eight Tornado IDS/GR.1 ground attack fighters, thirty BAe Hawk 65 trainers, thirty Pilatus PC-9 trainers, two Gulfstream aircraft, and air weaponry, ground support, and training services.

The Tornado ADV

The Tornado IDS/GR.1 proved to be a relatively successful strike aircraft, although it lacked a laser tracking system for the self-targeting of laser-guided bombs, advanced avionics for long-range attack missiles, and advanced electronic "stealth" features. In contrast, the Tornado ADV did not prove to be a successful air defense fighter for either the British Royal Air Force (RAF) or Saudi Arabia because it turned out to be underpowered. While its limited dogfight performance might not have been important in areas where long-range missile combat is critical, the short distances and reaction times affecting many potential threats to Saudi Arabia require dogfight superiority. Its radar warning receiver was not fully effective, and the Tornado's radar and air defense avionics experienced development and performance problems, as did efforts to fully integrate and qualify advanced air-to-air missiles with the aircraft.

Such "teething" problems are scarcely unusual in new aircraft, but they were severe enough in the case of the Tornado ADV to prompt the RAF to talk about converting its air defense Tornadoes to reconnaissance, strike, or electronic warfare missions, or to consider dropping them from service the moment it could obtain some form of Eurofighter. The RSAF's experience with the first eight Tornado ADVs was also negative. It converted some to reconnaissance, and converted the rest of its orders for ADVs to IDS strike-attack aircraft.

Orders for the Tornado Strike-Attack Fighter, Hawk, and Helicopters

At the same time, such problems did not prevent additional Saudi orders for British aircraft. In July 1988, Saudi Arabia signed a letter of intent for a second phase of al-Yamamah. According to Saudi sources, the second phase included forty-eight more Tornado strike-attack fighters, forty Hawk 100 and twenty Hawk 200 trainer-fighters, three to six Vosper Thorneycroft mine counter measure vessels, C[4]I systems, and additional weapons, spares, ground support, and training. Unlike the trainer version, the Hawk 200 has combat radars. It was also ordered with Sea Eagle antiship missiles. Munitions included the Skyflash, ALARM, Sea Eagle, and AIM-9L missiles, and JP-233 and BL-755 bombs.[24]

The new series of MOUs included the order for 80 Sikorsky Black Hawk helicopters for the Army discussed in Chapter 4. The RSAF had already ordered twelve Black Hawks through the United States, but these were transport versions of the aircraft and it was concerned that the U.S. Congress would not sell it armed or attack versions. Accordingly, it ordered the eighty-eight Black Hawks from Westland in Britain. According to some reports, it ordered them with TOW air-to-surface missiles.[25]

The total value of the memorandums of understanding that made up the second phase of al-Yamamah was approximately $18 billion. The deal included light transport aircraft (twelve BAe 125s and four BAe 146s) and two major military cities and air bases for the new Tornado forces, complete with British support.[26] The new British-built military cities and air bases were to be located at Taiba (about 290 kilometers southwest of Tabuk) and at al-Sulayyil (on the edge of the Empty Quarter). The air bases were to be equipped with at least twenty-five hardened multiple aircraft shelters. Saudi Arabia felt that its existing bases were adequate in the Eastern Province and near the PDRY, but were not suited for a force of nearly 400 combat aircraft. This brought the potential total value of the two phases of al-Yamamah to $60 billion, projected over a fifteen-year program.[27]

There were good reasons for the Saudi purchase of the first phase of the al-Yamamah package. Saudi Arabia's twelve BAC-167 trainers were only armed with 7.62 mm machine guns. They no longer could be used in anything other than light support functions. Saudi Arabia had bought its Lightning fighters from the UK under pressure from former Secretary of Defense Robert S. McNamara. The United States effectively forced Saudi Arabia to buy the Lightning as part of a then-covert three-cornered deal, in which the Lightning sale to Saudi Arabia was designed to allow the UK to buy the F-111 from the United States.[28] Even when first delivered, however, the Lightning never had the range, dual capability, and avionics Saudi Arabia needed. The investment in air bases was more questionable. While desirable, the cost was extremely high and Saudi Arabia soon found it faced serious funding constraints and that it had other priorities.

SAUDI MODERNIZATION AFTER THE GULF WAR

Saudi Arabia made significant new aircraft purchases as a result of the Gulf War. It purchased twenty-four additional F-15C/Ds from USAF stocks, eight C-130Hs, and two C-130H-30 aircraft and large numbers of Aim-9Ls and AIM-7Fs from the United States in late August 1990. It also bought the Falcon Eye electronic warfare aircraft, although it knew that this plane lacked the sophistication and capability of U.S. and Israeli ELINT aircraft.[29]

Saudi Arabia made these purchases because it felt it needed additional modern strike aircraft. Its F-5E-IIs and F-5Fs were relatively advanced models of the F-5E/F, equipped with INS, refueling probes, and the ability to fire Mavericks (the F-5F could also fire laser-guided bombs). The oldest of these F-5 aircraft, however, were nearing the end of their useful life, and the F-5 production line had long been closed. The F-5Es were not cost-effective to upgrade and required more than twice as much Saudi and foreign technical support manpower per plane as an F-15. The F-5E/Fs were also too short-ranged and limited in avionics and payload to cope adequately with the kind of advanced-threat aircraft being introduced into the region, or to deploy from one Saudi air base in support of another. As a result, the F-5Es were phased down into a training and light support role. Some 20% to 30% of Saudi Arabia's F-5 strength was already devoted to full-time training missions by 1990, and most aircraft gradually were deadlined during the 1990s.

The F-15C/D showed during the Gulf War that it could do an excellent job in air-to-air combat against the most advanced aircraft then in service in potential threat nations, and Iran and Iraq have not acquired more modern fighter types since that time. The Saudi F-15C/Ds, however, were configured as one-mission aircraft and could only be used for air combat. The USAF had recommended that the Saudi Air Force be given an advanced dual-capable fighter as early as 1977—when it conducted the original studies that led to the U.S. sale of the F-15—but the United States could not then obtain congressional permission to sell Saudi Arabia the bomb racks and attack systems necessary to make the F-15C/D effective in the air-to-ground role. As a result, a key part of Saudi Arabia's total first-line fighter strength was unable to perform effective attack missions, or provide attack support to Saudi land and naval forces.

The Search for Offensive Airpower and the F-15S Buy

The Gulf War showed the Saudi Air Force the importance of offensive air power, and demonstrated that it could use the Tornado in long-range strike missions. The RAF proved during Desert Storm that the Tornado could be an effective strike fighter, once it was equipped with new FLIR and laser designator pods. The Tornado delivered over 1,000 laser-guided bombs and ALARM missiles, and it was clear that it could help meet Saudi Arabia's need for a long-range deterrent to Iraq and Iran. However, the Tornado lacked the flexibility, maneuverability, and avionics to fly demanding missions using precision-guided munitions against advanced air defenses in the forward battle area, and did not meet all of Saudi Arabia's needs for a first-line strike aircraft.

Saudi Arabia reacted by buying seventy-two more F-15s in 1992. This purchase was possible because of the improvement in Saudi-Israeli relations and the strengthening of U.S. and Saudi ties during the Gulf War. The potential risk of the F-15S being used by an unfriendly regime in the event of some unforeseen coup is limited by the fact that Saudi Arabia accepted a reliance on U.S. technicians and technical support to keep the aircraft operating, knowing that this reliance would continue well beyond the year 2005. As Iran showed during the first weeks of the Iran-Iraq War, even a relatively sophisticated air force can lose much of its operational strength in a few days if it lacks sophisticated technical support. Iranian F-14s had even lost their ability to use the Phoenix missiles by the time the Iran-Iraq War started.[30]

These factors, and a U.S. commitment to provide Israel with enough technology superior to that of any potential Arab threat, allowed the Bush administration to move the sale forward. President Bush and Defense Secretary Cheney made such a commitment to provide advanced technology at the time they announced the sale of the F-15S, and Israel's new Labor government indicated that it did not pose the same objections to the sale as did the Likud. As a result, congressional leaders assured President Bush that they had the votes to ensure that Congress would not block the sale, and the president sent the proposed sale forward to Congress for approval on September 14, 1992.

Congress approved the sale on October 1, 1992, which removed the last obstacle to a sale that provided major strategic benefits for both the Royal Saudi Air Force and the United States. The Saudi order included seventy-two more F-15 aircraft, all of which were equipped with advanced avionics like LANTIRN, designated the F-15S, and dual-capable in both the air defense and strike/attack missions. The sale involved a total of $5 billion worth of aircraft and up to $4 billion worth of other arms and supplies—including $800 million worth of construction. It also included 24 spare engines, 48 targeting and navigation pods, 900 AGM-65D/G Maverick air-to-surface missiles, 600 CBU-87 bombs, 700 GBU-10/12 bombs, and special mission planning systems.[31]

The radars of all the F-15Ss were better than those on the F-15C/D, however, and had a resolution of 60 feet at twenty nautical miles versus resolution of 530 feet in the F-15C/D. They could use the same AIM-7F and AIM-7M radar-guided air-to-air missiles, used by existing Saudi F-15C/Ds, and the AIM-9S—the export version of the radar-guided AIM-9M air-to-air missiles. The F-15S also had the capability to be upgraded to use the advanced medium-range air-to-air missile (AMRAAM). In March 1999, the United States agreed to sell AMRAAM missiles to Saudi Arabia during a meeting with Saudi Defense Minister Prince Sultan. The missiles cost more than $380,000 each, but can be used to shoot enemy aircraft at ranges of over fifty miles.[32]

The F-15S variants of the F-15E Strike Eagle that were delivered to the Saudi Air Force were some of the world's most advanced combat aircraft, but differed from the USAF version of the F-15E in several ways. They used the AAQ-20 Path Finder navigation pods, the AAQ-20 Sharpshooter targeting pods, and a laser illuminator. The Path Finder pods have terrain-following radar, but have reduced ECCM capabilities that allow them to be tracked by U.S. types of fighters. The Sharpshooter pods for the F-15S only had limited cluster bomb delivery capability. They delivered the A/B version of the electro-optical Maverick and the D/G version of the IR Maverick, but did not have a missile boresight correlator. They only had a single-fire capability for Maverick, rather than multiple-fire capability, and were not equipped to deliver the HARM anti-radiation missile.

The United States also limited the offensive performance of the F-15S force. It did provide conformal fuel tanks for all of the aircraft, but without mounts to carry offensive air-to-ground weapons on these stations. The United States only provided forty-eight pod sets plus spares for the F-15Ss in order to limit the RSAF's ability to use the aircraft with smart air-to-ground munitions to only forty-eight fighters at any given time. Without the pods, the other aircraft could not use navigation and targeting pods or laser illuminators, and could only drop general-purpose bombs.

The F-15S had several other changes from the F-15E. It had a de-tuned version of the APG-70 radar on the 15E. The radar on the F-15S had only 60% of the bandwidth of the regular APG-70, and only had sixteen channels, rather than the regular thirty-two. It did not have a computerized mapping capability, and had a resolution of 60 feet at 15 nautical miles versus 8.5 feet at 20 nautical miles in the F-15E. The F-15S had altered software for the AWG-27 armament control system, lacked a data transfer module, and did not include the terrain following mode in its ASW-51 auto flight control. It also used a commercial-grade secure voice and global positioning system navigation system.

The F-15S's electronic warfare suite was missionized for use against non-U.S. aircraft and threats in the Gulf and Red Sea area. This meant substantial modifications to the ALQ-135 internal countermeasures set, the ALR-56C radar warning receiver, the ALE-45 countermeasures dispenser, and MX-9287 interference blanker set. The ALQ-135 initially supplied to Saudi Arabia did not have the capability to jam friendly aircraft by type, and the radar-warning receiver did not identify friendly aircraft by type.

There also were software issues as well. The performance of the F-15S is heavily affected by the software that its computer and other avionics use to recognize threats, launch air combat and attack munitions, counter enemy sensors and weapons, and navigate to target. The Saudis could not alter the software on the F-15S, and it had no software optimized to attack U.S. or Israeli air and air defense systems. The terms of the sale also meant the software could not be modernized to operate a new type of weapon or be optimized to deal with a new type of threat aircraft without U.S. approval.

This situation began to change in 1998–2000. The RSAF F-15S was supplied with conformal fuel tanks of the kind supplied on the F-15E, adding two extra tangential stores stations for carrying extra munitions and some of its ability to carry precision-guided weapons. The United States also agreed to deliver modern Mark IV IFF systems and Have Quick secure communications in the early 2000s. The F-15S's software has been steadily upgraded, however, as part of the USAF's multi-stage improvement programs (MSIPs) for the F-15. The United States has also granted access to the software codes for the F-16C to the UAE, and may eventually give the F-15 codes to the RSAF.

The end result is that the F-15S is now a far more advanced strike-fighter than any aircraft in service in Iran and Iraq, and could give Saudi Arabia a decisive edge over Iraq and Iran well beyond the year 2010. The F-15S fully meets Saudi Arabia's desire for an F-15E-like aircraft that can attack deep into Iraqi or Iranian territory, defend itself in air-to-air combat, and launch air-to-ground ordnance from outside the range of short-range air defense missiles. The F-15S can also be rapidly upgraded in an emergency if Iran or Iraq should acquire new types of fighters with advanced avionics.

In practice, however, the Saudi F-15 force has serious problems. These problems include inadequate funding for readiness, the lack of air and maintenance crews, inadequate offensive and joint warfare training, and the need for larger stocks of offensive munitions and more advanced types of munitions. Saudi Arabia is also developing a capability to conduct depot-level maintenance for either the overall aircraft or the APG-70 radar.

More Tornadoes

The Saudi Air Force also purchased additional Tornado and trainer aircraft. In April 1992, Britain announced that Saudi Arabia had agreed to a financing package for a $2.7 billion follow-on sale, and indicated that the deal would again be financed "off-budget," by shifting oil revenue directly to a London account. The purchase of the additional aircraft was made financially possible by Saudi Arabia's decision not to turn past MOUs into firm contracts. The Kingdom also took some cost-cutting measures: On August 24, 1992, Saudi Arabia cut the number of new air bases it would buy from two to one. This decision was a result of Saudi Arabia's discovery during the Gulf War that its existing facilities could sustain the buildup of some 500,000 foreign troops, and that they had substantial overcapacity. This decision saved Saudi Arabia $15.6 to $19.5 billion, and released funds it could use to complete the buy of forty-eight Tornado IDS/GR.1s.

Saudi Arabia signed a contract with Britain in early February 1993 to complete a buy of forty-eight Tornado IDS/GR/1s, which included shelters, maintenance, weapons, and training for the aircraft. The aircraft were to be delivered in configurations similar to those used by the RAF, and had Turbo-Union RB-199 engines, Sky Shadow ECM pods, and GEC-Marconi flight control systems, radars, and radar homing and warning receivers.[33]

The order did not include more Hawks and mine-countermeasure vessels, but negotiations continued on these purchases. When oil prices increased in 1994, Saudi Arabia ordered twenty more Hawk 65 jets and twenty more Swiss Pilatus PC-9 turboprop trainers, at a cost of $750 million. This purchase helped provide training for the new pilots but meant Saudi Arabia would not buy enough advanced Hawks to replace its F-5s and would rely more on the lower-performance, tandem-seat, Hawk 100 variant of the aircraft.[34]

The future status of al-Yamamah is in doubt. Crown Prince Abdullah was not included in the 1986 negotiations that led to the signing of the first part of al-Yamamah, and is said to be concerned with some aspects of the agreement. In particular, he may not favor the arrangement by which al-Yamamah is able to escape budgetary pressures while these constraints increased on other military forces, such as his National Guard.[35] He may oppose arrangements that grant Britain 400,000 to 600,000 bpd of Saudi oil to pay for al-Yamamah almost indefinitely into the future. If Abdullah becomes king, he might seek to make the al-Yamamah deal a regular part of the Saudi budget.[36]

Some Saudi officers and officials have expressed concern that the al-Yamamah program has gotten too broad and unwieldy. Many in the Saudi government now privately express their concern over allowing the Saudi MODA to operate the $3 billion program independent of normal budgetary constraints, particularly in view of Saudi Arabia's structural budget deficits. Political support for the al-Yamamah deal has also eroded as funds have grown progressively tighter, and many officials and some members of the royal family in civil ministries feel that the program has become wasteful, corrupt, and overambitious.

There are senior Saudis who feel that fully integrating all defense expenditures into a public national budget is a key step in bringing military spending under control, ensuring the proper trade-offs between military and civil expenditures, reducing corruption and favoritism, and building a popular consensus behind Saudi military efforts. At the same time, Saudi Arabia has a long tradition of secrecy and Prince Sultan is not likely to give up his prerogatives without a fight.[37]

Other factors are at work. A number of non-British firms have attempted to obtain part of the al-Yamamah funding. For example, Canadian Bell and Eurocopter have both sought to get money shifted to helicopter purchases and were recently successful.[38] Saudi Arabia chose to buy twelve Cougar Mark 2 search-and-rescue helicopters from Eurocopter in August 1996. The contract, valued at $590 billion, included training, logistics, and technical support and marks the first significant order of French equipment by the Saudi Air Force.[39]

An additional forty-four Canadian Bell-Boeing 412 search-and-rescue helicopters were expected to be purchased under the al-Yamamah deal by November 1997.[40] The new deal, however, encountered political and financing problems. The political problems related to British willingness to suppress the Saudi opposition. The Saudi government made it clear during the 1990s that its purchases of British equipment were dependent on a less hospitable climate for Saudi dissidents in Britain. The British government responded to a November 1995 car bombing in Riyadh by ordering the expulsion of Mohammed al-Mas'ari, the head of the CDLR, after he made statements seemingly condoning the bombing. This move was blocked in a British court, however, and the Saudi government threatened to halt further defense purchases as well as other major contracts. It was only after al-Mas'ari went bankrupt that Saudi Arabia made it clear it would not take political action.[41]

Saudi Arabia tightened its control over the al-Yamamah account at the end of 1996 by shifting responsibility for the daily sale of 650,000 barrels of oil to Aramco from Royal Dutch Shell and British Petroleum. The switch was a warning that the Kingdom felt the funds derived from petroleum sales should be used at the discretion of the MODA, rather than exclusively for the purchase of British equipment. In addition, these developments occurred at a time when Saudi Arabia faced serious budget deficits and the Saudi budget was strained by a sharp decline in oil prices that began in late 1997. The resulting drop in oil revenues also aggravated concerns elsewhere in the Saudi government over allowing the MODA to operate al-Yamamah independent of normal budgetary constraints. The Ministry of Finance made it clear that it would like to end all off-budget programs, including al-Yamamah.[42]

Looking Toward the Next Generation:
The F-5EII Replacement Problem

The next major procurement challenge the Saudi Air Force faces is how to deal with phasing out its aging F-5Es. The RSAF now has some eighty-seven F-5s of various types in storage, and Saudi Arabia has talked about replacing the F-5EII for years. At various times, it has considered buying entirely new aircraft—like F-16s and F-18s—as replacements for its F-5s. At other times, it has discussed the purchase of seventy-two F-15S aircraft, and forty-eight more Tornado IDS/GR.1s, plus some additional Hawks.

There were reports that Saudi Arabia would purchase 70 to 102 F-16C/D fighters to replace its F-5Es in the summer of 1996 and early 1997. Press reports appeared in January 1997 that Prince Sultan would announce such a purchase during a coming visit to Washington. These reports indicated that this announcement would be in part an effort to defuse the tension between the United States and Saudi Arabia over the investigation of the June 25, 1996, terrorist bombing of the Al-Khobar barracks. The sale was reported to have a potential value of up to $6 billion, and include a potential buy of the AIM-120 AMRAAM long-range air-to-air missile.[43]

The reports of such a sale were exaggerated, and the USAF privately indicated to the RSAF that it would be better off buying a smaller number of additional F-15Ss because of better commonality, lower manpower requirements, and economies of scale in maintenance and training. Nevertheless, these reports raised a number of issues. Israeli Prime Minister Netanyahu expressed concern over the sale on February 11, 1997, creating the possibility of a new round of congressional battles over arms sales to Saudi Arabia. Serious questions arose over Saudi Arabia's ability to fund the deal, given the fact it was already some $13 billion in debt to the United States for past arms buys and had previously agreed to limit its future debts to $10 billion. A number of U.S. military advisors privately indicated that Saudi Arabia was not yet ready to absorb such a purchase and had a higher priority for investments in training, readiness, and sustainability.[44] It is unclear whether Saudi Arabia ever planned to make such an announcement before press leaks triggered this debate, but no such announcement was made during Prince Sultan's visit.

There is no question that an export version of the F-16 C/D, Block 60, could have been an excellent replacement for the F-5—*if* it could have been properly financed and supported with the proper crews and readiness. It would then have been able to serve both Saudi and Western strategic interests by providing an advanced multi-role fighter that would be directly interoperable with USAF power projection forces and allow full integration into an advanced air battle management system using the AWACS, ̄TARS, and U.S. electronic warfare and intelligence systems. The F-16 also ̄ have provided a powerful new offensive capability against Iraq and

Iran that would compensate in part for the continuing weakness of the Saudi Army and Navy.

The same, however, would have been equally true of the purchase of a number of other types of combat aircraft, including more F-15s. More importantly, the key issues that Saudi Arabia face—and will continue to face—were not related to aircraft performance. The Kingdom's problems were money and the difficulties in converting an already inadequate maintenance, training, and sustainment base to an advanced new aircraft type. This has led to three very different views of how the Saudi Air Force should deal with the F-5EII replacement issue:

- Those who argue for a major new purchase feel a properly phased long-term buy of new fighters would ease Saudi Arabia's sustainability problems because such aircraft would be less of a maintenance burden than the F-5E, in spite of their greatly superior performance capabilities. They admit that trade-offs would have to be made with investment in improvements in other aspects of Saudi military capability, but feel that strengthening Saudi multi-role air capability would be the most effective investment that the Kingdom can currently make. They feel the main constraint in ensuring that such a purchase met Saudi Arabia's overall needs would be to schedule in ways in which the resulting payments did not place too large a burden on the Saudi budget.

- Those who argue against a major new purchase—and this group now includes most U.S. military advisors to Saudi Arabia—feel that Saudi Arabia already had enough problems in making its F-15s and Tornadoes fully combat-effective. They feel that Saudi Arabia does not have the money for such major aircraft buys, and that it either has higher military investment priorities or should concentrate its investment funds on the civil sector. They do not see a major air threat from either Iran or Iraq, and feel that Saudi Arabia cannot eliminate its de facto dependence on the United States in the event of a major regional war in any case.

- Those who argue for standardizing around the F-15 force and buying a limited number of F-15s to replace the F-5s. There have been reports that this is the course the RSAF will follow. In the spring of 2000, there were reports that Prince Sultan would announce that the Kingdom would buy twelve more F-15Ss, with a goal of eventually buying twenty-four. At the same time, there were reports that Boeing offered a major offset program that would potentially hire 3,000 Saudis and would give the Kingdom a depot-level maintenance and repair capability for its F-15s.[45] In any event, however, no such announcement took place.

There is no easy way to resolve the merits of this debate, and there is continuing outside pressure on the Kingdom to make a massive new arms buy. In fact, a Boeing Corporation executive "leaked" a plan in 2000 that would have called for a small buy of twelve to twenty-four F-15s to replace the F-5s, with the sweetener that Boeing would provide a depot-level maintenance facility for the aircraft. Other contractor efforts have been made to push the F-16 Block 60 and Eurofighter. What is clear, is that Saudi Arabia has gradually seen its F-5 force become almost inactive.

In any case, the sheer cost of any additional aircraft purchase has proven to be a key factor that has delayed any decision toward making any major new purchase as a follow-on to the F-5, although Saudi Arabia also faces serious problems in aircrew numbers, quality, and sustainment. Furthermore, the RSAF has found that major diseconomies of scale arise in trying to make a limited buy of a new advanced fighter like the F-16 or F-18. It takes about 50% to 100% more Saudi and foreign manpower to support a new type than it does to add an additional F-15 or Tornado. A new type also creates major problems in terms of additional facilities and maintenance stockpiles.[46]

THE READINESS AND WAR-FIGHTING CAPABILITIES OF THE SAUDI AIR FORCE

The Saudi Air Force has considerable experience with defensive operations. During the Iran-Iraq War, the Saudi Air Force worked closely with the USAF. They developed a patrol line called the Fahd Line near the center of the Gulf, a scramble line where aircraft on alert took off the moment an intruder came close, with inner defense lines covered by its Improved Hawk missiles. This air defense system was modified during the Gulf War to initially cover both the north and south because of the possible risk of hostile air attacks from Yemen and the Sudan. During the rest of the war, Saudi Arabia steadily refined its system, working with the USAF and other UN coalition forces to develop a layered system of land and airborne sensors and defense lines that could cover threats from Iraq as well as Iran.

The Lessons of the Gulf War

The first Saudi F-15C/Ds were operational in Dhahran by early 1983, a second squadron was formed at Taif by the end of 1983, and a third became operational at Khamis Mushayt in July 1984. Saudi aircraft attrition levels were significantly higher than those of the United States, but overall training levels were good. The Saudis began with an aircrew-to-aircraft ratio of 1.5:1 and the Saudi 34th Squadron became the most experienced F-15 squadron in the world, with pilots who had 700 to 900 hours each. Saudi pilots flew twenty-two to thirty-three hours per month versus eighteen hours in Israel and two-and-a-half hours in Egypt. Saudi live-firing exercises met NATO standards, and Saudi Arabia routinely fired off older missiles and munitions for training.

By late 1984 and early 1985, the Saudi Air Force was conducting exercises in both the Gulf and Red Sea areas, and conducting Red-Blue or aggressor exercises similar to those employed by the USAF. Saudi Arabia maintained these proficiency levels and began joint exercises with other members of the GCC. Its F-15 units scored first and second place in three exercises with NATO forces.

Saudi F-15C pilots performed well in air defense missions during Desert Storm, although they flew missions planned by the United States and supported by U.S. E-3As—electronic warfare and intelligence aircraft. The Saudi Air Force flew some 6,800 sorties during the Gulf War (January 17, 1991 to February 28, 1991), and some 2,000 sorties over the Kuwaiti Theater of Operations and Iraq. These sorties were largely counter-air. Saudi F-15C pilots proved to be competent and aggressive in air-to-air combat during the brief period when Iraq actively challenged Coalition fighters, and one Saudi pilot scored a double kill. Saudi Arabia was also the only Southern Gulf country that had a modern concept of air defense operations.

At the same time, the Gulf War showed that the RSAF still had some serious weaknesses:

- The ratio of qualified Saudi pilots to first combat aircraft was too low to maintain high sortie rates. Saudi Arabia could not reach the internationally accepted average ratio of 1:5, and its operational experience indicated that it needed 1:8 pilots per aircraft to maximize its sortie rates and combat efficiency.[47] Ironically, the Saudi Air Force now has only 0:9 aircrew per F-15 and only 0:5 effective maintenance crews per aircraft.

- The RSAF did well in flying air combat interdiction, airlift, and AWACS sorties, but it had weak mission planning and could not plan or control large-scale offensive operations. It had no force-on-force doctrine, jointness, or ability to operate beyond the squadron level. There were language, communications, inter-service cooperation, and mission-planning problems. Coordination problems often emerged between the RSAF and the MODA.

- The RSAF lacked the pilot numbers to operate all its British-supplied aircraft properly and British pilots flew some Saudi Tornadoes. Additional foreign technicians had to be brought in to maintain reasonable sortie rates with the F-15s and Tornadoes. The war showed that the RSAF will be dependent on such technicians for at least the next decade.

- The Saudi Air Force initially had difficulty in finding the manpower to operate its AWACS, and could not easily integrate AWACS data into its command operations center in Riyadh, and sector operating centers (SOCs) throughout the Kingdom. The Air Force operates these centers, although the Air Defense Force has responsibility for some functions and for the radars and equipment at surface-to-air missile sites and some other formations.

- The Saudi Air Force did not do well in electronic warfare and reconnaissance missions. The Saudi RF-5 force proved largely useless in seeking out targets and rapidly processing information, and Saudi Arabia was almost completely dependent on the United States for reconnaissance and intelligence.

- Saudi Arabia learned it needed the passive ELINT systems that are being fit to U.S. AWACS. These electronic intelligence systems are called the AN/AYR-1, and provide the ability to detect, locate, and identify the radar emissions of ships, aircraft, and ground systems—often indicating their precise type and location. Saudi Arabia may also need the upgraded CC-2E central computer, GPS navigation system, and Class 2H version of the secure Joint Tactical Information Distribution System (JTIDS). These upgrades to the E-3A, however, were only available for U.S. aircraft during 1995–1999, and have not yet been purchased by Saudi Arabia.

Saudi Air Force F-15, F-5, Tornado, and E-3A Readiness

Although Saudi Arabia's economic problems threatened its ability to take delivery on its new F-15Ss in the mid-1990s, Saudi Arabia gave a high priority to funding the F-15S, and the rescheduling of U.S. arms purchases discussed earlier eased its funding problems. As a result, the roll-out of the first F-15S took place in the United States in late September 1995, and the RSAF began to receive the F-15Ss at the rate of one squadron a year. The first full squadron of F-15Ss became operational in Saudi Arabia in 1996, the second in 1997, and the third in 1998.[48]

This Saudi operation of the F-15S has improved the potential interoperability of the U.S. and Saudi Air Forces, but there has been insufficient RSAF exercise activity since the mid-1990s to ensure that it can fully exploit the F-15S. Saudi Arabia has bought additional service and training facilities, munitions, spare parts, and specialized electronics facilities that could support both Saudi and USAF F-15 strike-attack aircraft—as well as Saudi and U.S. F-15 air defense fighters. Such facilities and munitions stocks could be used to improve U.S. rapid deployment capabilities in the Gulf in an emergency, and to help give the United States the ability to deploy and support well over seventy-two F-15E attack aircraft in a matter of days. More broadly, the Kingdom plans to create a depot maintenance capability that could improve the ability repair both RSAF and USAF combat stress and damage.

Nevertheless, the overall war fighting capability of the Saudi Air Force has deteriorated since the mid-1990s, and the RSAF now faces a crisis in readiness. Saudi Arabia has not been able to keep up with its force expansion, and even the lead elements in its F-15 force have lost readiness, reduced training standards, and experienced growing accident rates. Saudi Arabia now has only 0.9 aircrews and 0.5 ground crews per plane, something like one-third to two-thirds of its requirement for intense, "24-hour a day," sustained combat against a major Iraqi invasion. Its pilots fly an average of 3.5 to 5 hours of training per month versus a NATO standard of 20. This is roughly the same number of flight hours as a low-performance air force like Syria.

Accident rates have been high, and at least nine fatal accidents—five in 1999–2000—can be attributed to training and readiness problems. Proficiency levels have dropped from moderate to low, with particular problems in joint warfare and offensive missions. This decline has taken place even though large numbers of Saudi Arabia's F-5s have effectively been withdrawn from service. Although most estimates still show seventy-seven F-5E/Fs in Saudi Arabia's attack squadrons, ten RF-5Es in reconnaissance units, and fourteen F-5Bs in other combat units, experts indicate that up to eighty-seven F-5s are semi-operational or grounded.

This decline in the F-15 and F-5 force is partly the result of the Kingdom's cash-flow problems in the 1990s, partly the result of the pace of its expansion into highly sophisticated aircraft when the RSAF did not have time to recruit and train enough personnel, and partly the result of the Saudi failure to impose high training and proficiency standards on other Saudis. It is compounded by the Saudisation and language skill problems discussed earlier. It is also, however, the result of a serious crisis in top-level leadership that was compounded by corruption.

The problems in RSAF proficiency in using the Tornado have been similar. At least four Tornados crashed between November 2000 and July 2001—in the Beesha in November 2000, in the Eastern Province in March 2001, in the Southern Province in June 2001, and in the Eastern Province in July 2001.[49] The Tornado has not been upgraded in ways that impose as many new training and command and control requirements. The RAF only announced a comprehensive upgrade program for the Tornado in October 1997, and then cut back on many aspects of this program. It is unclear what aspects of the RAF program, if any, will be adopted by the RSAF.[50]

The RSAF now crews its five E-3A AWACS aircraft. The software for the E-3As has been updated, and infrared countermeasures were added to the engines. Although the upgrades to the E-3A are less advanced than originally planned, an improved mission computer with removable hard drives, new IFF hardware, and Mode IV interrogation capability will be added by the end of 2002. Secure communications, satellite communications, GINS, passive detection, improved radar, and additional consoles are now planned for another date, but are not currently funded. This will limit RSAF ability to carry out advanced attack missions and interoperability with U.S. forces until such improvements are funded and installed.[51]

Saudi Arabia has, however, failed to train its E-3A crews to properly support large-scale air battle operations, maritime surveillance missions, and joint warfare. It has also been slow to upgrade the overall C^4I/BM used by the Air Force and Navy to make full use of the capabilities of the E-3A. It has allowed its equivalent of a Rivet joint intelligence aircraft to become nearly useless and also has failed to develop the mix of training and exercise activity necessary to make full use of its modern combined air operations center (CAOC) without U.S. manning and assistance. This has compounded the impact of the much broader failure of the Saudi forces to develop effective combined operations, communication between the Air Force and National Guard, effective close support exercises between the Air Force and Army, and smooth interface between fighter air defense coverage and the land-based air defense coverage provided by the Air Defense Force. It would also force the USAF to segregate the operations of Saudi and U.S. E-3As into "boxes" with their own zones of responsibility.

The Air Force has also been slow to give its aircraft all of the advanced avionics and electronics, Mark IV identification of friend or foe (IFF) munitions, and secure communications capability they have needed, although U.S. delays in making key systems available have also caused problems. These systems—Mode IV IFF and secure communications systems like Have Quick—are "planned," but their availability, funding, and implementation status is unclear.[52] Saudi officers feel U.S. release problems are creating serious additional interoperability problems.

These readiness problems show that the Saudi Air Force is still very much an air force in transition. It has purchased several billion dollars worth of contractor and maintenance services from the United States to support its air defense and communications system, and signed a $2.5 billion contract to cover the period from June 1, 1997 to May 31, 2002.[53] It has since signed a series of contracts to support its aircraft purchases, such as contracts with Boeing to support the F-15. Nevertheless, Saudi Arabia has experienced serious problems in funding its maintenance contracts since the crisis in funding its arms purchases in 1995. These were worsened by the oil crash that began in 1997, and while spending recovered during the oil boom in 2000, problems still remain.

THE SAUDI AIR FORCE ENTERS THE TWENTY-FIRST CENTURY

Today, Saudi Arabia has the most modern air force in the Gulf. At the same time, it has scarcely solved all of its modernization problems and still faces funding problems. The Saudi Air Force must also make hard decisions over the next few years:

- Money remains a major problem. The F-15S sale alone cost nearly $9 billion, and the Tornado sale cost $7.5 billion. Saudi Arabia faces significant problems in funding the further modernization and expansion of its force structure and improved readiness, despite a slow payment schedule and some concessionary terms.[54] By the time the RSAF fully absorbs all its F-15S aircraft into its force structure by 1999, all of the Kingdom's F-5s will be over twenty years old, and its initial F-15C/Ds will be twelve to eighteen years old.[55]

- Overall, readiness and war fighting capability need improvement, which involves more than aircrew proficiency. It is one thing to train pilots, but another thing to try to reshape an entire air force to carry out an offensive and multi-mission warfare, achieve joint warfare capability, and adequately support the Saudi Navy. The purchase of the F-15Ss and additional Tornadoes requires the Saudi Air Force to focus on creating advanced offensive war-fighting capabilities. It has not yet made this conversion fully combat effective. The RSAF still needs to rethink many aspects of its command and control, reconnaissance and targeting, combined operations, offensive and joint warfare doctrine and training, and support and sustainability capabilities.

- Finally, Saudi Arabia's C⁴I/BM assets are still better structured for air defense than air offense. Saudi Arabia needs to rethink its C⁴I/BM needs for theater interdiction and large-scale attack missions comprehensively and acquire the necessary systems.

Saudi Air Force Capability for Effective Offensive and Joint Warfare

The RSAF has sought to upgrade some of its reconnaissance and targeting problems by improving the reconnaissance equipment on its aircraft, and by buying a relatively high-resolution satellite-imaging capability from the United States. This satellite-imaging service will be provided by Orbital Sciences of the United States, and will be the first time the United States has sold such precision imaging abroad.[56] The Saudi Air Force has also sought to improve its land-based C⁴I/BM system, and to acquire automated mission-planning support. Mission planning, however, remains a key weakness in Saudi operations, and the RSAF is still highly dependent on the United States.

The RSAF would also need U.S. support in missions like airborne warning and control. Saudi Arabia has found that flying a full air defense and air control and warning screen against a Northern Gulf state like Iraq or Iran can require up to four simultaneous orbits by AWACS aircraft, or a total of nine to twelve aircraft. Saudi Arabia can only fly two orbits with its current five E-3As, and has studied the purchase of four more AWACS aircraft, based on either a B-767 air frame or a modified Saudi B-707. Such a purchase would allow Saudi Arabia to support continuous air defense and maritime surveillance coverage over both coasts. The RSAF has found this plan to be too expensive, however, and must rely on the United States both for full coverage of Saudi Arabia and for coverage of its neighbors.[57]

The Gulf War showed that the Saudi Air Force needed far more extensive exercise training, equipment, and organization for offensive operations. The RSAF has since failed to make such improvements and its slow improvements in its training at the tactical and squadron levels are inadequate. It has failed to improve its training and organization at the mid- and high-command levels, and for joint operations at anything like the rate required—a serious, if not inexcusable, failure in military leadership.

The RSAF has made some improvements in its exercise activity since January 1996, when it held the Flag of Glory exercise. This exercise was one of the first force-wide exercises by any Gulf military service and involved 150 Saudi aircraft flying from bases at Dhahran, Khamis Mushayt, Tabuk, and Taif. It involved Saudi E-3As, F-5Es, F-15C/Ds, and Tornadoes, and concerned combined offensive and defensive maneuvers to deal with a threat like an Iraqi invasion. The Saudi Air Force also improved its performance in joint exercises with U.S. and Kuwaiti forces after 1995, and recent exercises have demonstrated that Saudi, Kuwaiti, and USAF aircraft could operate jointly using U.S. and Saudi E-3As, the US JSTARS, other U.S. C⁴I/BM systems, and digital data links. These efforts have declined, however, since the RSAF and USAF commands ceased to be collocated following the attack on the USAF barracks at Al Khobar.

Saudi Air Force Capability for Joint and Coalition Warfare

There are other areas in which the Saudi Air Force is not making significant progress. It needs to give still more emphasis to high-intensity, 24-hour-a-day operations against a threat like Iran and Iraq. It needs to raise its sortie rates sharply, and to improve its targeting and force-wide C⁴I/BM capabilities for offensive operations. This again may require more dynamic leadership at the top.

Nearly a decade after Desert Storm, the Saudi Air Force is not well organized to support the Saudi Army in the defense of Kuwait and the Kingdom's northern border. It found during the Gulf War that it lacked many of the capabilities it needed for joint operations with the Army and Navy. While the Saudi Air Force could fly against fixed, lightly defended, interdiction targets, it could only do so with foreign planning and support. The Saudi Air Force proved to have limited operational flexibility in adapting from range training to actual close air support missions, and communications between the Saudi Air Force and Army presented major problems.

The Saudi Air Force needs more extensive joint-training and joint-operations activity with the Saudi Army, although the lack of initiative and leadership in this area seems to be more the fault of the Army than the Air Force. The Air Force needs to develop a coordinated operational concept with the Saudi Navy, practice making more effective use of the maritime surveillance capabilities of the E-3A, and conduct joint training with the Navy. Here, however, the Air Force will have to wait until the Navy begins to transform its equipment strength into military effectiveness. At present, the Navy is more a showpiece than a force.

These weaknesses in RSAF war fighting capability must be kept in perspective. They indicate that Saudi Arabia will have major problems in defending against Iraq or Iran unless it has extensive foreign support. The RSAF will need at least a decade more of U.S. and British assistance to become an effective air force capable of force-on-force operations and combined operations. At the same time, such problems are common in even the best European air forces in the developing world and many air forces in

NATO. They do not prevent the Saudi Air Force from being the most effective air force in the Southern Gulf, and one of the most effective air forces in the Arab world. The RSAF not only has the most capable aircraft of any Southern Gulf or GCC air force, it is the only one with a fully modern command and control system and with the E-3A AWACS. Regrettably, this is unlikely to change until the GCC creates a fully modern and integrated air battle management, C⁴I, and strategic reconnaissance system and—as of 2001—its C⁴I integration consisted of little more than a glorified "hotline."

Hopefully, the appointment of Khalid bin Sultan as assistant defense minister will lead to the same effort to revitalize the Saudi Air Force that is beginning to take shape in the Army. It may also help lead to a new emphasis on training and readiness standards, merit-based promotion, and top-door integrity in every aspect of contracting—including construction. The Saudi Air Force still has a cadre of excellent personnel at every level, and great potential. It deserves the kind of leadership it needs.

NOTES

1. Unless otherwise specified, the military data quoted here are taken from the relevant country sections of various annual editions of the IISS, *Military Balance*; CIA, *The World Factbook*; JCSS, *The Middle East Military Balance*; and online editions of *Jane's Sentinel* series and *Periscope, Jane's Intelligence Review*, and *Jane's Defence Weekly*. The cut-off date for such material is January 2002.

Other sources include interviews with Saudi officials and military inside and outside of Saudi Arabia, U.S. experts, and British experts. These are not identified by source by request of those interviewed. They also include the author's publications and other sources mentioned at the start of the section on Saudi Arabia; Dr. Andrew Rathmell, "Saudi Arabia's Military Build-up—An Extravagant Error," *Jane's Intelligence Review* (November 1994), pp. 500–504; Andrew Rathmell, *The Changing Balance in the Gulf*, Whitehall Papers 38 (London: Royal United Services Institute, 1996); Edward B. Atkenson, *The Powder Keg* (Falls Church: NOVA Publications, 1996); USCENTCOM, *Atlas, 1996* (MacDill Air Force Base: USCENTCOM, 1997); *Jane's Land-Based Air Defense, 1997–1998* (London: Jane's Publishing); and various editions of *Jane's Air-Launched Weapons, Jane's Aircraft Upgrades, Jane's Avionics, Jane's All the World's Aircraft, Jane's World Air Forces, Jane's Air-Launched Weapons; Jane's Radar and Electronic Warfare Systems; Jane's Military Communications*; and *Jane's Unmanned Aerial Vehicles and Targets*.

2. Historical sources include James Bruce and Paul Bear, "Latest Arab Force Levels Operating in the Gulf," *Jane's Defence Weekly*, December 12, 1987, pp. 1360–1361; and various editions of the "Middle Eastern, North African, and South Asian Navies," sections of the March issue of *Proceedings*.

3. USCENTCOM, *Atlas, 1996*; IISS, *Military Balance, 1996–1997, 1999–2000, 2000–2001*, and *2001–2002*.

4. Ibid.

5. *Defense News*, September 9, 1996, p. 26.

6. USCENTCOM, *Atlas, 1996*; IISS, *Military Balance, 1996–1997, 1999–2000, 2000–2001,* and *2001–2002.*

7. *Washington Post,* July 30, 1991, p. A-12; Richard F. Grimmett, *Arms Sales to Saudi Arabia* (Washington: Congressional Research Service, IB91007, August 28, 1991), p. 4.

8. Eliot A. Cohen, *Gulf War Air Power Survey, Volume V* (Washington: U.S. Air Force/GPO, 1993), pp. 232, 279–287. Note that these data are not consistent from table to table.

9. Ibid., pp. 316–317, 335, 340, 343, 641, 653–654.

10. *Defense Daily,* July 31, 1991, p. 24.

11. *Defense Daily,* May 14, 1991, p. 258.

12. *Defense Daily,* February 2, 1993, p. 162.

13. *Defense Daily,* August 14, 1991, p. 258.

14. *Defense Daily,* July 31, 1991, p. 24.

15. *Business Wire,* September 23, 1996.

16. *Middle East Economic Digest,* February 26, 1993, p. 29.

17. *Defense Daily,* March 1995; October 3, 1995.

18. *Defense Daily,* September 17, 1993, p. 434; e-mail from Tom Cooper on January 23, 2002, 9:34.

19. *Defense Daily,* January 5, 1999.

20. *Defense News,* May 31, 1999, p. 1.

21. Ibid.

22. *Middle East Economic Digest,* January 19, 1996, p. 7.

23. *Jane's Defence Weekly,* August 14, 1996, p. 23.

24. *Jane's Defence Weekly,* February 13, 1993, p. 41; *Middle East Economic Digest,* January 19, 1996, p. 7.

25. *Jane's Defence Weekly,* February 13, 1993, p. 41.

26. *Jane's Defence Weekly,* July 9, 1988, p. 23, July 16, 1988, p. 59, July 23, 1988, pp. 111, 122–123, March 28, 1992, pp. 533–535; *Newsweek,* July 25, 1988, p. 47; *New York Times,* July 11, 1988, p. 1, July 12, p. 3.

27. *Jane's Defence Weekly,* July 9, 1988, p. 23, July 16, 1988, p. 59, July 23, 1988, pp. 111, 122–123, June 15, 1991, p. 998, October 26, 1991, p. 770, March 28, 1992, pp. 533–535; *Newsweek,* July 25, 1988, p. 47; *New York Times,* July 11, 1988, p. 1, July 12, p. 3.

28. See the author's, *The Gulf and the Search for Strategic Stability: Saudi Arabia, the Military Balance in the Gulf, and Trends in the Arab-Israeli Military Balance* (Boulder, CO: Westview, 1984), pp. 122–126.

29. Grimmett, *Arms Sales to Saudi Arabia*; *Defense News,* September 7, 1992, p. 7.

30. There are unconfirmed reports that Air Force officers loyal to the Shah ensured that the F-14s were not fully operational.

31. *Aviation Week,* September 21, 1992, p. 26; *New York Times,* September 12, 1992, p. A-1, September 15, 1992, p. A-1; *Defense News,* January 30, 1994, p. 32, June 26, 1994, p. 30, February 13, 1995, p. 21.

32. Reuters, March 7, 1999.

33. *Jane's Defence Weekly,* February 6, 1993, p. 6, February 13, 1993, pp. 38–42; *New York Times,* January 30, 1993, p. 3; *Defense News,* October 12, 1992,

p. 3; *Manchester Guardian*, October 25, 1992, p. 9; *Financial Times*, November 18, 1992, p. 10, January 29, 1993, p. 1.

34. *Financial Times*, January 29, 1993, p. 1; *Armed Forces Journal*, November 1994, p. 41.

35. *Defense News*, January 8–14, 1996, pp. 1, 20, March 24, 1997, pp. 1, 66.

36. *Jane's Defence Weekly*, August 14, 1996, p. 23.

37. *Defense News*, March 24, 1997, pp. 1, 66; *Washington Post*, April 19, 1996, p. A-31.

38. *Defense News*, March 24, 1997, pp. 1, 66.

39. *Jane's Defence Weekly*, August 7, 1996, p. 3.

40. *Defense News*, November 10, 1997.

41. *Middle East Economic Digest*, January 19, 1996, p. 7; *Wall Street Journal*, January 5, 1996, p. A6; Jane's *Pointer*, March 1997, p. 5; *Jane's Intelligence Review*, August, 1996; *Washington Post*, April 19, 1996, p. A-31.

42. *Defense News*, November 10, 1997, p. 60.

43. *Jane's Defence Weekly*, February 5, 1997, p. 3; *Wall Street Journal*, February 24, 1997, p. B-4; *Defense News*, February 3, 1997, p. 4.

44. *Defense News*, February 3, 1997, p. 4, March 2, 1997; Reuters, February 12, 1997, 1448; *Washington Times*, January 30, 1997, p. A-1, January 31, 1997, p. A-3, February 23, 1997, p. A-5; *Washington Post*, January 31, 1997, p. A-1.

45. Reuters, April 10, 2000, 0520, April 15, 2000, 0503.

46. *Signal*, August, 1991, p. 116; *Aviation Week*, December 5, 1988, p. 23; *Aerospace Daily*, October 28, 1991, p. 152.

47. *Defense News*, April 14, 1997, p. 3.

48. *Defense News*, January 24, 1994, p. 32; January 23, 1995, p. 1, February 13, 1995, p. 22; *Jane's Defence Weekly*, September 30, 1995, p. 19.

49. E-mail from Tom Cooper on January 23, 2002, 9:34.

50. *Jane's Defence Weekly*, October 22, 1997, p. 1.

51. Fax from Department of Defense, OSD/LA, January 11, 1987; *Baltimore Sun*, September 26, 1989, p. E-9; *Jane's Defence Weekly*, October 7, 1989, p. 744.

52. Information current as of January 15, 2002.

53. The contract involves the services of 25 U.S. government and 300 contract personnel. Associated Press, September 26, 1997, 1917.

54. The deal would be in addition to the $3.5 billion al-Yamamah I sale and bring total related sales to around $10 billion. *Jane's Defence Weekly*, April 11, 1992, p. 597; *Flight International*, April 21, 1992, p. 21; *Defense News*, August 31, 1992, p. 40.

55. *Defense News*, January 24, 1994, p. 32; January 23, 1995, p. 1, February 13, 1995, p. 22; *Jane's Defence Weekly*, September 30, 1995, p. 19.

56. *Baltimore Sun*, June 6, 1996, p. 20C.

57. Grimmett, *Arms Sales to Saudi Arabia*, p. 3; *Defense News*, September 7, 1992, p. 7.

Chapter 8

The Saudi Air Defense Force

The Saudi Air Force has significant air defense capabilities, and the Saudi Army has growing mobile air defenses to protect its forces. Saudi Arabia also has a separate Saudi Air Defense Force to provide fixed and mobile land-based air defense of key targets throughout the Kingdom. This force was created in 1984 to establish a separate professional service dedicated to the relatively high-technology air defense mission, and to reduce the manpower quality and leadership problems that emerged when these air defense forces were subordinated to the Army.

The Air Defense Force manages any use of the Saudi and U.S. Patriot air and Patriot missile defenses and its PRC-supplied CSS-2 surface-to-surface missiles. It is subordinate to the Air Force for C⁴I and battle management in time of war.[1]

THE CURRENT STRENGTH OF SAUDI LAND-BASED
AIR DEFENSE FORCES

A broad comparison of Saudi and other Gulf land-based air defense strength is shown in Table 8.1. Detailed estimates of the current strength and equipment of the Air Defense Force differ according to which specific surface-based air defense units are included in the total, and which forces are counted as being in the ADF versus the Air Force, Navy, and Army. It is clear that the Saudi Air Defense Force controls all of Saudi Arabia's Improved Hawk (IHawk) missiles and most of its medium surface-to-air missiles, but its exact lines of control are unclear. Some sources indicate that

Table 8.1
Gulf Land-Based Air Defense Systems, 2002

Country	Major SAM	Light SAM	AA Guns
Bahrain	8 IHawk	60 RBS-70 18 Stinger 7 Crotale	15 Oerlikon 35 mm 12 L/70 40 mm
Iran	16/150 IHawk 3/10 SA-5 45 HQ-2J (SA-2) ? SA-2	SA-7 HN-5 5/30 Rapier FM-80 (Ch Crotale) 15 Tigercat SA-7 Stinger (?)	1,700 Guns ZU-23, ZSU-23-4, ZSU-57-2, KS-19 ZPU-2/4, M-1939, Type 55
Iraq	SA-2 SA-3 SA-6	Roland 1,500 SA-7 (SA-8) (SA-9) (SA-13) (SA-14, SA-16)	6,000 Guns ZSU-23-4 23 mm, M-1939 37 mm, ZSU-57-2 SP, 57 mm 85 mm, 100 mm, 130 mm
Kuwait	4/24 IHawk 4/16 Patriot	6/12 Aspede 48 Starburst	6/2X35mm Oerlikon
Oman	None	Blowpipe 34 SA-7 14 *Javelin* 40 Rapier	10 GDF 35 mm 4 ZU-23-2 23 mm 12 L-60 40 mm

Qatar	None	10 Blowpipe 12 *Stinger* 9 Roland 20 SA-7, 24 Mistral	?
Saudi Arabia	16/128 IHawk 8/? Patriot	189 Crotale 400 Stinger 500 Mistral 500 *Redeye* 17/68 Shahine mobile 40 Crotale 73 Shahine static	— 50-73 AMX-30SA 30 mm 92 M-163 Vulcan 150 L-70 40 mm (in store)
UAE	5/30 IHawk Bty.	20+ Blowpipe *Mistral* 12 Rapier 9 Crotale 13 RBS-70 100 Mistral	42 M-3VDA 20 mm SP 20 GCF-BM2 30 mm
Yemen	SA-2, SA3, SA-6	*SA-7, SA-9, SA13, SA-14* 800 SA-7/9/13/14	50 M-167 20mm 20 M-163 Vulcan 20mm 100 ZSU-23-4 23 mm 150 M-1939 23 mm 120 S-60 37 mm KS-12 85 mm

Sources: Adapted by Anthony H. Cordesman from the IISS, *Military Balance; Military Balance; Periscope;* JCSS, *The Middle East Military Balance; Jane's Sentinel; Jane's Defence Weekly;* and material provided by U.S. experts. Some data adjusted or estimated by the author.

the Air Defense Force controls all mobile and crew-powered weapons, and that the Army controls all man-portable Mistral, Stinger, and Redeye teams. Other sources indicate the Army also controls Saudi Arabia's Crotale missiles. Control of given deployments of anti-aircraft guns is also unclear.

The Saudi Air Defense Force was reported to have a nominal strength of 16,000 men in 2002, and some thirty-three surface-to-air missile batteries. However, some sources indicate Saudi Arabia's total air defense manning was substantially smaller. Sources differed over the equipment of these forces:[2]

- Some reports indicated its total major surface-to-air missile strength included sixteen Improved Hawk batteries with 128 fixed and mobile fire units, nine Crotale batteries with forty-eight Crotale fire units (currently being modernized), sixteen air defense batteries with seventy-two Shahine fire units, and fifty AMX-30SA 30 mm self-propelled guns.

- In late 2001, the IISS reported a strength of sixteen Improved Hawk batteries with 128 fire units, seventeen air defense batteries with sixty-eight Shahine fire units and AMX-30SA 30 mm self-propelled guns, and seventy-three Crotale and Shahine fire units in static positions. It reported a total inventory of fifty AMX-30 SAs, 141 Shahine launchers, and forty Crotale launchers. It also reported ninety-two M-163 20 mm Vulcan anti-aircraft guns and fifty AMX-30SA anti-aircraft guns, plus seventy L/70 40 mm anti-aircraft guns in storage.

- USCENTCOM reported a total of thirty-three SAM batteries and seventy-three Crotale and Shahine fire units.

- *Periscope* reported in early 2002 that the Air Defense Force has thirty-three air defense batteries, with sixteen Hawk and seventeen Shahine batteries. It reported a weapons strength of eight MIM-104 Patriot launchers with 1,061 rounds (which seems far too high), 128 mobile and fixed MIM-23B IHawk fire units, four truck-mounted Otomat coastal defense batteries, and 141 Shahine fixed and mobile launchers with sixty Shahine II AMX-30-mounted launchers. It also reported holdings of 118 35 mm GDF 005 twin anti-aircraft guns plus 128 40 mm L/70 anti-aircraft guns in storage.[3]

Most of Saudi Arabia's Shahine units are deployed in fixed locations for the defense of air bases and key targets. All of the Shahine systems were being upgraded as the result of an agreement with France signed in 1991. These units provide close-in defense capability for virtually all of Saudi Arabia's major cities, ports, oil facilities, and military bases.

Total Saudi Army holdings of man-portable surface-to-air missiles include 500 to 700 Mistrals, 350 to 400 Stingers, and 500 to 600 Redeyes. The number and type of antiaircraft guns currently operational is uncertain. Some reports state it has thirty-five 35 mm Oerlikon-Contraves twin AA guns with Skyguard fire control systems, seventy-two 40 mm L-70 AA guns, fifty-three 30 mm AMX-30 DCA twin antiaircraft guns, and an unknown number of 20 mm Vulcan M163 guns. Other reports indicate it had had ninety-two M-163 Vulcan 20 mm anti-aircraft guns, thirty V-150s with Vulcan 20 mm guns, thirty towed 20 mm Vulcans, 128 35 mm AA guns, and 150 L/70 40 mm guns (most in storage).[4] These reports may mix the holdings of the Army and Air Defense Force.

Unclassified reports on the future buildup of a Saudi Patriot force are unclear. According to some reports, Saudi Arabia signed letters of agreement to purchase its first Patriot units on September 27, 1990, as part of its Gulf War arms package. Saudi Arabia signed a $1.03 billion contract for the first part of this force in December 1992. This contract included thirteen launchers, 671 missiles, and associated equipment. It then bought fourteen more Patriot fire units (with sixty-four Patriot long-range air defense missiles, one AN/MPQ-53 radar set, one engagement control station, and eight launcher stations each) to defend its sites, military bases, and major oil facilities.[5] Delivery of the first eight batteries, including two training batteries, began in 1993. Saudi Arabia signed a $580 million support contract for its new Patriots and its existing IHawks with Raytheon in March 1993.[6]

According to a report in the mid-1990s, Saudi Arabia's goal was to acquire 384 Patriot long-range air defense missiles, six AN/MPQ-53 radar sets, six engagement control stations, and forty-eight launcher stations. Another interview indicated that Saudi and U.S. Army studies showed that Saudi Arabia might eventually require a total of twenty-six launcher stations depending on the level of anti-tactical ballistic missile capability and anti-aircraft coverage desired. These same studies indicated Saudi Arabia was already committed to spending some $2.2 billion out of a total cost of $4 billion for the twenty to twenty-six batteries it would need.[7]

Reports differ over whether Saudi Arabia had two or three major operational Patriot fire units in early 2002, and there was one report that it had a fourth. The United States deployed an additional Patriot battalion near Riyadh in 2001, and some reports indicate equipment was pre-positioned for a second. Another source cites only eight active MIM-104 fire units. There seems to be agreement that operational readiness is limited. Live fire exercises only really began to improve in the fall of 2000, and mobile operations have taken years to develop. The first mobile deployment approaching a combat exercise was a road march from Dhahran to a site near King Khalid Military City in the fall of 2000.

U.S. experts indicated in early 2001 that they felt the Kingdom needed three to four major concentrations of Patriots to cover its major oil ports, Riyadh, and cities in the east and west. They noted, however, that no detailed assessment had been made of future requirements for Saudi anti-theater ballistic missile (ATBM) requirements and no detailed current plan existed for sizing an overall surface-to-air missile and ATBM force.

Regardless of what the Kingdom eventually does, Saudi and U.S. Patriot units have already improved Saudi Arabia's low- to high-level air defense capability along the Gulf coast and provided some defense against medium-range and theater ballistic missiles. The units Saudi Arabia has bought have improved software, radar processing capabilities, longer-range missiles, better guidance systems, and more lethal warheads. Unlike the Patriots used during the Gulf War, they are designed to kill short- to medium-range ballistic missiles at comparatively long ranges and to discriminate between warheads and decoys and parts of the missile body.

IMPROVING SAUDI AIR DEFENSE BATTLE MANAGEMENT

The Saudi Air Defense Force has many of the same readiness, joint warfare, training, and funding problems as the other services. As might be expected, some are matters of readiness, manpower quality, and training. Others are problems in command and control and battle management. The Air Defense Force still lacks the systems integration, battle management systems, and C^4I software and integration it needs for effective operation. Moreover, contractor efforts to improve the integration of the Saudi Air Defense Corps' IHawks, Shahines (Improved Crotale), anti-aircraft guns, and land-based radars and C^4I systems have not been fully effective, and the Saudi air defense system is not easy to restructure.

The Peace Pulse and Falcon Eye Programs

The Saudi air defense network was first developed in the 1960s and used U.S. and British radars—primarily the British T40 radar. Saudi Arabia then added a number of bits and pieces over the years. Its first major effort to create a modern integrated system took place in 1980 and was called the Peace Pulse program. The Kingdom bought a Thomson CSF air command and control system, and four Westinghouse AN/TPS-43 three-dimensional radars in 1980. It then ordered eleven Westinghouse AN/TPS-70 radars—relabeled as the TPS-72 to give it a unique Saudi identifier—as part of the Peace Pulse program in 1981. The radars came with related computers, software, communications systems, and systems integration capabilities.[8]

Although these systems improved Saudi capabilities, the Kingdom still was left with major communications and C^4I integration problems, which it attempted to solve by giving new contracts to Litton and Boeing.[9] The Litton contract involved a $1.7 billion effort to provide C^4I, sensors, and communications systems. It was also meant to handle the interface between missiles and other air defense systems, as well as build sites and train personnel. Key elements involved seventeen major communications links installed in S-280C militarized transportable shelters, and included both line-of-sight and tropospheric scatter links of seventy-two-channel capacity. The field phase involved thirty-four low-level and thirty-four high-level shelters. While there is some dispute as to responsibility, the system was not fully operational when the contract was due to be completed. Even today some parts of the Litton-supplied system seem to be experiencing problems, some of which may be the result of a lack of trained Saudi personnel.[10]

Saudi Arabia purchased another C⁴I/BM subsystem in March 1989, called Falcon Eye. Falcon Eye integrates data from ground radars and the E-3A force, and down-link data to the fourteen Skyguard/Gun King batteries in the Saudi Air Defense Force that are used for close-in defense of air bases and vital military installations. The system began to become fully operational in 1992.

The Peace Shield Program

The Boeing contract, which was called the "Peace Shield" program, had a total cost of $5.6 billion. It involved a far more ambitious effort to give Saudi Arabia a system of seventeen AN/FPS-117(V)3 long-range, three-dimensional radar systems fully netted with its existing nine AN-TPS-43 Dar/Litton ADF radars, eleven AN-TPS-72 radars, and four TPS-43s. (The Kingdom eventually acquired as total of six TPS-43s as part of Peace Pulse, but gave one each to Bahrain and Jordan.)

It was to have (a) a central command operations center (COC) at Riyadh, (b) five sector command centers (SCCs) at Dhahran, Taif, Tabuk, Khamis Mushayt, and Al-Kharj to cover the country, and (c) additional sector operations centers (SOCs) at each major air base. It was to use a tropospheric scattering and microwave communications system to integrate Saudi Arabia's surface-to-air missile defenses, some anti-aircraft gun units, its radars, its E-3A airborne warning and control systems (AWACS) aircraft and fighters, and six major regional underground operating centers and numerous smaller sites, all of which were to be managed by a command center in Riyadh.

This system was supposed to give Saudi Arabia the ability to provide battle management for high-intensity air combat and beyond-visual-range combat, and to provide the base for a system to integrate the six Southern Gulf countries in the GCC: Bahrain, Kuwait, Oman, Qatar, Saudi Arabia, and the UAE. However, the software and systems integration efforts required to make Peace Shield effective were years behind schedule at the time of the Gulf War. The U.S. Air Force found the performance of the contractor to be so bad that the USAF Electronic Systems Division issued a "show cause notice" and then terminated Boeing's work on the program in January 1991.

Part of the problem was the AN/FPS-117(V)3 radar. It was so unreliable that the RSAF was forced to leave TPS-72s collocated with the

AN/FPS-117(V)3s in several critical sites. This unreliable performance, however, had a number of causes, including a failure by the Kingdom to buy sufficient spares, a lack of qualified contract personnel, and a lack of qualified Saudi military personnel.

The situation was so bad that several senior U.S. advisors in Saudi Arabia regarded the combined failure of Boeing and the USAF to deliver a useful Peace Shield program as the worst-managed single arms sale in the history of the Gulf. One senior U.S. officer described it as "a disaster on the part of the contractor and the Air Force from start to finish. . . . A model of what should never happen." Boeing staff, in turn, blamed the USAF for problems in the contract specifications, program changes, and inadequate management.

In any case, Saudi Arabia had to begin again with a new contractor. It shifted the contract from Boeing to Hughes in July 1991, at a cost of $837 million; however, this time the program made solid progress.[11] The new Peace Shield system began to become operational in January 1995, and performed well in the Flag of Glory exercises that Saudi Arabia held in January 1996. The Peace Shield system uses Hughes AMD-44 workstations, Hughes HDP-6200 large-screen displays, a modern data-processing architecture, and far more advanced software. It is designed to have some 300 individual sites and integrate a mix of Saudi radars that some reports indicate was built-up to a total of twenty-eight AN/TPS-43s, seventeen AN/FPS-117s, and thirty-five AN/TPS-43s.

The core of the system consisted of the seventeen AN/FPS-117s, with three each under the control of centers at Khamis, Al Kharj, Dhahran, and Taif, and five under the control of Tabuk in the northwest. The system made extensive use of modern fiber-optic technology, although no provision was made for advanced data links to neighboring states like Bahrain and Kuwait. The system also failed to integrate the air defense units of the Saudi Air Defense Force with those of the Saudi Army.

Peace Shield finally became fully operational in 1996, some three years after the original target date of 1993. Like all of Saudi Arabia's more sophisticated air systems, it remains heavily dependent on U.S. technical assistance and the Saudi Air Defense Force will need such assistance in operating the system until well after the year 2010.[12] Saudi Arabia purchased the support necessary to make its system effective as part of the $2.5 billion contract for contractor and maintenance services discussed earlier. It also purchased $484 million worth of support and training services for its Patriots and IHawk units from Raytheon in May 1997. This contract has been renewed, but funding has been uncertain since the oil crash of 1997.[13]

The future of Saudi funding for the Peace Shield and Peace Sun projects was called into question in May 1999. Saudi Arabia had missed an FMS payment in March and the United States considered not renewing the

project. Saudi Arabia and the United States had to look for options to justify the renewal of the contract, including the assumption of loans by private
contractors involved in the project to cover a deferral of Saudi payments.
The Saudi government would then repay the loan with interest at a later
date. Although a payment was missed in March, the Kingdom has paid for
April and is expected to meet May's requirements. The delay in payments
is clearly a sign of Saudi Arabia's growing financial problems and may jeopardize its arms sales with the United States.[14]

Plans for integrated air defense systems are moving forward slowly. At
present, Saudi Arabia still does not have a truly integrated C^4I/BM system
for its land-based air defense units, which have to operate independently
or rely on limited data links and voice communications. It still has no plans
to integrate the land-based air defenses of the Saudi Air Defense Force and
the Saudi Army, and plans to create a GCC air defense system are oriented
more toward sharing data at the command level than true integration.

THE EFFECTIVENESS OF THE SAUDI AIR DEFENSE FORCE AND OPTIONS FOR GCC AND SOUTHERN GULF COOPERATION

The success of the Peace Pulse, Falcon Eye, and Peace Shield systems has
led to an improvement in the capability of the Saudi Air Defense Force, and
should be a major step in helping it to absorb and operate the Patriot missile. Saudi Arabia still, however, has a C^4I system with serious weaknesses
and only limited ability to deploy and operate layered air and land-to-air
defenses.

Saudi sources indicate that in a crisis or wartime, the Kingdom will establish a fighter patrol line like the Fahd Line near the center of the Gulf,
and use other fighters to cover the forward area on its borders, form a
scramble line where aircraft on alert take off the moment an intruder comes
close, and use inner defense lines covered by its IHawk and Patriot missiles. Saudi commanders in local operations and exercises are practicing this
system. Saudi junior officers are in command, although some workstations
are still foreign-manned. Saudi Arabia has also obtained twenty-seven
mission-planning systems from the Sanders Corporation to provide the
mission-planning support that the RSAF lacked during the Gulf War.

The Need for Integrated Air Defense at the National and Gulf Level

The most immediate problem Saudi Arabia now faces is the need to in-
tegrate the systems of the Saudi Air Defense Force with those of the Saudi
Army, to tighten coordination between the Saudi Air Defense Force and
RSAF, to develop an effective combined air defense and airborne maritime

patrol system and create joint air defense capabilities, and to create effective integrated defenses with the other Gulf states. This is crucial to both Saudi Arabia's future security and the ability of the West to reinforce Bahrain and Kuwait effectively, due to their small size and air space. Kuwait is particularly vulnerable because of its common border with Iraq and its proximity to Iran. It desperately requires a survivable air defense and land and maritime surveillance system. No Kuwaiti-based system can provide such characteristics unless it is integrated into a Saudi system, preferably with close links to Bahrain, Qatar, and the UAE.

The GCC is implementing a project called Hizam at-Ta'awun (HAT-Belt of Cooperation). This project is a two-tiered program meant to establish a telecommunications network linking the military headquarters of the GCC states, and then link the states' radar systems. Ericsson of Sweden was awarded a $70 million contract for the communications link, and U.S.-based Hughes Space and Communications won an $88 million contract for the radar link. The first phase of this program was completed in 2001.[15]

The resulting system does more to provide secure communications between the national air defense command and control centers of the GCC states than to actually integrate air defense, but it can provide early warning and some intercept and land-based air defense data in the event of an air attack by Iran or Iraq. (It would not necessarily provide useful data in a ballistic-missile or low-altitude air or cruise missile attack.) At least on paper, the resulting combination of a Raytheon-developed integrated air battle management system, and an Ericson secure optical fiber communications system should allow the GCC to finally develop capabilities that should have been in place well over a decade ago.

There has been some progress in creating such an integrated system.[16] Kuwait seems to be committed to purchasing a modern air defense system that could be integrated with the GCC and Saudi systems. In late 1997, Kuwait launched a $1.2 billion project to build a C⁴I network to eventually be integrated into similar networks in the other five GCC states. Ironically, the slow pace of the GCC-wide effort has hampered the Kuwaiti project. As of May 2000, the GCC had still not moved forward beyond the creation of fiber-optic data links designed to support communication between the leaders and high commands of the Southern Gulf states. Because the two systems are to be integrated, it is important that contractors have information about the GCC-wide system in order to make the Kuwaiti system compatible. The contract will involve the creation of a joint operations center, mobile command centers for each of the services, and battalion command centers.[17]

The air defense systems of Qatar, Oman, and the UAE need to be fully integrated with the Saudi air defense system, and airborne maritime patrol data needs to be added to the air defense sensor and battle management system to deal with potential threats from Iran and Yemen, and to enhance beyond-visual-range combat capability. The smaller Gulf states have no hope of providing effective air defense on a piecemeal basis or developing the kind of air combat training and exercise experience necessary to interoperate effectively with U.S. and Saudi fighters and E-3As. They need to standardize and exercise operational procedures and IFF capabilities and develop the kind of aggressor training needed to cope effectively with mass raids. In the long run, such cooperation will also be critical to linking the Patriot and follow-on ATBM systems that will be needed to deal with the risk of proliferation. The slow pace of the Kuwaiti and GCC efforts toward integrated air defense indicates that these plans may take years to be fully implemented.

Theater Missile Defense?

Saudi Arabia cannot ignore its potential need for theater missile defense. Iran's missile strike capabilities are slowly improving, and Iraq will not be under UN sanctions forever. Most of Saudi Arabia's energy facilities, and much of its population, is located near its Gulf coast. A single missile strike against its capital with a weapon of mass destruction might seriously weaken the regime or kill enough of its elite leaders to change the character of the Saudi state.

The United States signed a shared early warning agreement with Saudi Arabia in 1998. This agreement called for the United States to provide data on missile launches to the Kingdom that can be used to alert the Patriots and to provide some degree of warning for alert and civil defense purposes. It took the Kingdom nearly two years to sign a related shared secure communications agreement, however, and the U.S. early warning system still uses different data links from the Saudi Patriot and other land-based Saudi C^4I systems. As a result, the United States will have to pass all early warning data to the Air Defense Force through the more modern communications in the Saudi Navy.

More broadly, even Saudi Arabia's improved Patriots are not advanced anti-tactical ballistic missile systems, and even if the Kingdom buys the new Patriot 3, this will only provide adequate coverage against Scud-type missiles, not the more advanced types of missiles Iran has in development. At the same time, no more advanced system is currently available although the U.S. Navy and Army have such systems under development, and the U.S. Air Force is working on boost-phase defenses.

It is too soon for Saudi Arabia to make any investment in missile defenses beyond the limited point defenses provided by Patriot. At the same time, it must begin to consider the cost-benefits of a theater-wide system long before it makes an actual buy, particularly since such a system could take five to ten years to deploy and cost tens of billions of dollars.

One option is to seek the deployment of U.S. systems and U.S. sea-based systems that might offer suitable emergency protection without requiring full-time deployment. This, however, means establishing a new cooperative approach to theater missile defense, and one that so far is only in the discussion stage. The other option is for the Kingdom to buy such systems, but the United States so far has failed to brief the Saudis on its advanced ATBM systems and will not have any such systems to sell or deploy before 2008 at the earliest. The Saudis have no funds for a near-term buy in any case. Even the full PAC-3 upgrade of the Patriot may slip until well after 2003, and the most the United States can provide in the near-term is missile launch warning data that will allow Saudi Arabia to better use its existing Patriots and that may provide some degree of civil defense.

The Problem of Readiness and U.S.-Saudi Tensions

Finally, the tensions between Saudi Arabia and the United States since September 11, Saudi funding problems, and Saudisation are creating the same kind of problems for the overall readiness and training of the Saudi Air Defense Force as for the other Saudi services. Saudi Arabia does not have the technical base to provide the level of training and maintenance it needs without a major contract effort, and only the United States can provide the necessary skills and expertise for a U.S.-supplied system.

The U.S. contractor base has been underfunded since the mid-1990s, and Saudisation has put Saudis in roles for which they are not properly trained and qualified. The tensions between the United States and Saudi Arabia over September 11 and the Second Intifada have also had some effect in reducing the level of U.S.-Saudi cooperation, although military-to-military relations have remained good and the Saudi Air Defense Force and U.S. Army still work well together. The major operational problem might occur in any serious war in which the lack of integration and effective C^{4}I/BM capabilities of Saudi forces would present serious problems unless the United States provided the necessary skills, technical support, and intelligence/warning data to allow Saudi forces to make fully effective use of their assets and fight on an integrated basis.

NOTES

1. Unless otherwise specified, the military data quoted here are taken from the relevant country sections of various annual editions of the IISS, *Military Balance*; CIA, *The World Factbook*; JCSS, *The Middle East Military Balance*; and online editions of *Jane's Sentinel series* and *Periscope, Jane's Intelligence Review*, and *Jane's Defence Weekly*. The cut-off date for such material is January 2002.

Other sources include interviews with Saudi officials and military inside and outside of Saudi Arabia, U.S. experts, and British experts. These are not identified by source by request of those interviewed. They also include the author's publications and other sources mentioned at the start of the section on Saudi Arabia; Dr. Andrew Rathmell, "Saudi Arabia's Military Build-up—An Extravagant Error," *Jane's Intelligence Review* (November 1994), pp. 500–504; Andrew Rathmell, *The Changing Balance in the Gulf*, Whitehall Papers 38 (London: Royal United Services Institute, 1996); Edward B. Atkenson, *The Powder Keg* (Falls Church: NOVA Publications, 1996); USCENTCOM, *Atlas, 1996* (MacDill Air Force Base: USCENTCOM, 1997); *Jane's Land-Based Air Defense*; *Jane's Military Vehicles and Logistics*; *Jane's Radar and Electronic Warfare Systems*; and *Jane's C4I Systems*

2. For typical reporting see IISS, *Military Balance, 1996–1997, 1999–2000, and 2001–2002.* The Hawks are MIM-23Bs.

3. *www.periscope.ucq.com/docs/nations/mideast/saudiara/army*, accessed January 7, 2002.

4. See IISS, *Military Balance, 2001–2002*, and *www.periscope.ucq.com/docs/nations/mideast/saudiara/army*, accessed January 7, 2002.

5. DSAA, June 1996; Richard F. Grimmett, *Arms Sales to Saudi Arabia* (Washington: Congressional Research Service, IB91007, August 28, 1991), p. 3; *Defense News*, September 23, 1991, pp. 1, 36, March 1, 1993, p. 17, April 14, 1997, p. 3; *Washington Post*, November 12, 1991, p. C-1; *New York Times*, November 9, 1991, p. 3; *Jane's Defence Weekly*, October 19, 1991, p. 699, July 10, 1996, p. 33; *Washington Times*, October 24, 1991, p. A-4; *Defense Daily*, November 8, 1991, p. 223, November 11, 1991, p. A-14; *Wall Street Journal*, December 24, 1992, p. 2.

6. Raytheon background brief, February 1992; *Defense News*, September 23, 1991, pp. 1, 36, March 1, 1993, p. 17; *Aviation Week*, January 4, 1993, p. 25; *New York Times*, February 17, 1993, p. D-4; *Washington Post*, December 24, 1992, p. A-8.

7. *Defense News*, March 1, 1993, p. 17, April 14, 1997, p. 3; *Jane's Defence Weekly*, October 19, 1991, p. 699, July 10, 1996, p. 33.

8. *Jane's Radar: National and International Air Defense, 1994–1995*, pp. 24–25; *Jane's Air Defense Systems, 1994–1995*, pp. 805–806; *Jane's Command Information Systems, 1994–1995*, pp. 47, 127.

9. *Flight International*, July 23, 1991, p. 18; *Jane's Defence Weekly*, July 15, 1989, p. 57.

10. Ibid.

11. *Jane's Defence Weekly*, July 15, 1989, p. 57, January 19, 1991, July 20, 1991, p. 97; *London Financial Times*, July 5, 1991, p. 5; *Flight International*, July 23, 1991, p. 18.

12. *Jane's Defence Weekly*, January 19, 1991, July 20, 1991, p. 97; *London Financial Times*, July 5, 1991, p. 5; *Flight International*, July 23, 1991, p. 18.

13. The $2.5 billion contract involves the services of twenty-five U.S. government and 300 contract personnel. Associated Press, September 26, 1997, 1917; *Boston Globe*, May 21, 1997, D-7; *Jane's Defence Weekly*, May 28, 1997, p. 19; *Jane's Military Exercise and Training Monitor* (July–September 1996), p. 9.

14. *Defense Week*, May 31, 1999, pp. 1, 20.

15. *Jane's Defence Weekly*, December 3, 1997, p. 5.

16. Reuters, April 10, 2000, 0520, April 15, 2000, 0503.

17. *Defense News*, May 4, 1998, p. 3; interviews in Saudi Arabia in April 2000 and February 2001; Reuters, Kuwait, February 2001.

Chapter 9

Saudi Paramilitary and Internal Security Forces

Saudi Arabia has long fought its own battles against internal and external extremist movements. In fact, the Saudi regime has had to deal with a long series of internal challenges from Islamic extremists since the time of the Ikhwan in the 1920s, as well as from more secular movements supported by other Arab states. These struggles were particularly serious during the peak of Nasserism and Pan Arabism in the 1950s, and the first major Islamic backlash from oil wealth and modernization in the late 1970s. They have been a continuing problem since 1990 because of conservative Wahhabi hostility to a U.S. and Western military presence on Saudi soil.

During these battles, the Saudi government has quietly put pressure on the Saudi Ulema (Islamic clergy), has arrested a wide range of extremists, and publicly condemned terrorism. It cooperated with the United States in a number of cases, including the attack on the U.S.S. *Cole*. It also was careful to exploit the fact that the Saudi clergy is paid by the government, and that there are no Madrassas in Saudi Arabia providing religious education separate from the state educational system. The Ministry of Islamic Affairs is primarily organized for the purpose of religious administration, but it has always had an internal security element as well, and has been used to provide both carrots and sticks for internal security purposes. This role was given a higher profile during the Gulf War, when it became apparent that many hard-line Islamists opposed any Western presence on Saudi soil, and was slowly stepped up in the 1990s when Islamic extremists became more active. The Ministry of Interior and Saudi intelligence took similar steps, particularly after Osama bin Laden emerged as an opponent of the regime.

It is hardly surprising, therefore, that senior members of the Saudi royal family immediately expressed their sympathy for the United States after September 11, and condemned the terrorist attacks on the U.S. after the strikes on the World Trade Center and the Pentagon. The Saudi government issued a statement condemning the "regrettable and inhuman bombings and attacks," and strongly condemned such acts, "which contravene all religious values and human civilized concepts; and extended sincere condolences to the families of the victims, to U.S. President George W. Bush and to the U.S. people in general." The Saudi statement reiterated the Kingdom's position condemning all forms of terrorism, and its ongoing cooperation with the international community to combat it.

The Saudi Foreign Minister attacked terrorism in more depth in an interview in Okaz on September 16, 2001. The Minister of the Interior made similar statements on September 23. Saudi Arabia strongly condemned the terrorist Organization of the Islamic Conference meeting on October 11, and Minister of Foreign Affairs Prince Saud Al-Faisal issued a separate statement stressing that terrorism harmed the Islamic world and just Islamic causes. He also stated that terrorist acts have, for example, never advanced the Palestinian cause.

Senior Saudi religious and legal figures condemned the attacks with equal speed. The chairman of the Supreme Judicial Council, Sheikh Salih al-Luheidan, stated on September 14, "As a human community we must be vigilant and careful to oppose these pernicious and shameless evils, which are not justified by any sane logic, nor by the religion of Islam." Sheikh Abdulaziz Al-Sheikh, the cof the Senior Ulema and the mufti of Saudi Arabia, reemphasized Sheikh al-Luheidan's statements on September 15, stating, "The recent developments in the United States constitute a form of injustice that is not tolerated by Islam, which views them as gross crimes and sinful acts." Since that time, leading Saudi officials and clerics have repeatedly condemned the attack on the World Trade Center and the Pentagon, and other terrorist activities.[1]

THE SAUDI FAILURES THAT HELPED LEAD TO SEPTEMBER 11, 2001

Nevertheless, the events of September 11 have dramatized the fact that Saudi Arabia not only faces serious internal security issues but must now play a major role in the global struggle on terrorism. It not only must take new internal measures to deal with Islamic extremism and terrorism, but must also act to deal with a wide range of other internal security issues. In fact, the Saudi government has had to make repeated efforts since September 11 to tighten its control over the Saudi clergy, and deal with issues like sermons and literature that still contain anti-Semitic and anti-Christian content, as well as potential incitements to extremist or terrorist action.

Crown Prince Abdullah has repeatedly stated that Islam must be treated as a religion of tolerance and peace. On December 7, 2002, Sheikh Saleh al-Sheikh, a descendent of Muhammad Abd Al-Wahhab and minister of Islamic affairs, announced new restrictions had been put in place to prohibit "unauthorized persons" from making speeches at mosques and warned the speakers at mosques against "making provocative speeches and inciting people." The letter containing these instructions said, "mosques are meant only for prayer, guidance, and other pious activities and should not be used as political platforms . . . to make provocative speeches or incite people or exploit mosques by reciting poems in praise of some misguided people." The minister commended those imams (prayer leaders) and khatibs who fulfilled their religious duties in prayers by providing advice and guidance, and called upon them to "serve as models for others by spreading love and brotherhood." At the same time, he warned that violators of the new order would be subject to severe punishment, including removal from office.[2]

The fact that so many young Saudis were directly involved in September 11, as well as in the overall membership of Osama bin Laden's al Qaeda, reflects the fact that Saudi security efforts still have major weaknesses. Saudi Arabia has failed to come firmly to grips with its Islamic extremists at many levels. The Saudi government has tolerated problems and ultra-conservative forms of Wahhabi and Islamist teaching and text books in its educational system that encourages extremism. It has failed to properly track young Saudis who became involved with extremist movements outside the country. The government has carelessly provided funds and support for Wahhabi and other ultraconservative movements and activities outside Saudi Arabia that encouraged violence and extremism, and has failed to properly distinguish between support of legitimate Islamic causes and charities and involvement with violent movements.

Before September 11, the Saudi government was generally careful to monitor the activities of Islamic groups that directly criticize the Saudi government and royal family, but failed to monitor the flow of money to causes and groups outside the Kingdom with anything like the care and depth required. It often felt that it could export its problems to "safe" countries like Afghanistan and then buy off a regime like the Taliban to control Saudi dissidents. Saudi intelligence and diplomacy failed badly in dealing with al Qaeda and bin Laden in Afghanistan, and the security services failed to monitor the degree to which Saudis and Saudi money became involved in supporting al Qaeda and other extremist causes in Central Asia, Pakistan, Germany, and elsewhere long after incidents of terrorism reached a level in the mid-1990s that showed this should be a subject of serious concern.

These failures were compounded by other actions. The regime tolerated sermons, teaching, and textbooks with a strong xenophobic character—sometimes attacking Christians, Jews and other religions—as long as they did not attack specific political targets in Saudi Arabia or call for specific violent actions. It made relatively little effort to monitor the activities of "Islamic" groups in secondary schools and colleges if they did not directly oppose the regime, and made far too little effort to evaluate what Saudi and many foreign contract teachers were actually teaching their students. The regime did not oppose foreign and domestic efforts to raise money and obtain support for "pro-Islamic" movements in Bosnia, Kosovo, Afghanistan, and central Asia even when these represented extreme and sometimes violent causes. Little or no effort was made to monitor the extent to which foreign "charities" raised money for political movements in Europe, the Middle East, and Asia, that were far more extreme (and sometimes violent) than would have been tolerated in Saudi Arabia. The regime turned a blind eye to the flow of funds to movements like Hamas that mixed charitable activity with terrorist activities in Israel.

Somewhat ironically, Saudi Arabia's deep concern with religion and charity, and lack of an income tax, compounded its problems. Islam calls, for all those who can, to give Zakat, a religious donation of roughly 2.5% of their income, to charity. It also calls for those with land to give as much as a 5 to 10% Zakat, depending on the quality of their land. The fact that Saudi Arabia does not have an income tax and that it is still a highly patriarchical, tribal, and clan-oriented society dependent on personal patronage and charity, makes it a nation that places a heavy reliance on voluntary Islamic charity. As a result, large amounts of money have flowed out of the Kingdom from the king, other senior princes, and wealthy Saudis to groups and causes that would never have received the money if those asking for it had received proper review of what they were actually doing and saying. Senior members of the royal family, and wealthy Saudis, gave as if they had to meet a quota rather than care about a cause. They also often left the task to younger princes who either cared nothing about where the money actually went or had far too little political sophistication to evaluate the groups asking for money.

Extremists and terrorists learned to exploit this situation, using formal charities or personal requests to obtain money that they never would have gotten if they announced their real purpose in seeking funds. At the same time, some real charities had a strong political orientation and often supported extremist movements and some donors knowingly gave money to "charities" that were extremist fronts. This was particularly true after the beginning of the Second Intifada in the fall of 2000 with money going to Palestinian causes. Most Saudis saw Israel as an occupying nation constantly using excessive force against Palestinian freedom fighters—the opposite of how the Americans saw them. The end result was that massive amounts of money flowed out to extremists and terrorist movements through sheer negligence, fraud, or under the guise of charity.

In retrospect, both the Ministry of Interior and Saudi intelligence failed to pay attention to the "youth explosion" caused by Saudi Arabia's high birth rate. They were slow to monitor the movement and activities of young Saudis outside the Kingdom, and to closely to examine those Saudis that became involved in paramilitary training and movements in Afghanistan, Bosnia, Kosovo, and Chechnya. They paid too little attention to organizations like al Qaeda even though it took action against Osama bin Laden as early as 1994. They failed to distinguish between conservative Wahhabi teaching and the kind of extremist teaching and preaching that could lead to violence.

These failures were scarcely inevitable. While the exact organizations and chains of responsibility involved are unclear, Saudi Arabia learned just how threatening such developments could be during the Islamist extremist seizure of the Grand Mosque in 1979. Since that time, the security services have often been effective in monitoring the activities of those hard-line Saudi opposition groups overseas that attacked the regime, exploiting divisions within them, co-opting or bribing elements within them, and putting pressure on foreign governments to end their activities. They have been equally effective when dealing with Iranian, Yemeni, Iraqi, and Palestinian efforts to support Saudi opposition groups in Saudi Arabia.

One key problem is that Saudi intelligence activity has relied too much on human and communications intelligence. It has been weak in dealing with the financial aspects of intelligence and internal security, which helps explain why it failed to properly monitor the flow of money to Saudi charities, religious organizations, and individuals financing extremist groups other than those that posed a direct threat to the rule of the Saudi royal family.

In fairness, such monitoring is not easy. Saudi banking rules are relatively strict in terms of tracking and identifying individual accounts, but little effort was made before September 11 to track the flow of money inside or outside the country to extremist causes and factions. It should be noted however, that Saudi organizations and individuals have billions of dollars of privately held money in foreign banks. Effective surveillance of such holdings is difficult, if not impossible. The problem is further compounded by easy access to the financial institutions of other GCC countries, like the UAE. Many Gulf countries have financial institutions that make cash transfers extremely easy; tolerate high levels of money laundering, smuggling, and narcotrafficking; and have often been far more careless in allowing the flow of money to extremist causes than Saudi Arabia has been. The leaders and citizens of countries like Kuwait and the UAE have also been as careless in their donations to "charities" as Saudis.

More generally, Saudi Arabia has consistently failed in another major area of internal security. The level of corruption in Saudi Arabia is often exaggerated and used to make broad, undocumented charges against the government and royal family. Corruption is, however, a very real problem. Exaggerated perceptions of corruption can be as important as reality. Saudi

Arabia has been slow to reform civil law and regulation to create the legal basis for large-scale private and foreign investment and commercial operations that can be based on secure rights to property, conducting business without interference or reliance on agents, and revolving commercial disputes. There has been steady progress in these areas, but there has not been enough. Saudi internal security is growing increasingly dependent on the broad public and international perception that Saudi Arabia will rein in corruption, that members of the royal family and senior officials cannot intervene improperly in business affairs, and that investments and business activities are safe.

THE ROLE OF THE MINISTRY OF THE INTERIOR

Saudi Arabia has a complex mix of paramilitary and internal security forces, and an equally complex legal system for dealing with civil and security cases. There is no doubt that the Saudi security and criminal justice systems differ sharply from those in the West, and involve human rights abuses. At the same time, the Kingdom's internal security system is less repressive than many developing states', and relies more on detention than the physical punishment or exile of its opponents.[3] Co-option is used more than repression, and the security services rely more on family and tribal ties to pressure opponents than on direct arrests or punishments. While Saudi Arabia does not make use of formal exile procedures, it does force extremist and hostile elements out of the country, and deprives some security suspects of their citizenship.

As already noted, a number of civil ministries, like the Ministry of Islamic Affairs, play at least an indirect role in internal security because of their political impact. Others include the Ministry of Communications, the Ministry of Finance and National Economy, the Ministry of Information, the Ministry of Education, the Ministry of Higher Education, the Ministry of Justice, the Ministry of Petroleum and Mineral Resources, the Ministry of Pilgrimage and Islamic Trusts, and the Ministry of Post, Telephone, and Telegraph. This kind of indirect role in internal security is typical of similar ministries in virtually every country in the developing world, as well as a number of countries in Europe.

The Saudi security forces involve a mix of elements in the regular armed forces and the National Guard, and a range of internal security and intelligence services, most of which are under the Ministry of Interior. As discussed in previous chapters, the regular army provides external security, but is kept away from urban areas. The National Guard provides internal security under a different chain of command using both its regular forces and elements from the National Guard loyal tribes. It protects the territory of the Kingdom and the approaches to its cities and critical facilities, acts as reinforcement for the regular forces, and can serve as an urban security force in an emergency. It does, however, have an Intelligence Directorate that serves a broader purpose and which Crown Prince Abdullah uses for a variety of broader intelligence and internal security purposes.

The rest of the internal security forces and intelligence services are centralized under Prince Nayef bin Abdulaziz, the Minister of the Interior.[4] Prince Nayef is a major political power in the Kingdom. He is one of the strongest figures in the royal family and has long played a critical role in Saudi security. According to some reports, all of the security services report first to Prince Nayef, and even Crown Prince Abdullah must give his orders to the security services through Prince Nayef or his deputy Prince Ahmad.

As will be touched upon later, Prince Nayef is also a controversial figure. Some Saudis feel he is extremely conservative, and has become out of touch with the Kingdom's current security problems. These Saudis believe that he was far too slow to react to the growth of Islamic extremist movements outside the Kingdom and to the role the Kingdom played in supporting such movements with money and Saudi volunteers. They believe that Nayef felt outside pressure from the United States to crack down on such activities because of exaggerated U.S. fears that were partly the result of pressure from Israel.

These views do have some support from Prince Nayef's own words. Since September 11, Prince Nayef has made several political statements implying that the attacks were the product of the Egyptian Moslem Brotherhood and/or Israel. For example, he made such statements in an interview with the Kuwaiti newspaper *Al Siyasa* on November 29, 2002. In fairness, Prince Nayef did so in a long interview where he stressed the need to crack down on terrorism, that the government was putting pressure on Saudi religious figures and mosques, that the Kingdom has made numerous arrests, and that terrorism was fundamentally anti-Islamic. He was also reacting to a flood of poorly founded Western press that criticized Saudi Arabia, linking the wife of the Saudi Ambassador to the United States, who supposedly gave money to a family that *might* have been linked to terrorists.[5]

Nevertheless, Prince Nayef did say, "we put big question marks and ask who was committed to the events of September 11? Who benefited from the events of September 11? I think they (the Zionists) are behind these events." His view was that it was "impossible" that al Qaeda acted alone, or that 19 youths, of which 17 were Saudi, could have acted alone. He then went on to attack the Moslem Brotherhood saying, "All our problems come from the Moslem Brotherhood. We have given too much support to this group. . . . The Moslem Brotherhood has destroyed the Arab world." He attacked a multinational spectrum of Islamic politicians for turning their backs on Saudi Arabia, forgetting the favors it had given them, and launching attacks on the Kingdom. He singled out Hassan al Turabi of the Sudan as a case in point. He also mentioned Hamas, Jordan's parliamentary opposition, and the Islamic Action Front for their attacks on the Kingdom, and attacked Islamic scholars like Abdul Rahman Khalifa, Rashid Ghannouchi, Abdul Majeed Al-Zidani, and Necmettin Erbakan for supporting the Iraqi invasion of Kuwait. He stated there were no dormant al Qaeda cells remaining in Saudi Arabia and that this threat no longer existed.[6]

Some Saudi sources estimate the total internal security budget to be as high as $6 to $7 billion annually, with an open-ended capability to spend on any internal security purpose. Prince Nayef and Prince Ahmad are reported to pay massive bonuses to successful security officers, but also have a reputation for honesty and using the security budget only for the mission and not to enrich themselves.

The vice minister is the youngest full brother of the king. The assistant minister for security affairs is Prince Mohammad bin Nayef, Prince Nayef's son and the third-ranking individual in the ministry. The deputy positions include Dr. Ahmad al Salem, the deputy minister of the Interior who effectively runs the ministry and is the fourth-ranking individual. The deputy minister for security affairs in Saudi Arabia is General al Robayaan. He was formerly head of the minister's Research and Studies Bureau, and effectively reports to Mohammad bin Nayef. There is also a deputy minister for Regions, Dr. al Mazroe. There are also a couple of advisors to the Minister of the Interior who are part of the Office of the Minister of Interior.

The director generals of the respective services all report to the minister and vice minister and are directly responsible to the minister. These services include the director generals of General Security Service (GSS), Public Security Administration (all police forces fall under this service), Passports and Immigration Department, Frontier Guard, Coast Guard, and the Special Security Service. The security colleges fall under the Deputy Minister al Salem who runs the administration and management of the ministry. Prince Nayef also hired the former heads of a number of Arab security services (from Jordan, Morocco, Syria, and Egypt) as personal consultants, and pays them large retainers to remain at his disposal.

The Coast Guard, Civil Defense Administration, and Frontier Force are under one chain of command in the Ministry of the Interior. The Public Security, Special Security, Mujahideen, and GSS branches are under a separate chain of command. These organizations provide internal security at the political and intelligence levels, security inside cities dealing with limited problems that require crowd control and SWAT-like operations, and counterterrorist capabilities. They also provide the Kingdom's primary counterterrorist force, and played a major role in the bombings of the SANG headquarters and the USAF barracks at Al Khobar.

THE POLICE AND SECURITY SERVICES

The police and security forces are still somewhat traditional in character, but they have been steadily modernized over the years. Early in Saudi

Arabia's history, there were no formal police and local and tribal authorities administered justice. During the reign of Abd al-Aziz, more modern police, justice, and internal security organizations were developed. In 1950, he created a "general directorate" to supervise all police functions. He established the Ministry of Interior in 1951, which has since controlled police matters.

Saudi Arabia has received substantial technical advice from British, French, German, Jordanian, Pakistani, and U.S. experts. Substantial numbers of British and French advisors served in Saudi Arabia in the past, including seconded ex-government and military personnel, but it is unclear how many have continued to serve since the early 1990s.

The police security forces are now divided into regular police and special investigative police of the GSS, which are called the *mubahith* (secret police). The GSS conducts criminal investigations in addition to performing the domestic security and counterintelligence functions of the Ministry of Interior. The GSS has a large special investigation force, something like the British CID, but with political as well as criminal justice functions. The U.S. State Department reports that political detainees arrested by the GSS are often held incommunicado in special prisons during the initial phase of an investigation, which may last weeks or months. The GSS allows the detainees only limited contact with their families or lawyers.

There are approximately 35,000 paramilitary policemen in the Public Security Police equipped with small arms and some automatic weapons. They are assigned to provincial governors, and are under the aegis of the Minister of the Interior. The main Public Security College is in Riyadh, with another in Mecca. Police uniforms are similar to the khaki and olive drab worn by the army except for the distinctive red beret. Policemen usually wear side arms while on duty.

The Special Security Force is the Saudi equivalent of a special weapons assault team (SWAT). It reports directly to the Minister of Interior. It was organized in response to the poor performance of the National Guard during the revolt at the Grand Mosque in Mecca in 1979. The force is equipped with light armored vehicles, automatic weapons, and nonlethal chemical weapons. Its exact strength is unclear and its antiterrorism units have been steadily expanded since 1990. It is designed to deal with terrorism and hijacking and has SWAT capabilities and detachments in every major Saudi city and province. Saudi Special Forces include a regular Army airborne brigade, a Royal Guard Brigade, and a Marine Regiment.

The public security forces are recruited from all areas of the country, maintained police directorates at provincial and local levels. These forces, particularly the centralized Public Security Police, can be reinforced by the National Guard in an emergency or can get support from the regular armed forces. The director general for public security retained responsibility for police units but, in practice, provincial governors exercised considerable autonomy.

The focus of police and security activity has also changed over the years. Saudi Arabia is now a highly urbanized society and these formal state institutions carry out most internal security and criminal justice activity in urban areas. This has helped drive the effort to modernize the police and security forces. For example, new vehicles and radio communications equipment have enabled police directorates to operate sophisticated mobile units, particularly in the principal cities. Helicopters have been acquired for use in urban areas.

The Ministry of Interior now maintains a centralized computer system at the National Information Center in Riyadh. This computer network links some 1,100 terminals, and maintains records on citizens' identity numbers and passports, foreigners' residence and work permits, Hajj visas, vehicle registrations, and criminal records. Reports from agents and from the large number of informants employed by the security services are also entered. Officials of the Directorate of Intelligence have authority to carry out wiretaps and mail surveillance. The Ministry of the Interior has a large electronic intelligence and surveillance effort, with a budget well in excess of a billion riyals a year.

Some security activities do, however, continue to be enforced on a tribal level in tribal areas. The king provides payments or subsidies to key sheikhs and they are largely in charge of tribal affairs. Offenses and many crimes are still punished by the responsible sheikh. The National Guard acts as a support force to deal with problems that cannot be settled or controlled by the tribal authorities.

Border and coastline control have long been an important aspect of security operations. The paramilitary Frontier Force and Coast Guard are security forces with dedicated missions that can perform light combat functions. The 10,500-man Frontier Force covers Saudi Arabia's land and sea borders. It performs a host of patrol and surveillance missions, and can act as a light defensive screen. It is equipped with four-wheel-drive vehicles and automatic weapons. The Frontier Force did much of the fighting with Yemen in the past, and took casualties in doing so. It still must deal with the problem of smuggling and infiltration across the Saudi border. The 4,500 men in the Coast Guard are primarily concerned with smuggling, but do have a limited internal security mission.[7]

Saudi Arabia has considered building a border surveillance system that would use patrol aircraft, remotely piloted vehicles, and early warning systems to detect intruders and border crossings. This would involve a twelve-kilometer-deep security zone around all 6,500 kilometers of land and sea borders, with a mix of acoustic, seismic, radar, magnetic, and infrared sensors to detect movements of men and vehicles in the border area. It would be supported by small manned patrol aircraft, and unmanned remotely piloted vehicles, wherever some threat from an intruder might exist. Thomson CSF completed a $5 million feasibility study for this system in early 1990, and two consortiums—one led by E Systems and the other by Thomson CSF—submitted bids to Saudi Arabia in May 1991. The system was not funded in part because of its cost, and in part because of the ease with which given sections could be penetrated before an effective response would be possible. Its estimated cost was around $3 billion and it would have taken several years to complete.[8]

THE GENERAL INTELLIGENCE DIRECTORATE

Saudi Arabia has a General Intelligence Directorate (GID) with security, antiterrorism, and foreign liaison functions. The GID reports directly to the king, is part of the Royal Diwan, and has extensive funding. According to some sources, it is the most funded intelligence service in the Middle East, and has a larger budget than the Foreign Ministry, or the British SIS and French DGSE.

In theory, the GID is responsible for intelligence collection and analysis, and for the coordination of intelligence tasks and reporting by *all* intelligence agencies, including those of the Ministry of Defense and Aviation and the National Guard. In practice, there is no real Saudi intelligence "community." Intelligence sharing—or "fusion"—is weak, coordination is poor, and Saudi intelligence is filled with personal and bureaucratic rivalries and tensions. The problems are compounded by the fact that the research department of the GID is very weak, and Saudi intelligence relies too heavily on personal contacts and briefings, rather than systematic and structured analysis.

The GID has, however, been successful in dealing with many internal and foreign threats that have posed a direct threat to the region. It has a long history of cooperation with the CIA and other U.S. intelligence services, although it has generally opposed any Western efforts to introduce law enforcement organizations like the FBI into Saudi security issues in ways that could embarrass the Saudi government. This led to acute tensions between the GID and the FBI over the investigation of the Al-Khobar bombing, and helped lead to the charges that the Saudi government covered up Iranian involvement in the bombing.

In fairness to Saudi Arabia, the United States, Britain, and other Western countries have failed to cooperate with Saudi intelligence in a number of past cases because they felt that this might violate the rights of legitimate opposition movements or raise human rights issues. The United States and other Western intelligence services also turned a blind eye, or at least tolerated, Islamic extremist activity when it seemed to serve their interests in Afghanistan and Bosnia or acted as a counterbalance to Russian influence in Central Asia, and paid little attention to the potential threat posed by funds and manpower coming out of the Kingdom. If Saudi Arabia was slow to see the threat of extremism and terrorism and sometimes "exported" its problems, the United States, Britain, and other European intelligence and security services made equally serious mistakes in monitoring and characterizing "Islamic" movements.

THE OPERATIONS OF THE SAUDI SECURITY AND INTELLIGENCE SERVICES

Saudi Arabia has tended to deal with its security problems by trying to conceal them in a series of public denials. A number of members of the royal family do admit in retrospect, however, that the Saudi intelligence and security services failed to come to grips with the problems of Islamic extremism—although some believe the Foreign Ministry, Office of the King, and Office of the Crown Prince should have to accept equal or greater blame. Warning of the attacks occurred at least half a decade before September 11, 2001. The GID discovered after the National Guard and Al-Khobar bombings that approximately 8,000 to 15,000 young Saudi men had some contact with Islamic extremist groups, Afghanis, and paramilitary training facilities between 1979 and the mid-1990s.[9] While this represented a small fraction of young Saudi males, it was scarcely insignificant given the generally small size of Islamic extremist groups and terrorist cells in general.

The Saudi intelligence and internal security services paid far too little attention to the growing and highly visible ties between hard-line Pakistani extremists in the Pakistani ISI and religious schools, the impact of Saudi-financed activities in Pakistan and Central Asia, and the number of young Saudi men associated with Osama bin Laden and al Qaeda. Discussions with Saudi officials indicate that they had surprisingly little understanding of the difference between legitimate Islamic organizations in central Asia, China, and the Far East and highly political action groups that used Islam as an ideological weapon. They paid little attention to the fact that such groups were committed to the violent overthrow of governments in their region, and were strongly opposed to both modernization and reform, and broadly anti-Western in character. They also failed to monitor Wahhabi "missionary" and charity groups operating in Europe. Even though such groups showed little of the pragmatic tolerance and moderation common to mainstream Wahhabi practices in the Kingdom, they often took on an extremist character, particularly in Germany.

As touched upon earlier, they showed a tendency to turn a blind eye toward the flow of Saudi money to Palestinian groups like Hamas and Palestinian Islamic Jihad, and other hardline or violent Islamic elements in countries like Egypt. Furthermore, Saudi officials felt that Saudi support and financing of the Taliban and other governments acted as a way of containing Saudi extremists overseas, with the somewhat naive expectation that such governments would really rein in their activity or stay "bought."

Saudi Arabia has begun to make significant changes in its approach to these problems since September 11. It has quietly made significant arrests, and is making far more of an effort to understand the nature of Saudi activity in extremist groups and the flow of money outside the Kingdom. It is now making a major effort to track the activities of Saudi religious and charitable groups inside and outside the Kingdom, and is now giving special attention to Pakistan and central Asia. It is tightening security inside the Kingdom, and surveillance over young men with ties to extremist groups, as well as surveillance, religious figures that made hardline or extremist statements, and the activities of religious schools and teachers.

CHANGES IN THE GENERAL INTELLIGENCE DIRECTORATE

Developments have taken place within the GID since September 11 that are difficult to interpret. The GID had long been led by Prince Turki al-Faisal before he was replaced in 2001 by Crown Prince Abdullah's half brother, Prince Nawaf bin Abdalaziz.[10] This development was particularly striking because Prince Turki al-Faisal a son of King Faisal and a nephew of Nawaf, had spent some thirty years in intelligence. He began his career as deputy director at the age of twenty-three and was promoted to the top job in 1977. Prince Turki had long been the main contact point for the CIA, British Secret Intelligence Service, French intelligence and security services, among others. He had also been responsible for dealing with operations in Afghanistan and central Asia since the Soviet invasion in 1979, and was a key point of contact with the CIA-backed Mujahideen and Pakistani Intelligence, the various warring Afghan factions after the Soviet withdrawal, and with the Taliban and Osama bin Laden.[11]

The Saudi explanation for the change was that Prince Turki had resigned "at his own request." There are many different rumors and interpretations of what happened, and the very different views of Simon Henderson and John Duke Anthony illustrate the range of views involved. Simon Henderson explains the change as follows:[12]

Washington has been at a loss to explain what caused Turki to resign. One theory was that his wife was ill, and that he wanted more time for himself and his family. Another suggested that he had never completely recovered from an accident while camping in the desert in the mid-1980s, when he inhaled carbon monoxide from a defective heater. But these are just theories. He was sacked, and we don't know why, an indicator of how little is known about the closed Saudi society.

But Saudi watchers tend to be a diligent bunch. The involvement of Saudi-born terrorist bin Laden in the events of Sept. 11 made the resignation of Turki an issue that had to be resolved. The version now accepted as most likely is a baroque tale, combining dynastic tensions within the 30,000-strong royal family, Saudi relations with the Taliban, Saudi relations with the U.S., and the implication that the Saudis knew or suspected that bin Laden might carry out his hijacking outrages somewhere in the world in September.

The dramatis personae also include Prince Nayef, the interior minister. . . . The succession struggle, particularly fraught since late 1995—when King Fahd had the first in a series of strokes—has been played out against a background of internal political opposition, caused by poor government revenues from oil and resentment about princely corruption. There has also been long-standing tension between Turki and his uncle, Nayef, the interior minister, who was in charge of the domestic intelligence service. Theoretically, Turki answered to Nayef, but he had preserved a degree of independence.

The two men had a major falling out after the 1996 bombing of the Khobar Towers, attributed to minority Saudi Shiites with the backing of Iran. Turki had wanted full co-operation for the investigation with the FBI and the CIA; Nayef had refused, considering such co-operation an infringement of Saudi sovereignty. Turki's handling of the Afghanistan file was also judged faulty. Although the Taliban, like the Saudis, were Wahhabis, a puritanical interpretation of Sunni Islam, their support for bin Laden had clearly begun to harm the Kingdom's best interests. The regime had made a strategic mistake in backing the Taliban—their fellow Wahhabis—but now Turki was going to be the fall guy.

Nayef took the issue of his differences with Turki to Crown Prince Abdullah, the Kingdom's de facto ruler, who could not ignore the complaint. Along with Fahd, Abdullah and Sultan, Nayef is one of the four most powerful men in Saudi Arabia. Abdullah proposed a compromise. . . . Turki, he agreed, would go, but would be replaced by Abdullah's confidante and constant companion, Prince Nawaf.

The timing of Turki's removal—Aug. 31—and his Taliban connection raise the question: Did the Saudi regime know that bin Laden was planning his attack against the U.S.? The current view among Saudi watchers is probably not, but the House of Saud might have heard rumors that something was planned, although they did not know what or when. (An interesting and possibly significant detail: Prince Sultan, the defense minister, had been due to visit Japan in early September, but canceled his trip for no apparent reason less than two days before his planned departure.)

For Western diplomats and intelligence officers trying to achieve international cooperation in the hunt for bin Laden, Turki's forced departure seems like a cruel farce. The close personal relations they had developed over the years with a key player in Saudi Arabia are now worthless. U.S. officials find themselves dealing with Nayef, who doesn't want to cooperate, and Nawaf, the new intelligence chief, who is quite out of his depth. And it doesn't help that Crown Prince Abdullah is in a huff over President Bush's determination to wage war in Afghanistan.

As discussed earlier, Saudis have divided views over both what happened and the respective roles of Prince Nayef and Prince Turki. Many Saudis feel that Henderson's reporting is typical of the negative analysis that has come from outside analysts since September 11.

Few Saudis, however, seem to support Henderson's analysis of the facts, and many share the views of John Duke Anthony, who provides an explanation of why Prince Nawaf bin Abdalaziz al-Saud may have been chosen as Prince Turki's successor:[13]

The resignation this week of longtime Saudi Arabian Director of the General Intelligence Directorate HRH Prince Turki bin Faisal Al Sa'ud came to some as a surprise. Others familiar with the Minister's situation expected the resignation at some point—it was not a question of whether the Minister, who had served in his post for more than a quarter of a century, would step down, but when.

The timing was rooted in circumstances pertaining to the Minister's immediate family—and nothing more. . . . Despite rumors and speculations to the contrary, the resignation was not prompted, let alone validated, by the numerous ill-informed media reports that have appeared to date.

These include perceived intra-ruling family differences over the Ministry's handling of such matters as the June 1996 Al-Khobar Towers bombing investigations and the November 1995 explosions in Riyadh—phenomena dealt with more directly by other government agencies than the one that Prince Turki headed—and equally unfounded reports of squabbles pertaining to the Afghan Taliban, and/or potential scenarios related to succession.

In any case, many may ask, "What does the resignation mean? Does it signify that a policy change of some kind is imminent?" "If so, will our interests be affected?" Helping to assuage such anxieties is the following.

Prince Turki's successor, HRH Prince Nawwaf bin Abdalaziz Al Sa'ud, could hardly be closer to Heir Apparent Prince Abdallah bin Abdalaziz Al Sa'ud. The latter is known to have an exceptional measure of trust and confidence in this senior member of the ruling family.

. . . Among the new minister's challenges are those that pertain to establishing not so much credibility but as smooth a working relationship with other ministers as possible. Of greatest importance will be the need to forge effective inter-ministerial cooperation on matters that pertain to his portfolio and those that in some cases parallel or overlap with the portfolios of others.

In the latter instance, there will be a need for closest collaboration with the Ministry of Interior, especially on matters pertaining to security. But this should not be difficult. Prince Nawwaf, like Minister of Interior, Prince Nayif, share the same father, and he is nearer in age to Nayif than Prince Turki.

. . . On the external front, some of the more difficult challenges that the Kingdom faced during the long tenure of Prince Turki have either been settled, substantially modified, or become different and in some ways less arduous or complex than before.

Two examples are the ending of the Soviet invasion and occupation of Afghanistan and the termination of the Iran-Iraq war. Two more are the successful achievement of independence by the states along the Kingdom's eastern littoral, and the ending of the country's border disputes with virtually all of its neighbors.

There has also been a significant diminution of the kinds of threats to domestic security—the odd aircraft hijacking, Iranian-inspired disruptions during the annual Islamic pilgrimage, cross border forays from the south, and the occasional demonstration by religious minorities—that posed daunting challenges in years gone by.

. . . As for how quickly and easily the new Minister can be expected to settle into the day-to-day workings of his directorate, this will of course take time. Such things always do. But the process should prove to be less daunting and time-consuming than many unfamiliar with his background and previous experience might imagine.

The reasons are several. For nearly forty years, Prince Nawwaf has frequently been entrusted with exceptionally difficult challenges to the Kingdom's foreign policy objectives.

A case in point was during the period 1968–1971, when the British proceeded to abrogate the treaties by which, for more than a century, they had administered nine east Arabian principalities' defense and foreign relations. Throughout most of that period, it was Prince Nawwaf that the late King Faisal sent to work with these soon-to-be-independent rulers in pursuit of what he hoped would emerge as the most inclusive new Arab state possible. In the end, instead of a single federation, three states—Bahrain, Qatar, and the (seven-member) United Arab Emirates—were established.

Although many had wished for a larger union, such an outcome reflected accurately the then prevailing political realities. Since then, the results have proved to be positive. Compared to how most other Arab countries have fared over the same length of time, these three entities have survived and thrived. And this was not all. Much of the earlier distrust and suspicion between the Kingdom and the Emirate of Abu Dhabi was vitiated in the course of Prince Nawwaf's indefatigable efforts to help smooth the way to independence for these British-protected states.

In the process, Prince Nawwaf became exceptionally knowledgeable of the limits as well as the possibilities of Arab inter-state cooperation, coordination, and integration.

Certainly, few outside the Gulf sheikhdoms had more direct exposure to the steps that led to the formation of the United Arab Emirates in December 1971. And from that experience, no one in Saudi Arabia had more first hand awareness of the relevance of what the UAE represented for what would be the next successful effort in Arab intra-regional cooperation ten years later: namely, the six-country Gulf Cooperation Council that was formed in May 1981.

. . . Nor, with the exception of Princes Sa'ud and Turki, does any senior member of the ruling family have anywhere near as much direct experience in representing the Kingdom's interests within the 22-member League of Arab States, of which it was a co-founder in September 1944.

Prince Nawwaf's previous experience with Arab League issues is likely to prove propitious. Three reasons come to mind. One is the Kingdom's strong support for former Egyptian Foreign Minister Amr Moussa, who became the League's new Secretary-General this past April. The second is the resulting dynamism that has marked the League's deliberations from then until now.

The third is Saudi Arabian Foreign Minister Prince Sa'ud's completion in the past two weeks of visits to numerous League members. The goal of the latter exercise: to present a more united Arab front at the meetings of the UN General Assembly scheduled to begin next week in New York.

. . . In sum, the new Minister would be the first to agree with the observation that all in public life do little more than stand upon the shoulders of those that went before. In this instance, the shoulders of his predecessor were by all accounts exceptionally strong and broad. But, in their own way, the ones that Prince Nawwaf brings to the task of heading the Kingdom's intelligence directorate are also impressive.

Regardless of the exact explanation, Prince Nawaf has since had a stroke, and is now seen as little more than an ineffective figurehead. Without stronger, more modern, and more independent leadership, the future of Saudi internal security will not be shaped by the leadership of the GID alone, but rather by the overall effectiveness of the government and the royal family in dealing with the broader mix of political, economic, social, and demographic issues that threaten Saudi Arabia's internal security.

Saudi Arabia clearly needs to do more to expand and modernize some aspects of its intelligence operations. In the past, Saudi intelligence has tended to rely heavily on interpersonal relations and human intelligence (HUMINT), supplemented by limited usage of surveillance equipment and computerized records. It has worked closely with the CIA, British and French intelligence, and has had access to more advanced imagery and signal intelligence through these sources. Saudi intelligence has not, however, organized the kind of domestic and foreign surveillance efforts necessary to provide adequate coverage of small, dispersed Islamic terrorist groups and individual movements. It has tended to rely on information from traditional elites, and to have limited data on urbanized Saudis and Saudi young males that become affiliated with extremist movements inside and especially outside of Saudi Arabia. Surveillance of financial transfers, charitable organizations, and activities like money laundering has been particularly weak.

SAUDI SECURITY PROCEDURES

Saudi internal security efforts present broader problems than preserving internal stability and dealing with terrorism. They also affect the Kingdom's political evolution. Saudi security procedures vary according to the case and perceived threat to the government and state security. The application of such procedures can still be harsh, but enforcement has steadily eased over time and improved further during the 1990s. For example, royal decrees were announced in 1992 that included provisions calling for the Saudi government to defend homes from unlawful intrusions on the ground that the sanctity of family life and the inviolability of the home are among the most fundamental of Islamic precepts. The police generally must demonstrate reasonable cause and obtain permission from the provincial governor before searching a private home; however, warrants are not required.

The security forces have also been made more subject to the rule of law. King Fahd established boards of investigation and public prosecution, organized on a regional basis, in 1993. The members of these boards have the right to inspect prisons, review prisoners' files, and hear their complaints. It is unclear that they can deal with security cases, however, the government does not permit visits to jails or prisons by human rights monitors. Some diplomats have been granted regular access to incarcerated foreign citizens, although the U.S. State Department reports that impartial observers are not allowed access to specialized Ministry of Interior prisons where the government detains persons accused of political subversion, such as Al-Hair Prison south of Riyadh.

Problems in Saudi Security Procedures

Saudi Arabia is still a closed society in many ways, and there are clear boundaries as to what levels of political activity are permitted and what can and cannot be said. In broad terms, however, the Saudi government is now more tolerant of criticism and allows more dissent and media criticism. Saudis openly criticize members of the royal family in social situations with little regard to the security services. Individual religious figures and clerics often make criticisms of the government and even members of the royal family, and sometimes do so in sermons and public forums. Nevertheless, the Saudi government still reacts sharply to direct criticism of the royal family, and does not allow direct public criticism of the government's integrity and religious legitimacy.

There are both formal and unwritten "rules" that limit the scope of open criticism of the regime, and organized opposition is suppressed, but there are also many anonymous or indirect ways to criticize the government that range from religious poems to the use of faxes and the Internet.[14] Saudi technocrats, scholars, businessmen, religious figures, and even princes have to be careful of what they say in formal public forums, although they often are openly critical of various aspects of the government's behavior, organization, and use of money. The Saudi media is subject to strict censorship, although they have more latitude in publishing broad criticism of government activities than the media in many other Middle Eastern states.

A Saudi poet was arrested in 2002, for example, for publishing a poem in *Al-Madina* called "The Corruption on Earth" that referred to Islamic judges as corrupt and acting as tyrants who only cared about their bank accounts and the views of their rulers: "How many sacred verses and sayings you have slaughtered. . . . Your beards are smeared with blood. . . . You indulge a thousand tyrants and only the tyrant do you obey." Prince Nayef, the minister of the interior, also ordered that the editor be fired, and then censored another paper, *Al Hayat*, for publishing an article that dared to criticize such censorship.[15]

The U.S. State Department reports that there are few protections from government interference in privacy, family, home, or correspondence. Saudi Arabia shows little tolerance for hard-line or potentially violent opposition to the government, major deviations from Wahhabi orthodoxy, or any form of actual violence. The State Department report on human rights indicates that[16]

> [t]he Government commits and tolerates serious human rights abuses. Citizens have neither the right nor the legal means to change their government. Security forces continued to abuse detainees and prisoners, arbitrarily arrest and detain persons, and facilitate incommunicado detention; in addition there were allegations that security forces committed torture. Prolonged detention without charge is a problem. Security forces committed such abuses, in contradiction to the law, but with the acquiescence of the Government. Mutawa'in continued to intimidate, abuse, and detain citizens and foreigners. The Government infringes on citizens' privacy rights. The Government prohibits or restricts freedom of speech, the press, assembly, association, religion, and movement. Other continuing problems included discrimination and violence against women, discrimination against ethnic and religious minorities, and strict limitations on worker rights. The Government disagrees with internationally accepted definitions of human rights and views its interpretation of Islamic law as its sole source of guidance on human rights.

The State Department also reports that Saudi security forces detain prisoners for more than twenty-four hours without charge, conduct their own investigations, and fail to notify the public prosecutor. Security suspects can be held incommunicado for weeks or even months. Authorities usually detain suspects for no longer than three days before charging them, in accordance with a regulation issued by the Ministry of Interior in 1983, although serious exceptions have been reported. The regulation also has provisions for bail for less serious crimes. Also, detainees are sometimes released on the recognizance of a patron or sponsoring employer without the payment of bail. If not released, the accused are detained an average of one to two months before going to trial.

The State Department report on human rights is particularly critical of the Ministry of the Interior:[17]

> There were credible reports that the authorities abused detainees, both citizens and foreigners. Ministry of Interior officials are responsible for most incidents of abuse, including beatings and sleep deprivation. In addition, there were allegations of torture. Although the Government has ratified the Convention Against Torture and Other Cruel, Inhuman, or Degrading Treatment or Punishment, it has refused to recognize the authority of the Committee Against Torture to investigate alleged abuses. In April 1998, the Government

pledged to cooperate with UN human rights mechanisms. However, although the Government asks for details of reports of torture and other human rights abuses made by international human rights groups, it does not permit international observers to investigate them. The Government's general refusal to grant members of diplomatic missions access to the Ministry of Interior detention facilities, or allow members of international human rights groups into the country, hinders efforts to confirm or discount reports of abuses. The Government's past failure to criticize human rights abuses has contributed to the public perception that security forces can commit abuses with impunity.

Prison Conditions and Numbers of Detainees

Prison and jail conditions vary throughout the Kingdom. The State Department reports that prisons generally meet internationally accepted standards and provide air-conditioned cells, good nutrition, regular exercise, and careful patrolling by prison guards. However, some police station jails are overcrowded and unsanitary. The authorities generally allow family members access to detainees. The State Department also reports that the Saudi government conducts closed trials for persons who may be political prisoners and in other cases has detained persons incommunicado for long periods while under investigation. Although it rarely executes prisoners, charges of torture or poor prison conditions are much more rare than in many developing countries. The State Department also reports that the authorities often detain people who publicly criticize the government without charge, or charge them with attempting to destabilize the government. The State Department human rights report notes that,[18]

> [p]olitical detainees who are arrested by the General Directorate of Investigation (GDI), the Ministry of Interior's security service, commonly are held incommunicado in special prisons during the initial phase of an investigation, which may last weeks or months. The GDI allows the detainees only limited contact with their families or lawyers.

The total number of political detainees is impossible to determine because the government does not provide information on such persons or respond to inquiries about them; one NGO estimates that there are about 200, however. The government regularly releases prisoners under its annual Ramadan amnesty, and some seem to have a political background. In January 1999, it released over 7,000 prisoners and detainees, including over 3,000 foreigners convicted or held for minor offenses.[19]

DEALING WITH INTERNAL OPPOSITION AND TERRORISM

Saudi Arabia may have made serious mistakes in dealing with the past, but its support for Islamic fundamentalism has never meant tolerance for domestic movements that openly criticize the government, or violent forms of Wahhabi or Shi'ite extremism. The Saudi government has recognized the threat posed by independent religious groups ever since the time when King Abd al-Aziz was forced to use his troops to suppress the Ihkwan during the formation of Saudi Arabia as a modern state. It has taken repeated actions to suppress extremism and violence since the 1979 seizure of the Grand Mosque in Mecca, and the Shi'ite uprising in the Eastern Province in the early 1980s exposed the fact that Sunni and Shi'ite Islamic extremism remain a major internal threat.

The Saudi government has developed powerful tools to use in limiting the actions of the clergy. The Ministry of Islamic Affairs directly supervises, and is a major source of funds for, the construction and maintenance of almost all mosques in the country. The ministry pays the salaries of imams (prayer leaders) and others who work in the mosques. A governmental committee is responsible for defining the qualifications of imams. It has repeatedly used these tools to put pressure on the clergy to limit their political statements, condemn extremism, and support reform.

The Saudi government has tightened its control over the Ulema since September 11, 2001. Crown Prince Abdullah made it very clear to Saudi clerics after September 11 that the government would not tolerate even the indirect support of terrorism and extremism.[20] Leading Saudi clerics also strongly condemned such activity. For example, the imam of the Holy Mosque in Mecca, Sheikh Abdulrahman al-Sideis preached a sermon on September 28, 2001, explicitly condemning terrorism as disavowed by Islam and contrary to the ways of true Muslims.[21]

Nevertheless, Saudi Islamic extremists and terrorists remain a problem both inside and outside the country. The suppression of leading Islamic extremists inside Saudi Arabia does not mean that the Ulema does not still have advocates of such positions, or that they do not have strong popular support in some areas. Saudis participated in four major terrorist attacks on U.S. targets in Saudi Arabia, Kenya, Tanzania, and Yemen during 1995–2001, and Saudis received terrorist and paramilitary training in Afghanistan, Chechnya, Kosovo, and Bosnia. Those involved in such attacks included four Saudis arrested in the bombing of the National Guard training center in November 1995, Saudi Shi'ites arrested for the bombing the Al-Khobar barracks in June 1996, a Saudi arrested for the bombing of the U.S. embassy in Kenya, and what seems to have been the leader of the attack on the U.S.S. *Cole* in Yemen in October 2000.[22]

Fifteen of the men directly involved in the attacks on the World Trade Center and Pentagon on September 11, 2001, held Saudi passports, and the Saudi government has been slow to publicly acknowledge that they seem to have been Saudi citizens. As of early February 2002, it had also arrested at least 30 Saudis in Saudi Arabia with possible ties to the attacks, although some have already been released.[23] A large number of the volunteers fighting with al Qaeda in Afghanistan were Saudi. At least 600 to 1,000 Saudis were present in al Qaeda forces in Afghanistan in late December 2001, and Pakistani border forces captured some forty Saudis fleeing the battle over the Tora Bora caves in one day in January 2002. Since September 11, the Saudi government has arrested several Taliban fighters, and these arrests are evidence of the potential magnitude of future operations and the continuing problem the Saudi government will face regarding terrorism.[24]

At the same time some reports are exaggerated. For example, some sources reported that young Saudis carried out Islamic extremist attacks on women and Saudi families in Jeddah and Dammam during the Id in December 2001.[25] In practice, they were a group of youths using drugs and alcohol, and were captured and imprisoned for only a few weeks—although some seem to have been flogged in front of their families.

On June 18, 2002, Saudi Arabia announced the arrests of eleven Saudis, a Sudanese man, and an Iraqi for their attempts to carry out terrorist attacks on vital centers within the Kingdom. Evidence revealed that these operatives were linked to bin Laden and the al Qaeda network and were planning to target U.S. installations and forces in the region. One Saudi security source told officials that the Saudi operatives were given direct orders from al Qaeda to destroy all U.S. military targets in Saudi Arabia, as well as the Defense Ministry and the Interior Ministry. An unsuccessful attack against U.S. warplanes revealed al Qaeda's plans to use ground-to-air missiles as a tactic. The security source told the Saudi government that the operatives had smuggled two SAM-7 surface-to-air missiles and munitions into the Kingdom. The arrests also revealed that these Saudi citizens were planning an attack on U.S. warships in the Strait of Gibraltar.[26]

The basic causes of tension and extremism also remain. Direct and indirect unemployment among native young Saudi males consistently averages between 20 and 30%. The Saudi educational system and economy still need deep and fundamental reform. As Crown Prince Abdullah and other Saudi officials have repeatedly stated, these problems are reinforced by the broad conviction throughout Saudi Arabia that the United States is responsible for much of the suffering of the Palestinians in the Second Intifada. There is also a broad popular feeling in Saudi Arabia that the United States has shown far too little concern for the Iraqi people and has been more willing to use force against Islamic elements and states than it should be. These forms of anti-Americanism have no clear ties to Islamic extremism per se, but it does strengthen the hand of Islamic extremists in the Kingdom and gives Islamic terrorists far more popular sympathy than would otherwise be the case.

Saudi Treatment of Internal Extremist Movements

The fact that the intelligence and security services were slow to deal with the flow of funds and volunteers to extremist causes outside Saudi Arabia does not mean they have been slow to deal with overt opposition to the regime. The Saudi security forces cracked down on opposition movements like the CDLR and al Qaeda long before the events of September 11. They took action against leading clerical critics; for example, Salman al-Awdah and Safar al-Hawali are Muslim clerics who were arrested in September 1994 for publicly criticizing the government. Their detention that year sparked protest demonstrations that resulted in the arrest of 157 persons for antigovernment activities. At the end of 1996, at least nine persons were serving prison terms for their connections to the rigidly fundamentalist Committee for the Defense of Legitimate Rights (CDLR). All the prisoners have now been released, but Salman al-Awdah and Safar al-Hawali were not released until June 1999. The government only released al-Awdah after he moderated his views to support the Saudi government position. Even then, he was prohibited from preaching, lecturing at the university, and traveling abroad. Some sources indicate he has become considerably more moderate and may soon get his teaching job back.[27]

The government of Saudi Arabia has arrested and convicted many other Saudi and foreign terrorists when they committed acts of violence in Saudi Arabia. These include terrorists associated with the bombing of the Saudi National Guard Training Center and of the Al-Khobar Towers housing facility near Dhahran in June 1996. While Saudi authorities have arrested and detained several persons in connection with the attacks, they have reached no conclusions as to whether these bombings were solely the work of independent Islamic extremists or had some form of Iranian support. The U.S. and Saudi governments have cooperated in these investigations to the extent that the United States expelled Hani al-Sayegh, a Saudi national, to Saudi Arabia on October 11, 1999. Al-Sayegh originally was detained in Canada in March 1997, and documents submitted to the Canadian court alleged al-Sayegh, as a member of the Saudi Hezbollah, had participated in the Al-Khobar Towers bombing.

The Saudi government has rarely used forced exile, or revoked citizenship for political purposes, but it did revoke the citizenship of hard-line advocates of the overthrow of the government residing outside the country, such as Mohammed al-Masari. Long before September 11, it also revoked the citizenship of Osama bin Laden, because of his role in organizing terrorist activities, and as a suspect in the August 1998 bombings of the U.S. embassies in Kenya and Tanzania.[28]

Nevertheless, Saudi Arabia has tended to ignore Islamic extremist activity when it did not seem to pose a direct threat to the regime and has often issued large-scale amnesties. At the end of January 1999, for example, the government issued its annual Ramadan amnesty, and released over 7,000 prisoners and detainees, including over 3,000 foreigners convicted or held for minor offenses. At least some of those released were Islamic extremists, some senior Saudi Ulema, such as Sheikh Saleh al-Sadiaan, a preacher in the Princess Zohra Mosque, remain ambivalent about the support of

Islamic violence and some, like Sheikh Hamoud a-Shuaibi, have endorsed the September 11, 2001, attacks.[29]

Saudi Arabia chose rapprochement with Iran over dealing with Iranian ties to those involved in the bombing on the National Guard Training Center in 1995, and the Al-Khobar Towers housing facility.[30] The Kingdom maintained a dialogue with Libya while it was still under UN sanctions, and permitted Libyan aircraft to fly pilgrims to the Hajj. Saudi Arabia conspicuously failed to cooperate with the United States in arresting Imad Mughniyah on April 7, 1995. Mughniyah was a suspect in the killing of 241 U.S. Marines in a barracks in Lebanon in 1983, and the hijacking of an airliner in 1985 that resulted in the death of a U.S. Navy diver. Saudi Arabia did so in part because the United States attempted to have FBI agents arrest Mughniyah on Saudi soil with minimal notice and in spite of the fact that the United States and Saudi Arabia have no extradition treaty.[31]

Saudi Support of the Taliban and Islamic Extremists Outside Saudi Arabia

Although the Saudi government began to crack down on Osama bin Laden in 1994, it continued to provide worldwide support for Islamic fundamentalist causes and has played its own "Great Game" in central Asia in an effort to transform the Asiatic republics of the FSU into Islamic states. In the process it provided aid to Islamic movements and charities without properly examining their true character and then funneled the money into extremist causes or attempted to buy off movements like the Taliban in ways that ultimately led to the money being used in extremist causes. It also provided broader funding to elements of foreign governments like the Taliban in Afghanistan and the ISI in Pakistan, which then use the money to support Islamic extremist and violent movements.

Prince Turki has provided an important Saudi perspective on these issues in interviews he has given to *Arab News* and MBC television since he left the GID. He stated that the Saudi government's efforts to assist Afghanistan were designed "to help them to help themselves as far as possible. We provided them with financial, military and moral support during their struggle against the Soviets." He stated that Saudi Arabia had been worried that the Afghans would fight among themselves once Russia withdrew, and that King Fahd had directed him to try to put an end to this fighting between Afghan factions. He cited peace initiatives made by various leading Muslims, the Organization of the Islamic Conference (OIC), the Muslim World League and Pakistani government.[32]

When he addressed the subject of the Taliban, which Saudi Arabia had recognized and given aid, Prince Turki said, "At that time [when Saudi Arabia recognized the Taliban], the Taliban had not created any controversy. It was controlling 95 percent of the territory when the Kingdom recognized the regime in 1997. It was also providing security and stability in the regions. We recognized them several months after they captured Kabul." He said that another reason why the Kingdom recognized the Taliban regime was the prevailing agreement between the Kingdom and Pakistan since the time of President Zia ul-Haq to consult and coordinate on all matters concerning Afghanistan. It was as a result of this agreement and "the advice of our Pakistani brothers" that they recognized the Taliban.

As for the relationship between the Taliban and Osama bin Laden, Prince Turki stated,

> The Taliban . . . put themselves in a quandary. When they occupied the eastern city of Jalalabad in 1996, Bin Laden was there, being sheltered by Sheikh Yunus Khales, a former Mujahideen leader. The Taliban pledged that they would not allow Bin Laden to harm the Kingdom's interests, either in words or deeds, and they seemed to take their pledge seriously . . . but they failed to pressure Bin Laden into stopping certain of his activities that endangered security. If the Taliban were a sovereign government controlling the areas they allegedly ruled, we wanted to know how it exercised that control and sovereignty. If they were unable to exercise control and sovereignty, then they should have yielded to those who could.[33]

Prince Turki made it clear during these interviews that he did not see Islamic extremism as the only source of the problems the Kingdom faced with terrorism and hostility toward the United States. He focused on Arab-Israeli issues and the backlash from the Second Intifada. He dismissed charges that Wahhabism fostered violent extremism. He said:

> It is an unacceptable proposition invented by the smear-campaigners who seek to serve the Zionist cause. The Zionists would like to see, as would the perpetrators of the terror attacks in New York and Washington, the relationship between the United States and Arabs and Muslims severed. Each of them—the Zionists and the terrorist attackers—serves the interests of the other. . . . The very name of "Wahhabism" has been fabricated since Sheikh Muhammad ibn Abdul Wahhab launched a reformist movement, which expanded during the time of Imam Muhammad ibn Saud. It was even charged that Ibn Abd al-Wahhab and Ibn Saud invented a new school of thought in the religion.

When Prince Turki discussed other regional problems such as the Chechen issue and the breeding grounds for terrorism, he said, "Wherever Muslims are oppressed and ill-treated, we stand by them. The Chechens are an oppressed people." He also noted, however, that people affiliated with al Qaeda and bin Laden launched terrorist acts in Russia and "gave the Russian forces a pretext to launch a ferocious war on an innocent people, estimated at 2.5 million. The Russians employed weapons of massive destruction and killed 100,000 people and made a larger number of people refugees."

Osama bin Laden as a Case Study

Prince Turki has also provided insights into the Saudi regime's treatment of Osama bin Laden that make it a case study for the problems Saudi Arabia has had in dealing with terrorism and extremism. Osama bin Laden is the seventeenth son of construction magnate Muhammad bin Laden, a Saudi citizen of Yemeni origin. Osama bin Laden joined the Afghan resistance almost immediately after the Soviet invasion in December 1979 and played a significant role in financing, recruiting, transporting, and training Arab nationals who volunteered to fight in Afghanistan. During the war, bin Laden founded al Qaeda (the Base) to serve as an operational organization under his control, recruited Islamic extremists, and used his wealth to fund other hard-line Islamic extremist and terrorist groups.

After the end of the Afghan conflict, bin Laden directed his energy toward Islamic extremist causes in other countries, and increasingly turned toward terrorism. He also issued "fatwas" calling for terrorism using a front organization called the World Islamic Front for Jihad Against the Jews and Crusaders. The Saudi government reacted by revoking his citizenship in 1994, and his family officially disowned him that same year. However, Osama bin Laden had already relocated his operations to Yemen. He moved to Sudan in 1991, and international pressure on the Sudanese government forced him to move to Afghanistan in 1996.[34]

Bin Laden's ties to the bombings of the U.S. embassies in Nairobi, Kenya, and in Dar es Salaam, Tanzania, on August 17, 1998, do not seem to have involved any links to operations centered in Saudi Arabia. Like some other Islamic extremist movements, bin Laden and al Qaeda did receive some private financing from within Saudi Arabia, and there were extremist groups inside the Kingdom that supported him. Some of these groups continue to pose a threat to U.S. officials, military, and businessmen in Saudi Arabia. U.S. and British analysts estimate, however, that bin Laden and al Qaeda received at least as much support from Egyptian and South Asian groups as from Saudi ones. Al Qaeda also has contacts and subgroups in Afghanistan as well as Tajikistan, Bosnia, Chechnya, Somalia, Sudan, and Yemen. It has trained fighters from numerous other countries, including the Philippines, Egypt, Libya, Pakistan, and Eritrea.[35]

Prince Turki summarized the Saudi government's view of bin Laden as follows: "The statements and fatwas he [bin Laden] has issued over the past seven years give a good idea of how he thinks. In short, bin Laden wants to fight the whole world because he sees dishonesty and corruption in it." Prince Turki stated that bin Laden at first appeared to be an Islamist resisting the Soviets, rather than a threat. When he did emerge as a threat, Saudi Arabia had made repeated attempts to deal with him, forced him to leave the country, and revoked his Saudi citizenship.

The prince describes his first contact with bin Laden: "When jihad started in Afghanistan, I used to travel to Pakistan and sometimes to Afghanistan to follow up on the developments. It was there that I met him. Once or twice he was invited to the Saudi Embassy [in Islamabad]. The first time I met him was during one of these occasions. He was in the area supporting jihad."

Prince Turki said they talked "about the condition of the Mujahideen and what he [bin Laden] was doing to help them." He said neither bin Laden nor he had presented the other with any demands. "I did not know him thoroughly enough to judge him or expect any other thing from him. His behavior at that time left no impression that he would become what he has become." He said bin Laden's activities were welcomed at that time but denied bin Laden had ever enjoyed any official status or support.

He said that Saudi intelligence monitored bin Laden's activities, as it did with jihad activities in general. "As you know, at that time there were many volunteers, Saudis and non-Saudis, and he was one of them. He did not enjoy special status that made us focus on him." Prince Turki ruled out rumors that linked bin Laden with the CIA or any other American agency.

> His presence in the area and his activities did not call on him to have contacts with these bodies. We had no information that he had contacts with any foreign government agencies, except the Pakistanis. . . . From what was heard about him from those who went to join the jihad and met him in Afghanistan and Pakistan and then returned home, there were no fears regarding his conduct.

According to Prince Turki, Saudi intelligence did focus on the Afghan Arab Mujahideen after the Soviet withdrawal in 1989. "We were concerned with the return of Saudi citizens. Indeed, large numbers of Saudis returned. Attention was directed at those who stayed behind, including Bin Laden, and why they'd stayed. A number of organizations have been monitored trying to recruit these youths."

The prince said that bin Laden founded al Qaeda in 1989 for the defense of Muslims the world over against injustice.

> There was no goal for this organization after the end of the jihad in Afghanistan. . . . Bin Laden was not the sole leader of the Afghan Arabs, who were spread out in various parties in the region. The man was in constant contact with Sheikh Abdullah Azzam, as well as with Jalaluddin Haqqani, the Afghan leader who is currently the minister of tribal affairs in the Taliban government.[36]

Prince Turki said that bin Laden returned to Saudi Arabia shortly before the breakout of the Kuwait war. In August 1990, Iraq occupied Kuwait and Osama bin Laden met with a top Saudi official and offered to fight Saddam with a group of Arab volunteers.

> It was not he [bin Laden] alone who offered their services. Other personalities in the Arab world did the same, some with good and others with bad

intentions. They wanted to show that there are Arabs capable of fighting and defeating Saddam, especially after the Kingdom took the bold decision to bring together an international alliance to flush out the Iraqi forces.[37]

Prince Turki felt that it was at this time that there began to be signs of major changes in bin Laden's personality.

First, he believed that he was capable of preparing an army to challenge Saddam's forces. Second, he opposed the Kingdom's decision to call friendly forces. By doing so, he disobeyed the ruler and violated the fatwa of senior Islamic scholars, who had endorsed the plan as an essential move to fight injustice and aggression. . . . I saw radical changes in his personality as he changed from a calm, peaceful and gentle man interested in helping Muslims into a person who believed that he would be able to amass and command an army to liberate Kuwait. It revealed his arrogance and his haughtiness.[38]

Bin Laden does not have a strong reason to raise the issue [of U.S. and non-Islamic forces in the Kingdom]. We remember the hue and cry created by opponents of the move. They said the foreign forces would remain and become an occupying and colonizing force that would desecrate the Two Holy Mosques. Saddam used the same idea to try and foil the efforts to drive him out of Kuwait. People with subversive ideas also said that the move was against the teachings of Prophet Muhammad (peace be upon him), who had said that two religions could not meet in the Arabian Peninsula. I still remember, when I met a group of the so-called leaders of the Islamic work, who came to learn the Kingdom's stand before heading to Baghdad for mediation, that they also raised the same issue. Dr. Abdullah Al-Turki, who is now secretary-general of the Muslim World League, was present in that meeting. He explained to them that the Prophet had meant that no religion except Islam could dominate the Peninsula. The Jews and Christians were constantly coming to and leaving the region. Even after the Prophet had driven out the Jews from Medina and Khaiber some of them remained in the Peninsula, moving from one place to another. Those who have visited the Holy Places will find that Osama's claim was false.

Prince Turki stated that bin Laden started making public speeches without prior approval of the government agencies, and spoke at schools without the knowledge of the school authorities. When he was asked about these activities, bin Laden said that he was only discussing jihad and was campaigning for Afghans. Prince Turki noted, "Bin Laden did not undertake any subversive activities in the Kingdom at that time."[39]

Bin Laden was allowed to travel again in March 1992 because he was never banned from traveling, only required to get permission. He needed such permission because he had tried to engage in political activities in what was then South Yemen, and was told that he should inform officials when he wanted to leave the Kingdom. Ever since 1989, he had tried to launch a jihad in South Yemen, attempting to lure Yemeni youths into training camps in Afghanistan and beginning to campaign with the tribal leaders in southern Yemen.

Prince Turki denied that the Kingdom supported bin Laden in any of these activities:

> It was not possible for the Kingdom to assign any person to undermine any government. . . . The Kingdom's authorities warned him against doing such things and that he should desist from such acts. His role in Afghanistan was only aid supplies and nothing more. . . . The Kingdom will not try to topple any government or trigger any conflict or wars in any other country. And we expect the same from other countries in their dealings with Saudi Arabia.

In March 1992, Osama bin Laden was given permission to visit Pakistan. "He went there to work with other Islamic personalities who were trying to reconcile the Afghan Mujahideen, who differed on the setting up of a government. I saw him among those personalities," said Prince Turki, who was then making strenuous efforts with Pakistani Prime Minister Nawaz Sharif to unify Mujahideen ranks and bring them to an agreement before they entered Kabul.

He stated that Sudanese President General Omar al-Bashir made a "conditional offer" to hand over bin Laden before he returned to Afghanistan for the second time in 1996 after the Sudanese government asked him to leave, on condition that no legal action should be taken against him. However, the Saudis rejected the offer. "President Bashir asked for guarantees regarding Bin Ladin's prosecution. That he would not be tried by any legal authority in the Kingdom. He said that Bashir was told that no one is above the law and that we could not give such guarantees."[40]

Prince Turki discussed his two secret visits to Kandahar—the first one in June 1998.

> King Fahd and Crown Prince Abdullah sent me to meet Mullah Omar to persuade him to hand Bin Laden over to the Kingdom. This was because of some of his acts and statements and the Saudi move grew out of the Taliban's promise not to allow Bin Laden to harm the Kingdom's interests. I asked Mullah Omar to hand him over and he agreed. I was told their interests were with us and not with any individual. Mullah Omar asked me to inform the king and the crown prince that he wanted to set up a joint Saudi-Afghan committee to arrange procedures for the handover.[41]

The prince described a visit to Saudi Arabia by Abdul Wakeel, an adviser to Mullah Omar who later became the Taliban foreign minister. "He came to tell the Crown Prince that the Kingdom's request for Bin Laden had been approved and that a joint committee to oversee the handover was being set up." This visit came a few weeks before the bombings of the U.S.

embassies in Nairobi and Dar es Salaam, and stated that "One of the perpetrators of the attacks, a bin Laden supporter, confessed during interrogation in Pakistan that bin Laden had given the orders for the bombings and that the plans were made with his support and guidance."

Prince Turki said that he went to Kandahar again in September 1998, but that the Taliban were no longer cooperative:

> I wished I had not gone. After previously agreeing to hand the man over, I discovered Mullah Omar had reversed his decision and he was abusive about the Kingdom and its people. Under those circumstances, I had no choice but to break off negotiations. I still remember, however, that as I was leaving, I told Mullah Omar that one day he would regret his decision and that the unfortunate Afghan people would pay the price. . . . I saw that Mullah Omar made decisions arbitrarily and capriciously and once made, he was not interested in revising them. The decision to ban women's education is an example of what I am talking about. At first, we were told that the decision was made because of a lack of facilities but even after the United Nations and other organizations promised money for building schools, the ban was not lifted. . . . The Taliban were always the first to withdraw from the talks.
>
> . . . I met him [Mullah Omar] on two occasions. The first meeting lasted an hour, while the second ended after just half an hour. It was hard to understand a person in such a short time. I heard from his associates that he was very brave, fought against the Russians and was deeply religious. On the other hand, his opponents said he was an introvert who holds extreme religious views. He never tolerated any criticism of his decisions and never swerved from a decision under any circumstances, whatever risks it involved. This is what I learned about him from both his friends and foes.
>
> . . . In my first meeting with Mullah Omar, he was very cordial, but in the second meeting he turned hysterical in his attacks on the Kingdom. [In the first meeting, Prince Turki was accompanied by Dr. Abdullah Al-Turki, present secretary-general of the Muslim World League.] Mullah Omar did not object to Sheikh Al-Turki's arguments on the extradition of the Al-Qaida chief to the Kingdom and I thought he agreed with Al-Turki's arguments on the basis of Shariah law. In the second meeting Mullah Omar was not in a mood to listen to anyone.[42]

Prince Turki also stated that bin Laden used someone else to issue edicts for him. "Some may say that if you don't commit the act yourself, you are innocent. You may not have crashed the plane into the building or put the bomb into the car but you are responsible for those who did. And those people who follow this line of reasoning think bin Laden has a way out. But he doesn't; God will punish him."

The prince noted, "The presence of international terrorism which affects everyone plus an organization such as al-Qaeda which threatens the entire world undoubtedly demands a response from the Kingdom. It must offer all its resources and whatever information it has to control the cancer which will spiral out of control if left unchallenged." At the same time, Prince Turki reacted angrily to claims by American analysts that Saudi Arabia breeds terrorism. "This is totally unacceptable. Let them look at what they have, at the terrorist organizations in their own country. In the United States there are 200 terrorist organizations, targeting not only domestic interests, but those of the entire world. Instead of highlighting a very small minority of bad people, they should look at the thousands of others who are the peaceable and peace-loving majority."[43]

Putting the Issue in Perspective

Some of Prince Turki's remarks have considerable justification. Saudis have reason to criticize the extent to which the United States and other Western media have exaggerated the Kingdom's role in supporting terrorism since September 11, 2001. Western media have often ignored the role of other countries and their citizens in focusing on Saudi Arabia, and ignored the importance of U.S. domestic terrorists, in spite of indications that the anthrax attacks that followed September 11 were the work of U.S. terrorists. There has often been a broad anti-Islamic and anti-Arab character to such reporting, and many editorials have been as ethnocentric and prejudiced in their own way as sermons and writings of the more extreme Saudi preachers.

At the same time, the fact remains that the Saudi government did provide funding for Islamic education without carefully monitoring how the money was used or paying proper attention to educational material and what was being taught. It allowed funds to go to many groups that were Islamic extremist rather than fundamentalist—such as Madrassas in Pakistan that educate their students to carry out violent acts and to hate non-Muslims and even members of non-Sunni sects of Islam.[44] Thousands of young Saudi men became involved in terrorist and military elements of al Qaeda and other organizations in cells scattered throughout Europe, the Middle East, and United States.

The costs of these failures became all too clear after September 11. NATO security officers raided the Saudi High Commission for Aid to Bosnia—which is under the patronage of King Fahd and which was founded by Prince Alman bin Abdulaziz in October 2001—and found maps of the U.S. embassies in Kenya and Tanzania, as well as maps of U.S. facilities and equipment for forging false IDs. The Saudi-sponsored Mercy International Relief Organization was used as a front in the 1998 bombings of the U.S. embassies, as was the International Islamic Relief Organization and Muslim World League. The al-Wafa Humanitarian Organization was a major source of funds for al Qaeda, and some suspect organizations like the World Assembly of Muslim Youth and Quranic Literacy Organization may also have been used as fronts.[45]

Controlling the Flow of Saudi Funds

Serious questions exist about the activities of other major Saudi charities like the al-Haramain Islamic Foundation, which the U.S. Treasury has
treated as an active supporter of Islamic extremism and terrorism, and
whose funds the United States blocked on March 11, 2002.[46] It should be
noted, however, that charities like the al-Haramain Islamic Foundation had
some forty field offices and may not have understood where all of its funding was going.

Once again, such Saudi activity, as well as the Saudi government's ability
to control it, must be kept in perspective. As has been touched on earlier,
Saudi funding for such activities was only part of a much broader flow of
funds from within the Arab and Islamic world. Funds from non-Saudi individuals, non-Saudi Islamic charities, and from other governments like
those of Libya, Pakistan, Syria, Iran, and Iraq have all played a major role
in the flow of financial support to extremist causes. The dispersal of most
private Saudi money is beyond governmental control. Many private organizations are largely self-financing, and the real-world costs of extremism
and terrorism are relatively low. The vast amount of private Saudi capital
outside the Kingdom is outside the government's control, as is the capital
of non-Saudis funding such groups in Kuwait, the UAE, and many other
countries—including the United States. In broad terms, controlling or preventing movements of capital and individuals is impossible for Saudi Arabia.

Nevertheless, the Kingdom must come to grips with its internal and external problems in dealing with Islamic extremists with far more firmness
than in the past. It took nearly four months for the Saudi government to
freeze the assets of some 150 suspected terrorist accounts after the September 11 attacks, if only because the same organizations that attacked the
United States also opposed the Saudi government. Similarly, it should not
have taken until March 2002 for Saudi Arabia to order all charity organizations to inform the authorities of their overseas projects and take steps
to ensure that funds did not flow to terrorist causes.[47]

Controlling the Activities of Young Saudis

The problem raised by the training and participation of young Saudis
in terrorist and extremist groups is far from over. Many of the al Qaeda
activists captured in Afghanistan have been Saudi. There have been significant arrests of Saudis in Europe, the United States, the Middle East, and
in Saudi Arabia. A number of European intelligence services, notably
Germany's, are deeply concerned about the extremist character, sermons,
and publications of Wahhabi activities in their countries that cannot be tied
to terrorist activities per se. As of July 2002, however, far more young Saudi
males who are part of al Qaeda have escaped into Pakistan or are dispersed
in other countries; also many Saudi extremists have ties to other movements.

New, largely Saudi-manned terrorist plots to attack U.S. and British ships involving at least five Saudis were detected in Morocco in June 2002.[48] Attempts were made to use SA-7 manportable surface-to-air missiles to shoot down U.S. fighters operating out of Prince Sultan Air Base,[49] which were carried out by a Sudanese but planned and managed by Saudis in an al Qaeda cell in Saudi Arabia.[50] This led to the arrest of thirteen Saudis in Saudi Arabia, although Saudi intelligence did not allow them to be interrogated by U.S. or other intelligence services.[51] Significant numbers of young Saudis still operate in al Qaeda cells that fled into Afghanistan and at least seem to have ties to attacks on Western targets in Pakistan.[52]

There have been several bombing attacks that may be related to Islamic extremism. For example, a package bomb gravely injured Gary Hatch, an American physical therapist, in May 2001.[53] Other attacks have since taken place. The Kingdom also has never fully explained a series of bomb plot arrests following bombings that struck at British and Irish workers in the Kingdom on November 17, 2000 and November 22, 2000. It claims these were related to purely Western alcohol smuggling, however, and has arrested a Belgian, Canadian, and five Britons for the crimes.[54] The Britons arrested for the bombings have retracted their confessions, however, and the facts remain uncertain.[55]

It is important that the West understand that some aspects of progress will not be quick. A large part of al Qaeda remained intact after the defeat of the Taliban in Afghanistan. There is a legacy of young Saudi men with military and terrorist training. The broad process of Islamic extremism in central Asia, the Middle East, and elsewhere is also driven by forces that have nothing to do with developments inside Saudi Arabia. The resentments inside the Islamic and Arab worlds that come from the rapid pace of global secularization, the backlash from the Second Intifada, and problems like the suffering of the Iraqi people will continue to present problems for the West regardless of any actions by Saudi Arabia, and can only be addressed in very different ways.

There is a certain irony to a Western call for tight Saudi government control of students who may be radical. It is far from clear that some of the most anti-U.S. students are Islamists, as opposed to being anti-Israel because of the Second Intifada or anti-U.S. because of its support of Israel. Like most of the Saudi population, Saudi students have been heavily polarized by constant broadcasts of Palestinian suffering, which come from outside the Kingdom, and by Western media and politicians that have launched broad attacks on the Kingdom's politics, social customs, and the Wahhabi interpretation of Islam, rather than focusing on extremists. Such critics often seem to be deliberately dodging the massive political backlash against Israel and the United States arising from the Second Intifada, and grossly exaggerating a very real—but relatively limited—threat from actual Islamic extremists.

There is also a danger in pressing for control without considering the impact on internal reform. While the government does carry out surveillance over teachers and students, it has become increasingly tolerant in ways that encourage reform. No political science professor has been called in for questioning, regarding what he teaches in his classes, for a decade. Extremely sensitive subjects for Islamists, like the writings of Freud, have quietly been introduced in some courses in institutions like King Saud University. Some courses actually teach the pros and cons of democracy versus monarchy, and term papers are written split on the subject. Counterterrorism must never become anti-freedom or anti-civil liberties, or be used as an excuse to condemn different social and religious practices.

Saudi Shi'ites

There are other significant security problems in Saudi Arabia. The Saudi Shi'a Muslim minority (which the U.S. embassy estimates at roughly 500,000 of nearly 14 million actual citizens) presents special security and legal problems. The Shi'ites live mostly in the Eastern Province. The Saudi government permits Shi'a Muslims to use their own legal tradition to adjudicate noncriminal cases within their community.

The U.S. State Department has long reported, however, that Shi'ites remain the objects of officially sanctioned political and economic discrimination. The Saudi government seldom permits private construction of Shi'a mosques. The Shi'a have also declined government offers to build state-supported mosques because the government would prohibit the incorporation and display of Shi'a motifs in any such mosques. The State Department reports that Saudi security forces arrest Shi'ites on the smallest suspicion, hold them in custody for lengthy periods, and then release them without explanation.

In November 1998, several Mutawaa'in attacked and killed an elderly Shi'a prayer leader in Hofuf for repeating the call to prayer twice (a traditional Shi'a practice). The government still punishes Shi'a who travel to Iran without permission from the Ministry of the Interior, or those suspected of such travel, by confiscating passports for up to two years.

The State Department does report, however, the Saudi discrimination against Shi'ites seems to be easing in some respects, in part because of actions by Prince Muhammad bin Fahad, the governor of the Eastern Province, and Crown Prince Abdullah. More Shi'ites are being allowed into government jobs and some areas in the military. There is one Shi'a on the Consultative Council, or Majlis Ash-Shura, and the government has appointed its first Shi'a ambassador. Prior to 1990, the government prohibited Shi'a public processions during the Islamic month of Muharram and restricted other processions and congregations to designated areas in the major Shi'a cities. Since 1990 the authorities have permitted marches on the Shi'a holiday of Ashura, provided that the marchers do not display banners or engage in self-flagellation. Ashura commemorations take place during the year, generally without incident.

Open acts of Shi'ite terrorism receive serious punishments, although the Kingdom has never publicly discussed the extent to which Iran provided support for terrorist acts by Saudi Shi'ites. The 1996 bombing of the USAF barracks at Al-Khobar, which killed nineteen U.S. servicemen, led to a major series of arrests of Saudi Shi'ites. These arrests did lead to formal Saudi government denials that bin Laden and al Qaeda were involved, but never led to any disclosure of the extent to which Iranian officials were involved.[56] Many, including some senior Saudis, believe Iran did play a role in the Al-Khobar bombings and several other successful and failed attacks, and that the Saudi government and Saudi intelligence covered this up because of Saudi Arabia's rapprochement with Iran and desire to use Iran as a counter-balance to Iraq.

The State Department reports that the Saudi government still holds an unknown number of Shi'a in jail that were arrested in the aftermath of the AlKhobar bombing. It also reports that the Saudi internal security services continue to detain, interrogate, and confiscate the passports of a number of Shi'a Muslims suspected of fundamentalist tendencies or Iranian sympathies.

Non-Muslims

Non-Muslims have not presented a security threat in the past, but Saudi insistence on religious conformity has serious security implications. The Saudi government does not permit public non-Muslim religious activities. Saudi politics do not permit such tolerance, which might provoke extensive violence by the religious police and Saudi traditionalists. While the government discourages the most extreme sermons and religious writings, some Wahhabi Ulema and teachers show little tolerance of other religions or even other Islamic practices. Non-Muslim worshippers risk arrest, lashing, and deportation for engaging in overt religious activity that attracts official attention.

The State Department reports that the government's tolerance of private worship is uncertain and there is sporadic harassment of other faiths. High-level Saudi authorities have stated that the government's policy allows for private non-Muslim worship and that the government does not sanction investigation or harassment of such private worship services. A senior Saudi leader stated publicly in 1997 that the government does not "prevent" private non-Muslim religious worship in the home and such private non-Muslim worship occurs on a wide scale through the country, including on the premises of several embassies. However, there have been arrests and deportations for private worship. The government ascribes some of this harassment of private worship services to individuals and organizations acting on their own authority and in contradiction of government policy. Representatives of many Christian denominations present in the country report that the Government is not interfering with their private worship services.

Treatment of Foreign Workers

While foreign labor has not been a source of significant political unrest to date, the security services closely monitor the activities and movements of foreign workers. The U.S. State Department reports that foreigners are normally allowed to reside or work in Saudi Arabia only under the sponsorship of a Saudi national or business. The government requires foreign residents to carry identification cards and does not permit foreigners to travel outside the city of their employment or change their workplace without their sponsor's permission. Foreign residents who travel within the country may be asked by the authorities to show that they possess letters of permission from their employer or sponsor.

Saudi Arabia does not tolerate political activity by foreign nationals. It is tolerant of casual social criticism, but generally expels activists almost immediately and provides tight surveillance of known foreign intelligence operatives in embassies and consulates.

The security forces have never shown any tolerance for any hostile political activity by foreign labor, whether Islamic or secular, and many brokers providing labor from developing countries are ex-military or have some ties to the security services in their countries. The Saudi military justice system also does not tolerate political or Islamic extremist activity by Saudi military personnel, who are tried by court-martials.[57]

There is no established procedure for providing detainees the right to inform their family of their arrest. The authorities may take as long as several months to provide official notification of the arrest of foreigners, if at all. If asked, the authorities usually confirm the arrest of foreigners to their country's diplomats. In general, foreign diplomats only learn about such arrests through informal channels. Foreigners have been tried and executed in the past in both civil and security cases without notification of their arrest ever having been given to their government's representatives.

The State Department reports that such measures also lead to significant human rights abuses. Employers have significant control over the movements of foreign employees, which gives rise to situations that sometimes involve forced labor, especially in remote areas where individuals are unable to leave their place of work. Some sponsors prevented foreign workers from obtaining exit visas to pressure them to sign a new work contract or to drop claims against their employers for unpaid salary. In another pressure tactic, some sponsors refused to provide foreign workers with a "letter of no objection" that would allow them to be employed by another sponsor.

Some foreign nationals who have been recruited abroad have complained that after their arrival in Saudi Arabia they were presented with work contracts that specified lower wages and fewer benefits than originally promised. Other foreign workers reportedly have signed contracts in their home countries and later were pressured to sign less favorable contracts on arrival. Some employees report that at the end of their contract service, their employers refuse to grant permission to allow them to return home. Foreign employees involved in disputes with their employers may find their freedom of movement restricted. Some female domestic servants often were subjected to abuse.

The labor laws do not protect domestic servants. There are credible reports that female domestic servants sometimes were forced to work twelve to sixteen hours per day, seven days a week. There were numerous confirmed reports of runaway maids. The authorities often returned runaway maids to their employers against the maids' wishes. There have been many reports of workers whose employers refused to pay several months, or even years, of accumulated salary or other promised benefits. Nondomestic workers with such grievances have the right to complain before the labor courts, but few do so because of fear of deportation.

The enforcement of work contracts is difficult and generally favors employers. Labor courts, while fair, can take months or over a year to reach a final appellate ruling, during which time the employer may prevent the foreign laborer from leaving the country. An employer also may delay a case until a worker's funds are exhausted and the worker is forced to return to his home country.

The State Department reports that sponsors have additional leverage because they generally retain possession of foreign workers' passports. Foreign workers must obtain permission from their sponsors to travel abroad. If sponsors are involved in a commercial or labor dispute with foreign employees, they may ask the authorities to prohibit the employees from departing the country until the dispute is resolved. Some sponsors use this as a pressure tactic to resolve disputes in their favor or to have foreign employees deported. There were numerous reports of the government prohibiting foreign employees involved in labor disputes from departing the country until the dispute was resolved. The government seizes the passports of all potential suspects and witnesses in criminal cases and suspends the issuance of exit visas to them until the case is tried or otherwise concluded. As a result, some foreign nationals are forced to remain in the country for lengthy periods against their will.

Treatment of Iraqi Exiles and Prisoners of War

The Saudi 1992 Basic Law provides that "the state will grant political asylum if the public interest mitigates" in favor of it. The language does not specify clear rules for adjudicating asylum cases. In general, the authorities regard refugees and displaced persons like other foreign workers: they must have sponsors for employment or risk expulsion.

The State Department reports that none of the 33,000 Iraqi civilians and former prisoners of war allowed refuge in Saudi Arabia at the end of the Gulf War have been granted permanent asylum in the country. The Saudi government has, however, paid the entire cost of providing safe haven to the Iraqi refugees, and it continues to provide excellent logistical and administrative support to the United Nations High Commissioner for Refugees (UNHCR) and other resettlement agencies. In early 2000, approximately 27,000 of the original 33,000 Iraqi refugees had been resettled in other countries or voluntarily repatriated to Iraq. Most of the approximately 6,000 remaining refugees are restricted to the Rafha refugee camp. The UNHCR has monitored over 3,000 persons voluntarily returning to Iraq from Rafha since December 1991 and found no evidence of forcible repatriation.

Representatives of the UNHCR are present at the Rafha refugee camp, which houses former Iraqi prisoners of war and civilians who fled Iraq following the Gulf War. According to UNHCR officials, there was no systematic abuse of refugees by camp guards. When isolated instances of abuse have surfaced in the past, the authorities have been responsive and willing to investigate allegations and reprimand offending guards. The State Department reports that the camp receives a high level of material assistance and is comparatively comfortable and well run.

BORDER AND COASTAL SECURITY

Saudi Arabia has dealt with foreign threats to its internal security in a relatively sophisticated manner. It has taken diplomatic steps to greatly reduce its problems and tensions with Iran and Yemen, and particularly to reduce Iranian efforts to exploit Saudi Arabia's problems with its Shi'ites and use the Hajj as a propaganda forum. It has steadily improved its monitoring of foreign nationals and ability to track their movements and activities. Nevertheless, Saudi Arabia does face major challenges in providing security for its borders and coastlines.

Smuggling is endemic, even across the Saudi border with Iraq. Saudi border guards arrested 777 smugglers crossing the border during 2001, and seized nearly three tons of hashish, more than 5,700 bottles of alcohol, more than 450 weapons, and 43,680 rounds of ammunition.[58] While Saudi Arabia does not announce the fact publicly, it regularly has to deal with Iraqi patrols that cross into Saudi territory, and it is clear that some Iraqi intelligence officers have entered the Kingdom.

It is virtually impossible for Saudi Arabia to secure either its Gulf or Red Sea coast against smuggling and infiltration by small craft. The traffic is simply too high in both areas, the coasts are too long, and sensors cannot track movements by dhows and small craft. The Saudi Navy, Coast Guard, and National Guard might be able to provide adequate security screening for key ports, desalination facilities, and petroleum export facilities with roughly two weeks of warning. Coverage is generally very limited in peacetime. At least some smuggling by sea occurs in areas where it seems doubtful that this could occur without the knowledge and tolerance of some elements of the Saudi security forces.

Saudi Arabia had serious problems with Iranian intelligence agents and support of Shi'ite extremists after the fall of the Shah in 1979 until it reached an accommodation with the Iranian government in the late 1990s. Weapons and explosives were intercepted in the Eastern Province and there were numerous small acts of sabotage related to Iranian-sponsored activities. Iran trained a number of Saudi Shi'ites in low-intensity warfare and covert operations in Iran and Lebanon, and regularly disrupted the Hajj to make political protests. As has been mentioned earlier, the most serious case of Iran-related activity seems to be the Al-Khobar bombing, although the exact level of Iranian involvement remains unknown. Iranian activity seems to have sharply diminished since the Saudi-Iranian rapprochement, but Saudi intelligence officials note that Iran continues to maintain a significant intelligence presence in the Kingdom, monitor U.S. military activity in the Kingdom, and provide political, paramilitary, and religious training for at least some Saudi Shi'ites.

Similar problems exist along the border with Yemen, although the border clashes that used to take place between Yemeni and Saudi security forces seem to have largely ended following the settlement of the Saudi-Yemeni border. The main problems are now smuggling and inter-tribal violence, which are still endemic. The Saudi borders with Kuwait, Bahrain, the UAE, and Oman are stable and secure except for smuggling. The movement of alcohol and narcotics is still a problem.

SECURITY AND THE ROLE OF THE JUDICIAL SYSTEM

The Saudi civil and criminal legal system has slowly been modernized, but presents problems both in terms of efficient internal security operations and human rights. It is traditional, religious in character, and based on Shari'a as interpreted by Islamic practice under the Wahhabi order, which adheres to the Hanbali School of the Sunni branch of Islam. The Shari'a courts exercise jurisdiction over common criminal cases and civil suits regarding marriage, divorce, child custody, and inheritance. These courts base judgments largely on the Koran and on the Sunna, another Islamic text. Cases involving relatively small penalties are tried in Shari'a summary courts; more serious crimes are adjudicated in Shari'a courts of common pleas. Appeals from Shari'a courts are made to the courts of appeal. The

Saudi government permits Shi'a Muslims to use their own legal tradition to adjudicate noncriminal cases within their community. Other civil proceedings, including those involving claims against the government and enforcement of foreign judgments, are held before specialized administrative tribunals, such as the Commission for the Settlement of Labor Disputes and the Board of Grievances.[59]

Human rights groups and the media often are harsh critics with regard to the operations of the Saudi judicial system and exaggerate its failings and use of harsh punishments, including executions. Once again, the U.S. State Department provides a more balanced set of criticism. It reports that the independence of the judiciary is prescribed by law and usually is respected in practice; however, judges occasionally accede to the influence of the executive branch, particularly members of the royal family and their associates, who are not required to appear before the courts. In general, members of the royal family, and other powerful families, are not subject to the same rule of law as ordinary citizens. For example, judges do not have the power to issue a warrant summoning any member of the royal family. Moreover, the Ministry of Justice exercises judicial, financial, and administrative control of the courts.[60]

The Operation of the Judicial System in Ordinary Civil Cases

Civil and criminal trial procedures are very different than in the West. Defendants usually appear without an attorney before a judge, who determines guilt or innocence in accordance with Shari'a standards. Defense lawyers may offer their clients advice before trial or may attend the trial as interpreters for those unfamiliar with Arabic. The courts do not provide foreign defendants with translators. Public defenders are not provided. Individuals may choose any person to represent them by a power of attorney filed with the court and the Ministry of Justice. Most trials are closed. However, in a highly publicized 1997 case involving two foreign women charged with murder, the Saudi court conducted preliminary matters with relatively open and transparent procedures, including more effective use of counsel, increased consular presence, and increased family access.

The State Department reports that a woman's testimony does not carry the same weight as that of a man. In a Shari'a court, the testimony of one man equals that of two women. In the absence of two witnesses, or four witnesses in the case of adultery, confessions before a judge almost always are required for criminal conviction—a situation that repeatedly has led prosecuting authorities to coerce confessions from suspects by threats and abuse.

Criminal penalties and sentencing are not uniform. Foreign residents sometimes receive harsher penalties than citizens. Under Shari'a, as interpreted and applied in Saudi Arabia, crimes against Muslims receive harsher penalties than those against non-Muslims. In the case of wrongful death, the amount of indemnity or "blood money" awarded to relatives varies with the nationality, religion, and sex of the victim.

A sentence may be changed at any stage of review, except for punishments stipulated by the Koran. In a case that was known widely but was not reported in the press, a member of the royal family, who shot and killed two Mutawaa'in who had entered his property without permission in October 1998, was allowed to pay "blood money" to the family members of the Mutawaa'in instead of being charged with murder.

The Judicial System and Internal Security

The judicial system works differently when it deals with internal security issues. The Saudi government is still deeply concerned about the security of the military forces—although there have been almost no recent cases of active opposition within either the regular military forces or the paramilitary and security forces. The military justice system has jurisdiction over uniformed personnel and civil servants who are charged with violations of military regulations. The minister of defense and aviation and the king review the decisions of courts-martial and it is clear that serious cases get the direct attention of the royal family. Similarly, the Saudi government conducts closed trials for persons who may be political prisoners, and in other cases has detained persons incommunicado for long periods while under investigation.

The State Department reports that there are several bodies that perform higher legal review functions:

- The Supreme Judicial Council is not a court and may not reverse decisions made by a court of appeals. However, the council may review lower court decisions and refer them back to the lower court for reconsideration. Only the Supreme Judicial Council may discipline or remove a judge. The king appoints the members of the council.

- The Council of Senior Religious Scholars is an autonomous body of twenty senior religious jurists, including the minister of justice. It establishes the legal principles that guide lower-court judges in deciding cases.

- Provincial governors have the authority to exercise leniency and reduce a judge's sentence.

- The king and his advisors review cases involving capital punishment. The king has the authority to commute death sentences and grant pardons, except for capital crimes committed against individuals. In such cases, he may request the victim's next of kin to pardon the murderer—usually in return for compensation from the family or the king.

Saudi Enforcement of Islamic Justice

One of the ironies in Saudi Arabia is that the security services are often more humane in dealing with the opposition than those in most other Middle Eastern states, but the criminal justice system practices the severe physical punishment of criminals. Western human rights groups often strongly object to such traditional punishments, and the State Department reports that[61]

> [t]he Government punishes criminals according to Islamic law, or Shari'a. Punishments include flogging, amputation, and execution by beheading, stoning, or firing squad. The authorities acknowledged 100 executions during the year, a substantial increase from 25 in 1998, but less than the 134 reported in 1997. Executions included 36 men for murder (29 Saudis and 7 foreigners), 40 men for narcotics-related offenses (2 Saudis and 38 foreigners), 3 men for gang-related activities (2 Saudis and 1 foreigner), 8 men for rape (7 Saudis and 1 foreigner), 10 men for armed robbery (7 Saudis and 3 foreigners), and 3 women for narcotics-related offenses (all foreigners). The men were executed by beheading and the women were executed by firing squad. There were no executions by stoning. In accordance with Shari'a, the authorities may punish repeated thievery by amputation of the right hand. There were two reports of multiple amputations (right hand, left leg) for the crime of highway robbery during the year. The amputations were carried out against two Saudi men. Persons convicted of less serious offenses, such as alcohol related offenses or being alone in the company of an unrelated person of the opposite sex, sometimes were punished by flogging with a cane.

Western critics of this aspect of Saudi justice should, however, keep three factors in mind. First, the percentage of the Saudi population tried or convicted of crimes is probably less than 10% of that subject to trial or conviction in the United States. Second, Saudi prison sentences are generally much shorter and Saudi prison conditions are usually substantially better. Whether Saudi draconian punishments are cumulatively harsher than the treatment of U.S. prisoners over time is questionable. Third, at least some Saudi government officials point out that giving "traditionalists" power over criminal punishment is both popular with the vast majority of Saudis and an area where the government can make concessions with the least damage to the modernization of the Kingdom.

THE MUTAWAA'IN (RELIGIOUS POLICE)

Saudi Arabia has a religious police called the Mutawaa'in, which is a semi-autonomous force organized under the king in conjunction with the Islamic clergy (Ulema). It is known in English as the "Organization to Prevent Vice and Promote Virtue" or "Committees for Public Morality." It is primarily responsible for ensuring compliance with the precepts of Wahhabism, but performs some minor security functions in the surveillance religious extremists.[62] The Mutawaa'in enforce the public observances of religious practices, such as the closure of public establishments during prayer times. They have been known to exceed their authority with both

Saudi and expatriate alike by undue harassment of both men and women in public places and the trespassing into private homes.

The Mutawaa'in have the authority to detain persons for no more than twenty-four hours for violations of the strict standards of proper dress and behavior. However, they sometimes exceed this limit before delivering detainees to the police. Current procedures require a police officer to accompany the Mutawaa'in at the time of an arrest, and the Mutawaa'in generally comply with this requirement. In the more conservative Riyadh district, however, there are continuing reports received of Mutawaa'in accosting, abusing, arresting, and detaining persons alleged to have violated dress and behavior standards.

The State Department reports that

> Mutawaa'in practices and incidents of abuse varied widely in different regions of the country, but were most numerous in the central Nejd region. In certain areas, both the Mutawaa'in and religious vigilantes acting on their own harassed, assaulted, battered, arrested, and detained citizens and foreigners. The Government requires the Mutawaa'in to follow established procedures and to offer instruction in a polite manner; however, Mutawaa'in did not always comply with the requirements. The Government has not criticized public abuses by Mutawaa'in and religious vigilantes, but has sought to curtail these abuses.

It also reports that the Mutawaa'in enforce strict standards of social behavior, including the closing of commercial establishments during the five daily prayer observances, insisting on compliance with strict norms of public dress, and dispersing gatherings of women in public places. The Mutawaa'in frequently reproach Saudi and foreign women for failure to observe strict dress codes, and arrest men and women found together who are not married or closely related. In November 1998, several Mutawaa'in attacked and killed an elderly Shi'a prayer leader in Hofuf for repeating the call to prayer twice (a traditional Shi'a practice). Mutawaa'in attempts to cover up the killing were unsuccessful. The State Department reports that the government reportedly investigated the incident, but did not make public the results of any investigations involving Mutawaa'in personnel.

The level of Mutawaa'in activity has varied over time and is difficult to predict. The government appointed a new and more compliant leader for the religious police after a series of raids on rich and influential Saudis in 1990, but their power grew strikingly after the Gulf War as Saudi traditionalists reacted to the presence of U.S. and other Western forces; it seems to have peaked in the mid-1990s. The number of reports of harassment by the Mutawaa'in during the late 1990s remained relatively low in comparison with previous years, but the Mutawaa'in continue to intimidate, abuse, and detain citizens and foreigners of both sexes.

Some Saudi officials go so far as to describe the Mutawaa'in as a form of disguised unemployment for religious Saudis, and state that it is sharply overstaffed in some areas. One senior Saudi official went so far as to say the Mutawaa'in as a religious labor union were "more interested in their benefits than anything else." Other Saudis are more divided in their reaction. Some feel the Mutawaa'in perform a useful function in limiting the secularization of the Kingdom. Others see it as an outdated and over-conservative annoyance.[63] Serious questions also remain about the degree to which the attitudes of organizations like the Mutawaa'in affect the safety of Saudi girls' schools and did or did not interfere in a school fire that killed fifteen Saudi girls in March 2002. Certainly, religious conservatism was a factor that led to the gross overcrowding of some aspects of the school, which allowed 800 students to occupy a space designed for 300.[64]

In late November 2002, Prince Nayef was sufficiently disturbed over continuing problems with the Mutawaa'in that he publicly took action to try to improve the conduct of the Department of Virtue Propagation and Vice Prevention. He called upon the department to "hire well-qualified people and people of limited qualifications who act recklessly" to "gently deal with the people and avoid harshness, especially with young people." He announced a training institute was being set up, and that the Mutawaa'in would operate with better training and discipline.[65]

In general, the Mutawaa'in seem to be more of a Saudi internal security problem than part of the solution. Saudis do not seem to be able to cite any examples of cases where the Mutawaa'in have played a role in limiting the activities of Islamic extremists and defending the core values of Islam against extremism. They cannot cite cases in which the force played a role in defending religious values while aiding modernization and reform. To be blunt, they have been a "gentler and kinder" Taliban. They have carried out rote enforcement of Saudi religious practices while acting as a tacit endorsement of efforts to force compliance with Islam rather than persuade. As such, they at least indirectly endorse Islamic extremism while lacking the intellectual depth, training, and experience to truly defend one of the world's great religions.

It should be noted, however, that the "Mujahideen," whose operations are centered in Riyadh, patrol at night as a kind of religious vice squad. This force is much more professional than the "Mutawaa'in," and is rarely seen or talked about.

ENFORCEMENT OF ISLAMIC NORMS, CENSORSHIP, AND CONTROL OF THE MEDIA

The State Department reports that the Saudi government enforces most social and Islamic religious norms, which are matters of law. The authorities do not tolerate criticism of Islam, the ruling family, or the government.

However, the authorities allow the press some freedom to criticize governmental bodies and social policies through editorial comments and cartoons. Persons whose criticisms align them with an organized political opposition are subject to arrest and detention until they confess to a crime or sign a statement promising not to resume such criticisms, which is tantamount to a confession.

Internal Security and Surveillance of Ordinary Citizens

While the Saudi government may have failed to come to grips with Islamic extremism and terrorism, the State Department reports that there are few barriers to religious censorship and the security force's access to private communications. Customs officials routinely open mail and shipments to search for contraband, including material deemed pornographic and non-Muslim religious material. Officials confiscate censored materials considered offensive, including Christian Bibles and religious videotapes. The authorities also open mail and use informants and wiretaps in internal security and criminal matters.

The Saudi internal security forces rarely intrude visibly in day-to-day life, but they do use wiretaps against both Saudi citizens and foreigners, and do so even for relatively limited crimes such as alcohol-related offenses. Neighborhood mayors (known as umdas) report "seditious ideas" or antigovernment activity in their neighborhoods to the Ministry of the Interior.

The State Department reports that academic freedom is restricted. The authorities prohibit the open, formal study of evolution, Freud, Marx, Western music, and Western philosophy. Some professors believe that informers monitor their classroom comments and report to government and religious authorities. Others, however, comment that they have comparative freedom to hold private discussion sessions, and that the restrictions on formal teaching activity do not apply to criticisms of the way in which the government operates, the allocation of budget resources, the value of government programs, or other kinds of criticism that are not directed specifically at the legitimacy of the regime.

The State Department notes that the Saudi government strictly limits freedom of assembly. It prohibits public demonstrations as a means of political expression. For example, the Saudi government arrested several clergymen and ninety-seven other Saudis for protesting against the U.S. military presence in Saudi Arabia in 1994. It stopped public protests in Riyadh supporting the Palestinians in October 2000, and arrested several of those who participated. The Ministry of the Interior issued a public warning in April 2002 that such meetings were forbidden after another spontaneous protest arose against Israel's treatment of the Palestinians by some 150 Saudi citizens in northern Saudi Arabia.[66] Unless meetings are sponsored by diplomatic missions or approved by the appropriate governor, foreign residents who seek to hold nonsegregated meetings risk arrest and deportation.

According to the State Department, the Saudi authorities monitor large gatherings of persons, especially of women. The Mutawaa'in disperse groups of women found in public places, such as restaurants. Government policy permits women to attend cultural and social events at diplomatic chanceries and residences only if a father, brother, or husband accompanies them. The State Department reports, however, that the Saudi police implement the policy in an arbitrary manner. On many occasions during the year, authorities actively prohibited women from entering diplomatic chanceries or residences to attend cultural events and lectures. However, in May 2001, for the second year in a row, authorities allowed unescorted Saudi women to attend a women-only cultural event hosted at a diplomatic mission.

Even so, Saudis do routinely hold large social gatherings, and frank—if not brutal criticism—of the government is almost a social sport. While Saudis generally seem to avoid criticism of the legitimacy of the regime, they can be very critical of members of the royal family even when other members of the royal family are present, and criticism of ministers is common. Few educated Saudis seem to exhibit any concern about monitoring by the security services at social events.

Internal Security and Control of the Media

The government uses censorship as another way of strengthening internal security. The print media are privately owned but publicly subsidized. A 1982 media policy statement and a 1965 national security law prohibit the dissemination of criticism of the Saudi government. The media policy statement urges journalists to uphold Islam, oppose atheism, promote Arab interests, and preserve the cultural heritage of Saudi Arabia. The State Department reports that the Ministry of Information appoints, and may remove, editors in chief. It also provides guidelines to newspapers on controversial issues. The Saudi government owns the Saudi Press Agency (SPA), which expresses official government views.

According to the State Department, newspapers typically publish news on sensitive subjects, such as crime or terrorism, only after it has been released by the SPA or when a senior government official has authorized it. Two Saudi-owned, London-based dailies, *Ash-Sharq al-Awsat* and *Al-Hayat*, are widely distributed and read in Saudi Arabia. Both newspapers tend to practice self-censorship in order to comply with government restrictions on sensitive issues. However, any reader of these publications, and other Saudi newspapers, will recognize that they still can be highly critical of Saudi government activities. The Ministry of Information compiles and updates a list of publications that are prohibited from being sold in the country.

The Saudi government normally tightly restricts the entry of foreign journalists into the Kingdom, uses visas to select the reporters it admits, and tries to influence their coverage. It often provides escorts for and monitors the movements of foreign journalists. The State Department reports that the Saudi authorities also continue to censor stories about Saudi Arabia in the foreign press. Censors may remove or blacken the offending articles, glue pages together, or prevent certain issues of foreign publications from entering the market. The Saudi government owns and operates the television and radio companies. Government censors remove any reference to politics, religions other than Islam, pork or pigs, alcohol, and sex from foreign programs and songs. The Ministry of Information has, however, continued to relax its blackout policy regarding politically sensitive news concerning Saudi Arabia reported in the international media, although press restrictions on reporting of domestic news remain very stringent.

The State Department reports that the Saudi government's policy is motivated in part by pragmatic considerations: Saudi access to outside sources of information, especially the Cable News Network (CNN), Al Jahzirha, and other satellite television channels, is increasingly widespread and may now reach as much 70% of the population. The State Department estimates that there are well over one million satellite receiving dishes in the country that provide citizens with foreign broadcasts, although the legal status of these devices is ambiguous. The government ordered a halt to their importation in 1992 at the request of religious leaders who objected to foreign programming being made available on satellite channels. In 1994 the government banned the sale, installation, and maintenance of dishes and supporting devices, but the number of dishes continues to increase and residents legally may subscribe to satellite decoding services that require a dish.

Other changes in technology, however, are making censorship less and less effective. Access to the Internet is available through Saudi servers or through servers in other Gulf countries and may now be available to over 40% of native Saudis. The government attempts to block all Web sites that it views as presenting hostile opposition views and that have sexual, pornographic, or otherwise offensive or un-Islamic content. However, visits to Saudi Arabia confirm the State Department judgment that virtually all Web site search engines are now readily accessible to experienced users of the Internet from within the country. Public access to the Internet is expanding at a geometric rate, and Saudi attempts to limit access to various sections of the Net are largely ineffective. Saudi students find it easy to work around government controls, as do any groups seeking to use the Internet for political purposes or communication.

LOOKING TOWARD THE FUTURE

As has been discussed earlier, Saudi Arabia has taken a number of steps to improve its internal security and support the war on terrorism since September 11, 2001. Saudi intelligence and the foreign ministry have conducted a detailed review of Saudi companies and charities operating in Pakistan and central Asia. Saudi Arabia and the other GCC countries agreed to take new steps to control the flow of funds and money laundering at the GCC summit meeting on December 31, 2001.[67] Saudi Arabia has also made the Combined Aerospace Operations Center (CAOC) at Prince Sultan Airbase available for U.S. use in supporting the war in Afghanistan.[68]

The Saudi government has arrested a number of individuals the United States suspects of supporting Osama bin Laden, as well as cracked down on its more extreme Islamists. While it has acted slowly because of the sensitivity Saudis show to any outside pressure, and rising public anger over the Second Intifada, it issued orders blocking the assets of sixty-six persons, companies, groups, and charities on the United States' watch list for entities linked to global terrorism in late October 2001.[69] Saudi Arabia agreed to sign the 1999 UN anti-terrorism convention aimed at blocking the financial support of terrorists in early November 2001.[70] The foreign minister, Prince Saud Faisal, promised to punish Saudis criminally involved in al Qaeda terrorism in December 2001.[71]

The government has acted to freeze bank accounts linked to suspected terrorists, and Saudi intelligence is now monitoring at least 150 accounts for terrorist activity. The Saudi Chamber of Commerce established a task force in January 2002 to develop a financial and administrative system for Saudi charities to ensure that their funds would not go to extremist causes, and the Saudi Arabian Monetary Agency is assisting Saudi banks to develop and computerize systems to track money laundering. The Saudi government is also drafting new laws to limit money-laundering activity.[72]

Saudi Arabia issued a full list of such actions in early December 2002, and U.S. officials have confirmed the validity of this list. These measures are summarized in Table 9.1.[73]

These are important steps in coming to grips with both the problems exposed by the events of September 11, and the long-standing struggle between the Saudi government and Islamic extremists. It is clear, however, that the Saudi government must do more if it is to ensure its own internal security as well as fight global terrorism. It is equally clear that the government must now take much broader steps in areas like education, and expand employment opportunities for young Saudis to come to grips with security problems like Islamic extremism, while it simultaneously continues to liberalize its overall internal security arrangements and create and enforce a more modern version of the rule of law.

There is no reason that Saudi Arabia should always copy Western approaches to internal security and law enforcement as it makes these changes.

Table 9.1
Saudi Measures to Fight Terrorism and Improve Internal Security Since September 11, 2001

International Cooperation

- Supporting and implementing UN Security Council Resolution 1267 by freezing the funds and financial assets of the Taliban. Freezing the funds of the individuals listed in Security Council Resolution 1333. Signing the International Convention for Suppression and Financing of Terrorism based on Security Council Resolution 1373 and reporting on the implementation of the rules and procedures pertaining to this resolution; reporting to the Security Council on the implementation of Resolution 1390. Supporting and implementing Security Council Resolution 1368, of September 12, 2001, limiting the financing of terrorist activities.

- Maintaining a Counterterrorism committee with the United States comprised of intelligence and law enforcement personnel who meet regularly to share information and resources and to develop action plans to root out terrorist networks. Saudi Arabia has sought to strengthen cooperation between the Kingdom and the United States through reciprocal visits.

- Encouraging Saudi government departments and banks to participate in international seminars, conferences, and symposia on combating terrorist financing activities. Saudi Arabia has hosted seminars, conferences, and symposia on combating terrorism and is a member of the GCC Financial Action Task Force (FATF).

- Completing and submitting the Self-Assessment Questionnaire regarding the 40 recommendations of the FATF. Saudi Arabia has also submitted the Self Assessment Questionnaire regarding the 8 Special Recommendations of the FATF.

- Having the Saudi Arabian Monetary Authority (SAMA) exchange information on money-laundering–related activities with other banking supervisory authorities and with law enforcement agencies. SAMA has created a Committee to carry out a self-assessment for compliance with the recommendations of the FATF and these self-assessment questionnaires have been submitted. Saudi Arabia has invited the FATF to conduct a Mutual Evaluation in April 2003.

- Signing a multilateral agreement under the auspices of the Arab League to fight terrorism.

- Submitting a report every 90 days on the initiatives and actions the Kingdom has taken to fight terrorism to the UN Security Council committees dealing with terrorism.

- Establishing formal communication points between the Ministry of Foreign Affairs and the Permanent Representative to the UN.

Arrests and Questioning of Suspects

- Saudi Arabia has questioned over 2,000 individuals fort possible ties to al Qaeda. Many of these people fought in Afghanistan during the Soviet invasion as well as in Bosnia and Chechnya.

continued

Table 9.1 (Continued)

- Detaining up to 200 suspects out of this total for questioning and interrogation. Well over 100 were still held in detention in December 2002.
- Saudi intelligence and law enforcement agencies identified and arrested a cell composed of seven individuals linked to al Qaeda who were planning to carry out terrorist attacks against vital sites in the Kingdom. The cell leader was extradited from the Sudan. This cell was responsible for the attempt to shoot down American military planes at Prince Sultan Airbase using a shoulder-launched surface-to-air missile.
- Saudi Arabia successfully negotiated with Iran for the extradition of 16 suspected Al Qaeda members. These individuals are now in Saudi custody and are being questioned. The Iranian authorities handed over the al Qaeda fugitives, all Saudis, knowing that whatever intelligence was obtained from them during interrogation in Saudi Arabia would be passed on to the United States for use in the war against terrorism.
- Asking Interpol to arrest 750 people, many of whom are suspected of money laundering, drug trafficking, and terror-related activities. This figure includes 214 Saudis whose names appear in Interpol's database and expatriates who fled Saudi Arabia.
- Helping to identify a network of more than 50 shell companies that Osama bin Laden used to move money around the world. The companies were located in the Middle East, Europe, Asia, and the Caribbean. A sophisticated financial network that weaved through more than 25 nations was uncovered and virtually shut down.

Legal and Regulatory Actions and Freezing Terrorist Assets and Combating Money Laundering

- Signing and joining the United Nations Convention against Illicit Trafficking of Narcotics and Psychotropic Substances in 1988.
- Freezing assets of Osama bin Laden in 1994.
- Establishing Anti–Money-Laundering Units at the Ministry of Interior, SAMA, and Commercial Banks in 1995.
- Having SAMA issue "Guidelines for Prevention and Control of Money Laundering Activities" to Saudi Banks to implement "Know your Customer Rules," maintain records of suspicious transactions, and report them to law enforcement officials in SAMA in 1995.
- Adopting 40 recommendations of the Financial Task force relating to banking control of money laundering that grew out of the G-7 meeting in 1988.
- Saudi banks to identify and freeze all assets relating to terrorist suspects and entities per the list issued by the United States government on September 23, 2001. Saudi banks have complied with the freeze requirements and have initiated investigation of transactions that suspects linked to al Qaeda may have undertaken in the past.
- Investigating bank accounts suspected to have been linked to terrorism. Saudi Arabia froze 33 accounts belonging to 3 individuals that total about $5,574,196.

Table 9.1 (Continued)

- Establishing a Special Committee with personnel from the Ministry of Interior, Ministry of Foreign Affairs, the Intelligence Agency, and the Saudi Arabian Monetary Agency (SAMA) to deal with requests from international bodies and countries with regard to combating terrorist financing.

- Reorienting the activities of the GCC Financial Action Task Force (FATF) to deal with terrorism and creating a Committee to carry out a self-assessment for compliance with the recommendations of the FATF.

- Joining Finance Ministers and Central Bank Governors of the G-20 in order to develop an aggressive action plan directed at the routing-out and freezing of terrorist assets worldwide.

- Having the Saudi Arabian Monetary Authority (SAMA) instruct Saudi banks to promptly establish a Supervisory Committee to closely monitor the threat posed by terrorism and to coordinate all efforts to freeze the assets of potential terrorists. The Committee is composed of senior officers from banks responsible for Risk Control, Audit, Money-Laundering Units, Legal, and Operations. The committee meets regularly in the presence of SAMA officials.

- Requiring Saudi banks to put in place mechanisms to respond to all relevant inquiries, both domestically and internationally, at the level of their Chief Executive Officers, as well as at the level of the Supervisory Committee. To ensure proper coordination and effective response, all Saudi banks route their responses and relevant information via SAMA.

- Having the Ministry of Commerce issue Regulation 1312 aimed at preventing and combating money laundering in the non-financial sector. These regulations are aimed at manufacturing and trading sectors and also cover professional services such as accounting, legal, and consultancy services.

- Creating an institutional framework for combating money laundering, including the establishment of Anti–Money-Laundering units, with a trained and dedicated specialist staff. These units work with SAMA and law enforcement agencies. The government has also encouraged banks to bring Money-Laundering–related experiences to the notice of various bank committees (Chief Operations Officers, Managing Directors, Fraud Committee, etc.) for exchange of information and joint actions.

- Creating specialized Financial Intelligence Unit (FIU) in the Security and Drug Control Department of the Ministry of Interior. This unit is specially tasked with handling money-laundering cases. A new liaison group dealing with terrorist finances has been established between SAMA and the Ministry of the Interior.

- Carrying out regular inspection of banks to ensure compliance with laws and regulations. Any violation or non-compliance is cause for serious actions and is referred to a bank's senior management and the Board. Furthermore, the government has created a permanent Committee of Banks' compliance officers to review regulations and guidelines and recommend improvements, and to ensure all implementation issues are resolved.

- Freezing bank accounts suspected of links to terrorists.

continued

Table 9.1 (Continued)

- Use of the interbanking system in Saudi Arabia to identify possible sources of funding of terrorism.
- Supporting UN resolutions, such as UN Security Council Resolution 1368 to limit the financing of terrorist activities.
- Working with the United States and other countries to block more than $70 million in possible terrorist assets in Saudi Arabia and other countries.
- Quietly providing data on suspect private Saudi accounts in Switzerland, Liechtenstein, Luxembourg, Denmark, and Sweden.
- Directing SAMA to issue rules "Governing the Opening of Bank Accounts" and "General Operational Guidelines" in order to protect banks against money-laundering activities in May 2002. For instance, Saudi banks are not permitted to open bank accounts for non-resident individuals without specific approval from SAMA. Banks are required to apply strict rules and any non-customer business has to be fully documented.
- Carrying out regular inspection of banks to ensure compliance with laws and regulations. Any violation or non-compliance is cause for serious actions and is referred to a bank's senior management and the Board. Creating a Permanent Committee of Banks' compliance officers to review regulation and guidelines and recommend improvements, and to ensure all implementation issues are resolved.
- Making significant new efforts to train staff in financial institutions and the Security and Investigation departments in the Ministry of Interior as well as others involved in compliance and law. Special training programs have been developed for bankers, prosecutors, judges, customs officers, and other officials from government departments and agencies. Furthermore, training programs are offered by the Prince Nayef Security Academy, King Fahd Security Faculty, and Public Security Training City.
- Establishing a Permanent Committee of representatives of seven ministries and government agencies to manage all legal and other issues related to money-laundering activities.
- Directing SAMA to organize a conference with the Riyadh Interpol for the First Asian Regional meeting in cooperation with law enforcement agencies and financial institutions on January 28–30, 2002.
- Having the Council of Saudi Chambers of Commerce and Industry in cooperation with SAMA conduct an International Conference on Prevention and Detection of Fraud, Economic Crimes, and Money Laundering on May 13–14, 2002.
- Directing Saudi banks and SAMA to computerize reported cases to identify trends in money-laundering activities to assist in policymaking and other initiatives.

Actions Taken in Regard to Charitable Organizations

- Creating a High Commission for the Oversight of Charities to look at ways to regulate charities, help them put financial control mechanisms and procedures in place, require that charities conduct audits, and review them. A department

Table 9.1 (Continued)

will be set up that will grow out of the High Commission for the Oversight of Charities to maintain suitable review and controls. This will compensate for the fact that Saudi Arabia does not have an income tax and does not have the same tax-related review of expenditures common in the West.

- Requiring that charitable activities that extend outside Saudi Arabia be reported to the Saudi government and be routinely monitored, and that charitable activities outside Saudi Arabia be reported to the Foreign Ministry.

- Taking joint action with the United States to freeze the assets of Wa'el Hamza Julaidan, a Saudi fugitive and a close aide of bin Laden, who is believed to have funneled money to al Qaeda. Julaidan served as the director of the Rabita Trust and other organizations.

- Establishing a High Commission for oversights of all charities, contributions, and donations is in the final process of setting up Operational Procedures to manage contributions and donations to and from the charities.

- Auditing all charitable groups to ensure there are no links to suspected organizations since September 11, 2001.

- Issuing new guidelines and regulations, including financial control mechanisms to make sure terrorist and extremist organizations cannot take advantage of legitimate charities.

- Setting up the Higher Saudi Association for Relief and Charity to oversee the distribution of donations and guarantee they are channeled to the needy.

- Strengthening the role of the Saudi Arabia and U.S. counterterrorism committee comprised of intelligence and law enforcement personnel who meet regularly to share information and resources on the misuse of charities and charitable funds and develop plans of action to root out terrorist networks.

- Freezing bank accounts involving the flow of charitable funds that are suspected of being linked to terrorism.

- Working with the U.S. Treasury Department to block the accounts of the Somalia and Bosnia branches of the Saudi Arabia–based Al-Haramain Islamic Foundation in March 2002. While the Saudi headquarters for this private charitable entity is dedicated to helping those in need, the United States and Saudi Arabia determined that the Somalia and Bosnia branches of Al-Haramain Islamic Foundation engaged in supporting terrorist activities and terrorist organizations such as al Qaeda, AIAI (Al-Itihaad Al-Islamiya), and others.

Other Initiatives Related to Fighting Terrorism

- Signing a multilateral agreement under the auspices of the Arab League to fight terrorism.

- Participating in G-20 meetings and signing various bilateral agreements with non-Arab countries.

- Preparing and submitting a report on the initiatives and actions taken by the Kingdom, with respect to the fight against terrorism, to the UN Security Council Committees every 90 days.

continued

Table 9.1 (Continued)

- Establishing communication points between the Ministry of Foreign Affairs and the Permanent Representative to the United Nations.
- Supporting and meeting the requirements of various UN resolutions related to combating terrorism.
- Freezing funds and other financial assets of the Taliban regime based on UN Security Resolution 1267.
- Freezing funds of listed individuals based on UN Security Council Resolution 1333.
- Signing the International Convention for Suppression and Financing of Terrorism based on UN Security Council Resolution 1373 on reporting to the UN Security Council's committee regarding the implementation of the Rules and Procedures pertaining to 1373.
- Reporting to the UN Security Council the implementation of Resolution 1390.
- Embassy of Saudi Arabia, *Initiatives and Actions Taken by the Kingdom of Saudi Arabia in the Financial Area to Combat Terrorism*, December 3, 2002.

The Kingdom can preserve its Islamic character and still take the necessary steps to end support for violent Islamic extremism both within and outside Saudi Arabia. Similarly, Saudi Arabia can also do much to liberalize and improve human rights without giving up its own national cultural traditions and still act to suppress terrorist and extremist activity.

Nevertheless, Saudi economic and political reform cannot take place without sufficient social and religious reform, and without sufficient tolerance of modern media and communications. To allow Saudi Arabia to compete in global economic terms, the Kingdom must become a more open society, one in which its young men and women are fully prepared to compete in the marketplace with global efficiency. This is not based on the moral and ethical need to improve human rights—valid as such issues are—but is a pragmatic need that is vital to Saudi Arabia's future development and growth.

The dividing line between Islam and terrorism is clear, and one that has already been publicly stated by Crown Prince Abdullah, many other senior Saudi officials, and many senior members of the Saudi clergy. No one can argue with Saudi advocacy of Islam and the conservative practices of the Wahhabi sect when these are so clearly the choice of the Saudi people. Everyone can argue with the thesis that extremists can use God to advocate violence, terrorism, and actions that kill innocent civilians. The same is true of halting religious practices that teach intolerance and hatred, regardless of whether such practices are defended in the name of Islam,

Judaism, Christianity, or any other faith. The Saudi government needs to aggressively and consistently enforce its own policies in those areas.

There is no dilemma between improving intelligence and the security services and liberalization. More modern security and legal procedures can improve the quality of investigations intelligence-gathering, warning without preventing reductions in censorship and government controls, more tolerance of the Saudi Shi'ites and practices of foreigners on Saudi soil, and methods of arrest and trial that guarantee more rights. Past progress in these areas has also shown that the necessary rate of progress can be made on Saudi terms and in ways that preserve Saudi custom.

Most importantly, Saudi security is best preserved by progress and reform, and not by the activities of the internal security and intelligence services. The state of the Saudi economy, and coming to grips with the Kingdom's problems with education, Saudisation, youth employment, and demographics, are the true keys to internal security. So is a level of political progress that expands the role ordinary Saudis can play in government and makes further reductions in sources of social unrest like corruption. Even the best counterterrorist operations can only deal with the small fraction of the Saudi population who are violent extremists. True internal security is based on popular support.

NOTES

1. Associated Press, NY, December 30, 2001, 1928; Reuters, December 29, 2001, 1802; *Saudi Arabia*, Vol. 18, No. 10, October 2001, pp. 1–4.

2. Press release, "Mosques Not to Be Used as Political Platforms," Embassy of Saudi Arabia, December 7, 2002.

3. Some elements of the report are paraphrased from reporting in the U.S. State Department report on Human Rights, particularly the 1999 edition: *1999 Country Reports on Human Rights Practices*, U.S. Department of State, February 25, 2000 *http://www.state.gov/www/global/human_rights/1999_hrp_report/saudiara.html*, released by the Bureau of Democracy, Human Rights, and Labor. The author looked extensively at various NGO reports on human rights in the Kingdom, but does not believe that they have the objectivity or reliability of the State Department report. He did, however, ask a wide range of Saudis, inside and outside Saudi Arabia, and Western legal and internal security experts to review his extensive restructuring of the State Department report, and the text has sometimes been modified accordingly. The reader should be fully aware that the credit for most of the analysis of Saudi legal, censorship, and human rights development in this analysis belongs to State Department personnel, and that no outside analyst can report as reliably on these aspects of developments in the Kingdom.

4. Prince Nayef is 68 years old. Like Fahd, Abdullah, and Nawaf, he is a son of King Abdul Aziz.

5. These comments are based on an English transcript and summary provided in e-mail form by the Saudi Embassy in Washington on December 5, 2002.

6. These comments are based on an English transcript and summary provided in e-mail form by the Saudi Embassy in Washington on December 5, 2002.

7. This analysis draws heavily on interviews; various annual editions of the IISS, *Military Balance*; and *Jane's Sentinel: The Gulf States, 1997* (London: Jane's Publishing, 1997).

8. *Defense News*, November 11, 1991, p. 36; *Washington Technology*, September 24, 1992, p. 1.

9. Interviews in Saudi Arabia in 2000.

10. Prince Nawaf is a son of King Abd al-Aziz. Prince Turki is brother of Prince Saud al-Faisal, the foreign minister and a brother of Turki and son of the late King Faisal.

11. See Simon Henderson, "The Saudis: Friend or Foe?," *Wall Street Journal*, October 22, 2001, as provided by e-mail in *publications@washingtoninstitute.org*. Also see *The Estimate*, Vol. XIII, No. 16, September 7, 2001, p. 1.

12. Simon Henderson, "The Saudis: Friend or Foe?," *Wall Street Journal*, October 22, 2001, p. A-18 and similar article provided by e-mail in *publications@washingtoninstitute.org*; Joseph A. Kechichian, *Succession in Saudi Arabia* (New York: Palgrave, 2001), pp. 9, 30, 52, 75, 111.

13. John Duke Anthony, "A Changing of the Guard in Saudi Arabia, A Personal Perspective," *Gulf Wire—Perspectives*, September 3–9, 2001, *http://arabialink.com/GulfWire/GULFWIRE.htm*.

14. The historical data draw on work by the Congressional Research Service, specifically by Helen Chapin Metz in *Saudi Arabia, A Country Study* (Washington: Congressional Research Service, December 1992), *http://lcweb2.loc.gov/cgi-bin/query/r?frd/cstdy:@field(DOCID+sa0000)*, and the U.S. State Department report on Human Rights, particularly the *2000 Country Reports on Human Rights Practices*, U.S. Department of State, February 25, 2000, *http://www.state.gov/www/global/human_rights/2000_hrp_report/saudiara.html*, released by the Bureau of Democracy, Human Rights, and Labor.

15. Associated Press, March 20, 2002, 1013; March 23, 2002, 1418.

16. U.S. State Department, *Country Report on Human Rights Practices*, *http://www.state.gov/www/global/human_rights/1999_hrp_report/saudiara.html*, and U.S. State Department, *1999 Country Reports on Human Rights Practices*, "Saudi Arabia," Released by the Bureau of Democracy, Human Rights, and Labor, U.S. Department of State, February 25, 2000.

17. U.S. State Department, *Country Report on Human Rights Practices*, *http://www.state.gov/www/global/human_rights/1999_hrp_report/saudiara.html*, and U.S. State Department, *1999 Country Reports on Human Rights Practices*, "Saudi Arabia," Released by the Bureau of Democracy, Human Rights, and Labor, U.S. Department of State, February 25, 2000.

18. U.S. State Department, *Country Report on Human Rights Practices*, various editions.

19. U.S. State Department, *Country Report on Human Rights Practices*, various editions, especially U.S. State Department, *1999 Country Reports on Human Rights Practices*, "Saudi Arabia," Released by the Bureau of Democracy, Human Rights, and Labor, U.S. Department of State, February 25, 2000.

20. *The Estimate*, December 28, 2001, p. 9.

21. *Saudi Arabia*, Vol. 18, No. 10, October 2001, p. 3.

22. Douglas Jehl, "Holy War Lured Saudis as Rulers Look Away," *New York Times*, December 27, 2001, pp. A-1, B-4–B-5.

23. *Washington Times*, February 7, 2002.

24. Reuters, January 3, 2002, 0731; *New York Times*, December 27, 2001, p. A-1.

25. *The Estimate*, December 28, 2001, p. 9.

26. Howard Schneider, "Saudis Suspect Al Qaeda Plot Against US Military, Arrest 13," *The Washington Post*, June 19, 2002, p. A-15.

27. Douglas Jehl, "Holy War Lured Saudis as Rulers Look Away," *New York Times*, December 27, 2001, pp. A-1, B-4–B-5.

28. Douglas Jehl, "Holy War Lured Saudis as Rulers Look Away," *New York Times*, December 27, 2001, pp. A-1, B-4–B-5.

29. Douglas Jehl, "Holy War Lured Saudis as Rulers Look Away," *New York Times*, December 27, 2001, pp. A-1, B-4–B-5.

30. For additional sources, see *Washington Times*, July 14, 1996, p A-4, June 16, 1997, p. A-11; *Washington Post*, January 26, 1997, p. A-22, January 23, 1997, p. A-8, March 23, 1997, p. A-28, May 9, 1997, p. A-31; Reuters, November 1, 1996, 1635, February 20, 1997, 0143; *Baltimore Sun*, February 28, 1997, p. 1A, June 16, 1997, p. 7A; *Chicago Tribune*, March 31, 1997, p. 4; *USA Today*, June 16, 1997, p. 12A.

31. *New York Times*, April 22, 1995, p. A-5; *Los Angeles Times*, April 21, 1995, pp. A-9, A-26; *USA Today*, April 26, 1995, p. 11A; *Washington Post*, April 22, 1995, p. A-24; *Washington Times*, April 22, 1995, p. A-8, April 24, 1995, p. A-11, May 3, 1995, p. A-12.

32. Jamal Khashoggi, Deputy Editor in Chief, "Kingdom has a Big Role to Play in Afghanistan," *Arab News*, Jeddah, November 4, 2001.

33. Ibid.

34. U.S. State Department, *Patterns of Global Terrorism: 1999*, "Middle East Overview," *http://www.state.gov/www/global/terrorism/1999report/mideast.html#Arabia*.

35. U.S. State Department, *Patterns of Global Terrorism: 1999*, "Middle East Overview," *http://www.state.gov/www/global/terrorism/1999report/mideast.html#Arabia*; Trifin J. Roule, Jeremy Kinsell, and Brian Joyce, "Investigators seek to break up Al-Qaida's financial structure," *Jane's Intelligence Review*, November 2001, pp. 8–11.

36. Jamal Khashoggi, Deputy Editor in Chief, "Kingdom has a Big Role to Play in Afghanistan," *Arab News*, Jeddah, November 6, 2001. Similar interviews and reports have appeared in a number of sources, including the *New York Times* and *Washington Post*. Also see Reuters transcript of interview on Middle East Broadcasting network, November 6, 2001, 1556 and Reuters, November 3, 2001, 1609; Scott Macleod, "The Near Misses," *Time*, November 12, 2001, p. 45; Douglas Jehl, "Holy War Lured Saudis as Rulers Look Away," *New York Times*, December 27, 2001, pp. A-1, B-4–B-5.

37. Jamal Khashoggi, Deputy Editor in Chief, "Kingdom has a Big Role to Play in Afghanistan," *Arab News*, Jeddah, November 6, 2001.

38. Jamal Khashoggi, Deputy Editor in Chief, "Kingdom has a Big Role to Play in Afghanistan," *Arab News*, Jeddah, November 6, 2001.

39. Jamal Khashoggi, Deputy Editor in Chief, "Kingdom has a Big Role to Play in Afghanistan," *Arab News*, Jeddah, November 6, 2001.

40. Jamal Khashoggi, Deputy Editor in Chief, "Kingdom has a Big Role to Play in Afghanistan," *Arab News*, Jeddah, November 6, 2001.

41. Jamal Khashoggi, Deputy Editor in Chief, "Kingdom has a Big Role to Play in Afghanistan," *Arab News*, Jeddah, November 4, 2001.

42. Jamal Khashoggi, Deputy Editor in Chief, "Kingdom has a Big Role to Play in Afghanistan," *Arab News*, Jeddah, November 6, 2001.

43. Jamal Khashoggi, Deputy Editor in Chief, "Kingdom has a Big Role to Play in Afghanistan," *Arab News*, Jeddah, November 4, 2001.

44. Arnaud de Borchgrave, "Bullets of Saudi Gold," *Washington Times*, October 22, 2001, p. A-18; Roule, Kinsell, and Joyce, "Investigators seek to break up Al-Qaeda's financial structure," pp. 8–11; *Wall Street Journal*, February 5, 2002; *Washington Times*, February 5, 2002, pp. 18–19; *The Washington Post*, December 8, 2001, p. A-3; Douglas Farah, "Al Qaida's Road Paved with Gold," *The Washington Post*, February 17, 2002, pp. A-1, A-32; Reuters, November 29, 2001, 1219, January 23, 2002, 1016, January 31, 2002, 0704; Bruce Crumley, "Follow the Money," *Time*, November 19, 2001, p. 47; "Bin Laden Wealth Overestimated," *CNN.com*, November 5, 2001; Associated Press, NY, October 28, 2001, 1559; Jehl, "Holy War Lured Saudis as Rulers Look Away," pp. A-1, B-4–B-5.

45. Matthew Levitt, "Tackling the Financing of Terrorism in Saudi Arabia," *Policywatch* no. 609, March 11, 2002.

46. Reuters, March 11, 2002, 1745, March 12, 2002, 1310.

47. Reuters, March 20, 2002, 0520.

48. *International Herald Tribune*, June 25, 2002, p. 3; *Time*, June 15, 2002.

49. *New York Times*, June 14, 2002.

50. *Washington Post*, June 14, 2002, p. 11.

51. *Washington Post*, June 19, 2002, p. 15; *Baltimore Sun*, June 20, 2002.

52. *New York Times*, Web edition, June 14, 2002; *Los Angeles Times*, June 11, 2002, p. 1; *Washington Post*, June 18, 2002, p. 1.

53. Associated Press, 1852, May 6, 2001; *The London Times*, May 3, 2001, p. 14.

54. *The Estimate*, February 9, 2001, p. 9.

55. Reuters, March 14, 2002, 1649.

56. Associated Press, NY, October 29, 2001, 0747.

57. U.S. State Department, *Country Report on Human Rights Practices*, various editions.

58. *Arab News*, July 8, 2001, Jeddah, *http://www.arabnews.com/article.asp?ID=3823*.

59. This text is modified from text provided in the U.S. State Department, *Country Report on Human Rights Practices*, *http://www.state.gov/www/global/human_rights/1999_hrp_report/saudiara.html*, and U.S. State Department, *1999 Country Reports on Human Rights Practices*, "Saudi Arabia," Released by the Bureau of Democracy, Human Rights, and Labor, U.S. Department of State, February 25, 2000.

60. U.S. State Department, *Country Report on Human Rights Practices*, *http://www.state.gov/www/global/human_rights/1999_hrp_report/saudiara.html*, and U.S. State Department, *1999 Country Reports on Human Rights Practices*, "Saudi Arabia," Released by the Bureau of Democracy, Human Rights, and Labor, U.S. Department of State, February 25, 2000.

61. Ibid.

62. U.S. State Department, *Country Report on Human Rights Practices*, various editions, especially U.S. State Department, *1999 Country Reports on Human Rights Practices*, "Saudi Arabia," Released by the Bureau of Democracy, Human Rights, and Labor, U.S. Department of State, February 25, 2000.

63. The Ministry of Islamic Affairs funds the Mutawaa'in, and the general president of the Mutawaa'in holds the rank of cabinet minister. The ministry also pays the salaries of imams and others who work in the mosques. During 1999, foreign imams were barred from leading worship during the most heavily attended prayer times and were prohibited from delivering sermons during Friday congregational prayers. The government claims that its actions were part of its Saudisation plan to replace foreign workers with citizens.

64. Associated Press, NY, March 18, 2002, 0650, March 25, 2002, 1225; Reuters, March 12, 2002, 0430.

65. These comments are based on an English transcript and summary provided in e-mail form by the Saudi Embassy in Washington on December 5, 2002.

66. Reuters, April 4, 2002, 0526.

67. *Wall Street Journal*, February 5, 2002.

68. *The Estimate*, January 25, 2002, p. 4.

69. Reuters, October 31, 2001, 1255.

70. Associated Press, NY, November 6, 2001, 0617.

71. *Washington Post*, December 8, 2001, p. A-3.

72. *Washington Times*, February 8, 2002, p. 18; *Wall Street Journal*, February 5, 2002.

73. Embassy of Saudi Arabia, *Initiatives and Actions Taken by the Kingdom of Saudi Arabia in the Financial Area to Combat Terrorism*, December 3, 2002.

Chapter 10

Proliferation and Saudi Missile Capabilities

Saudi Arabia already faces major challenges from proliferation in Iran and Iraq, and these challenges are likely to become steadily more serious in the future. Iran and Iraq are both deeply involved in the developing of chemical, biological, radiological and nuclear weapons, and are pursuing a wide range of delivery systems. So far, Saudi Arabia's response has been limited. The Kingdom has supported arms control treaties that limit biological, chemical, and nuclear weapons, and there have been few indications that it has actively sought weapons of mass destruction or funded significant efforts to acquire them.[1]

During the Iran-Iraq War, Saudi Arabia reacted to missile exchanges in the "war of the cities" between Iran and Iraq by purchasing the Chinese CSS-2 (DF-3) long-range surface-to-surface missiles, which it deployed as part of the Air Defense Force. The Saudis bought a package of fifty to sixty missiles, ten to fifteen mobile launchers, and support from the PRC at a cost of about $3 billion to $3.5 billion.[2]

Saudi Arabia has now begun to seek a replacement for the CSS-2, and it is hardly coincidental that Prince Sultan visited China in late October and November 2000 and inspected a missile factory. Some feel that other Saudi visits to Pakistan indicate that the Saudis may be looking at Pakistani missile programs and possibly even Pakistani nuclear weapons, although senior Saudi officials deny this. They also deny that Saudi planners are beginning to seriously discuss whether Saudi Arabia needs its own deterrent and retaliatory capability, or can rely on a mix of U.S. strength, Saudi air and missile defenses, and U.S. and international arms control and counter-proliferation programs.

IRAQ AND WEAPONS OF MASS DESTRUCTION

As was discussed in Chapter 1, both Iran and Iraq pose CBRN threats to Saudi Arabia. Iraq, however, has a much more serious history of both proliferation and using weapons of mass destruction than Iran. The scale of these threats is shown in detail in Appendix 10.1. It has seen proliferation as a counter to Israel's conventional superiority since the late 1960s, and as a key weapon that could give it a decisive edge in dealing with its neighbors. It sought weapons of mass destruction long before the Gulf War showed it what the "revolution in military affairs" and U.S. conventional superiority could accomplish.

Since 1991, Iraq has been unable to obtain significant imports of conventional weapons; it is incapable of producing its own. As a result, it is scarcely surprising that Iraq sees proliferation as its key potential method of countering the U.S. advantage in conventional forces and has been willing to pursue such options in the face of massive economic costs, UNSCOM and IAEA efforts to destroy its remaining capabilities, and the extension of UN sanctions. Iraq's possession of weapons of mass destruction has also become the key rationale for possible U.S. and British military action to overthrow Saddam Hussein's regime.

For these reasons, it seems worth focusing on Iraqi capabilities in more detail. Iran may ultimately pose the more serious mid- and long-term threat, but the Iraqi threat offers a much higher near-term probability of actual conflict—one that the Kingdom cannot ignore.

Iraqi Missile Developments and Possible Capabilities

Iraq may face serious limits on its imports and overt activities, but it successfully forced an end to the UN inspection effort in December 1988, and it is all too clear that Iraq may have made significant increases in its CBRN capabilities since the active UNSCOM and IAEA inspections efforts ended. It is known to have continued to import precursors for chemical weapons and may have increased its holdings of biological growth agents. No one can dismiss the risk that Iraq does have weapons with very high real-world lethalities.

Missiles remain a threat as well. UNSCOM inspectors note that UNSCOM's claims to have identified 817 out of 819 Scud imports are extremely soft and may well have an error of sixty weapons, and that no accurate count exists of Iraqi-produced components. This could give Iraq a range of twenty to eighty operational Scuds, and Iraq has shown in the past that it can produce its own TEL launchers. Iraq also continues development work on shorter-range missiles, since missiles with ranges of 150 kilometers or less are permitted under the terms of the ceasefire.

U.S. intelligence reporting provides the following assessment of Iraq's capabilities in this area. A CIA report in August 2000 summarized the state of Iraqi CBRN and missile development as follows:

- Since the Gulf War, Iraq has rebuilt key portions of its chemical production infrastructure for industrial and commercial use, as well as its missile production facilities. It has attempted to purchase numerous dual-use items for, or under the guise of, legitimate civilian use. This equipment—in principle subject to UN scrutiny—also could be diverted for WMD purposes. Since the suspension of UN inspections in December 1998, the risk of diversion has increased.

- Following Desert Fox, Baghdad again instituted a reconstruction effort on those facilities destroyed by the U.S. bombing, including several critical missile production complexes and former dual-use CW production facilities. In addition, it appears to be installing or repairing dual-use equipment at CW-related facilities. Some of these facilities could be converted fairly quickly for production of CW agents.

- Iraq continues to pursue development of two SRBM systems that are not prohibited by the United Nations: the liquid-propellant Al-Samoud, and the solid-propellant Ababil-100. The Al-Samoud is essentially a scaled-down Scud, and the program allows Baghdad to develop technological improvements that could be applied to a longer-range missile program. We believe that the Al-Samoud missile, as designed, is capable of exceeding the UN-permitted 150-kilometer range restriction with a potential operational range of about 180 kilometers. Personnel previously involved with the Condor II/Badr-2000 missile—which was largely destroyed during the Gulf War and eliminated by UNSCOM—are working on the Ababil-100 program. If economic sanctions against Iraq were lifted, Baghdad probably would attempt to convert these efforts into longer-range missile systems, regardless of continuing UN monitoring and continuing restrictions on WMD and long-range missile programs.

A Department of Defense report in January 2001 reported that

- Iraq likely retains a limited number of launchers and Scud-variant SRBMs capable of striking its neighbors, as well as the components and manufacturing means to assemble and produce others, anticipating the reestablishment of a long-range ballistic missile force sometime in the future. Baghdad likely also has warheads capable of delivering chemical or biological agents. While Iraq's missile-production infrastructure was damaged during the December 1998 strikes, the country retains domestic expertise and sufficient infrastructure to support most missile component production, with the exception of a few critical subelements.

- The Department of Defense also noted the development of the Al-Samoud and Ababil-100 missile systems in 1999. It concurs that the Al-Samoud missile, as designed by the Iraqis, has an inherent potential to exceed the 150-kilometer range restriction imposed under UNSCR 687.

- Iraqi personnel involved with pre–Desert Storm ballistic missile efforts are working on the Ababil-100 SRBM program. Once economic sanctions against Iraq are lifted, unless restricted by future UN monitoring, Baghdad probably will begin converting these efforts into longer-range missile systems. Despite the damage done to Iraq's missile infrastructure during the Gulf War, Desert Fox, and subsequent UNSCOM activities, Iraq may have ambitions for longer-range missiles, including an ICBM.

- Iraq also has a variety of fighter aircraft, helicopters, artillery, and rockets available as potential means of delivery for NBC weapons, although their operational status is questionable due to the cumulative effects of the UN arms embargo. However, Iraq has continued to work on its UAV program, which involves converting L-29 jet trainer aircraft originally acquired from Eastern Europe. These modified and refurbished L-29s may be intended for the delivery of chemical or biological agents. In the future, Iraq may try to use its research and development infrastructure to produce its own UAVs and cruise missiles or, should the UN arms embargo be lifted, it could try to purchase cruise missiles.

A CIA report issued in January 2002 stated that a military parade in December 2000 showcased Iraq's Al-Samoud missiles, which were deployed on new transporter-erector-launchers (TELs). The liquid-propellant Al-Samoud SRBM probably will be deployed soon. It projected future Iraqi capabilities as follows:

- Iraq is likely to use its experience with Scud technology to resume production of the pre–Gulf War 650-kilometer-range Al-Hussein, the 900-kilometer-range Al-Abbas, or other Scud variants, and it could explore clustering and staging options to reach more distant targets. Iraq *could* resume Scud-variant production—with foreign assistance—quickly after UN prohibitions ended.

- With substantial foreign assistance, Baghdad *could* flight-test a domestic MRBM by mid-decade. This possibility presumes rapid erosion of UN prohibitions and Baghdad's willingness to risk detection of developmental steps, such as static engine testing, earlier. An MRBM flight test is *likely* by 2010. An imported MRBM *could* be flight-tested within months of acquisition.

- For the first several years after relief from UN prohibitions, Iraq probably will strive to reestablish its SRBM inventory to pre–Gulf War numbers, continue developing and deploying solid-propellant systems, and pursue MRBMs to keep pace with its neighbors. Once its regional security concerns are being addressed, Iraq may pursue a first-generation ICBM/SLV.

- Although Iraq *could* attempt before 2015 to test a rudimentary long-range missile based on its failed Al-Abid SLV, such a missile almost certainly would fail. Iraq is unlikely to make such an attempt. After observing North Korean missile developments the past few years, Iraq would be more likely to pursue a three-stage TD-2 approach to an SLV or ICBM, which would be capable of delivering a nuclear weapon–sized payload to the United States.

- Some postulations for potential Iraqi ICBM/SLV concepts and timelines from the beginning of UN prohibition relief include: (i) If Iraq could buy a TD-2 from North Korea, it *could* have a launch capability within a year or two of a purchase; (ii) It *could* develop and test a TD-1-type system within a few years; (iii) If it acquired No Dongs from North Korea, it *could* test an ICBM within a few years of acquisition by clustering and staging the No Dongs— similar to the clustering of Scuds for the Al-Abid SLV; (iv) If Iraq bought TD-2 engines, it *could* test an ICBM within about five years of the acquisition, and (v) Iraq *could* develop and test a Taepo Dong-2-type system within about ten years of a decision to do so.

Foreign assistance is key to Iraqi efforts to quickly develop longer-range missiles. Iraq relied on extensive foreign assistance before the Gulf War and will continue to seek foreign assistance to expand its current capabilities.

Iraq continues to work on UCAVs and drones and has experimented with the modification of trainers and MiG-21s in this role. It developed crude "sprayer" tanks and systems to deliver chemical and biological weapons using its aircraft and helicopters before the Gulf War, and may since have developed more effective ways of releasing chemical and biological agents in "line source" deliveries that would be an order of magnitude more lethal than release through conventional bombs and shells.

Recent Iraqi CBRN Developments and Possible Capabilities

Recent U.S. intelligence reporting notes that it is not possible to collect detailed information on Iraq's CBRN programs, but that the programs almost certainly are advancing and are being given high priority. A CIA report in August 2000 summarized the state of biological weapons proliferation in Iraq as follows:[3]

- Since Operation Desert Fox in December 1998, Baghdad has refused to allow United Nations inspectors into Iraq as required by Security Council Resolution 687. Although UN Security Council Resolution (UNSCR) 1284, adopted in December 1999, established a follow-on inspection regime to the United Nations Special Commission on Iraq (UNSCOM) in the form of the United Nations Monitoring, Verification, and Inspection Committee (UNMOVIC), there have been no UN inspections during this reporting period. Moreover, the automated video monitoring system installed by the UN at known and suspect WMD facilities in Iraq has been dismantled by the Iraqis. Having lost this on-the-ground access, it is difficult for the UN or the United States to accurately assess the current state of Iraq's WMD programs.
- Since the Gulf War, Iraq has rebuilt key portions of its chemical production infrastructure for industrial and commercial use, as well as its missile production

facilities. It has attempted to purchase numerous dual-use items for, or under the guise of, legitimate civilian use. This equipment—in principle subject to UN scrutiny—also could be diverted for WMD purposes. Since the suspension of UN inspections in December 1998, the risk of diversion has increased.

- Following Desert Fox, Baghdad again instituted a reconstruction effort on those facilities destroyed by the U.S. bombing, to include several critical missile production complexes and former dual-use CW production facilities. In addition, it appears to be installing or repairing dual-use equipment at CW-related facilities. Some of these facilities could be converted fairly quickly for production of CW agents.

- UNSCOM reported to the Security Council in December 1998 that Iraq continued to withhold information related to its CW and BW programs. For example, Baghdad seized from UNSCOM inspectors an Air Force document discovered by UNSCOM that indicated that Iraq had not consumed as many CW munitions during the Iran-Iraq War in the 1980s as had been declared by Baghdad. This discrepancy indicates that Iraq may have an additional 6,000 CW munitions hidden.

- We do not have any direct evidence that Iraq has used the period since Desert Fox to reconstitute its WMD programs, although given its past behavior, this type of activity must be regarded as likely. We assess that since the suspension of UN inspections in December of 1998, Baghdad has had the capability to reinitiate both its CW and BW programs within a few weeks to months, but without an inspection-monitoring program, it is difficult to determine if Iraq has done so. We know, however, that Iraq has continued to work on its unmanned aerial vehicle (UAV) program, which involves converting L-29 jet trainer aircraft originally acquired from Eastern Europe. These modified and refurbished L-29s are believed to be intended for delivery of chemical or biological agents.

A Department of Defense report issued in January 2001 stated,

Iraq's continued refusal to disclose fully the extent of its biological program suggests that Baghdad retains a biological warfare capability, despite its membership in the BWC. After four and one-half years of claiming that it had conducted only "defensive research" on biological weapons Iraq declared reluctantly, in 1995, that it had produced approximately 30,000 liters of bulk biological agents and/or filled munitions. Iraq admitted that it produced anthrax, botulinum toxins and aflatoxins and that it prepared biological agent–filled munitions, including missile warheads and aerial bombs.

However, UNSCOM believed that Iraq had produced substantially greater amounts than it has admitted—three to four times greater. Iraq also admitted that, during the Persian Gulf War, it had deployed biological agent–filled munitions to airfields and that these weapons were intended for use against Israel and coalition forces in Saudi Arabia. Iraq stated that it destroyed all of these agents and munitions in 1991, but it has provided insufficient credible evidence to support this claim. The UN believes that Baghdad has the ability to reconstitute its biological warfare capabilities within a few weeks or months, and, in the absence of UNSCOM inspections and monitoring during 1999 and 2000, we are concerned that Baghdad again may have produced some biological warfare agents.

In his February 6, 2002, testimony before the Senate Select Committee on Intelligence, Director of Central Intelligence George J. Tenet stated that "Iraq continues to build and expand an infrastructure capable of producing WMD. Baghdad is expanding its civilian chemical industry in ways that could be diverted quickly to CW production. We believe it also maintains an active and capable BW program; Iraq told UNSCOM it had worked with several BW agents."

John R. Bolton, under secretary for arms control and international security described Iraq's status as follows in a speech on May 6, 2002:

> Foremost is Iraq. Although it became a signatory to the BWC in 1972 and became a State Party in 1991, Iraq has developed, produced, and stockpiled biological warfare agents and weapons. The United States strongly suspects that Iraq has taken advantage of more than three years of no UN inspections to improve all phases of its offensive BW program. Iraq also has developed, produced, and stockpiled chemical weapons, and shown a continuing interest in developing nuclear weapons and longer range missiles.

Any assessment of Iraq's progress in weaponizing its CBRN assets must be speculative, but Iraq does have cluster bomb technology and the theoretical engineering capability to use non-explosive release mechanisms like air bags to release chemical and biological munitions. Before the Gulf War, Iraq developed crude parachute-release designs for its missile warheads, systems that would be substantially more effective than the primitive contact-fuse warheads and bombs it had at the time of the war, and that might well have produced negligible weapons effects if they had ever been used. Iraq must realize that its crude contact fusing and chemical/biological warhead/bomb designs drastically limited the effectiveness of its CBRN weapons. It has had strong incentives to correct these problems, but experts are deeply divided over the probability that Iraq has done so.

Similar critical uncertainties exist in other areas of Iraqi CBRN war fighting. It has experimented with the conversion of biological agents into dry, coated micropowders that can be two orders of magnitude or more lethal than slurries of wet agents. Such biological weapons can achieve the lethality of simple nuclear fission weapons, and are far better suited to use in bombs, missile warheads, and covert attacks.

Several UNSCOM inspectors believe that Iraq created new parallel chemical and biological weapons design efforts that were unrelated to its prewar efforts no later than 1995, and may have been able to develop better VX weapons, more lethal forms of anthrax and other non-infectious agents, and possibly weaponize smallpox. Once again, Iraq has had strong incentives to correct the problems in its previous CBRN weapons, but experts are deeply divided over the probability that Iraq has done so.

IAEA and U.S. intelligence experts privately put little or no faith in the claims of various Iraqi defectors that Iraq retains the ability to make fissile material, has extensive covert production facilities, and has workable bomb designs small enough to be used in missile warheads. IAEA experts note that the Iraqi diffusion effort was never effective, that the Calutron designs fell far short of meeting specification, that Iraq's centrifuge designs proved to be far less effective during laboratory review than they initially estimated, and that Iraq does not seem to have understood the technical problems in using centrifuges to enrich fissile material beyond 90%. They note that cascades of centrifuges are relatively easy to conceal in multistory buildings, but that Iraq is extremely dependent on imports to create such a facility and would probably need outside technical support.

Iraq did, however, have at least two workable implosion designs that could be used in large bombs at the time of the Gulf War, had solved the technical problems in making and triggering high explosive lenses for nuclear weapons, and had workable neutron initiators. If it could obtain fissile material, it could probably make a large explosive device relatively quickly, but not fit one to a missile warhead or build a bomb that any of its aircraft other than its bombers and MiG-24s could deliver at long distances, particularly in low-altitude penetration missions. Iraq might be much more successful in arming any actual nuclear weapon it could obtain, particularly because of the relatively crude PAL systems fitted to many FSU weapons and the duplicative code sequences used to arm them.

A Current War-Fighting Capability "Guesstimate"

These uncertainties make it extremely difficult to assess Iraq's war-fighting capabilities. As a guesstimate, Iraq's present holdings of delivery systems and chemical and biological weapons seem most likely to be so limited in technology and operational lethality that they *currently* do not severely constrain U.S. military freedom of action or seriously intimidate Saudi Arabia and Iraq's other neighbors. Iraq has not fired any Scud variants in nearly twelve years. There are no public reports that it has tested dry-storable biological weapons, or has made major advances in its weaponization of nerve gas. Furthermore, it seems unlikely that Iraq can openly build up major production and deployment capabilities without having them detected and targeted, and without provoking strong U.S. counterproliferation programs, including preemptive or retaliatory strike capabilities.

Barring classified intelligence to the contrary, this means that *current* Iraqi CBRN capabilities must be taken seriously but do not seem great enough to change Saudi, U.S., British, Iranian, Israeli, and/or Southern Gulf perceptions of risk to the point where they would limit or paralyze Saudi willingness to defend the Kingdom, limit military action by a U.S.-led coalition, or limit Israeli retaliatory strikes on Iraq.

Nevertheless, Iraq's possession of even moderately effective CBRN weapons already affects some aspects of Saudi, U.S., British, Iranian, Southern Gulf, and Israeli perceptions of the risks inherent in attacking Iraq. Iraqi and Iranian proliferation are major factors that reinforce Saudi dependence on the United States; however, the Saudi rapprochement with Iran defers urgent Saudi concern over the Iranian threat. Saudi Arabia has the time to consider such options as relying on extended deterrence by the United States, acquiring its own CBRN weapons, and/or acquiring missile defenses.

It the case of Iraq, Saudi Arabia faces the more immediate risk that it might become a target in any war in which Saddam Hussein felt the existence of his regime was threatened or was willing to take extreme risks for other political reasons. This makes the Kingdom heavily dependent on U.S. military actions and capabilities. Any major U.S. and British air and missile attack on Iraq would almost certainly target suspect Iraqi CBRN and delivery facilities immediately after the beginning of such an attack. The United States also has the option of using its advanced ISR and other targeting capabilities and air and missile power to carry out a massive preemptive strike on Iraq's CBRN and delivery capabilities at the first sign of any major crisis or as a prelude to an invasion to overthrow Saddam.[4]

It is impossible to estimate the success of such U.S. attacks, or how much U.S. intelligence, targeting, and strike capability has improved since Desert Fox. The Bush administration has begun to talk about preemption, but talk about preemption is much cheaper than acquiring the ability to execute it.[5] Iraq has had decades in which to improve its use of deception, dispersal, decoys, and other countermeasures to U.S. ISR and strike capabilities.

In spite of claims to the contrary, the United States was unable to detect and target most Iraqi CBRN and missile capabilities during the Gulf War. U.S. and British Special Forces failed to locate and target Iraqi missiles and CBRN weapons. Additionally, the massive U.S. intelligence and air strike effort following the beginning of Iraqi missile strikes on Saudi Arabia and Israel failed to characterize the changes in Iraqi facilities and capabilities made during the course of the war, and had no meaningful successes against dispersed missiles. The U.S. and British air and missile strikes during Desert Fox failed to find and strike significant Iraqi CBRN facilities. At most, they had several successes in hitting large Iraqi missile production facilities, and these were known, overt targets because they were permitted under the terms of the UN ceasefire. It is unclear that other raids had any useful impact, particularly because most critical equipment could be rapidly dispersed or sheltered. There seem to be good reasons why the U.S. military has never released any meaningful damage assessment data on Desert Fox, and it is all too possible that future attacks would be equally unsuccessful.

Preemption—and any other form of U.S.-led air and missile strikes—would also have more limited effectiveness if Iraq has created some kind of launch on warning force, or deploys one the moment it detects the fact the United States is preparing to launch a preemptive strike on Iraq's CBRN and missile capabilities, or is preparing a major land attack and coalition effort to overthrow the ruling regime and/or occupy the country. No reports have surfaced so far that Iraq has such a capability in place. However, it is possible that a covert capability does exist. During the Gulf War, Iraq dispersed missiles and bombs to create a crude retaliatory strike capability to deliver CB weapons if the regime collapsed or lost the ability to command Iraq forces. It took major risks in collocating CB and conventional weapons, and in dispersing such weapons without security protection.

It is unlikely that the United States can count on detecting and accurately targeting most of a mobile Iraqi launch on warning (LOW), launch under attack (LUA), or retaliatory force for the delivery of CBRN weapons once it is deployed. The United States might well not detect the initial deployment of such a capability unless Iraq chose to signal this for deterrent purposes. However, U.S. intelligence and air strike capabilities may well have advanced to the point where the United States might destroy many important fixed equipment items and facilities and disrupt some aspects of Iraqi operations.

A continuing series of U.S. and British strikes might be able to severely limit or even suppress Iraqi ability to sustain CBRN operations over time—if the United States organized and sustained a major effort to provide continuing surveillance and strike capability over probable launch areas and any suspected Iraqi CBRN facilities and infrastructure. Unfortunately, it is less clear that U.S. or British Special Forces have made effective efforts to improve their wide area coverage to support such an effort. The real-world capabilities of the improved Patriot and Arrow also present major uncertainties about the level of anti-ballistic missile (ATBM) defense that would be available, and much would depend on the readiness and deployment of such ATBM forces.

It seems likely, therefore, that Iraq could succeed in launching some CBRN strikes against U.S. Coalition forces, targets in Saudi Arabia and other neighboring states, and/or Israel. If so, Iraq would face the problem that it would be using weapons it has had no way to operationally test. At the same time, the targeted forces and countries would be confronted with CB agents of unknown character, weaponization quality, and operational lethality. As a result, the defender could only characterize the weapon after it struck, which could take hours or days in the case of biological weapons, and would not be able to characterize dissemination firmly except by observing the lethal effects.

This situation could have the following military effects:

- The U.S. must currently plan to deploy the best available ATBM defenses, and suitable passive defenses, to Saudi Arabia and the Gulf region in a crisis, to deal with CB attacks on ports, airfields, major U.S. staging facilities, allied cities, and key oil facilities. While highly lethal Iraqi attacks now seem unlikely, they are possible (and Iraqi capabilities are likely to steadily increase with time).

- In the best case, Saudi Arabia, U.S. Coalition forces, and neighboring states could ride out an Iraqi CBRN attack that would not be lethal enough to force massive retaliation.

- In the more likely case, an Iraqi CBRN attack would at least have enough political impact to force the same major diversion of U.S. and other air strike and intelligence assets as Iraqi missile attacks did during the Gulf War. This would not save the Iraqi regime, but does mean the United States must size its air and missile forces to cover this contingency. This would require major theater-wide air capabilities in excess of those needed for conventional war fighting. It also would not prevent some Iraqi CBRN strikes on targets in Saudi Arabia.

- In the worst case, the United States might be forced to threaten Iraq with a massive offensive response to any use of CBRN weapons, and then execute it. The question then would be: Would the resulting destruction of Iraq's economy and infrastructure be rapid and drastic enough to persuade the loyalist elements operating the Iraqi force to stop? The same question would apply to any U.S. threat or use of nuclear weapons, albeit at a far more drastic level.

Future Risks and Breakout Problems

If UN sanctions on Iraq are lifted or are sharply weakened, Iraq may be able to rebuild its strategic delivery capabilities relatively quickly, and any sustained conflict involving weapons of mass destruction could have drastic consequences. This would be particularly true if Iraq could develop advanced biological weapons with near-nuclear lethality, or assemble nuclear devices with weapons-grade fissile material bought from an outside source. There might be little or no warning of such strategic developments, and the United States might not be willing to counter by extending theater nuclear deterrence to protect its Southern Gulf allies.

As mentioned in Chapter 1, there are several other developments that might allow Iraq to use proliferation to pose a near-term threat to U.S. conventional capabilities in the region:

- *A successful Iraqi attempt to buy significant amounts of weapons-grade material.* This could allow Iraq to achieve a nuclear breakout capability in a matter of months. Both the United States and the region would find it much harder to adjust to such an Iraqi effort than to the slow development of nuclear weapons by creating fissile material within Iraq. It seems likely that the United States could deal with the situation by extending a nuclear umbrella over the Gulf, but even so, the Southern Gulf states might be far more responsive to Iraqi pressure and intimidation. Most, after all, are so small that they are virtually "one-bomb states."

- *A change in U.S. and regional perceptions of biological weapons.* Biological weapons are now largely perceived as unproven systems of uncertain lethality. Regardless of their technical capabilities, they have little of the political impact that the possession of nuclear weapons has. Iraq might, however, conduct live animal tests to demonstrate that its biological weapons have near-nuclear lethality, or some other power might demonstrate their effectiveness in another conflict. The successful mass testing or use of biological weapons might produce a rapid "paradigm shift" in the perceived importance of such weapons and of Iraq's biological warfare programs.
- *Iraq might break out of UN sanctions and reveal a more substantial capability than now seems likely.* Paradoxically, such an Iraqi capability would help to legitimize Iran and Israel's nuclear, biological, and chemical programs and the escalation to the use of such weapons.
- *Iraq might use such weapons through proxies, or in covert attacks with some degree of plausible deniability.* Terrorism and unconventional warfare would be far more intimidating if they made use of weapons of mass destruction.

IRAN AND WEAPONS OF MASS DESTRUCTION

Iraq does not seem to pose a major current CBRN threat to Saudi Arabia, although overt or tacit Iranian threats are at least possible in any crisis between Iran and the United States, dispute over oil and gas rights in the Gulf, or confrontation of Abu Musa and the Tunbs. It should be clear from Appendix 10.2, however, that Iran already has the military capabilities to pose at least the same CBRN threat to the Kingdom as Iraq. Moreover, Iran may well be deploying its new long-range Shehab 3 missile, may have dry storable biological weapons, and may well obtain nuclear weapons sooner than Iraq.

THE CSS-2

Saudi Arabia's present CSS-2 missiles are not a meaningful response to either the Iranian or Iraqi CBRN threat, and are largely an exercise in political symbolism and have only token war-fighting capability. The CSS-2 missiles are extremely large seventy-ton systems, and have a special, large conventional warhead. They are nearly seventy-ton missile/launcher systems but they are semi-mobile, and one-third are supposed to be kept armed and near-launch-ready on transporters, one-third are kept half fueled, and one-third are normally empty and being serviced. Saudi sources indicate that actual readiness rates are normally far lower.

The missiles are deployed in two battalions. One is located at the As-Sulayyil Oasis, roughly 475 kilometers south to southwest of Riyadh. As-Sulayyil will also be the site of one of Saudi Arabia's new air bases for its Tornado fighter-bombers. A second battalion is located at Al-Juaifer near the Al-Kharj air base south of Riyadh. A further training facility that may have a launch capability seems to exist in southwestern Saudi Arabia at Al-Liddam.[6]

Commercial satellite photos of the site at As-Sulayyil show a headquarters and transportation complex with sixty buildings or tents, a transportation center, a command and control complex with roughly forty buildings and tents, a secure area, a construction area, a bunker which may be a fixed launcher site, other launch areas with bunkers for missile storage, an additional launch area, and three 150-meter-long white buildings that may be missile assembly facilities.[7] Saudi Arabia has only a very limited technological base to support such programs, although it has begun to experiment with short-range artillery systems.

None of the Saudi missiles are now armed with weapons of mass destruction. Saudi Arabia is a signatory of the Non-Proliferation Treaty, and Saudi Arabia and the PRC have provided U.S. officials with assurances that the missiles will remain conventional. The Saudi government has issued a written statement asserting that "nuclear and chemical warheads would not be obtained or used with the missiles." U.S. experts believe that Saudi Arabia has largely kept its word, although the Saudis have refused a U.S. request to inspect the missile sites in Saudi Arabia, and the Kingdom's visits to nations like China and Pakistan do raise questions about their future intention.[8]

Saudi Arabia has no capability to produce its own long-range ballistic missiles or weapons of mass destruction. The most it has done is develop an unguided rocket. In July 1997, Saudi Arabia test-fired its first domestically produced surface-to-surface artillery rocket or missile at the Al-Kharj complex. Defense Minister Prince Sultan stated that the missile has a range of between thirty-five kilometers and sixty-two kilometers.[9]

The Saudis cannot maintain or fire their CSS-2 missiles without Chinese technical support, and Chinese technicians are operating the missiles under Saudi supervision. Ballast Nedam, a subsidiary of British Aerospace, has recently extended the runway at the As-Sulayyil air base to 3,000 meters. There are some signs that Saudi Arabia may be deploying surface-to-air missiles to defend the facility.[10]

Saudi Arabia claimed that it bought the CSS-2 to "propagate peace," but it really bought them for a number of other reasons.[11] Its efforts to buy arms from the United States had reached a low point when the purchase was made, and Saudi Arabia felt the purchase would be a major demonstration of its independence. Equally, the Kingdom felt threatened by the fact that Iran and Iraq had long-range surface-to-surface missiles and Yemen then had the SS-21, and Saudi Arabia did not. Saudi Arabia was particularly interested in acquiring systems that could hit Tehran while being deployed outside the range of Iranian surface-to-surface missiles.

There are good reasons to question the military value of such missiles, however, as long as they are only equipped with conventional warheads.[12] The CSS-2s deployed in the PRC are all nuclear-armed missiles. Each can carry one to three megaton warheads. They have a maximum range of about 2,200 miles, an inertial guidance system, and a single-stage, refrigerated liquid fuel rocket motor. The version of the CSS-2 that the PRC has sold to Saudi Arabia is very different. It is heavily modified and has a special large conventional warhead that weighs up to 3,500 to 4,000 pounds. This added warhead weight cuts the maximum range of the missile to anywhere from 1,550 nautical miles to 1,950 nautical miles.

A conventional warhead of this size is more effective than the warhead on a Scud, but is hardly a weapon of mass destruction, or even an effective conventional weapon. Assuming an optimal ratio of HE to total weight, the warhead of the CSS-2 could destroy buildings out to a radius of 200 to 250 feet, seriously damage buildings out to a radius of 300 to 350 feet, and kill or injure people with projectiles to distances of up to 1,000 feet.[13] This is the damage equivalent of three to four 2,000-pound bombs, or about the same destructive power as a single sortie by a modern strike fighter.

The CSS-2 has other limitations that led Saudi Arabia to examine possible replacements beginning in the mid-1990s. It is an obsolete missile that was first designed in 1971. While an improved version has been deployed, most experts still estimate that the missile has a CEP of nearly two to four kilometers, and lacks the accuracy to hit anything other than large area targets like cities or industrial facilities. Even with the improved warhead, each missile would still only have the effective lethality of a single 2,000-pound bomb. It requires large amounts of technical support and ground equipment, and takes hours to make ready for firing.[14]

It is also far from clear that the CSS-2 missile can be properly calibrated for targeting purposes, and be kept truly operational, without more frequent test firings and without test firings conducted at long ranges along the axis it would have to be fired in an actual strike. Saudi Arabia has never conducted a meaningful operational test of the CSS-8, and is incapable of conducting the tests necessary to refine the missile's targeting using the derived-aim point method.[15]

The Saudi purchase of the CSS-2 thus raises serious issues on several grounds:

- A very costly weapons system is being procured in very small numbers with relatively low lethality.
- As now configured, the missile system may do more to provoke attack or escalation than to deter attack or provide retaliatory capability. This point be-

came clear to the Saudis during the Gulf War. King Fahd rejected advice to retaliate against Iraqi strikes because he felt that strikes that simply killed civilians would have a provocative, rather than a deterrent effect.

- On the other hand, Saudi acquisition of chemical or nuclear warheads would radically improve the value of the system as a deterrent or retaliatory weapon.

At best, the CSS-2 acts as a low-level deterrent and a symbol of Saudi Arabia's willingness to retaliate against Iraqi and Iranian strikes. At worst, the missiles are a potential excuse for Iranian or Iraqi missile strikes, and their use could trigger a process of retaliation against which Saudi Arabia would have little real defense capability. Israel, which initially showed concern about the system, no longer seems to perceive it as any kind of direct threat. Israel has the capability to launch air strikes against the Saudi missile sites, but is unlikely to consider preemptive strikes unless radical changes take place in Saudi Arabia's political posture or regime.

The CSS-2 does, however, symbolize the risk that Saudi Arabia will buy much more capable missiles and seek weapons of mass destruction. Long-term Saudi motives will remain uncertain to its neighbors despite Saudi pledges, foreign intelligence reports, and any inspection agreements. Such concerns have already led to fears that Saudi investments in imaging satellites might be used for intelligence and targeting purposes.[16] While nations like India, Iran, Iraq, Israel, Libya, and Syria are the major proliferators in the region, Saudi possession of the CSS-2 also gives other countries an added incentive and excuse to join the missile arms race, acquire weapons of mass destruction, or preempt in a conflict.

Saudi Arabia seems to rely on the United States to deter attacks using weapons of mass destruction, and as a potential source of theater missile defenses. As previously stated, the most Saudi Arabia seems to have done to date to acquire weapons of mass destruction is to quietly examine its options for acquiring chemical and biological weapons and hold preliminary discussions with China and Pakistan. Saudi Chief of Staff Lieutenant General Saleh Mohaya and Prince Khalid Bin Sultan also seem to have begun discussing replacement of the CSS-2 with China in 1995. However, there has been no visible progress to date.[17]

Similarly, in 1999, after Pakistan's nuclear tests, Prince Sultan and other Saudi military officials toured Pakistan's nuclear weapons facilities. There was no firm evidence, however, that they intended to buy an "Islamic bomb." While there have been reports of a much more extensive Saudi nuclear program, the "evidence" advanced to date has been tenuous at best and the charges seem to be more political in character and directed at trying to break up the U.S.-Saudi military relationship than inspired by any facts or actual knowledge. The main disturbing aspect of Saudi talks with Pakistan is that some estimates indicate that Pakistan's production of fissile material will begin to exceed its domestic military requirements at some point around 2005. Similarly, there is no convincing data available on whether Saudi Arabia has had any discussions with China about the possible purchase of weapons of mass destruction.

WHAT COMES NEXT? MISSILES, MISSILE DEFENSES, CIVIL DEFENSE, COUNTERPROLIFERATION, COUNTERTERRORISM, AND DETERRENCE

Saudi Arabia's CSS-2 missiles have already aged to the point where they need to be replaced. The need to find a new system is becoming steadily more pressing. At the same time, Saudi Arabia does not have any good options for acquiring its own capabilities. It has three basic choices in dealing with the CSS-2: (1) to establish a program with China to extend the life of the CSS-2, (2) to get a new MRBM, preferably a solid-fuel system like the CSS-5 that would eliminate all of the problems in using liquid fuels and the need for Chinese operators, and (3) to use Pakistan as a source of other missiles. One problem is that, in theory, China cannot make new sales of long-range missiles without openly violating its agreements relating to the Missile Technology Control Regime (MTCR), and Russia and the other FSU states are bound by both the MTCR and the limits of the IRBM Treaty. Pakistan's missile programs are still in development, as are those of North Korea.

Saudi Arabia also faces broader concerns as to whether it should invest in a symbolic and ineffective deterrent, buy new missiles armed with weapons of mass destruction, trust in extended deterrence by the United States, and/or invest in areas like theater missile defense, civil defense, and counterterrorism. A few Saudi planners do advocate buying modern missiles and arming them with chemical, biological, or nuclear weapons. They believe that buying long-range missiles without such weapons has little purpose. It is unclear, however, that such thinkers as yet have any broad support from Saudi leaders and policymakers, or that Saudi Arabia really does have better options to acquire weapons of mass destruction than it does to buy missiles. It does not have the industrial base to produce biological and nuclear weapons or to compete in producing chemical weapons. It is very difficult to purchase "turnkey" production capabilities and/or finished weapons abroad, and such purchases might well cut off Saudi Arabia from U.S. and other Western supplies of conventional arms.

Saudi Arabia faces additional problems. Such a purchase would certainly seriously jeopardize U.S.-Saudi security arrangements and could make Saudi Arabia a target for Israel. Even if Saudi Arabia could find ways to join Iran, Iraq, and Israel in proliferating, it is also not clear whether it would reduce its vulnerability or simply raise the threshold of any attack on the Kingdom. Mere possession of weapons of mass destruction may be adequate for the purposes of prestige in peacetime, but they must be carefully structured to avoid encouraging preemption and escalation in wartime and accelerating the efforts of neighboring states to acquire even more chemical, biological and nuclear arms.

Although Saudi Arabia is concerned with regional proliferation, it does not express the acute overt concern over Iranian and Iraqi WMD programs that U.S. policymakers do. In an interview with *Al Sharq al-Awsat*, Crown Prince Abdullah defended Iran's right to arm itself, as well as the right of others to do so: "Iran has every right to develop its defense capabilities for its security without harming or damaging the rights of others. We also do the same. All countries follow the same policy." He also expressed concern about Israeli armament and weapons programs. Although Saudi views differ from those held by Washington, Saudi Arabia is not likely to enter any arrangements or relations with Iran that would compromise their defense links with the United States and the West.[18]

At the same time, measures like buying improved theater missile defense, civil defense, and counterterrorism may well not be enough to deal with the creeping proliferation in Iran and Iraq. The United States has agreed to share missile early warning data with Saudi Arabia and other friendly Arab states, but it is unclear what this warning is worth. The Saudi and U.S. Patriot PAC-2 missiles deployed in Saudi Arabia have only limited missile intercept capability against advanced Scud missiles. While the Patriot PAC-3 should provide more effective defense against such missiles—when and if the Patriot PAC-3 becomes available—it has only limited effectiveness against more advanced missiles with higher closure speeds. Iran is already testing such missiles, and Iraq is almost certain to develop them if it can break out of sanctions.

Developmental anti-theater ballistic missile (ATBM) U.S. systems like the Navy Theater Wide, Navy Area Defense, and U.S. Army THAAD systems are designed to provide such defense capabilities—as are additional boost-phase intercept weapons—but these programs are lagging and deeply troubled. The United States currently has no ability to tell Saudi Arabia when it will be able to sell such weapons, and what their cost, effectiveness, and delivery dates will be.

As a result, Saudi Arabia may eventually come to believe that it needs some much stronger form of deterrence, as do the other Southern Gulf states. If so, the main options for Saudi Arabia would likely be to create a major long-range strike capability that combines the assets of the Saudi Air Force with modern strike systems like cruise missiles—systems Saudi Arabia might arm with either conventional warheads or some imported weapon of mass destruction—and Saudi de facto or formal reliance on U.S. extended deterrence and counterproliferation capabilities.

The first option, however, raises serious questions as to whether the Kingdom can either create conventional strike capabilities that are a credible deterrent to weapons of mass destruction or obtain weapons of mass destruction on its own. The second option requires a major rethinking of U.S. strategy as well as that of Saudi Arabia. Extended deterrence is not a casual affair, and it cannot be separated from efforts to develop some form of regional arms control and integrated missile defense, civil defense, and counterterrorism defenses for the Southern Gulf.

These issues are not urgent as long as Iran's proliferation remains at low levels and Iraq remains under UN sanctions. However, there scarcely is any guarantee that these conditions will hold true long after the year 2002. If the United States and Britain do not force Iraq to give up its weapons of mass destruction, and put firm limits to Iraq's actions, dealing with these issues may be one of Saudi Arabia's most difficult challenges in the years to come. Furthermore, U.S. efforts like the agreement to provide early warning of enemy missile launchers, and discussing the potential sale of theater missile defense systems, offer little near- to mid-term security. At best, warning can have limited benefits in improving civil defense if it is not backed by active missile and air defense or retaliation in kind. The United States will not possess wide-area theater missile defenses until well after 2010, and their future cost, effectiveness, and delivery schedule is unclear. At least, at present, the proliferator is likely to acquire major offensive capabilities that outstrip any near-term options for defense.

APPENDIX 10.1: IRAQ'S SEARCH FOR WEAPONS OF MASS DESTRUCTION

Delivery Systems

- Prior to the Gulf War, Iraq had extensive delivery systems incorporating long-range strike aircraft with refueling capabilities and several hundred regular and improved, longer-range Scud missiles, some with chemical warheads. These systems included:
- Tu-16 and Tu-22 bombers.
- MiG-29 fighters.
- Mirage F-1, MiG-23BM, and Su-22 fighter attack aircraft.
- A Scud force with a minimum of 819 missiles.
- Extended-range Al Husayn Scud variants (600-kilometer range) extensively deployed throughout Iraq, and at three fixed sites in northern, western, and southern Iraq.
- Developing Al-Abbas missiles (900-kilometer range), which could reach targets in Iran, the Persian Gulf, Israel, Turkey, and Cyprus.
- Long-range superguns with ranges of up to 600 kilometers.
- Iraq also engaged in efforts aimed at developing the Tamuz liquid-fueled missile with a range of over 2,000 kilometers and a solid-fueled missile with a similar range. Clear evidence indicates that at least one design was to have a nuclear warhead.

- Iraq attempted to conceal a plant making missile engines from the UN inspectors. It only admitted this plant existed in 1995, raising new questions about how many of its missiles have been destroyed.

- Iraq had design work underway for a nuclear warhead for its long-range missiles.

- The Gulf War deprived Iraq of some of its MiG-29s, Mirage F-1s, MiG-23BMs, and Su-22s. Since the end of the war, the UN inspection regime has also destroyed many of Iraq's long-range missiles: A State Department summary issued on November 16, 1998, indicates that UNSCOM has supervised the destruction of:

  - 48 operational missiles;

  - 14 conventional missile warheads;

  - 6 operational mobile launchers; 28 operational fixed launch pads;

  - 32 fixed launch pads;

  - 30 missile chemical warheads;

  - other missile support equipment and materials, and a variety of assembled and non-assembled supergun components.

  - 38,537 filled and empty chemical munitions;

  - 90 metric tons of chemical weapons agent;

  - more than 3,000 metric tons of precursor chemicals;

  - 426 pieces of chemical weapons production equipment; and,

  - 91 pieces of related analytical instruments.

- The UN estimates that it is able to account for 817 of the 819 long-range missiles that Iraq imported in the period ending in 1988:

  - Pre-1980 expenditures, such as training   8

  - Expenditures during the Iran-Iraq War (1980–1981), including the war of the cities in February–April 1988   516

  - Testing activities for the development of Iraq's modifications of imported missiles and other experimental activities (1985–1990)   69

  - Expenditures during the Gulf War (January–March 1991)   93

  - Destruction under the supervision of UNSCOM   48

  - Unilateral destruction by Iraq (mid-July and October 1991   83

  - UNSCOM's analysis has shown that Iraq had destroyed 83 of the 85 missiles it had claimed were destroyed. At the same time, it stated that Iraq had not given an adequate account of its proscribed missile assets, including launchers, warheads, and propellants.

  - UNSCOM also reports that it supervised the destruction of 10 mobile launchers, 30 chemical warheads, and 18 conventional warheads.

- Iraq maintains a significant delivery capability consisting of:

  - HY-2, SS-N-2, and C-601 cruise missiles, which are unaffected by UN ceasefire terms.

- FROG-7 rockets with 70 kilometer ranges, also allowed under UN resolutions.
- Multiple rocket launchers and tube artillery.
- Experimental conversions such as the SA-2.
- Iraq claims to have manufactured only 80 missile assemblies, 53 of which were unusable. UNSCOM claims that 10 are unaccounted for.
- U.S. experts believe Iraq may still have components for several dozen extended-range Scud missiles.
- In addition, Iraq has admitted to:
  - Hiding its capability to manufacture its own Scuds.
  - Developing an extended-range variant of the FROG-7 called the Laith. The UN claims to have tagged all existing FROG-7s to prevent any extension of their range beyond the UN imposed limit of 150 kilometers for Iraqi missiles.
  - Experimenting with cruise missile technology and ballistic missile designs with ranges up to 3,000 kilometers.
  - Flight testing Al Husayn missiles with chemical warheads in April 1990.
  - Developing biological warheads for the Al Husayn missile as part of Project 144 at Taji.
  - Initiating a research and development program for a nuclear warhead missile-delivery system.
  - Successfully developing and testing a warhead separation system.
  - Indigenously developing, testing, and manufacturing advanced rocket engines to include liquid-propellant designs.
  - Conducting research into the development of remotely piloted vehicles (RPVs) for the dissemination of biological agents.
  - Attempting to expand its Ababil-100 program designed to build surface-to-surface missiles with ranges beyond the permitted 100–150 kilometers.
  - Importing parts from Britain, Switzerland, and other countries for a 350 mm "supergun," as well as starting an indigenous 600 mm supergun design effort.
- Iraq initially claimed that it had 45 missile warheads filled with chemical weapons in 1992. It then stated that it had 20 chemical and 25 biological warheads in 1995. UNSCOM established that it had a minimum of 75 operational warheads and 5 used for trials. It has evidence of the existence of additional warheads. It can only verify that 16 warheads were filled with Sarin, and 34 with chemical warfare binary components, and that 30 were destroyed under its supervision—16 with Sarin and 14 with binary components.
- In November 1995, Iraq was found to have concealed an SS-21 missile it had smuggled in from Yemen.
- Jordan found that Iraq was smuggling missile components through Jordan in early December 1995. These included 115 gyroscopes in 10 crates and mate-

rial for making chemical weapons. The shipment was worth an estimated $25 million. Iraq claimed the gyroscopes were for oil exploration but they are similar to those used in the Soviet SS-N-18 SLBM. UNSCOM also found some gyroscopes dumped in the Tigris.

- The CIA reported in January 1999 that Iraq is developing two ballistic missiles that fall within the UN-allowed 150-kilometer-range restriction. The Al-Samoud liquid-propellant missile—described as a scaled-down Scud—began flight-testing in 1997.

- A State Department report in September 1999 noted that:

  - Iraq has refused to credibly account for 500 tons of Scud propellant, over 40 Scud biological and conventional warheads, 7 Iraqi-produced Scuds, and truckloads of Scud components.

  - Iraq refuses to allow inspection of thousands of MODA and Military Industries Commission documents relating to biological and chemical weapons and long-range missiles.

- The DCI Nonproliferation Center (NPC) reported in February 2000 that Iraq has continued to work on the two SRBM systems authorized by the UN: the liquid-propellant Al-Samoud, and the solid-propellant Ababil-100. The Al-Samoud is essentially a scaled-down Scud, and the program allows Baghdad to develop technological improvements that could be applied to a longer-range missile program. We believe that the Al-Samoud missile, as designed, is capable of exceeding the UN-permitted 150-kilometer-range restriction with a potential operational range of about 180 kilometers. Personnel previously involved with the Condor II/Badr-2000 missile—which was largely destroyed during the Gulf War and eliminated by UNSCOM—are working on the Ababil-100 program. Once economic sanctions against Iraq are lifted, Baghdad probably will begin converting these efforts into longer-range missile systems, unless restricted by future UN monitoring.

- Defense intelligence experts say on background that Iraq has rebuilt many of the facilities the United States struck in Desert Fox, including 12 factories and sites associated with missile construction and the production of weapons of mass destruction. These are said to include the missile facilities at Al Taji.[19]

- In late June 2000, Iraq was reported to have carried out eight tests of the Al-Samoud missile.

- A CIA report in August 2000 summarized the state of missile development in Iraq as follows:

  - Since the Gulf War, Iraq has rebuilt key portions of its chemical production infrastructure for industrial and commercial use, as well as its missile production facilities. It has attempted to purchase numerous dual-use items for, or under the guise of, legitimate civilian use. This equipment—in principle subject to UN scrutiny—also could be diverted for WMD purposes. Since the suspension of UN inspections in December 1998, the risk of diversion has increased.

  - Following Desert Fox, Baghdad again instituted a reconstruction effort on those facilities destroyed by the U.S. bombing, to include several critical missile production complexes and former dual-use CW production facilities. In addition, it appears to be installing or repairing dual-use equipment at CW-related facilities. Some of these facilities could be converted fairly quickly for production of CW agents.

- Iraq continues to pursue development of two SRBM systems that are not prohibited by the UN: the liquid-propellant Al-Samoud and the solid-propellant Ababil-100. The Al-Samoud is essentially a scaled-down Scud, and the program allows Baghdad to develop technological improvements that could be applied to a longer-range missile program. We believe that the Al-Samoud missile, as designed, is capable of exceeding the UN-permitted 150-kilometer-range restriction with a potential operational range of about 180 kilometers. Personnel previously involved with the Condor II/Badr-2000 missile—which was largely destroyed during the Gulf War and eliminated by UNSCOM—are working on the Ababil-100 program. If economic sanctions against Iraq were lifted, Baghdad probably would attempt to convert these efforts into longer-range missile systems, regardless of continuing UN monitoring and continuing restrictions on WMD and long-range missile programs.

- A Department of Defense report in January 2001 reported:

- Iraq likely retains a limited number of launchers and Scud-variant SRBMs capable of striking its neighbors, as well as the components and manufacturing means to assemble and produce others, anticipating the reestablishment of a long-range ballistic missile force sometime in the future. Baghdad likely also has warheads capable of delivering chemical or biological agents. While Iraq's missile production infrastructure was damaged during the December 1998 strikes, Iraq retains domestic expertise and sufficient infrastructure to support most missile component production, with the exception of a few critical subelements.

- During 1999, Iraq continued to work on the two short-range ballistic missile systems that fall within the 150-kilometer-range restriction imposed by the UN: the liquid-propellant Al-Samoud and the solid-propellant Ababil-100. The Al-Samoud is essentially a scaled-down Scud, and work on it allows Baghdad to develop technological capabilities that could be applied to a longer-range missile program. We believe that the Al-Samoud missile, as designed by the Iraqis, has an inherent potential to exceed the 150-kilometer-range restriction imposed under UNSCR 687.

- Iraqi personnel involved with pre–Desert Storm ballistic missile efforts are working on the Ababil-100 SRBM program. Once economic sanctions against Iraq are lifted, unless restricted by future UN monitoring, Baghdad probably will begin converting these efforts into longer-range missile systems. Despite the damage done to Iraq's missile infrastructure during the Gulf War, Desert Fox, and subsequent UNSCOM activities, Iraq may have ambitions for longer-range missiles, including an ICBM.

- Depending on the success of acquisition efforts and degree of foreign support, it is possible that Iraq could develop and test an ICBM capable of reaching the United States by 2015.

Cruise Missiles and Other Means of Delivery

- Iraq may have a very limited stockpile of land-launched short-range anti-ship cruise missiles and air-launched short-range tactical missiles that it purchased from China and France prior to the Gulf War. These are potential means of delivery for NBC weapons.

  - Iraq also has a variety of fighter aircraft, helicopters, artillery, and rockets available as potential means of delivery for NBC weapons, although their operational status is questionable due to the cumulative effects of the UN arms embargo. However, Iraq has continued to work on its UAV program, which involves converting L-29 jet trainer aircraft originally acquired from Eastern Europe. These modified and refurbished L-29s may be intended for the delivery of chemical or biological agents. In the future, Iraq may try to use its research and development infrastructure to produce its own UAVs and cruise missiles or, should the UN arms embargo be lifted, it could try to purchase cruise missiles.

- A CIA report in January 2002 estimated that:

- Baghdad's goal of becoming the predominant regional power and its hostile relations with many of its neighbors are the key drivers behind Iraq's ballistic missile program. Iraq has been able to maintain the infrastructure and expertise necessary to develop missiles, and the IC believes it has retained a small, covert force of Scud-type missiles, launchers, and Scud-specific production equipment and support apparatus. For the next several years at least, Iraq's ballistic missile initiatives probably will focus on reconstituting its pre–Gulf War capabilities to threaten regional targets and probably will not advance beyond MRBM systems.

  - Prior to the Gulf War, Iraq had several programs to extend the range of the Scud SRBM and became experienced working with liquid-propellant technology. Since the Gulf War, despite UN resolutions limiting the range of Iraq's missiles to 150 kilometers, Baghdad has been able to maintain the infrastructure and expertise necessary to develop longer-range missile systems.

  - A military parade in December 2000 showcased Al-Samoud missiles on new transporter-erector-launchers (TELs). The liquid-propellant Al-Samoud SRBM probably will be deployed soon.

  - The IC assesses that Iraq retains a small covert force of Scud-variant missiles, launchers, and conventional, chemical, and biological warheads.

- We cannot project with confidence how long UN-related sanctions and prohibitions will remain in place. They plausibly will constrain Iraq during the entire period of this estimate. Scenarios that would weaken the prohibitions several years from now also are conceivable, allowing Iraq to reconstitute its missile infrastructure and begin developing long-range missiles before the end of the decade. The discussion that follows addresses developments that could and are likely to occur should UN prohibitions be significantly weakened in the future.

- Iraq is likely to use its experience with Scud technology to resume production of the pre–Gulf War 650-kilometer-range Al-Hussein, the 900-kilometer-range Al-Abbas, or other Scud variants, and it could explore clustering and staging options to reach more distant targets. Iraq could resume Scud-variant production—with foreign assistance—quickly after UN prohibitions ended.

- With substantial foreign assistance, Baghdad could flight-test a domestic MRBM by mid-decade. This possibility presumes rapid erosion of UN prohibitions and Baghdad's willingness to risk detection of developmental steps, such as static engine testing, earlier. An MRBM flight test is likely by 2010. An imported MRBM could be flight-tested within months of acquisition.

- For the first several years after relief from UN prohibitions, Iraq probably will strive to reestablish its SRBM inventory to pre–Gulf War numbers, continue developing and deploying solid-propellant systems, and pursue MRBMs to keep pace with its neighbors. Once its regional security concerns are being addressed, Iraq may pursue a first-generation ICBM/SLV.

- Although Iraq could attempt before 2015 to test a rudimentary long-range missile based on its failed Al-Abid SLV, such a missile almost certainly would fail. Iraq is unlikely to make such an attempt. After observing North Korean missile developments the past few years, Iraq would be more likely to pursue a three-stage TD-2 approach to an SLV or ICBM, which would be capable of delivering a nuclear weapon–sized payload to the United States. Some postulations for potential Iraqi ICBM/SLV concepts and timelines from the beginning of UN prohibition relief include:

  - If Iraq could buy a TD-2 from North Korea, it could have a launch capability within a year or two of a purchase.

  - It could develop and test a TD-1-type system within a few years.

  - If it acquired No Dongs from North Korea, it could test an ICBM within a few years of acquisition by clustering and staging the No Dongs—similar to the clustering of Scuds for the Al-Abid SLV.

  - If Iraq bought TD-2 engines, it could test an ICBM within about five years of the acquisition.

  - Iraq could develop and test a Taepo Dong-2–type system within about ten years of a decision to do so.

- Most agencies believe that Iraq is unlikely to test before 2015 any ICBMs that would threaten the United States, even if UN prohibitions were eliminated or significantly reduced in the next few years. Some believe that if prohibitions were eliminated in the next few years, Iraq would be likely to test an ICBM probably masked as an SLV before 2015, possibly before 2010. In this view, foreign assistance would affect the timing and the capability of the missile.

- Foreign assistance is key to Iraqi efforts to quickly develop longer-range missiles. Iraq relied on extensive foreign assistance before the Gulf War and will continue to seek foreign assistance to expand its current capabilities.

Chemical Weapons

- Iraq is the only major recent user of weapons of mass destruction. U.S. intelligence sources report the following Iraqi uses of chemical weapons:

Date	Area	Type of Gas	Approximate Casualties	Target
August 1983	Haij Umran	Mustard	Less than 100	Iranians/ Kurds
October– November 1983	Panjwin	Mustard	30,000	Iranians/ Kurds
February– March 1984	Majnoon Island	Mustard	2,500	Iranians
March 1984	Al Basrah	Tabun	50–100	Iranians
March 1985	Hawizah Marsh	Mustard/Tabun	3,000	Iranians
February 1986	Al Faw	Mustard/Tabun	8,000–10,000	Iranians
December 1986	Umm ar Rasas	Mustard	1,000s	Iranians
April 1987	Al Basrah	Mustard/Tabun	5,000	Iranians
October 1987	Sumar/Mehran	Mustard/Nerve Agents	3,000	Iranians
March 1988	Halabjah	Mustard/Nerve Agents	100s	Iranians/ Kurds

Note: Iranians also used poison gas at Halabjah and may have caused some of the casualties.

- In revelations to the UN, Iraq admitted that prior to the Gulf War, it:
  - Procured more than 1,000 key pieces of specialized production and support equipment for its chemical warfare program.
  - Maintained large stockpiles of mustard gas, and the nerve agents Sarin and Tabun.
  - Produced binary Sarin-filled artillery shells, 122 mm rockets, and aerial bombs.
  - Manufactured enough precursors to produce 70 tons (70,000 kilograms) of the nerve agent VX. These precursors included 65 tons of choline and 200 tons of phosphorous pentasulfide and di-isopropylamine.
  - Tested Ricin, a deadly nerve agent, for use in artillery shells.
  - Had three flight tests of long-range Scuds with chemical warheads.
  - Had a large VX production effort underway at the time of the Gulf War. The destruction of the related weapons and feedstocks has been claimed by Iraq, but not verified by UNSCOM. Iraq seems to have had at least 3,800 kilograms of V-agents by time the of the Gulf War, and 12 to 16 missile warheads.
- The majority of Iraq's chemical agents were manufactured at a supposed pesticide plant located at Muthanna. Various other production facilities were also

used, including those at Salman Pak, Samara, and Habbiniyah. Though severely damaged during the war, the physical plant for many of these facilities has been rebuilt.

- As of February 1998, UNSCOM had supervised the destruction of a total of:
  - 40,000 munitions, 28,000 filled and 12,000 empty.
  - 480,000 liters of chemical munitions.
  - 1,800,000 liters of chemical precursors.
  - Eight types of delivery systems including missile warheads.
- U.S. and UN experts believe Iraq has concealed significant stocks of precursors. Iraq also appears to retain significant amounts of production equipment dispersed before, or during, Desert Storm and not recovered by the UN.
- UNSCOM reports that Iraq has failed to account for:
  - Special missile warheads intended for filling with chemical or biological warfare agent.
  - The material balance of some 550 155 mm mustard gas shells, the extent of VX programs, and the rationale for the acquisition of various types of chemical weapons.
  - 130 tons of chemical warfare agents.
  - Some 4,000 tons of declared precursors for chemical weapons.
  - The production of several hundred tons of additional chemical warfare agents, the consumption of chemical precursors.
  - 107,500 empty casings for chemical weapons.
  - Whether several thousand additional chemical weapons were filled with agents.
  - The unilateral destruction of 15,620 weapons, and the fate of 16,038 additional weapons Iraq claimed it had discarded. "The margin of error" in the accounting presented by Iraq is in the neighborhood of 200 munitions.
  - Iraq systematically lied about the existence of its production facilities for VX gas until 1995, and made "significant efforts" to conceal its production capabilities after that date. Uncertainties affecting the destruction of its VX gas still affect some 750 tons of imported precursor chemicals, and 55 tons of domestically produced precursors. Iraq has made unverifiable claims that 460 tons were destroyed by Coalition air attacks, and that it unilaterally destroyed 212 tons. UNSCOM has only been able to verify the destruction of 155 tons and destroy a further 36 tons on its own.
- Iraq has developed basic chemical warhead designs for Scud missiles, rockets, bombs, and shells. Iraq also has spray dispersal systems.
- Iraq maintains extensive stocks of defensive equipment.
- The current status of the Iraqi program is as follows (according to U.S. intelligence as of February 19, 1998, and corrected by the National Intelligence Council on November 16, 1998):

Agent	Declared	Potential Unaccounted for	Comments
Chemical Agents	*(Metric Tons)*	*(Metric Tons)*	
VX Nerve Gas	3	300	Iraq lied about the program until 1995.
G Agents (Sarin)	100–150	200	Figures include weaponized and bulk agents.
Mustard Gas	500–600	200	Figures include weaponized and bulk agents.
Delivery Systems	*(Number)*	*(Number)*	
Missile Warheads	75–100	2–25	UNSCOM supervised destruction of 30.
Rockets	100,000	15,000–25,000	UNSCOM supervised destruction of 40,000, 28,000 of which were filled.
Aerial Bombs	16,000	2,000–8,000	High estimate reflects the data found in an Iraqi Air Force document in July 1998.
Artillery shells	30,000	15,000	
Aerial Spray Tanks	?	?	

- UNSCOM reported to the Security Council in December 1998 that Iraq continued to withhold information related to its CW and BW programs.

  - For example, Baghdad seized from UNSCOM inspectors an Air Force document discovered by UNSCOM that indicated that Iraq had not consumed as many CW munitions during the Iran-Iraq War in the 1980s as had been declared by Baghdad. This discrepancy indicates that Iraq may have an additional 6,000 CW munitions hidden.

  - We do not have any direct evidence that Iraq has used the period since Desert Fox to reconstitute its WMD programs, although given its past behavior, this type of activity must be regarded as likely. We assess that since the suspension of UN inspections in December of 1998, Baghdad has had the capability to reinitiate both its CW and BW programs within a few weeks to months, but without an inspection-monitoring program, it is difficult to determine if Iraq has done so. We know, however, that Iraq has continued to work on its unmanned aerial vehicle (UAV) program, which involves converting L-29 jet trainer aircraft originally acquired from Eastern Europe. These modified and refurbished L-29s are believed to be intended for delivery of chemical or biological agents.

- A State Department report in September 1999 noted that:
  - In July 1998, Iraq seized from the hands of UNSCOM inspectors an Iraqi Air Force document indicating that Iraq had misrepresented the expenditure of over 6,000 bombs that may have contained over 700 tons of chemical agent. Iraq continues to refuse to provide this document to the UN.
  - Iraq continues to deny weaponizing VX nerve agent, despite the fact that UNSCOM found VX nerve agent residues on Iraqi Scud missile warhead fragments. Based on its investigations, international experts concluded that "Iraq has the know-how and process equipment, and may possess precursors to manufacture as much as 200 tons of VX. . . . The retention of a VX capability by Iraq cannot be excluded by the UNSCOM international expert team."
  - The DCI Nonproliferation Center (NPC) reported in February 2000, "We do not have any direct evidence that Iraq has used the period since Desert Fox to reconstitute its WMD programs, although given its past behavior, this type of activity must be regarded as likely. The United Nations assesses that Baghdad has the capability to reinitiate both its CW and BW programs within a few weeks to months, but without an inspection monitoring program, it is difficult to determine if Iraq has done so."
  - It also reported that, "Since Operation Desert Fox in December 1998, Baghdad has refused to allow United Nations inspectors into Iraq as required by Security Council Resolution 687. As a result, there have been no UN inspections during this reporting period, and the automated video monitoring system installed by the UN at known and suspect WMD facilities in Iraq has been dismantled by the Iraqis. Having lost this on-the-ground access, it is difficult for the UN or the US to accurately assess the current state of Iraq's WMD programs."
  - Since the Gulf War, Iraq has rebuilt key portions of its chemical production infrastructure for industrial and commercial use, as well as its missile production facilities. It has attempted to purchase numerous dual-use items for, or under the guise of, legitimate civilian use. This equipment—in principle subject to UN scrutiny—also could be diverted for WMD purposes. Following Desert Fox, Baghdad again instituted a reconstruction effort on those facilities destroyed by the U.S. bombing to include several critical missile production complexes and former dual-use CW production facilities. In addition, it appears to be installing or repairing dual-use equipment at CW-related facilities. Some of these facilities could be converted fairly quickly for production of CW agents.
  - The UNSCOM reported to the Security Council in December 1998 that Iraq continued to withhold information related to its CW and BW programs. For example, Baghdad seized from UNSCOM inspectors an Air Force document discovered by UNSCOM that indicated that Iraq had not consumed as many CW munitions during the Iran-Iraq War in the 1980s as declared by Baghdad. This discrepancy indicates that Iraq may have an additional 6,000 CW munitions hidden. This intransigence on the part of Baghdad ultimately led to the Desert Fox bombing by the United States.

- Iraqi defector claims in February 2000 that Iraq had maintained a missile force armed with chemical and biological warheads that can be deployed from secret locations, and that warheads are stored separately near Baghdad and have been deployed to the missiles in the field in exercises.[20]
- A CIA report in August 2000 summarized the state of chemical weapons proliferation in Iraq as follows:
  - Since Operation Desert Fox in December 1998, Baghdad has refused to allow United Nations inspectors into Iraq as required by Security Council Resolution 687. Although UN Security Council Resolution (UNSCR) 1284, adopted in December 1999, established a follow-on inspection regime to UNSCOM in the form of the UN Monitoring, Verification, and Inspection Committee (UNMOVIC), there have been no UN inspections during this reporting period. Moreover, the automated video monitoring system installed by the UN at known and suspect WMD facilities in Iraq has been dismantled by the Iraqis. Having lost this on-the-ground access, it is difficult for the UN or the United States to accurately assess the current state of Iraq's WMD programs.
  - Since the Gulf War, Iraq has rebuilt key portions of its chemical production infrastructure for industrial and commercial use, as well as its missile production facilities. It has attempted to purchase numerous dual-use items for, or under the guise of, legitimate civilian use. This equipment—in principle subject to UN scrutiny—also could be diverted for WMD purposes. Since the suspension of UN inspections in December 1998, the risk of diversion has increased.
  - Following Desert Fox, Baghdad again instituted a reconstruction effort on those facilities destroyed by the U.S. bombing to include several critical missile production complexes and former dual-use CW production facilities. In addition, it appears to be installing or repairing dual-use equipment at CW-related facilities. Some of these facilities could be converted fairly quickly for production of CW agents.
- A Department of Defense report in January 2001 reported:
  - Since the Gulf War, Baghdad has rebuilt key portions of its industrial and chemical production infrastructure; it has not become a state party to the CWC. Some of Iraq's facilities could be converted fairly quickly to production of chemical warfare agents. Following Operation Desert Fox, Baghdad again instituted a rapid reconstruction effort on those facilities to include former dual-use chemical warfare–associated production facilities destroyed by U.S. bombing. In 1999, Iraq may have begun installing or repairing dual-use equipment at these and other chemical warfare–related facilities. Previously, Iraq was known to have produced and stockpiled mustard, tabun, sarin, and VX, some of which likely remain hidden. It is likely that an additional quantity of various precursor chemicals also remains hidden.
  - In late 1998, UNSCOM reported to the UN Security Council that Iraq continued to withhold information related to its chemical program. UNSCOM cited an example where Baghdad seized from inspectors a document discovered by UNSCOM inspectors, which indicated that Iraq had not

consumed as many chemical munitions during the Iran-Iraq War as had been declared previously by Baghdad. This document suggests that Iraq may have an additional 6,000 chemical munitions hidden. Similarly, an UNSCOM discovery in 1998 of evidence of VX in Iraqi missile warheads showed that Iraq had lied to the international community for seven years when it repeatedly said that it had never weaponized VX.

- Iraq retains the expertise, once a decision is made, to resume chemical agent production within a few weeks or months, depending on the type of agent. However, foreign assistance, whether commercial procurement of dual-use technology, key infrastructure, or other aid, will be necessary to completely restore Iraq's chemical agent production capabilities to pre–Desert Storm levels. Iraqi doctrine for the use of chemical weapons evolved during the Iran-Iraq War, and was fully incorporated into Iraqi offensive operations by the end of the war in 1988. During different stages of that war, Iraq used aerial bombs, artillery, rocket launchers, tactical rockets, and sprayers mounted in helicopters to deliver agents against Iranian forces. It also used chemical agents against Kurdish elements of its own civilian population in 1988.

Biological Weapons

- Iraq had highly compartmented "black" program before the Gulf War with far tighter security regulations than chemical program.
- It had 18 major sites for some aspect of biological weapons effort before the Gulf War. Most were nondescript and had no guards or visible indications they were a military facility.
- Iraq systematically lied about biological weapons effort until 1995. First stated that had small defensive efforts, but no offensive effort. In July 1995, admitted had a major defensive effort. In October 1995, finally admitted major weaponization effort. Iraq, however, has continued to lie about its biological weapons effort since October 1995. It has claimed the effort was headed by Dr. Taha, a man who only headed a subordinate effort. It has not admitted to any help by foreign personnel or contractors. It has claimed to have destroyed its weapons, but the one site UNSCOM inspectors visited showed no signs of such destruction and was later said to be the wrong site. It has claimed only 50 people were employed full time, but the scale of the effort would have required several hundred.
- Since July 1995, Iraq has presented three versions of FFCDs and four "drafts."
- Iraq has not admitted to the production of 8,500 liters of anthrax, 19,000 liters of Botulinum toxin, 2,200 liters of Aflatoxin.
- UNSCOM reports indicate that Iraq tested at least 7 principal biological agents for use against humans.
  - Anthrax, Botulinum, and Aflatoxin are known to be weaponized.
  - Looked at viruses, bacteria, and fungi. Examined the possibility of

weaponizing gas gangrene and Mycotoxins. Some field trials were held of these agents.

- Examined foot and mouth disease, hemorrhagic conjunctivitis virus, rotavirus, and camel pox virus.

- Conducted research on a "wheat pathogen" and a Mycotoxin similar to "yellow rain" defoliant.

- First produced "wheat smut" at Al-Salman, and then put in major production during 1987–1988 at a plant near Mosul. Iraq claims the program was abandoned.

- The August 1995 defection of Lieutenant general Husayn Kamel Majid, formerly in charge of Iraq's weapons of mass destruction, revealed the extent of this biological weapons program. Lieutenant General Kamel's defection prompted Iraq to admit that it: Imported at least 39 tons of growth media (31,000 kilograms or 68,200 pounds) for biological agents obtained from three European firms. According to UNSCOM, 3,500 kilograms (7,700 pounds) remain unaccounted for. Some estimates go as high as 17 tons. Each ton can be used to produce 10 tons of bacteriological weapons.

- Other reports indicate that Iraq obtained nearly 40 tons of the medium to grow anthrax and botulinum bacterium for its biological weapons program from Oxoid Ltd., and other suppliers in the UK in 1988.

  - Imported type cultures from the United States that can be modified to develop biological weapons. Tried to import the Ames strain of anthrax from the United States but does not seem to have succeeded. Did import the Sterne and A-3 strains of anthrax from the Institut Pasteur in France, and two Vollum strains and five other strains of anthrax from the American Type Culture collection, located near Manassas, Virginia. Vollum 1B is the strain of anthrax the United States developed for its own biological weapons program before it signed the BWC.

  - Had a laboratory- and industrial-scale capability to manufacture various biological agents including the bacteria that cause anthrax and botulism; Aflatoxin, a naturally occurring carcinogen; clostridium perfringens, a gangrene-causing agent; the protein toxin ricin; tricothecene Mycotoxins, such as T-2 and DAS; and an anti-wheat fungus known as wheat cover smut. Iraq also conducted research into the rotavirus, the camel pox virus and the virus which causes hemorrhagic conjunctivitis.

  - Created at least seven primary production facilities including the Sepp Institute at Muthanna, the Ghazi Research Institute at Amaria, the Daura Foot and Mouth Disease Institute, and facilities at Al-Hakim, Salman Pak Taji, and Fudaliyah. According to UNSCOM, weaponization occurred primarily at Muthanna through May 1987 (largely botulinum), and then moved to Al-Salman (anthrax). In March 1988 a plant was opened at Al-Hakim, and in 1989 an Aflatoxin plant was set up at Fudaliyah.

  - Had test site about 200 kilometers west of Baghdad, used animals in cages and tested artillery and rocket rounds against live targets at ranges up to 16 kilometers.

- Took fermenters and other equipment from Kuwait to improve effort during the Gulf War.
- Iraq had least 79 civilian facilities capable of playing some role in biological weapons production still in existence in 1997.
- The Iraqi program involving Aflatoxin leaves many questions unanswered.
  - Iraqi research on Aflatoxin began in May 1988 at Al-Salman, where the toxin was produced by the growth of fungus aspergilus in 5.3-quart flasks.
  - The motives behind Iraq's research on Aflatoxin remain one of the most speculative aspects of its program. Aflatoxin is associated with fungal-contaminated food grains, and is considered non-lethal. It normally can produce liver cancer, but only after a period of months to years and in intense concentrations. There is speculation, however, that a weaponized form might cause death within days and some speculation that it can be used as an incapacitating agent.
  - Iraq moved its production of Aflatoxin to Fudaliyah in 1989, and produced 481 gallons of toxin in solution between November 1988 and May 1990.
  - Produced 1,850 liters of Aflatoxin in solution at Fudaliyah.
  - It produced a total of at least 2,500 liters of concentrated Aflatoxin (1,850 liters filled into munitions).
  - It developed 16 R-400 Aflatoxin bombs and two Scud warheads. Conducted trials with Aflatoxin in 122 mm rockets and R-400 bombs in November 1989 and May and August 1990. Produced a total of 572 gallons of toxin and loaded 410.8 gallons into munitions.
  - UNSCOM concluded in October 1997, that Iraq's accounting for its Aflatoxin production was not credible.
- Total Iraqi production of more orthodox biological weapons reached at least 19,000 liters of concentrated botulinum (10,000 liters filled into munitions); and 8,500 liters of concentrated anthrax (6,500 liters filled into munitions). It manufactured 6,000 liters of concentrated botulinum toxin and 8,425 liters of anthrax at Al-Hakim during 1990; 5,400 liters of concentrated botulinum toxin at the Daura Foot and Mouth Disease Institute from November 1990 to January 15, 1991; 400 liters of concentrated botulinum toxin at Taji; and 150 liters of concentrated anthrax at Salman Pak.
  - Iraq acknowledged to UNSCOM that it had produced at least 19,000 liters of botulinum toxin, using more than half to fill at least 116 bombs and missile warheads.
  - Filled at least 50 bombs and missile warheads with a wet anthrax agent using the Vollum strain, or one very similar.
  - Some Al-Hussein warheads were found at the Al-Nibal missile destruction site with traces of wet anthrax agent, similar to the Vollum strain.
  - Vials were found with a dry, freeze-dried anthrax agent of the Vollum strain; reports differ as to whether Iraq weaponized a dry, clay-coated version of the particle size most lethal for delivering inhaled anthrax, and clay-coated the particles to eliminate the electrostatic charge and ensure optimal dispersion.

- Iraq is also known to have produced at least:
  - 340 liters of concentrated clostridium perfringens, a gangrene-causing biological agent, beginning in August 1990.
  - 10 liters of concentrated ricin at Al-Salam. Claim abandoned work after tests failed.
- Iraq weaponized at least three biological agents for use in the Gulf War. The weaponization consisted of at least:
  - 100 bombs and 16 missile warheads loaded with botulinum.
  - 50 R-400 air-delivered bombs and 5 missile warheads loaded with anthrax.
  - 4 missile warheads and 7 R-400 bombs loaded with Aflatoxin, a natural carcinogen.
  - The warheads were designed for operability with the Al-Hussein Scud variant.
- Iraq had other weaponization activities:
  - Armed 155 mm artillery shells and 122 mm rockets with biological agents.
  - Conducted field trials, weaponization tests, and live firings of 122 mm rockets armed with anthrax and botulinum toxin from March 1988 to May 1990.
  - Tested ricin, a deadly protein toxin, for use in artillery shells.
  - Iraq produced at least 191 bombs and 25 missile warheads with biological agents.
  - Developed and deployed 250-pound aluminum bombs covered in fiberglass. Bombs were designed so they could be mounted on both Soviet- and French-made aircraft. They were rigged with parachutes for low-altitude drops to allow efficient slow delivery and aircraft to fly under radar coverage. Some debate over whether bombs had cluster munitions or simply dispersed agent like LD-400 chemical bomb.
  - Deployed at least 166 R-400 bombs with 85 liters of biological agents each during the Gulf War. Deployed them at two sites. One was near an abandoned runway where it could fly in aircraft, arm them quickly, and disperse with no prior indication of activity and no reason for the UN to target the runway.
  - Filled at least 25 Scud missile warheads and 157 bombs and aerial dispensers with biological agents during the Gulf War.
- Iraq developed and stored drop tanks ready for use for three aircraft or RPVs with the capability of dispersing 2,000 liters of anthrax. Development took place in December 1990. Claimed later that tests showed the systems were ineffective.
  - The UN found, however, that Iraq equipped crop-spraying helicopters for biological warfare and held exercises and tests simulating the spraying of anthrax spores.
  - Iraqi Mirages were given spray tanks to disperse biological agents.
    - Held trials as late as January 13, 1991.

- The Mirages were chosen because they have large, 2,200-liter belly tanks and could be refueled by air, giving them a longer endurance and greater strike range.
- The tanks had electric valves to allow the agent to be released and the system was tested by releasing simulated agent into desert areas with scattered petri dishes to detect the biological agent. UNSCOM has videotapes of the aircraft.

- Project 144 at Taji produced at least 25 operational Al-Hussein warheads. Ten of these were hidden deep in a railway tunnel, and 15 in holes dug in an unmanned hide site along the Tigris.
- Biological weapons were only distinguished from regular weapons by a black stripe.
- The UN claims that Iraq has offered no evidence to corroborate its claims that it destroyed its stockpile of biological agents after the Gulf War. Further, Iraq retains the technology it acquired before the war and evidence clearly indicates an ongoing research and development effort, in spite of the UN sanctions regime.
- UNSCOM reported in October 1997 that:
  - Iraq has never provided a clear picture of the role of its military in its biological warfare program, and has claimed it only played a token role.
  - It has never accounted for its disposal of growth media. The unaccounted-for media is sufficient, in quantity, for the production of over three times more of the biological agent—anthrax—Iraq claims to have produced.
  - Bulk warfare agent production appears to be vastly understated by Iraq. Expert calculations of possible agent production quantities, either by equipment capacity or growth media amounts, far exceed Iraq's stated results.
  - Significant periods when Iraq claims its fermenters were not utilized are unexplained.
  - Biological warfare field trials are underreported and inadequately described.
  - Claims regarding field trials of chemical and biological weapons using R-400 bombs are contradictory and indicate that "more munitions were destroyed than were produced."
  - The Commission is unable to verify that the unilateral destruction of the BW-filled Al-Hussein warheads has taken place.
  - There is no way to confirm whether Iraq destroyed 157 bombs of the R-400 type, some of which were filled with botulin or anthrax spores.
  - "The September 1997 FFCD fails to give a remotely credible account of Iraq's biological program. This opinion has been endorsed by an international panel of experts."
- The current status of the Iraqi program is as follows (according to U.S. intelligence as of February 19, 1998):

Agent	Declared Concentrated Amount		Declared Total Amount		Uncertainty
	Liters	Gallons	Liters	Gallons	
Anthrax	8,500	12,245	85,000	22,457	Could be 3–4 times declared amount
Botulinum	19,400	NA	380,000	NA	Probably twice declared toxin amount; some extremely concentrated
Gas Gangrene, Clostridium, Perfingens	340	90	3,400	900	Amounts could be higher
Aflatoxin	NA	NA	2,200	581	Major uncertainties
Ricin	NA	NA	10	2.7	Major uncertainties

- A State Department report in September 1999 noted that:
  - Iraq refuses to allow inspection of thousands of Ministry of Defense and Military Industries Commission documents relating to biological and chemical weapons and long-range missiles.
  - In 1995, Iraqis who conducted field trials of R-400 bombs filled with biological agents described the tests to UNSCOM experts in considerable detail, including the use of many animals. These field trials were reflected in Iraq's June 1996 biological weapons declaration. Yet, amazingly, Iraq now denies that any such trials were conducted at all.
  - In September 1995, Iraq finally declared the existence of two projects to disseminate biological agents from Mirage F-1 and MiG-21 aircraft, yet there is no evidence that the prototype weapons and aircraft were ever destroyed. There is also no evidence that the 12 Iraqi helicopter-borne aerosol generators for biological weapon delivery were ever destroyed.
  - Apart from one document referring to a single year, no Iraqi biological weapon production records have been given to the UN—no records of storage, of filling into munitions, or of destruction. This is why UNSCOM refers to Iraq's biological weapons program—which deployed Scud missile warheads filled with anthrax and botulinum toxin to be ready for use against Coalition forces—as a "black hole."
  - The Iraqis have repeatedly changed their story about their biological weapons warheads. Iraq has revised several times its declarations regarding the precise locations of warhead destruction and the fill of warheads. The movements of concealed warheads prior to unilateral destruction, claimed by Iraq, have been proven to be false.

- A CIA report in August 2000 summarized the state of biological weapons proliferation in Iraq as follows:[21]

  - Since Operation Desert Fox in December 1998, Baghdad has refused to allow United Nations inspectors into Iraq as required by Security Council Resolution 687. Although UN Security Council Resolution (UNSCR) 1284, adopted in December 1999, established a follow-on inspection regime to the United Nations Special Commission on Iraq (UNSCOM) in the form of the United Nations Monitoring, Verification, and Inspection Committee (UNMOVIC), there have been no UN inspections during this reporting period. Moreover, the automated video monitoring system installed by the UN at known and suspect WMD facilities in Iraq has been dismantled by the Iraqis. Having lost this on-the-ground access, it is difficult for the UN or the United States to accurately assess the current state of Iraq's WMD programs.

  - Since the Gulf War, Iraq has rebuilt key portions of its chemical production infrastructure for industrial and commercial use, as well as its missile production facilities. It has attempted to purchase numerous dual-use items for, or under the guise of, legitimate civilian use. This equipment—in principle subject to UN scrutiny—also could be diverted for WMD purposes. Since the suspension of UN inspections in December 1998, the risk of diversion has increased.

  - Following Desert Fox, Baghdad again instituted a reconstruction effort on those facilities destroyed by the U.S. bombing to include several critical missile production complexes and former dual-use CW production facilities. In addition, it appears to be installing or repairing dual-use equipment at CW-related facilities. Some of these facilities could be converted fairly quickly for production of CW agents.

  - UNSCOM reported to the Security Council in December 1998 that Iraq continued to withhold information related to its CW and BW programs. For example, Baghdad seized from UNSCOM inspectors an Air Force document discovered by UNSCOM that indicated that Iraq had not consumed as many CW munitions during the Iran-Iraq War in the 1980s as had been declared by Baghdad. This discrepancy indicates that Iraq may have an additional 6,000 CW munitions hidden.

  - We do not have any direct evidence that Iraq has used the period since Desert Fox to reconstitute its WMD programs, although given its past behavior, this type of activity must be regarded as likely. We assess that since the suspension of UN inspections in December of 1998, Baghdad has had the capability to reinitiate both its CW and BW programs within a few weeks to months, but without an inspection monitoring program, it is difficult to determine if Iraq has done so. We know, however, that Iraq has continued to work on its unmanned aerial vehicle (UAV) program, which involves converting L-29 jet trainer aircraft originally acquired from Eastern Europe. These modified and refurbished L-29s are believed to be intended for delivery of chemical or biological agents.

- A Department of Defense report stated in 2001 that Iraq's continued refusal to disclose fully the extent of its biological program suggests that Baghdad retains a biological warfare capability, despite its membership in the BWC. After four and one-half years of claiming that it had conducted only "defensive research" on biological weapons, Iraq declared reluctantly, in 1995, that it had produced approximately 30,000 liters of bulk biological agents and/or filled munitions. Iraq admitted that it produced anthrax, botulinum toxins and aflatoxins and that it prepared biological agent-filled munitions, including missile warheads and aerial bombs. However, UNSCOM believed that Iraq had produced substantially greater amounts than it has admitted—three to four times greater. Iraq also admitted that, during the Persian Gulf War, it had deployed biological agent-filled munitions to airfields and that these weapons were intended for use against Israel and coalition forces in Saudi Arabia. Iraq stated that it destroyed all of these agents and munitions in 1991, but it has provided insufficient credible evidence to support this claim. The UN believes that Baghdad has the ability to reconstitute its biological warfare capabilities within a few weeks or months, and, in the absence of UNSCOM inspections and monitoring during 1999 and 2000, we are concerned that Baghdad again may have produced some biological warfare agents.

Nuclear Weapons

- Inspections by UN teams have found evidence of two successful weapons designs, a neutron initiator, explosives and triggering technology needed for production of bombs, plutonium processing technology, centrifuge technology, Calutron enrichment technology, and experiments with chemical separation technology. Iraq had some expert technical support, including at least one German scientist who provided the technical plans for the URENCO TC-11 centrifuge.
- Iraq's main nuclear weapons–related facilities were:
  - Al-Atheer—center of nuclear weapons program. Uranium metallurgy; production of shaped charges for bombs, remote-controlled facilities for high explosives manufacture.
  - Al Tuwaitha—triggering systems, neutron initiators, uranium metallurgy, and hot cells for plutonium separation. Laboratory production of UO_2, UCL_4, UF_6, and fuel fabrication facility. Prototype-scale gas centrifuge, prototype EMIS facility, and testing of laser isotope separation technology.
  - Al-Qa Qa—high explosives storage, testing of detonators for high explosive component of implosion nuclear weapons.
  - Al-Musaiyib/Al-Hatteen—high explosive testing, hydrodynamic studies of bombs.
  - Al Hadre—firing range for high explosive devices, including FAE.
  - Ash Sharqat—designed for mass production of weapons-grade material using EMIS.
  - Al Furat—designed for mass production of weapons-grade material using centrifuge method.

- Al Jesira (Mosul)—mass production of UCL_4.
- Al Qaim—phosphate plant for production of U308.
- Akashat uranium mine.
- Iraq had three reactor programs:
  - Osiraq/Tammuz I 40 megawatt light-water reactor destroyed by Israeli air attack in 1981.
  - Isis/Tammuz II 800 kilowatt light water reactor destroyed by Coalition air attack in 1991.
  - IRT-5000 5 megawatt light water reactor damaged by Coalition air attack in 1991.
- Iraq used Calutron (EMIS), centrifuges, plutonium processing, chemical diffusion and foreign purchases to create new production capability after Israel destroyed most of Osiraq.
- Iraq established a centrifuge-enrichment system in Rashidya and conducted research into the nuclear fuel cycle to facilitate development of a nuclear device.
- After invading Kuwait, Iraq attempted to accelerate its program to develop a nuclear weapon by using radioactive fuel from French- and Russian-built reactors. It made a crash effort in September 1990 to recover enriched fuel from its supposedly safe-guarded French and Russian reactors, with the goal of producing a nuclear weapon by April 1991. The program was only halted after Coalition air raids destroyed key facilities on January 17, 1991.
- Iraq conducted research into the production of a radiological weapon, which disperses lethal radioactive material without initiating a nuclear explosion.
- Orders were given in 1987 to explore the use of radiological weapons for area denial in the Iran-Iraq War. Three prototype bombs were detonated at test sites—one as a ground-level static test and two others were dropped from aircraft. Iraq claims the results were disappointing and the project was shelved but has no records or evidence to prove this.
- UNSCOM believes that as of 1998, Iraq's nuclear program has been largely disabled and remains incapacitated, but warns that Iraq retains substantial technology and established a clandestine purchasing system in 1990 that it has used to import forbidden components since the Gulf War. The major remaining uncertainties were:
  - Iraq still retains the technology developed before the Gulf War and U.S. experts believe an ongoing research and development effort continues, in spite of the UN sanctions regime.
  - Did Iraq conceal an effective high-speed centrifuge program?
  - Are there elements for radiological weapons?
  - Is it actively seeking to clandestinely buy components for nuclear weapons and examining the purchase of fissile material from outside Iraq?
  - Is it continuing with the development of a missile warhead suited to the use of a nuclear device?

- A substantial number of declared nuclear weapons components and research equipment have never been recovered. There is no reason to assume that Iraqi declarations were comprehensive.

- Work by David Albright indicates that Iraq still holds approximately 1.7 metric tons (MT) of low-enriched uranium (LEU) and several hundred MT of natural uranium. He estimates that if Iraq should master one of the uranium enrichment technologies that it was pursuing before the Gulf War, its LEU stock would provide a means to rapidly make enough HEU for at least one nuclear weapon, and that the natural uranium could become the feedstock for many more. This uranium remains in Iraq because the UN Action Team did not have a mandate under resolution 687 to "remove, destroy or render harmless" this uranium. Without further enrichment or irradiation in a nuclear reactor, it is not "weapons-usable nuclear material."

- Dr. Khidhir Hamza, a highest-ranking Iraqi scientist who defected from Iraq, claims Iraqi scientists were commanded to build one nuclear bomb immediately after Saddam invaded Kuwait in 1990, and that the resulting device was crude and untested and might even fall apart. In an April 2, 2001, edition of *Middle East Forum Wire*, he says that:

  - Iraq still runs its nuclear program and distributes its nuclear program infrastructure among dozens of small corporations, as it does with biological and chemical weapons.

  - One group was responsible for enrichment of uranium by diffusion, and did this under the front of a large refinery in Baghdad. A refinery and a uranium enrichment plant require similar piping, structures, compressors, and handling of gases. He says his assistant, who designed bombs under Hamza, is now running the program while also doing seismic prospecting for oil maps. Apart from designing weapons, he engineers underground explosions that generate seismic waves in order to locate oil. When an inspector visits, all programs relating to the bomb design are put aside, and replaced with seismic prospecting maps. The bomb designer is a real expert at seismic prospecting, so he is very convincing to the inspectors.

  - In a 1998 *New York Times* interview, he stated that Iraq was three years away from nuclear capability. Sadly, inspections ceased that same year. Three years have passed, and Saddam is undoubtedly on the precipice of nuclear power.

  - He now estimates that Iraq will have between three to five nuclear weapons by 2005. Iraq now has 12 tons of uranium and 1.3 tons of low enriched uranium. This is enough for at least 4 bombs already.

- A Department of Defense report in January 2001 stated:

  - Despite these severe pressures on its economy, Saddam Hussein's government continues to devote Iraqi resources to rebuilding certain portions of its development program that were focused on building an implosion-type device. The program was linked to a ballistic missile project that was the intended delivery system. From April 1991 to December 1998, Iraqi nuclear aspirations were held in check by IAEA/UNSCOM inspections and monitoring. All known weapons-grade fissile material was removed from the country.

- Although Iraq claims that it destroyed all of the specific equipment and facilities useful for developing nuclear weapons, it still retains sufficient skilled and experienced scientists and engineers as well as weapons design information that could allow it to restart a weapons program.
- Iraq would need 5 or more years and key foreign assistance to rebuild the infrastructure to enrich enough material for a nuclear weapon. This period would be substantially shortened should Baghdad successfully acquire fissile material from a foreign source.
- The CIA estimated in January 2002 that Baghdad had a crash program to develop a nuclear weapon for missile delivery in 1990, but coalition bombing and IAEA and UNSCOM activities significantly set back the effort. The intelligence community estimates that Iraq, unconstrained, would take several years to produce enough fissile material to make a weapon. Iraq has admitted to having biological and chemical weapons programs before the Gulf War and maintains those programs.

APPENDIX 10.2: IRAN'S SEARCH FOR WEAPONS OF MASS DESTRUCTION

Delivery Systems

- Air delivery systems include:
  - Su-24 long-range strike fighters with range-payloads roughly equivalent to US F-111 and superior to older Soviet medium bombers.
  - F-4D/E fighter-bombers with capability to carry extensive payloads to ranges of 450 miles.
- Can modify HY-2 Silkworm missiles and SA-2 surface-to-air missiles to deliver weapons of mass destruction.
- Iran has made several indigenous long-range rockets:
  - The Iran-130, or Nazeat, since the end of the Iran-Iraq War. The full details of this system remain unclear, but it seems to use commercially available components, a solid-fuel rocket, and a simple inertial guidance system to reach ranges of about 90–120 kilometers. It is 355 millimeters in diameter, 5.9 meters long, weighs 950 kilograms, and has a 150-kilogram warhead. It seems to have poor reliability and accuracy, and its payload only seems to be several hundred kilograms.
  - The Shahin 2. It too has a 355-mm diameter, but is only 3.87 meters long, and weighs only 580 kilograms. It evidently can be equipped with three types of warheads: A 180 kilogram high-explosive warhead, another warhead using high-explosive submunitions, and a warhead that uses chemical weapons.
  - Iranian Oghab (Eagle) rocket with 40+-kilometer range.

- New SSM with 125-mile range may be in production, but could be modified FROG.

- Large numbers of multiple rocket launchers and tube artillery for short range delivery of chemical weapons.

- Iran has shorter missile range systems:

  - In 1990, Iran bought CSS-8 surface-to-surface missiles (converted SA-2s) from China with ranges of 130–150 kilometers.

  - Has Chinese sea- and land-based anti-ship cruise missiles. Iran fired 10 such missiles at Kuwait during Iran-Iraq War, hitting one U.S.-flagged tanker.

- The Soviet-designed Scud B (17E) guided missile currently forms the core of Iran's ballistic missile forces.

  - Iran acquired its Scuds in response to Iraq's invasion. It obtained a limited number from Libya and then obtained larger numbers from North Korea. It deployed these units with a special Khatam ol-Anbya force attached to the air element of the Pasdaran. Iran fired its first Scuds in March 1985. It fired as many as 14 Scuds in 1985, 8 in 1986, 18 in 1987, and 77 in 1988. Iran fired 77 Scud missiles during a 52-day period in 1988, during what came to be known as the "war of the cites." Sixty-one were fired at Baghdad, 9 at Mosul, 5 at Kirkuk, 1 at Takrit, and 1 at Kuwait. Iran fired as many as 5 missiles on a single day, and once fired 3 missiles within 30 minutes. This still, however, worked out to an average of only about 1 missile a day, and Iran was down to only 10–20 Scuds when the war of the cities ended.

  - Iran's missile attacks were initially more effective than Iraq's attacks. This was largely a matter of geography. Many of Iraq's major cities were comparatively close to its border with Iran, but Tehran and most of Iran's major cities that had not already been targets in the war were outside the range of Iraqi Scud attacks. Iran's missiles, in contrast, could hit key Iraqi cities like Baghdad. This advantage ended when Iraq deployed extended-range Scuds.

  - The Scud B is a relatively old Soviet design that first became operational in 1967, designated as the R-17E or R-300E. The Scud B has a range of 290–300 kilometers with its normal conventional payload. The export version of the missile is about 11 meters long, 85–90 centimeters in diameter, and weighs 6,300 kilograms. It has a nominal CEP of 1,000 meters. The Russian versions can be equipped with conventional high-explosive, fuel air explosive, runway penetrator, submunition, chemical, and nuclear warheads.

  - The export version of the Scud B comes with a conventional high explosive warhead weighing about 1,000 kilograms, of which 800 kilograms are the high explosive payload and 200 are the warhead structure and fusing system. It has a single stage storable liquid rocket engine and is usually deployed on the MAZ-543 eight-wheel transporter-erector-launcher (TEL). It has a strap-down inertial guidance, using three gyros to correct its ballistic trajectory, and uses internal graphite jet vane steering. The warhead hits at a velocity above Mach 1.5.

- Most estimates indicate that Iran now has 6–12 Scud launchers and up to 200 Scud B (R-17E) missiles with 230–310-kilometer range.
- Some estimates give higher figures. They estimate Iran bought 200–300 Scud Bs from North Korea between 1987 and 1992, and may have continued to buy such missiles after that time. Israeli experts estimate that Iran had at least 250–300 Scud B missiles, and at least 8–15 launchers on hand in 1997.
- U.S. experts also believe that Iran can now manufacture virtually all of the Scud B, with the possible exception of the most sophisticated components of its guidance system and rocket motors. This makes it difficult to estimate how many missiles Iran has in inventory and can acquire over time, as well as to estimate the precise performance characteristics of Iran's missiles, since it can alter the weight of the warhead and adjust the burn time and improve the efficiency of the rocket motors.
- Iran has new long-range North Korean Scuds with ranges near 500 kilometers.
  - The missile is more advanced than the Scud B, although many aspects of its performance are unclear. North Korea seems to have completed development of the missile in 1987, after obtaining technical support from the People's Republic of China. While it is often called a "Scud C," it seems to differ substantially in detail from the original Soviet Scud B. It seems to be based more on the Chinese-made DF-61 than on a direct copy of the Soviet weapon.
  - Experts estimate that the North Korean missiles have a range of around 500 kilometers, a warhead with a high explosive payload of 700 kilograms, and relatively good accuracy and reliability. While this payload is a bit limited for the effective delivery of chemical agents, Iran might modify the warhead to increase payload at the expense of range and restrict the use of chemical munitions to the most lethal agents such as persistent nerve gas. It might also concentrate its development efforts on arming its Scud C forces with more lethal biological agents. In any case, such missiles are likely to have enough range-payload to give Iran the ability to strike all targets on the southern coast of the Gulf and all of the populated areas in Iraq, although not the West. Iran could also reach targets in part of eastern Syria, the eastern third of Turkey, and cover targets in the border area of the former Soviet Union, western Afghanistan, and western Pakistan.
  - Accuracy and reliability remain major uncertainties, as does operational CEP. Much would also depend on the precise level of technology Iran deployed in the warhead. Neither Russia nor the People's Republic of China seems to have transferred the warhead technology for biological and chemical weapons to Iran or Iraq when they sold them the Scud B missile and CSS-8. However, North Korea may have sold Iran such technology as part of the Scud C sale. If it did so, such a technology transfer would save Iran years of development and testing in obtaining highly lethal biological and chemical warheads. In fact, Iran would probably be able to deploy far more effective biological and chemical warheads than Iraq had at the time of the Gulf War.
  - Iran may be working with Syria in such development efforts, although Middle Eastern nations rarely cooperate in such sensitive areas. Iran served

as a transshipment point for North Korean missile deliveries during 1992 and 1993. Some of this transshipment took place using the same Iranian B-747s that brought missile parts to Iran. Others moved by sea. For example, a North Korean vessel called the Des Hung Ho, bringing missile parts for Syria, docked at Bandar Abbas in May 1992. Iran then flew these parts to Syria. An Iranian ship coming from North Korea and a second North Korean ship followed, carrying missiles and machine tools for both Syria and Iran. At least 20 of the North Korean missiles have gone to Syria from Iran, and production equipment seems to have been transferred to Iran and to Syrian plants near Hama and Aleppo.

- Iran has created shelters and tunnels in its coastal areas which it could use to store Scud and other missiles in hardened sites and reduce their vulnerability to air attack.

- Iran can now assemble Scud and Scud C missiles using foreign-made components. It may soon be able to make entire missile systems and warhead packages in Iran.

- A U.S. examination of Iran's dispersal, sheltering, and hardening programs for its anti-ship missiles and other missile systems indicates that Iran has developed effective programs to ensure that they would survive a limited number of air strikes and that Iran had reason to believe that the limited number of preemptive strikes Israel could conduct against targets in the lower Gulf could not be effective in denying Iran the capability to deploy its missiles.

- Iran is developing an indigenous missile production capability with both solid- and liquid-fueled missiles.

  - The present scale of Iran's production and assembly efforts is unclear. Iran seems to have a design center, at least two rocket and missile assembly plants, a missile test range and monitoring complex, and a wide range of smaller design and refit facilities.

  - The design center is said to be located at the Defense Technology and Science Research Center, which is a branch of Iran's Defense Industry Organization, and located outside Karaj, near Tehran. This center directs a number of other research efforts. Some experts believe it has support from Russian and Chinese scientists.

  - Iran's largest missile assembly and production plant is said to be a North Korean–built facility near Isfahan, although this plant may use Chinese equipment and technology. There are no confirmations of these reports, but this region is the center of much of Iran's advanced defense industry, including plants for munitions, tank overhaul, and helicopter and fixed wing aircraft maintenance. Some reports say the local industrial complex can produce liquid fuels and missile parts from a local steel mill.

  - A second missile plant is said to be located 175 kilometers east of Tehran, near Semnan. Some sources indicate this plant is Chinese-built and began rocket production as early as 1987. It is supposed to be able to build 600–1,000 Oghab rockets per year, if Iran can import key ingredients for solid-fuel motors like ammonium perchlorate. The plant is also supposed to produce the Iran-130.

- Another facility may exist near Bandar Abbas for the assembly of the Seer-sucker. China is said to have built this facility in 1987 and is believed to be helping the naval branch of the Guards to modify the Seersucker to extend its range to 400 kilometers. It is possible that China is also helping Iran develop solid-fuel rocket motors and produce or assemble missiles like the CS-801 and CS-802. There have, however, been reports that Iran is developing extended-range Scuds with the support of Russian experts, and a missile called the Tondar 68, with a range of 700 kilometers.

- Still other reports claim that Iran has split its manufacturing facilities into plants near Pairzan, Seman, Shiraz, Maghdad, and Islaker. These reports indicate that the companies involved in building the Scuds are also involved in Iran's production of poison gas and include Defense Industries, Shahid, Bagheri Industrial Group, and Shahid Hemat Industrial Group.

- Iran's main missile test range is said to be further east, near Shahroud, along the Tehran-Mashhad railway. A telemetry station is supposed to be 350 kilometers to the south at Taba, along the Mashhad-Isfahan road. All of these facilities are reportedly under the control of the Islamic Revolutionary Guards Corps.

- Iran is developing a new Shahab system:

  - The missile flew for a distance of up to 620 miles, before it exploded about 100 seconds after launch. U.S. intelligence sources could not confirm whether the explosion was deliberate, but indicated that the final system might have a range of 800–940 miles (a maximum of 1,240 kilometers), depending on its payload. The test confirmed the fact that the missile was a liquid-fueled system.

  - General Muhammad Bagher Qalibaf, head of the Islamic Revolutionary Guards Corps' air wing, publicly reported on August 2, 1998, that the Shahab-3 is a 53-foot-long ballistic missile that can travel at 4,300 miles per hour and carry a one-ton warhead at an altitude of nearly 82,000 feet. He claimed that the weapon was guided by an Iranian-made system that gives it great accuracy: "The final test of every weapon is in a real war situation but, given its warhead and size, the Shahab-3 is a very accurate weapon."

  - Other Iranian sources reported that the missile had a range of 800 miles. President Khatami on August 1, 1998, stated that Iran was determined to continue to strengthen its armed forces, regardless of international concerns: "Iran will not seek permission from anyone for strengthening its defense capability."

  - Martin Indyck, the U.S. assistant secretary for Near East affairs, testified on July 28 that the U.S. estimated that the system needed further refinement but might be deployed in its initial operational form between September 1998 and March 1999.

  - Iran publicly displayed the Shahab-3 on its launcher during a parade on September 25, 1998. The missile carrier bore signs saying, "The US can do nothing" and "Israel would be wiped from the map."

- There are some reports of a Shahab-3B missile with extended range and a larger booster.

- The resulting system seems to be close to both the No Dong and Pakistani Ghauri or Haff-5 missile, first tested in April 1998, raising questions about Iranian–North Korean–Pakistani cooperation.

- North Korean parades exhibiting the Tapeo Dong in September 1999 exhibited a missile with rocket motor and nozzle characteristics similar to those of the Shahab-3.

- The Shahab-3 was tested in a launch from a transporter-erector-launcher (TEL) from a new air base of the Islamic Revolutionary Guards at Mashad on February 20, 2000, and successfully demonstrated the integration of the engine and missile subsystems. Iran tested the system again in July 2000, at a nominal range of 810 miles. The missile underwent further tests in 2001 and 2002.

- Iranian sources indicate that the missile has an inertial navigation system with a CEP of 3 kilometers, making it so inaccurate that it can only be lethal against area targets using a weapon of mass destruction.

- Iran's Defense Minister Admiral Ali Shamkhani has said a larger missile, Shahab-4, was in production as a vehicle for launching satellites into space.[22]

  - U.S. experts indicated that they estimated the missile had a range of 1,300 kilometers, making it capable of hitting Israel, and that the Shahab-3 was modeled mainly on North Korea's No Dong 1, but has been improved with Russian technology. The U.S. intelligence community is divided whether Iran will sustain its current programs, and actually deploy a system capable of striking the United States.[23]

  - Iran tested a solid-state missile it called the Shahab D on September 20, 2000. The Iranian deputy defense minister, Vice Admiral Ali Shamkani, claimed that it was part of a peaceful program for launching satellites.

  - In spite of these developments, a number of U.S. intelligence officials feel the NIC report was politicized by pressure from the policy level to support the NMD program, and to not disagree with the results of the Rumsfeld Commission. They feel that Iran still faces problems in its program to build the Shahab-3, which some feel is a missile with a range of only 780 miles. At least one official has been quoted on background as stating that, "There is an Iranian threat to U.S. forces in the region, not to the continental United States."

- Israeli and U.S. intelligence sources have reported that Iran is developing the Shahab-4, with a range of 2,000 kilometers (1,250 miles), a payload of around 2,000 pounds, and a CEP of around 2,400 meters. Some estimates indicate that this system could be operational in 2–5 years.

- The U.S. Assistant Secretary for Near East Affairs testified on July 28, 1998, that the United States estimated that the system still needed added foreign assistance to improve its motors and guidance system.

- Some reports indicate that the Shahab-4 is based on the Soviet SS-4 missile.

Others that there is a longer range Shahab-5, based on the SS-4 or Tapeo Dong missile. Reports saying the Shahab is based on the SS-4 say it has a range of up to 4,000 kilometers and a payload in excess of one ton.

- It seems clear that Iran has obtained some of the technology and design details of the Russian SS-4. The SS-4 (also known as the R-12 or "Sandal") is an aging Russian liquid-fuel design that first went into service in 1959, which was supposedly destroyed as part of the IRBM Treaty. It is a very large missile, with technology dating back to the early 1950s, although it was evidently updated at least twice during the period between 1959 and 1980. It has a CEP of 2–4 kilometers and a maximum range of 2,000 kilometers, which means it can only be lethal with a nuclear warhead or a biological weapon with near-nuclear lethality.

- At the same time, the SS-4's overall technology is relatively simple and it has a throw weight of nearly 1,400 kilograms (3,000 pounds). It is one of the few missile designs that a nation with a limited technology base could hope to manufacture or adapt, and its throw weight and range would allow Iran to use a relatively unsophisticated nuclear device or biological warhead. As a result, an updated version of the SS-4 might be a suitable design for a developing country.

  - U.S. officials agree that Iran is considering developing a rocket that can put satellites in orbit, but note that the development of such a booster would give Iran significantly enhanced capabilities to develop an intercontinental ballistic missile.[24] U.S. Defense Department spokesman Ken Bacon stated, "From everything we can tell, it was a successful firing. It is another sign they are determined to build longer-range weapons of mass destruction."

  - In September 1999, the Revolutionary Guard exhibited another missile called the Zelzal, which it stated was "now in mass production." The missile was said to have taken four and one-half years to develop and to be derived from the Zelzal 2, which the IRGC had exhibited earlier. Some estimates indicate that it can carry a warhead of 500 kilograms for up to 900 kilometers. However, the missile exhibited in Tehran was a rocket on a truck-mounted launch rail that seemed more likely to have a range of 150–200 kilometers.

  - Russia has been a key supplier of missile technology.

  - Russia agreed in 1994 that it would adhere to the terms of the Missile Technology Control Regime and would place suitable limits on the sale or transfer of rocket engines and technology. Nevertheless, the CIA has identified Russia as a leading source of Iranian missile technology, and the State Department has indicated that President Clinton expressed U.S. concerns over this cooperation to President Yeltsin. This transfer is one reason the president appointed former ambassador Frank Wisner, and then Robert Galluci, as his special representatives to try to persuade Russia to put a firm halt to support of Iran.

  - Some sources have indicated that Russian military industries have signed contracts with Iran to help produce liquid-fueled missiles and provide specialized wind tunnels, manufacture model missiles, and develop specialized computer software. For example, these reports indicate that the Russian Central Aerohydrodynamic Institute is cooperating with Iran's Defense Industries Organization (DIO) and the DIO's Shahid Hemmat Industrial Group (SHIG). The Russian State Corporation for Export and Import or Armament and Military Equipment (Rosvoorouzhenie) and Infor are also reported to be involved in deals with the SHIG. These deals are also said to include specialized laser equipment, mirrors, tungsten-coated graphite material, and managing steel for missile development and production. They could play a major role in helping Iran develop long-range versions of the Scud B and C, and more accurate variations of a missile similar to the No Dong.

- On July 15, 1998, the Rumsfeld Commission reported that Iran had engines or engine designs for the Russian RD-214 rocket engine used in both Russian SS-4 and SL-7 space launch vehicles.

- Russian firms said to be helping Iran included the Russian Central Aerohydrodynamic Institute which developed a special wind tunnel; Rosvoorouzhenie, a major Russian arms-export agency; Kutznetzov (formerly NPO Trud) a rocket motor manufacturer in Samara; a leading research center called the Bauman National Technical University in Moscow, involved in developing rocket propulsion systems; the Tsagi Research Institute for rocket propulsion development; and the Polyus (Northstar) Research Institute in Moscow, a major laser test and manufacturing equipment firm. Iranians were also found to be studying rocket engineering at the Baltic State University in St. Petersburg and the Bauman State University.

- Russia was also found to have sold Iran high-strength steel and special foil for its long-range missile program. The Russian scientific and production center Inor concluded an agreement as late as September 1997 to sell Iran a factory to produce four special metal alloys used in long-range missiles. Inor's director, L. P. Chromova worked out a deal with A. Asgharzadeh, the director of an Iranian factory, to sell 620 kilograms of a special alloy called 21HKMT, and provide Iran with the capability to thermally treat the alloy for missile bodies. Iran had previously bought 240 kilograms of the alloy. Inor was also selling alloy foils called 49K2F, CUBE2, and 50N in sheets 0.2–0.4 millimeters thick for the outer body of missiles. The alloy 21HKMT was particularly interesting because North Korea also uses it in missile designs. Inor had previously brokered deals with the Shahid Hemat Industrial Group in Iran to supply maraging steel for missile cases, composite graphite-tungsten material, laser equipment, and special mirrors used in missile tests.

- Reports on Chinese transfers of ballistic missile technology provide less detail:
  - There have been past reports that Iran placed orders for PRC-made M-9 (CSS-6/DF-15) missiles (280–620 kilometers range, launch weight of 6,000 kilograms).
  - It is more likely, however, that PRC firms are giving assistance in developing indigenous missile R&D and production facilities for the production of an Iranian solid-fueled missile.
  - The United States offered to provide China with added missile technology

if it would agree to fully implement an end of technology transfer to Iran and Pakistan during meetings in Beijing on March 25–26, 1998.

- Iran has, however, acquired much of the technology necessary to build long-range cruise missile systems from China.

- Such missiles would cost only 10% to 25% as much as ballistic missiles of similar range, and both the HY-2 Seersucker and CS-802 could be modified relatively quickly for land attacks against area targets.

- Iran reported in December 1995 that it had already fired a domestically built anti-ship missile called the Saeqe-4 (Thunderbolt) during exercises in the Strait of Hormuz and Gulf of Oman. Other reports indicate that China is helping Iran build copies of the Chinese CS-801/CS-802 and the Chinese FL-2 or F-7 anti-ship cruise missiles. These missiles have relatively limited range. The range of the CS-801 is 8–40 kilometers, the range of the CS-802 is 15–120 kilometers, the maximum range of the F-7 is 30 kilometers, and the maximum range of the FL-10 is 50 kilometers. Even a range of 120 kilometers would barely cover targets in the Southern Gulf from launch points on Iran's Gulf coast. These missiles also have relatively small high explosive warheads. As a result, Iran may well be seeking anti-ship capabilities, rather than platforms for delivering weapons of mass destruction.

  - A platform like the CS-802 might, however, provide enough design data to develop a scaled-up, longer-range cruise missile for other purposes, and the Gulf is a relatively small area where most urban areas and critical facilities are near the coast. Aircraft or ships could launch cruise missiles with chemical or biological warheads from outside the normal defense perimeter of the Southern Gulf states, and it is at least possible that Iran might modify anti-ship missiles with chemical weapons to attack tankers—ships that are too large for most regular anti-ship missiles to be highly lethal.

  - Building an entire cruise missile would be more difficult. The technology for fusing CBW and cluster warheads would be within Iran's grasp. Navigation systems and jet engines, however, would still be a major potential problem. Current inertial navigation systems (INS) would introduce errors of at least several kilometers at ranges of 1,000 kilometers and would carry a severe risk of total guidance failure—probably exceeding two-thirds of the missiles fired. A differential global positioning system (GPS) integrated with the inertial navigation system (INS) and a radar altimeter, however, might produce an accuracy of 15 meters. Some existing remotely piloted vehicles (RPVs), such as the South African Skua claim such performance. Commercial technology is becoming available for differential GPS guidance with accuracies of 2–5 meters.

  - There are commercially available reciprocating and gas turbine engines that Iran could adapt for use in a cruise missile, although finding a reliable and efficient turbofan engine for a specific design application might be difficult. An extremely efficient engine would have to be matched to a specific airframe. It is doubtful that Iran could design and build such an engine, but there are over 20 other countries with the necessary design and manufacturing skills.

- While airframe-engine-warhead integration and testing would present a challenge and might be beyond Iran's manufacturing skills, it is inherently easier to integrate and test a cruise missile than a long-range ballistic missile. Further, such developments would be far less detectable than developing a ballistic system if the program used coded or low-altitude directional telemetry.
- Iran could bypass much of the problems inherent in developing its own cruise missile by modifying the HY-2 Seersucker for use as a land-attack weapon and extending its range beyond 80 kilometers, or by modifying and improving the CS-801 (Ying Jai-1) anti-ship missile. There are reports that the Revolutionary Guards are working on such developments at a facility near Bandar Abbas.
- The CIA reported in September 2001 that entities in Russia, North Korea, and China continued to supply crucial ballistic missile–related equipment, technology, and expertise to Iran. Tehran is using assistance from foreign suppliers and entities to support current development and production programs and to achieve its goal of becoming self-sufficient in the production of ballistic missiles. Iran already is producing Scud short-range ballistic missiles (SRBMs) and is in the late stages of developing the Shahab-3 medium-range ballistic missile (MRBM). Iran has built and publicly displayed prototypes for the Shahab-3 and has tested the Shahab-3 three times—July 1998, July 2000, and September 2000. In addition, Iran has publicly acknowledged the development of a Shahab-4, originally calling it a more capable ballistic missile than the Shahab-3, but later categorizing it as solely a space launch vehicle with no military applications. Iran's Defense Minister also has publicly mentioned plans for a Shahab-5. Such statements, made against the backdrop of sustained cooperation with Russian, North Korean, and Chinese entities, strongly suggest that Tehran intends to develop a longer-range ballistic missile capability.
- The CIA reported in January 2002 that:
  - Iran's missile inventory is among the largest in the Middle East and includes some 1,300-kilometer-range Shahab-3 MRBMs, a few hundred SRBMs, and a variety of unguided rockets. Tehran's long-standing commitment to its ballistic missile programs—for deterrence and war fighting—is unlikely to diminish.
  - The 1,300-kilometer-range Shahab-3 MRBM—based on the North Korean No Dong—is in the late stages of development.
  - In addition to SRBM and MRBM development, Iran is likely to develop space launch vehicles to put satellites into orbit and to establish the technical base from which it could develop IRBMs/ICBMs capable of delivering payloads to Western Europe and the United States. Iran is likely to test these vehicles initially as SLVs and not as ballistic missiles to demonstrate an inherent IRBM/ICBM capability without risking the potential political and economic costs of a long-range missile test. Iran certainly is aware of the North Korean SLV/missile program and the benefits Pyongyang has tried to gain from the inherent ICBM capability posed by the Taepo Dong 1 and 2.
  - All agencies agree that Iran could attempt to launch an ICBM/SLV about mid-decade, although most agencies believe Iran is likely to take until the

last half of the decade to do so. One agency further judges that Iran is unlikely to achieve a successful test of an ICBM before 2015.

- Iranian acquisition of complete systems or major subsystems—such as North Korean TD-2 or Russian engines—could accelerate its capability to flight-test an ICBM/SLV.

- If Iran were to acquire complete TD-2 systems from North Korea, it could conduct a flight test within a year of delivery, allowing time to construct a launch facility. Iran is unlikely to acquire complete ICBM/SLV systems from Russia.

- In contrast, a halt or substantial decrease in assistance would delay by years the development and flight-testing of these systems.

- Foreign assistance—particularly from Russia, China, and North Korea—will remain crucial to the success of the Iranian missile program for the duration of this Estimate.

Chemical Weapons

- Iran purchased large amounts of chemical defense gear from the mid-1980s onward. Iran also obtained stocks of nonlethal CS gas, although it quickly found such agents had very limited military impact since they could only be used effectively in closed areas or very small open areas.

- By 1986–1987, Iran developed the capability to produce enough lethal agents to load its own weapons. The director of the CIA and informed observers in the Gulf made it clear that Iran could produce blood agents like hydrogen cyanide, phosgene gas, and/or chlorine gas. Iran was also able to weaponize limited quantities of blister (sulfur mustard) and blood (cyanide) agents beginning in 1987, and had some capability to weaponize phosgene gas, and/or chlorine gas. These chemical agents were produced in small batches, and evidently under laboratory scale conditions, which enabled Iran to load small numbers of weapons before any of its new major production plants went into full operation.

- These gas agents were loaded into bombs and artillery shells, and were used sporadically against Iraq in 1987 and 1988.

- Reports regarding Iran's production and research facilities are highly uncertain:

  - Iran seems to have reached completion of a major poison gas plant at Qazvin, about 150 kilometers west of Tehran. This plant is reported to have been completed between November 1987 and January 1988. While supposedly a pesticide plant, the facility's true purpose seems to have been poison gas production using organophosphorous compounds.

  - It is impossible to trace all the sources of the major components and technology Iran used in its chemical weapons program during this period. Mujahideen sources claim Iran also set up a chemical bomb and warhead plant operated by the Zakaria Al-Razi chemical company near Mahshar in southern Iran, but it is unclear whether these reports are true.

- Reports that Iran had chemical weapons plants at Damghan and Parchin that began operation as early as March 1988, and may have begun to test-fire Scuds with chemical warheads as early as 1988–1989, are equally uncertain.

- Iran established at least one large research and development center under the control of the Engineering Research Centre of the Construction Crusade (Jahad e-Sazandegi), and had established a significant chemical weapons production capability by mid-1989.

- Post–Iran-Iraq War estimates of Iran chemical weapons production are uncertain:

  - U.S. experts believe Iran was beginning to produce significant mustard gas and nerve gas by the time of the August 1988 cease-fire in the Iran-Iraq War, although its use of chemical weapons remained limited and had little impact on the fighting.

  - Iran's efforts to equip plants to produce V-agent nerve gases seem to have been delayed by U.S., British, and German efforts to limit technology transfers to Iran, but Iran may have acquired the capability to produce persistent nerve gas during the mid-1990s.

  - Production of nerve gas weapons started no later than 1994.

  - Iran began to stockpile cyanide (cyanogen chloride), phosgene, and mustard gas weapons after 1985. Recent CIA testimony indicates that production capacity may approach 1,000 tons annually.

  - Weapons include bombs and artillery. Shells include 155 mm artillery and mortar rounds. Iran also has chemical bombs and mines. It may have developmental chemical warheads for its Scuds, and may have a chemical package for its 22006 RPV (doubtful).

- There are reports that Iran has deployed chemical weapons on some of its ships.

- Iran is seeking to buy more advanced chemical defense equipment, and has sought to buy specialized equipment on the world market to develop indigenous capability to produce advanced feedstocks for nerve weapons.

- CIA sources indicated in 1996 that Iran obtained 400 metric tons of chemical for use in nerve gas weapons from China—including carbon sulfide. Another report indicated that China supplied Iran with roughly two tons of calcium-hypochlorate in 1996, and loaded another 40,000 barrels in January or February of 1997. Calcium-hypochlorate is used for decontamination in chemical warfare.

- Iran placed several significant orders from China that were not delivered. Razak Industries in Tehran, and Chemical and Pharmaceutical Industries in Tabriz ordered 49 metric tons of alkyl dimethylamine, a chemical used in making detergents, and 17 tons of sodium sulfide, a chemical used in making mustard gas. The orders were never delivered, but they were brokered by Iran's International Movalled Industries Corporation (Imaco) and China's North Chemical Industries Co. (Nocinco). Both brokers have been linked to other transactions affecting Iran's chemical weapons program since early 1995, and Nocinco has supplied Iran with several hundred tons of carbon disulfide, a chemical used in nerve gas.

- Another Chinese firm, only publicly identified as Q. Chen, seems to have supplied glass vessels for chemical weapons.

- The United States imposed sanctions on seven Chinese firms in May 1997 for selling precursors for nerve gas and equipment for making nerve gas—although the United States made it clear that it had "no evidence that the Chinese government was involved." The Chinese firms were the Nanjing Chemical Industries Group and Jiangsu Yongli Chemical Engineering and Import/Export Corporation. Cheong Yee Ltd., a Hong Kong firm, was also involved. The precursors included tionyl chloride, dimethylamine, and ethylene chlorohydril. The equipment included special glass-lined vessels, and Nanjing Chemical and Industrial Group completed construction of a production plant to manufacture such vessels in Iran in June 1997.

- Iran sought to obtain impregnated Alumina, which is used to make phosphorous-oxychloride—a major component of VX and GB—from the United States. It has obtained some equipment from Israelis. Nahum Manbar, an Israeli national living in France, was convicted in an Israeli court in May 1997 for providing Iran with $16 million worth of production equipment for mustard and nerve gas during the period from 1990 to 1995.

- CIA reported in June 1997 that Iran had obtained new chemical weapons equipment technology from China and India in 1996. India is assisting in the construction of a major new plant at Qazvim, near Tehran, to manufacture phosphorous pentasulfide, a major precursor for nerve gas. The plant is fronted by Meli Agrochemicals, and the program was negotiated by Dr. Mejid Tehrani Abbaspour, a chief security advisor to Rafsanjani.

- A report by German intelligence indicates that Iran has made major efforts to acquire the equipment necessary to produce Sarin and Tabun, using the same cover of purchasing equipment for pesticide plants that Iraq used for its Sa'ad 16 plant in the 1980s. German sources note that three Indian companies—Tata Consulting Engineering, Transpek, and Rallis India—have approached German pharmaceutical and engineering concerns for such equipment and technology under conditions where German intelligence was able to trace the end user to Iran.

- Iran ratified the Chemical Weapons Convention in June 1997.
  - It submitted a statement in Farsi to the CWC secretariat in 1998, but this consisted only of questions in Farsi as to the nature of the required compliance.
  - It has not provided the CWC with details on its chemical weapons program.
- A Department of Defense report in January 2001 summarized Iranian developments as follows:
  - Iran has acceded to the Chemical Weapons Convention (CWC) and in a May 1998 session of the CWC Conference of the States Parties, Tehran, for the first time, acknowledged the existence of a past chemical weapons program.

Iran admitted developing a chemical warfare program during the latter stages of the Iran-Iraq War as a "deterrent" against Iraq's use of chemical agents against Iran. Moreover, Tehran claimed that after the 1988 cease-fire, it "terminated" its program. However, Iran has yet to acknowledge that it, too, used chemical weapons during the Iran-Iraq War.

- Nevertheless, Iran has continued its efforts to seek production technology, expertise, and precursor chemicals from entities in Russia and China that could be used to create a more advanced and self-sufficient chemical warfare infrastructure. As Iran's program moves closer to self-sufficiency, the potential will increase for Iran to export dual-use chemicals and related equipment and technologies to other countries of proliferation concern.

- In the past, Tehran has manufactured and stockpiled blister, blood, and choking chemical agents, and weaponized some of these agents into artillery shells, mortars, rockets, and aerial bombs. It also is believed to be conducting research on nerve agents. Iran could employ these agents during a future conflict in the region. Lastly, Iran's training, especially for its naval and ground forces, indicates that it is planning to operate in a contaminated environment.

- The CIA reported in September 2001 that:

  - Iran remains one of the most active countries seeking to acquire WMD and ACW technology from abroad. In doing so, Tehran is attempting to develop a domestic capability to produce various types of weapons—chemical, biological, and nuclear—and their delivery systems. During the reporting period, the evidence indicates determined Iranian efforts to acquire WMD- and ACW-related equipment, materials, and technology focused primarily on entities in Russia, China, North Korea, and Western Europe.

  - Iran, a Chemical Weapons Convention (CWC) States party, already has manufactured and stockpiled chemical weapons—including blister, blood, choking, and probably nerve agents, and the bombs and artillery shells for delivering them. During the second half of 2000, Tehran continued to seek production technology, training, expertise, equipment, and chemicals that could be used as precursor agents in its chemical warfare (CW) program from entities in Russia and China.

  - Prior to the reporting period, Chinese firms had supplied dual-use CW-related production equipment and technology to Iran. The U.S. sanctions imposed in May 1997 on seven Chinese entities for knowingly and materially contributing to Iran's CW program remain in effect. Evidence during the current reporting period shows Iran continues to seek such assistance from Chinese entities, but it is unclear to what extent these efforts have succeeded.

Biological Weapons

- An Iranian weapons effort was documented as early as 1982. Reports surfaced that Iran had imported suitable type cultures from Europe and was working on the production of mycotoxins—a relatively simple family of biological agents that require only limited laboratory facilities for small-scale production.

- U.S. intelligence sources reported in August 1989 that Iran was trying to buy two new strains of fungus from Canada and the Netherlands that can be used to produce mycotoxins. German sources indicated that Iran had successfully purchased such cultures several years earlier.

- The Imam Reza Medical Center at Mashhad Medical Sciences University and the Iranian Research Organization for Science and Technology were identified as the end users for this purchasing effort, but it is likely that the true end user was an Iranian government agency specializing in biological warfare.

- Many experts believe that the Iranian biological weapons effort was placed under the control of the Islamic Revolutionary Guards Corps, which is known to have tried to purchase suitable production equipment for such weapons.

- Since the Iran-Iraq War, Iran has conducted research on more lethal active agents like anthrax, hoof and mouth disease, and biotoxins. In addition, Iranian groups have repeatedly approached various European firms for the equipment and technology necessary to work with these diseases and toxins.

  - Unclassified sources of uncertain reliability have identified a facility at Damghan as working on both biological and chemical weapons research and production, and believe that Iran may be producing biological weapons at a pesticide facility near Tehran.

  - Some universities and research centers may be linked to biological weapons programs.

  - Reports surfaced in the spring of 1993 that Iran had succeeded in obtaining advanced biological weapons technology in Switzerland and containment equipment and technology from Germany. According to these reports, this led to serious damage to computer facilities in a Swiss biological research facility by unidentified agents. Similar reports indicated that agents had destroyed German biocontainment equipment destined for Iran.

  - More credible reports by U.S. experts indicate that Iran has begun to stockpile anthrax and botulinum in a facility near Tabriz, can now mass manufacture such agents, and has them in an aerosol form. None of these reports, however, can be verified.

  - The CIA has reported that Iran has "sought dual-use biotech equipment from Europe and Asia, ostensibly for civilian use." It also reported in 1996 that Iran might be ready to deploy biological weapons. Beyond this point, little unclassified information exists regarding the details of Iran's effort to "weaponize" and produce biological weapons.

  - Iran may have the production technology to make dry storable and aerosol weapons. This would allow it to develop suitable missile warheads and bombs and covert devices.

  - Iran may have begun active weapons production in 1996, but probably only at a limited scale suitable for advanced testing and development.

  - CIA testimony indicates that Iran is believed to have weaponized both live agents and toxins for artillery and bombs and may be pursuing biological warheads for its missiles. The CIA reported in 1996, "We believe that Iran holds some stocks of biological agents and weapons. Tehran probably has investigated both toxins and live organisms as biological warfare agents. Iran has the technical infrastructure to support a significant biological weapons program with little foreign assistance."

- The CIA reported in June 1997 that Iran had obtained new dual-use technology from China and India during 1996.

- Iran announced in June 1997 that it would not produce or employ chemical weapons including toxins.

- The CIA estimated in January 1999 that Iran continued to pursue purchasing dual-use biotechnical equipment from Russia and other countries, ostensibly for civilian uses. Its biological warfare (BW) program began during the Iran-Iraq War, and Iran may have some limited capability for BW deployment. Outside assistance is both important and difficult to prevent, given the dual-use nature of the materials and equipment being sought and the many legitimate end uses for these items.

- Russia remains a key source of biotechnology for Iran. Russia's world-leading expertise in biological weapons makes it an attractive target for Iranians seeking technical information and training on BW agent production processes.

- The DCI Nonproliferation Center (NPC) reported in February 2000 that Tehran continued to seek considerable dual-use biotechnical equipment from entities in Russia and Western Europe, ostensibly for civilian uses. Iran began a biological warfare (BW) program during the Iran-Iraq War, and it may have some limited capability for BW deployment. Outside assistance is both important and difficult to prevent, given the dual-use nature of the materials, the equipment being sought, and the many legitimate end uses for these items.

- A Department of Defense report in January 2001 reported that Iran has a growing biotechnology industry, significant pharmaceutical experience and the overall infrastructure to support its biological warfare program. Tehran has expanded its efforts to seek considerable dual-use biotechnical materials and expertise from entities in Russia and elsewhere, ostensibly for civilian reasons. Outside assistance is important for Iran, and it is also difficult to prevent because of the dual-use nature of the materials and equipment being sought by Iran and the many legitimate end uses for these items. Iran's biological warfare program began during the Iran-Iraq War. Iran is believed to be pursuing offensive biological warfare capabilities and its effort may have evolved beyond agent research and development to the capability to produce small quantities of agent. Iran has ratified the BWC.

- The CIA reported in September 2001, "Tehran continued its efforts to seek considerable dual-use biotechnical materials, equipment, and expertise from abroad—primarily from entities in Russia and Western Europe—ostensibly for civilian uses. We judge that this equipment and know-how could be applied to Iran's biological warfare (BW) program. Iran probably began its offensive BW program during the Iran-Iraq War, and it may have some limited capability for BW deployment."

Nuclear Weapons

- The Shah established the Atomic Energy Organization of Iran in 1974, and rapidly began to negotiate for nuclear power plants.

- He concluded an extendible ten-year nuclear fuel contract with the United States in 1974, with Germany in 1976, and France in 1977.

- In 1975, he purchased a 10% share in a Eurodif uranium enrichment plant being built at Tricastin in France that was part of a French, Belgian, Spanish, and Italian consortium. Under the agreement the Shah signed, Iran was to have full access to the enrichment technology Eurodif developed, and agreed to buy a quota of enriched uranium from the new plant.

- He created an ambitious plan calling for a network of 23 power reactors throughout Iran that was to be operating by the mid-1990s, and sought to buy nuclear power plants from Germany and France.

- By the time the Shah fell in January 1979, he had six reactors under contract, and was attempting to purchase a total of 12 nuclear power plants from Germany, France, and the United States. Two 1,300-megawatt German nuclear power plants at Bushehr were already 60% and 75% completed, and site preparation work had begun on the first of two 935-megawatt French plants at Darkhouin that were to be supplied by Framatome.

- The Shah also started a nuclear weapons program in the early to mid-1970s, building upon his major reactor projects, investment in URENCO, and smuggling of nuclear enrichment and weapons-related technology from the United States and Europe.
  - 5-megawatt light water research reactor operating in Tehran.
  - 27-kilowatt neutron-source reactor operating in Isfahan.
  - Started two massive 1,300-megawatt reactor complexes.
  - The Shah attempted to covertly import controlled technology from the United States.
  - U.S. experts believe the nuclear weapons research program was centered at the Amirabad Nuclear Research Center. This research effort included studies of weapons designs and plutonium recovery from spent reactor fuel.

- In 1984, Khomeini revived the nuclear weapons program begun under the Shah.

- Some experts feel that the IRGC moved experts and equipment from the Amirabad Nuclear Research Center to a new nuclear weapons research facility near Isfahan in the mid-1980s, and formed a new nuclear research center at the University of Isfahan in 1984—with French assistance. Unlike many Iranian facilities, the center at Isfahan was not declared to the IAEA until February 1992, when the IAEA was allowed to make a cursory inspection of six sites that various reports had claimed were the location of Iran's nuclear weapons efforts.

- Iran received significant West German and Argentine corporate support in some aspects of nuclear technology during the Iran-Iraq War.

- It has received limited transfers of centrifuge and other weapons-related technology from PRC, possibly Pakistan.

- It has a Chinese-supplied heavy water, zero-power research reactor at Isfahan Nuclear Research Center, and two Chinese-supplied sub-critical assemblies— a light water and graphite design.

- It has stockpiles of uranium and mines in the Yazd area. It may have had a uranium ore concentration facility at University of Tehran, but status unclear.

- Iran may have opened a new uranium ore processing plant close to its Shagand uranium mine in March 1990, and it seems to have extended its search for uranium ore into three additional areas. Iran may have also begun to exploit stocks of yellow cake that the Shah had obtained from South Africa in the late 1970s while obtaining uranium dioxide from Argentina by purchasing it through Algeria.

- Iran began to show a renewed interest in laser isotope separation (LIS) in the mid-1980s, and held a conference on LIS in September 1987.

- Iran opened a new nuclear research center in Isfahan in 1984, located about 4 kilometers outside the city and between the villages of Shahrida and Fulashans. This facility was built at a scale far beyond the needs of peaceful research, and Iran sought French and Pakistani help for a new research reactor for this center.

- The Khomeini government may have obtained several thousand pounds of uranium dioxide from Argentina by purchasing it through Algeria. Uranium dioxide is considerably more refined than yellow cake, and is easier to use in irradiating material in a reactor to produce plutonium.

- The status of Iran's nuclear program since the Iran-Iraq War is highly controversial, and Iran has denied the existence of such a program.

  - On February 7, 1990, the speaker of the Majlis publicly toured the Atomic Energy Organization of Iran and opened the new Jabir Ibn al Hayyan laboratory to train Iranian nuclear technicians. Reports then surfaced that Iran had at least 200 scientists and a work force of about 2,000 devoted to nuclear research.

  - Iran's Deputy President Ayatollah Mohajerani stated in October 1991, that Iran should work with other Islamic states to create an "Islamic bomb."

  - The Iranian government has repeatedly made proposals to create a nuclear-free zone in the Middle East. For example, President Rafsanjani was asked if Iran had a nuclear weapons program in an interview the CBS program *60 Minutes* in February 1997. He replied, "Definitely not. I hate this weapon."

  - Other senior Iranian leaders, including President Khatami have made similar categorical denials. Iran's new Foreign Minister, Kamal Kharrazi, stated on October 5, 1997, "We are certainly not developing an atomic bomb, because we do not believe in nuclear weapons. . . . We believe in and promote the idea of the Middle East as a region free of nuclear weapons and other weapons of mass destruction. But why are we interested to develop nuclear technology? We need to diversify our energy sources. In a matter of a few decades, our oil and gas reserves would be finished and therefore, we need access to other sources of energy . . . Furthermore, nuclear technology has many other utilities in medicine and agriculture. The case of the United States in terms of oil reserve is not different from Iran's. The United States also has large oil resources, but at the same time they have nuclear power plants. So there is nothing wrong with having access to nuclear technology if it is for peaceful purposes."

- The IAEA reports that Iran has fully complied with its present requirements, and that it has found no indications of nuclear weapons effort, but IAEA only inspects Iran's small research reactors.

  - The IAEA visits to other Iranian sites are not inspections, and do not use instruments, cameras, seals, etc.—they are informal walk-throughs.

  - The IAEA visited five suspect Iranian facilities in 1992 and 1993 in this manner, but did not conduct full inspections.

  - Iran has not had any 93+2 inspections and its position on improved inspections is that it will not be either the first or the last to have them.

- These are reasons to assume that Iran still has a nuclear program:

  - Iran attempted to buy highly enriched fissile material from Kazakhstan. The United States paid between $20 million and $30 million to buy 1,300 pounds of highly enriched uranium from the Ust-Kamenogorsk facility in Kazakhstan that Iran may have sought to acquire in 1992. A total of 120 pounds of the material—enough for two bombs—cannot be fully accounted for.

  - Iran has imported maraging steel, sometimes used for centrifuges, by smuggling it in through dummy fronts. Britain intercepted a 110-pound (50 kilogram) shipment in August 1996. Seems to have centrifuge research program at Sharif University of Technology in Tehran. IAEA "visit" did not confirm.

  - Those aspects of Iran's program that are visible indicate that Iran has had only uncertain success. Argentina agreed to train Iranian technicians at its Jose Balaseiro Nuclear Institute, and sold Iran $5.5 million worth of uranium for its small Amirabad Nuclear Research Center reactor in May 1987. A CENA team visited Iran in late 1987 and early 1988, and seems to have discussed selling Iran the technology necessary to operate its reactor with 20% enriched uranium as a substitute for the highly enriched core provided by the United States, and possibly uranium enrichment and plutonium reprocessing technology as well. Changes in Argentina's government, however, made it much less willing to support proliferation. The Argentine government announced in February 1992 that it was canceling an $18 million nuclear technology sale to Iran because it had not signed a nuclear safeguards arrangement. Argentine press sources suggested, however, that Argentina was reacting to U.S. pressure.

  - In February 1990, a Spanish paper reported that Associated Enterprises of Spain was negotiating the completion of the two nuclear power plants at Bushehr. Another Spanish firm called ENUSA (National Uranium Enterprises) was to provide the fuel, and Kraftwerke Union (KWU) would be involved. Later reports indicated that a 10-man delegation from Iran's Ministry of Industry was in Madrid negotiating with the director of Associated Enterprises, Adolofo Garcia Rodriguez.

- Iran negotiated with Kraftwerke Union and CENA of Germany in the late 1980s and early 1990s. Iran attempted to import reactor parts from Siemens in Germany and Skoda in Czechoslovakia. None of these efforts solved Iran's problems in rebuilding its reactor program, but all demonstrate the depth of its interest.

- Iran took other measures to strengthen its nuclear program during the early 1990s. It installed a cyclotron from Ion Beam Applications in Belgium at a facility in Karzaj in 1991.

- Iran conducted experiments in uranium enrichment and centrifuge technology at its Sharif University of Technology in Tehran. Sharif University was also linked to efforts to import cylinders of fluorine suitable for processing enriched material, and attempts to import specialized magnets that can be used for centrifuges, from Thyssen in Germany in 1991.

- In 1992, Iran attempted to buy beryllium from a storage site in Kazakhstan that also was storing 600 kilograms of highly enriched uranium. These contacts then seem to have expanded to an attempt to try the material. In 1994, they helped lead the United States to buy the enriched material and fly it out of the country.

- It is clear from Iran's imports that it has sought centrifuge technology ever since. Although many of Iran's efforts have never been made public, British customs officials seized 110 pounds of maraging steel being shipped to Iran in July 1996.

- Iran seems to have conducted research into plutonium separation and Iranians published research on uses of tritium that had applications to nuclear weapons boosting. Iran also obtained a wide range of U.S. and other nuclear literature with applications for weapons designs. Italian inspectors seized 8 steam condensers bound for Iran that could be used in a covert reactor program in 1993, and high technology ultrasound equipment suitable for reactor testing at the port of Bari in January 1994.

- Other aspects of Iran's nuclear research effort had potential weapons applications. Iran continued to operate an Argentine-fueled 5-megawatt light water highly enriched uranium reactor at the University of Tehran. It is operated by a Chinese-supplied neutron source research reactor, and sub-critical assemblies with 900 grams of highly enriched uranium, at its Isfahan Nuclear Research Center. This center has experimented with a heavy water zero-power reactor, a light water sub-critical reactor, and a graphite sub-critical reactor. In addition, it may have experimented with some aspects of nuclear weapons design.

- Iran claims it eventually needs to build enough nuclear reactors to provide 20% of its electric power. This Iranian nuclear power program presents serious problems in terms of proliferation. Although the reactors are scarcely ideal for irradiating material to produce Plutonium or cannibalizing the core, they do provide Iran with the technology base to make its own reactors, have involved other technology transfer helpful to Iran in proliferating and can be used to produce weapons if Iran rejects IAEA safeguards.

- Russia has agreed to build up to 4 reactors, beginning with a complex at

Bushehr—with two 1,000–1,200 megawatt reactors and two 465-megawatt reactors, and provide significant nuclear technology. Russia has consistently claimed the light water reactor designs for Bushehr cannot be used to produce weapons-grade plutonium and are similar to the reactors the United States is providing to North Korea. The United States has claimed, however, that Victor Mikhaliov, the head of Russia's Atomic Energy Ministry, proposed the sale of a centrifuge plant in April 1995. The United States also indicated that it had persuaded Russia not to sell Iran centrifuge technology as part of the reactor deal during the summit meeting between Presidents Clinton and Yeltsin in May 1995.

- It was only after U.S. pressure that Russia publicly stated that it never planned to sell centrifuge and advanced enrichment technology to Iran, and Iran denied that it had ever been interested in such technology. For example, Muhammad Sadegh Ayatollahi, Iran's representative to the IAEA, stated that, "We've had contracts before for the Bushehr plant in which we agreed that the spent fuel would go back to the supplier. For our contract with the Russians and Chinese, it is the same." According to some reports, Russia was to reprocess the fuel at its Mayak plant near Chelyabinsk in the Urals, and could store it at an existing facility, at Krasnoyarsk-26 in southern Siberia.

- Russia indicated that it would go ahead with selling two more reactors for construction at Bushehr within the next five years.

- The first 1,000-megawatt reactor at Bushehr has experienced serious construction delays. In March 1998, Russia and Iran agreed to turn the construction project into a turnkey plant because the Iranian firms working on infrastructure had fallen well behind schedule. In February, Iran had agreed to fund improved safety systems. The reactor is reported to be on a 30-month completion cycle.

- The CIA reported in January 1999 that Russia remained a key supplier for civilian nuclear programs in Iran and, to a lesser extent, India. With respect to Iran's nuclear infrastructure, Russian assistance would enhance Iran's ability to support a nuclear weapons development effort. Such assistance is less likely to significantly advance India's effort, given that India's nuclear weapons program is more mature. By its very nature, even the transfer of civilian technology may be of use in the nuclear weapons programs of these countries.

- The CIA warned in January 2000 that Russia might have sold Iran heavy water and graphite technology.

- The control of fissile material in the FSU remains a major problem:

  - U.S. estimates indicate the FSU left a legacy of some 1,485 tons of nuclear material. This includes 770 tons in some 27,000 weapons, including 816 strategic bombs, 5,434 missile warheads, and about 20,000 theater and tactical weapons. In addition, there were 715 tons of fissile or near-fissile material in 8 countries of the FSU in over 50 sites: enough to make 35,000–40,000 bombs.

  - China is reported to have agreed to provide significant nuclear technology transfer and possible sale of two 300-megawatt pressurized water reactors in the early 1990s, but then to have agreed to halt nuclear assistance to Iran after pressure from the United States.

- Iran signed an agreement with China's Commission on Science, Technology, and Industry for National Defense on January 21, 1991, to build a small, 27-kilowatt research reactor at Iran's nuclear weapons research facility at Isfahan. On November 4, 1991, China stated that it had signed commercial cooperation agreements with Iran in 1989 and 1991, and that it would transfer an electromagnetic isotope separator (Calutron) and a smaller nuclear reactor, for "peaceful and commercial" purposes.

- The Chinese reactor and Calutron were small research-scale systems and had no direct value in producing fissile material. They did, however, give Iran more knowledge of reactor and enrichment technology, and U.S. experts believe that China provided Iran with additional data on chemical separation, other enrichment technology, the design for facilities to convert uranium to uranium hexaflouride to make reactor fuel, and help in processing yellow cake.

- China pledged in October 1997 not to engage in any new nuclear cooperation with Iran but said it would complete cooperation on two ongoing nuclear projects, a small research reactor and a zirconium production facility at Isfahan that Iran will use to produce cladding for reactor fuel. The pledge appears to be holding. As a party to the Nuclear Nonproliferation Treaty (NPT), Iran is required to apply IAEA safeguards to nuclear fuel, but safeguards are not required for the zirconium plant or its products.

- The United States put intense pressure on China to halt such transfers. President Clinton and Chinese President Jiang Zemin reached an agreement at an October 1997 summit. China strengthened this pledge in negotiations with the United States in February 1998.

- In March 1998, the United States found that the China Nuclear Energy Corporation was negotiating to sell Iran several hundred tons of anhydrous hydrogen fluoride (AHF) to Isfahan Nuclear Research Corporation in central Iran, a site where some experts believe Iran is working on the development of nuclear weapons. AHF can be used to separate plutonium, help refine yellow cake into uranium hexaflouride to produce U-235, and as a feedstock for Sarin. It is on two nuclear control lists. China agreed to halt the sale. Iran denied that China had halted nuclear cooperation on March 15, 1998. Even so, the United States acting under secretary of state for arms control and international security affairs stated that China was keeping its pledge not to aid Iran on March 26, 1998.

- The CIA reported in January 1999 that China continued to take steps to strengthen its control over nuclear exports. China promulgated new export control regulations in June 1998 that cover the sale of dual-use nuclear equipment. This follows on the heels of the September 1997 promulgation of controls covering the export of equipment and materials associated exclusively with nuclear applications. These export controls should give the Chinese government greater accounting and control of the transfer of equipment, materials, and technology to nuclear programs in countries of concern.

- U.S. estimates of Iran's progress in acquiring nuclear weapons have changed over time.
  - In 1992, the CIA estimated that Iran would have the bomb by the year 2000. In 1995, John Holum testified that Iran could have the bomb by 2003.
  - In 1997, after two years in which Iran might have made progress, he testified that Iran could have the bomb by 2005–2007.
  - In 1999, the NIE on proliferation estimated that Iran could test a missile that could reach the United States by 2010, but did not change the 1997 estimate or when Iran might acquire a bomb.
  - In early 2000, the *New York Times* reported that the CIA had warned that Iran might now be able to maker a nuclear weapon. The assessment stated that the CIA could not monitor Iran closely enough to be certain whether Iran had acquired fissile material from an outside source.
  - U.S. experts increasingly refer to Iran's efforts as "creeping proliferation" and there is no way to tell when or if Iranian current efforts will produce a weapon, and unclassified lists of potential facilities have little credibility.
  - Timing of weapons acquisition depends heavily on whether Iran can buy fissile material—if so it has the design capability and can produce weapons in 1–2 years—or must develop the capability to process plutonium or enrich uranium—in which case, it is likely to be 5–10 years.
  - George Tenet, the director of the CIA, testified before the Senate Foreign Relations Committee on March 20, 2000, and stated, "We are concerned about the potential for states and terrorists to acquire plutonium, highly enriched uranium, and other fissile materials, and even complete nuclear weapons. . . . Iran or Iraq could quickly advance their nuclear aspirations through covert acquisition of fissile material or relevant technology."
- A Department of Defense report in January 2001 reported:
  - Although a signatory to NPT and the CTBT, Iran also is seeking fissile material and technology for weapons development through an elaborate system of military and civilian organizations. We believe Iran also has an organized structure dedicated to developing nuclear weapons by trying to establish the capability to produce both plutonium and highly enriched uranium. Iran claims to desire the establishment of a complete nuclear fuel cycle for its civilian energy program. In that guise, it seeks to obtain whole facilities that could be used in numerous ways in support of efforts to produce fissile material for a nuclear weapon. The potential availability of black market fissile material also might provide Iran a way to acquire the fissile material necessary for a nuclear weapon.
  - Iran's success in achieving a nuclear capability will depend, to a large degree, on the supply policies of Russia and China or on Iran's successful illicit acquisition of adequate quantities of weapons-usable fissile material. Russia is continuing work on a 1,000-megawatt power reactor at Bushehr. Although Russian officials have provided assurances that Russian cooperation with Iran will be limited to the Bushehr reactor project during the period of its construction, the U.S. government is aware that a number of

Russian entities are engaged in cooperation with Iran that goes beyond this project. One of Iran's primary goals is the acquisition of a heavy water-moderated, natural uranium-fueled nuclear reactor and associated facilities suitable for the production of weapons-grade plutonium. Although Bushehr will fall under IAEA safeguards, Iran is using this project to seek access to more sensitive nuclear technologies from Russia and to develop expertise in related nuclear technologies. Any such projects will help Iran augment its nuclear technology infrastructure, which in turn would be useful in supporting nuclear weapons research and development.

- In the past, Chinese companies have been major suppliers of nuclear-related facilities and technology albeit under IAEA safeguards. China pledged in 1997 that it would not undertake any new nuclear cooperation with Iran and that it would close out its two existing projects—a small research reactor and a zirconium production facility, which will produce cladding for nuclear fuel—as soon as possible. (Neither of these two projects poses a significant proliferation concern.) China also agreed to terminate cooperation on a uranium conversion project. This project would have allowed Iran to produce uranium hexafluoride or uranium dioxide, which are the feedstock materials for the manufacture of weapons-grade plutonium. In addition, China announced new export controls in June 1998 that cover the sale of dual-use nuclear equipment. China appears to be living up to its 1997 commitments.

- The CIA reported in September 2001:

  - Iran sought nuclear-related equipment, material, and technical expertise from a variety of sources, especially in Russia. Work continues on the construction of a 1,000-megawatt nuclear power reactor at Bushehr that will be subject to International Atomic Energy Agency (IAEA) safeguards. In addition, Russian entities continued to interact with Iranian research centers on various activities. These projects will help Iran augment its nuclear technology infrastructure, which in turn would be useful in supporting nuclear weapons research and development. The expertise and technology gained, along with the commercial channels and contacts established—particularly through the Bushehr nuclear power plant project—could be used to advance Iran's nuclear weapons research and development program.

  - Beginning in January 1998, the Russian Government took a number of steps to increase its oversight of entities involved in dealings with Iran and other states of proliferation concern. In 1999, it pushed a new export control law through the Duma. Russian firms, however, faced economic pressures to circumvent these controls and did so in some cases. The Russian Government, moreover, failed to enforce its export controls in some cases regarding Iran. A component of the Russian Ministry of Atomic Energy (MINATOM) contracted with Iran to provide equipment clearly intended for Atomic Vapor Laser Isotope Separation (AVLIS). The laser equipment was to have been delivered in late 2000 but continues to be held up as a result of U.S. protests. AVLIS technology could provide Iran the means to produce weapons quantities of highly enriched uranium.

- The Russian Government's commitment, willingness, and ability to curb pro-liferation-related transfers remain uncertain. The export control bureaucracy was reorganized again as part of President Putin's broader government re-organization in May 2000. The Federal Service for Currency and Export Controls (VEK) was abolished and its functions assumed by a new depart-ment in the Ministry of Economic Development and Trade. VEK had been tasked with drafting the implementing decrees for Russia's July 1999 export control law; the status of these decrees is not known. Export enforcement continues to need improvement. In February 2000, Sergey Ivanov, then Sec-retary of Russia's Security Council, said that during 1998–1999 the gov-ernment had obtained convictions for unauthorized technology transfers in three cases. The Russian press has reported on cases where advanced equip-ment is simply described as something else in the export documentation and is exported. Enterprises sometimes falsely declare goods to avoid govern-ment taxes.

- China pledged in October 1997 to halt cooperation on a uranium conver-sion facility (UCF) and not to engage in any new nuclear cooperation with Iran but said it would complete cooperation on two nuclear projects: a small research reactor and a zirconium production facility at Isfahan that Iran will use to produce cladding for reactor fuel. As a party to the Nuclear Non-proliferation Treaty (NPT), Iran is required to apply IAEA safeguards to nuclear fuel, but safeguards are not required for the zirconium plant or its products. Although the Chinese appear to have lived up to these commit-ments, we are aware of some interactions between Chinese and Iranian entities that have raised questions about its "no new nuclear cooperation" pledge. According to the State Department, the Administration is seeking to address these questions with appropriate Chinese authorities.

- Iran has attempted to use its civilian energy program, which is quite modest in scope, to justify its efforts to establish domestically or otherwise acquire assorted nuclear fuel-cycle capabilities. But such capabilities can also sup-port fissile material production for a weapons program, and we believe it is this objective that drives Iran's efforts to acquire relevant facilities. For example, Iran has sought to obtain turnkey facilities, such as the UCF, that ostensibly would be used to support fuel production for the Bushehr power plant. But the UCF could be used in any number of ways to support fissile material production needed for a nuclear weapon—specifically, production of uranium hexafluoride for use as a feedstock for uranium enrichment operations and production of uranium compounds suitable for use as fuel in a plutonium production reactor. In addition, we suspect that Tehran most likely is interested in acquiring foreign fissile material and technology for weapons development as part of its overall nuclear weapons program.

- The CIA estimated in January 2002 that the U.S. "Intelligence Community judges that Iran does not yet have a nuclear weapon. Most agencies assess that Tehran could have one by the end of the decade, although one agency judges it will take longer. All agree that Iran could reduce this time frame by several years with foreign assistance. Iran has biological and chemical weapons programs."

Missile Defenses

- Seeking Russian S-300 or S-400 surface-to-air missile system with limited anti-tactical ballistic missile capability.

NOTES

1. The discussion of Saudi attitudes and many of the details of the Saudi effort are based largely on interviews in Saudi Arabia in 2000 and 2001, and discussions with U.S. experts.

2. Associated Press, May 12, 1997, 0251; *Defense News*, April 8, 1991, p. 1; *Defense and Foreign Affairs Weekly*, November 28, 1988, p. 1; *Washington Post*, September 20, 1988, p. A-8; *Jane's Defence Weekly*, October 1, 1988, pp. 744–755.

3. CIA, August 10, 2000, "Unclassified Report to Congress on the Acquisition of Technology Relating to Weapons of Mass Destruction and Advanced Conventional Munitions, 1 July Through 31 December 1999," Internet edition.

4. According to some reports, General Tommy Franks, the commander of USCENTCOM, has made such preemptive strikes part of his contingency planning. See John Henderson, "In Iraq, US Faces New Dynamics," *Los Angeles Times*, July 6, 2001, p. 1.

5. For a discussion of some of these issues, see Christopher J. Bowie, "Destroying Mobile Ground Targets in an Anti-Access Environment," Analysis Center Papers, Northrup Grumman, December 2001; and Vernon Loeb, "US Gains in Attacking Mobile Arms," *Washington Post*, July 5, 2002, p. A-14.

6. Associated Press, May 12, 1997, 0251; *Jane's Defence Weekly*, July 30, 1997, p. 17.

7. *Jane's Defence Weekly*, October 1, 1988, pp. 744–755, July 30, 1997, p. 17; Associated Press, May 12, 1997, 0251.

8. *Washington Times*, October 4, 1988, p. A-2; *Christian Science Monitor*, October 8, 1988, p. 2.

9. *Jane's Defence Weekly*, July 30, 1997, p. 17.

10. *Jane's Defence Weekly*, October 1, 1990, pp. 744–746.

11. Associated Press, May 12, 1997, 0251.

12. Shuey, Lenhart, Snyder, Donnelley, Mielke, and Moteff, *Missile Proliferation: Survey of Emerging Missile Forces* (Washington, DC: Congressional Research Service, Report 88-642F, February 9, 1989), pp. 64–65.

13. The warhead could also be enhanced with submunitions, a proximity fuse to detonate before impact to give an optimum burst pattern and widen the area covered by shrapnel, and a time delay fuse to allow the warhead to fully penetrate a building before exploding. Shuey, Lenhart, Snyder, Donnelley, Mielke, and Moteff, *Missile Proliferation: Survey of Emerging Missile Forces*, pp. 23–24.

14. U.S. experts have never monitored a test of the conventional version of the missile. CEP stands for "circular error probable," and is an indication of a missile's

accuracy. The figure represents the radius of a circle in which half the warheads are expected to fall. It should be noted, however, that the theoretical figures apply only to missiles that operate perfectly up to the point that the missile has left the launcher and at least its first booster and guidance system are operating perfectly. Operational CEPs can only be "guesstimated," but will be much lower. Missiles generally do not have fail-safe warheads. A substantial number will have partial failures and deliver their warhead far from their intended targets. *Jane's Defence Weekly*, October 1, 1990, pp. 744–746; Fred Donovan, "Mideast Missile Flexing," *Arms Control Today* (May 1990), p. 31; Shuey, Lenhart, Snyder, Donnelley, Mielke, and Moteff, *Missile Proliferation: Survey of Emerging Missile Forces*.

15. *Jane's Defence Weekly*, October 1, 1990, pp. 744–746, July 30, 1997, p. 17; Donovan, "Mideast Missile Flexing," p. 31; Shuey, Lenhart, Snyder, Donnelley, Mielke, and Moteff, *Missile Proliferation: Survey of Emerging Missile Forces*.

16. *Defense News*, October 17, 1994; Letter to Honorable Rondal H. Brown, October 6, 1994, by sixty-three U.S. senators.

17. *Defense News*, March 17, 1997, p. 3; Associated Press, May 12, 1997, 0251; *Jane's Defence Weekly*, July 30, 1997, p. 17.

18. *Jane's Defence Weekly*, June 16, 1999, p. 14.

19. *New York Times*, February 1, 2000.

20. London *Sunday Times,* February 21, 2000.

21. CIA, August 10, 2000, Unclassified Report to Congress on the Acquisition of Technology Relating to Weapons of Mass Destruction and Advanced Conventional Munitions, 1 July Through 31 December 1999; Internet edition.

22. Associated Press, July 15, 2000, 0935; Reuters, July 15, 2000, 0714.

23. Associated Press, July 15, 2000, 0935; Reuters, July 15, 2000, 0714.

24. Elaine Sciolino and Steven Lee Myers, "U.S. Study Reopens Division Over Nuclear Missile Threat," *New York Times*, July 4, 2000.

Chapter 11

Saudi Arabian Security at the Start of the Twenty-First Century

Saudi Arabia faces major security problems as it enters the twenty-first century. These problems include a wide range of external challenges such as Iran and Iraq, proliferation, Islamic extremism, counterterrorism, the threat of asymmetric warfare, improving cooperation with the Southern Gulf states, and restructuring the Kingdom's alliance with the United States and the West. At the same time, Saudi Arabia must preserve its internal security and cope with the ongoing challenges of force transformation in a climate where funding constraints are becoming steadily more serious.

The previous chapters have shown that Saudi Arabia must redefine many aspects of its security structure to meet these challenges. It must find ways to bring the Saudi force posture into better balance, to improve Saudi planning, and to ensure that modernization does not outpace readiness and sustainability. However, Saudi Arabia needs to do more than make its military forces more effective; it needs to continue to explore the possibility that Iran may emerge as a moderate and pragmatic state, and it must look beyond the containment of Iraq. It cannot ignore the problems posed by Iranian and Iraqi conventional forces and proliferation. It needs to strengthen the GCC, and focus on stronger joint security efforts and interoperability with Bahrain and Kuwait. It needs to create a more stable partnership with the United States that is less sensitive to the level of the U.S. presence in the Kingdom and the backlash from the Arab-Israeli conflict and Second Intifada.

At the same time, the previous chapters have also shown that the Kingdom should be able to cope with all of its security challenges if it pursues the right policies. While significant, the threats and security problems the Kingdom faces can all be dealt with over time. Saudi Arabia needs to change its military posture in some areas and tighten its strategic focus in others, but it is scarcely a fragile state or one without strengths and allies.

SAUDI MILITARY DEVELOPMENT

Saudi Arabia has succeeded in using its wealth to create modern military forces, ones that fought effectively against first-line Iraqi forces in the Gulf War. Saudi Arabia is by far the strongest and most modern military power in the Southern Gulf, and the only force large enough to provide the support, training, C^{4}I/BM, and other specialized capabilities necessary to sustain modern land-air combat and provide the infrastructure for effective regional cooperation. Its military forces are now strong enough to deal with many low-intensity contingencies and limit the amount of U.S. reinforcements needed in low-intensity contingencies.

Yet Saudi Arabia does remain vulnerable to threats from Iran and Iraq. It badly needs to strengthen its cooperative defense arrangements with its Southern Gulf neighbors. Even then, it must continue to rely on U.S. support to secure itself against an all-out Iraqi attack. The Gulf War has left Iraq a revanchist state, with much of its army intact and the capability to overrun Kuwait's military forces in a matter of days regardless of Kuwait's present force-improvement plans.

Iran may be moving toward moderation, but Saudi Arabia cannot ignore its conventional military capabilities or efforts to proliferate. Saudi Arabia is within five to seven minutes flying time from Iran, from the earliest point of detection by an AWACS to over-flying key Saudi targets on the Gulf coast. Missile attacks would offer even less warning and present more problems for defense. While Iran cannot bring the bulk of its land power to bear without major increases in amphibious lift, it can bring naval and air pressure to bear on tanker and air traffic through the Gulf and threaten Saudi Arabia in other ways. "Wars of intimidation" will generally offer Iran more prospects of success than actual fighting, and Iran's ability to intimidate will increase as it develops its missile forces, and chemical, biological, radiological, and nuclear warfare capabilities.

FORCE TRANSFORMATION AND MISSION-ORIENTED PROCUREMENT PRIORITIES

The time is past when the Kingdom could spend its way out of its military development problems, or could excuse the lack of overall balance and effectiveness in its forces on the grounds. Saudi Arabia needs to give its force development efforts far more focus in order to develop a program of force transformation that can better meet its future needs. In doing so, it must focus on procuring interoperable and/or standardized equipment to provide the capability to perform the following missions:

- Heavy armor, artillery, attack helicopters, and mobile air defense equipment for defense of the upper Gulf.
- Interoperable offensive air capability with standoff, all-weather precision weapons and anti-armor/anti-ship capability.
- Interoperable air defense equipment, including heavy surface-to-air missiles, BVR/AWX fighters, AEW and surveillance capability, ARM and ECM capability (with growth to ATBM and cruise missile defense capability).
- Maritime surveillance systems and equipment for defense against maritime surveillance, and unconventional warfare.
- Mine detection and clearing systems.
- Improved urban, area, and border security equipment for unconventional warfare and low-intensity conflict.
- Advanced training aids.
- Support and sustainment equipment.

ELIMINATING THE GLITTER FACTOR

Money is already a critical issue and will become steadily more important in the future. Saudi Arabia signed nearly $25 billion worth of new arms agreements between 1993 and 2000, and took delivery on $66 billion worth of military imports.[1] This is more than the Kingdom can afford, and Saudi Arabia needs to consolidate its modernization programs to reduce its number of different suppliers and major weapons types. It also needs to establish much more strict limits to its defense spending and make its spending more effective. One key is the emphasis on mission capabilities just discussed; another is to give proper priority to readiness, training, and sustainability.

Realistic Limits on Military Spending and Arms Purchases

Saudi Arabia needs to set firm and realistic limits on its military procurement spending. The goal for Saudi Arabian military procurement should not be simply to buy the best or most possible equipment, but rather to improve the overall holdings of combat forces in a balanced and evolutionary manner. It should be to reach the maximum possible interoperability with the power projection capabilities of U.S. land and air forces, and to procure the training, munitions, and support facilities to deal with the threat from Iran and Iraq.

This Kingdom needs to recognize that it can no longer afford military procurement efforts that emphasize political considerations and/or high technology "glitter" over military effectiveness. Saudi Arabia needs long-term force plans and planning, programming, and budget systems that create stable and affordable force development and defense spending efforts. It needs to bring its manpower quality and sustainment capabilities into balance with its equipment and needs to recognize that its effectiveness is heavily dependent on interoperability with U.S. and Kuwaiti forces.

Reducing Future Waste

There should never be another set of massive arms package deals with the United States or Europe of the kind that took place during the Gulf War, or a purchase like al-Yamamah. Barring a future major war, purchases should be made and justified on a case-by-case basis, off-budget and oil barter deals should be illegal, and all offset deals subject to annual public reporting with an independent accountant and auditor.

Saudi Arabia must also take every possible step to eliminate the waste of funds on:

- Unique equipment types and one-of-a-kind modifications.
- "Glitter factor" weapons; "developmental" equipment and technology.
- Arms buys made from Europe for political purposes, where there is no credible prospect that the seller country can project major land and air forces.
- Non-interoperable weapons and systems.
- Submarines and ASW systems.
- Major surface warfare ships.
- Major equipment for divided or "dual" forces.
- New types of equipment that increase the maintenance, sustainability, and training problem, or layer new types over old.
- New types of equipment that strain the financial and manpower resources of Saudi Arabia, and overload military units that are already experiencing absorption and conversion problems in using the equipment they possess or have on order.

RESHAPING DEFENSE PLANNING, PROGRAMMING, BUDGETING, AND TRANSPARENCY

More broadly, Saudi Arabia needs to make fundamental reforms in the way it shapes its defense plans, budgets, and purchases. Secrecy does not aid effective planning or preserve the Kingdom's security; it instead encourages poor planning and budgeting, as well as corruption and cronyism. It encourages the failure to insist on plans that force the various military services to develop joint plans, demonstrate their effectiveness, and convince the Saudi people that they get the security their money should buy. Secrecy also makes it impossible to explain the need for the Kingdom's alliances, and the nature of the threats the Kingdom faces.

The creation of public defense plans, programs, and program budgets is one way to help reform Saudi Arabia's defense planning, programming, and budgeting system; to set a sustainable level of defense spending, and to build public confidence and trust. The Kingdom should also begin to issue white papers explaining major defense purchases, real-world progress in offset efforts, and other major security actions—another way to build that trust and reduce political pressure from outside countries over issues like major arms purchases.

COOPERATION WITH OTHER SOUTHERN GULF STATES

The lack of effective military cooperation between the Kingdom, other moderate Gulf states, and its Arab neighbors outside the Gulf presents major problems for Saudi Arabia that are not easy to solve. Saudi Arabia cannot turn to the rest of the Arab world for meaningful military support. The failure of the Damascus Declaration to give Saudi Arabia any credible guarantee of Egyptian and Syrian reinforcements was the result of far more than Arab politics and Egyptian and Syrian demands for money. Neither Egypt nor Syria is organized to project effective combat forces. They lack most of the technological advantages of U.S. forces and are not equipped and trained to provide the Saudi Air Force and Saudi Army with the mix of interoperable capabilities they need. Although they are Arab and Muslim, they also are states with separate interests, regional ambitions, and strategic objectives that often differ from those of Saudi Arabia.

The Need for Real-World Progress in Cooperation with Kuwait, Bahrain, and the GCC

Saudi Arabia badly needs to strengthen its cooperation with Bahrain, Kuwait, and the GCC. So far, however, there has been more progress in political and economic areas than in military areas. Efforts to create a GCC-wide C⁴I system for air defenses are making progress, but are still in the early stages of development, and the GCC has only made serious progress in a few areas of military exercise training like air combat and mine warfare. The GCC's long-standing failure to agree on effective plans for cooperation, interoperability, and integration has left the military role of the council a largely symbolic one.

Rhetoric is not a substitute for reality. The GCC will only play a major role in regional security once it can develop integrated air defenses, integrated mine warfare and maritime surveillance capabilities, an ability to deal with Iranian surface and ASW forces, rapid reaction forces that can actually fight, and the ability to defend Kuwait and eastern Saudi Arabia against land attack.

Priorities for Action

Saudi Arabia needs to look beyond its own military modernization program and take tangible steps to expand military cooperation with the GCC. Even if this is not possible on a GCC-wide basis, Saudi Arabia must focus on finding ways to strengthen the defense of its northern border area and Kuwait. At a minimum, Saudi Arabia must work to:

- Create an effective planning system for collective defense, the creation of interoperable forces with common C^{4}I/BM capabilities, and interoperable infrastructure and sustainability.

- Provide the infrastructure, transportation, sustainability, training and C^{4}I systems to rapidly deploy Saudi forces to support the joint land defense of the Kuwaiti/northwestern Saudi borders and to reinforce other Gulf states like Oman in the event of any Iranian amphibious or airborne action.

- Create joint air defense and air attack capabilities with an emphasis on Saudi-Kuwaiti-Bahraini cooperation.

- Integrate the Saudi C^{4}I and sensor nets for air and naval combat, including BVR and night warfare, and link them to Kuwait, Bahrain, and the other Southern Gulf states.

- Create joint air and naval strike forces to deal with threats from Iran and Iraq.

- Develop a joint war-fighting capability to provide minesweeping, naval-based air and anti-ship missile defenses to protect Gulf shipping, offshore facilities, ports, and coastal facilities.

- Establish effective cross-reinforcement and tactical mobility capabilities throughout the Kingdom with special emphasis on the defense of Kuwait and the Saudi-Iraqi border. Emphasize forward defense and active maneuver warfare.

- Prepare for rapid over-the-horizon reinforcement by the United States and other Western powers. Seek a solution to the lack of U.S. Army prepositioning in Saudi Arabia.

- Set up joint training, support, and infrastructure facilities with the other Southern Gulf states.

- Create common advanced training systems that develop a brigade and wing-level capability for combined arms and joint warfare, and that can support realistic field training exercises for Saudi and allied Southern Gulf forces of the kind practiced by U.S. and Israeli forces.

- Develop a common capability to provide urban and urban area security and to fight unconventional warfare and low-intensity combat.

- Begin development of a broadly based counterproliferation program.

Saudi Arabia is the only GCC state that can serve as the central focus for such activities. At least for the next decade, there is no other Southern Gulf state that will be able to use heavy armored forces, modern air control and warning systems, maritime forces and surveillance systems, minesweeping forces, integrated air defense and anti-tactical ballistic missile defenses, heliborne assault and other rapid reaction forces, and C⁴I/BM systems in ways that can provide an effective deterrent and defense against large-scale Iranian and Iraqi attacks.

CHANGING SAUDI ARABIA'S MILITARY RELATIONS WITH THE UNITED STATES AND THE WEST

Saudi Arabia has long played a critical role as a regional ally of the United States and in supporting U.S. and other Western power projections. The United States and Saudi Arabia cooperated closely in setting up combined air and naval defenses against Iran beginning in 1983, when Iraq came under serious military pressure from Iran. The two countries conducted joint exercises, and cooperated in establishing the "Fahd Line," which created an Air Defense Identification Zone and forward air defense system off the Saudi coast. Saudi Arabia and the United States have jointly operated E-3A AWACS units in the Kingdom ever since, and Saudi Arabia and the United States also cooperated closely during the tanker war of 1987–1988.

Saudi Arabia took the lead in organizing the Arab world's effort to force Iraq to leave Kuwait in 1990, and worked closely with the United States in first developing effective defenses against further Iraqi aggression and then liberating Kuwait. Saudi Arabia supported the United States in deploying massive land and air forces to the Kingdom during the Gulf War, and jointly commanded UN Coalition forces with the United States during Desert Storm. Saudi Arabia also provided the United States with $12.809 billion in direct aid during the Gulf War, and $4.045 billion in goods and services, for a total of $16.854 billion.[2]

Since the Gulf War, Saudi Arabia has recognized that the United States is the only power that can provide Saudi Arabia with the kind of land and air reinforcements that can fight "24-hour-a-day" intensive combat, launch highly maneuverable armored counter-offensives, strike deep and repeatedly with long-range precision air attacks, check and deter missile and air attacks with weapons of mass destruction, and provide "force multipliers" like satellite intelligence and targeting, advanced electronic warfare capabilities, and sophisticated battle management and C⁴I systems.

Saudi cooperation with the West, however, has not been easy nor without risks. The United States is also Israel's closest ally. The outbreak of new fighting between Israel and Palestine in September 2000 has shown that U.S. ties to Israel can present real risks in terms of the Saudi domestic reaction, hostility from other Arab states, and Israeli and pro-Israeli pressure on the United States.

Moreover, the events of September 11, 2001, have shown that Islamic extremism and terrorism are no longer regional problems and have led to serious additional tensions between the Kingdom and the United States.

They interact with the fact that any kind of U.S. or Western military presence on Saudi soil is opposed by a significant number of Saudis, not all of whom are Islamists. Finally, the debates between the Kingdom's leaders and the Bush administration over the possible U.S. use of force to overthrow Saddam Hussein and policy toward Iran have shown that serious differences can arise over whether the United States can use Saudi bases and facilities to pursue its own security policies.

The Need for New Forms of U.S. and Saudi Cooperation

The events of September 11 and the tensions of the Second Intifada have made it clear that the United States must continue to readjust its forward presence in Saudi Arabia. At the same time, there are limits to what the United States can do. Saudi Arabia needs to assume far more of the burden of explaining to its people that:

- The United States does not have any forces near Mecca and Medina,
- A limited U.S. presence is a powerful deterrent to Iran, Iraq, or any other enemy,
- Such U.S. presence greatly improves the speed at which the United States can project power into the region and the quality of joint training and interoperability with Saudi forces, and
- Such U.S. presence is essential to provide the training and maintenance aid Saudi forces need to properly absorb and maintain well over $60 billion worth of advanced U.S. military equipment, and which involved nearly $28 billion worth of new FMS sales agreements between 1990 and 2000. The United States delivered $32.2 billion worth of FMS arms sales plus roughly $300 million in commercial sales.[3]

At the same time it is far too easy to push reductions in the U.S. presence to the level at which they begin to create serious security problems for both Saudi Arabia and the United States. At some point the alliance needs to be justified and explained rather than simply made less visible and weakened.

Saudi Arabia and the United States need to consult much more closely on military options. No-fly zones and U.S. threats of cruise missile and air attacks will not contain Iraq indefinitely. Iraq has already begun to resume massive oil exports and revenues, and gradually to reassert its political and military power. Sound strategic cooperation cannot be based on a divided policy toward Iraq in which the United States advocates overthrow and the Kingdom advocates containment. There is no decisive way to defend one position over the other, but it is all too clear that divisions between the United States and Saudi Arabia make it difficult, if not impossible, to pursue either overthrow or containment effectively.

Similarly, Saudi Arabia and the United States need to develop a better-coordinated policy toward Iran. In practice, the United States needs to be more tolerant of Saudi political successes in dealing with Iran, while both states need to work together to firmly deter any Iranian efforts to use its military capabilities.

Proliferation presents a growing challenge that further reinforces some degree of Saudi strategic dependence on the United States. Long-range missiles—and chemical, biological, and nuclear weapons—present a major new challenge for U.S. and Saudi military cooperation. Saudi Arabia must redefine its security arrangements with the United States to deal with the problem of creeping proliferation in Iran and Iraq. Saudi Arabia must consider missile defenses and civil defense, but it will still need some form of extended deterrence from the United States, as will the other Southern Gulf states. The main option open to the Kingdom seems to be de facto or formal reliance on U.S. deterrent and counterproliferation capabilities. This, however, requires a rethinking of U.S. strategy as well as that of Saudi Arabia. As the U.S. Nuclear Posture Review of 2002 has concluded, extended deterrence is not a casual affair, and it cannot be separated from efforts to develop some form of regional arms control and develop integrated missile defense, civil defense, and counterterrorism defenses for the Southern Gulf.

ISLAMIC EXTREMISM AND TERRORISM

Saudi Arabia and the United States—as well as the Arab world and Europe—must continue to work together to reduce Islamist resentment of the United States' military role and presence in Saudi Arabia and to help prevent further attacks by Sunni and Shi'ite extremists. The United States can minimize the vulnerability of its personnel by isolating them, restricting their numbers, and taking additional security measures, as it has already done.[4] Neither Saudi Arabia nor the United States can afford, however, to let their military agendas be dictated by terrorists or the nations that support them. There also is no strategic alternative that offers anything approaching the same advantages as a significant, forward-deployed U.S. strategic presence in Saudi Arabia.

This requires more effective security cooperation between Saudi Arabia and the United States in counterterrorism. Saudi Arabia needs to modernize and improve its security services and make even stronger efforts to bring Islamic extremism under control. On the other hand, the United States needs to provide highly professional teams of area specialists that can work quietly and discreetly with the Saudi security services, that understand Saudi culture and politics, and that are fluent in Arabic. It may be that this is a function that belongs in the CIA and with the relevant intelligence and security services of the Department of Defense.

The Saudi and U.S. governments also need to deal with the causes of terrorism in the Kingdom. They need to communicate more openly and frankly with the Saudi people about the reasons why U.S. forces are in Saudi Arabia. The Saudi government can no longer deal with the Saudi people by ignoring them, and the United States cannot rely on silence. If the Saudi and U.S. governments do so, they simply leave the ground free for exaggerated charges and criticism.

Public diplomacy has a military dimension. The United States needs to do more to make it clear to the Saudi people that it is not a mercenary, that its military presence is comparatively limited, that it works in close cooperation with the Saudi military, and that it limits the role of U.S. forces to missions vital to the defense of Saudi Arabia. The U.S. military forces in Saudi Arabia have helped make these points to the Saudis they work with, but this is hardly a public-information campaign. At this point in time, it is far too easy for extremists to criticize the U.S. presence in the most exaggerated terms with little fear of rebuttal. Even generally friendly Saudis know so little about the facts that they often accept some of these charges.

Saudi Arabia and the United States cannot ignore the impact of the Arab-Israeli conflict and the Second Intifada. Far more Saudis resent U.S. ties to Israel than a U.S. military presence in Saudi Arabia. At the same time, Americans find it difficult to understand how the Kingdom can support Palestinian and Islamic causes that they associate with terrorism.

Saudi Arabia and the United States approach the issues involved from a different perspective and with different biases, but Crown Prince Abdullah and Presidents Clinton and Bush have made it clear, however, that the leaders of both countries are united in a search for peace. Saudi and U.S. cooperation in a highly visible and enduring effort to create a just peace for both the Palestinians and Israel—as well as between Israel, Lebanon, and Syria—is another key step in both counterterrorism and strengthening the U.S-Saudi alliance.

ARMS SALES AND SECURITY ASSISTANCE

Both the Saudi government and its arms suppliers need to recognize that the majority of educated Saudis already ask serious questions about the value of Saudi Arabia's arms imports and the honesty of the procurement and delivery process. This questioning comes from senior Saudi officials and some junior members of the royal family as well as the public, and is one of the few areas where Saudi Arabia's most progressive businessmen and technocrats and Islamic extremists agree in criticizing the Saudi government. The time has passed when the government could deal with these problems with secrecy and silence; it needs to make its programs more public, bring them openly on budget, and demonstrate that it has accounting procedures that limit favoritism and commissions to levels that are broadly acceptable in Saudi society.

Effective arms buys also require hard choices and well-planned trade-offs, and Saudi Arabia is long past the point where it simply can throw money at the problem. It needs a stable long-term procurement plan that spends no more than 60% to 70% of what the Kingdom has averaged since the Gulf War, that limits total outstanding orders to $7 to$8 billion, focuses on its highest priorities for standardization and interoperability with the United States, and ensures that Saudi Arabia does not buy a series of partly incompatible systems when it buys from other countries.

The West must be careful in pressing for military sales, or aid, in ways that do not meet vital Saudi security needs and that do not take Saudi Arabia's domestic economic problems and social needs into account. Saudi Arabia has long been one of the largest single customers for U.S. and European military exports. Saudi purchases had the benefit of increasing interoperability and sustainability with British, French, and U.S. forces, and reduced the unit cost of equipment purchased by Western forces. It is clear, however, that Saudi Arabia faces serious long-term constraints on what it can buy in the future, and that it will often have to make hard choices between the military desirability of standardization with Western power projection forces and the political need to buy arms from a range of friendly states.

Defense contractors will be defense contractors—they exist to sell regardless of need or merit. Governments, however, must act as governments and think first of their strategic interests. It is time that governments of Europe and the United States make it clear to the Saudi people that they emphasize Saudi security, military readiness, and effectiveness rather than exports and sales. They need to make it clear that they are not pressuring Saudi Arabia to buy unnecessary arms, recognize Saudi Arabia's need to limit its purchases to the level the Kingdom can afford, act to prevent corruption, and ensure that arms buys are part of packages that include the proper support, training, munitions stocks, and sustainability.

NOTES

1. Richard F. Grimmett, *Conventional Arms Transfers to Developing Nations, 1993–2000* (Washington: Congressional Research Service, RL31083, August 16, 2001), pp. CRS-47, 48, 58, 59.

2. Stephen Dagget and Gary J. Pagliano, *Persian Gulf War: US Costs and Allied Financial Contributions* (Washington: Congressional Research Service, IB91019, September, 21, 1992), pp. 11–13.

3. The United States also sold over $1 billion in foreign military construction services, U.S. Department of Defense, *DSCA (Facts Book)—Foreign Military Sales,*

Foreign Military Contruction Sales, and Military Assistance Facts (Washington: OSD[PA], September 30, 2000), unpaged computer printout.

4. See *Jane's Defence Weekly*, July 10, 1996, p. 10; *USA Today*, July 15, 1996, p. 7A; *Baltimore Sun*, July 15, 1996, p. 1A.

Bibliography

Abir, Mordechai. *Oil, Power, and Politics: Conflict in Arabia, the Red Sea and the Gulf*. London: Frank Cass, 1974.

———. *Saudi Arabia: Government, Society and the Gulf Crisis*. London: Routledge, 1993.

———. "Saudi Security and Military Endeavor." *The Jerusalem Quarterly*, no. 33 (Fall 1984), 79–94.

Aburish, Said K. *The Rise, Corruption, and Coming Fall of the House of Saud*. New York: St. Martin's/Griffin, 1996.

Aerospace Daily, various editions.

Air Force, various editions.

Ajami, Fouad. "The Sentry's Solitude." *Foreign Affairs* (November/December 2001), 2–16.

Albright, David, Frans Berkhout, and William Walker. *Plutonium and Highly Enriched Uranium, 1996—World Inventories, Capabilities, and Policies*. Oxford: SIPRI-Oxford Press, 1997.

Amery, Hussein A. and Aaron T. Wolfe. *Water in the Middle East: A Geography of Peace*. Austin: University of Texas Press, 2000.

Anthony, John Duke. "A Changing of the Guard in Saudi Arabia, A Personal Perspective." *Gulf Wire–Perspectives* (September 3–9, 2001), *http://arabialink.com/GulfWire/GULFWIRE.htm*.

———. "The GCC's 21st Summit, Part Two: Defense Issues." *Gulf Wire* (January 2001).

———. "Saudi-Yemeni Relations: Implications for U.S. Policy." *Middle East Policy*, vol. 7, no. 3 (June 2000), 78–96.

Arab News, various editions.

Armed Forces Journal, various editions.

Arquilla, John, and David Ronfeldt, eds. *Networks and Netwars: The Future of Terror, Crime and Militancy.* Santa Monica, CA: RAND, National Defense Research Institute, 2001.

Atkenson, Edward B. *The Powder Keg.* Falls Church, VA: NOVA Publications, 1996.

Aviation Week and Space Technology, various editions.

Baltimore Sun, various editions.

Baram, Amatzia. "The Iraqi Armed Forces and Security Apparatus." In *Conflict Security Development,* 113–123. London: Centre for Defense Studies, King's College, 2001.

Barnaby, Frank. *The Invisible Bomb.* London: I. B. Taurus, 1989.

Bass, Gail, and Bonnie Jean Cordes. *Actions Against Non-Nuclear Energy Facilities: September 1981–September 1982.* Santa Monica, CA: Rand Corporation, 1983.

Beling, Willard A., ed. *King Faisal and the Modernization of Saudi Arabia.* Boulder, CO: Westview Press, 1980.

Belyakov, Rostislav, and Nikolai Buntin. "The MiG 29M Light Multirole Fighter." *Military Technology,* 8/94, 41–44.

Bitzinger, Richard. "The Globalization of the Arms Industry." *Foreign Policy* (Summer 1995), 170–182.

Blechman, Barry M., and Stephan S. Kaplan. *Force Without War.* Washington, DC: The Brookings Institution, 1978.

Bligh, A., and S. Plant. "Saudi Modernization in Oil and Foreign Policies in the Post-AWACS Sale Period." *Middle East Review,* 14 (Spring–Summer 1982).

Bonds, Ray. *Modern Soviet Weapons,* New York: ARCO, 1986.

Boston Globe, various editions.

Bowie, Christopher J. "Destroying Mobile Ground Targets in An Anti-Access Environment." Analysis Center Papers, Northrup Grumman, December 2001.

Bruce, James, and Paul Bear. "Latest Arab Force Levels Operating in the Gulf." *Jane's Defence Weekly* (December 12, 1987), 1360–1361.

Bruner, Dale. "US Military and Security Relations with the Southern Gulf States." Washington, DC: NSSP, Georgetown University, May 8, 1995.

Bulletin of Atomic Scientists, various editions.

Byman, Daniel. "After the Storm: U.S. Policy Toward Iraq Since 1991." *Political Science Quarterly,* vol. 115, no. 4.

Carus, W. Seth. *The Genie Unleashed: Iraq's Chemical and Biological Weapons Production.* Policy Papers, Number 14. Washington, DC: The Washington Institute for Near East Policy, 1989.

Carus, W. Seth, and Hirsh Goodman. *The Future Battlefield and the Arab-Israeli Conflict.* London: Transaction Press, 1990.

Carver, Michael. *War Since 1945.* London: Weidenfeld and Nicholson, 1980.

Chicago Tribune, various editions.

Christian Science Monitor, various editions.

Central Intelligence Agency (CIA). *Unclassified Report to Congress on the Acquisition of Technology Relating to Weapons of Mass Destruction and Advanced Conventional Munitions,* various editions.

———. *World Factbook,* various editions.

Clawson, Patrick. *Iran's Challenge to the West: How, When, and Why.* Policy

Papers, Number 33. Washington, DC: The Washington Institute for Near East Policy, 1993.

Cleron, Jean Paul. *Saudi Arabia 2000.* London: Croom Helm, 1978.

Codevilla, Angelo M. *Missiles, Defense, and Israel.* Papers in Strategy, Number 5. Washington, DC: IASP, November 1997.

Cohen, Avner. *Israel and the Bomb.* New York: Columbia University Press, 1998.

Cohen, Eliot A. *Gulf War Air Power Survey.* Washington, DC: US Air Force/ Government Printing Office, 1993.

Cohen, Eliot A., Michael J. Eisenstadt, and Andre J. Bacevich. *Knives, Tanks, and Missiles.* Washington, DC: Washington Institute, 1998.

Cohen, Michael J. *Fighting World War Three from the Middle East.* Portland, OR: Frank Cass Publishers, 1997.

Collins, John M., and Clyde R. Mark. *Petroleum Imports from the Persian Gulf: Use of U.S. Armed Force to Ensure Supplies.* Issue Brief IB 79046. Washington, DC: Library of Congress, Congressional Research Service, 1979.

Collins, John N. *Military Geography.* Washington, DC: National Defense University, 1998.

Congressional Budget Office. *Limiting Conventional Arms Transfers to the Middle East.* Washington, DC: A CBO Study, September 1992.

Cordesman, Anthony H. "After AWACS: Establishing Western Security Throughout Southwest Asia." *Armed Forces Journal* (December 1981), 64–68.

———. *After the Storm: The Changing Military Balance in the Middle East.* Boulder, CO: Westview, 1993.

———. *The Arab-Israeli Military Balance and the Art of Operations.* Washington, DC: University Press of America-AEI, 1987.

———. *Bahrain, Oman, Qatar and the UAE: Challenges of Security.* Boulder, CO: Westview, 1997.

———. "The Changing Military Balance in the Gulf." *Middle East Policy,* vol. 6, no. 1 (June 1998), 25–43.

———. "Defense Planning in Saudi Arabia." In *Defense Planning in Less-Industrialized States,* ed. Stephanie Neuman. Lexington, MA: Lexington Books, 1984.

———. *The Gulf and the Search for Strategic Stability.* Boulder, CO: Westview, 1984.

———. *The Gulf and the West.* Boulder, CO: Westview, 1988.

———. *Iran in Transition: Conventional Threats and Weapons of Mass Destruction.* Westport, CT: Praeger, 1999.

———. *Iraq and the War of the Sanctions: Conventional Threats and Weapons of Mass Destruction.* Westport, CT: Praeger, 1999.

———. *Kuwait: Recovery and Security After the Gulf War.* Boulder, CO: Westview, 1997.

———. "The New Balance of Gulf Arms." *Middle East Policy,* vol. 6, no. 4 (June 1999), 80–103.

———. *Peace and War.* Westport, CT: Praeger, 2001.

———. *Saudi Arabia, AWACS and America's Search for Strategic Stability.* International Security Studies Program, Working Paper Number 26A. Washington, DC: Wilson Center, 1981.

———. *Saudi Arabia: Guarding the Desert Kingdom.* Boulder, CO: Westview, 1997.

————. "The Saudi Arms Sale: The True Risks, Benefits, and Costs." *Middle East Insight*, vol. 4, nos. 4 and 5, 40–54.

————. *The Threat from the Northern Gulf.* Boulder, CO: Westview, 1994.

————. *Transnational Threats from the Middle East.* Carlisle, PA: U.S. Army War College, 1999.

————. *US Forces in the Middle East: Resources and Capabilities.* Boulder, CO: Westview, 1997.

————. *Weapons of Mass Destruction in the Middle East.* London: Brassey's/RUSI, 1991.

————. *Western Strategic Interests and Saudi Arabia.* London: Croom Helm, 1986.

Cordesman, Anthony H., and Abraham R. Wagner. *The Lessons of Modern War, Volume II: The Iran-Iraq Conflict.* Boulder, CO: Westview, 1990.

————. *The Lessons of Modern War, Volume IV: The Gulf War.* Boulder, CO: Westview, 1995.

Dagget, Stephen T., and Gary J. Pagliano. *Persian Gulf War: US Costs and Allied Financial Contributions.* Congressional Research Service IB 91019, September 21, 1992.

Dawisha, Adeed I. *Saudi Arabia's Search for Security.* Adelphi Paper Number 158. London: International Institute for Strategic Studies, Winter 1979–1980.

Defense and Foreign Affairs Daily, various editions.

Defense Daily, various editions.

Defense News, various editions.

Dekmejian, R. Harir. *Islam in Revolution: Fundamentalism in the Arab World,* 2nd ed. Syracuse, NY: Syracuse University Press, 1995.

Denoeux, Guilain. "The Forgotten Swamp: Navigating Political Islam." *Middle East Policy*, vol. 9, no. 2 (June 2002), 56–81.

DMS/FI Market Intelligence Reports database.

Dolotrar, Mostafa, and Tim S. Gray. *Water Politics in the Middle East: A Context for Conflict or Cooperation.* Houndsmill, Basingstoke, and Hampshire: Macmillan Press; New York: St. Martin's Press, 2000.

Donovan, Fred. "Mideast Missile Flexing." *Arms Control Today* (May 1990), 31.

Drake, C.J.M. *Terrorist's Target Selection.* New York: St. Martin's Press, 1998.

The Economist, various editions.

Economist Intelligence Unit, various country reports.

EIA. *Persian Gulf Factsheet.* March 2002, *http://www.eia.doe.gov/cabs/pgulf.html.*

Eisenberg, Laura Zittrain. "Passive Belligerence, Israel and the 1991 Gulf War." *Journal of Strategic Studies*, vol. 15, no. 31 (September 1993), 304–330.

Eisenstadt, Michael. *Like a Phoenix from the Ashes? The Future of Iraqi Military Power.* Washington, DC: The Washington Institute, 1993.

————. "Syria's Strategic Weapons," *Jane's Intelligence Review* (April 1993), 168–171.

The Estimate, various editions.

Executive News Service, Online database.

FBIS. "King Fahd on Iran Ties, Hajj, Missiles, Hijack." FBIS-NES-88-084, May 2, 1988, 18.

Feldman, Shai. *Nuclear Weapons and Arms Control in the Middle East.* Cambridge, MA: MIT Press, 1997.

Financial Times, various editions.

Flight International, various editions.

Foreign Intelligence Service of the Russian Federation. *A New Challenge After the Cold War: The Proliferation of Weapons of Mass Destruction, Moscow, 1993.* Available in a February 1993 FBIS translation from the Government Operations Committee of the U.S. Senate.

Fromkin, David. *A Peace to End All Peace: The Fall of the Ottoman Empire and the Creation of the Modern Middle East.* New York: Avon Books, 1989.

Gabriel, Richard A. *Fighting Armies: Antagonists in the Middle East, A Combat Assessment.* Westport, CT: Greenwood Press, 1983.

Gause, F. Gregory, III. *Oil Monarchies: Domestic and Security Challenges in the Arab Gulf States.* New York: Council on Foreign Relations Press, 1994.

General Dynamics. *The World's Missile Systems*, 8th ed. Pomona: General Dynamics, 1988.

Grimmett, Richard F. *Conventional Arms Transfers to the Third World.* Washington, DC: Congressional Research Service, CRS-93-656F, various editions.

Hameed, Mazher. *An American Imperative: The Defense of Saudi Arabia.* Washington, DC: Middle East Assessments Group, 1981.

Hart, Parker T. *Saudi Arabia and the United States: Birth of a Security Partnership.* Bloomington: Indiana University Press, 1998.

Held, Colbert. *Middle East Patterns.* Boulder, CO: Westview, 1989.

Helms, Christian Moss. *The Cohesion of Saudi Arabia.* Baltimore, MD: John Hopkins University Press, 1981.

Hersh, Seymour M. *The Samson Option, Israel's Nuclear Arsenal and American Foreign Policy.* New York: Random House, 1991.

Holden, David, and Richard Johns. *The House of Saud.* London: Sidgwick and Jackson, 1981.

Inside Defense Electronics, various editions.

Inside the Army, various editions.

Inside the Navy, various editions.

Inside the Pentagon, various editions.

Insight, various editions.

International Institute of Strategic Studies (IISS). *Military Balance, 2001–2002.*

International Monetary Fund (IMF). *Direction of Trade Statistics*, various editions.

———. *Direction of Trade Yearbook*, various years.

Isby, David C. *Weapons and Tactics of the Soviet Army, Fully Revised Edition.* London: Jane's, 1987.

Jaffee Center for Strategic Studies. *The Middle East Military Balance.* Tel Aviv: Tel Aviv University, various editions.

Jane's Air Defence Systems, various editions.

Jane's Aircraft Upgrades, various editions.

Jane's Air-Launched Weapons, various editions.

Jane's All the World's Aircraft, various editions.

Jane's All the World's Armies, various editions.

Jane's Armor and Artillery, various editions.

Jane's Avionics, various editions.

Jane's Battlefield Surveillance Systems, various editions.

Jane's C4I Systems, various editions.

Jane's Command Information Systems, various editions.

Jane's Defence Weekly, various editions.

Jane's Fighting Ships, various editions.

Jane's Helicopter Markets and Systems, various editions.

Jane's Infantry Weapons. London: Jane's Publishing, various editions.

Jane's Intelligence Review, various editions.

Jane's International Defence Review, various editions.

Jane's Land-Based Air Defence, various editions.

Jane's Military Communications, various editions.

Jane's Military Exercise and Training Monitor, various editions.

Jane's Military Vehicles and Logistics, various editions.

Jane's Pointer, various editions.

Jane's Radar: National and International Air Defense, URL: *http://www.state.gov/ www/global/human_rights/1999_hrp_report/saudiara.html*.

Jane's Radar and Electronic Warfare Systems, various editions.

Jane's Sentinel: The Gulf States. London: Jane's Publishing, various editions.

Jane's Sentinel series—Eastern Mediterranean, Gulf States, and North Africa.

Jane's Sentinel Security Assessment, Online edition.

Jane's Strategic Weapons Systems. London: Jane's Publishing, various editions.

Jane's Unmanned Aerial Vehicles and Targets, various editions.

Jane's World Air Forces, various editions.

Jerichow, Anders. *The Saudi File: People, Power, Politics*. New York: St. Martin's Press, 1998.

Johnson, Maxwell Orme. *The Military as an Instrument of U.S. Policy in Southwest Asia: The Rapid Deployment Joint Task Force, 1979–1982*. Boulder, CO: Westview, 1983.

Jones, Rodney W., March C. McDonough, Toby F. Dalton and Gregory D. Koblentz. *Tracking Nuclear Proliferation*. Washington, DC: Carnegie Endowment, 1998.

Journal of Electronic Defense, various editions.

Kalicki, Jan H. "A Vision for the U.S.-Saudi and U.S.-Gulf Commercial Relationship." *Middle East Policy*, vol. 5, no. 2 (May 1997), 73–78.

Kan, Shirley A. *Chinese Proliferation of Weapons of Mass Destruction, Background and Analysis*. Library of Congress, CRS-96-767F, September 13, 1996.

Kaplan, Stephen S. *Diplomacy of Power*. Washington, DC: The Brookings Institution, 1981.

Katzman, Kenneth. *Iran: Arms and Technology Acquisitions*. Library of Congress, CRS-97-474F, October 1, 1997.

Keegan, John. *World Armies*. New York: Facts on File, 1979.

———. *World Armies*, 2nd ed. London: Macmillan Publishers, 1983.

Kelly, J. B. *Arabia, the Gulf and the West: A Critical View of the Arabs and Their Oil Policy*. New York: Basic Books, 1980.

Kemp, Geoffrey. *The Control of the Middle East Arms Race*. Washington, DC: Carnegie Endowment, 1991.

Kemp, Geoffrey, and Robert E. Harkavy. *Strategic Geography and the Changing Middle East*. Washington, DC: Carnegie Endowment/Brookings, 1997.

Khalid bin Sultan, Prince. *Desert Warrior: A Personal View of the Gulf War by the Joint Forces Commander*. Written with Patrick Seale. New York: HarperCollins, 1995.

Kronsky, Herbert, and Stephen Weissman. *The Islamic Bomb.* New York: Times Books, 1981.

Lacey, Robert. *The Kingdom.* London: Hutchinson and Company, 1981.

Laffin, John L. *The Dagger of Islam.* London: Sphere, 1979.

———. *The World in Conflict*, or *War Annual.* London: Brassey's, various editions.

Lambeth, Benjamin S. *Moscow's Lessons From the 1982 Lebanon Air War.* Santa Monica, CA: Rand Corporation, 1984.

Lesch, Ann M. "Osama bin Laden: Embedded in the Middle East Crisis." *Middle East Policy*, vol. 9, no. 2 (June 2002), 82–91.

London Financial Times, various editions.

London *Sunday Times*, various editions.

Long, David E. *The Kingdom of Saudi Arabia.* Gainesville: University Press of Florida, 1997.

Looney, Robert E. *Saudi Arabia's Development Potential.* Lexington, MA: Lexington Books, 1982.

Mansur, Abdul Kasim (pseud.). "The American Threat to Saudi Arabia." *Armed Forces Journal International* (September 1980), 47–60.

Maoz, Zeev. *Regional Security in the Middle East.* Portland, OR: Frank Cass Publishers, 1997.

Mark, Clyde R. "Middle East and North Africa: US Aid FY1993, 1994, and 1995." CRS 94-274F, March *Jane's Defence Weekly*, July 12, 1995, p. 19.

Martin, David. *Ballistic Missile Defense Overview.* Washington, DC: Ballistic Missile Defense Office, Department of Defense, March 3, 1999.

Matinuddin, Kamal. *The Taliban Phenomenon: Afghanistan 1994–1997.* New York: Oxford University Press, 1999.

Mauroni, Albert J. *Chemical-Biological Defense.* Westport, CT: Praeger, 1998.

McDonald, John, and Clyde Burleson. *Flight from Dhahran.* Englewood Cliffs, NJ: Prentice-Hall, 1981.

McLaurin, R.D., and Lewis W. Snider. *Saudi Arabia's Air Defense Requirements in the 1980s: A Threat Analysis.* Alexandria, VA: Abbott Associates, 1979.

McMillan, Joseph, Anthony H. Cordesman, Mamoun Fandy and Fareed Mohamedi. "The United States and Saudi Arabia: American Interests and Challenges to the Kingdom in 2002." *Middle East Policy*, vol. 9, no. 1 (March 2002), 1–28.

Metz, Helen Chapin. *Saudi Arabia, A Country Study.* Washington, DC: Congressional Research Service, December 1992, Available from: *http://lcweb2.loc.gov/cgibin/query/r?frd/cstdy:@field(DOCID+sa0000.*

Middle East Economic Digest, various editions.

Middle East Policy (formerly *Arab-American Affairs*), various editions.

Military Technology, various editions.

Military Technology, World Defense Almanac, various editions.

The Naval Institute Guide to the Combat Fleets of the World: Their Ships, Aircraft, and Armament. Annapolis, MD: U.S. Naval Institute, various editions.

New York Times, various editions.

Newhouse, John. "The Diplomatic Round, Politics and Weapons Sales." *New Yorker*, June 9, 1996.

Newsweek, various editions.

Niblock, Tim, ed. *State, Society, and the Economy in Saudi Arabia*. London: Croom Helm, 1982.

Nimir, S.A., and M. Palmer. "Bureaucracy and Development in Saudi Arabia: A Behavioral Analysis." *Public Administration and Development* (April–June 1982).

Noyes, James H. *The Clouded Lens*. Stanford, CA: Hoover Institution, 1982.

Obaid, Nawaf E. *The Oil Kingdom at 100: Petroleum Policymaking in Saudi Arabia*. Washington, DC: The Washington Institute for Near East Policy, 2000.

O'Ballance, Edgar. *The Electronic War in the Middle East, 1968–1970*. Hamden, CT: Archon, 1974.

Ochsenwald, William. "Saudi Arabia and the Islamic Revival." *International Journal of Middle East Studies*, vol. 13, no. 3 (August 1981), 271–286.

Organization of Petroleum Exporting Countries (OPEC). *Annual Report*, Vienna, various years.

Philadelphia Inquirer, various editions.

Policywatch, various editions.

Quandt, William B. "Riyadh between the Superpowers." *Foreign Policy*, no. 44 (Fall 1981).

———. *Saudi Arabia in the 1980s: Foreign Policy, Security and Oil*. Washington, DC: The Brookings Institution, 1982

Rashid, Ahmed. *Taliban: Militant Islam, Oil and Fundamentalism in Central Asia*. New York: Yale/Nota Bene, 2000.

Rathmell, Andrew. *The Changing Balance in the Gulf*. Whitehall Papers 38. London: Royal United Services Institute, 1996.

———. "Saudi Arabia's Military Build-up—An Extravagant Error." *Jane's Intelligence Review* (November 1994), 500–504.

Rekhess, Elie. "The Terrorist Connection—Iran, the Islamic Jihad, and Hamas." *Justice*, vol. 5 (May 1995).

Reuters, Online access.

Roule Trifin J., Jeremy Kinsell, and Brian Joyce. "Investigators seek to break up Al-Qaida's financial structure." *Jane's Intelligence Review* (November 2001), 8–11.

Royal Embassy of Saudi Arabia. "Government Official's Biographies: His Royal Highness Prince Sultan bin Abdulaziz Al Saud." Available from: *http://www.saudiembassy.net/gov_profile/bio_sultan.html*. Accessed on May 30, 2002.

Sabini, John. *Armies in the Sand: The Struggle for Mecca and Medina*. New York: W.W. Norton, 1981.

Safran, Nadav. *Saudi Arabia: The Ceaseless Quest for Security*. Cambridge, MA: Belknap Press of Harvard University Press, 1985.

Salameh, Mamdouh G. "A Third Oil Crisis?" *Survival*, vol. 43, no. 3 (Autumn 2001), 129–144.

Saudi Arabia, various editions.

Scarlott, Jennifer. "Nuclear Proliferation After the Gulf War." *World Policy Journal* (Fall 1991), 687–695.

Schmid, Alex P. *Soviet Military Interventions Since 1945*. New Brunswick, NJ: Transaction, 1985.

Shadid, Anthony. *Legacy of the Prophet: Despots, Democrats, and the New Politics of Islam*, Boulder, CO: Westview, 2001.

Shaw, John A., and David E. Long. *Saudi Arabian Modernization*. Washington Papers, 89. New York: Praeger, 1982.

Shuey, Lenhart, Snyder, Donnelley, Mielke, and Moteff. *Missile Proliferation: Survey of Emerging Missile Forces*. Report 88-642F. Washington, DC: Congressional Research Service, February 9, 1989.

Signal, various editions.

Spector, Leonard S., Mark G. McDonough, and Evan S. Medeiros. *Tracking Nuclear Proliferation*. Washington, DC: Carnegie Endowment, 1995.

Stockholm International Peace Research Institute. *World Armaments and Disarmament: SIPRI Yearbook*. London: Oxford Press, various editions.

Survival, various editions.

Taecker, Kevin. "Saudi Arabia and the GCC in a Troubled Global Economy." *Middle East Policy*, vol. 6, no. 2 (October 1998), 29–35.

Tanks of the World (Bernard and Grafe), various editions.

Teitelbaum, Joshua. *Holier than Thou: Saudi Arabia's Islamic Opposition*. Washington, DC: The Washington Institute for Near East Policy, 2000.

Tillema, Herbert K. *International Conflict Since 1945*. Boulder, CO: Westview, 1991.

Turner, Louis, and James M. Bedore. *Middle East Industrialization: A Study of Saudi and Iranian Downstream Investments*. London: Saxon House, 1979.

U.S. Congress, House of Representatives, Committee on Appropriations, Foreign Assistance and Related Programs Appropriations for 1982. Part 7: *Proposed Airborne Warning and Control Systems (AWACS), F-15 Enhancement Equipment, and Sidewinder AIM 9L Missiles Sales to Saudi Arabia*, 97th Congress, 1st Session, Hearings.

U.S. Congress, House of Representatives, Committee on Foreign Affairs. *Activities of the U.S. Corps of Engineers in Saudi Arabia*, 96th Congress, 1st Session, 1979.

U.S. Congress, Senate, Committee on Armed Services. *Military and Technical Implications of the Proposed Sale of Air Defense Enhancements to Saudi Arabia. Report of the Hearings on the Military and Technical Implications of the Proposed Sale of Air Defense Enhancements to Saudi Arabia, Based Upon Hearings Held before the Committee in Accordance with Its Responsibilities under Rule XXV (C) of the Standing Rules of the Senate*, 97th Congress, 1st Session.

U.S. Congress, Senate, Committee on Foreign Relations. *Arms Sales Package to Saudi Arabia—Part 2*, 97th Congress, 1st Session, 1981.

U.S. General Accounting Office. *Perspectives on Military Sales to Saudi Arabia*, Report to Congress, October 2, 1977.

U.S. Library of Congress, Congressional Research Service, Foreign Affairs and National Defense Division. *Saudi Arabia and the United States: The New Context in an Evolving "Special Relationship."* Report prepared for the Subcommittee on Europe and the Middle East, Committee on Foreign Affairs, U.S. House of Representatives, 1981.

———. *Western Vulnerability to a Disruption of Persian Gulf Oil Supplies: U.S. Interests and Options*. 1983.

United Nations. Note by the Secretary General, "Report of the Secretary-General on the Activities of the Special Commission," S/1997/774, October 6, 1997.

———. *Report on the Eighth IAEA Inspection in Iraq Under Security Council Resolution 687*, S/23283 (English). New York: United Nations, November 11–18, 1991.

U.S. Arms Control and Disarmament Agency (ACDA). *World Military Expenditures and Arms Transfers*. Washington, DC: GPO, various editions.

U.S. Central Intelligence Agency (CIA). *Prospects for Further Proliferation of Nuclear Weapons*. DCI NIO.

U.S. Defense Intelligence Agency (DIA). *The Scud Missile: An Unclassified Overview for Policy Makers*. Forwarded under U-3,148/SVI-FOIA, October 22, 1997.

———. *Soviet Chemical Weapons Threat*. DST-1620F-051-85, 1985, p. 8.

U.S. Defense Security Assistance Agency (DSAA). Foreign Military Sales, *Foreign Military Construction Sales, and Military Assistance Facts*. Washington, DC: Department of Defense, various editions.

U.S. Department of Defense (DOD). *DSCA (Facts Book)—Foreign Military Sales, Foreign Military Contruction Sales, and Military Assistance Facts*. Washington, DC: OSD (PA), various editions.

———. "Notice Pursuant to Section 62(A) of the Arms Export Control Act, Transmittal Number 9-93," July 19, 1993.

———. *Report on Allied Contributions to the Common Defense*. Report to the U.S. Congress by the Secretary of Defense, March 2001.

———. "Sale of Abrams Tanks to Saudi Arabia." Background Information. November 1, 1989.

U.S. Department of State. *Annual Report on Military Expenditures*. Submitted to the Committee on Appropriations of the U.S. Senate and the Committee on Appropriations of the U.S. House of Representatives, in accordance with section 511(b) of the Foreign Operations, Export Financing, and Related Programs Appropriations Act, 1993, various editions.

———. *Congressional Presentation: Foreign Operations*, various editions.

———. *Congressional Presentation for Security Assistance Programs, Fiscal Year 1996*. Washington, DC: U.S. Department of State, 1995.

———. *Patterns of Global Terrorism*, various years.

———. *World Military Expenditures and Arms Transfers*. Washington, DC: GPO, various editions.

U.S. Director of Central Intelligence. *The Acquisition of Technology Relating to Weapons of Mass Destruction and Advanced Conventional Munitions, July–December, 1996*. Washington, DC: CIA, June 1997.

U.S. National Intelligence Council. *Foreign Missile Developments and the Ballistic Missile Threat to the United States Through 2015*. Washington, DC: NIC, September 1999.

U.S. Naval Institute database.

U.S. Office of Technology Assessment. *Global Arms Trade: Commerce in Advanced Military Technology and Weapons*. Washington, DC: OTA, U.S. Congress, June 1991.

U.S. Office of the Secretary of Defense. *Proliferation: Threat and Response*. Washington, DC: Department of Defense, various editions.

US SDIO. *Ballistic Missile Proliferation: An Emerging Threat, 1992.* Washington, DC: SDIO, October 1992.

U.S. Secretary of Defense. *Report on Forces for the Common Defense, Report to the US Congress.* Washington, DC: Department of Defense, various editions.

U.S. State Department. *Country Report on Human Rights Practices.* Available from: *http://www.state.gov/www/global/human_rights/l*, various editions.

———. *Patterns of Global Terrorism.* Available from: *http://www.state.gov/www/global/terrorism/*, various editions.

USA Today, various editions.

USCENTCOM. *Atlas.* MacDill Air Force Base: USCENTCOM, various editions.

von Pikva, Otto. *Armies of the Middle East.* New York: Mayflower, 1979.

Warplanes of the World (Bernard and Grafe), various editions.

Washington Post, various editions.

Washington Times, various editions.

Weyer's Warships (Bernard and Grafe), various editions.

Wiley, Marshall W. "American Security Concerns in the Gulf." *Orbis*, vol. 28, no. 3 (Fall 1984), 456–464.

Wolfe, Ronald G., ed. *The United States, Arabia, and the Gulf.* Washington, DC: Georgetown University Center for Contemporary Arab Studies, 1980.

World Bank. *Atlas*, various editions.

World Bank. *World Development Indicators*, various editions.

Yodfat, Aryeh Y. *The Soviet Union and the Arabian Peninsula: Soviet Policy towards the Persian Gulf and Arabia.* New York: St. Martin's Press, 1983.

Index

Note: Page numbers in *italics* refer to illustrations.

About the Author

ANTHONY H. CORDESMAN is a Senior Fellow and the Arleigh A. Burke Chair in Strategy at the Center for Strategic and International Studies, and a military analyst for ABC News. The author of numerous books on Middle Eastern security issues, he has served in senior positions for the office of the Secretary of Defense, NATO, and the U.S. Senate.